600   words

Embattled Glory

STATE AND SOCIETY IN EAST ASIA
Series Editor: Elizabeth J. Perry

Embattled Glory

Veterans, Military Families, and the Politics of Patriotism in China, 1949–2007

Neil J. Diamant

ROWMAN & LITTLEFIELD PUBLISHERS, INC.
Lanham • Boulder • New York • Toronto • Plymouth, UK

ROWMAN & LITTLEFIELD PUBLISHERS, INC.

Published in the United States of America
by Rowman & Littlefield Publishers, Inc.
A wholly owned subsidary of The Rowman & Littlefield Publishing Group, Inc.
4501 Forbes Boulevard, Suite 200, Lanham, Maryland 20706
www.rowmanlittlefield.com

Estover Road
Plymouth PL6 7PY
United Kingdom

British Library Cataloguing in Publication Information Available

Library of Congress Cataloging-in-Publication Data:

Diamant, Neil Jeffrey, 1964–
  Embattled glory : veterans, military families, and the politics of patriotism in China,
1949–2007 / by Neil J. Diamant.
    p. cm.
  Includes bibliographical references and index.
  ISBN-13: 978-0-7425-5766-6 (cloth : alk. paper)
  ISBN-10: 0-7425-5766-9 (cloth : alk. paper)
  ISBN-13: 978-0-7425-5768-0 (electronic)
  ISBN-10: 0-7425-5768-5 (electronic)
  1. Veterans—China—Social conditions. 2. Veterans—China—Political activity—
History. 3. Families of military personnel—China—Social conditions. 4. Patriotism—
Political aspects—China—History. 5. China—Social conditions—1949– I. Title.
  UB359.C6D53 2009
  305.9'0697095109045—dc22   2008032620

Printed in the United States of America

⊗™ The paper used in this publication meets the minimum requirements of American
National Standard for Information Sciences—Permanence of Paper for Printed Library
Materials, ANSI/NISO Z39.48-1992.

For my family

Table of Contents

Preface

This book is the culmination of years of thinking about the meanings of a war I had to join, a tax I had to pay, and the sex I wanted to get—in short, the three three-letter words that have long preoccupied the minds of millions of men.

Allow me to explain. In 1977 my family picked up and moved from a comfortable middle-class life in Westchester, New York, to a collective agricultural settlement in Israel—what is called a kibbutz in Israel and a commune in the United States and the People's Republic of China. Then and even now, the path to a respectable manhood in the kibbutz passed through the military: the older teenage *kibbutzniks* we looked up to all served in elite units in the Israeli Defense Forces, with mysterious names like "669" in the Air Force, "Sayeret Matkal" (the General Staff's anti-terror unit), "Shayetet 13" (Naval commandos), and "Raven"—the paratrooper's "tank-hunting" squads. On weekends these soldiers would come home, bronzed from the sun, each sporting a young woman on his arm. When it came time for me to begin my own military service in 1982, there was little doubt in my mind that I would serve in a combat unit as well: it was what was done, and it was the surest way to secure the attention of young women who might be attracted to a soldier returning from the field caked with dirt and grime.

Unluckily for me, my years of service (1982–1985) coincided with Israel's first large-scale war in Lebanon. Not long after completing basic training, we were sent to relieve soldiers on the Syrian front. When we were not training in the Golan Heights, we were in forward outposts conducting patrols, three-hour shifts of guard duty, all-night ambushes, and live-fire exercises. And, like the teenagers before me, my chest was puffed out just a little bit further when I walked into the communal dining hall during weekend leaves. For a kid from Westchester, this was great stuff—I felt Israeli. Whether this was true or not, whatever success I had with women at the time, I (surely mistakenly!) attributed to having "become a man" by serving in a combat unit. At the time, I was not particularly attuned to the controversies surrounding the Lebanon War, now considered the most illegitimate and ill-conceived exercise of military force in Israel's history, even though I was well aware of its cost. One soft-spoken young man (three years my elder) who served in the Golani Brigade was killed in the summer of '82. So, when told in briefings that it was necessary to be in telescope (and artillery) range of Damascus "in order to protect the north of Israel," I didn't think too much about it. Only when Israel pulled back from Lebanon's north to occupy a 40-kilometer "security strip" along the southern border, just as I was completing my service and getting ready to enter Hebrew University, did I scratch my head and think, "What about all those briefings about the necessity of being stationed on the Syrian border?" Not long after this, Defense Minister Ariel Sharon was forced out of his job after being condemned by an independent state commission examining the massacre of Palestinians in the Sabra and Shatila refugee camps near Beirut, and a massive demonstration against him took place in the heart of Tel Aviv.

Even though I ended my compulsory service in 1985, the military continued to require sacrifices from its former combat soldiers. Every year at Hebrew University, often during exam time, the telltale brown envelope from the army would come, informing me of upcoming reserve duty. When the first Palestinian *intifada* broke out, it was not uncommon to serve three or more weeks in the reserves. But this was not all. The war in Lebanon still had to be paid for. The government instituted a new tax for this purpose: $100 for all Israelis who exited the country, whether for business, pleasure, or visiting sick relatives abroad. Even though the war remained controversial and the tax was not particularly fair—why should former combat troops have to pay the same as soldiers who spent their service living it up in Tel Aviv?—people paid it without too much brouhaha. The tax was finally cancelled roughly seven years later, when I was already a graduate student at Berkeley.

It was this experience in the military and as a citizen of Israel that left me intellectually unprepared for "wartime" in the United States, where I now teach. Even though this country has been at war in Iraq and Afghanistan for close to six years already (a war that has been described as a battle for the future of Western civilization) and the military is suffering from manpower shortages, there is little discussion of a draft, a war tax, the sale of war bonds, or some form of compulsory national service; American citizens who are not serving in the military do not have to sacrifice anything, and they have not been asked to. Nevertheless, bumper stickers proclaiming "support for the troops" abound, and politicians, few of whom have any children in the military, compete with each other in their professed support for the soldiers. Even though the war in Iraq is deeply unpopular, there have been few large-scale public protests, and many opponents of the war have been intimidated by the mere intimation that not supporting the president's policies is "unpatriotic." I have had a very difficult time wrapping my mind around these things. Personally, as a citizen, and as a matter of public policy, I find the disjuncture between the highfalutin rhetoric and the lack of national mobilization very puzzling.

This contrast constitutes the intellectual and personal baggage I bring to this book on China (in comparative perspective). It has propelled my interest in the legitimacy of wars as well as the meanings, values, costs, and rewards attached to "heroic" military service, patriotism, nationalism, and citizenship—concepts that, for the most part, originated in the West but have been used in the Asian context for more than a century. How can we assess the legitimacy of a war and, by implication, the state? Exactly what constitutes "sacrifice" that deserves to be rewarded, and who determines what form of military service is important to the state and society? To what extent is military service considered a path to upward mobility (and sexual attractiveness)? What is the meaning of citizenship with and without sacrifice or a sharing of costs? Can there be a sense of nationhood without shared experiences? Who gets to be recognized as "patriotic" or not in the context of war and peace, and why? These are, admittedly, big questions that cannot have very tidy answers, but they are ones well worth asking. Over the last three centuries, wars have created states and destroyed empires, and states have mobilized citizens with appeals to patriotism and nationalism. War-making has produced new groups of people with powerful claims for recognition and status as well as those who refuse to accept the legitimacy of these demands. How these claims and counterclaims play out in state bureaucracies, neighborhoods, the workplace, and more everyday encounters should be of interest not only to students of politics but also to more casual observers of the contemporary political scene. Who will be blamed for the problems in Iraq and Afghanistan? Who will be able to claim success if the outcome is more favorable? Whose patriotism will be impugned and whose will be bolstered by the war's outcome? And how will all this affect those who actually did the fighting and endured numerous sacrifices?

In my pursuit of answers to these questions, I have been a very grateful recipient of grants and fellowships from several foundations as well as the support of academic institutions on three continents. Travel, research, and writing support were generously provided by the Ford Foundation, Chiang Ching-kuo Foundation, Freeman Foundation, the Fulbright Scholarship

Board, the Research and Development Committee of Dickinson College, the East Asian Institute of South Korea, and the George and Eliza Gardner Foundation. I also benefited from research and scholarly support from four intellectual homes in the past decade: Tel Aviv University in Israel, the University of Pittsburgh, Dickinson College, and the Shanghai Academy of Social Sciences, whose director of scholarly exchange, Li Yihai, provided the crucial support that made my research (considered quite sensitive in China) possible. I am also extremely grateful to archivists at the Shanghai Municipal Archives, Qingpu District Archives (near Shanghai), Dongcheng District Archives (Beijing), Shandong Provincial Archives, Ministry of Justice Archives (Taiwan), and the Israel Defense Forces and State Archives in Israel (for material in chapter 6). Like all academics, I am highly indebted to the diligence and expertise of librarians. At the University of Pittsburgh, Zou Xiuying and Zhang Haihui alerted me to new sources, as did Susan Xue and Wu Yifeng at the Center for Chinese Studies Library at UC Berkeley and Song Yongyi and Ye Yunshan at Dickinson College. A special note of thanks goes to Ayelet Harel, my research assistant for two years in Israel, who became a versatile and intrepid researcher in her own right, as well as to student researchers at Dickinson College: Kim Gabriel, Devi Bengfort, Micah Hostetter, and Caitlin Steirman. As a visiting scholar at Dickinson College for two semesters, Professor Fei Changkang from the Shanghai Academy of Social Sciences helped me puzzle through many hard-to-decipher texts from rural China. I owe a special thanks to my uncle, Bob Rothenberg, for his sharp proofreading eye when he read the entire manuscript, as well as to Adrienne Su for help with the title of the book. Of course, as author, I remain solely responsible for error of fact and interpretation.

As a project that has been in gestation for a long time, I have also benefited from many formal meetings and informal exchanges with colleagues, some of whom have sacrificed valuable time and effort to read a chapter or two of the manuscript. I am that much wiser, thanks to exchanges with Liz Perry, Dave Strand, Kevin O'Brien, Robert Culp, Tim Weston, Michelle Rivkin-Fish, Mark Frazier, Bill Hurst, Fei Chengkang, Azar Gat, Yossi Shain, Gil Merom, Yoav Peled, Xia Guomei, Chen Yung-fa, Shen Guoming, Stephan Haggard, Stephan MacKinnon, Matt Sommer, Woody Goldberg, Tia Thornton, Andy Rudelevige, Doug Stuart, Mark Ruhl, Russ Bova, Harry Pohlman, Rae Yang, Ann Hill, and Zhou Minglang. Audiences at Dickinson College, the Center for Naval Analysis (CNA Corp.), University of Pittsburgh, University of Washington, Tel Aviv University, University of Michigan, University of Pennsylvania, Stanford University, Columbia University, National Taiwan University, the Shanghai Academy of Social Sciences, Tokyo University, and the East Asian Institute in Seoul all provided very helpful comments. I am very grateful to the organizers of these workshops, conferences, and lecture series.

This book also benefitted from the strong support of Susan McEachern at Rowman & Littlefield Publishers. Susan was very enthusiastic about the project from the get-go and provided much needed encouragement as the book went through the review and production process. I am very proud to be included in the "stable" of Rowman & Littlefield authors. That I even got to this point was largely due to a meeting with Liz Perry, the editor of the "State and Society in East Asia" series. Liz immediately took the book under her wing, and by sheer force of her personal example, made sure that I finished it. As anyone who has worked with Liz knows, she is a great scholar, critic, editor, and colleague. Being included in her series (that now includes so many wonderful books) is also a source of pride. Doug English, senior production editor at the press, expertly guided the manuscript into its currently polished form and patiently dealt with all of my detail-oriented queries. After having dealt with university presses in my previous publications, Rowman & Littlefield was a very welcome change.

Last, but, of course, not least, I have been blessed with a very supportive family. During the year I wrote this book, my son Aviv, meaning "Spring" in Hebrew, was created. As he learned to crawl, walk, and babble, he was a constant reminder to keep things in perspective and to pay attention to the wonders of parenthood. His sister, Lani, and brother, Eli—a baby himself when I began this project, supported me by being such a big help with Aviv. Finally, my wife, Debbey, has been at my side since my freshman year as an undergraduate at Hebrew University of Jerusalem, where she was a junior in the university's study abroad program. I did not know how to type at the time, and she helped me with my very first papers; now, 20 years of marriage later, she has witnessed the publication of my second book (which I was able to type myself!). For her support, patience, and grit (especially when I made my solo China trips), I will be forever grateful.

1

Introduction

Storytelling, on my mind a lot these days because I have several young children, has much in common with the social sciences: the attempt to explain—using what will hopefully be intelligible and moderately compelling language—phenomena large and small, mundane and seemingly miraculous, and peopling these narratives with protagonists, heroes, and villains. Workers' struggles against capitalists were at the core of theories of revolution and the development of the welfare state; peasants' politics have been central to studies of rebellion in the developing world, resistance to capitalism, and the downside of globalization; the experiences of women and minorities (sexual and ethnic) and other marginalized groups were foundational in postcolonial, "subaltern," and postmodern scholarship; the middle class has been a key protagonist in theories of democratic development or the lack thereof; African-Americans' experiences during the Civil Rights Movement in the United States have provided key concepts for theories of collective action; and bureaucratic elites and technocrats were key actors in theories of state-led economic development. I could go on.

This book continues this venerable tradition, with a twist. It places front and center a group that arguably has been "the most influential interest group of the twentieth century" but has not yet been "given its due" in the social sciences, and in political science in particular.[1] I am, in fact, referring to veterans. Evidence for their significance is ubiquitous in the historical record, so a sampling will have to suffice. The failure of the Roman Senate to provide for "regular grants" to veterans was an important cause of the fall of the Republic, since the men "gave their support to those who would obtain something for them—or would promise to do so."[2] In the United States, disillusioned veterans of the Revolutionary War living a hardscrabble life in western Pennsylvania rebelled against a new tax on whiskey. These veterans, "organized in disciplined militias and comfortable with danger," attacked tax collectors and federal agents, prompting the first major assertion of federal power in the United States; the so-called "Whiskey Rebellion" was the first "war for the American soul," according to William Hogeland.[3] Shays' Rebellion (1786–1787) in western Massachusetts was led by former Continental Army officers, and rank-and-file veterans represented one-third to one-half of the participants. Upset that they received little recognition for their service, that some were thrown in jail for their inability to pay back loans, and that the General Court did not cut them any slack, the veterans "took up arms and began closing down courthouses in order to prevent the courts from enacting judgments in collection suits."[4] Fearful that local authorities would not possess the power to suppress such uprisings, local elites, who had vigorously objected to the expansion of federal power, were a "more pliable group" in the Constitutional Convention that took place the following year.[5] As Susan Browne notes, veterans' "interventions as a political pressure group tipped the balance between nationalists and localists toward the formation of a national state."[6] In the post–Civil War period, Union veterans, organized as the "Grand Army of the Republic," pressed for, and received, pensions that between 1882 and 1900 never fell below 20 percent of all federal expenditures (peaking in 1893 at 41.6 percent),[7] leading some scholars to argue that the United States had a de facto welfare state well prior to the New Deal;[8] in 1932, thousands of disgruntled World War I veterans protested, this time in the capital, for a promised bonus. Well-disciplined and organized, the veterans were soon suppressed by the military (led by Douglas MacArthur and a young Dwight Eisenhower), but the impact opened a wider path for World War II veterans. Fearing tangling with them again after the war, Congress passed the GI Bill in 1944, which created the largest expansion of economic opportunity for the working class in American history, a long stretch of civic activism, and post-war economic growth.[9] African-American veterans of that war "formed the vanguard of new recruits who swelled the ranks of the ranks of the civil rights movement,"[10] and disabled veteran organizations "helped to ignite the disability rights movement" after WWII.[11]

Across the Atlantic, veterans have lodged themselves in key political junctures. French veterans of the American Revolutionary War "were in the vanguard" of their own revolution in 1789[12] and played key roles in the neo-Jacobin movement in the late 1790s and in pacifist groups in the interwar period.[13] In Germany after WWI, many veterans (including Hitler), embittered by what they perceived as the ingratitude of the Weimer Republic and ordinary German civilians, joined various paramilitary organizations (often under the command of their former officers) and contributed to the rise of the Nazis.[14] In Italy, "rowdy" provincial war veterans were recruited by Mussolini as he built his party between 1919 and 1921; four days after commemorating his "March on Rome" (which led to his ascension to power), Italians celebrated Veteran's Day.[15] In the USSR, according to Amir Weiner, WWII "redefined the party according to the ethos of veterans' sacrifices."[16] Serbian veterans of the lost war in Kosovo, upset about unpaid wages, the lack of jobs, and the disparity between propaganda and their experiences in the field, played a critical role in the ouster of President Slobodan Milošević in 1999.[17] Non-European struggles for independence were also linked to veterans' wartime and post-war experiences. In Vietnam, veterans who fought in France during WWI returned as "changed men" and were involved in various forms of social disturbances throughout the 1920s and 1930s and contributed to the radicalization of Vietnamese politics (which French colonial authorities found intolerable). Veterans' activism, according to Greg Lockhart, aligned the course of mid-20th-century Vietnamese history along "the revolutionary path."[18] In Africa, post-independence conflicts in Mozambique and Angola were "in part attributable to frustrated veterans, disappointed at government failures to fulfill promises."[19] In China, the failure of the Guomindang (Nationalist Party) to plan for the demobilization of its veterans after the end of WWII resulted in roughly 500,000 soldiers becoming available for service in the Communist military during the Civil War of 1946–1949.[20]

Scholarship in the social sciences has not kept up with this impressive record of veteran activism or, in a broader sense, the question of what happens to politics, society, and culture when large armies are demobilized into society.[21] Even a cursory survey of major journals and books in political science, history, and sociology reveals an odd discrepancy between the scarcity of articles devoted to veterans in politics and their political clout.[22] In Chinese history—the largest subfield in Asian Studies—scholars of intellectual, social, labor, and women's history far outnumber those interested in military history, despite the acknowledged importance of warfare in Chinese history.[23] In the study of Chinese politics, fewer than ten articles or book chapters have been published on veterans since 1980, even though millions of veterans have been discharged since then and China has become far more accessible to foreign scholars.[24] The journal *Armed Forces and Society*, where one would expect a great deal of attention to veteran issues, has published only twenty original articles since 1974, representing roughly three percent of its content.[25] Even scholars whose research focuses on the role of war in "making states" and nations tend to neglect the role of veterans in the development of the state and how demobilization shapes political stability and the post-war economy.[26]

The precise reasons for this rather large gap in scholarship are not clear. Some have speculated that it is due to post–Vietnam War anti-militarism among the intellectual left who migrated into academia;[27] others feel that "the immediacy" of the Vietnam conflict has deterred scholars from looking at "the macroscopic implications of social change"[28] or that many social scientists are reluctant to place war and its social ramifications front and center because of their preference (following Marx) for economic explanations; and others attribute it to certain "ideological and methodological biases" (such as the view that war is an "aberration" and that things return to normal after it, and their unwillingness to admit that anything positive, such as welfare institutions, can be traced to a terrible thing like war).[29] My own guess is that the absence of the draft has resulted in a fairly wide chasm between civilians and the uniformed military as well as a more general "schema" among academics associating the military with conservative, "non-progressive" values. Regardless of the exact reason, the result is clear: a group that has toppled and created regimes, inspired national holidays, elected presidents, and organized mass protests and powerful interest groups has not been a dominant "actor" in theories in comparative politics (particularly compared to the "mountains of research on labor politics"[30]), international relations, or political theory. This is also reflected in the composition of political science departments. Even though most scholars readily acknowledge that modern states have been founded on force and that the military plays a powerful role in politics, very few hire specialists on military matters.

This is also the case in other disciplines. As noted by the military historian John Lynn, between 1977 and 1997 *The American Historical Review*, the flagship journal of the profession, "failed to publish a single research article focused on the conduct of the Hundred Years' War, the Thirty Years' War, the Wars of Louis XIV, the War of American Independence, the Revolutionary and Napoleonic Wars, World War I and World War II," and during that period the journal published only one article on the United States Civil War. The "new wisdom," he acerbically complains, "decrees that . . . the reshaping of the world by warfare from 1937 to 1945 falls short of a single article in nearly two decades because apparently more important matters had to be discussed."[31] Similarly, social historians interested in veterans complain about the lack of scholarship on their social and legal status;[32] prominent sociologists claim that "sociology has paid only minimal attention to the military, despite its touching more lives and intersecting with more sectors of society than do most institutions" and that military service and its relationship to citizen obligation is a topic "most sociologists merely avoid or neglect."[33] Historians of the American Civil War—probably the most extensively researched period in American history—have paid scant attention to what James Marten calls "adjustment problems" among its veterans. "With a few exceptions," he writes, "historians have ignored the transition to civilian life."[34] Another "path generating" social movement in the United States—the 1932 Bonus March—has received scant attention in historical scholarship or in theories of collective action.[35] It does say something about the politics of choosing topics in academia that there are departments, majors, programs, foundations, institutes, and centers devoted to the study of ethnic groups, rights, law, gender, women, and labor but none solely devoted to the humanistic or social-science–oriented study of veterans (except in the context of medicine, rehabilitation, social work, and psychiatry). While this book cannot hope to close this gap, I hope it will draw greater attention to their overall significance and potential contribution to scholarship.

Although my main "case" is China, I will be arguing that the study of the social and political predicament of veterans in post-war periods sheds some light on many issues in the social sciences in general and politics in particular. How could it not! In the era of mass warfare and citizen armies, veterans, whether they want to or not, are often identified with the state, a particular regime, concrete and symbolic benefits, claims for higher social and political status, the meaning and legitimacy of wars, and the abstract causes for which they served ("patriotism," "democracy," "nationalism," "racial purity," "revolution," "equality," "justice," and the like). Veterans' position in the state and society, I suggest, can serve as a proxy for gauging both the legitimacy of the state and its policies and the public's willingness to accept the official (or social scientific) definitions of the causes for which they fought. We can draw conclusions about the legitimacy of a war (or revolution) and a state's "narrative" of that conflict when veterans of that war are feted in the press, offered generous benefits, and gain widespread respect in society, or when there is a large discrepancy between rhetoric and everyday interactions. We can learn something about the concrete meaning of "patriotism" by studying how veterans—who are often portrayed as embodying this virtue—are treated. Veteranhood also has been closely linked, sometimes causally, to claims for citizenship, social and political recognition, and entitlements. In numerous cases throughout history (including the United States, continental Europe, Japan, Russia, Bolivia, and Brazil, among others), military service has been a very clear demonstration of patriotism and served as a basis for demanding higher status and more rights (sometimes in the form of citizenship status).[36] We can certainly learn a lot about power. Throughout history, veterans who have returned from war or even regular military service have fought for, and sometimes received, tangible rewards, such as preferential treatment in jobs, health care, pensions, access to important decision makers, and political representation, as well as symbolic benefits not afforded to most of the population. These could include lofty speeches by politicians about patriotism and sacrifice, monuments, museums, statues, holidays, street-namings, medals and decorations, and military parades. But rarely have such large-budget allocations been uncontested. Other groups in society (for example, women who bear the brunt of war on the home front or workers who were denied raises during the war) feel that they, too, are "worthy," "served," "sacrificed," "participated," or "suffered" and demand to receive their share of recognition and credit. Under what circumstances are veterans likely to receive more or less credit for their military service? To what extent will fellow citizens, but particularly elites who control scarce resources (symbolic and material), allow veterans to "cash in" military experiences for social recognition as a patriot and citizen? Is military service seen as a legitimate, widely accepted path toward improved legal, social, or political status? All of these battles—over language, power, rights, and resources—occur even before the guns of war have been silenced but intensify as soon as the "boys come home."

China, contrary to its popular image nowadays as a rising but politically troubled economic powerhouse, provides particularly fertile ground for such an exploration. Three decades of rapid economic development and Westernization have shifted the fulcrum in China scholarship away from the study of elites and military-related issues toward those dealing with political economy and state–society relations. Given the burgeoning interest in China among the lay public, corporations, lawyers, students, and civic groups, this shift was probably inevitable and, to some extent, necessary. But it comes with a price. It has become a little too easy to forget what might be called "foundational" issues in the establishment of the state, among these, the relevance of war, which historically has had a critical impact on political, economic, and social institutions, demography, and gender relations. The Chinese Communists succeeded largely because of a more effective military, not economy; China's status in world politics was raised because of its ability to reach a stalemate with the United Nations Forces in Korea in the early 1950s and to defeat India in the early 1960s, well before its economic boom; the strengthening of the central government and the reestablishment of political sovereignty and stability in the early to mid-1950s were also byproducts of military success. Because of all of this warfare, by 1956 China had roughly five million veterans who were trying to reintegrate into society, politics, and the economy (and by 1959, close to seven million). In 1979, just as the period of "reform and opening up" was beginning, China went to war once again, this time against Vietnam, producing yet another generation of veterans. How these veterans were treated after their demobilization—and what this tells us about patriotism, the status of the military, and state legitimacy—are the framing questions of this study.

This work's central finding, which is based on a treasure trove of recently declassified archival sources in several cities and rural areas in China and Taiwan, is that a very substantial number of these veterans, irrespective of which war they fought in—the "victorious" wars against the Nationalists, Americans, and Indians or the far more problematic one against Vietnam— were frequently mistreated and not given much credit for the military or political successes by state officials and society. Even urban-educated elites (with the exception of teenage students between 1963 and 1969) who were otherwise "proud" of the People's Liberation Army (PLA) and appreciated political stability and the rise in international stature that China enjoyed after 1949 frequently looked upon veterans with disdain and treated them accordingly. Ostensibly heroes of the revolution who had good class status because they contributed to the Chinese Communist Party's (CCP's) victory, many veterans nonetheless suffered abuse (verbal and physical), widespread neglect, and discrimination in places of employment, hospitals, clinics, government offices, and many other "everyday" circumstances; many officials and ordinary people heavily discounted their contributions to the establishment of "New China." Veterans expected to be treated well, or at least given what we might call a "fair shake" in employment, residential rights, housing, and overall standard of living after their discharge from years of service, but these hopes dimmed almost immediately after their discharge, even as they saw themselves as highly patriotic citizens who had a great deal to contribute to the state and who were entitled to be treated with respect. As we will see, the phrase veterans used to describe their situation evoked the rural setting from which many of them came: "We're treated like a donkey slaughtered after having finished grinding the wheat" (*momian shalü*). Throughout the 1950s, 1960s, and well into the reform period (which has supposedly witnessed a surge of patriotism and significant state investment in war-related museums, martyrs shrines, and "patriotic education"[37]), veterans attempted to reverse this treatment by protesting both peacefully and violently; traveling to county seats, provincial capitals, and Beijing; writing letters to low-level clerks and national-level leaders; organizing independent veterans associations; posting big-character posters; whistleblowing; and calling attention to their plight by committing suicide.

Are these findings significant, or do they merely add to the well-worn "charge sheet" drawn up against Communist regimes? The case of the Soviet Union, China's political "teacher" for many years and another "winner" of WWII, suggests that the lack of appreciation and the abuse of veterans are not universal to these regime types. According to Amir Weiner's pathbreaking research on the impact of WWII, Red Army veterans had very high status, with combat service and active resistance to the Nazis in occupied areas a virtual litmus test for Communist Party membership (in Ukraine). Unlike Chinese veterans, Russian and Soviet-era veterans have been allowed to form national and local veterans associations.[38] In post-war Vietnam, the government has allowed the publication of several books and movies about the problems facing its veterans, but the cultural czars in the People's Republic of China (PRC) government have refused to allow filmmakers and authors to delve into this sensitive topic.[39] A similar question of significance can be raised from a public policy perspective. Why is it necessarily interesting that the implementation of programs to benefit veterans did not go smoothly? After all, even in the highly successful case of the American GI Bill, many African-Americans, particularly those in the Deep South, could not take advantage of their rights.[40] My argument is that such failings, which occurred over the entire course of CCP history in both urban and rural areas, cannot be dismissed as "politics as usual." They are the manifestations of a weak and limited sense of what I call "everyday" patriotism and nationalism—twin concepts that I believe have had an exaggerated and ultimately distorting role in the analysis of Chinese politics and history;[41] a failure, despite many decades of effort beginning from the 1860s, to convince many officials (especially those who are better educated) and ordinary people that demands for appreciation, sympathy, respect, and higher status stemming from service in an organized military are as legitimate and worthy as civilian or cultural claims to citizenship; and the very complicated and virulently contested nature of legitimacy of the party, military, and China's twentieth-century conflicts.

Taken together, this study suggests that some of the key tropes scholars have employed to make sense of China in the last 50 years should be reassessed. For instance, if Chinese patriotism and nationalism have been on the rise since 1949, if Chinese take pride in many of the key results of military success, why would there be widespread and persistent discrimination against many of the veterans who were involved in bringing about these outcomes? Why would military and martyr families sell their blood to support themselves? If the revolution was supposed to benefit the revolutionaries the most, and if the PLA was a highly respected organization (it has been said to have risen to "exceptional heights" during the Korean War[42]), why would its veterans be called "People's Liberation Army trash," "scum," or "used and discarded goods," or refer to themselves as "tossed away dirty socks"? Why would a veteran tell party officials, "When the Party wanted me, I was pulled along like a cow, but after my return home, I'm treated not that much differently than a counter-revolutionary"? Why were wives and fiancées of mobilized soldiers raped by village officials at the height of the "militarization" of society prior to the Cultural Revolution?[43] Why were there uprisings against the CCP led by Korean War veterans in the early 1950s?[44] Why has the state devoted massive resources to commemorate the heroic tales of "revolutionary martyrs" and established a special day for labor, women, and children but not a "Veteran's Day" or even a single street, avenue, or highway with the word *veteran* in it?[45] (This cannot be attributed to "Asian" or Confucian culture"; as early as 1947, North Vietnam declared July 27 "War Invalids and Martyrs Day.")[46] Why doesn't Beijing have a central war memorial or cenotaph commemorating unknown PLA soldiers (again, unlike Hanoi)?[47] Why weren't groups of veterans included in state-sponsored parades there when workers, artists, and even athletes were?[48] If veterans "have always been treated as a privileged group in China,"[49] were defined by the state as ideally representing the "social basis of the revolution," constituted the "institutional core of the revolutionary regime,"[50] and were the "most important" source of new rural leadership,[51] and service in the PLA was "regarded as prestigious" (until the late 1970s),[52] why would more than 4,000 of them commit suicide in the first five years after the "glorious" victory over Japan and the Nationalists, and why were the most crucial battles of the war ignored in state propaganda? If the PLA troops who entered China's coastal cities were welcomed by intellectuals, students, and business people,[53] and if the "army was heralded for winning the revolution and making the nation independent,"[54] and the years 1949–1957 were the "honeymoon period" or golden age of CCP legitimacy,[55] then why did many of its favored sons—the revolutionaries themselves—make their way to Beijing to file petitions, lay down on railway tracks, or mount street parades holding aloft the picture of Mao? If patriotic status (demonstrated through military service in many democracies and non-democracies) has helped generate a certain measure of *respect* from fellow citizens, why would many veterans not receive much "credit" for this from their fellow citizens in China? If veterans benefited from state patronage in allocation of jobs (in fact, only a minority received positions), why would some of them say, only partly in jest, "At least if I were a counterrevolutionary in labor reform I would have something to eat!"? Clearly the prestige that was attached to the small number of Long March (1934–1935) veterans was not evenly distributed among those discharged from the PLA in later years. The questions that emerge from these empirical findings require that we dig a bit deeper for answers.

Many of the answers to these questions are buried fairly deep in the political history of China's revolutions and wars. The Chinese Communist Party was established in Shanghai in 1921 but was allied with its rival Nationalist Party, which had its stronghold in South China between 1923 and 1927. After the Nationalists attacked the CCP in 1927 during the "Northern Expedition," the bulk of the CCP sought refuge in the countryside, transforming into a nearly decimated, rural-based political party; it was during this time that it began to build its own military force. From 1927 on, top CCP

leaders—many of whom were from relatively well-off families and had opportunities to study Marxist theory abroad—sought to mobilize poor peasants to conquer Nationalist-held cities. From 1927 to 1937, the Nationalists,
more of an amalgam of factions and warlords than a real "party," struggled
to consolidate their control of urban areas but had even less success establishing "infrastructural power" in the countryside; much like the CCP,
returned overseas students, rather than trained military personnel, occupied
the top ranks in the party and army (in 1930, 67 percent of its generals and
39 percent of its lieutenant and major generals were returned students, far
higher figures than graduates of regular and auxiliary military academies).[56]
Not long after Japan invaded large areas in the North—much of the South,
Northwest, and Southwest were not under their direct control even during
WWII, more than half of the population did not live under the occupation,
and those who chose to remain in such cities as Beijing, Shanghai, Canton,
and Tianjin "lived in relative peace and comfort"[57]—the Nationalists, under
intense political pressure, agreed to a second "United Front" with the CCP
to fight against Japan (see Figure 1.1).

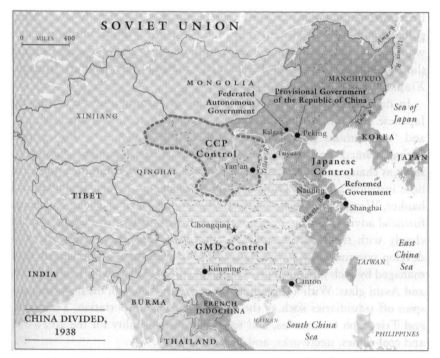

**Figure 1.1. China in 1938. From *The Search for Modern China* by Jonathan Spence.
Copyright ©1990 by Jonathan D. Spence. Used by permission of W.W. Norton & Company, Inc.**

Even with this political window of opportunity, the Nationalists' fighting capacity was severely weakened by their inability to recruit educated elites (including the wealthy and physicians) and ordinary civilians to perform military service, their inability to enforce conscription at the local level (among all the allied powers, China had the lowest rate of conscription per available population), and the tendency of field commanders to draw their staff from among their relatives and schoolmates.[58] (In contrast, during the successive wars against France in the 18th century, 40 percent of British officers came from landed background.)[59] During this time of political polarization, the Nationalists were officially allied with the United States and other Western powers against the Axis, but collaboration with Japan was not very unusual at the level of local elites and national-level leaders.[60] The Communists, taking advantage of Japan's attacks against the Nationalist government, expanded their control over Northwest China, organized or co-opted rural militias (roughly 2 million men), formed guerrilla units and regular military forces (estimated at 900,000), fought against the Japanese army and "puppet" forces (on a limited scale and in small unit actions, especially after 1940), and infiltrated unions, the police, and workers' armed militias in the urban underground—all while struggling to maintain control over scattered base areas in the East.[61] After Japan's surrender in 1945 (an event for which the CCP implausibly claims primary, if not sole, credit[62]), the Nationalist Army attacked the CCP-controlled territory (some generals, but particularly Yan Xishan in the Northwest, used veterans of the defeated Japanese Imperial Army for this purpose[63]), but even though it benefited from American military advisors and equipment, it was routed by the PLA in the Civil War of 1946–1949. Like Chiang Kai-shek and his allies, the CCP, while waving the banner of nationalism, also used a considerable number of Japanese troops for key battles in the Northeast; for instance, in the battle of Tianjin in 1949, "most of the artillery employed by the Communists was manned by Japanese gunners."[64] Its goal of encircling the cities from the countryside fulfilled, the CCP rapidly shifted its priorities back to cities, depending heavily upon the educated elite to staff key civilian party, government, and economic institutions, while its military continued to depend upon "good class" poor and middle-class peasants.[65] Less than a year after taking over power and long before it had full control of the country's population, the CCP (or, more precisely, Mao Zedong, against the counsel of his colleagues[66]) was at war again—this time against China's wartime ally against Japan: the United States in coalition with UN Forces. Other significant CCP military engagements were mostly against countries with which it had had *positive* relations in the past: India was an "ally" in the Non-Alignment Movement in the mid-1950s, the Soviet Union was its ally between 1950 and 1961, and Vietnam had been an ideological ally of the CCP since the 1920s.

This "stylized," abbreviated, and uncontroversial historical review of revolutions and war provides much explanatory clout for the problems many veterans faced in the post-war period. China's modern revolutions and wars, I argue, were simply *too long*; they allowed too many people to lay claim to patriotic status in the victory of 1949. Mao famously said, "Out of the barrel of a gun grows political power," but this was a tremendous simplification of the role of armed force. During the CCP's long march to power between 1921 and 1949, myriad organizations (militias, intelligence agencies, police, the Red Army, etc.) possessed and used different kinds of guns (and other weapons, such as clubs to kill landlords). Whose "gun barrel" should get the most credit for capturing political power? For the majority of war veterans, war also ended *too late*: by the time they returned home after the Civil and Korean wars, most political positions in the country (with some exceptions in certain provinces) were already occupied by non-veterans, and land reform had already occurred in their absence, leaving them with nothing. China's wars were also *too complicated*; when wars were fought, it was never entirely clear to many ordinary citizens and officials who was responsible for victory or defeat, or why the enemy was the enemy. For example, who should get the most patriotic credit for defeating Japan? Was it the United States, the Nationalists who claimed to govern "China" at the time, CCP guerrillas, violence-prone rural militias, civilian party members, peasants, workers, the "patriotic" students who engaged in propaganda work, PLA regulars, or "the Chinese people" generally speaking?[67] Who could be considered "heroic" when military units that fought valiantly against the Japanese between 1937 and 1945 then battled the CCP during the Civil War and were "mopped up" as "bandits" in the early 1950s?[68] Complicating this further was the historically inconvenient fact, acknowledged even by Mao in his talks with Kakuei Tanaka, a former war criminal who served as Japan's prime minister, that the CCP would not have been as successful as it was without Japan's invasion of China; Japan's "success" in China was also the CCP's. Similar questions can be raised about the Civil War. Why was the CCP allied with Nationalists not once but twice, but then fought a battle to the death and "almost entirely denied or neglected" its contribution to the war effort against Japan until the mid-1980s (but even here it was mainly for reasons of state legitimization after the Cultural Revolution)?[69] The same applies to post-1949 wars. Why was the United States the "enemy" in 1950, when many people knew that it helped "China" (under the Nationalists) defeat Japan? Moreover, who won the war? Having demobilized millions of Civil War veterans in the early 1950s, many new recruits (probably more than one million) in the People's Volunteers in

Korea after 1951 were provided by militias from whom a "certain proportion" entered the regular PLA.[70] Confusing matters even further, entire units of the former Nationalist Army, including some that only recently had been involved in fighting the CCP in the Southwest, as well as large groups of "reeducated" bandits, were dispatched to the war.[71] Then, in 1979, the PRC went to war against Vietnam. But why was Vietnam an enemy, when state propaganda of more than two decades had hailed that country as an ally of China in the international battle against imperialism? All these twists and turns had a negative impact on veterans as well as on the families of soldiers and martyrs. In contrast to WWII in the USSR, in China, notes Arthur Waldron, "neither during the Second World War nor after did China produce an unequivocally collective and therefore 'national' commemoration of the war dead."[72] A simple question—"What did the Korean or Vietnam wars do for us?"—could not be easily answered by most urban and rural residents in China.[73]

Finally, China's official ideology, wars, and military were *too narrow* in terms of their politics and social composition. In Marxist–Leninist political theory, veterans are completely missing in action as a status group; there are only "soldiers," "workers," "peasants," "capitalists," the "bourgeoisie," and the like. Militarily, unlike the modern United States, Japan, France, Korea, Taiwan, Singapore, Soviet Union, and many Western European states (most of which served as models for Chinese elites at one point or another), no modern Chinese state has effectively implemented near-universal conscription for men or fought in the context of a mass army in a total war that had a high degree of popular consensus against a hated foreign foe; most of its wars were *limited* engagements.[74] Both traditionally and more contemporarily, the military recruited its soldiers primarily from among the peasantry (most veterans were from peasant background), but because of either the weakness of the state in the Nationalist period or the confinement of the CCP to "base areas" in North and East China between 1936 and 1945, *a national scale draft into a functioning military never occurred*. As a result, regional warlords had armies and fought wars, and political parties had armies (and still do) and fought wars, but China never fought as a nation-in-arms, and its wars never served a critical state-, nation-, or citizenship-building role, as was the case of Britain, France, Prussia, Japan, Russia, and the United States, among others.[75] Mao, much like Chiang Kai-shek, understood war not as mobilized armies of nation-states but as a "rush of people" against enemies—which in itself would form a nation. He found the idea of protracted warfare "fundamentally uncongenial"[76] and was far more enamored of militias than a standing army (much like Thomas Jefferson, but in contrast to European militaries where militias were more marginal[77]). Notwithstanding the CCP's political vocabulary of "campaigns," "fronts," and the like, Mao's governing style after 1949 was that of a guerilla leader, not the executive of a modern state and military.[78] These four facets of China's wars, revolution, and ideology (too long, late, complicated, and narrow) account for the poor treatment very many PRC veterans (and military and martyr families) received upon their discharge as well as their political vulnerability and difficulties translating official rights and status as patriotic heroes into positive interactions with ordinary citizens and officials.

When we look at the development of patriotism and nationalism in comparative perspective—and I stress *development* because none of these sentiments, or any behavior that flows from them, is "natural" or inevitable—a very strong case can be made that they depend a great deal on the advent of large, *integrated* armies (fighting legitimate wars) that produce significant, socially leveling experiences grounded in action and a shared sense of sacrifice as well as respect and appreciation of the valor, masculinity, and "worthiness" of the lower classes in each post-war period. Nationalism, patriotism, and martial citizenship, particularly in the sense I define below, will be far more truncated in states that have never experienced being a "nation-in-arms" in a legitimate war, and wars will have no significant leveling effect if social participation in them is very limited.[79] While the "nationalist" and "patriotic" activities, views, musings, and writings of educated elites are interesting and important, they are ultimately less consequential than *lived experience between classes*, which, rather unfortunately, has at least a reasonable chance of emerging from near-universal conscription (but could also emerge from other sorts of intensive cross-class experiences, such as national service).[80] In the Nationalist Army, draftees were drawn almost exclusively from among the "huge unlettered masses" in the countryside—in 1930 only 13 percent of soldiers were capable of writing a letter—and were often "treated as military coolies" (only 2.2 percent of enlisted men received commissions at the rank of second lieutenants to captains).[81] The CCP, largely owing to the rural-to-urban dynamic of its revolution and its class bias in recruiting, clearly had a "mass" army in terms of numbers, but also a poorly integrated one, particularly at the level of the operational combat units, which tend to have more equality and informality than those further in the rear.[82] Thus, military service that in many Western and Asian contexts led to a slow rise in the status of ordinary men as valued citizens, thanks to their being championed by elite veteran officers (who served with them in the trenches) both in rhetoric and in policies (such as far-reaching welfare programs), did not happen in China, whose elites show scant appreciation for any sacrifice (military or economic) of the lower classes, including poor military families.[83] To be sure, military service in the PRC did account for some upward mobility when the central state, frustrated by local resistance, took a very proactive role in placing veterans in jobs (usually those who were already privileged by urban status), but these efforts were accepted reluctantly and grudgingly. If veterans (and military dependents) had a very difficult time asserting claims to patriotic status in the Maoist period when wars and war-induced "nationalism" and "patriotism" were supposedly more salient, the reform period has produced an even more challenging political environment. Since 1978, the power of the military has rapidly declined, ideology has been all but abandoned, the Vietnam War did not end particularly well, a market culture and individualism have gained more traction, and inequality has increased. At the same time, Chinese will no longer share any sort of cross-class experiences; a youth in contemporary urban China, unlike the Cultural Revolution generation, whose elites have been a bit more sympathetic to the peasantry,[84] might never meet a villager in his or her lifetime. In the absence of shared cross-class experiences, it is unlikely that military service will become a path for gaining appreciation, respect, status, and sympathy (or martial citizenship), even if it remains a source of minimal upward mobility for very poor villagers, or that patriotism or "rising nationalism" will result in much action for the good of the nation—bombastic bursts of rhetoric attacking Taiwan, Japan, or the United States notwithstanding.

The absence of a more simplified and agreed-upon narrative about who contributed the most to "victory," or of a relatively short, legitimate, and successful war with near-universal conscription, also helps explain the surprisingly low status of most veterans in China. As we will see as we look at a number of comparative cases, veterans have been more likely to gain political clout and social respect when they were given primary patriotic credit for victory (in the U.S. military, few doubted that the combat soldier's contributions outweighed those in the rear; many civilians were willing to take credit but still gave more respect to those in combat[85]) and when they were allowed to establish feisty organizations with a critical mass of cross-class membership. In China, the party-state, which remains dominated by urban, educated, and civilian elites, has persistently denied veterans, most of whom come from the countryside, the capacity to organize (unlike the USSR and many other authoritarian governments) or forge links to other groups in society. Thus, it is not surprising that China, despite winning, or at least claiming to have won, several wars, does not have a "Veterans" or a "Memorial" day. Neither does it have a cabinet-level Department of Veteran Affairs (United States) or regional "Patriots and Veterans Affairs" offices (South Korea) or anything comparable to the "GI Bill of Rights" in the United States or the USSR's Demobilization Law of 1945.[86] Bizarrely, Civil Affairs, the bureaucracy responsible for many of their affairs, also handles flood relief, minority issues, religious organizations, local elections, senior citizen homes, mental institutions, orphanages, and the disabled. While women in China have benefited from several Marriage Laws and have an organization that represents their interests to some extent (the Women's Federation), youth and the disabled have their own organizations, and workers' interests were taken into account in a new Labor Law, a "Veteran's Law" is not even on the political agenda, and veterans are not represented by any corporate body.

Because this study will make their central claims about veterans' status in politics and society—that evidence of widespread abuse, neglect, and disrespect are indicative of (a) the highly contested claims over patriotic status and the rewards that are supposed to flow from this; (b) the lack of support for demands for martial-based citizenship; and (c) the problematic legitimacy of the revolution, war, and the state itself—it is important to clarify what I mean by these terms. This is not only because they are somewhat abstract but also because they are somewhat puzzling. Veterans were often abused, yet PRC politics have sometimes been described as highly *militaristic*: peasants were organized into "brigades"; violence against various "enemies" was common; one of the most famous model citizens was a soldier (Lei Feng); the PLA was venerated in books, art, countless plays, movies, and television programs; and during the Cultural Revolution youth marched—military style and in uniform—through major cities (wielding pens rather than weapons). Furthermore, for more than a decade scholars, journalists, and citizens of countries neighboring China have worried about the rise, or at least the growing significance, of Chinese nationalism and patriotism. To suggest that very little of this mattered much to most veterans does not "sit" very well on our stored body of literature. These findings make much more sense, however, if we try to think a bit differently about patriotism, nationalism, and legitimacy.

TWO DIMENSIONS OF PATRIOTISM AND NATIONALISM

How would one know to what extent people in China, or anywhere for that matter, are "patriotic"? Any assessment of this question must begin with at least a rudimentary effort to define the term. This isn't easy: *patriotism* (and the concept often linked to it, *nationalism*) is a value-laden and politicized term. Despite eminent political theorist George Kateb's warning that patriotism is "inherently disposed to disregard morality" and a "grave moral error" whose source is "typically a state of mental confusion,"[87] American surveys repeatedly show that most people (either despite or because of their alleged confusion) consider themselves to be "patriotic,"[88] probably because its antonym connotes treasonous or dishonorable behavior; few people savor being labeled "unpatriotic," even if they do not agree with government policies. Political baggage, however, should not deter us from trying to get a better sense of what patriotism involves; it should not be any different from other key concepts in comparative politics that scholars debate, such as "democracy," "authoritarianism," "inequality," or "corruption." A reasonable place to begin is the most common and seemingly straightforward definition of it (and the one that was translated into Chinese from the Japanese): "love of country." "Love" is sometimes padded with qualities such as loyalty and pride, "an attitude of sentiment and devotion" to a state or nation,[89] an "acquired sentiment,"[90] "a sense of one's country as an entity that can legitimately demand contributions and to which loyalty should be given,"[91] "ongoing civic concerns" for fellow citizens,[92] or "identification with others in a particular common enterprise"[93] or with "an actual or potential nation-state."[94] Maurizio Viroli suggests that historically *patriotism* has been used to strengthen or invoke "love of political institutions and the way of life that sustain the common liberty of a people,"[95] while Walter Berns argues that patriots in the traditional ("Spartan") sense are "citizens who love their country simply because it is their country."[96]

From my perspective, all of these definitions and characterizations are problematic. First, to the extent that "love," "sense," "sentiments," and "devotion" are all emotions, it is fairly commonsensical that *all* emotions vary in intensity across time and with the "object" of desire or affection. What do they actually mean in the context of states or nations? Is it similar to "love" or "devotion" between boyfriend and girlfriend (passionate but often fleeting), husband and wife (secure but often less passionate), or perhaps parent and child (unconditional, but still prone to bouts of frustration)? Second, and much more problematically, they all embody *excessively low thresholds* for claiming or assigning patriotic status to any individual, group, or institution. If we look at the ideology of patriotism (or nationalism) in its *human incarnation*—the "patriot" or the "nationalist"—is it really enough for someone to simply express sentiments such as "I love my country" or "I am devoted to it" to be considered patriotic?[97] "Loyalty" is too simple and too easy. Too simple because most people have multiple, and sometimes competing, loyalties; too easy because, as Morton Grodzins argued more than fifty years ago, the overwhelming majority of citizens are "loyal" simply because they do not actively join ranks with a country's sworn enemies and becomes spies.[98] Loyalty is a *passive* sentiment (which, of course, always makes charges of "unpatriotic" behavior or "disloyalty" highly suspect and partisan). On a day-to-day basis, love, loyalty, and sentimentality do not *demand* any sort of behavior from citizens; its excessively low threshold is somewhat comparable to a regime that claims to be a "democracy" just because people have rights in the constitution or to a "government" with a seat in the United Nations but without effective control over territory or population.

This problem also applies to the concept of "nationalism," particularly when scholars adopt, either implicitly or explicitly, Benedict Anderson's (wildly popular in anthropology, history, and cultural studies) definition of it as an "imagined political community" based on the perception of some sort of shared identity[99]—a "recognition of similarity" in the Chinese word for "identity" (*rentong*). Imagination, like identity, essentially is a *cognitive* process—it "tells" us that we share some sort of commonality with fellow citizens, much like "emotions" and "sentiments" also occur at this "intracranial" level. Even among scholars who question whether Anderson's causal argument (which focuses on the development of print capitalism) can be applied to an underdeveloped country like China, or whether his singular focus on the "nation" as the sole object of loyalty and identity is sufficient given the prominence of regionalism in many areas of the world,[100] few have noted this "threshold" problem: one can become a "nationalist" either through an "act" of imagination, by suggesting, usually in speech or writing, that one possesses this shared will with others (or what Adam Smith, in *A Theory of Moral Sentiments*, called "fellow feeling" with other citizens), that "our" fellow feeling is different or opposed to those of other states, or through "advocating" that other citizens *should* "rejuvenate," "awaken," or embrace a higher degree of cultural, linguistic, or ethnic homogeneity.[101] To this we might add the complexities of pinning down identity, let alone shifts in it, over time and place. How can we know that an identity has been established, shed temporarily or permanently, and fragmented or consolidated if many people hold multiple forms of it? It was for this reason that the anthropologist John Kelly—who traces this problem back to "the scholarly communities' extraordinary enthusiasm for Benedict Anderson's emphasis on memory and modalities of homogenizing"—proposed to "banish the very concept of identity."[102] Given the professional stakes involved, few have taken up this suggestion, and this has had fairly predictable methodological consequences: to "find" nationalism as a form of imagination or identity, scholars have tended to focus on the short-term protests of elites[103] (such as editors, politicians, journalists, students, and intellectuals) or their sentiments, ideas, ideals, and ideology, since they are the only ones who leave coherent records of their musings.[104] Jonathan Unger, for example, argues that Chinese peasants "had little *notion* of China as a whole, let alone being *attuned* to the nationalist *sentiments* that were developing among the educated classes in China's urban areas."[105] The rise of "nationalist sentiments" or "popular nationalism" in China has become the conventional wisdom in much of the recent work on China's international relations, and it is one of the intellectual wellsprings of the idea that China will be a threat to the international order, even though very little evidence is presented that Chinese demonstrate much "fellow feeling" or "recognize similarity" with their national cohabitants except in a superficial sense ("we're all Han Chinese").

Peter Gries's best-selling *China's New Nationalism: Pride, Politics, and Diplomacy* and even some of the reviews of his book exemplify the problems of this approach.[106] In this study, Gries examines sporadic incidents of outrage against Japan and the United States and the writings of a new cohort of young, fourth-generation "nationalist" intellectuals, some of whom also wrote best-selling books with such bombastic titles as *China Cannot Be Insulted!*, *China Cannot Be Bullied!*, and *China That Can Say No*. Arguing that "to understand Chinese nationalism, we must listen to the Chinese" and not only state-generated discourse, Gries offers a number of interesting historical and social–psychological explanations for the high-octane "nationalist" discourse that emerged in the press and public demonstrations in the mid-1990s, among them an overwrought sense of "face" and victimization.[107] While reviewers challenged his use of social psychology and the motives he attributed to Chinese writers and protesters, neither Gries nor his critics questioned the extent to which penning a book or participating in a short-lived, virtually risk-free protest should qualify someone as a "nationalist" or "patriot." Is it really enough to have a strong sense of corporate identity juxtaposed to another's, or strong "sentiments" against them (especially in China, which is ethnically very homogenous)? That his study only looked at a relatively small cohort of urban writers and other elites is also problematic in a book that tries to explain *popular* nationalism.[108] In some respects, *China's New Nationalism* zeroes in on a phenomenon that exists only if we adopt a fairly low threshold for considering a person a patriot or nationalist. That reviewers failed to notice this issue even as they called attention to other methodological problems attests to the rather amorphous standards we use in evaluating claims to nationalistic or patriotic status.[109]

In my view, to be even moderately meaningful and useful, concepts must include *and exclude* certain behaviors, qualities, and attitudes. Self-definition, claims of love, devotion, and loyalty are insufficient since they tend to include most everybody. I would suggest the following. To be meaningful, patriotism should incorporate at least two of the following four criteria: *sustained action or commitment*, a certain degree of *courage*, moderate to long-term *commitment of resources*, and what a "reasonable person"[110] would consider a *sacrifice* (not just a "willingness" or "readiness" to sacrifice, which many can claim too easily[111]). These dimensions of patriotism are not new by any stretch of the imagination, maybe just unfashionable in an age that is highly materialistic, focused on the rights of individuals and groups, and largely devoid of any integrative experience such as conscription or some other form of national service. Often promoted by military leaders in the context of mass, protracted wars,[112] they hark back to a long tradition of *republican* or *martial patriotism* which stresses the notions of "self-sacrifice for the good of all,"[113] a "framework of duty"[114] that treated military service as a critical component of citizenship and rights.[115] Much like the emphasis on *ma'asim* (deeds) in Scripture or the old idea that "actions speak louder than words," it implies that speech, cognition, right-minded thinking, sentiments, love, and imagination do not a functioning society, nation, or state make. Political theorist Michael Walzer, for example, argues that "men are bound by their significant actions, not by their feelings or thoughts; *action is the crucial language of moral commitment.*"[116] Like Walzer, Carole Pateman critiques liberal political theory for not providing an adequate intellectual basis for political obligations. In her view, the citizen voluntarism that is at the heart of social contract theory (and the basis for civil society) is only "hypothetical"; there is no requirement to commit.[117] But such "obligations" cannot be fleeting. "The nation's existence is a *daily plebiscite*," noted French theorist Ernest Renan in "What Is a Nation?" which he defines largely in terms of *actions* and the *memories* created around them, especially shed blood: "the culmination of a long past of endeavors, sacrifice, and devotion."[118] A similar conception took hold in the United States *after* the mass mobilization of the Civil War. Ralph Waldo Emerson wrote in 1864, "Before the war our patriotism was a firework, a salute, a serenade for holidays and summer evenings, but the reality was cotton thread and complaisance." With the death of hundreds of thousands, American patriotism was finally "real." Another New Englander, Horace Bushnell, echoed this theme: "We had not bled enough . . . to . . . make us a proper nation."[119] Roughly a century later, John F. Kennedy famously asked citizens to think about what *they* could do for their country—which contributed to a wave of civic activism at home and abroad. This perspective is not necessarily Western or American. Koreans at the turn of the century penned eloquent essays on such "virtues" as bravery in action and the "sacrificial spirit," which they saw in both Western civilization (citing figures as diverse as Jesus Christ, Peter the Great, and Bismarck) and Asian civilization (the general Zhuge Liang and the Song dynasty loyalist Wen Tianxiang).[120] One of the most revered figures in Chinese civilization, Qu Yuan (c. 340–278 BC), achieved iconic status as a "patriotic poet" because he sacrificed himself for the principle of loyalty and opposing corruption in government; Yue Fei, a Song dynasty general (1103–1142 AD), is currently revered as a patriot because of his loyalty and for devoting years of his life and taking significant risks in combat for the state; contemporary memorials and shrines to revolutionary martyrs in the PRC and Taiwan emphasize action and sacrifice (the Nationalist general Zhang Zizhong, killed in combat against Japan, is a good case in point).[121] Chinese republican political theorists (Liang Qichao, for instance) have long been influenced by the militarized, Continental versions of patriotism and nationalism (including conscription and military training in schools), arguing that "the new citizens of China had to be civic-minded, disciplined, capable of self-sacrifice, aggressive and rational."[122] Official biographies of martyrs in the PRC made repeated use of the terms *duty*, *devotion*, and *sacrifice*.[123] Few, to my knowledge, object to this behaviorist principle. In short, most things we consider valuable would not exist without citizens' sacrifice, action, and long-term commitment. This perspective weakens the claims to patriotic (or even elite) status of those who speak but do not follow up with action; who act, but only for the moment; or who might contribute, but not what a reasonable person would consider any personal sacrifice.

In many societies throughout history (here we return to the issue of veterans), those who served in successful militaries have demanded, and sometimes received, a greater "claim" on patriotic status than those who have not, and from this derives their political influence. As much as this bothers those with ambivalent attitudes toward the military as an institution, both empires and many modern states have provided wide-ranging benefits to veterans and fewer (or none at all) to other groups. There is a fairly wide consensus, accepted even in more Confucian-influenced countries that had traditionally discriminated against soldiers, such as China and South Korea,[124] that national policies should at least pay lip service to the idea that enlistment with the knowledge of potential danger, years of military service, risking one's life by fighting wars or in dangerous training, and losing limbs (even when the motives for service, enlistment, or even heroism are not "pure"[125]) are more important sacrifices than, say, cutting gas consumption, working overtime on the home front, or paying somewhat higher taxes—even though the latter could, and have, claimed otherwise.[126] It is also why veterans, as well as civilians who have made significant sacrifices, are often accorded higher political and moral authority than those who have not, at least in official discourse. The Nixon White House, for example, found it fairly easy to repel the attacks of student anti–Vietnam War protesters, calling them "spoiled" kids, but became extremely worried when criticized by veterans; two of them—John Kerry and John McCain—later became senators and presidential candidates based mainly on their heroics in war.[127] Throughout history, many states have been worried about veteran protest—not only because they have been trained to use weapons, but also because, having served, they have more legitimacy and more solid "patriotic standing" to question and criticize state policy (what Chinese call *fayanquan*—the right to speak up).

These sorts of claims, and the political reverberations they have caused, have not been adequately reflected in many of the social science disciplines and the humanities. This, in combination with a fairly widespread shunning of the military as a "sexy" subject in many academic disciplines, has, I believe, resulted in definitions of patriotism and nationalism that stress the abstract and emotive ("love," "imagination") rather than the *institutional* (impressive scholarship suggests that few institutions have been more important to fostering nationalism and patriotism than the state and its military[128]) and *behavioral* (action and sacrifice as opposed to thinking and feeling). Methodologically, this definition will tend to privilege elite sources, since the educated strata are in a much better position to leave coherent records of their emotional states (as well as their friends') in publications, rather than smaller-scale actions of the lower classes. This study, by using a different conceptualization of patriotism and nationalism, requires different sources as well. These sources allow us to complicate the official narrative about veterans and national pride or various "patriotic" social movements and moments (as gripping as these may be[129]) by looking at how the real, flesh-and-blood people behind patriotic discourse were treated in more mundane, "everyday" circumstances: in villages when disabled veterans needed help with the harvest, in factories when an old wound flared up, in government offices when they requested housing or when they needed time off from work to go to a hospital. If patriotism can be conceptualized as Renan's "daily plebiscite" that involves action, sacrifice, and commitment of resources, and nationalism requires *actual exhibitions* of "fellow feeling" and "recognizing the similar" among compatriots, we should be able to get a better sense of their internal dynamics by examining documents that both hone in on and explain any gap between veterans' official patriotic status and how they were treated in "everyday" interactions with fellow citizens. The reason for this is simple enough: veterans are a historically "problematic" population owing to their experiences in war and long time away from family and civilian society, which makes interaction with them difficult. Moreover, fulfilling promises to them always involves some personal or institutional *costs* in material resources, symbolic recognition, and administrative time and effort. While there is no standard "measurement" for patriotism—and readers are certainly free to think up their own definitions—I argue that, on the whole, this is a better gauge of its substance than studying a dozen urban residents writing books and articles about China's position in the world, flag waving at the Olympics or soccer games, or even a "movement" involving hundreds of them marching on the streets, only to disband and return home several hours later after stopping off for a caffe latte at Starbucks or buying Japanese-made products.[130] For a discipline recently addicted to "hard" quantitative measures, it is rather odd (and somewhat amusing) that mushy concepts such as *love* or *pride* could be a critical part of a definition! For example, if scholars claim that contemporary "nationalism" is based on "pride" in China's economic growth, fancy high rises, export volume, and modernization, we could examine how those who have contributed to these successes (low-wage migrant workers, workers in township and village enterprises, foreign capitalists, etc.) are treated by elites. In any case, even if one chooses a different population by which to measure patriotism, the criteria should at least include, and hopefully emphasize, the behavioral as well as the rhetorical, emotional, and cognitive. This also applies to the United States. For all the talk about improved civic attitudes in the United States in the immediate wake of the attacks of September 11, 2001, patterns of civic *engagement*—the more important standard in my view—did not change in any significant way—with the exception of TV viewing.[131]

MARTIAL CITIZENSHIP

Does this problem with patriotism "carry over" to how we assess the political and social status of different social groups in society (including veterans and military families)? One large body of literature dealing with this question focuses on the concept of *citizenship*, which also has benefited from the outpouring of scholarship in recent years. Sometimes prompted by the emergence of transnational entities such as the European Union (what does citizenship in such an entity actually mean, for example?) or the emergence of politically active groups demanding the same legal status given to other citizens (gays and lesbians who claim the right to marry), scholars have documented both the contested quality of citizenship—achieving full citizenship status is often the result of political struggle—and the extent to which even the granting of citizenship does not necessarily result in the complete actualization of citizen rights, benefits, or higher status: rights on paper are not rights in practice. Dorothy Solinger's prize-winning book on rural migrants in Chinese cities, for example, demonstrates how state policy has systematically discriminated against migrants—all "citizens" in law—by not affording them the same access to health care, education, and residence, sometimes deporting them back to their hometowns when convenient, and also how migrants have tried to assert claims on the state by virtue of their citizenship.[132] Citizenship as a claim to certain entitlements or state commitments—in the Chinese case, these have been generally more oriented toward social welfare and subsistence than demands to participate in the exercise of power—has been the guiding intellectual tradition in this scholarship.[133] In reviewing recent literature on citizenship in her study of the impact of the GI Bill, for example, Suzanne Mettler writes that academic and political conversations about citizenship tend to cluster around the "citizens themselves and the extent to which they participate—or, more likely, fail to participate—in civic and political life. The other focuses on government and the extent to which it bestows—or fails to bestow—rights on citizens in the form of social, civil, and political guarantees."[134] Ronald Krebs, in *Fighting for Rights*, views citizenship in terms of nationality and rights: "Citizenship establishes a permanent home for some, declares some probationary residents, and fully excludes still others, and citizens alone are entitled to particular rights and subject to particular duties . . . to challenge another's citizenship is to challenge his or her place in the community."[135] Since modern citizenship in democracies has been defined more by a slow, and often conflict-ridden, broadening of rights (from propertied men to all men, free men to slaves, men to women, whites to minorities, majorities to minorities) than an expansion of duties (witness the decline in conscription in industrialized democracies), the rights-oriented conceptualization of citizenship makes a great deal of sense, has provided an opportunity for scholars to document the struggle for and barriers to rights among a wide variety of groups in different regimes, and has served as a rough gauge of just how far states have "progressed" vis-à-vis these groups. When peasants in rural China scrawl on a wall, "We're citizens. Return us our citizenship rights,"[136] we know for certain that the rights-based conception of citizenship has spread very far indeed.

The rights-oriented conceptualization of citizenship (sometimes called "liberal") is difficult to argue with on a normative level—after all, who among us doesn't want more rights?—but, as Morris Janowitz noted more than 25 years ago, "the long-term trend has been to emphasize and elaborate citizen rights without simultaneously clarifying the issues of citizen obligation."[137] This may be an overstatement, since to most citizens it's clear what they do for the government: they pay taxes, obey the law, and, in some cases, serve in the military. Don't these all count as "obligations"? What Janowitz seems to be calling attention to is a "discursive imbalance" between proliferating "rights talk" and relatively muted public debates about exactly how citizen obligations should be manifested if there is already a sense of "paying" for rights in the form of taxes. Does citizenship, like many religions, also involve particular *obligations* toward fellow citizens? Janowitz raises this point by citing a small section of the classic study of the progression of citizenship as the evolutionary expansion of different kinds of rights in Europe, T. H. Marshall's "Class, Citizenship and Social Development":

If citizenship is invoked in the defense of rights, the corresponding duties of citizenship cannot be ignored. Those do not require a man to sacrifice his individual liberty or to submit without question to every demand made by government. But they do require that his acts should be inspired by a lively sense of responsibility towards the welfare of the community.[138]

Marshall does not elaborate on whether this "lively sense" of responsibility requires action or sacrifice, but one senses in this passage that citizenship should not be understood only in terms of the individual (does the citizen vote?, for instance) and his or her relationship to the government (what rights does the individual demand and the state "bestow"?), but also *horizontally* in terms of political and social *practices*: how should citizens treat one another? If, in addition to the awarding of rights, citizenship is also embedded in interactions *between* people, how can progress, or the lack thereof, be gauged?

This issue is also raised by conservative political theorists who otherwise gripe about "excessive" demands for rights (and excessive litigation) among liberals. Walter Berns notes, for example, that citizenship, more than a legal status, is

a sentiment or state of mind, an awareness of sharing an identity with others to whom one is related by nationality, if not by blood, a sense of belonging to a community for which one bears some responsibility.[139]

In this passage Berns, much like Marshall, appears to believe that he is correcting the liberal emphasis on liberal rights. Still, are "sentiments," "awareness," or "senses" of anything sufficient to make a citizen? What exactly constitutes "some responsibility"? Still, the general point made by Bern, Janowitz, and Marshall (and many others concerned about the "democratic deficit" in developed democracies) is a good one. Taken together, they suggest that 1) citizenship has to involve a balance of rights and obligations, in public debates and in public policy, and 2) obligations are not limited to the state but also encompass fellow citizens. To this list we might add that a good gauge of the *quality of citizenship* or the attainment of higher status in a polity is the extent to which citizens fulfill reasonable obligations and treat fellow citizens with a reasonable degree of sympathy, recognition, and respect. Citizenship, notes James Burk, is "whether we enjoy recognition and respect *from our fellow citizens* as *worthy* members of the political community."[140] It is in the sometimes silent nod of respect, the kind word, the gesture of decency, and the helping hand that "citizenship" status can best be discerned and assessed.

This is, admittedly, a tall order, since it requires not only that government grant rights where none existed—something that in itself requires political

struggle—but also that certain actions, either small- or large-scale, take place
between people. Higher political status cannot be said to have been achieved
only when certain benefits or rights are conferred, say, after the Chinese migrant is allowed to send his child to an urban school or if a factory accepts
veterans into the workforce because it has no choice in the matter, but when
other, already established urbanites afford the newcomer some sympathy and
respect. Law and public policy can have powerful effects by incorporating
new groups as citizens in the formal sense (the guest worker gets her pass-
port) or granting new rights and benefits to weaker groups in society who
are already formally citizens (the GI Bill to African-American veterans), but
these have significant limitations in the second, more horizontal dimension
of status.

This is where we have to return to the role of the military. Particularly in
Continental Europe after French revolutionaries, thinking that "war was to be
a total effort, in which all members of the community had a role," showed
the world the power of a conscripted citizen-army,[141] full citizenship status
for males was very closely connected to military service.[142] For those who
already had established "citizenship" in a polity (involving rights and respect), military service has often enhanced, or "turbocharged," their claim to
patriotic status,[143] seen most clearly in the important political role veterans
have played in many countries. Even in the early history of the United States,
where large-scale conscription was fairly limited owing to the traditional
Anglo-Saxon antipathy to standing armies, military service was *conceptually*
connected to the development of male citizenship and nation building:

> Participation in the war effort would be a testament to one's membership in
> the American nation. . . . It would dramatize and publicly signify the political
> contribution of all soldiers—gentry, freeholder, mechanic or pauper—to the war
> which they as citizens had to win in order to build their "more perfect union."
> The result would be to bind citizens as solders more tightly to the regime, and
> its fate to their actions as one nation.[144]

This ideal, to be sure, was never achieved: provisions for bounties for
substitutes ensured that most regular soldiers came from the lower classes.[145]
But the principle remained: citizenship, or least "community recognition
of who you are, where you belong, what is expected of you, and what you
can expect in return,"[146] could be *activated* and *proven*, and social respect
could possibly be attained, *if* men demonstrated courage, and sacrifice, and
comported themselves with honor in difficult circumstances—all traits that
came under the more general rubric of "patriotism." In other words, for those
on the margins of society, patriotic behavior could trump, or help offset,
more fixed boundaries, such as sex, class, ethnicity, or age.[147] Despite its

historical significance, the role of martial-based claims to citizenship status has received far less attention in the social sciences than rights or law-based approaches. When it has been considered, it has often been in a critical light, as either concealed or overt nativism, jingoism, a barrier to those who were not allowed to serve (women and the disabled, for instance), or the assertion of hyper-masculine ideals and warmongering.[148] This sort of critique, notes Linda Colley in the British case, has prompted more scholarship of dissenting voices during wartime at the expense of "the other, apparently more conventional voices of those far greater numbers of Britons who . . . supported these successive war efforts [against France in the 18th century]." Such voices were "much more than visceral chauvinism, or simple-minded deference, or blinkered conservatism."[149]

In contrast to these sorts of critiques, minorities and other politically or socially marginalized groups have accepted, or perhaps tolerated, the exchange, or "cashing in," of patriotic military service for more rights, appreciation, and respect in society. Military service has led to more than just the conferring of formal rights upon veterans; in some cases, it has, over time and after political struggle, led to more equitable treatment. "War," notes American historian Lucy Salyer, "has often been critical to nation building and particularly to the expansion of civil and political membership,"[150] and Rogers Smith points out that major wars (the Revolutionary War, the Civil War, WWI, and WWII) produced the most liberal and inclusive citizenship policies.[151] It is surely not a coincidence that those who opposed welfare for the masses *also* opposed military training for them, warning that "he who serves the state with his life has also a claim on it for his support."[152] Take as an example the case of Japanese-Americans between WWII and the 1950s. During WWI, the government offered naturalization to any alien who served in the armed forces during the war. This statute, however, clashed with those that denied citizenship for Asians on the basis of race, thus pitting two concepts of political membership against each other: martial and racial. During the 1920s, when nativism peaked, the racial conception was dominant, despite the war-born assertiveness of Asian veterans who argued that their wartime patriotism placed upon the government and society a moral obligation to treat them with greater respect. In 1935, however, Congress, under pressure from the American Legion (which argued that "these Japanese boys are veterans just like the rest of us"), passed the Nye-Lea Act, which awarded citizenship (in the formal sense) to Asian veterans of that war. "The powerful appeal of militaristic patriotism," Salyer notes, "provided an unexpected opening for Asians who fought in the world war and supplied the only successful argument for their naturalization before the racial prerequisite for citizenship was repealed in 1952."[153] Formal citizenship, however, did not prevent the interning of

Japanese-Americans during WWII, but that war, like the first, provided yet another opportunity to demonstrate loyalty and courage, which was publicly acknowledged by President Harry Truman, a veteran himself. By the early 1950s, thanks in large part to the battlefield successes of Japanese-American units in Europe (to which Japanese-American leaders repeatedly called attention), all racial barriers to citizenship fell.[154]

The cases of African-Americans in the United States and the impact of conscription in Japan and Russia also demonstrate the important, and arguably indispensable, role military service (with its attendant hardships, sacrifices, and long-term commitment of resources) has played in improving the status of weaker groups, fighting discrimination, and nation building in democratic and non-democratic states. In the United States, African-American men, whose social status was not altogether dissimilar to poor veterans from Northwest China, have long sought to perform military service to demonstrate their patriotism and masculine worthiness as citizens.[155] As many as 5,000 African-Americans fought against the British to gain their freedom, "or, if free, to enhance their standing in the community."[156] Many Northern blacks and former slaves served with great courage during the Civil War (for many, proving their manhood was one of the key motivations to serve, in addition to rights and equality[157]), impressing many of their white officers who previously doubted their patriotism, courage, and masculinity. After the war, when racism and orchestrated attacks against blacks (both physical and in "scientific theories" of racial inferiority) grew in scale and intensity, "some of the greatest defenders of black soldiers were their former commanders," even though many of them "yielded all or in part to [racist] public sentiment" and found it quite easy to part ways with them after the war.[158] Among a small group of Northerners, racism was merely "softened" by blacks' wartime patriotism.[159] Even so, it became "an article of faith" among blacks that "military service during wartime represented a path toward freedom and greater postwar opportunity."[160] Service often led to a much stronger sense of identity, demands for "full citizenship," organization, and less willingness to tolerate abuse.[161] Not all agreed with such sentiments: in the immediate post-war years, returning veterans from WWII suffered "endless bouts of discrimination"; many were harassed, beaten, and murdered by white civilians and police authorities, who feared their claims to patriotism would result in higher political and social status.[162] Still, military service in WWII and the beginning of the Cold War (veterans repeatedly called attention to the hypocrisy of promoting democracy and anti-Communism abroad and the racism they encountered upon their return) finally spurred President Truman's decision to integrate African-Americans into the military (1947). In the late 1940s, the military did not fully enforce Truman's order, but with the sudden onset of the Korean War and its attendant manpower demands for combat units, the military finally enforced the 1947 decision on a much wider scale. Today, the U.S. military has been at the "forefront" of the effort to end the stigma attached to race. Blacks and other minorities enlist in large numbers, and it is one of the few institutions in American society where large numbers of minorities (male and female) routinely command whites without significant controversy.[163] It is, of course, impossible to know what would have happened had these wars not occurred, and there is a lively but still generally inconclusive debate about whether and under what conditions minorities' service in the military alongside whites improves the racial "attitudes" of whites, but it would not be that far-fetched to imagine that the state of race relations would be far worse than it is today.

This relationship between war, patriotism, and political and social status is not only relevant in democracies, which place a premium, if not in practice then at least in rhetoric, on rights issues. In Meiji Japan, for example, the 1873 law requiring military service of young men led to the conferring of rights as well, since a "blood tax" on people could not be demanded in the absence of a constitutional system. By 1890, Roger Hackett argues, "the obligation of military service for qualified males was accompanied by the right to vote for males over twenty-five who met certain property qualifications," but over time the room for exemptions narrowed and the franchise broadened. National military service also reduced social stratification (according to a 1921 study, peasants and the "laboring classes" looked up to veterans because of their rigorous military training and more worldly experiences) and "heightened feelings of identification with the state" (in light of WWII, how one feels about this identification is a separate issue).[164] Since discharged soldiers also served in the reserves, the 1911 comment of Tanaka Gi'ichi (a veteran of the Sino-Japanese War, one of the founders of the Imperial Military Reserve Association, and prime minister in the late 1920s) that "all citizens are soldiers" reflected a very different conceptualization of civil–military relations.[165] During the 1930s, organized veterans played a key role in the cultivation of patriotism and were involved in a wide range of community services in villages and towns (including providing aid to families of men on active duty and the poor).[166] Russia in the late czarist and early Soviet periods demonstrates this point as well. There, research by Joshua Sanborn shows, military officials in the army high command, worried about the security of their country, argued for a very broad extension "of military service and citizenship" by means of the Universal Military Service Law (passed in the 1870s). As late as 1894, military officials explicitly argued for the "citizen-building role of the military," since few institutions besides the military would be able to weaken "tribal differences" among Russians.[167] It was also the military, not urban intellectual elites, which argued for a conception of citizenship in which people can and should expect something in return from the state for their military service. Even though the autocracy fell not long after this, the Bolsheviks (the model party for the Chinese Communists and Nationalists), building on this military conception of citizenship, generated a "discourse that finally incorporated the idea that soldiers acquired rights when they performed their national duty." This conception, Sanborn suggests, was in part a response to a "dialogue between military officials and conscripts" that resulted in new expectations: soldiers wanted the state to take care of their families while they were away, "respect" their contributions, and grant them privileges in relation to their "nonwarrior fellow citizens."[168] The Bolsheviks succeeded in capturing power and maintaining it against significant odds in the 1920s largely due to the "consensus" it reached with young men about the "duties and rights" of the state and citizen "in relationship to military service."[169] Ultimately, however, the *military-led* creation of the new identity of "national citizen"—a product more of wars than revolutions and of officers more than humanist intellectuals—undermined both the czarist and Bolshevik regimes, since it both contested the notion of "subject" and class-based political identity.[170]

China, it turns out, was substantially different in this respect. We will see that most Chinese veterans, much like many marginalized and poor Asian-American, African-American, and Russian veterans, experienced a heightened sense of status after their service: as former fighters they expected at least equal or better treatment because they served. In the Chinese case, however, these expectations have not yet been met (even remotely in many cases). It is the case that some veterans enjoyed more "rights" than other members of society, were provided with better employment opportunities, and were designated as "heroes" in government propaganda. But, to the extent that their position in society can also be gauged by the quality and content of interactions between people—the respectful nod and gesture, the pat on the back—most Chinese veterans did not enjoy a boost in status. Respectful treatment, particularly by elites, was not forthcoming despite the facts that both of China's major political parties modeled themselves, as well as their militaries, on the nation-states of Continental Europe, Japan, and the Soviet Union, China fought several foreign wars, and veterans were "red" in terms of revolutionary credentials.[171] Even when veterans managed to secure a respectable position in the economy, it was mostly because of skills and education acquired before their military service; their status as *veterans* did not provide much of a boost to their prospects. Often the opposite was the case.

These problems with citizenship and military service have been noted before. Reformers in the late 19th century, concerned about China's weakness vis-à-vis the West, repeatedly called attention to deficits in the conception of citizenship and patriotism, particularly in the realm of taxes and military service; one early Chinese word for "citizen" *guomin,* or "nationals"—suggested that a key problem was a failure to identify with the state, while another word, *shimin* ("city person"), explicitly denies citizenship status to peasants. Failure to appreciate military service and martial values (unless they were very closely linked to civil virtues) was seen as another, but unconnected, problem.[172] However, upon closer inspection, few of these circumstances were unique to China. Identification with the local more than the national has been problematic in many countries, including the United States prior to the Civil War and in France as late as the 1880s, where the army was increasingly considered "a school in which French youth acquired basic principles of citizenship"[173] and "an agency for acculturation . . . as potent in its way as the schools."[174] Russia, much like China, was an agrarian society with relatively low levels of literacy and high social stratification; until the 19th century, the status of the land forces was quite low in Great Britain. Its veterans, who came from the lower classes, were despised.[175]

What best explains China's continued weakness in this respect is the exceptionally limited role the military has played as an institution that, in many other contexts, made more significant contributions to nation- and state-building and as an experience that elevated the status of marginalized groups in society by highlighting "classical" masculine virtues. Educated urban elites in China, unlike critical masses of elites in Japan, Korea, Russia, the United States, or France (among others), still do not show much support for the notion of martial citizenship, a critical mechanism by which veterans from lower-status groups have raised their position in society to the benefit of their class, ethnicity, or race. In part, this is because veterans in China have not been able to organize and form alliances; in other countries, *cross-class* veterans organizations have promoted the legitimacy of exchanging military service for higher status and respect, as well as a civil religion centered on notions of sacrifice. In China, in contrast, conceptions of citizenship have been dominated by such civilians as students, intellectuals, editors, and journalists, who, according to Robert Culp, "sought to associate themselves with the ideal of the active citizen, which was produced through the articulation of discourses of political participation, social order, and national membership, *as a way to claim social privilege and political agency*";[176] citizenship did not imply a recognition of the status, rights, and "deservedness" of the lower classes. The other element is the absence of any connection in China between military service and positive *masculine* values. In the West, as well as in Japan, South Korea, and Russia, the "glue" that connected military service to worthiness as patriots and full-fledged citizens was that military service proved that one was a good or "real" man: brave, willing to sacrifice, and tough. Even though the Chinese government expended considerable resources in mimicking the aesthetic ideal of bold and aggressive masculinity in its art (statues, memorials, paintings), its educated elites as well as the business class, both of whom rarely serve in the military, never shared this conception of manliness; it did not constitute a basis for "fellow feeling." One important result of this is that veterans who otherwise might have benefited from educated elites' recognition of the value of their service (not only in rhetorical forms), or at least their masculine qualities, remain subject to multiple forms of discrimination in policy and in their everyday treatment in society. The lack of support or respect for veterans is also manifested in the lack of respect and support for peasants, the class that "supplies" most of them: if veterans were better respected, I suggest, peasants would be, too—just as the recognition of Japanese-American veterans' sacrifices in WWII contributed to the improvement of their status and reputation in American society. The lack of respect for the military, I suggest, helps explain one of China's most "durable" and significant inequalities—the gap between town and country.

LEGITIMACY

By some criteria, it would seem that veterans in China were one of the primary beneficiary groups of the Communist Revolution. Many PLA veterans assumed posts in the new state administration. Veterans also had high-level political patronage—Zhou Enlai served as a director of the National Veterans Committee, which had branches all the way down to local governments. The Ministry of Interior and two units within the Civil Affairs bureaucracy were specifically tasked with handling veterans' most pressing problems: resettlement and disability.[177] The State Council, China's "cabinet," produced thousands of policy directives, decisions, clarifications, and regulations on veteran affairs when it became clear that there were problems at lower levels. It also dispatched investigation teams to get to the source of problems that were becoming intractable. At the symbolic level, veterans would seem to have been the beneficiaries of a "halo effect" emanating from rituals surrounding Army Day (August 1) and Spring Festival, when schoolchildren, state officials, and representatives from various organizations fanned out to help military families (*junshu*) and relatives of revolutionary martyrs (*lieshu*)—and the campaign to canonize military figures such as Lei Feng in the early 1960s. Now there is even a military MTV channel that often features veterans! This sort of treatment stands out even more when one considers the neglect of veterans under the Nationalists and the fate of various regime enemies throughout the Maoist years: millions were killed, sent to labor reform camps, and persecuted in countless other ways. It would seem, then, that the PRC government fulfilled its part of a political "bargain" that has become increasingly common in nation-states: in return for their service (whether voluntary or conscripted), veterans (and the families of soldiers) have been awarded certain benefits in the post-war period, whether material (land, education, health care) or symbolic. By both a comparative measure of justice (how have groups fared vis-à-vis other groups?) and a "distributive" one (are rewards commensurate with the contribution?), veterans and military families appear to have fared well. By most accounts that divvy up how various groups fared under the CCP (and other authoritarian regimes), veterans and military personnel are generally considered among the "winners."

This study, however, is less concerned with any actual benefits that veterans' and military families may have received from the state (for reasons that will be discussed shortly) than with the actual treatment many received in everyday interactions with officials and ordinary members of society and what this treatment can tell us about the larger questions in Chinese politics. I assume that it makes a very big difference *how* political gifts are awarded: money thrown on the floor has the same monetary value as money handed over in a nice envelope, but its meaning has changed in the gesture. In the context of veterans, I argue that these sorts of interactions and people's comments on them can serve as a very useful proxy for gauging the legitimacy of the wars, causes, and states for which they fought or served. As Suzanne Mettler suggests in her study of the GI Bill in the United States, everyday encounters between beneficiaries and the state "may tell them [the former] a great deal about whether government is legitimate, how well it functions, how people like them are regarded in the political community, what their rights are, and what their obligations are."[178] If we are to believe the accounts of some prominent Chinese intellectuals, the CCP was *highly* legitimate, at least until 1957.[179] If this was the case, however, why would veterans of the revolution be subject to frequent discrimination and abuse, and why would they write impassioned letters to the National People's Congress about their poor treatment? Is it possible that many state officials, including those who were highly educated, did not view veterans as legitimate and worthy recipients of benefits—that they did not *deserve* them? If this was the case, their value would be significantly reduced; a sense of justice is unlikely to result from a material benefit when *others* (fellow workers, villages, family members, neighbors) do not view the granting of it as legitimate in the first place. This assessment of the legitimacy of the reward or benefit, or the extent of worth or "deservedness," I argue, reflects a still larger, and politically far more consequential, evaluation of the legitimacy of the *cause* veterans (and military families) represent. When people disparage veterans and military families'

[handwritten margin notes: "Assumption"; "mistreating veterans is to question the legitimacy of the cause?"]

deservedness, they are, in effect, indirectly commenting on the legitimacy and rightness of the cause they represent.

Comparative historical research on veteran politics suggests that much can be gained by looking at issues of state legitimacy from the perspective of veterans in their communities and interactions with multiple levels of the state (even in China, the state is not monolithic).[180] Deborah Cohen, in *The War Come Home: Disabled Veterans in Britain and Germany, 1914–1939*, found that even though German war disabled received far better material benefits than their British counterparts—German employers, for example, were forced to hire them, while their British counterparts were only encouraged to—they still became alienated from the state that granted these benefits and defected in large numbers to the Nazis; British veterans, who suffered because of a tight-fisted British treasury, protested against the state in the early 1920s but otherwise did not participate in many anti-state activities. The main reasons for this, Cohen suggests, were political and social. In Germany, the state, fearing rampant fraud, monopolized welfare and did not allow private charities to help veterans; in Britain, the government encouraged civil society to contribute. As a result, in Germany society "disengaged" from veterans, who, in turn, turned their anger against civilians for forsaking them and against the state for the small injustices they experienced dealing with benefit claims. They found succor in the rhetoric of sacrifice, elaborate rituals, and symbols proffered by the Nazis, who did *not* increase budget allocation to disabled veterans. In Great Britain, in contrast, disabled veterans felt a much stronger embrace by society, and this compensated for miserly benefits.[181] In other words, the concept of "treatment" appears to be equally proportioned between material benefits (the disabled still need crutches) and the *experiences* veterans have when interacting with members of society and state officials. The political consequences of many negative experiences, even if the benefits are generous both in absolute numbers and in comparison to other groups, could be far-reaching. As noted earlier, whether veterans are disaffected or successfully integrated into post-war regimes shapes the very nature of the state (the impact of the Whiskey Rebellion, for instance) and the economy (the post-war boom in the United States spurred in part by the successful integration of veterans through the GI Bill).

Cohen's comparative study is illuminating, particularly in its emphasis on the need to examine veterans' interactions with both the state and society. There could be, however, other explanations for the differences between German and British veterans. Germany, not Britain, lost the war, so its veterans represented defeat and a discredited state, and all the propaganda about wartime heroism could not change that. As noted by historian Morton Sosna, "obviously, it matters greatly whether a conflict ends in victory or defeat, or is inconclusive."[182]

The state provided resources, but society did not show much appreciation because there was not much to appreciate; the illegitimacy of the war was reflected back on the way veterans were treated. The British were part of the willing coalition of WWI, and this victory contributed to a more positive treatment of veterans. Some preliminary research on German and Japanese veterans—representatives of defeated powers in WWII—also shows how their poor treatment resulted from the fact that they symbolized defeat and that the regime lacked legitimacy.[183] In other words, how society assesses the legitimacy of a conflict (or, in the case of China, conflict*s*) will have a substantial impact on veterans' interactions with those around them.

Of the three countries mentioned above, the PRC would appear to least resemble Germany and Japan, simply because its wars are officially considered victories, not humiliating defeats, the causes for which it fought generally legitimate, especially anti-imperialism, and three important outcomes—stability, sovereignty, and greater international prestige—highly desirable. If the comparative record is any guide, PRC veterans should have been treated more along the lines of their British, not German, counterparts—but this frequently was not the case, as we will see. To be sure, the PRC's record is not one of unmitigated failure: the government was very successful in integrating veterans in terms of making sure they did not pose a dire threat to the party, as was the case in interwar Germany (where most of the leaders of the paramilitary organizations that helped bring down Weimer were former frontline officers[184]), or rove the countryside in bandit organizations, as was the case earlier in the century and during several dynasties.[185] However, the CCP's concern for veterans (or rather, fear of them) did not go much beyond the interest in regime survival. As a result of this conception, Chinese veterans frequently experienced poor treatment, and their comments (to the press, to investigators, in letters to each other and other officials) revealed widespread discontent with their status in the state and society.

Why? Many Chinese veterans, I will argue, were victimized both by the virulently contested legitimacy of the causes for which they served and fought and by the very nature of the Communist Revolution. First, most veterans in China were peasants. To them, it was only fair that, having united the country after years of internal and foreign strife, they should be able to choose their place of residence. Usually, this meant moving to a city, something neither urbanites nor policymakers wanted. Second, veterans wanted an income equal to or more than those who did not serve, but given their background, physical problems, and lack of consensus about the extent to which they were worthy of higher status, this was also difficult to attain. Finally, there is history—in particular, the basic fact that the Chinese Communist revolution and its wars (against Japan and the Nationalists) took a great deal of time.

Unlike the relatively brief period of 4–6 years of WWI and WWII, it took 28 years for the CCP to secure victory. What this meant, in practice, was that, in addition to military veterans, millions of other people could claim to have "participated" in the revolution from 1921 to 1949 or "socialist construction" (after 1949) in one capacity or another; the revolution, as it were, had to have very many cooks because the pot simmered for so long. As a result, those who wrote articles, worked underground, left an arranged marriage, took a couple of shots at the Japanese army while serving in a militia, or beat up a landlord during land reform were all praised for having made glorious contributions to the cause, and they made it a point to say so. Naturally, they also wondered why veterans (and military families) should get the benefits they did. Veterans' legitimacy as patriotic "agents of memory" of the successful revolution was thus heavily diluted by the flood of rhetoric that poured forth from state propaganda that praised millions of others and legitimized their claims; unlike the USSR after WWII, there was no consensus that "fighting for the community was more important than other activities and that it entitled those who engaged in the task of soldiering to special treatment."[186] Thanks to successful military education, many veterans did gain a much stronger sense of patriotic identity because of their participation in the People's Liberation Army, but for many educated Chinese—whose Confucian biases against military service have already been mentioned—this contribution was seen as no more patriotic than joining a union or penning an article. Because veterans lacked a grassroots organization to support their version of what counted as a truly worthy patriotic sacrifice until the pre–Cultural Revolution years, "glory" was sliced and diced into millions of little pieces and distributed widely, leaving many veterans vulnerable to political attacks against their status. This phenomenon is not unusual—some veterans in the United States after WWII were also frustrated by the extent to which civilians claimed a share of victory—but in China, because the revolution was so long and so many veterans were poor and not very educated, there were that many more people who had far greater "cultural capital" who could, and did, claim authorship of its victorious narrative.

SOURCES AND METHODOLOGY

This study argues that a very useful way to understand the politics of patriotism, citizenship, and legitimacy is to zero in on localized, everyday interactions between veterans and the state and ordinary citizens. This is not to deny that formal rules (about benefits, status, political worthiness, rights) are important or that the "discourses" surrounding the meaning of patriotism *legitimacy of a cause* [handwritten annotation]

among elites are not important, but to state that the more meaningful and telling indicators of these concepts often occur well beyond the reach of more mainstream sources. In my view, the heart of patriotism can be better gauged by looking at how people react when disabled veterans need some time off from work to go to a hospital, for instance, than the writings of intellectuals *about* patriotism or China's place in world politics. We can best understand the legitimacy of a cause by examining how a representative of that cause is treated in more mundane circumstances. We can grasp how military service affected political and social status by studying the reactions of people to those who claimed higher status and political worthiness because they served in the military. For the purposes of understanding the construction of national "narratives" of history and historical memory, or even the content of patriotic education in schools, elite sources, open or confidential, might suffice; there have been a number of interesting studies relying on this type of evidence. But for the more ordinary sort of interactions that, taken together, constitute the *politics* of patriotism, citizenship, and legitimacy, we need to look elsewhere—to the locales where people actually live their lives surrounded by others who are in a position to assess their "patriotic worthiness" and the extent to which they deserve preferential treatment or reward for "services rendered."

Thanks to China's "reform and opening up" policy, we now have access to sources that allow us to burrow quite deeply into this sort of conceptual terrain: archives. Since the mid-1980s or so, Chinese archives covering the late imperial, Republican, and Communist periods have slowly opened up to scholars, and the result has been a series of small and large tremors across both the social sciences and, to a greater extent, history. Most archival sources were never intended for public consumption and cover all sorts of mundane official and social affairs that otherwise would not merit publication. Already, scholars have used this material to challenge the conventional wisdom about the role of law and lawyers in China,[187] the meaning and regulation of homosexuality and polyandry,[188] the impact of the Marriage Law of 1950,[189] the origins of the work unit system and the evolution of state-owned enterprises,[190] the role of labor during the Cultural Revolution and worker militias,[191] campaigns against counterrevolutionaries in the 1950s,[192] and the status of teachers,[193] among others. Still, this research is the tip of the iceberg when considering the vast number of archives in China (every county government has one, as do all cities) and the possibility of new knowledge that can be gained from them. As much as the generation of "theory" has become the proverbial pot at the end of the rainbow for many disciplines (despite the disappointingly few cases of *successful* predictions, which is supposed to be a defining attribute of "theory"), there is still much to be said for the (question-driven) discovery of new facts and data, particularly in a field as "new" (in terms of sources that are becoming available) as Chinese politics, sociology, and history. We are still immature as a field in terms of basic knowledge of key events: what we think we know now about key events in the PRC—land reform, elite politics, the Great Leap Forward, the origins of township and village enterprises, for example—will almost certainly undergo revision the more scholars plunge into archives.

The bulk of this study, covering the years 1949–2007, is based on archival findings from several locations (Shanghai, Beijing, Qingpu, Shandong, Taiwan, and Israel for the comparisons on disability in Chapter 6); newspaper articles; county, city, and district gazetteers (*xian*, *shi*, and *qu zhi*); and other "open" sources about veterans, such as a collection of State Council documents concerning veterans published in the early 1980s. Shanghai is a key industrial city that attracted both veterans and intellectuals, its residents were exposed to a great deal of state propaganda and "patriotic sentiments," and because of its status it was also copied on thousands of reports concerning veterans within its own jurisdiction as well as many national-level reports circulated by the State Council. Nonetheless, a study based entirely on Shanghai sources, no matter how revealing, would obviously not be remotely generalizable. To broaden my perspective, I spent a good deal of time in Qingpu, which in 2007 was roughly an hour from Shanghai by car but in the 1950s and 1960s was still quite rural, albeit still connected to Shanghai thanks to convenient water transportation. Both Shanghai and Qingpu, however, are in East China. Even more problematically, most veterans (from the 1940s and more contemporarily) hailed from *northern* provinces, particularly Shandong, Henan, Anhui, and Shanxi. Did veterans in northern provinces, particularly those that had a longer history of serving as the recruiting pool of the PLA *and* which had CCP "base areas" prior to 1949, experience a very cool reception as well?

To try to find out, colleagues at the Shanghai Academy of Social Sciences and I wrote to four archives—Shandong, Anhui, Jiangxi, and Shanxi—but received a positive answer only from Shandong (see Chapter 8 for why this was the case). Expecting to find that Shandong veterans would be treated better than their Shanghai counterparts, I was surprised when the limited number of materials I was allowed to peruse suggested that very many of them experienced similar treatment. Still, because of the limited geographic scope of this work (I, for one, would be very interested in a large study comparing two provinces, counties, or even townships, since there were probably important local variations) and the often-vague language in many documents (which, in most cases, do not allow us to differentiate between veterans of different wars), this study should be seen as a "first cut" at a very interesting and important population. There are, after all, dozens of books about veterans in the United States and Europe, all of which cover different ground. Certainly there is much room to expand this topic into other disciplines, regions (minority veterans), or gender. Much will depend on whether China will allow greater access to written sources and unsupervised interviews with its veterans from different wars.

In each archive I visited, I tried to draw from as wide a range of sources as possible. By virtue of its administrative jurisdiction over veteran resettlement, Civil Affairs offices processed most of the paperwork concerning veteran issues or were furnished reports compiled by other agencies. These reports covered matters ranging from employment, strikes, suicides, political problems, and requests for disability payments to criminal activities involving veterans. Some of these were "summaries" of a year or six months' worth of work (*zongjie baogao*) that were often filled with "bureaucratese" (or "empty talk," as the Chinese say), while others were special investigation reports (*diaocha baogao*) that were ordered by the State Council in response to reports of widespread problems. The latter sources were particularly useful because they included interviews with veterans and local officials, each of whom reported their side of the story. In addition to Civil Affairs' records, I also gathered materials from the bureaucracies in charge of labor issues, health, commerce, housing, local veterans committees, and ad hoc committees (to support the Korean War, for example). Ideally, I would have liked to complement these materials with those from the People's Liberation Army, the archives of the central government, and oral histories, but the former two are still inaccessible to most foreign scholars and the latter too sensitive during a period of widespread veteran protest. I would have also liked to be able to construct a standardized comparison of veteran benefits in China to those in other countries. To the best of my knowledge, there is no officially recognized international standard or ranking of these benefits (unlike poverty, education, unemployment, gender equality, etc.) or those provided to military families, perhaps because of constantly changing laws and regulations over time and region. In theory, one could compare state budget allocations, but this does not necessarily reflect what veterans and military families actually receive. In China, the use of more quantitative measures is even more problematic. As we will see, a very large percentage of center-allocated funds were never spent by provincial and county authorities, many benefits were selectively enforced at the local level but then exaggerated to emphasize success (for instance, Civil Affairs might report that 90 percent of veterans were "resettled" but not that a week later, quite a few left their jobs), and the figures in documents were often missing numbers and, in any case, are very difficult to confirm.

THE ORDER OF THINGS

In contrast to many studies of the PRC that are organized either chronologically or around the various political campaigns that punctuated the period,
this work studies veterans' status in politics and society through the prism of
their experiences after their discharge from the military; I try, as far as possible given the limitations of sources, to step into their shoes to see what they
saw of the political and social world around them. To be sure, some of these
experiences were shaped by political campaigns—such as the "Resist America, Support Korea" campaign, the Three Antis (targeting corruption), and the
Cultural Revolution—but because most veterans had good class status in the
regime, they were less affected than more vulnerable groups, such as intellectuals, whose experiences are the most well known to Western readers (thanks
to hundreds of memoirs they have written in the last 30 years). Rather than
campaigns, veterans were most affected by a host of other issues. State policies could determine where they worked and lived; other citizens could determine the extent to which they felt appreciated; speaking with other veterans
could embolden them to take action against those who discriminated against
them; women could determine their future as successful men in Chinese
society. Few of these topics would be a good fit for the usual chronology.[194]
Thus, Chapter 2 deals with the main policy that shaped the post-war veteran
experience and sense of their place in politics: the state's demand that they
return to the countryside after their discharge. How did veterans react to this
policy, given the wide differential between city and countryside in China?
Chapter 3 examines veterans' complicated identities, focusing in particular
on the clash between heightened expectations (raised by military service that
was praised as patriotic and worthy of support, respect, and appreciation) and
the lack of consensus over their contribution and value to society. Chapter 4
analyzes veterans' experiences in the workforce (in factories, mines, fields),
and Chapter 5 takes a look at the interactions between veterans (and military
families) and the state agencies responsible for their discharge and job placement. In Chapter 6, I turn to the relationship between politics, health, sex,
and marriage; many veterans returned from service with poor health, and
quite a few had not yet married. They placed many "demands" on budgets,
administration, and society's tolerance for those who had "special needs," to
use contemporary lingo. Chapter 7 explores the relationship between military
families (and, to a lesser extent, families of revolutionary martyrs) and the
state and ordinary people. Were they respected? What happened to them
when their sons or husbands were in the military? In Chapter 8, I take a close
look at the status of veterans after the 1978 reforms and the problematic 1979
war against Vietnam. Veterans have led, and have been involved in, numer-

ous protests from the late 1970s until today. Why is this? Throughout the text, I draw upon a wide range of comparative literature on veterans in order to see how Chinese veterans fared in relation to their counterparts around the globe at different historical junctures and to try to tease out those factors that appear to have made a significant difference in how they were treated. In the background are the questions I have highlighted in the introduction: Under what circumstances did veterans receive more or less credit for their contributions to the state (usually described as patriotic)? How did officials and citizens treat veterans, beyond rhetorical flourishes? How did military service affect social status? To what extent was state discourse about the meaning of patriotism accepted by ordinary people? Answering these questions does not provide a "neat" model of politics. Veterans' experiences were complex, as were citizens' reactions to them; some policies affecting them changed, and others did not. Capturing these experiences and reactions, providing a reasonably plausible explanation for them, and relating these to large themes in politics and the comparative literature are the main goals of this study.

NOTES

1. For this argument, see Gregory Kasza, *One World of Welfare: Japan in Comparative Perspective* (Ithaca: Cornell University Press, 2006), 51.
2. J. C. Mann, "The Settlement of Veterans in the Roman Empire," 15.
3. William Hogeland, *The Whiskey Rebellion*, 7–8.
4. Susan Browne, "War-Making and U.S. State Formation," 234, 248.
5. Ibid., 234.
6. Ibid., 232–33.
7. Richard Bensel, "Politics Is Thicker than Blood," 257.
8. Theda Skocpol, *Protecting Soldiers and Mothers*.
9. Suzanne Mettler, *Soldiers to Citizens: The G.I. Bill and the Making of the Greatest Generation*.
10. Jennifer Brooks, *Defining the Peace*: *World War II, Veterans, Race and the Remaking of the Southern Political Tradition*, 7; Neil McMillen, "How Mississippi's Black Veterans Remember World War II," 110.
11. Doris Zames Fleischer and Frieda Zames, *The Disability Rights Movement*, 176.
12. Forrest McDonald, "The Relation of the French Peasant Veterans of the American Revolution to the Fall of Feudalism in France, 1789–1792," 344–47.
13. Mark van Ells, *To Hear Only Thunder Again*, 6; Stephen Ward, "Introduction," in James Diehl and Stephen Ward (eds.) *The War Generation*: *Veterans of the First World War*, 3.
14. Ernest Doblin and Claire Pohly, "The Social Composition of the Nazi Leadership," 46; Deborah Cohen, *The War Come Home: Disabled Veterans in Britain*

and Germany, 1914–1939, 63. In contrast, after WWII, former Wehrmacht officers, believing that "comradeship would provide the model for a democratic Germany," were key players in the rise of stable representative democracy. Most officers were content to lobby for pensions and other forms of recognition. See Jay Lockenour, *Soldiers as Citizens,* 10.

15. Mabel Berezin, *Making the Fascist Self,* 76.

16. Amir Weiner, *Making Sense of War,* 7.

17. Blaine Harden, "Reservists a Crucial Factor in Effort against Milosevic," *New York Times,* July 9, 1999.

18. See his "In Lieu of the Levée en masse: Mass Mobilization in Vietnam," 219–20.

19. Rosemary Preston, "Integrating Fighters after War," 459.

20. F. F. Liu, *A Military History of China, 1924–1949,* 7.

21. Two Canadian scholars call demobilization of large armies "one of the most ignored" topics among social scientists. See Desmond Morton and Glenn Wright, *Winning the Second Battle: Canadian Veterans and the Return to Civilian Life, 1915–1930,* viii.

22. I conducted a search on JSTOR, looking for articles with *veteran, military service,* and *servicemen* in their titles and *veteran politics* as a keyword anywhere in them. *The American Political Science Review,* in its history of more than 100 years, includes fewer than 10 articles expressly devoted to veterans' politics. *Comparative Politics* has none.

23. Hans van de Ven notes that "how war has shaped China is not yet at all clear," even though "it is plain that China's history has in fact been at least as violent as Europe's." See "War in the Making of Modern China," *Modern Asian Studies,* 737.

24. See Gordon White, "The Politics of Demobilized Soldiers from Liberation to the Cultural Revolution," 187–213; Yitzhak Shichor, "Demobilization: The Dialectics of PLA Troop Reduction," 336–59. There have been book chapters by June Dreyer, John Dixon, and Maryanne Kivlehan-Wise, and parts of chapters on the PLA (John Gittings, *The Role of the Chinese Army*).

25. Paul Camacho and Paul Atwood, "A Review of the Literature on Veterans Published in *Armed Forces and Society,* 1974–2006," 351; Camacho, "Veterans and Veterans' Issues," (same volume), 314.

26. Charles Tilly, the best-known proponent of the critical role of war making in state making, does not look at what happens after war. Linda Colley, who places war and military service at the very forefront of her study of British patriotism, mentions in passing that 200,000 soldiers were demobilized after the Seven Years' War, most of whom were poor and "some of them mutilated," but has nothing to say about what happened to them after their discharge. See *Britons: Forging the Nation, 1707–1837,* 101.

27. Maris Vinovskis, "Have Social Historians Lost the Civil War?" 1–2, 11, 29.

28. Modell and Haggerty, "The Social Impact of War," 205.

29. Gregory Kasza, "War and Comparative Politics," 355–73.

30. Kasza, *One World of Welfare,* 51.

31. John A. Lynn, "The Embattled Future of Academic Military History," 780–81.

32. Elise Wirtshafter, "Social Misfits: Veterans and Soldiers Families in Servile Russia," 216.

33. David Segal, "Citizenship and Military Service," 186; Morris Janowitz, "Observations on the Sociology of Citizenship," 6; Miguel Centeno, *Blood and Debt: War and the Nation-State in Latin America*, 10.

34. James Marten, "Exempt from the Ordinary Rules of Life," *Civil War History*, 59.

35. Paul Dickson and Thomas Allen call the Bonus March "a major historical event and a catalyst for social change" that has been "lost in the margins of history." See *The Bonus Army: An American Epic*, 7.

36. Janowitz, "Military Institutions and Citizenship in Western Societies," 185–204.

37. On these new memorials, see Kirk Denton, "Museums, Memorial Sites and Exhibitionary Culture in the People's Republic of China," 565–86. In Western sources, this newfound patriotism is usually called "rising *nationalism*," even though this term (*minzu zhuyi*) is infrequently invoked in the PRC.

38. Weiner, *Making Sense of War,* Chapter 1.

39. See Mark P. Bradley, "Contests of Memory," in Hue-Tam Ho Tai (ed.), *The Country of Memory,* 196–202, 208–12; Hue-Tam Ho Tai, "Faces of Remembering and Forgetting," in the same volume, 183–85.

40. David Onkst, "First a Negro . . . Incidentally a Veteran," 517–43.

41. Here I am in basic agreement with Arthur Waldron, whose study of the post–Cultural Revolution rehabilitation of WWII military hero Zhang Zizhong led him to wonder "to what extent such concepts [patriotism and nationhood]—at least in a form available to political exploitation—really exist at all." He notes that Chinese patriotism is not really about a *patria* at all—there is no word that corresponds to it in classical Chinese—but, rather, about the celebration of "a kind of character, and of death in which the full human potential for moral meaning is attained." This sense is "very different from the modern Western one that China today seeks to import." See "China's New Remembering of WWII: The Case of Zhang Zizhong," 947, 960, 962–63.

42. John Gittings, *The Role of the Chinese Army*, 200.

43. Citations for most of these quotes are in Chapters 3, 4, and 7. For the cow reference, see Qingpu Archives (QA), 48-2-105 (1957), 139.

44. For "nationalist" pride in China's victory, see Peter Gries, *China's New Nationalism: Pride, Politics and Diplomacy*, 56–58.

45. China does have an "Army Day" (August 1), but its primary focus has been on military dependents, martyr families, and soldiers, not veterans. What is significant here is that veterans are not *singled out* for any special recognition.

46. Malarney, "Fatherland," 54.

47. There is a monument to the Unknown Soldier at the Memorial Museum of the Chinese People's Resistance against Japan in Wanping County, a trip that takes several hours from Beijing. There is also a statue at the Longhua Martyrs Park in Shanghai. There are museums that commemorate the military, but these tend to focus on *generals* who were born in a particular province and rose to high status. In Xingguo County, Jiangxi Province, there is a large museum honoring dozens of PLA generals who were "produced" by the county. Ordinary soldiers do not make an appearance,

and officers from Jiangxi who fought against the Japanese (with the Guomindang) and then fled to Taiwan do not appear, either. I am not sure when these commemorations were erected. Personal communication from Elizabeth Perry.

48. Chang-tai Hung, "Mao's Parades: State Spectacles in China in the 1950s," 417–18.

49. Shichor, "Demobilization," 338.

50. White, "Politics of Demobilized Soldiers," 191.

51. Ezra Vogel, *Canton under Communism,* 145.

52. Dreyer, "The Demobilization of PLA Servicemen," 300.

53. This was noted by foreign observers such as Derk Bodde (in *Peking Diary*) and A. Doak Barnett (*China on the Eve of Communist Takeover*).

54. Edward Friedman, Paul Pickowicz, and Mark Selden, *Revolution, Resistance and Reform in Village China,* 139.

55. Joseph Esherick, "War and Revolution: Chinese Society during the 1940s," 26; Friedman, Pickowicz, and Selden, *Revolution, Resistance and Reform,* 23, 162.

56. The comparable figures for generals and lieutenant to major generals among regular and auxiliary military academies are 0 percent and 16.2 percent. However, 16.67 percent of generals came from other types of military schools. See F. F. Liu, *A Military History of China, 1924–1949,* 146. According to Michael Mann, infrastructural power is "the capacity of the state actually to penetrate civil society, and to implement logistically political decisions throughout the realm." During the 1930s, 1940s, and the Korean War, neither the CCP nor the Nationalists had this power. See "The Autonomous Power of the State," 113. According to F. F. Liu, a former Nationalist officer, the GMD enjoyed "at best a precarious unity" and therefore was "not organized well enough at all levels to provide that general mobilization of all resources which *total* war, by the very nature of its name, demands." See *A Military History,* 108, 222. Unsurprisingly, during the Korean War, the CCP relied on mass campaigns to recruit soldiers, but even these efforts were improvised. See Gittings, *The Role of the Chinese Army,* 84–85.

57. Stephen MacKinnon, "Conclusion: Wartime China," in MacKinnon, Lary, and Vogel (eds.), *China at War,* 343. He writes that "the idea of a shared experience by the Chinese population during the China War . . . has its purposes, but historically it is a myth" (p. 335).

58. China's "conscription index" (the average number of men mobilized per year as a percentage of the population) was 0.4 percent, which compared to 1.3 percent for Japan, 1.4 percent for the United Kingdom, 2.4 percent for the United States, and 3.0 percent for the USSR. China "could not catch the rich" and "had difficulty in mobilizing the best brains from all walks of life when the military called for their assistance," Liu notes. Between 1940 and 1945, only 791 physicians were recruited into the GMD military, even though between 1939 and 1945 China had 5,119 medical school graduates. See F. F. Liu, *Military History,* 108, 135–36, 140, 151.

59. Colley, *Britons,* 183–84.

60. On collaboration at the local level in the Yangzi Delta, see Timothy Brook, *Collaboration: Japanese Agents and Local Elites in Wartime China*; Ralph Thaxton, Jr., *Catastrophe and Contention in Rural China,* Chapter 2.

61. On the limited scale of CCP engagement with the Japanese, see Arthur Waldron, "China's New Remembering," 948, 971. In the Taihang Base area, CCP cadre misbehavior included "forced recruitment for military service." See David S. G. Goodman, *Social and Political Change in Revolutionary China*, 57. The figures on militia and regular army forces are cited in Tang Tsou, *America's Failure in China, 1941–1950,* 301.

62. As noted by Parks Coble, "the Party mandated a historical narrative which privileged the revolution and the leadership of the Communist Party and consigned other players and memories to historical oblivion." See "China's 'New Remembering,'" 395–96. The Japanese military, however, credited neither the CCP guerrillas nor the Nationalists with their defeat. See Ronald Spector, *In the Ruins of Empire,* 39.

63. Donald Gillin (with Charles Etter), "Staying On: Japanese Soldiers and Civilians in China, 1945–1949," 500–502.

64. Ibid., 511–13.

65. White, "The Politics of Demobilized Soldiers," 191.

66. MacFarquhar, *The Origins of the Cultural Revolution, Vol. 3,* 70.

67. Most CCP accounts focus on the last item in this list. In a 1991 article, Luo Huanzhang, a "historian" at the PLA Military Institute, insisted that China's role in defeating Japan was far greater than that of the United States. "The Chinese people were *the key determining influence* in defeating Japanese imperialism." Cited in Peter Gries, *China's New Nationalism,* 76. According to Ralph Thaxton's study of Da Fo village in Henan, "the political culture that formed among CCP-led militia activists during the war years gave rise to cadres who proclaimed themselves heroes and who attributed *all* of the successes of the revolutionary struggle to themselves, and hence expected that their interests would take priority over those of the community." This sense of heroism was "imagined," however, since "few of Da Fo's militia activists fought shoulder to shoulder with the PLA." See *Catastrophe and Contention*, 87, 82–83. Emphasis in original. On students' focus on propaganda work, see Peter Merker, "The Guomindang Regions of Jiangxi," 296–97; Frederic Wakeman Jr., "Cleanup," 36; Jeremy Brown, "From Resisting Communists to Resisting America: Civil War and Korean War in Southwest China, 1950–1951," 110.

68. Units from Guangxi Province, for example, offered some of the fiercest resistance to the Japanese but then followed their leader (General Bai Chongxi) in combating the CCP until the bitter end. According to Diana Lary, despite their heroism against Japan, the troops "were part of a defeated army fleeing for its life." For the next 40 years, "tens of thousands of men who died during the war [against Japan] were soon forgotten heroes, their memories obliterated." See "One Province's Experience of War: Guangxi, 1937–1945," in *China at War*, 330.

69. Waldron, "China's New Remembering," 948.

70. Archival evidence from the Korean War describes this confusion. See Chapter 3. On the role of the militia, which provided the "mass element in recruitment," see John Gittings, *The Role of the Chinese Army*, 78–79.

71. Jeremy Brown, "From Resisting Communists," 120, 126–27.

72. Waldron, "China's New Remembering," 965.

73. I thank Robert Culp for this formulation.

74. By "mass army" and "total war," I rely on Barry Posen's and Miguel Centeno's definitions. Posen argues that *mass* refers to both size and "its ability to maintain its size in the face of the rigors of war" and its ability to retain its combat power. See his "Nationalism, the Mass Army, and Military Power," 83. For instance, during the Sino-Japanese War conscripts often had to walk hundreds of miles to join their units and often suffered from the lack of food, shelter, or warm clothing en route. According to General Joseph Stilwell, who worked closely with the Nationalist Army during the early 1940s, only 56 percent of all recruits reached their assigned units—the rest either died or "went over the hill" on the way. F. F. Liu notes that in 1943 almost three-quarters of a million recruits "were lost in this way." See *A Military History of China*, 137. Centeno suggests that *total wars* are characterized by (1) increased lethalness of the battlefield, (2) civilian targets, (3) a moral and ideological crusade that demonizes the enemy, (4) the involvement of significant parts of the population in either direct combat or support roles, and (5) militarization of society in which social institutions are increasingly oriented toward military success and judged in their contribution to a war effort. The Anti-Japanese and Korean wars partially fit the first two of Centeno's categories, largely because of the overwhelming firepower on the part of Japan and the United States. During the Sino-Japanese War, the Japanese were demonized, but collaboration with them was widespread and Chiang Kai-shek considered them less of a "demon" than the CCP; Mao also saved his firepower for the fight against the Nationalists. For both sides, it was also legitimate to use the "demons" in the Civil War. The CCP's "crusade" against the United States during the Korean War did not last more than several months. Equally important, in all these cases, the state could not, or chose not to, mobilize significant parts of society (and regions) in support roles or in direct combat, and the status of the military remained low. Centeno's category of *limited war* seems to have more applicability: the duration is relatively short (this could include the Korean War and the conflicts against India, Vietnam, and the USSR in the early 1970s), the fighting is limited to relatively small geographic areas, and battles are fought primarily by draftees from the lower classes. The wars begin as border clashes and involve states with a shared ideological or cultural profile (Japan was not ideologically so different from China, and India, the USSR, and Vietnam were not, either). See Centeno, *Blood and Debt*, 21–22.

75. The problematic structure of the Chinese military was noted early on in the Whampoa Academy, China's first "modern" military academy in the early 1920s. At the opening ceremony, Sun Yat-sen noted that "the military was to be regarded as the strong right arm of the party, but under the guidance of the non-military, political head." He called the 3,000 men and officers who graduated from Whampoa "the Party Army" (*dang jun*). His idea was to place the control of the armed forces "securely in the hands of the party and prevent it from falling into the hands of the warlords." The whole army, he stressed, "is subservient to the ends of the party." See F. F. Liu, *A Military History*, 10, 15. On the role of war and the military in French nationalism, see Rogers Brubaker, *Citizenship and Nationhood in France and Germany*, 8; Barry Posen, "Nationalism, the Mass Army, and Military Power," 94. For the emergence of the British nation-in-arms (in response to Napoleon), see Linda Colley, *Britons*, esp. 285–91, 318.

76. According to F. F. Liu, Chiang's military thought was strongly influenced by "traditional philosophies of Chinese warfare," such as Sunzi, Hu Ningyi, and Zeng Guofan. See *A Military History of China, 1924–1949*, 12; on Mao, see Waldron, "From Jaurès to Mao," 205.

77. Washington, who had much experience with the actual operation of militias, rejected this view. See Browne, "War-Making," 238. In Prussia, for example, military reformers (after their defeat by Napoleon in 1807) introduced general conscription to create a formal mass army but also combined it with a militia element, the *Landwehr*, which was less rigid and populist. However, it was understood that the reformed mass army was more important than the militia. See Alfred Vagts, *A History of Militarism*, 59–60. As late as 1964, Mao favorably compared militias to the PLA in his transcribed "talks" with his nephew Mao Yuanxin. See Stuart Schram (ed.), *Chairman Mao Talks to the People: Talks and Letters, 1956–1971*, 244–45.

78. MacFarquhar, *Origins, Vol. 3*, 326–27.

79. For this hypothesis, see Stanislav Andreski, *Military Organization and Society* (London: Routledge and Kegan Paul, 1967), 20–39. The basic argument is that mass war tends to have a leveling effect on class differences. See Kasza, in *One World of Welfare*, 44.

80. Ronald Krebs, in *Fighting for Rights: Military Service and the Politics of Citizenship*, calls this the "contact hypothesis." According to this perspective, "the armed forces may bring together individuals of various backgrounds in common cause and in a collaborative spirit, providing a setting seemingly well suited to breaking down dividing lines based on race, ethnicity, religion, or class." This model of the military as the "school of the nation" was prominent in the United States, Italy, Brazil, Japan, and other states. It is based on the assumption, common in social psychology, that face-to-face contact with other groups can dispel ignorance and prejudice. Krebs is skeptical of the contact hypothesis because of the possibility that increased contact with others might produce more hostility: the more I know about someone, the more I may *not* like him. Krebs acknowledges that "numerous studies have reported a positive correlation between interaction with out-group members and friendly attitudes towards that group" but also notes that "it remains possible that these positive views are the reason for high levels of interaction rather than the consequence" (p. 10).

81. Liu, *A Military History*, 146, 222.

82. Elizabeth Perry and Li Xun note the "heavily peasant and proletarian composition of the army." See "Revolutionary Rudeness: The Language of Red Guards and Rebel Workers in China's Cultural Revolution," *Indiana East Asian Working Paper Series on Language and Politics in Modern China*, 5; Maurice Meisner, *Marxism, Maoism and Utopianism: Eight Essays*, 177; Shichor, "Demobilization," 338; and June Dreyer, "The Demobilization of the PLA Servicemen," 307. During the Korean War, it would appear that more "students" entered the PLA. Roughly 1.75 million was the "rough upper limit" for recruitment, which added to approximately four million in Field Armies and Garrison Armies. Students were recruited to serve, but the goal of the recruitment campaign was to "skim the *technical and political cream* of China's student and working class population for the armed forces." Students from technical schools with specialized qualifications (chemistry, engineering, etc.) were

"particularly sought after." In the Southwest, workers were not recruited into the military, owing to the poor economic conditions. In a second recruitment campaign in June 1951, no workers were recruited. Some 4,000 Shanghai railway men served, although it is not clear in what capacity. See Gittings, *The Role of the Chinese Army*, 80–83.

83. John Keegan argues that the emergence of the post-WWI welfare state in Great Britain can be partially explained by the fact that middle-class officers gained sympathy for their working-class soldiers during the war. See *The Face of Battle: A Study of Agincourt, Waterloo and the Somme*, 220–21. For another argument on the impact of WWI on European welfare systems, see Bruce Porter, *War and the Rise of the State: The Military Foundations of Modern Politics*, 179–91; Richard M. Titmuss, *Essays on 'The Welfare State,'* 79–80; and Linda Colley, *Britons*, 287, 304, 316–17.

84. On the impact of the Cultural Revolution on the current generation of leadership, see Li Cheng, *China's Leaders: The New Generation*, 188–94.

85. Samuel Stouffer et al., *The American Soldier: Combat and Its Aftermath*, vol. 2, 309. After the war there was virtually no groundswell of opposition to the GI Bill. See Gerald Linderman, *The World within War,* 334.

86. On the benefits of this law, see Mark Edele, "Soviet Veterans as an Entitlement Group, 1945–1955," 124. Among the benefits were access to housing loans and construction material and "a job equal to or higher than the one they had had before the war."

87. See "Is Patriotism a Mistake?" *Social Research*, 901, 909. Kateb also acknowledges that patriotism is "an inevitable mistake . . . almost no one can help being a patriot of some kind and to some degree."

88. In a 2003 survey (1,200 people contacted by phone) conducted by the Institute of Politics at Harvard University, almost 90 percent of Americans considered themselves to be either "somewhat" or "very" patriotic. The results were the same in 2002. These rates may have been higher than in previous years because of 9/11. A Harris poll from 1998 found that 77 percent of Americans rank their level of patriotism from 7 to 10 on a scale of 1–10. See http://poll.orspub.com.

89. George Fletcher, *Loyalty: An Essay on the Morality of Relationships*, 17, 140; patriotism is referred to as an "acquired *sentiment*."

90. Daniel Druckman, "Social–Psychological Aspects of Nationalism," 58.

91. Margaret Levi, *Consent, Dissent and Patriotism,* 42–43.

92. Yael Tamir, "Reflections on Patriotism," 32–33, 37.

93. Charles Taylor, "Cross-Purposes: The Liberal Communitarian Debate,"166.

94. Alan Knight, "Peasants into Patriots," 138.

95. Maurizio Viroli, *For Love of Country: An Essay on Patriotism and Nationalism*, 1.

96. See his *Making Patriots*, 10, 65.

97. By these criteria, the war profiteer who discriminates against veterans and says "I love my country" or claims to "feel patriotic" is defined as "patriotic" on par with the commando on the front risking his life or the civilian who devotes years to working on behalf of impoverished citizens in remote areas—a proposition most reasonable people would reject, I would argue. It raises the question: what degree of

hypocrisy can we tolerate before it becomes appropriate to exclude certain individuals from the patriotic or nationalist category?

98. *The Loyal and the Disloyal: Social Boundaries of Patriotism and Treason*, 3–35.

99. For an application of this notion to American patriotism, see John Bodnar (ed.), *Bonds of Affection: Americans Define Their Patriotism*.

100. See many of the contributions to Jonathan Unger (ed.), *Chinese Nationalism* (Armonk: M.E. Sharpe, 1996). Also see Bryna Goodman, "Networks of News: Power, Language and the Transnational Dimensions of the Chinese Press, 1850–1949," 1–10.

101. Knight, "Peasants into Patriots," 139. Viroli argues that *nationalism* focuses on defending or reinforcing the "cultural, linguistic and ethnic oneness" of a people (p. 1).

102. John D. Kelly, "Diaspora and World War, Blood and Nation in Fiji and Hawai'i," 486–87.

103. It is very common in Chinese history to speak of *patriotic movements* or protests much like Chinese demands for democracy are often expressed in movements rather than in institutions. See David Strand, "Protest in Beijing: Civil Society and the Public Sphere in China," 1–19.

104. For a sophisticated approach to nationalism using intellectuals' writings, see John Fitzgerald, *Awakening China: Politics, Culture, and Class in the Nationalist Revolution*; Lei Guang, "Realpolitik Nationalism: International Sources of Chinese Nationalism," 487–514.

105. Unger, *Chinese Nationalism*, xv. Emphases mine. Linda Colley agrees with the connection between urbanization and patriotism but does not find that the *most educated* city folk were the most willing to serve in the volunteer corps. See *Britons,* 298, 302. *Tradesmen* were more likely to join, in part because they saw opportunities for profit.

106. It was "best selling" at the University of California Press, not the *New York Times*.

107. Journalists have also adopted this "trope" of rising nationalist "sentiment" uncritically. See "Balancing Act; A Survey of China," *The Economist*, March 25, 2006.

108. Gries appears to make claims both about "popular" nationalism *among* elites and also the (unverified) impact of these elites on ordinary Chinese. "Popular" seems to refer to actions that were not supported by the state rather than actually supported by the "masses."

109. Yan Sun's review in *Perspectives on Politics* (March 2005) praises Gries for his argument that "Chinese nationalism involves the Chinese people, not just the party and elites," but it does not point out that Gries' writers are, by virtue of their education and tacit government sponsorship, "elites." Likewise, Womack (*Journal of Asian Studies*, vol. 64, no. 3) notes that Gries "makes a thoroughly convincing argument that the demonstrations . . . expressed genuine *popular* sentiment" without questioning the paucity of evidence showing that 1) the sentiments were *widespread* and 2) these views were significantly or consistently distinct from the official view at that time.

110. The notion of what a "reasonable person would consider" is a standard criterion in legal reasoning in common law. Sacrifice should have this standard; otherwise, a $100 contribution from a millionaire "counts" the same as a contribution from someone with more meager resources.

111. Druckman, "Social–Biological Aspects of Nationalism," 58.

112. See Bruce Porter, *War and the Rise of the State*.

113. Bodnar, *Bonds of Affection*, 7; Krebs, *Fighting*, 28.

114. As per Israel's first prime minister, David Ben-Gurion. Cited in Uri Ben-Eliezer, "A Nation-in-Arms: State, Nation, and Militarism in Israel's First Years," 265.

115. Krebs, *Fighting*, 4.

116. Michael Walzer, *Obligations: Essays on Disobedience, War and Citizenship* (Cambridge: Harvard University Press, 1970), 98. Emphasis mine. Early Chinese Marxists accepted the notion that action is a necessary component of patriotism but stressed the state as the sole recipient of citizen actions. They, too, did not specify what sort of "love" was involved between citizen and state. See John Fitzgerald, "The Nationless State: The Search for a Nation in Modern Chinese Nationalism," in Unger (ed.), *Chinese Nationalism*, 70.

117. Carole Pateman, *The Problem of Political Obligation: A Critical Analysis of Liberal Theory*, 1, 163.

118. Cited in Cecilia O'Leary, *To Die For: The Paradox of American Patriotism*, 4–5. Emphasis mine. John Kelly argues that for Renan, memory of shed blood is more important to nationalism than any blood of "race." See his "Diaspora and World War," 477.

119. Emerson and Bushnell are both cited in Melinda Lawson, *Patriot Fires: Forging a New American Nationalism in the Civil War North*, 3. This quote does not suggest that fireworks and parades are unimportant but that they are in themselves *insufficient* to make patriotism meaningful.

120. Vladimir Tikhonov, "Masculinizing the Nation," 1030.

121. Personal observations; on Zhang's military record, see Waldron, "China's New Remembering."

122. Han van de Ven, "War in the Making of Modern China," 748. Also see Robert Culp, *Articulating Citizenship: Civic Education and Student Politics in Southeastern China, 1912–1940*, 104–7.

123. Chang-tai Hung, "The Cult of the Red Martyr," 288.

124. This discrimination was encapsulated in the saying "good people do not serve in the army." But if this were still the case, the PRC would not even have an "Army Day" or any preferential policies for veterans and South Korea or Taiwan would not have established a government agency for "patriots and veterans." Indeed, one of the successes of modern Chinese patriotism has been said to be the elevation of the status of the military and the importance of military power.

125. If governments and societies required "pure motives," we would be forced to eliminate most of those who died for their countries from receiving any sort of recognition. Many serve because it is the law and they are drafted. We generally recognize *actions*, not "correct" or pure thoughts or motives, in many fields. Many

societies honor millionaire businessmen and lawyers who might be motivated by a desire to improve their image or gain status in the community or tax breaks. Most all political leaders (even the noble George Washington) recognized that patriotism works best when it is tied to some form of self-interest. Washington wrote of soldiers: "The few . . . who act on principle of disinterestedness, are, comparatively speaking, no more than a drop in the Ocean" (cited in Browne, "War-Making and State Formation," 238).

126. On these benefits in the Roman Empire, see Keppie, *Colonisation and Veteran Settlement in Italy, 47–14 B.C.*, 39–40, 74; Richard Alston, *Soldier and Society in Roman Egypt: A Social History*, 6, 48; for Imperial Russia, Elise Wirtschafter, "Social Misfits," 226; Theda Skocpol, *Protecting Soldiers and Mothers*, on Civil War pensions in the United States. According to Gregory Kasza, "unlike the mixed response to labor groups that press for social reform, every political camp ordinarily recognizes the legitimacy of a veteran's claim to a better life." See *One World of Welfare*, 51. In China, this is *not* the case, I will argue.

127. Andrew Hunt, *A History of Vietnam Veterans against the War*.

128. See, for instance, Charles Tilly, *Coercion, Capital, and European States, AD 990–1992*, 115–16. For France and Prussia, see Omer Bartov, "The Nation in Arms: German and France, 1789–1939," 29, 31.

129. For a sophisticated treatment of the import of such emotionally charged moments, see Aristide Zolberg, "Moments of Madness," 183–207.

130. By this standard, being an "economic nationalist" would require one to pay a higher price for a domestic-made product even though its quality might be inferior. Merely talking about this, or expressing a hypothetical willingness to pay a higher price, would not qualify a person as a nationalist of this sort.

131. On the contrast between attitudes and behavior after 9/11, see Theda Skocpol, "Will 9/11 and the War on Terror Revitalize American Civic Democracy?" 539–40.

132. Dorothy Solinger, *Contesting Citizenship in Urban China*.

133. Elizabeth J. Perry, "Chinese Conceptions of 'Rights': From Mencius, to Mao and Now" *Perspectives on Politics* 6, no. 1 (March 2008), 38. According to R. Bin Wong, in China people could not exercise claims vis-à-vis the government since there was no possibility of third-party enforcement of these claims. The government "made commitments to people" who were not "citizens" in the way most Westerners think of this concept. Like Perry, Wong also notes that in China there was "no notion of rights or privileges" that could be negotiated over between state and society. Even during the 1920s and 1930s, "the kinds of citizenship associated with political rights in European traditions were never established." At the same time, it was possible to demand "entitlements" (not "rights"). See "Citizenship in Chinese History," 98–101.

134. See Mettler, *Soldiers to Citizens*, 119.

135. Krebs, *Fighting*, 11.

136. Kevin J. O'Brien, "Villagers, Elections and Citizenship," 212.

137. See "Observations on the Sociology of Citizenship: Obligations and Rights," 1.

138. Janowitz, "Observations," 4.

139. *Making Patriots*, 11.

140. James Burk, "Citizenship Status and Military Service: The Quest for Inclusion by Minorities and Conscientious Objectors," 503. Emphasis mine.

141. Alan Forrest, "La Patrie en danger," 14. According to Forrest, prior to the levée, "the social status of soldiering was low" and the "incentive to become an infantryman was poor." Soldiers could not claim "civic rights and even privileges," either (pp. 9, 11).

142. This link is quite old in the West. It can be found in some of the city-states of ancient Greece and Rome as well, in addition to writings of Machiavelli and Hegel. See Michael Geyer, "War and the Context of General History in an Age of Total War," 152–53.

143. Janowitz, "Observations," 14.

144. Meyer Kestnbaum, "Citizenship and Compulsory Military Service: The Revolutionary Origins of Conscription in the United States," 25.

145. Ibid., 28.

146. When citizenship was not formally encoded in laws, improved interactions with others were the hallmark of what Isaac Land calls "street citizenship." See "Bread and Arsenic: Citizenship from the Bottom Up in Georgian London," 90.

147. The clearest and most forceful articulation of this argument (for the British case) is Linda Colley, *Britons: Forging the Nation, 1707–1837.* Colley writes, "Being a patriot was a way of claiming the right to participate in British public life, and ultimately a means of demanding a much broader access to citizenship" (p. 5).

148. O'Leary, *To Die For.*

149. Colley, *Britons*, 4.

150. See Salyer, "Baptism by Fire: Race, Military Service and U.S. Citizenship Policy, 1918–1935," 849.

151. Rogers Smith, *Civic Ideals: Conflicting Visions of Citizenship in U.S. History*, 16. This was the case in the United Kingdom and in Germany. The war, notes Bruce Porter, generated "intense pressures for franchise reform." See *War and the Rise of the State*, 173.

152. This is attributed to German historian Leopold von Ranke. Cited in Kasza, *One World of Welfare*, 31. As noted by Linda Colley, the French Revolution and the Napoleonic Wars, which dictated "mass arming on an unprecedented scale," caused "considerable anxiety and bewilderment among the propertied classes about the social and political repercussions of such extraordinary levels of mobilization." See *Britons*, 283.

153. Salyer, "Baptism By Fire," 848–49.

154. Krebs, *Fighting*, 170.

155. Wray Johnson, "Black American Radicalism and the First World War: The Secret Files of the Military Intelligence Division," 29, 33.

156. Burk, "Citizenship Status," 506.

157. Donald Shaffer, *After the Glory: The Struggles of Black Civil War Veterans.*

158. Joseph Glatthaar, *Forged in Battle: The Civil War Alliance of Black Soldiers and White Officers*, 257, 260. White officers also assisted former soldiers in fights over pensions (p. 262).

159. Shaffer, *After the Glory*, 96.

160. Burk, "Citizenship Status," 506.

161. Robert F. Jefferson, "Enabled Courage: Race, Disability and Black World War II Veterans in Postwar America," 1105.

162. Ibid., 1109–10.

163. Burk, "Citizenship Status," 508.

164. Roger Hackett, "Japan," in *Political Modernization in Japan and Turkey*, 336, 350.

165. Theodore Cook, "The Japanese Reserve Experience: From Nation-in-Arms to Baseline Defense," 271.

166. Richard J. Smethurst, *A Prewar Basis for Japanese Militarism: The Army and the Rural Community*, Chapter 5.

167. Sanborn, *Drafting the Russian Nation*, 9, 12, 18.

168. Ibid., 5, 50.

169. Ibid., 50.

170. Ibid., 5.

171. Han van de Ven notes that China's Leninist parties and their relationship to society were modeled on the military. See "War in the Making of Modern China," 749.

172. For late Qing and early Republican views of the importance of *shangwu* (respecting the martial), see Hans van de Ven, *War and Nationalism in China, 1925–1945*, 13.

173. See Richard Challener, *The French Theory of the Nation in Arms, 1866–1939*, 47.

174. Eugen Weber, *Peasants into Frenchmen: The Modernization of Rural France, 1870–1914*, 302. For the Civil War in the United States, see Stuart McConnell, "Reading the Flag," 102–7. For the role of "movement of men in wartime" and wartime experiences in contributing to a new sense of personal and national identity, see Linda Colley, *Britons*, 313–14.

175. Peter Reese, *Homecoming Heroes*, 44.

176. Culp, *Articulating Citizenship*, 11. Emphasis mine.

177. In each Bureau of Civil Affairs, there was a Resettlement Division (*anzhi chu*) and Preferential Treatment Division (*youfu chu*).

178. Mettler, *Soldiers to Citizens*, 60.

179. Yue Daiyun, a Peking University professor, writes that intellectuals of the 1950s saw in the Communist Party China's savior—a pure, powerful, and incorruptible political party. "Full of confidence and enthusiasm for the Communist Party," she writes, intellectuals had a love for the party that "permeate[d] every aspect of the way they conduct[ed] themselves and the way they treat[ed] others." See *Intellectuals in Chinese Fiction*, 110. Looking back at the early 1950s after the Anti-Rightist campaign, Liu Binyan wrote, "Most people felt nostalgic for 1956 and regarded it as the best period in the history of the People's Republic." See *A Higher Kind of Loyalty*, 61. For other examples of this perspective on state legitimacy, see Perry Link, *Evening Chats in Beijing: Probing China's Predicament*, 140–42.

180. On "disaggregating" the state, see my *Revolutionizing the Family*; and Joel Migdal, "The State in Society," 16.

181. Deborah Cohen, *The War Come Home: Disabled Veterans in Britain and Germany, 1914–1939.*

182. See "Introduction," in Neil R. McMillen (ed.), *Remaking Dixie,* xiii.

183. See John Dower, *Embracing Defeat,* 58–60. At the same time, however, only 18 percent of 3,000 veterans who were surveyed by the *Hokkoku Mainichi* in 1946 reported that "the cold attitude of the people" was what impressed them the most after they returned. Instead, veterans were far more taken by the demoralization of society and food shortages. See National Archives, Record Group 331, Box 05897. After the war in Germany, "nearly every major newspaper printed angry letters to the editor denouncing officers as militarists, warmongers, and elitists and blaming them for Germany's current suffering." See Lockenour, *Soldiers as Citizens,* 5–6.

184. George L. Mosse, *The Fascist Revolution: Toward a General Theory of Fascism,* 18.

185. Bandit groups were sometimes augmented by veterans. See R. Bin Wong, "Citizenship in Chinese History," 107.

186. Edele, "Soviet Veterans," 134.

187. See, in particular, the studies by Philip C. C. Huang and Kathryn Bernhardt of UCLA's History Department.

188. See Matthew Sommer, *Sex, Law and Society in Late Imperial China.*

189. See Neil J. Diamant, *Revolutionizing the Family: Politics, Love, and Divorce in Urban and Rural China, 1949–1968.*

190. Mark Frazier, *The Making of the Chinese Industrial Workplace: State, Revolution, and Labor Management.*

191. Elizabeth Perry and Li Xun, *Proletarian Power: Shanghai in the Cultural Revolution*; Elizabeth Perry, *Patrolling the Revolution.*

192. Julia Strauss, "Paternalist Terror: The Campaign to Suppress Counterrevolutionaries and Regime Consolidation in the People's Republic of China, 1950–1953," 80–105.

193. Eddy U, "The Making of *zhishifenzi*: The Critical Impact of the Registration of Unemployed Intellectuals in the Early PRC," 100–121.

194. On the need to question the usual periodization, see Julia Strauss, "Introduction: In Search of PRC History," 7–9.

2

To the City or Bust:
Veterans and the Quest for Urban Citizenship

VETERANS, LAND, AND COMMUNITY

Service to a state or a revolutionary cause rarely goes completely unrecognized or unacknowledged, even if the motivations for such service have been less than pure or altruistic. In the contemporary United States, veterans are considered worthy of receiving a host of benefits—ranging from extra points on applications to institutions of higher education and assistance with tuition to beneficial terms in loans for housing—even if many join the armed services because of limited career options. Requiring "pure motives" as the quid pro quo for worthiness would not only be impractical (people could easily lie, and how would impure motives be uncovered?) and counterproductive (it would deter people from serving), but it would also be unfair: pure motives are not expected of any other sector of society that benefits from government largesse. So entrenched is the understanding that some form of recognition (whether material or symbolic) is due for military service that denying it outright would not only be seen in legalistic terms—a break in a "contract" between former soldier and the state—but as a travesty of justice as well. One could scarcely imagine informing soldiers returning from Iraq, "Sorry, we canceled your benefits under the GI Bill; budget constraints, you know." As noted in the introduction, even those who are not sympathetic to the military have rarely called for the reduction or cancellation of veteran benefits or for the abolishment of government agencies or organizations in civil society that cater to their needs and promote their interests. Even at the height of the Republican "revolution" in the mid-1990s, it was merely the Department of Education's budget that some proposed to slash, not that of Veterans Affairs. One way to gauge the way veterans are treated by the state and society is to

55

How to assess

"measure" (even crudely) the extent to which their service is rewarded and state promises to them are fulfilled. A plausible approach here would be to focus on political elites (since they decide upon rewards), the communities where veterans live after demobilization, and veterans themselves: how do they assess the reward or incentive offered by elites?

In the West, one of the most common and attractive rewards for military service has been the land grant, sometimes accompanied by cash payments. By some indications, the Roman Republic (and later Empire) established the precedent for this. Soldiers discharged from service after the Second Punic War (218–201 BC, against Hannibal) received land grants in Italy as part of the consolidation of Roman power on the peninsula. According to military historian Azar Gat, most regular soldiers came from the "poor rural proletariat" and were "politically almost disenfranchised," which surely made the promise of land quite appealing. Since the Republic never quite figured out a pension system for veterans of Rome's wars during the second century BC, successful and ambitious generals found it easy to persuade them to march on Rome by promising them "land upon retirement."[1] J. C. Mann, who studied the resettlement of Roman veterans, notes that many discharged soldiers "desired to settle on the land" and had pressed generals and politicians for land grants "from the time of [Gaius] Marius" (Consul of Rome in 107 BC, 104–100 BC, and 86 BC). This was not a coincidence: Marius was not from an aristocratic family and rose to power largely due to his military prowess and his support among veterans—but even then was not accepted by Roman elites, who also took no initiative to resettle veterans.[2] Even though Marius was not able to secure land in Italy, poor and rural veterans were nevertheless "prepared to make the move of their own free will" to places such as Sardinia and Africa.[3] Land for service did become more formalized, however. In 103 BC, Saturninus drafted legislation that granted land in northern Africa to some of the veterans from Marius's war in Numida; Julius Caesar's father was one of the commissioners appointed to oversee its implementation. In 70 BC, Pompey also sought to "secure grants of land to the discharged veterans of his armies" but did not succeed until 56 BC (owing to the objections of a politician who resented him for divorcing his half sister).[4] At the time, land was not conceived as a recognized right per se, and not all veterans settled on the land, preferring instead to use it as capital,[5] but by Caesar's time (101–44 BC), it was "almost taken for granted" that if a general wanted to enhance the benefits for his men, it would be in the form of land grants. Caesar, who spent a great deal of time with his soldiers (he trained and marched with them), did not disappoint his veterans after his triumph in 46 BC. Intending "to satisfy the discharged veterans," he provided each soldier 5,000 denarii, more than a soldier would earn if he "served a full 16-year term in the army," and, importantly, more than he expected. Faced with growing demands from his veterans for land and compensation, in the fall of 46 BC, he began his program "to provide farms for his veteran soldiers," a compensation plan that required a great deal of effort and involved surveyors, investigators, and staff to hear "pleas from interested parties."[6] Some evidence suggests that Caesar had tried to avoid displacing landowners "at least on a large scale" but, rather, to make use of available public lands or to buy land "at a fair rate," which could then be used for his veterans. He also confiscated land from vanquished enemies (like Pompey) and their supporters for this purpose,[7] and to make room for veterans in overcrowded Rome, he settled members of the urban lower classes in colonies overseas.[8] After Caesar, however, land confiscations to benefit veterans became even more widespread and aggressive. In the early part of the reign of his adopted son Octavian (Augustus), eighteen cities in Italy, many known for their "proven fertility," lost land "for the benefit of veterans" (those who fought with him as well as for those who "came over to his side" after fighting with Antony and Cleopatra in the battle of Actium[9]). When land was not enough for veterans in a town, the emperor took from adjacent ones by force.[10]

The decision to grant land, however, was only the first step in making this reward a socially meaningful one as far as veterans were concerned. The communities from which land was taken or purchased did not always welcome the newcomers. Relations between veterans and townspeople could be tense. Having spent many years away from civilian life (as many as 25 years), veterans were often considered "uncouth boors" who would lower agricultural productivity because they lacked agricultural competence (a perception we will see in China as well); few held public office or played an important role in the communities they joined.[11] Street fighting between veterans and civilians was not unheard of, and family relations were surely complicated.[12] This was the case in Italy, where large groups of veterans (sometimes 3,000 in a single town, or several hundred in other cases) were resettled in already existing communities as well as in more distant colonies, such as Egypt, where veterans experienced "continual conflict with the nome (a district or province) authorities who were interested in suppressing veteran privilege."[13] One solution to this problem, more prevalent in Italy than in Egypt, was resettling veterans in their own new colonies. Pursued mainly in Italy by Augustus, who "wished to be seen as maintaining a close bond as *patronus* with individual veterans," some fifty towns became veteran colonies. Veterans, for their part, would sometimes host their emperor in their homes.[14] According to several accounts, in all forms of settlement, veterans were allowed a significant degree of autonomy, as befitted their martially gained status as "citizens" of the Empire. Settled "in strict military formation," they had their own leaders and spokesmen and were able to maintain a "spirit of comradeship" in their colonies.[15] Equally important, there is little evidence, either from this period or later in the Empire, that veterans were forcibly resettled on land if they did not want to farm; Mann repeatedly refers to veterans' "choices" and "preferences" in deciding where to move after service.[16]

The role of political patronage and veteran–community interactions about land issues can be seen in the history of many other demobilizations. In Great Britain, for example, some 4,000 veterans and their families were resettled in Nova Scotia in 1749, and in 1763, after the Seven Years' War, veterans were settled in Quebec, Florida, and Grenada. As was the case during the Roman Empire, rank generally determined land holdings: a major might receive 5,000 acres, a private only fifty. Simply awarding land, however, was not enough: veterans often lacked the capital and skills to work it.[17] In Russia, during a roughly comparable period, legislation was passed under Alexander I that "required cities to assign soldiers plots of urban land where they could build a house and maintain a garden" and provided veterans with 50 rubles for this purpose.[18] Such legislation was likely prompted by reports noting that landlords, native villages, and urban communities were not particularly eager to see them return, since by law they were exempt from taxes and "could become dependent on public assistance." As in Rome, disputes over land occurred whenever veteran–settlers moved into established communities.[19]

In the United States until quite recently, land grants were also the principal way the government rewarded veterans. The Continental Congress and some of the colonies promised bounties of land for military service during the Revolutionary War. The Military Land Bounty Acts of 1811–1812 "set aside a special Military Tract between the Illinois and Mississippi Rivers."[20] Land grants were also offered to veterans of the War of 1812, Mexican–American War, and various conflicts with Indians in the 1850s; by 1855, "any veteran of any war from the Revolution on, or his heirs, could obtain a warrant for 160 acres of land anywhere in the surveyed public domain."[21] As was often the case in Rome, land was both "available" and "almost universally desired."[22] Still, these grants were problematic. As was the case in early periods, many veterans could not successfully till the land and ended up selling the warrants on the open market. Land speculation often accompanied land grant programs for veterans. By 1858, the United States stopped issuing military land warrants, but under the Homestead Act of 1862, veterans still had preferential access to land—they were allowed to deduct time served from the five-year residency requirements of the act (down to a minimum of one year). After WWI, several states "had some rather unfortunate experiences with soldier settlement," particularly California, Washington, and Minnesota, so that under the GI Bill of 1944, veterans who "were determined to farm" (estimated in 1944 as roughly 8.7–13.9 percent of white enlisted men[23]) were provided with loan guarantees, not loans or grants. To prevent abandonment of the land, the government provided funds (tuition and stipends) for veterans (some 1.5 million veterans came from farms) to attend education programs to improve their farming skills; before the war was over, agricultural economics and rural sociology professors—some of whom rotated between government service and universities—encouraged the government to create local boards to dispense sage advice about farm management and urged the communities to form ad hoc veteran resettlement councils and be patient with them.[24]

Nevertheless, owing to past experience, the widely recognized income differentials between city and farm, and the "city delights" that have attracted rural folk since large-scale urbanization began, rural experts were quite sanguine about the prospects for a massive "back-to-the-land" movement after the war.[25] American veterans who chose to return to the land—and there were probably 150,000 of them after WWII—needed to be prepared for hardship. "It must be drawn to the veterans' attention that he will be forced to lower his standard of living and that in all probability he will be socially and economically isolated for a number of years," warned rural sociologist Douglas Marshall. "Settling every veteran and war-worker in agriculture," he warned, "would be sheer folly."[26] Similar programs, and warnings about the vital role of a welcoming community, were put in place in Canada as well (after WWI). In addition to being available, land was seen as a way to rehabilitate the veteran—agriculture, nature, and the fresh air would help cleanse him of the muck of war and the damage it caused to his psyche.[27]

The Roman model, to be sure, was not confined to North America. Australia and New Zealand also rewarded veterans with land, setting up "soldier settlements" composed of WWI veterans.[28] In the Australian case, the central government provided the money for loans and the individual states gave the land, but few were under the illusion that farming by itself could generate enough income for veterans to live on; Australian veteran programs emphasized "smallholding types of enterprises, like pig raising" and "cooperative buying and selling." New Zealand "provided a wider range of farming opportunities," according to one study.[29] The African experience varied more widely. "Resettlement communities" for Nigerian veterans who fought with the British in WWI failed; many of them, unwelcomed in their native places and lacking jobs and marketable skills, "returned to the army."[30] Like American and Canadian veterans of WWI, Ghanaian veterans who returned to their villages encountered drought and low prices for crops. "Many" briefly returned to their farms, then left "to try and become watchmen or policemen in urban centres"; others "reenlisted in the army, or found jobs as laborers in the mines or in public works." An official commission later found "a great deal of discontent" among "a large section of ex-servicemen.[31] This was not universal among WWI veterans in Africa. Among the Nandi of Kenya, a welcoming community appears to have made a significant difference in how veterans fared after the war, offsetting the meager rewards for military service. According to Lewis Greenstein, the Nandi never received pensions (only back wages) from the British but were "warmly welcomed" by local communities when they returned home, got their former positions back, and used their money to purchase cattle, bride wealth to get married, and then land, which they highly desired. Successful reintegration into villages resulted in the "absence" of veteran-inspired political activity after the war.[32] Community and veterans' positive evaluation of "home" and "land" also played an important role in the smooth reintegration of rural German veterans of WWI. Unlike Commonwealth countries, these veterans did not receive land grants after their demobilization, but they returned to till the land anyway. When the war was finally over, they "demanded a swift return home" and were eager and happy to "till the earth once again." Despite Germany's defeat, between 1918 and 1919 there were celebrations welcoming them back home.[33]

Demobilizations in Chinese history have not been researched particularly intensively, but it is still possible to note the confluence of political concerns, community reception, and the relative value of land. During the Ming dynasty (1368–1644), benefits for service were quite limited. Conscription was limited to hereditary military families, who, by law, were expected "to furnish a soldier for active service at all times" (even so, registration was never "put on a sound basis even at the founding of the dynasty").[34] Those who were settled in military colonies benefited from tax-free land, but few remained on the land for long. According to Huang, "desertion and absconding started as soon as the military colonies were organized";[35] there was never a self-sustaining veteran community as was the case in Rome. In later centuries, at least some veterans were able to convert the land into cash, but how many these were and how they fared afterwards is not known. Civilian officials, who might have written about this, lacked "intrinsic and professional interest in the affairs of the army."[36] In the Qing dynasty (1644–1911), the ruling Manchus considered their conquest of China as one involving "perpetual full-time mobilization" and never instituted a demobilization process; there were no "veterans" as such.[37] Instead, the Manchus constituted themselves as a hereditary military caste (similar to the samurai of Tokugawa Japan), whose soldiers, the bannermen, enjoyed exclusive state benefits such as land grants, stipends in silver and rice, and affirmative action policies for the civil service examination, among others. At the same time, the court forced bannermen and their families to live in segregated residential compounds outside Chinese cities (to keep them free of Chinese influence and to deter disturbances), and they were banned from other occupations (such as trade) and had to work the land even though they "were not inclined to farm."[38] With the stipends not increasing in proportion to the growth of the size of the banner population (the absolute number of stipends was fixed in the late 17th century), many sank into poverty and even banditry; in 1692, some 5,000 bannermen protested the inadequacy of their silver stipends in the capital, and during the Qianlong reign (1736–1795), strikes and riots among poor bannermen on state farms were "endemic." Some poor bannermen illegally fled the garrisons, a highly risky action given that capture would probably result in enslavement in the Northeast and excommunication from clan spirits.[39] In China, it appears, emperors, much like their Roman counterparts, supported the notion that military service should be rewarded, but these benefits were confined to a far narrower stratum. Moreover, military service was not connected to a broader notion of citizenship. Equally important, there is little evidence that veterans (or bannermen) in China chose to settle on the land or in garrisons, unlike in the West, where veterans, even when financially pressed, were often allowed to decide for themselves whether or not to take advantage of land grant programs. Finally, although some Chinese emperors did deal with veteran issues (more likely at the beginning of the dynasty), there is little evidence that veterans ever enjoyed the same political status (as "citizens") and level of political patronage as did Roman veterans with successive emperors (especially Caesar and Augustus). Part of the reason for this was the dominant role of Confucian elites. These elites, much like their aristocratic counterparts in Rome who besmirched the military and its veterans in order to preserve their own status,[40] produced an ideology that placed soldiers and soldiering in a low position of the social hierarchy. Confucian scholars were able to make sure that "cultural" capital, rather than military prowess, remained the preferred path to upward mobility. It is not clear that the supposed rise in Chinese nationalism in the 19th and 20th centuries changed this. Few modern-day "nationalists" joined the army, trained troops, or joined them in marches like Caesar and other generals.[41]

Even if history made for a tenuous connection between veteran status and land in China, modern circumstances made rural resettlement (with or without land grants) even less attractive. From the mid-19th century on, large swaths of China's countryside were ravaged by wars and natural disasters, following the historical pattern of dynastic decline after 150 years of consecutive rule (the Qing dynasty had ruled China from 1644). From the 1850s to 1870s, China was racked by several homegrown rebellions (the Taiping, Nian, Muslim, among others) that, together, destroyed thousands of acres of farmland and caused large refugee flows to safer and wealthier areas, such as Shanghai.

Wars with the West and Japan in the 19th century were less damaging to the environment,[42] but Japan's invasion of China in 1937, which covered most of the eastern seaboard, ravaged the countryside. The four-year civil war between the Nationalists and Communists (1945–1949) was fought mainly in North China, but large-scale battles also took place in Central China and the Southwest, where the Nationalist remnants fled. The refugee flight from Japan's invasion in 1937–1938 was staggering—one 1946 survey put the total number of people who were on the move from villages, towns, and cities during the war at more than 95 million—but most of the flight came from poorer, north and central provinces such as Henan, Shanxi, Hunan, and Hebei rather than the coastal trade centers such as Shanghai, Fuzhou, and Xiamen, which remained "economically viable under the Japanese and lost relatively little population";[43] most of southern China, not occupied by Japan, did not experience this dislocation, either. In contrast, the United States, Canadian, and Australian heartlands were untouched by the devastation of WWII. During the revolution in the USSR, cities bore more of the brunt of warfare than the countryside. Communist rule was solidified after a four-year period of conflict (1917–1921) that witnessed a massive outflow of refugees from cities to the countryside, not vice versa (in China, rural refugees often sought shelter in cities). "The cities," writes Diane Koenker, "instead of representing the attractions of modernity and culture, became after 1917 places from which to flee."[44] Importantly, this urban-to-rural shift also affected cities' population of skilled workers and the social composition of the Red Army. Most skilled workers were "full-time urbanites" (rather than recent migrants to cities) considered by the regime as the very backbone of the proletariat. In Moscow, the "overwhelming majority" of them were "lost to the Red Army itself" because they, like other full-time city residents, had "no place to go."[45] Migrant workers also returned to the countryside during these years, but for a different reason: "to make sure they would share in the expected redivision of land."[46]

Wars were not the only large-scale events that made land a less-than-attractive reward for military service in China. The opening of Western-dominated "treaty ports" along China's coast, coupled with the development of industries in these areas, helped to create, and then widen, an urban–rural divide. Even though many peasants who moved to cities were often "sojourners" rather than full-time residents—much like the Russian migrants noted above—factory wages still paid far more than agriculture. And unlike the Russian case where urban areas witnessed a rapid decline prior to and during early Soviet rule, in China the urban population increased rapidly during the latter half of the 19th and first half of the 20th centuries, as did the attractiveness of city living—a phenomenon also noted in the U.S. case but, according to Koenker, largely absent from the USSR between 1917 and 1921. The discourse of "modernization"—a key trope of Chinese intellectuals' writings in the 20th century—emphasized the progressive nature of cities and their elites and the backwardness of the countryside. Marxism added yet another layer to this anti-rural bias; Marx did not think particularly highly of life in a rural community, to put it mildly, and Lenin despised peasants.[47] That the Nationalist Party's power base was in cities and its elites emphasized urban and industrial development certainly contributed to the sense that the city—not towns, and definitely not the countryside—was "the place to be." Being a "city person" meant the coincidence of not only living in a particular spatial setting—with large buildings, cars, telephone poles, and the like—but also having higher status and association with desired values. Not coincidently, when it was time to decide on a translation for the word *citizen*, intellectual elites coined the term *shi min*, "city person."

The problematic relationship between "veteranhood" and land (as both a resource and marker of a particular status in a community) was particularly acute in the case of the Chinese Communist Revolution. The People's Liberation Army, much like the CCP after its expulsion from cities after 1927, drew very heavily, but not exclusively, upon the peasantry, particularly in its lower ranks; it never had a large-scale influx of skilled urban workers, as was the case in the early years of the Red Army in Russia.[48] Conducting a rural-based revolution that surrounded the cities from the countryside,[49] the overwhelming majority of PLA veterans were rural dwellers.[50] According to Nationalist intelligence reports, many of the soldiers recruited for the Korean War joined during the high tide of land reform, conducted in the late 1940s and early 1950s.[51] This was generally true, if a bit simplified, since the PLA's recruits generally came from specific rural locales, mainly poorer regions of North and Northwest China, where they had more secure base areas and land reform had already taken place.[52] These areas tended to coincide geographically with those that experienced harsh warfare as well. After 1949, PLA manpower policy also favored recruiting among the peasantry (in Shandong, officials told me that several counties were well known for providing many PLA recruits), who were considered more politically reliable than the urbanites who lived in Nationalist-controlled areas. Unlike WWI and WWII veterans in the United States, England, Russia, and France, who were recruited from cities, small towns, and villages and returned to their communities after the war without considering that living in the countryside was a step down in status, PLA veterans saw their main "reward" for service in more narrow, "spatial" terms. Urban residence and status—not land grants, returning home to till the good soil, veteran colonies, or even the promise of tilling the land for future generations—would constitute one of the main "markers" of their status as victors and heroes of the successful revolution.

REGULATIONS

Despite the CCP's well-deserved reputation for frequent, and sometimes extreme, policy oscillations during the 1950s and 1960s, its resettlement policy for veterans was remarkably consistent: veterans were either "collectively" demobilized or "resettled in their native place" (*yuan ji an zhi*); sometimes this latter policy was referred to as "you go back to where you came from" (*cong nali lai, hui dao nali qu*). In the former scenario, reminiscent of both Roman and Chinese military colonies, an entire brigade or division would demobilize together, leaving the command structure essentially intact; military rank was converted to a civilian pay scale. In the latter, veterans, equipped with discharge papers and a little bit of money, would simply return to the village, town, or city from which they hailed, usually as individuals or a small group rather than as part of a larger collective. According to a 1957 report by Defense Minister Peng Dehuai to the State Council, thirty-one divisions and eight regiments had been collectively demobilized. Most of these units were composed of PLA veterans who had previously served with the Nationalists but switched to the PLA during the Civil War (these "politically problematic" veterans will be discussed at greater length in the next chapter), but others were veterans of the Korean War. Located primarily in Xinjiang and Qinghai in the Northwest and the Northeast, these veterans worked in railway construction, opening up agricultural wasteland, oil exploration, and other large-scale civil engineering projects. In some cases, veterans built their villages from scratch. Little is known about everyday life in these units, but some sources suggest that it could be quite harsh, probably somewhat comparable to British veterans demobilized to remote Nova Scotia in the 17th century. In 1950, for instance, a unit of 20,000 soldiers under the command of Tao Zhiyue became a "construction brigade" in the arid and virtually barren Northwest. Lacking any form of housing, the veterans built shacks out of grass and protected themselves from the winds and rain by constructing earthen walls. With subsequent aid from the USSR, this unit ended up growing cotton and winter grains. In Qinghai Province, also in the Northwest, veterans were the "main" (*zhuyao*) workforce; 2,000 were assigned to one well alone, constituting some 70 percent of the workforce; in a Xinjiang oil field, veterans represented some 50 percent of the workforce. Some managed to establish families thanks to the importing of young women from other provinces (many of whom were poor, had problematic family backgrounds, or were divorced or widowed). Other units, however, worked exclusively in agriculture. A very large contingent of veterans (together with their family members) was ordered to Hainan Island in the South, where they established two agricultural farms, growing crops like sugarcane, coffee, and peppers.[53]

Whether working in engineering, oil, or agricultural projects, many of these veterans did not have much contact with ordinary citizens, since the areas where they settled were sparsely populated and remote from urban centers, and life within these units was highly regimented. Some veterans protested these circumstances: a 1957 report issued by the State Council noted "20 significant protests" involving veterans "in the last several years." Among these, four were initiated by "collectively demobilized" veterans, involving roughly 1,880 people.[54]

Those veterans who were not demobilized collectively—and my sources suggest that most were not—fell under the *yuan ji an zhi* regulation of returning to one's native place. In the case of the PLA, this usually meant returning to the countryside.[55] At least officially, there were some exceptions: veterans who had special technical skills and could find employers willing to hire them might be able to attain urban residence. In addition, there was variation over time—in some counties not a single rural veteran was permitted to move to a city in the mid- to late 1950s, but in the years just prior to the Cultural Revolution, when the PLA was "in vogue" and its soldiers were promoted as national models, more veterans were allowed to move there.[56] The exact origins of this policy are not clear, but the main thrust of it was quite similar to the collective demobilization policy: disperse veterans and keep them as far away as possible from the capital, cities, and industrial centers. Some Roman emperors had the same idea when they established veteran colonies on the periphery of the empire. One key difference, however, was that in the Chinese case, with the exception of some pre-1949 base areas in the North, most Chinese veterans under the *yuan ji an zhi* policy rarely went in with many comrades-in-arms to any particular village, they were not given any choice in the matter, and they did not enjoy meaningful autonomy or independent leadership. And unlike Roman, American, Canadian, Australian, or Nandi veterans in Kenya, the overwhelming majority of Chinese veterans did not want to settle down, farm, and live a quiet life. In China, martial citizenship—veterans' expectations of appreciation, respect, support, and higher status after their military service—was infused with demands for urban citizenship (*shimin*), since this connoted higher pay and status. The *yuan ji an zhi* policy flatly contradicted this aspiration.

On the face of it, the *yuan ji an zhi* policy made sense: why wouldn't soldiers want to go "home," after all? But in the context of the war-torn and poor countryside, this regulation, particularly as a public policy that affected millions of individuals with complex circumstances, was a stupendous simplification. Take the concept of "native," for instance. Wars frequently lead to social dislocation, refugee flows, and long-term family separation. Did "native" mean where one was born, or where one lived for many years during the war? "Place" could be equally problematic. Wars also lead to a great deal of physical destruction—entire villages were bombed and burned by the Japanese during their occupation, and hundreds of villages were destroyed by the intentional flooding of the Yellow River in 1938 as part of a doomed Nationalist effort to halt the Japanese advance. What if there was no "place" to return to? County gazetteers report cases of veterans who moved into non-native villages because of war-related problems,[57] but even in better scenarios rural China suffered from excess rural labor. On the surface, "resettlement" (*an zhi*) appears to be a simple concept, but it wasn't. Wars in China resulted in massive civilian casualties. What if an entire family was killed or some of them were wounded? How could a veteran who returned to an empty or damaged home be celebrated as a returning war hero? None of the inevitable chaos and complexity of war, let alone rural veterans' desire for urban residence, was taken into consideration in the *yuan ji an zhi* policy.[58]

Unsurprisingly, implementing the *yuan ji an zhi* policy was problematic, just as a comparable policy was in Namibia after its independence in 1989. There, as in China, it was "assumed that integration would be unproblematic and no programmed development was envisaged: people would return to their places of origin and resume the lives they had led before the war."[59] Moreover, given the stakes involved, there is little evidence of serious deliberation about its potential effectiveness, dangers, or complexities. In all of the time he spent writing theoretical, diplomatic, and other instructions from his relatively safe haven in Yanan, Mao did not devote a single essay to demobilized veterans (as a result, policy documents did not cite his thoughts on the subject).[60] In addition, I can find no hints of input from veterans in the "mass line" style of policy formulation or from various local experts on the Chinese rural economy, as was the case in many Western countries in the run-up to major legislation affecting rural-bound veterans.[61] This is indicative of either a significant "gap" between Chinese educated elites (who constituted the leadership of the CCP) and veterans in terms of sympathy and concern, which would be in line with historical evidence about their elitism and disdain for the military;[62] the CCP's desire to severely weaken a potential source of opposition; an overly sharp differentiation between "military" and "civil" policymaking; a more general tendency (also noted in the United States) of policymakers to neglect administration;[63] or simply the result of our inability to gain access to key archival records. It may, in fact, have been the case that experts from Nankai University (just to give a possible scenario) consulted with CCP leaders about the *yuan ji an zhi* policy, but we cannot be sure of this until more archives are opened.

County gazetteers, much like the hundreds of documents reiterating this basic regulation, give us a rather glossy and uncomplicated summary of how the resettlement was implemented. These gazetteers, published in the 1980s and 1990s, all include sections on veteran resettlement, including information on how many veterans were resettled in agriculture. Even though I am dubious about the reliability of these data for any one county, a random selection of hundreds of the gazetteers reveals the extent to which the *yuan ji an zhi* policy was pursued since 1950. Some samples of these data from different provinces give a pretty good flavor of the social origins of PLA soldiers and the veterans' post-war predicament but are silent about why men became soldiers in the first place. (Did many join because they had no other prospects? Because they were provided with land prior to recruitment before collectivization?)[64] The Civil Affairs section of Anhui's provincial gazetteer notes that from 1950 to 1958, the province took in 224,344 veterans, among whom 198,448 (88.5 percent) were returned to the countryside from which they came.[65] In Shandong Province, approximately 50,000 demobilized soldiers arrived in the first six months of 1957. Of these, "the absolute majority" (*jueda duoshu*) returned to the countryside, generally close to 80 percent.[66] In Nanling County, 3,233 out of 3,990 veterans (90 percent) became peasants once again.[67] This was also the case in Huaiyuan because "in our county most all soldiers come from the countryside."[68] (In contrast, Huangpu District in Shanghai, which had almost a quarter million residents in 1956, took in only 576 veterans between 1951 and 1956.)[69] In Songjiang County near Shanghai, with the exception of those who were seriously disabled after 1972, "all" veterans whose family remained in the countryside returned there after military service (*dou hui xiang*).[70] In Henan Province, of the 130 veterans sent to Fan County in 1954, 128 ended up in the countryside, with only two in enterprises.[71] In Yi County, Hebei Province, 97.6 percent of returning veterans were sent to villages between the years 1950 and 1957; in Ningyang, "all" veterans in 1954 returned to agriculture, and in 1955, 95 percent did.[72] In Wangdu County, the figure was roughly 93 percent for every year between 1953 and 1963.[73] Prospects improved in some areas during the years of the industrialization push of the Great Leap Forward (only 84 percent of veterans in Wangdu and 50 percent in Ningyang had to return to the village[74]), but this was not the case in other counties during that year; in Taihe, Anhui, the figure was still 91 percent (512 of 559). It was only during the Cultural Revolution, or, more precisely, between 1970 and 1971, when veterans appear to have gotten what they wanted. The gazetteer of Wei County (Hebei Province) reported that only 22 percent and 5 percent of veterans discharged in those years, respectively, returned to the village;[75] in Yihua County, every single veteran was assigned to an enterprise in those years. In 1972, however, "civilian order" was restored, and only 4 out of 425 veterans (1 percent) were assigned to an enterprise.[76]

Leaving aside for the moment the question of whether or not veterans "assigned" to work in agriculture actually stayed in the countryside in the short or long term, the general thrust of the data suggests that a very large majority of them returned to (and stayed in) the countryside. If this is the case, it would mean that only a minority of rural veterans would be able to secure positions in the local political structure, while those few who benefited from state patronage would see their interests aligned with the state, rather than other returning veterans.* This would be a double blow to veterans since, in addition to "becoming urban," getting an official post (zuo guan) has long been a marker of higher status. To return to the countryside after service without any increase in status was a serious loss of face, particularly when others in leadership positions did little to boost their post-service status. In Yelong Township in Qingpu, veteran Dong Jianliang told officials at a meeting convened during the Hundred Flowers Movement, "Civil Affairs doesn't educate the cadres and peasants enough, so when we returned here and had to go back to farming, they all look down upon us, thinking that we're all good-for-nothings. There's great pressure on us, which makes us very depressed (kumen). It's hard for us to work. That's why we request job transfers."[77]

Gazetteer and other data bear out veterans' minority status in local political administration and the limited opportunities for upward mobility. In Yi County, Hebei, 21 percent of returned veterans had positions at the village and township levels,[78] with a similar figure in Jinzhai County in Anhui;[79] Jixi County in Anhui had a slightly higher proportion (26.7 percent).[80] Undoubtedly, these fortunate veterans—like those of the Long March, who also enjoyed many political privileges—were grateful to the CCP and viewed their military experience very positively—but it appears that most were less lucky and could not secure political jobs, especially those that were considered more rewarding, such as village party secretary or township party secretary.[81] In some areas, the percentage of beneficiaries could have been considerably less. In Pinghe County in Fujian province, only 5 percent joined the political establishment between 1950–1958 (115 out of 2,306).[82] In Dongping County, Shandong (1950–1981), 17 percent of returning veterans (3,100 out of 17,842) were cadres in production teams and brigades.[83] The gazetteers are also usually silent on their precise status in the hierarchy, generally noting that they were "cadres" but not whether they were village or township "heads" (*zhang*) or how long they remained in that status; in the Henan village studied by Ralph Thaxton, veterans who returned from war in 1953 and 1955 "faced a party leader who could thwart any threat to his power."[84] Province-wide, the

---

* In rural China, the lowest administrative level is the village, followed by the township and then the county. Above the county is the province. In some places, the "district" was positioned between the township and county.

Henan situation may have been better. A detailed investigation of 483 veterans in 35 townships (in 19 counties) found that 20.7 percent of them were "major" (*zhuyao*) officials.[85] In Qingpu County, however (circa 1951), only one of the 38 returned veterans was a village chief, two were militia platoon (*fendui*) leaders, and one-third were militiamen.[86] (Whether militia service was a sought-after post is not at all clear; evidence from militias in rural Germany after WWI suggests that veterans were "tired of new military activities" and therefore reluctant to join the Volkswehr.)[87] Two years later in Qingpu, among 28 returned veterans, only one secured a position at the township level (as deputy chief) and one as village chief, which was roughly comparable to the low level of political leadership in rural Japan after WWII, where veterans-turned-village chiefs appear to have been few and far between.[88] According to a 1956 report, only 10 percent of veterans were heads of anything (82 of 758),[89] and a statistical spreadsheet on 683 Qingpu veterans showed that only a few more (14 percent) were in the CCP and 25 percent were in the Communist Youth League (CYL);[90] this percentage rose to 45 percent in the CCP in 1962 (with 8 percent in the CYL).[91] A transcript of a 1957 meeting with Qingpu veterans during the Hundred Flowers Movement hints that one cause of the earlier low figure was that some Qingpu officials may have suppressed veteran membership in the CCP. A veteran surnamed Huang, for example, said, "I want to enter the party but it's been delayed for a very long time. It's especially hard with local officials: whenever they see a veteran they just shake their heads. Nowadays, keys don't open any locks." Fellow veterans agreed. One said, "In the army I was a prospective party member, but after my discharge township officials ignore me, so the problem of party membership is still unresolved"; according to another, "In the army, our commanders were concerned about us, but it's very different with local cadres. I filled out my party membership application in 1954 but still [three years later] haven't heard anything about it."[92] As bad as this seemed to veterans in Qingpu, it may have been far worse elsewhere. In the Southwest, there were cases of bandit leaders, landlords, and secret society members who received official posts in the bureaucracy (even district chief). In one district, some 40 percent of militia members were members of secret societies in the early years of the PRC.[93] Even in Wugong Village in Hebei Province—a "model" community—a key militia position was awarded to a female relative of a party official, not a veteran.[94]

A 1957 report from the National Veterans Commission lends some support to these county data on local leadership patterns, noting that 30 percent of veterans were "local level cadres,"[95] a percentage that did not appear to change significantly in the next six years, and that 42.4 percent of veterans were CCP or CYL members.[96] In Shandong Province circa 1963, 30 percent of all "basic-level rural cadres" (*nongcun jiceng ganbu*) were veterans and disabled revolutionary soldiers (without noting their precise status),[97] and in Chongming County near Shanghai (1961), 31.7 percent of the 410 returning veterans were either "basic level cadres" or "advanced producers,"[98] but the latter term does not necessarily suggest any political clout. The remainder, it appears, were cadres whose profile differed very substantially from that of veterans. According to Roderick MacFarquhar, "between 50 and 60 per cent of all basic-level cadres were youngsters who had not been tempered in the class struggle of land reform" or in war or military service.[99] My estimate is that most lower-ranking veterans (sergeant and below) could not secure many political positions and rarely went above the township level if they did. Equally important to notice is that these figures represent county-wide and national averages; it is possible that in some villages there were only three veterans among many other types of cadres (for instance, those who were promoted for activism in land reform, militias, and other political campaigns).

As official sources, gazetteers are edited with a fairly heavy hand and thus have certain limitations. They provide us with a first cut at what happened in a particular place, but they rarely flesh out the whole story. It would be a mistake to deduce that just because the state provides data telling us that 80 percent of veterans "returned to agricultural production," these veterans would actually be in the villages, or even "producing" for that matter; we have already seen evidence from rural resettlement schemes elsewhere in the world that veterans did not easily acclimate to agricultural labor. To get a much better sense of what happened and why, we have to turn to the archives. Archival documents, unlike gazetteer data, undergo far less editing since they were never intended for widespread distribution (many are handwritten first drafts). What these reveal is a broad pattern of veteran migration (sometimes successful) into cities, urban resistance to this migration, and veterans' determination to parlay military service into claiming urban status despite the odds.

CITY HO!

State officials, or more precisely, officials literate enough to write reports that ended up in the archives, generally wrote in condescending tones toward veterans seeking to gain residency status commensurate with their status as veterans of the successful revolution. Rarely did they use a neutral term, such as moving or even migrating. Rather, veterans were almost always described as "aimlessly" or "recklessly wandering" (*mangmu wailiu*) into cities, even if subsequent sections of reports included a detailed exploration of their motives. This term was used in the earliest reports about this sizable migration, which began immediately after the founding of the PRC in 1949, as well as in those from the 1960s. For urban officials, veterans' desires for, and claims to, urban residence were always framed as problems that required some form of administrative solution (such as limiting their number, cracking down on rural officials who allowed them to come, or persuading them to go back). I have found no evidence that veterans ever felt welcomed by urban denizens.

In the literature on the PRC's early years, the period 1950–1956 is often characterized as the era of "consolidating of state power" after years of revolution and war. It is certainly true that the state built or expanded its institutions and dismantled rival ones, staffed bureaucracies, and cracked down extremely hard on various "anti-Communist elements." For veterans, as for many others, however, this period was characterized more by mobility and fluctuation than order, an opportunity to shift identities (for instance, peasant to worker, veteran to official, low status to higher status) before state administrative procedures became more bureaucratic and its power to penetrate deeply into society grew stronger.

The phenomenon of veterans' *mangmu wailiu* very quickly caught the attention of wary urban officials, not a few of whom apparently thought that "cities cannot resettle veterans" (*dou shi bu neng anzhi fuyuan junren*).[100] The exact reasoning behind this assessment is not clear, especially considering that there were high-ranking PLA officers who already had assumed leadership positions in the city[101] and that the biographical profile of some of the first PLA veterans to arrive mirrored their "own" skilled workforce in terms of native place. One of the first analyses of veterans in that city—a group of 51 "non-Shanghainese" who arrived in 1950—found that almost half (25) of them came from the "south Yangzi" region (Sunan), which was, in broad terms, associated with higher levels of "skill" and "culture"; only 10 from this group hailed from areas north of the river, which had a poorer reputation in the eyes of city folk.[102] Perhaps a better reason for the negative assessment was the profile of many veterans who arrived later in 1950 and early 1951. By this time, roughly 150 veterans each month were making their way to Shanghai, but most of them hailed from areas north of the Yangzi. According to officials, the region's topography was partly the reason: as a major port and industrial city surrounded by many waterways, transportation to the city was convenient.[103] More criticism, however, was leveled at rural officials in the veterans' native locales. "Despite the fact that the Center and the Political–Military Commission of Eastern China have repeatedly emphasized that, under present conditions, veterans who are not native to cities are not permitted to move there for resettlement," rural officials nonetheless issued them "letters of introduction." Just how the city could house, feed, and employ a seemingly unlimited supply of northern veterans was obviously a great concern,[104] even though veterans represented an extremely small proportion of the overall population, as indicated in the district-level gazetteers. In early 1952, with several thousand "registered" unemployed veterans on their hands,[105] Shanghai officials pleaded with the Center to do more to prevent veterans from entering the city. Veterans who have come to Shanghai, they complained, "do not want to go back to their native place." Some said that they "would rather die" than return to the countryside.[106] A 1952 report confirmed that, indeed, the numbers were increasing; in a six-month period, some 700 veterans had arrived, "the most coming from north of the Yangzi," including some areas that were well known for their poor environment and poverty.[107] Shanghai officials were also perturbed by what they considered carelessness on the part of the PLA, which did not investigate veterans' claims that "they were from Shanghai" but still gave them letters of introduction. Even worse, the PLA discharge officers, perhaps overestimating the legitimacy of the CCP takeover, told them that they would be welcomed with open arms and with jobs. When this did not materialize, they bitterly complained about the gap between "theory and practice."[108] Authors of a summary report of veterans' letters noted that owing to a constant "back and forth of correspondence" between Shanghai officials and those in their native places, "non-Shanghai veterans are processed too slowly. As a result, they can't find permanent residence and can't find work for a very long period, which causes great distress."[109]

Regardless of how it was classified, the documents do demonstrate that *mangmu wailiu* was not limited to greater Shanghai. Other cities may not have had lights as bright as Shanghai's, but they were cities nonetheless. Much like Shanghai tended to draw veterans from poor or war-torn surrounding provinces, northeastern cities also became beacons for veterans sent "home" under the *yuan ji an zhi* policy. Shandong Province, on China's eastern seaboard, was one of the main areas of conflict in the recent wars against Japan and the Nationalists. After the wars, thousands of veterans refused to go home, spilling into near and faraway cities. Deeming the problem of mangmu wailiu "very serious" (*hen yanzhong*), Shandong officials wrote, "Almost every large city in the country has veterans from Shandong who are blindly (*mangmu*) looking for work," with most of them concentrating in the north.[110] In 1954, the Shandong Provincial government, unable to ignore the fact it was rapidly becoming an impressive "exporter" of veterans, issued a special report on this "problem," which in its view was "getting more serious day-by-day." Certainly the numbers suggested that a large-scale movement of veterans was under way; in a three-month period in 1954, a year that saw shortfalls in agricultural production, close to 3,000 veterans departed the province and "headed northeast," often after having sold off their farm material and personal possessions (whatever land rights they may have received as an inducement to join the military had already lost their value due to collectivization, a fact never mentioned in the reports). The city of Harbin alone took in 600 veterans in March and April of that year.[111] As was the case among veterans from Anhui and Jiangsu who made their way to Shanghai, Shandong veterans came equipped with paperwork ("letters of introduction" and "migration authorization") from village and township governments. For instance, officials in Xue Family Village in Chunan County, "using the authority of the local security office," sent eleven veterans to the city of Dalian "to seek employment." This story was confirmed in correspondence between local authorities in Dalian and other cities in the province: "Most veterans who come to the city have 'change of official residence' papers issued by the public security office." When confronted by urban officials and asked to leave the city and return home, veterans brandished these official documents, as well as those that were issued by the PLA, and claimed that they were authorized to live there.[112] One Shanghai official was so frustrated with a veteran who refused to leave Shanghai that he locked him in his office.[113]

Efforts to roust them do not appear to have been very successful. Take, for instance, the case of Zhou Mingbao, a veteran discharged from the political department of an anti-aircraft unit who left Shandong and moved to Shanghai. Zhou's family consisted of a grandfather, father, and mother, all of whom received government aid in Shandong. Because he "had family" there, Shanghai officials complained, "He should return home to work in agricultural production." The problem, they noted, was that his military unit provided him with all the proper documentation for moving to Shanghai. Apparently, however, this was not enough to stay. Pressed again, Zhou claimed that he had an uncle in the city. Shanghai officials were not persuaded and once again tried to get him to return to Shandong. Zhou, "with a bad attitude," then "raised a ruckus at the district government" and still refused to leave. In the report, they remarked that the "material" they received on Zhou from the military indicated a longer-term problem with "obeying orders" as well as a history of illicit relations with women. Cases such as this one "happen every day," authors of the report lamented.[114] Unsurprisingly, these efforts to restrict veterans from living in urban areas were not appreciated, perhaps not very surprising in a country with a long history of labor mobility and sojourning in cities part-time. Veterans were "angry" at Shanghai policies, a 1952 document noted.[115]

Some of these problems, to be sure, could certainly be attributed to the lack of coordination in the early years of the state between government agencies, particularly the PLA, whose officers may have wanted to "reward" their soldiers with urban residence, and municipal officials who would rather have done without them. *Mangmu wailiu*, however, did not end after the government had more time to "gets its act together" further into the decade. On the contrary, owing to the Korean War, the PLA was able to demobilize on a massive scale only toward the mid-1950s. This, together with collectivization, contributed to an even greater flow of veterans toward cities and added to the number of earlier migrants who, according to a 1955 State Council report, "are unwilling to leave cities or go to impoverished areas to work."[116] The number of discharged veterans was large, but not relative to the overall population. A 1957 "situation report" issued by the National Veterans' Work Conference in Beijing noted that "in the last several years," 5.26 million veterans had been demobilized, averaging roughly 700,000 per year.[117] Unlike those discharged in the early 1950s who mainly fought or served in the wars against Japan and the Nationalists, most of these veterans had been recruited between 1951 and 1953 and fought against a foreign enemy—the United States; only "a minority" had served in the Civil War and apparently none in the Anti-Japanese War—the shortest length of service was four years (indicating a 1953 recruitment); the longest was ten (1947 recruitment). According to this report, which agrees with Nationalist intelligence sources, most veterans clearly represented the state and party; most had been "basic level cadres" in the countryside; some 62.3 percent were party members; and 26 percent were members of the Communist Youth League (CYL).[118] However, in their desire to avoid resettlement back "home" in the countryside, these veterans were exactly like their early 1950s counterparts. "Very many" (*xu duo*) of these "old soldiers," the PLA noticed, "are unwilling to return to the countryside" and expected the government to assign them jobs in urban areas or in government offices.[119]

Not only the veterans expected this. Prior to their discharge, soldiers received letters from their families instructing them to either "stay in the army or work for the government, just don't come back!"[120] Since the former was extremely difficult and "government work" was assigned to fewer than 40 percent at even the lowest levels of the political structure, many veterans heeded the last part of this advice by briefly returning to the countryside, getting a letter from local authorities, and moving to the city, letting the chips fall where they may. Even a national-level meeting on "veteran work" did not produce a report very favorable to veterans. Despite their poverty and hardships, veterans were expected to sympathize with the plight of city residents: government agencies and the military, its authors suggested, should "explain to veterans the importance of agricultural production" and the difficulties created for the cities in terms of jobs and provisions. If veterans had a hard time working in agriculture, at the very least they could be engaged in "protecting production" by "capturing paratroopers and secret agents" sent from Taiwan.[121] Local officials, for their part, should stop "casually issuing documentation," but if it was already too late, they should "try to get them to come home; once home, they should take the initiative to help them solve any problem they might have."[122]

Coming to veterans' aid, however, was unlikely to happen, if only because other state policies in the late 1950s guaranteed that local officials would be kept busy doing other things. The rapid pace of the collectivization of rural land after 1956, and then the radical policy experiment called the "Great Leap Forward" (which caused a massive famine in large swaths of rural China in the early 1960s), made it abundantly clear to veterans that cities were far more attractive destinations than the countryside. A 1959 investigation report on veterans in eleven counties near Shanghai reveals how desperate "not a few" veterans, and their families, had become.[123] Chongming County, for instance, received 177 veterans in early 1959. From March 22 until April 27 of that year, 115 of them had "come to the county government" on 230 separate occasions "to request work in industry." The record was held by a veteran who came three times in one month. Some veterans in Chuansha County no longer wanted to work in agriculture but were not permitted to change their household registration. Often pressured by family, they left, anyway, headed for the northern port city of Tianjin and the interior city of Hankou.[124] In Qingpu, the county veteran committee issued a (handwritten) report in 1957 describing the case of a veteran surnamed Jin from nearby Kunshan County who married a Qingpu woman who was a party member. After his discharge, Jin returned to Qingpu but was holed up at a local hostel because "he could not do agricultural labor and wanted to be assigned other work." Eventually he relented, since the local government leaned heavily on his wife and she got him to agree.[125]

Mangmu wailiu showed no sign of abating during the early 1960s. Much like it did in the early 1950s, in 1964 the Shanghai Municipal government shot off letters to the State Council complaining about non-Shanghainese veterans "coming to Shanghai after their service." Once again the PLA was blamed, since they failed to conduct a rigorous investigation of veterans' actual native place. Shanghai reported on veterans who were neither drafted in Shanghai nor had family there but "were discharged to Shanghai," anyway. Urban officials again pleaded with the Center to make sure that veterans "whose native place is not Shanghai" went home, but they were indifferent to what would happen to them after their return.[126] The Shanghai Garrison echoed these sentiments in 1963: "every (*yi lü*) veteran from the suburbs and the countryside should return there."[127] Similarly, 1965 resettlement regulations jointly issued by the Garrison, Labor, and Civil Affairs bureaus reiterated this hard-line position,[128] even though in the interim years the PLA was promoted as the model of revolutionary proletarian virtues for the rest of the country. Since a

1961 report on veteran problems noted that "no veteran wants to return to the countryside," it is highly unlikely that the spate of policy documents stopped the flow, much like household registration did not stop peasants from migrating in the millions during the Great Leap Forward–induced famine years or even the Cultural Revolution (1966–1976).[129] A "top secret" investigation report on Qingpu's 1,007 veterans (absorbed between 1951 and 1962) by the Qingpu Garrison and sent to the county party committee and other military addressees suggests precisely this. Some veterans "refused" to work in the collective rural economy and "even let their own plots remain barren." Others "do not have sufficient understanding of the importance of agricultural production, and are unwilling to return to the countryside." Some refused assignment on more than four occasions, using "excuses" such as "I'm not familiar with agricultural labor" or "I'm not strong enough" to avoid going back. One of these veterans, Wu Longqing from Shengang commune, was typical. Wu made his money gambling, perhaps because he refused to work in "collectivized agriculture." When accosted by local cadres who tried to mend his erring ways, Wu shot back, "I've been abroad (Korea)! What makes you think you're so great?" (*nimen you shenma liaobuqi*).[130] Unfortunately, the report does not mention what happened after this, but it would seem unlikely that Wu would settle down on the land and slowly fade away, content with knowing that he had served his country.

THE PUSH FROM THE VILLAGE, THE PULL OF THE CITY

Studies of migration have long focused on "push" and "pull" factors to explain migration and immigration. "Pull" factors can include relative safety, higher wages, or better prospects for children; people can be "pushed" out by poverty, famine (think of the Irish immigration to the United States after the potato famine), or violence (pogroms in Russia). Research on China's large-scale internal migration to cities since the reform period have generally highlighted economic factors—it is far easier earning money in the city than raising crops in the countryside—as well as demographic ones—China has a surplus of rural labor, which the construction boom in cities and their suburbs helps alleviate.[131] To what extent were these factors present in the case of veterans in the more collectivized economy of the 1950s and 1960s? Like their more contemporary counterparts, the so-called "floating population," most veterans are also from rural areas. Unlike them, however, veterans, by the state's own reckoning and propaganda, have a greater claim to status, appreciation, support, and privilege because of their service. How did this play out when veterans acted upon their desires?

Table 2.1. Migrant Veterans' Occupations in Shanghai, 1957

Occupation	%	Explanation
Full-time factory worker	1.9	These positions generally included extensive medical and insurance benefits.
Temporary workers	37.3	Some of these were in factories; others were in construction, docks, or the service sector. Some were engaged in "mobile" manual labor in the service sector, such as carpenters, haircutters, hair washers, cobblers, and cement mixers
Peddlers	21.3	These veterans were also "mobile" within the city, selling vegetables, firewood, peanuts, and used odds and ends.
Unemployed	2.5	These veterans had no income and were said to be relying on family and friends.
Welfare recipients	6.4	Aid was generally provided by the Bureau of Civil Affairs based on need.
"Illicit activities"	8.1	Generally refers to theft.

Source: "Guanyu mangmu laihu de waiji fuyuan junren qingkuang yu chuli yijian de baogao," SMA B168-1-633 (1957), 100-101.

Thankfully, the archival documents do provide us with some reasonably fleshed-out answers. Urban officials were concerned about the *mangmu wailiu* phenomenon, as seen above, and so sought to understand veterans' motives as well. In Shanghai, an interagency work team was established and wrote a detailed investigation report based on 469 "non-native" veterans out of approximately 1,000 in the city.[132] Confirming earlier migratory trends, and reflecting the prominence of CCP "base areas" in these provinces prior to 1949, almost 80 percent of these veterans (the bulk of whom arrived in Shanghai in 1956–1957) were from poorer areas in Jiangsu and Anhui provinces (76.6 percent from Jiangsu, 2.6 percent from Anhui). Veterans' family situations also reflected wartime losses and dislocation: 26 percent of the veterans had no family back home. Generally ill-educated, poor, and lacking technical skills, these veterans were located at the very low end of the urban workforce, especially in terms of stability and income, as we can see in the table above.

Interestingly, most of these veterans did not come directly to Shanghai but, rather, followed orders and returned to their native place after their discharge. It was only after "not getting settled" that they made their way to the city. Moreover, while marginal in terms of occupation, much like their Jiangsu and Anhui civilian counterparts, most were not marginal or "reckless" in terms of abiding by laws and regulations. Most (80 percent) had official residency documentation. Like the migrants in the early 1950s, quite a few came equipped with "letters from the township committee or cooperative" or other proof of identity (*zhengming shu*).[133]

Statistics, by their very nature, give little sense of how these veterans managed to get by in these low-paying occupations. The report makes it quite evident that life was very difficult, a far cry from their officially high status. Some veterans, for example, were not provided with enough cloth to make another set of clothes, so they walked around in their dirty uniforms. The authors of the report were clearly disturbed by veterans, who, in a transparent tactic to gain public sympathy, went out to "polish shoes, sell peanuts and pickled vegetables" wearing their military uniforms with "a bunch of medals and decorations on them." For those who could not get by selling these items, begging and cutting down expenses were the main urban survival strategies:

> Because some do not have any money, they have to go begging, roaming the streets, stealing food or picking scraps out of garbage. Some live in police pillboxes and next to sewers. Others, lacking any work, or, in the case of temporary workers who have been dismissed, are seriously contemplating suicide.[134]

But even begging had a "martial" element to it. Apparently anticipating the lack of sympathy from Shanghai's civilian denizens, veterans targeted a potentially more sympathetic population. Some went to the train station to beg for money from PLA officers or wandered around the streets looking for homes and people they recognized as either "martyr families" or "family members of military dependents," thinking that, of all people, those who sacrificed for the revolution and state would be willing to lend them a hand.[135]

Given this reception—which probably spread by word of mouth or letters—why did these veterans come to Shanghai? The chances for securing a permanent job in a factory were bleak (see Chapter 4) and surely it was not pleasant to hawk peanuts wearing a uniform festooned with medals. The materials from Shanghai and other areas suggest three main factors. One might be classified as a classic "pull"—the higher wages of the city and its exciting life—while two were in the "push" category—natural disasters, which primarily affected agricultural production, and rural politics surrounding land.

Peasants' attraction to cities certainly is no news to anyone who studies the developing world, industrialization, and social change. What makes the Chinese situation with veterans fairly unique, I suggest, is that state policies, particularly regarding rural-based demobilization and rapid industrialization under the "Soviet Model" of development, as well as more deeply entrenched patterns of discrimination against those with less education, often had the effect of accentuating veterans' rural background and identity at the expense of their military or political credentials. Unlike militaries mobilized for total, mass war which required deep urban conscription, the PLA was a predominantly rural force. As a result, policies regarding industry and urban develop-ment would have even greater impact on their prospects than had the PLA been better integrated. As early as 1951, urban officials complained about veterans who "love big-city life" and refuse to return home.[136] Among the veterans in the 1957 Shanghai sample, shedding themselves of peasant status and earning more money were critical factors in their decision to move to the city. Veterans, having come from the north, invariably described agricultural life as "very bitter," quite unlike "the good life" (*haohun*) in Shanghai. Wang Ruiying, for example, was a CCP member and former sergeant in the PLA. He was discharged in 1954, after nine years in the service. Asked by inter-viewers why he left the countryside, he said,

> As a temporary worker on the docks I can make around two yuan per day, or 60 yuan a month. In the countryside you'd eat bitterness for a year and the most you'd make wouldn't be more than 200 yuan.

With income more than three times higher than rural wages, Wang was able to bring his wife and child to Shanghai, where they lived in a working-class district.[137] In the relatively developed Shanghai suburbs, veterans were very aware of the difference between wages in agriculture and industry. In a meeting of veterans in Qingpu, some complained, largely correctly, that state food-purchasing policies were impoverishing the countryside while allowing Shanghai residents to "eat as much as they want to"; wondered why policies were so biased toward the city; and told attending officials that the CCP was no better than Chiang Kai-shek when it came to veterans' livelihood. More than fourteen veterans shouted their approval when a veteran surnamed Huang said, "The difference between peasants' and workers' standard of living is just too large: a worker makes 70–80 yuan a month, but a peasant can make 100 yuan in a year. That's why peasants are itching to leave the countryside. Workers' salaries should come down a bit."[138] A 1959 investiga-tion report complained about their "commonly held view" of "loving the city, hating the village; loving industry, hating agriculture" (*xicheng yanxiang, xigong, yannong*).[139]

During a meeting of representatives of veterans, martyr families, and military dependents from Qingpu County, veterans vented some of these sentiments in even harsher tones. "Veterans from rural areas," the summary report noted, "are convinced that there is no future in agriculture." Others complained that land was in short supply and there were "too many people" already working on it. Veterans who were older (early 30s) could not work as hard or long as younger peasants, so they earned fewer work points and less money. The countryside was considered "backward," even among these "rep-resentatives" who were selected for their political reliability. Of the fifty-six veterans present at the meeting, twenty-three openly stated that they were "not at ease" in the countryside. The demand for urban jobs was acute: in Dianshan Township, the chair of the meeting was approached by seven veterans who demanded that he "go to the government to get them work in industry." As they were departing the meeting, the seven warned him: "If you can't arrange for our jobs, we'll withdraw our support for you as a representative."[140]

In all likelihood, there was little the chair could do to help them out, for reasons that will be explained in Chapter 5. His probable course of action would be to pen a letter to the Bureau of Civil Affairs, which during these years was responsible for placing veterans in jobs, on behalf of the seven. In its summary report of 1956, Qingpu Civil Affairs noted that, "on average," roughly ten veterans per day paid them a visit, the majority requesting industrial employment. "Prior to military service," they noted, "the veterans were engaged in agricultural work, so after their discharge they were sent back to the countryside (some became local officials)." The report stated that these veterans "looked down" on agriculture and had "bad relations" with rural officials. The report writers, sitting in their offices in the county seat, criticized these veterans for being "too picky" and not having enough wherewithal to "overcome difficulties," but they also acknowledged that, from an "objective standpoint," the "very large gap" between the quality of life in cities/towns and rural areas was a critical cause as well.[141] In a 1957 summary of a veterans meeting at the county seat, officials tallied 639 complaints (among them 256 focused on work, 124 on relations with village cadres, 97 on food supply, 47 on resettlement policy, and 82 on Civil Affairs) and deemed 86 percent as "reasonable."[142] Shanghai may have been an extreme case, but other cities in China—Beijing, Canton (in Guangdong Province), and Ningbo (Zhejiang)—also experienced veterans who were unable to adjust to working the land and "blindly" moved away to cities.[143]

Quality-of-life issues, frustrating for returned rural veterans in normal times, became direr when land was not only in short supply but also plagued with locusts or covered with water from the flooding of rivers and their tributaries. A long-time concern in rural China, and the cause of much violence and rebellion, environmental problems did not end in 1949. In the early to mid-1950s, northern Jiangsu Province was afflicted with several floods, which severely affected the harvests. Migration to better, more secure locales long had been in the repertoire of responses to these disasters, and these continued unabated—but with an important difference. Unlike during the pre-1949 period when those affected by disaster were "mere" peasants, now CCP propaganda had elevated hundreds of thousands of poor peasants from the north into heroes of the revolution. This included veterans as well as family members of martyrs and PLA soldiers. The dilemma was this: how could their high status be maintained if they appeared as poor and bedraggled as previous waves of refugees from stricken rural areas?

Reports from the early and mid-1950s attest to the movement of "high-status" migrants from poverty-stricken areas in the north to the relatively secure south Yangzi region. In Qingpu, martyr and military dependent families from Jiangsu and Shandong could be found begging for food in the street, in part because they were "not treated well by their families." "We can't take all of them into this region," officials complained.[144] A 1953 report in *Internal Reference*, a limited-circulation official publication, noted that there were some 30,000 of this group in Shanghai, and "not a few have barely anything to eat."[145] Veterans were likewise affected by the environment. The investigation report on 469 "non-Shanghai" veterans found that, among those who arrived in 1956–1957 (422 of them), roughly 75 percent were simply escaping natural disasters, "especially in the north Yangzi area."[146] This level of detail is not available in the Shandong reports I have at my disposal, but the *Shandong Administrative Bulletin* also noted that "their" veterans and martyr and military dependents' families were migrating to cities because of "real economic difficulties or because they were victims of natural disasters and cannot find any other solution."[147]

In theory, veterans and other elite populations who were affected by natural disasters were entitled to government assistance. When push came to shove, however, "the government" could be quite capricious when it came to deciding who actually received funds. Take, for instance, the case of Jiang Kaiqing. Jiang, demobilized in 1952, was from "north of the Yangzi" and had been working back in his township for four years when natural disaster struck in 1956. Unable to eat for three days, Jiang was upset that township and village cadres "never came by to see if he was alright." According to the report, these cadres "did not like him beforehand" and used their access to emergency funds and food to teach him a lesson. Jiang "sought revenge" for this slight but eventually reasoned that it was better just to leave the village than to fight it out. Last seen, Jiang was working in a Shanghai barbershop.[148]

These last couple of cases hint at the second major "push" factor, in addition to natural disasters, for veteran migration into cities. Kaiqing Jiang ended up in the barbershop because of two intersecting events: the natural disaster in the area and his poor relationship with village officials who offended his sense of honor and kept his stomach empty for three days. Jiang's case was not simply quirky or, in statistical terms, an "outlier." Numerous reports from the 1950s and 1960s (and the reform period) point to a difficult, tense, and sometimes outright hostile relationship between returning veterans and local cadres, many of whom had risen to their status through non-military careers (see Chapter 3

for more on this topic). Land, power, and other resources were highly contentious issues, much as they were when Nigerian, Roman, Ghanaian, and other
veterans were demobilized back to the countryside, and in the battles over
them (who got good land and jobs working on it) veterans generally found
themselves in a weaker position. In Shandong, for example, a report noted that
"lack of land" was a "problem" for returning veterans.[149] This was a whopping
understatement when we consider a hand-transcribed report of a meeting of
county officials in the province, many of whom were alarmed by "uprisings"
against the government led by veterans and former prisoners of war who lacked
land and housing.[150] In some cases, village cadres prevented veterans from assuming political posts. Not a few were punched, kicked, and otherwise abused
by village cadres.[151] *People's Daily* reports from the mid-1950s also attest to
rural cadres "discriminating" against returned veterans and being insufficiently
concerned with their well-being.[152] In Qingpu, veterans complained that the
only time local cadres were concerned with their welfare was when they were
needed; otherwise, they were ignored (*bu yong bu cai*).[153] One veteran put it
this way: "In the army we talked about everything, but back in the village the
cadres just ignore us (*bu licai*), as if we're not members of the mutual aid team.
In the army, we felt welcomed, but here the treatment is always cold (*shui qing
shui leng*). How can we be enthusiastic about our work?" This military–civilian
transition problem was seconded by another: "In the army I was a platoon commander; I led men. Now others lead me. The township party secretary doesn't
even talk or listen to me. What's more, he looks down on me (*qiaobuqi*)! I can't
take it (*kanbuguai*)."[154] According to a township-level investigation, some veterans reciprocated this treatment: "You ignore me, so I'll ignore you." "Mutual
condescension" (*huxiang qiaobuqi*) was common.[155]

   In part, this problem can be attributed to veterans' minority status in
most villages, with the exception of those in some of the pre-1949 base
areas. But more problematic from veterans' perspective was bad timing:
land reform, which was completed in most areas by 1953, usually took
place before they arrived on the scene. By 1954–1957, by which time
roughly 5.26 million veterans had been discharged,[156] the rural economy
was already undergoing collectivization. Veterans, who had been away
from the fields for a very long time, had rusty agricultural skills and tended
to be older; some, as we will see in Chapter 6, also had physical ailments.
Moreover, few of them were enthusiastic about their return to the land in
the first place—it was not their choice. As such, they were generally seen
as a "burden" on local resources, much like during the Roman Empire when
villagers derided veteran–farmers for their poor agricultural skills and generally had poor relations with them.[157] Although there is scant evidence on
veterans' income relative to that of other villagers (which in itself varied

widely), it's highly plausible (given the many complaints about "livelihood problems" scattered throughout the sources) that their incomes were somewhat lower than their age cohorts who did not serve in the military.[158] In relatively commercialized areas such as Qingpu, difficulties working the land, while irksome, were not extremely problematic, since veterans might be employed in shops, local industry, or fisheries or in trades like blacksmithing.[159] There were also fewer of them, since areas south of the Yangzi supplied fewer soldiers to the PLA than more northern provinces. It was a different story, however, for veterans demobilized to rural locales that were poorer and less commercialized and whose officials had little appreciation for veterans' return.

Several disturbing cases in Guangxi Province in China's southwest,[160] while perhaps extreme, demonstrate just how problematic this combination could be. These cases, unlike many others that involved run-of-the mill discrimination, were extensively investigated by Guangxi officials and sent on to the State Council in December 1955. The State Council, in turn, distributed them nationwide as part of a larger effort to draw attention to problems affecting demobilized soldiers. Located largely in Guangxi's Xing'an and Anfu counties, these cases, the government concluded, were the clear result of local authorities' "neglect" of the dire economic straits of returned veterans—a serious charge, but not enough to warrant criminal prosecution. The first case involved Liu Jinya, who was discharged in the early 1950s and lived in Yang Township. Said to have developed a "mild" mental illness in the army, Liu was greatly disturbed when he discovered that his father had died of illness. Unable to work the land, Liu rented out his family's property and sold off his farm equipment and one cow. According to the investigators, "township officials not only did not help or educate him, they also halted his grain provisions and threatened him." Liu tried to make a living selling firewood, but the proceeds from this were only enough to buy vegetables, which constituted his entire diet. In mid-July 1955, Liu was on his way back home from collecting firewood and happened to see a corpse; where it came from is not clear in the report. Next to it laid a bowl of rice, which Liu promptly ate. With his stomach a bit fuller, Liu gathered his strength and dragged the corpse back to the village, where he washed, cooked, and ate it. Village authorities got word of his meal and arrested him—on exactly what charge is not clear in the report. What happened to him after his arrest is also undetermined, although the judicial authorities may have been lenient, given that they established that "he ate the corpse because he was close to starvation."[161]

Other veterans took comparably desperate measures to feed themselves. A veteran surnamed Xie, who lived in Tangtou Township with several family members, fell into debt (50 yuan) after paying for his father's funeral costs. Ignored by officials, Xie sold his son to repay the money. But even after collecting the proceeds from this sale, he was unable to dig himself out of debt. He and his wife hung themselves but were rescued before they died. In a similar case in Jintian Township, Anfu County, a veteran suffered from pain in his hips and was unable to do strenuous labor in the fields. Because of this, his income was quite low. To get by, he requested that the head of the township "arrange for the sale of his five year-old son." According to the investigators, the township chief "not only did not help him [with government funds] but assisted with the sale," which netted 230 yuan.[162]

How widespread these practices were is difficult to determine, given the reluctance of archivists in poorer areas to declassify these materials. But this reluctance in itself is probably telling: an archive director in Shandong told me that he feared that his province would "lose face" if more materials were opened up. What does seem to be clear from the available sources is that the challenge of rural poverty was exacerbated among veterans who were discharged relatively late and found themselves on the margins of the rural political structure. Without much assistance from local officials, veterans often faltered in an economy that placed a high premium on physical and taxing labor. Rural politics, or, rather, veterans' relatively weak position in it, explains many veterans' desire to move to cities, as well as the fact that many of them arrived with official documentation: local officials were quite pleased to see them leave.

In the comparative literature, there is only fragmentary evidence of this sort of "political push." Officials of rural communities may have derided veterans' poor agricultural skills and allegedly "boorish" behavior during the Roman Empire, but veterans' status protected them from widespread abuse at their hands. Like many rural Chinese veterans, French veterans of the Napoleonic Wars (some were drafted in 1793 and were still fighting through 1814) "admitted that they felt increasingly alienated from civilian life" and did not think that they could find a "niche for themselves back in the village or on the family farm," but there is little evidence that they were expelled from their communities because they were not wanted there.[163] I have found no evidence of returning white Civil War veterans in the United States—Union or Confederate—who were maltreated by rural communities in this manner. German prisoners of war who were repatriated to East and West Germany by the Soviet Union in the 1950s were welcomed by key institutions in society, despite their defeat in WWII.[164] There are, however, interesting counterexamples. Japanese veterans of WWII did not receive a warm welcome back home—but Japan lost WWII, whereas the CCP allegedly elevated its status at home and in the world after its wars.

More telling examples, and ones that I will draw upon in subsequent chapters, are American Revolutionary War veterans and African-Americans in the United States. In the former case, there is little evidence that they were welcomed home as heroes; on the contrary, even in a very revolutionary state such as Massachusetts, "civilians were suspicious of the Continentals, and the back country resisted paying veterans their settlements." Some soldiers resorted to begging as they made their way home.[165] In the case of another celebrated war—World War II—African-American veterans, unlike whites, were often abused, killed, and discriminated against when they returned to rural communities from the Civil War and WWII.[166] Like Chinese veterans, many southern African-American veterans migrated to northern cities after encountering this treatment.[167] While somewhat counterintuitive, northern Chinese peasant–veterans and African-Americans shared many characteristics: low education and literacy levels, rural background, poverty, poor prospects in their local communities, and widespread ideas about their inferiority (albeit for different reasons). The main difference, of course, is that in the United States, African-Americans are a demographic minority, whereas in China peasants have always (even today) been the majority and are considered as "Han Chinese" as the Shanghai intellectual.

THE BATTLE TO REMAIN URBAN

National regulations for resettling veterans were based on the simple premise of requiring them to return to their native place (*yuan ji an zhi*). At the same time, national leaders were not so naïve as to expect that this would be easy, especially given the lure of higher salaries, status, and excitement that was associated with urban living. The Center instructed cities that, should veterans remain in cities despite the *yuan ji an zhi* policy, local officials should "patiently" try to convince them to return, "teach them about the policy," and "stress the importance of agricultural production."[168] Urban officials immediately recognized just how difficult it would be to enforce these mandates; they understood that veterans' circumstances in the city were "complicated." It would be better, they recommended, to handle veterans "on a case-by-case basis and avoid uniform solutions for everyone."[169] Setting out their strategy after having researched a sizable sample of non-Shanghai veterans, Shanghai officials decided that it would be best to start ousting those who "have not succeeded in the city and have no way to get by," since they were a drain on resources and could at least be tempted by the prospect of farming for a living. The next candidates for removal would be veterans who were "dependent on friends and relatives in the city, but the latter are poor themselves." Representing some 40 percent of the veteran migrant population, these former soldiers were generally employed as barbers and peddlers of one thing or another. Even less amenable to rural repatriation were those veterans (50 percent) who had "temporary residence permits" and who managed to get by without family assistance by being employed as temporary workers in factories, service sector employees, and "manual laborers whose income is relatively good." With this group, urban officials should conduct repeated and extensive "educational work" to get them to leave, but the prospects for this were not great. Some veterans, however, were allowed to remain in the city: "the minority" who already had established formal residence, who had found "stable" employment, or who "truly have no family or work capacity in their native place."[170]

The inclusion of the word "truly" in this municipal guideline is telling. Urban officials had long been trying to get migrant veterans to leave the city but were often confounded by veterans' resort to trickery, which, as it turns out, was fairly easily accomplished given that the Bureau of Civil Affairs had a weak investigative apparatus and the security organs had other priorities. A letter from the Shanghai Bureau of Civil Affairs to the Ministry of the Interior (1954) complained that "many veterans [from Anhui, Shandong, Fujian, Jiangsu, and Zhejiang] come to Shanghai falsely claiming they have relatives here" and even "tell us that their acquaintances are their relatives." In one case, a veteran's "uncle" was actually "his army buddy who was discharged at the same time." Other veterans told officials that they were born in Shanghai and "lived in the city for several years" before being moved by their parents elsewhere in the country. One veteran, for instance, was, in fact, born in Shanghai but moved to Guiyang, the capital of Guizhou Province, in 1932. Naturally, he claimed his native place as "Shanghai," but Shanghai officials based their definition on where his family was located (still in Guiyang) and joined the PLA (Guiyang). Even Shanghai wives could be invented! A veteran surnamed Wang, who served in naval logistics in the East China Military Region, was originally from Huang County in Shandong, where he still had parents and brothers. Wang was one of many soldiers from Shandong who participated in the final battle for Shanghai. After 1949, he stayed on to defend the city's coastal areas. On leave he happened to meet a married woman, with whom he "became close, causing a divorce." Prior to his discharge, Wang falsely claimed to his unit that "his wife" lived in Shanghai, hoping that this would persuade officials to grant him permanent residency.[171] This sort of trickery continued well into the 1950s and early 1960s. A 1960 "Summary Report" on veteran resettlement noted cases of forgery of party member status, native place, and military status. One veteran even managed to get into the Shanghai Academy of Social Sciences by falsifying his records.[172] Some of these efforts failed, which the summary report emphasized, but it is highly probable that many veterans managed to fly in under the radar, particularly when verifying claims of relatives' residence required correspondence with faraway provinces. A document from 1953 admitted that some units did not conduct "serious investigation of native place."[173]

Nevertheless, the effort to get veterans to depart the city—what veterans called "Shanghai's policy"—irked them a great deal. Veterans were reportedly "very angry" when confronted by the police and other authorities demanding documents and information or when forced to listen to urban officials offering vagaries such as "rural resettlement is in accordance with the current demands of development and is helping local reconstruction."[174] Thinking in terms of a national state rather than just cities and countryside—a characteristic also noted among veterans of the American Revolutionary War[175]—one veteran said, "Now we have a unified government, so we should be able to go wherever we want!" Others shot back: "If you don't take me in, where will you get me a job?" "Where will you send me back to?" "My document clearly says: 'Native Place: Shanghai.'" Some—by one 1953 account, the "majority"[176]—flat-out refused to leave, "convinced that it will be easy to find a job,"[177] or cited official approval for staying: "The army has allowed me to come to Shanghai; I'm just following orders; why don't you resettle me?"[178] In 1959, a veteran from Fengtai County in the Shanghai suburbs circumvented the mandated employment process (which required that veterans be "introduced" to jobs through the Bureau of Civil Affairs) by not reporting to Fengtai after his discharge, getting a job by himself, and only then going to the county for a predated "letter of introduction," just to make it official.[179] Just how pervasive this practice was is difficult to determine, however.

When trickery and "talking back" did not work, veterans were quite willing to do what people in many countries do when they don't get what they want: make a nuisance of themselves. In Shanghai, veterans took their bedding to the reception offices of local authorities and refused to leave.[180] In Qingpu, veterans made repeated visits to the Bureau of Civil Affairs, often getting into heated arguments with its officials.[181] To each other they said, "You're a fool and idiot if you don't fight with government officials," and when reprimanded for their behavior, they remarked, "Party, Government—I don't give a damn!" which prompted county officials to write, "Veterans like this should be punished, not just 'talked to.'"[182] Another veteran, however, threatened to "take my discharge certificate and go to Beijing to beg" (thinking that this would evoke sympathy) because his problems were not being addressed locally.[183] Some wrote letters—often more than one—requesting the opportunity to study and work in industry:[184]

Dear Section Chief:

When we were demobilized and returned to the village, we heard through the news that the State Council would solve employment and other concrete problems. Will veterans who have returned to the countryside have the opportunity to go to school? Before going into service I worked on a boat. After participating in the revolution I was sent back to work in agriculture. My thinking is that because I already worked in agriculture, now you could help introduce me to working in industry. Is that possible? Please reply (you didn't reply to previous letters).

Soldier xxx

This request was denied. The section chief responded (untruthfully) that they can make exceptions only for those with rural backgrounds "who have needed skills." Other veterans tried at levels higher than a mere section chief, whose power to procure a job in industry was highly limited in any case (see Chapter 4). In Shanghai, some migrant veterans wrote to the city government and party committee, others to Chairman Mao or Marshal Zhu De, the founder of the Red Army.[185] Mao, however, was not Caesar, a general who was in frequent contact (including training and marching) with his former soldiers; there is little evidence of personal and sustained attention to veterans' problems after 1949 on the part of Mao, whose sympathies, much like his fellow romantic revolutionary Thomas Jefferson, seemed to be with militias and the notion of a people's war rather than with veterans of the main standing army.

Complaining and letter writing were probably among the milder methods to obtain urban citizenship. Some threatened suicide, one veteran telling officials, "I'll kill myself if you send me back! The Huangpu [river] will be my home!", a warning that he would drown himself,[186] and others actually carried out their threats.[187] Others said that they would "starve themselves to death in Shanghai" in hunger strikes rather than return to their native place.[188] Some violence was not self-directed: reports mentioned veterans who "beat cadres" and "create disturbances."[189] Efforts were also made to evoke public sympathy:

After arrival veterans are approached by the Residence Committee, Police, Bureau of Civil Affairs and district committee for their residence permit. If they don't have it, they get into heated arguments with the cadres and rail (*manma*) against the government. In public, they grumble, "You're an upright person and still end up like this; you go home and can't make a living and Shanghai doesn't give you any work!"[190]

Public remonstrations, however, could also assume a very different, and for the regime potentially more dangerous, dynamic when they brought together veterans from different areas who were willing to engage in collective action. In late January 1957, for instance, the head of the National Veterans' Committee, Fu Qiutao—a former general with the New Fourth Army—reported that a naval unit sent 140 veterans back to Hubei Province. When they arrived at the train station of the provincial capital of Wuhan, however, the veterans "refused to go to the countryside" and demanded other work. When the veterans threatened to mount a street protest, municipal authorities stepped in and prevented any further action.[191] This national-level report may have downplayed the seriousness of this incident. That this might have been the case is suggested by a classified report from Guomindang Intelligence, which was monitoring the veteran situation on the mainland fairly closely. According to one report, also from 1957, the Xian train station was the scene of a violent incident between veterans and the local police. Apparently, a group of northern veterans was dispatched to the far northwest—probably Qinghai or Xinjiang—but they were so unhappy with the conditions there they returned together to Xian and demanded free tickets back "home." Station officials refused and dispatched security personnel to prevent any problems. Undeterred, the veterans clobbered them and used stones to damage the station's equipment. Outnumbered, the station security team called for reinforcements. In the ensuing melee, four people at the station were seriously injured, one of whom died on the way to the hospital; more than twelve were slightly injured. The veterans did not relent, however, and refused to leave if they were forced to pay for tickets.[192] Problems involving veterans who refused to move to the interior and other rural areas were noted in 1960 (blamed on "excessive individualism")[193] and 1965 as well.[194]

Shandong and other provinces also experienced the wrath of angry veteran groups. Mentioned in an internally circulated government report that found its way to the provincial archive, some unemployed veterans "gathered together" and created a ruckus in government offices. In the cities of Harbin and Dalian, government offices were occasionally "closed for business" because of collective protests. In the city of Fushun, several veterans hooked up with former comrades-in-arms from Hebei Province and mounted a street "parade" carrying aloft the image of Mao as well as a sign that read (rhyming in Chinese): "The government doesn't care, so we have to beg" (*zhengfu bu guan, woman zhi hao tao fan*). Other Shandong veterans, probably in a faux-suicide ploy, lay down on railway tracks to make a statement about their treatment.[195] Other veterans took their complaints directly to provincial and national authorities.[196]

Northern cities and provinces appear to have been main loci of veteran protests over settlement policy, but they were not the only ones. Tao Zhu, provincial party secretary of Guangdong in the far south, wrote in a May 5,

1957, article in *Nanfang Daily* that among the twelve "contradictions" [difficult problems] in the province, "veteran contradictions" ranked as number nine, even though Guangdong did not absorb many veterans. Noting problems in "very many" areas and in government institutions, various incidents involving veterans were commonplace. Citing a number of causes, including the veterans' sense that protesting was "their capital" (*benqian*), or entitlement, Tao placed most of the blame on "resettlement work" that was not being implemented properly, not the policy itself.[197]

Tao's observation was astute, but it also ignored the larger issues, as he was likely aware. Regardless of how well policy was implemented on the ground, it would be unlikely to shift the overwhelming sentiment among veterans that the future was in industry and in cities and that rural areas would forever remain poor and backward. An observation in a 1959 report that the "biggest problem in resettlement is that veterans hope to enter industry and are not at ease working in agriculture"[198] remained as consistent throughout PRC history as the state's determination, through the *yuan ji an zhi policy*, to severely limit the number of veterans able to realize these hopes; as one veteran from the Shanghai suburbs said in 1962, "after three years in the army there's no way I'm returning to the countryside."[199] For veterans who had a strong sense of China as a national state and who assessed their status in society in spatial terms—whether or not they could live in a city and work in a factory—returning them "back home" to the countryside, regardless of how impoverished it was or how the nature of its economy had changed in the interim, was a source of tremendous frustration and resentment. That the state refused this basic demand severely tarnished its legitimacy in their eyes.

The history of veteran resettlement, however, can tell us much more than just the outcome of land-based reward programs, important as these were to veterans' sense of justice. Many states have also tried to reward veterans with higher status, moral authority, an empowered identity, and political clout—in addition to the more "concrete" reward of land or money. Moreover, veterans have taken status, identity, and power-related issues as key "measures" of whether their service is rewarded and appreciated by their government and society at large. The modern Chinese state was different from the West in its conception of "land for service" but did share with it the notion (at least officially) that veterans, by virtue of their patriotic service, should have a higher status and more respect in society as well as a greater role in politics. Did veterans in China have the sense of political empowerment because of their service? Did society concur with the Center's articulation of the terms of this exchange? How did these issues play out in everyday interactions between veterans and officials and other citizens? It is to these questions that I turn in the next chapter.

NOTES

1. Azar Gat, *War in Human Civilization*, 319.
2. J. C. Mann, "The Settlement of Veterans in the Roman Empire," 13–15.
3. Ibid., 14.
4. Adrian Goldsworthy, *Caesar: Life of a Colossus*, 29, 156, 254.
5. Mann, "Settlement of veterans," 14.
6. Ibid., 17; Goldsworthy, *Caesar*, 473–74.
7. Keppie, *Colonisation and Veteran Settlement in Italy,* 55; Goldsworthy, *Caesar*, 473.
8. Mann, "Settlement of veterans," 17.
9. Ibid., 19.
10. Keppie, *Colonisation*, 60–61, 89. According to Mann, "the triumvirs . . . did not hesitate to confiscate land . . . [and] the land of 18 Italian cities was destined to be divided among veterans" ("Settlement of veterans," p. 22).
11. Mann, "Settlement of veterans," 80, 82, 86. Emphasis mine.
12. Keppie, *Colonisation*, 101.
13. Richard Alston, *Soldier and Society in Roman Egypt,* 66. Mann notes that in Egypt in the second and third centuries, the title *veteranus* "was recognized as an important distinction, without regard to the type of unit from which the individual veteran has been discharged" ("Settlement of veterans," p. 290).
14. Keppie, *Colonisation*, 113.
15. Ibid., 110; Mann, "Settlement of veterans," 292.
16. Mann, "Settlement of veterans," 64, 81, 82, 85, 232, 333–34, 344.
17. Peter Reese, *Homecoming Heroes,* 39, 42.
18. Elise Wirtshafter, "Social Misfits: Veterans' and Soldiers' Families in Servile Russia," 226.
19. Ibid., 227.
20. John Black and Charles Hyson, "Postwar Soldier Settlement," 3.
21. Ibid.
22. Carl Taylor, "The Veteran in Agriculture," 48.
23. Ibid., 53.
24. See Douglas Marshall, "Soldier Settlement in Agriculture," 277.
25. Taylor, "Veteran in agriculture," 48. Emphasis mine. Taylor served in the Bureau of Agricultural Economics in the U. S. Department of Agriculture and was also a professor of agriculture.
26. Marshall, "Soldier settlement," 275, 278.
27. For the most comprehensive account of Canadian resettlement, see Robert England, *Discharged: A Commentary of Civil Reestablishment of Veterans in Canada*; for veteran rehabilitation by working the land, see Desmond Morton and Glenn Wright, *Winning the Second Battle,* xi, 10, 100.
28. Pam and Brian O'Connor, *In Two Fields: Soldier Settlement in the South East of South Australia.*
29. Black and Hyson, "Postwar soldier settlement," 8.

30. James Matthews, "Clock Towers for the Colonized: Demobilization of the Nigerian Military," 266–67.

31. Adrienne Israel, "Ex-Servicemen at the Crossroads," 361–62, 366.

32. Lewis Greenstein, "The Impact of Military Service in World War I on Africans: The Nandi of Kenya," 499–500, 503.

33. Benjamin Ziemann, *War Experiences in Rural Germany*, 213–15.

34. Ray Huang, *1587: A Year of No Significance*, 160.

35. Ibid., 160.

36. Ibid., 162.

37. Pamela K. Crossley, *Orphan Warriors: Three Manchu Generations and the End of the Qing World*, 51.

38. Ibid., 23, 49, 51, 56. For the notion of the Qing as a military caste, see Edward Rhoads, *Manchus and Han: Ethnic Relations and Political Power in Late Qing and Early Republican China 1861–1928*. According to Mark Elliot, the compounds were conceptualized as "a tiger poised on a hill." See Mark Elliot, *The Manchu Way: The Eight Banners and Ethnic Identity in Late Imperial China*, 129–32.

39. Crossley, *Orphan Warriors*, 56.

40. Alston (*Soldier and Society*, p. 54) notes that the view of the veteran as a swaggering bully rests "primarily on the interpretation of literary texts . . . produced by the elite of the Roman Empire who were, by their very nature, hostile to any group that threatened or that they perceived to threaten their aristocratic power." The army was the biggest threat to aristocratic government, so the "rise in privileges granted to soldiers and veterans was condemned." The hostility of the "literary elite," he argues, "shapes our sources and influences the modern view."

41. There were, to be sure, regional variations in this general pattern. In practice, elites in frontier areas tended to rely more on controlling the gun than their cultural cultivation but did not completely ignore the importance of studying Confucian texts. See Joseph Esherick and Many Rankin (eds.), *Chinese Local Elites and Patterns of Dominance*. Arthur Waldron notes that "the passionately nationalistic and populist Chinese writers of the early twentieth century were not notable for the numbers of them that actually joined armies—a reflection of the traditionally low status according military service in China, which has persisted right down to the present, despite all intervening national and revolutionary ferment." See "Looking Backward: The People in Arms and the Transformation of War," 257.

42. The Opium War was fought largely on the southern coast; the war of 1894–1895 with Japan was fought mainly in Korea, not on the Chinese mainland.

43. Stephen MacKinnon, "Refugee Flight at the Outset of the Anti-Japanese War," 122.

44. Diane Koenker, "Urbanization and Deurbanization during the Russian Revolution and Civil War," 428.

45. Ibid., 442.

46. Ibid., 437.

47. Jan Meijer, "Town and Country in the Civil War"; Richard Pipes, "The Origins of Bolshevism: The Intellectual Evolution of Young Lenin."

48. As noted by Ray Huang (*Year of No Significance*, p. 171), General Ch'i in

the Ming dynasty preferred rural residents, as did Zeng Guofan. I thank David Strand for this reference.

49. This does not suggest that the revolution did not have an urban component; the CCP did conduct revolutionary activities in cities after being routed in 1927. See Patricia Stranahan, *Underground: The Shanghai Communist Party and the Politics of Survival*; Elizabeth Perry, *Patrolling the Revolution*, Chapter 3.

50. This is easily discerned in the statistics on veterans' resettlement. Since the policy was to return veterans to their hometowns and, in most cases, 85–95 percent of veterans "returned to the countryside," it stands to reason that these veterans came from the countryside as well.

51. *Zhu-Mao feijun fuyuan gongzuo zhi yanjiu* (1957), 33. Bureau of Investigation Archives 590.808/814. n.p.

52. These provinces included Shandong, Anhui, Jiangsu, Shaanxi, Shanxi, and Henan.

53. *Zhu-Mao feijun fuyuan gongzuo zhi yanjiu* (1957), 33. Bureau of Investigation 590.808/814, 36–39. These reports were all culled from the PRC press (e.g., *Beijing Dagong Bao, Xinhua*). Also see Greg Rohlf, "Dreams of Oil and Fertile Fields: The Rush to Qinghai in the 1950s," 467. For evidence on the importation of young women, see James Gao, "The Call of the Oases: The 'Peaceful Liberation' of Xinjiang, 1949–1953," 198–99.

54. SMA B1-2-1958, 31.

55. In Shandong, it was estimated that roughly 80 percent of veterans "returned to agriculture," with the "minority" in factories and government offices. See *Zhu-Mao*, citing the Shandong Veteran Resettlement Committee in 1957 (p. 33).

56. See, for instance, the Taihe County gazetteer (Anhui Province). In 1956, 94 percent of veterans returned to the countryside, but "only" 80 percent in 1964 and 87 percent in 1965 returned. *Taihe xian zhi* (Hefei: Huangshan, 1993), 268–69. In Wei County, Hebei Province, every single veteran supposedly returned to the countryside in 1950, 1954–1955, 1960, and 1962, but only 52 percent in 1956 and 87 percent in 1965 returned. See *Wei xian zhi* (Beijing; Sanxia, 1995), 497.

57. *Wuqiang xian zhi* (Beijing: Fangzhi chubanshe, 1996), 416. Wuba County, located on the Hebei-Shandong border, also took in homeless veterans. See *Wuba xian zhi* (Beijing: Fangzhi chubanshe, 1998), 581.

58. In the United States, which did not experience war on its home front, the concept "home" had far more positive associations. See Alfred Shuetz, "The Homecomer," 370.

59. Rosemary Preston, "Integrating Fighters after War," 463.

60. Mao did mention veterans in a written report to the Third Plenum of the Seventh CCP Central Committee on June 6, 1950, but devoted only one sentence to veteran resettlement. See "Struggle for a Fundamental Turn for the Better in the Financial and Economic Situation in the Country," in Michael Y. M. Kau and John K. Leung (eds.), *The Writings of Mao Zedong, 1949–1976*, Vol. 1, 100.

61. The "mass line" stipulated that policy decisions should include public input ("from the people") but that the party would systemize these ideas and then implement them ("to the people"), as seen in the Veterans' Advisory Boards in Canada and

the input of social scientists in its Veterans' Land Act of 1942 as well as the advisory roles American agricultural experts played in the GI Bill.

62. Stephen MacKinnon points out that very few intellectuals told the story of poor refugees from the Anti-Japanese War. See "Refugee Flight," 119.

63. See Martha Derthick, *Agency under Stress: The Social Security Administration in American Government,* 181. Derthick writes: "Persons who would presumably give painstaking attention to instructions on how to use a pasta machine . . . make major policy decisions with virtually no thought to whether a complex organization of human beings can reasonably be expected to execute their commands" (p. 175).

64. The unfavorable land–population ratio in rural China would suggest that there would be an ample supply of poor, unmarried male peasants ("bare sticks") who could be recruited into service. Other evidence suggests that the CCP had to work hard to pry recruits out of villages and that one way of doing this was providing them with land (See Chen, *Making Revolution*, p. 383). With collectivization, land was no longer a benefit of recruitment.

65. *Anhui sheng zhi: minzheng zhi* (Hefei: Anhui renmin chubanshe, 1993), 140.

66. *Zhu-Mao*, citing a report from *Xinhua*, 13, 33.

67. *Nanling xian zhi* (Hefei: Huangshan chubanshe, 1994), 499.

68. *Huaiyuan xian zhi* (Shanghai: Shanghai kexue yuan chubanshe, 1990), 394.

69. *Huangpu qu zhi* (Shanghai: Shanghai kexue yuan chubanshe, 1996), 115, 1088.

70. *Songjiang xian zhi* (Shanghai: Renmin chubanshe, 1991), 284.

71. *Fan xian zhi* (Zhengzhou: Henan renmin chubanshe, 1993), 514.

72. *Yi xian difang zhi* (Beijing: Zhongyang bianyi, 2000), 360, 362; *Ningyang xian zhi* (Beijing: Zhongguo shuji chubanshe, 1994), 258.

73. *Wangdu xian zhi* (Beijing: Fangzhi chubanshe, 2000), 601.

74. In Pingyuan County, Shandong, the best year for veterans was 1958, when 71 percent of veterans were allowed into enterprises. The following year, however, it fell to 1 percent but rose to 20 percent in 1960. See *Pingyuan xian zhi* (Jinan: Jilu, 1993), 556.

75. *Wei xian zhi* (Zhongguo sanxia chubanshe, 1995), 497.

76. *Yihua xian zhi* (Hebei renmin chubanshe, 1993), 716.

77. QA 48-2-105 (1957), 4. General Fu Qiutao, head of the National Veterans Committee, reported that "some families think their son or husband is good-for-nothing if they return to the countryside." See SMA A54-2-49, 43.

78. *Yi xian zhi* (Beijing: Zhongyang bianyi chubanshe, 2000), 360.

79. *Jinzhai xian zhi* (Shanghai: Renmin chubanshe, 1992), 527.

80. *Jixi xian zhi* (Hefei: Huangshan shu she, 1998), 632.

81. Because I was not able to secure access to archives in other provinces (such as Henan, Anhui, or Jiangxi), I have not been able to systemically compare veterans' wages, occupations, or residence status (*hukou*) in order to assess the extent to which there were different patterns of upward mobility in different regions. The information provided by gazetteers does hint at some provincial variation (generally in the range of 20–35 percent securing political positions) but does not provide greater detail.

82. *Heping xian zhi* (Beijing: Qunzhong chubanshe, 1993), 575.

83. *Dongping xian zhi* (Jinan: Shandong renmin chubanshe), 373.

84. Thaxton, *Catastrophe and Contention*, 82–83.

85. DDA 11-7-89 (1954), 150. Veterans were recruited into militias, although it is not clear whether they were the "primary source" of personnel or formed their "mainstay," as Victor Nee suggests. I have little evidence that many veterans were in charge of militias. In any event, militias were controlled by village and township leaders, most of whom were not returned veterans. See Nee, "Between Center and Locality: State, Militia, and Village," 230, 241. In Shenxiang Township in Qingpu, among 24 returning veterans, there were 18 who "participated" in the militia, but only six of these had any sort of leadership position. Only three of the 24 became either CCP or CYL members after their return. See QA 48-2-109 (1957), 51.

86. QA 48-2-31, 30.

87. Benjamin Ziemann, *War Experiences in Rural Germany,* 229–31.

88. QA 48-2-53. A 1956 report provided the following breakdown on the discharge rank of 692 veterans: 464 privates, 182 corporals, 14 sergeants (*fu paizhang*), 25 master sergeants, and 7 lieutenants and lieutenant colonels (battalion commanding officers). See QA 48-2-88 (1956). On rural Japan, see Soda Cultural Research Institute, "Investigation of Life of Demobilized Soldiers in Agricultural Villages," September 30, 1946. National Archives, Record Group 331, Box 05743.

89. QA 48-2-109, 37.

90. QA 48-2-88 (1956); a 1957 township-level investigation of veterans found that among 21 veterans, four (19 percent) were party members. Among these, two entered the party after they returned to the township. See QA 48-2-109, 72.

91. QA 48-2-156 (1962), 18.

92. QA 48-2-105 (1957), 136.

93. Jeremy Brown, "From Resisting Communists to Resisting America," 111, 114.

94. Friedman, Pickowicz, and Selden, *Revolution, Resistance and Reform in Village China*, 49.

95. *Zhu-Mao*, 13.

96. SMA B1-2-1958 (1957), 24.

97. See *People's Daily*, January 17, 1963. The only areas where the percentage was significantly higher (60 percent) were in some of the pre-1949 revolutionary "base areas."

98. SMA B127-1-846, 25.

99. See *Origins of the Cultural Revolution, Vol. 3,* 337.

100. SMA B168-1-600 (1951), 126.

101. Perry and Li, *Proletarian Power*, 67. They note that these northern veterans were "soldiers" who had "stayed on to assume top political posts in the new municipal government," but it is more likely that they had much higher rank and were educated.

102. SMA B168-1-600 (1951), 113. For discrimination against these northerners, see Emily Honig, *Creating Chinese Ethnicity: Subei People in Shanghai, 1850–1980*.

103. SMA B168-1-600 (1951), 111.

104. Ibid.

105. SMA B169-1-607 (1952), 50.

106. Ibid.

107. Ibid., 75.

108. Ibid., 49–50.

109. SMA B168-1-628 (1956), 135.

110. SA A20-1-109 (1953), 48. Other provinces also called attention to veterans moving to cities. See *Guangxi tongzhi: minzheng zhi* (Nanning: Guangxi renmin chubanshe, 1996), 74.

111. *Shandong xingzheng gongbao*, 12/1954 (SA), 13. According to the Anhui gazetteer, Anhui veterans left the province for Nanjing, Beijing, and Xi'an as well. These trips outside the province included 362 visits to Beijing to petition central authorities between July and November 1956. See *Anhui sheng zhi: minzheng zhi*, 140.

112. *Shandong xingzheng gongbao*, 13.

113. SMA B168-1-619 (1955), 30.

114. SMA B168-1-605 (1952), 80.

115. SMA B168-1-607 (1952), 50.

116. This was noted in the 1955 State Council "Decision" regarding veterans' resettlement. See SMA B127-1-811, 17.

117. SMA B1-2-1958 (1957), 21. In the United States, roughly 9.5 million were discharged between 1945 and 1947.

118. Ibid., 26.

119. Ibid.

120. Ibid.

121. Ibid., 28.

122. Ibid., 29.

123. SMA B168-1-645, 41.

124. Ibid., 41–42.

125. QA 48-2-109 (1957), 13. For more Qingpu evidence on this, see QA 48-2-156, 21.

126. SMA B168-1-658 (1964), 43–44.

127. SMA B168-1-209 (1963), 7.

128. SMA B127-1-869 (1965), 10.

129. See MacFarquhar and Schoenhals, *Mao's Last Revolution*, 374.

130. QA 48-2-155 (1962), 24.

131. Several important studies of migration and migrants include Li Zhang, *Strangers in the City: Reconfigurations of Space, Power and Social Networks within China's Floating Population*; Dorothy Solinger, *Contesting Citizenship in Urban China: Peasant Migrants, the State and the Logic of the Market*; and Rachel Murphy, *How Migrant Labor Is Changing Rural China*.

132. Given that these veterans had not yet settled down, tracking their numbers was an imprecise science, as Public Security officials admitted. See SMA B168-1-633 (1957), 100.

133. Ibid., 100–101.

134. Ibid., 102; in Qingpu see QA 48-2-105, 136.

135. SMA B168-1-633 (1957), 102.

136. SMA B168-1-600 (1951), 109–10.

137. SMA B168-1-633 (1957), 101.

138. QA 48-2-105 (1957), 134, 140.

139. SMA B168-1-645 (1959), 21.

140. QA 48-2-27 (1956), 46, 48.

141. QA 48-1-35 (1956), 15.

142. QA 48-2-105 (1957), 4. The rest were deemed miscellaneous. Veterans were said to object to the unified purchasing system for agricultural products, which had the effect of subsidizing urban food at the expense of the countryside.

143. *People's Daily*, January 27, 1954, and May 6, 1954.

144. QA 48-2-2 (1949), 23.

145. SMA B168-1-609 (1953), 4.

146. SMA B168-1-633 (1957), 102.

147. *Shandong xingzheng gongbao*, December 1954, 13 (SA).

148. SMA B168-1-633 (1957), 101.

149. SA A20-1-109, 5.

150. SA A20-1-41 (1952), 69. These uprisings were said to have taken place "in every county" in one administrative region (*zhuanqu*) and in Tai'an, Changqing, Xintai, and five other counties. These veterans lost contact with their families and were suddenly demobilized to the village, but after returning they found there was no land left after land reform and no reserve housing for them. The township government could not place them. Some were living at the District Government, others with relatives. Others committed suicide. It is difficult to assess what sorts of veterans were involved in these uprisings. Some may have been frontline troops who were veterans of the PLA during Civil War. Others may have been former Nationalist Army soldiers who switched over to the Communist side in the late 1940s who were then dispatched to fight in Korea. On the participation of ex-Nationalist troops in Korea, see John Gittings, *The Role of the Chinese Army*, 77.

151. For a typical report, see DDA 11-7-96, 5. The amount of land distributed to each veteran is difficult to gauge, since conditions varied widely across the country. In Tongcheng County in central Anhui, which was probably fairly typical of North China, veterans received about four *mou* each, which is roughly two-thirds of an acre. See *Tongcheng xian zhi* (Hefei: Huangshan, 1995), 507.

152. *People's Daily*, April 18, 1956.

153. QA 48-2-141 (1957), 13; QA 48-2-46 (1953), 76.

154. QA 48-2-105 (1957), 135, 139–40.

155. QA 48-2-109 (1957), 75.

156. SMA B1-2-1958 (1957), 21. The average was roughly 700,000 a year.

157. Keppie, *Colonisation and Veteran Settlement in Italy*, 101.

158. QA 48-2-27 (1957), 48.

159. QA 48-1-35 (1956), 13. The county received 80 veterans. Of these, 40 percent were *not* resettled into agriculture.

160. According to Diana Lary, Guangxi, already a very poor province, was hit particularly hard by the Anti-Japanese War because it contributed so many soldiers to the war effort. During the war, it suffered an acute labor shortage and food shortages were

very serious. See "One Province's Experience of War: Guangxi, 1937–1945," 319.

161. SMA B168-1-628 (1956), 166.

162. Ibid.

163. See Alan Forrest, "La Patrie en danger," 30.

164. Frank Biess, *Homecomings: Returning POWs and the Legacies of Defeat in Postwar Germany.*

165. Susan Browne, "War-Making and U.S. State Formation," 244.

166. David Onkst, "First a Negro . . . Incidentally a Veteran," 517–34.

167. Neil McMillen, "How Mississippi's Black Veterans Remember WWII," 106.

168. SMA B168-1-633 (1957), 103.

169. Ibid.

170. Ibid., 103–4.

171. SMA B1-2-1519 (1954), 1–2.

172. SMA B168-1-649 (1960), 18–19.

173. SMA B168-1-611 (1953), 125.

174. SMA B1-2-1519 (1954), 4.

175. Browne, "War-Making and U.S. State Formation," 232.

176. SMA B168-1-611 (1953), 125.

177. SMA B1-2-1519, 4.

178. SMA B168-1-611 (1953), 125.

179. SMA B168-1-645 (1959), 21.

180. SMA B168-1-633 (1957), 102.

181. QA 48-2-27 (1956), 47; QA 48-1-35 (1956), 15.

182. QA 48-2-156, 21.

183. QA 48-2-105 (1957), 139.

184. This collection was transcribed for me by Qingpu archivists, so personal names were excluded. They also did not include archive reference numbers.

185. SMA B1-2-1519 (1954), 4.

186. SMA B1-2-1519, 4.

187. SMA B168-1-600 (1951), 111.

188. SMA B168-1-633 (1957), 102.

189. Ibid.

190. Ibid.

191. SMA B1-2-1958 (1957), 55.

192. *Zhu-Mao*, 42.

193. SMA B127-1-1036 (1960), 134.

194. SMA 127-1-869 (1965), 10.

195. *Shandong xingzheng gongbao*, December 1954, 13.

196. *People's Daily*, August 6, 1956.

197. *Zhu-Mao*, 42.

198. SMA B168-1-645 (1960), 42.

199. SMA B127-1-846 (1961), 24.

3

The Complications of Veteran Identities

In the 1992 film *Hero*, Dustin Hoffman portrays Bernie LaPlante, a down-on-his-luck man and petty thief who just happens to be on a bridge when an airliner crashes right in front of him. After some hesitation, he meanders into the burning airplane and manages to rescue many of the surviving passengers. He then leaves the scene. One of the rescued passengers, a television reporter (played by Geena Davis), is determined to track down the identity of the anonymous hero. After she offers a generous reward, a handsome-but-homeless Vietnam War veteran (played by Andy Garcia) comes forward to claim it; a friend of Hoffman's character, he is able to convince the reporter that he was the one who rescued the passengers. LaPlante agrees to this: he's a "cash kind of guy" and recognizes his unsuitability for "heroic" status. After getting cleaned up and donning a new suit, the veteran, playing his "patriotic hero" role to a tee, fast becomes a media darling; he is what the media, public officials, and public expect and want their heroes to look and act like. As is typical in a Hollywood movie, the reporter starts to fall in love with him as well. The veteran, to be sure, feels somewhat guilty about the deceit but is trapped by the role assigned to him.

Unlike some other films that portray the heroism of ordinary people (the film borrows heavily from the director Frank Capra, but with a twist), *Hero* can be seen as a fairly realistic depiction of the deliberate manufacturing of model citizens and the difficulties that the media (and the state) face when confronted with untidy details and complexities of history (LaPlante is a petty thief) and biography (LaPlante is not attractive, did not serve in the military, and does not speak well). Although produced at the end of the Cold War, the movie's basic and well-worn argument—that a heroic narrative requires simplification—is just as relevant today. In the Iraq War, the state and the media created the perfect patriotic hero out of Corporal Pat Tillman because he was a handsome white soldier in a Special Forces unit who volunteered for the war and sacrificed a highly lucrative career in professional football. Like the veteran in *Hero*, he was perfect for the part—until it became known that he was killed by friendly fire and not the Taliban. To sustain public interest in war and to boost their own legitimacy, governments strive to create a positive aura among those who fight for their causes. They pick heroes among soldiers and veterans (in WWI, Sergeant York; in WWII, the soldiers who raised the flag at Iwo Jima) as symbols and role models, but they do so at their peril, since truth has to be distorted and simplified to convey it to large audiences. This effort can also be risky to those placed on a pedestal, particularly if their personalities, family backgrounds, histories, and behavior do not square with society's "cognitive frame" of what constitutes honorable or heroic status.[1] Bernie LaPlante presciently recognized this problem and took steps to avoid the spotlight.

By most any measure, veterans in the PRC had the high status that is often associated with combatants and victors in war; they were among the many heroes of the regime's narrative of revolution, liberation, and state strengthening. Not only did they have access to institutional support and preferential policies that were supposed to ease their way back into civilian life, but the state's propaganda machinery (*sans* Geena Davis!) mounted successive campaigns to remind the Chinese population that sacrifices were made, and continue to be made, on behalf of the common good. Particularly when compared with the lot of those who opposed the regime, or were suspected of opposing the regime because of their class background (education, ties to the West, wealth, ownership of land, etc.), veterans, having served on the side of the victors, were in a clearly favored position. This view has been articulated implicitly or explicitly by political scientists, sociologists, and feminist scholars[2] and has been reinforced by much of the memoir literature from the PRC. Often penned by sons and daughters of intellectuals after the Cultural Revolution, much of this literature focuses on their victimization at the hands of "good class" party members. Even though China does not have much of a civil religion focused on veterans per se, at least in the more formal sense of policies, legislation, and administrative practices, martial citizenship was a reality in China, much as it is in the United States and many other countries, where veteran status entitles one to receive benefits, honors, and rights that other groups do not.[3] Like the revolutionary proletariat and poor peasants, veterans—many being poor peasants as well—were said to have a "flesh and blood connection" to the revolution.[4]

But was this the case on the more interactive, practice-oriented, "horizontal" dimension of martial citizenship discussed in the introduction? In the Soviet Union, perhaps the country most comparable to China in terms of its political system, veterans in the post-WWII period dominated the scene politically and culturally: war novels, memoirs, and parades and honors galore were bestowed upon the victors in the "Great Patriotic War." There was no status higher than a decorated and wounded combat veteran; those not serving in combat were marginalized in the Communist Party.[5] Was this the case in China? Did veterans see themselves as embodying and deserving of patriotic and heroic status, or were they more like the central character in *Hero*, who, because of his class and past, tried to conceal his heroism and avoid the spotlight? In day-to-day life, did preferential policies and laudatory propaganda translate into *other* citizens and scores of lower- and mid-level officials treating veterans like heroes, or at least like individuals who deserve and are worthy of empathy, courtesy, and respect (what Anne Schneider and Helen Ingram have called the "social construction of entitlement"[6])? Because veterans' identities were bound up with state policies and its most important political narratives (about wartime patriotism, legitimacy, conscription, and military service), answering these questions can tell us a great deal about the nature of political power and the very meaning of war and revolution in China. To use a more theatrical metaphor, if a culture or society is very ambivalent about the virtues of the main characters and disagrees with the story, the narrative will fall flat, and the characters will be left wondering what happened. Substantial evidence suggests that this is what happened to many veterans in China.

This chapter consists of four parts. In the first, I take a look at the way veterans understood their own role in the revolution, how they expected to be treated after their service, as well as other, more problematic facets of their identity. I also look at how local officials responded to political claims asserted by veterans after their return home. In the following two sections, I explore the phenomenon of veteran "whistleblowing" (about sex, corruption, and waste), state retaliation against them, and the reasons why retaliation was often successful. This will include material on PRC veterans who served in the Nationalist Army and had bad family backgrounds as well as popular reactions to early 1950s campaigns to entice people to sign "patriotic compacts," support the Korean War, and register for the draft (1956). The final section turns to the comparative record. In what ways were Chinese veterans' experiences shared with counterparts elsewhere in the world, and how were they significantly different?

VETERAN IDENTITIES

Broad assertions about individual identity, let alone identity in a group numbering in the hundreds of thousands, will always be fraught with conceptual and methodological difficulties. Individual identity is multifaceted and changes over the course of the life cycle and in response to different circumstances; people often assume different identities when interacting with different people. Identity *change* is a particularly hard nut to crack, even in optimal research conditions with sophisticated methodologies and excellent data, but it is ever more so when dealing with large numbers with a limited "data set." How is it possible to get a good "sense" of Chinese veterans' identity (this is the best we can hope for) some 40 years ago, or today, for that matter, if ordinary veterans have not written about their experiences in a free political environment and we cannot administer questionnaires, do longitudinal surveys, or conduct interviews in an unsupervised setting? Despite these methodological difficulties, the question of veteran identities is critically important: it shaped the nature and quality of everyday interactions between veterans and fellow community members and state officials; it had direct impact on veterans' expectations of what they thought they deserved, both in terms of material and symbolic resources—their "just rewards," so to speak. When veterans asserted their identity as *worthy veteran*—rather than as "poor peasant" or "worker" or simply "man"—it was a cue ball shot at the body politic. Everyone was forced to react in some way: scatter, get out of sight, resist, stay close or far; veterans could not easily be ignored. Even though we do not have access to the sorts of materials that have resulted in excellent studies of veterans in the United States (including all minority groups), Europe, and the former Soviet Union,[7] scores of investigations into veteran issues from three different areas of China provide a reasonably nuanced sense of how veterans thought of themselves, how they viewed others, and vice versa. A clue can be found in the silences in these reports: there is not a single document from any area describing them as shy, fearful, retiring, or meek. We have already seen glimpses of this in the second chapter: many veterans did whatever they could to stay in the city despite discriminatory state policies.

Inasmuch as the rural part of veterans' biographical profiles complicated their efforts to get urban residence, we might expect that another "slice" of their identity would work to their advantage. In addition to being peasants, veterans were on the winning side of the revolution. They took on Japan and a world superpower; they were celebrated in articles and political rituals centered around the heroics of the PLA, martyrs, and others who sacrificed for the revolution (for the relationship of martyr families to the state, see Chapter 7). To what extent did this second, more heroic, part of their identity matter, and to whom? Were veterans any more respected in the urban areas most exposed to "patriotic sentiment" than the rural areas from which they hailed?

Despite their low socioeconomic status, or, rather, *because* of it, veterans did, in fact, see themselves as the beneficiaries of China's peasant-led revolution, if not in policy then in terms of their heightened sense of citizenship based upon martial contributions to the cause. Veterans took to heart the government's and the military's education and propaganda that their sacrifices were heroic and their contributions patriotic. One of the more frequent complaints and observations about veterans in both urban and rural China was their confidence, which report writers—who were generally more educated—often negatively characterized as prideful arrogance (*jiao'ao*) or a "hero" mentality (*gongchen ziju sixiang*). A report from Shanghai as early as 1951, for example, noted that veterans had "a great deal of confidence immediately upon their discharge from the military,"[8] and in 1955 another report noted the "problem" of "some veterans who think of themselves as important heroes" getting into heated arguments over jobs and status in factories and other places of employment.[9] In 1957, a confidential Ministry of Defense report on veteran resettlement warned that veterans needed to do more to prevent "any arrogant/prideful attitude" to surface in their relations with other cadres and the population at large.[10] The Defense Ministry's warning was likely a response to comparable reports bubbling up from lower levels that year. Veterans in Shanghai were called "arrogant," "unruly," (*tiaopi*) and thinking of themselves as "special" in their interactions with others on more than one occasion during 1957–1959,[11] and in Shandong—seemingly a more hospitable environment for them—veterans were also taken to task for an overwrought sense of entitlement in the late 1950s and mid-1960s.[12]

We need to take these reports with a grain of salt, however, since any sign of "uppity" behavior stood in marked contrast to the official ideology of egalitarianism and "service to the people" and thus came to the attention of the state's chroniclers. It is also possible that a "Shanghai bias" crept into these reports, since those committing the sin of prideful arrogance were often not locals and came from poor rural areas to boot. Reports from rural areas, therefore, are a better gauge of the pervasiveness of veterans' confidence, since in villages they interacted with those from the same locale and socioeconomic background.

As was the case in Shanghai, veterans in rural Qingpu and Shandong were also charged with an excessive sense of self-worth that emerged from their military experiences and official status. In the early 1950s, unedited reports on veteran affairs noted with some dismay that veterans were a bit too "full of themselves," citing as evidence veterans' public comments such as "We're veterans; we don't commit any big mistakes, only small ones, so what can the government do to us?"[13] Some clearly felt that they were entitled to govern because they were the main force of the revolution and were quite upset as they felt power slipping out of their hands into those of intellectuals who contributed less: "We captured power in war, but now intellectuals are in control" (*zhishifenzi zuo tianxia*), one griped in a 1954 meeting of representatives of local military and martyr families and "honored veterans."[14] Given their propensity to speak publicly about sensitive issues, it was not long before veterans developed a reputation among peasants—"strong personalities" and "saying whatever they want to say" (*you sa jiang sa*, in Qingpu dialect) were said to be their "special characteristics";[15] this personality trait was also noted in the person who, during the Cultural Revolution, would become China's most famous veteran (deputy chairman of the CCP), Wang Hongwen,[16] and is vividly portrayed in the 2007 film *Assembly* (*Jijie hao*), where Captain Gu Zidi fearlessly rails and curses party officials sent to investigate the battle in which he lost all of his "brothers."[17] Township and district officials complained in a 1957 meeting that "as soon as veterans come home—no matter who—they are always 'hard to lead' (*nan lingdao; nan gao*), 'difficult to get along with' (*bu hao xiang chu de ren*),"[18] and arrogant because they "treated their honor like capital . . . [and] they think they've made a contribution to the revolution."[19] Some veterans did earn their respect, however, a reaction that was far rarer (in the available documentation) in the allegedly more nationalistic and patriotic cities; a rule of thumb civilian officials used in dealing with them (in Shandong as well) was "respect them, but keep them at a distance" (*jing er yuan*).[20] In part, this was because many veterans experienced events that changed their self- and national identities—few people return from war and military service unchanged—but it was also because veterans, by their own testimonies and the reactions of others, felt fairly secure in their status and confident that others would recognize their contributions and reciprocate with a modicum of respect.

This turbocharged sense of identity, status, and the expectations of reciprocity it generated turned out to be highly problematic in a polity and society that (we will see in this and other chapters) had scant appreciation, understanding, empathy, or interest in veterans; these are emotions and concerns that do not come naturally—they are more likely to emerge after shared experiences and extensive contact between military personnel from different class backgrounds who share a common cause. Veterans, quite unlike Mencius's famous example of a baby stuck in a well whose rescue demonstrates innate human goodness,[21] were not, and never have been—as we will see later in this chapter—an easy population. Shifting identity is most always disruptive to societies, whether it occurs among women demanding divorce, minorities learning about rights, or teenagers acquiring a stronger sense of self. Veterans were no different, only perhaps more extreme given their officially high status and difficult experiences in the military. In the archival documents, examples of "veterans behaving badly" abound, as do examples of flummoxed officials, workers, and peasants. Take, for instance, the cases of Fei Suisheng and Zhao Yikang. Fei was demobilized in 1954 and then assigned by the Bureau of Civil Affairs to be an apprentice in a factory in Shanghai.

Unhappy with his job, he frequently disobeyed orders, took off from work at random times, visited prostitutes, and flirted with many women. The factory tried to "educate" him on three different occasions but soon expelled him. Last heard from, Fei had stolen a rickshaw and absconded. Zhao Yikang was assigned to be a supervisor for meat and dairy products in the Health Department but after several days faked an illness, took off from work, and sought out prostitutes. Unlike Fei, he did not have the gumption to steal a rickshaw, so he was caught by the Public Security Bureau and arrested—a "very bad influence," the report noted. In assessing this sort of behavior, administrators placed partial blame on veterans' "prideful arrogance" and their "believing that they have rendered an outstanding service to the revolution," but the primary blame was on the excessively sharp transition between the military and civilian life and the absence of any "follow-up" work.[22] Because the state did not successfully institutionalize a demobilization process, veterans were often unceremoniously "dumped" in factories and back in villages after their discharge (there were no parades and only occasional welcome signs, music, greetings, and the like).

Fei and Zhao, to be sure, were not the only problematic veterans. Like any good police force, the Shanghai Public Security Bureau (PSB) tabulated crime statistics, and veterans were found among them. In a review of veteran placement between 1950 and 1955, the PSB reported that they had handled 157 criminal cases involving veterans. Of these, 25 percent involved "counterrevolutionary" activities, 19 percent were sex-related (soliciting prostitutes, adultery, and rape), and 52 percent were economic (theft and embezzlement of property).[23] This pattern was also noted among veterans in Taiwan at roughly the same time. According to Yu-Wen Fan, in the small town of Tongshi in central Taiwan, some veterans "joined local criminals to take control of illegal brothels and gambling houses," and others blocked traffic with boulders, "extorting those wishing to pass through." Other veterans, however, were arrested only because their poverty and poor dress made them appear suspicious.[24]

This crime pattern is not random, as any Durkheimian sociologist or criminologist worth his or her salt would confirm. The charge of "counterrevolution" was *politically motivated*—most veterans, after all, had documents attesting to their participation in the revolution because they served in the PLA; most were assigned to apprenticeships and were therefore poor (hence the prevalence of economic crimes); and many were young men who had not been able to have sex with women during war (notice all the "flirting" and solicitation). While some Bureau of Civil Affairs officials expressed sympathy for the veterans (see Chapter 5 on Civil Affairs and other state agencies dealing with veterans), other officials did not. In 1954, a task force led by the Shanghai procuratorate investigated the veteran situation in Hongkou District, a working-class area. Noting "a lot of problems," the investigators called specific attention to the case of a veteran named Wang Hongnian, a worker at the Shenghua pharmaceutical factory. Wang, they noted, was known to be "creative" in his job and was chosen as a district-level veteran representative. During work one day, he caused a work accident that resulted in several hundred yuan of damage. Shenghua, however, reported to the Public Security Bureau (PSB) that Wang "intentionally" caused 7,600 yuan worth of damage during a "counterrevolutionary incident." In October 1954, Wang was arrested and stayed in prison without a hearing until November 1955, when the Hongkou District Court sentenced him to two years. Wang appealed the verdict to the Shanghai Intermediate Court, which investigated and then cleared him of all charges. Factory officials, however, refused to reemploy him. Suffering from dire poverty and stress, Wang was said to have lost his mind.[25] Wang was not alone in having the cards stacked against him in court. In a 1957 review of 223 arrested veterans, 43 (21 percent) were "harshly convicted for relatively minor offenses and got their sentences reduced" (after how long is not clear) and six (2 percent) had their verdicts overturned completely.[26] Even though a small minority of veterans became entangled in the city's criminal justice system—according to 1958 statistics, there were 17,900 veterans in Shanghai, but only 300 were ever charged with a criminal offense (1.6 percent)[27]—their reputation among urbanites suffered as a result. This was also the case among their counterparts in Taiwan. There, very few veterans became involved in crime, but those who did stigmatized the rest: "one rat's excrement spoils a pot of soup."[28]

Rural areas were not immune from problematic veterans. In a preview of more current scandals in China involving corruption and orphanages (the latter are run by the Bureau of Civil Affairs), in 1962 a Bureau of Civil Affairs cadre in Qingpu named Kang A'tao completed a hat trick of crimes often associated with veterans. Kang "frequently went to an orphanage to steal food, had feasts (*da chi da he*) and illicit sex with an accountant." Unlike Wang Hongnian, however, he received only "intra party" disciplinary measures, probably a reflection of his association with a "pro-veteran" organization like Civil Affairs rather than a factory.[29] Others were involved in more serious crimes. In Huaihua County in Hunan, a veteran surnamed Tian had been a bandit prior to joining the PLA. He served in combat during the Civil War, but after his discharge he returned to banditry. In 1950 he was caught and sent to labor reform but reenlisted in 1951, serving for another year. Apparently unable to disavow his bandit ways, he was sent to labor reform yet again. Banned from local political organizations, Tian reportedly maintained "close relations" with a bankrupt landlord who was under state supervision and "threatened cadres and activists" demanding land, which he apparently lacked; during land reform, the above chronology suggests, he was away from the village, and local officials did not reserve any for him.[30]

The conflict between Tian and other local cadres and activists (probably from land reform) hints at a broader and deeper problem related to veterans' sense of status, boldness, and confidence; not everyone had the courage to threaten cadres or have a public relationship with a former landlord! Well before the Cultural Revolution, when conflicts between military and civilian officials broke out into the open, veterans and local officials were at loggerheads over just who could claim the mantle of revolutionary citizenship and patriotism. In Qingpu, for example, veterans "looked down upon local cadres" (*kanbuqi jiceng ganbu*) and did not hesitate to yell at them but then found themselves "isolated" in the village;[31] a township chief confessed to having a "hostile" (*choushi*) attitude toward them.[32] In Tiansheng Township, a veteran confessed at a meeting that he "used to think that local cadres can only talk a lot, but can't get much done; that's why I disrespected them,"[33] a complaint which echoed Soviet WWII veterans' anger at "laid back bureaucrats" and fueled their desire to "cut through red tape" with an "iron will."[34] In Shandong, reports noted that veterans held local officials in "disdain" (*kanbuguan*); mutual "estrangement" (*ge he*) was common. This animosity (which was also noted in Guangdong and Sichuan provinces during these years[35]) spread to their respective families as well—the relationship between veterans' families and those of other cadres was described as "bad."[36] Veterans were instructed to "respect basic-level cadres" in a nationally circulated 1957 Ministry of Defense document;[37] *People's Daily* critiqued veterans on this account,[38] as did Marshal Peng Dehuai in a speech to a large meeting of "activists" among martyr and military families and veterans,[39] but the available documents do not point to much change. A two-month-long investigation of veteran issues in Qingpu (1957) discovered 47 veterans who were quite "arrogant" and "looked down upon village cadres." Most of their offenses (22) involved "improper" sex with "class enemies" (including former landlords' daughters who were married) but also included beating peasants (10) and stealing money, collective property, rice, and a watch (15).[40]

Local officials, however, could give as well as they could take, and thanks to their powerful position in most local governments and party branches, and veterans' very fragile support structure, they usually had the upper hand. In this respect, the Chinese post-war situation was quite different from that in the USSR. There, a "harsh battle" took place between partisans and the Red Army veterans over "what the legacy of the war should be," but *the former* went down in a resounding defeat.[41] In China, however, sources speak of a vicious cycle developing: veterans expected to be greeted as returning heroes upon their return from war; when they were not, they continued to assert their superiority through "prideful arrogance" and purposeful violation of class boundaries and petty theft, which further inflamed local officials, who then retaliated. Maltreatment, abuse, cold shoulders, and icy attitudes were commonplace. An investigation by *People's Daily* in 1956 noted that basic-level cadres in villages "do not see any positive qualities" among veterans, and this resulted in discrimination and "rejection" of them. "After encountering the arrogance of veterans [including the disabled]," local officials "ignored" and "embarrassed" them, telling reporters, "They were better than us in battle on the front line, but they can't beat us running a cooperative."[42] In Funning County in Hebei Province, party members in Chengguan district beat veterans.[43] In Xu'an Township in Qingpu, PLA veteran Han Desheng was said to be a good worker but drank too much. District and township officials called him "army riff-raff" (*bing pi*) and refused to allow him to enter a cooperative, a decision that received the blessings of the organization department of the Qingdong District Party Committee, who considered him "beyond education" (*wufa jiaoyu*). The decision was reversed only after repeated interventions by Civil Affairs officials,[44] who most likely included this item in their report because it demonstrated their effectiveness. In a village in the Shanghai suburbs, a veteran surnamed Chen was "usually active in work, but lacked education and made mistakes." He was also poor and relied on welfare. The deputy party secretary told him, "You think you've made a big contribution, but who can see it? How can you be so proud and self-satisfied when you have to get in line for welfare at the Civil Affairs office?"[45] In Qingpu, civilian officials denigrated the contributions of veterans to the revolution by telling them that "the revolution would've succeeded without you."[46]

Lack of empathy for veterans and disrespect for military experience were also common among officials with more education, such as those who worked in health departments. In the early 1950s medical personnel from Shanghai were mobilized to help cure military personnel of waterborne parasitic infections. The physicians were willing to help out but had mixed feelings about the PLA. Some appreciated the PLA, but in a parochial, localist sense: "We appreciate that the PLA liberated *our Shanghai* and then left for the suburbs to reduce urban expenditures," while others were afraid: "The PLA comrades have guns, they're soldiers and are tough and unreasonable. . . . if there's some sort of difficulty and we make a mistake, they'll box our ears and slap us in the face." Evidently, these worries proved groundless—after three months, the physicians reportedly "returned with high enthusiasm" to Shanghai.[47] Veterans working at a Tuberculosis Prevention Center in Qingpu commented on the "cold" attitude and demeanor of their bosses compared to the "warmth" shown by their PLA commanders. When one veteran surnamed Lu requested a table for food for his wedding, the deputy director of the prevention center agreed, but he was overridden by the director. Few hid their views from investigators: "The PLA's always bad" (*jiefang jun zongshi bu hao de*). They also ridiculed veterans, calling them "Mr. Army-man'" (*nimen dou shi jiefang jun shushu*).[48]

Shanghai unions shared many of these sentiments. Veterans who wanted to join unions also found that their martial contributions were disparaged by other workers who, despite not enduring years of war, were nevertheless able to draw upon China's long, multiregional revolutionary process to prevent their ascension. At the Hongxiangxin boat repair factory, cadres told veterans: "It took 30 years of bloody struggle for our working class to establish the union. You can't enter just like that to enjoy power and benefits."[49] At the #3 Textile Mill, investigators quizzed an engineer about workers' views of veterans. According to the engineer, "all the workers say that veterans are just like the Guomindang [Nationalist Party]."[50] At the Shenxin #1 Mill, veterans had their applications to join unions delayed for years. When one veteran wanted to transfer to a different factory, his workshop boss told him, "I can tell you to push a vehicle your whole life! Let's see what you can do about it. You're pretty naïve—you'll do whatever I tell you to do!"[51] Reports of this sort of treatment spread to the PLA, which prompted many to try to avoid demobilization altogether.[52]

Veterans who were exposed to these sorts of challenges to their political and personal identities realized that political language was a flexible and powerful resource in the hands of their enemies, who were themselves threatened by veterans' sense of martial accomplishment and patriotism and the state's rhetorical draping of them in deep red. Unlike the Nationalists in Taiwan for whom "nationalism was associated with the notion to particularize the status of *rongmin* [veterans] and make this group exclusive,"[53] in the PRC, union officials, township cadres, and activists of all colors could, quite legitimately as far as official discourse was concerned, pat themselves on the back for *their* "glorious" patriotic contribution to victory, liberation, socialist construction, struggle against the imperialists, and the like—and at the same time denigrate veterans as Guomindang (GMD) imitators and army riffraff. Lasting as long as it did, the revolution had many authors, contributors, heroes, and bit players; it could not really be otherwise (unlike a quick *coup d'état*). Veterans were well aware of this linguistic slippage. Take, for example, a letter written by a disabled veteran (formerly a junior officer in the PLA) to the minister of the interior.[54] It is worth quoting at length since it reveals veterans' awareness of the propaganda tricks being played on them as well as deep frustration with their predicament.

August 5, 1956

Dear Minister of the Interior,

I'm a disabled revolutionary soldier. I participated in the Anti-Japanese War and the War of Liberation, serving as a scout for the company C.O. After discharge I've worked very hard, and, with the guidance and leadership of the party, I'm now a section chief, Grade 16. This should be considered quite good.

Recently, we were contacted by the Conscription Bureau (*bingyi ju*) notifying us that xx unit authorized our appointment as reserve duty officers, and that this is a glorious (*guangrong*) duty to fulfill.

Glory, glory, glory, really glorious. To our ears, "glory" is a hollow, meaningless, and detestable word because we've had far too many "glories." When we signed up during the war, which was "glorious"; fighting is "glorious"; sacrifice is "glorious"; shedding blood is "glorious." After discharge we were beneficiaries of the free supply system (*gonggei zhi*) and that was also "glorious." Then, when this was changed to the salary system, it was even more glorious that our salaries were lower than a comparable grade section chief or someone who participated in the revolution later but who is blessed with a glib tongue. In the future there will be a war and we will reenlist and risk our lives and that will be our "special glory." This is glory's meaning; this is how it is interpreted.

What I don't quite understand is how is it that those comrades in the army making 100–200 yuan a month aren't "glorious" as well; and what about cadres in units on the home front—especially those who are educated—aren't they "glorious" too? And what about ordinary folks with fathers, mothers, wives, and children who can eat their fill and clothe themselves warmly—aren't they "glorious"? Or is it only parents whose son has been killed and who are now going hungry? I think you're pretty well versed on this point. When someone makes a pointed inquiry, "glory" is the magic weapon (*fabao*) that is supposed to resolve everything.

It is possible that some people will say that the problems are not as serious as I make them out to be, that these problems have disappeared after the wars ended. If a war breaks out, though, I'm afraid that these problems will get even worse. What I am writing to you now I do not discuss with others, or in any public place, even though I can speak very well. If I were to take this letter and read it out loud to the masses, no one would believe that it's me speaking these words. This is the main reason why those bureaucrats can't find out about these problems.

Still, we hereby resolve that if a war breaks out, we will definitely not fight in it.

The veterans in our unit recently convened a meeting, in accordance to some Interior Ministry directive. At the meeting everyone said "very good, very good"—what else could we say?—and the party secretary is happily preparing a report to send to the higher authorities. But after the meeting we spoke and everyone said things are really bad. Every province and every city has veteran representatives. These people can only speak superficially; if they didn't no one would want them. If you speak frankly, you would be deemed "backwards."

This is what I propose: convene a meeting of veteran representatives and look for some of these "backward" people to help you understand the situation better. I also propose that if you are truly interested in understanding these problems you need to investigate directly; if you go through veteran organizations you won't understand.

I am now approaching six years since my discharge. On the outside, people think I'm OK, but on the inside I am growing bitterer by the day. Because there is no place where we can speak the truth, we have to go on pretending. Nevertheless, when people like me get together we can talk, at length and without stopping.

But no matter. Telling you might be useless as well.

(Signed),

A Backward Person

This threat may not have been idle; all 80 veterans in Factory #501 (in Shandong), for instance, "refused to register for reserve duty" in 1957.[55] In addition to calling attention to the sense in which "glory" was diluted to the point of meaninglessness, the letter calls attention to yet another feature of veteran identity: despite everything, they were willing to speak out and call attention to their predicament. Unlike intellectuals who often veered between fear of the regime and an intense desire to serve it, veterans, feeling more secure in their status and already predisposed to a certain degree of frankness, frequently appealed to higher levels of the state. In addition to writing angry letters (sometimes cursing in them) or asking PLA marshals to come to their counties to investigate[56]—veterans went to district and county governments to demand job transfers, usually in response to discrimination,[57] remonstrated at provincial governments,[58] argued loudly with local officials,[69] and complained and grumbled[60]—their discontent was hardly a secret. Of course, all this writing, complaining, and running around did not endear them to local officials, who took it as more evidence of their "arrogance" and overwrought sense of entitlement, confirming their view that veterans were a "burden," "troublesome," and "demanding and difficult to deal with" (*nanruo nanchan, nan nong*), with few redeeming qualities.[61]

THE WHISTLEBLOWERS

One excellent gauge of the Chinese state's (and society's) ability to accommodate veterans' demands for martial citizenship and recognition of their patriotism is to examine the politics surrounding "whistleblowing"—an act that is often motivated by the desire to do good but which is also threatening to authority; it is also an act that requires courage, since the risk of retaliation is high. In their study of whistleblowing in the United States, Myron Glazer and Penina Migdal Glazer found that whistleblowers tend to be "conservative people devoted to their work and their organizations. . . . They believed that they were defending the true mission of their organization by resisting illicit practices." This defense usually comes at a steep price. Regardless of how well justified the complaint or the motivations of employees, government and industry showed a "consistent pattern of harsh reprisals—from blacklisting, dismissal, or transfer, to personal harassment."[62] Despite this, whistleblowing can pay off in the United States, and the whistleblowers are not without recourse. Under the False Claims Act, a whistleblower who exposes fraud against the government can collect up to 30 percent of the amount the government recovers; some high-level politicians support them, and there are advocacy groups willing to lend a helping hand.

While the term *whistleblowing* does not have a lexical equivalent in Chinese, the concept is not foreign. In the Confucian tradition, it was the literati's obligation to gather up their courage and call attention to immorality, injustice, and corruption in government; in more modern times, intellectuals and educated youth have generally claimed this mantle, whistleblowing against the regime during the 100 Flower Movement (1956–1957), "revisionism," corruption and sexual immorality during the Cultural Revolution, and leftist radicalism and injustice in its aftermath (during the Democracy Wall movement). But when we have sources that allow us to shift our attention away from educated urban elites, "movements," and "campaigns," it becomes clear that in everyday life it was often veterans, not intellectuals, who "blew the whistle" on corruption, injustice, and "immorality" in the state and society. In Maoist China, the most famous whistleblower was probably Marshal Peng Dehuai, who, after criticizing Mao for some of the failures of the Great Leap Forward, was quickly denounced, abandoned, and ousted by Mao and the civilian leadership.[63] Many veterans took seriously at least some of the public-minded ideals they had been taught and experienced in the military. Like some American WWII veterans in the Deep South who ran for office on "clean government" platforms because they were disgusted by the waste and corruption they witnessed around them,[64] Chinese veterans, with their strong personalities, courage, frankness, and conviction that they were protected by their status (unlike most intellectuals), were behind an outpouring of complaints, petitions, protests, strikes, and sarcastic letters addressed to civilian officials throughout the Maoist years, even during the early 1950s, when the regime was supposedly in its "honeymoon years." As it turned out, they generally suffered the same fate as most of their American whistleblowing counterparts.

As in the United States, the press was where whistleblowing often surfaced. In 1957, Zhang Zhengfei penned an essay that appeared in *People's Daily* under the title "In the End, Is Complaining a Lot Good or Bad?"[65] In it, he recalled the following incident:

> In the fall of 1953 I was at a meeting in the Shanxi government. I overheard a personnel official in the General Office proclaiming that "there are very many veterans who have come to Taiyuan [the provincial capital], and there are some units in the city that think that veterans raise too many objections (*ti yijian*) and refuse to hire them. We're now supposed to rectify this mistake."

This brief account does not delve into details about what sorts of issues veterans raised, but it does show that as early as 1953, veterans had a reputation for complaining. References to veterans "habitually" (*ai ti yijian*) or "readily" (*hao ti yijian*) raising objections to various practices abound in the archival sources as well. The summary report from a national-level meeting of veterans in Beijing in 1956 noted that "some areas and work units think that veterans always complain . . . and are a pain in the neck for their leaders."[66] State Council reports also noted veterans' courage in criticizing "unreasonable phenomena" in their units, complaints which outside investigators found to be "absolutely correct" in "very many instances."[67] Interestingly, this praise was often paired with complaints about the difficulty in "leading" veterans (*bu hao lingdao*) and retaliation (*baofu*) against them. These issues, as the whistleblowing literature would have predicted, were connected: veterans' claims to status, dissatisfaction, and tendency to speak out did make it difficult to "lead" them, and retaliation usually followed complaints. The topic of complaints varied over the years but tended to focus on several issues: morality, corruption, work methods, theft, and waste, as the following abbreviated examples show.

Morality

Evidence from Qingpu suggests that veterans brought with them to civilian life a rather austere sense of official morality, even though quite a few of them, for reasons that will be discussed more extensively in Chapter 6, failed to maintain the ideals of a "socialist family." A case in Zhaidong Township involved a veteran named Tao Baoqing, who was discharged in 1950. Upon his return, Tao was upset to discover that Zhang Yongzhen, a member of Siyi Village's Women's Committee, was having an illicit relationship with Zhao Borong, a village cadre. He repeatedly yelled and cursed at Zhang and Zhao, who naturally came to despise him. In 1951, village cadre Zhao refused to supply water for Tao Baoqing's field, causing a loud argument between them.

Zhao and Zhang then attempted to mobilize the village women to struggle against him, but this plan was nixed by the township organization committee. Tao had yet another argument with township and village cadres in 1952; the latter all claimed that Tao was "unruly" and "lacked authority" among the villagers. As for Tao, he was said to be "very dissatisfied" with village and township authorities and did not hesitate to complain about them. "A very negative influence," the report noted.[68]

Village sexual relations or, more precisely, the abuse of power to procure sex (perhaps at their expense) also came up at a meeting of Qingpu veterans and military dependents in 1957. In Xujing Township, a veteran stood up and said, "Those who violate the Marriage Law are almost all township cadres. In Zhaidong Township, villagers caught the party secretary having illicit sex with another female official, but up until now nothing has been done to him." This tale inspired a soldier's mother to talk: "Cadres' class standpoint is very muddled: they want to take landlords' daughters [who were generally reputed to be pretty] as their lovers, but look down upon (*kanbuqi*) revolutionary families. No one takes care of military families and families of revolutionary martyrs anymore." Huang Qilin, a veteran, also called attention to rather "chaotic" sexual relations in villages. "Xinqiao Township officials frequently have illicit sex," he complained. Among thirty cadre families, eleven were having some sort of sex-related impropriety, which led to a rash of divorces involving both cadres and ordinary peasants. In a single day, he pointed out, 37 couples were divorced, among whom four were party members, and nine were cadres. Among those having illicit sex was a member of the township's investigation committee, who ordinarily might be involved in imposing "party discipline" on these cadres.[69]

Corruption, Work Methods, Theft, and Waste

These all were more serious charges than illicit affairs, as the CCP had specifically targeted them in political campaigns throughout the 1950s and 1960s. The conventional wisdom about these campaigns is that veterans-turned-officials were the primary perpetrators of corruption: they entered the city, got power, and were seduced by urban materialism. Some of this was undoubtedly true, but it also may reflect an urban bias against the newcomers. Since *most* veterans did *not* have access to power and valuable resources, it stands to reason that more may have complained about corruption than perpetrated it. Veteran complaints against corruption were very threatening, and the retaliation against them could be harsh. In Qingpu, for example, a veteran surnamed Lu worked at a cooperative and witnessed the director falsely reporting inventory and then selling the extra goods at a higher price on the private market. Lu "exposed" him and was promptly fired and reassigned to a factory that employed only veterans. "If you raise objections, only misfortune befalls you," veterans noted.[70] This was true. A handwritten report on Qingpu veterans (1956) noted a case involving three veterans—Shen Yanmin, Wang Rong, and Di Ren—who were employed as temporary workers in an organization of fishermen that was paid by the county to sell fish in the marketplace. Di Ren, however, had a chronic lung disease, which impaired his productivity. County officials were unwilling to shoulder the expense of treatment, so they sent him back to the village to become an ordinary peasant once again. Upset at this treatment, and dissatisfied with their own prospects of getting a permanent position, Shen Yanmin and Wang Rong penned a letter exposing the corruption of the fishermen organization's leader. The county then dismissed the two and sent them to work in a paper factory that exclusively employed veterans.[71] In other cases in Qingpu, veteran Lu Tujin exposed corruption at the Jinze Cooperative (involving shady budgeting and false reporting) and was immediately kicked out of his job,[72] and in Liantang District, Zhenghe Township, the head of a production team took some melons from a field, but a veteran caught him red-handed. The veteran charged that officials could not just walk into a field and take whatever they felt like (this was a strict rule in the PLA). As a result, the production team leader told other officials that the veteran was "an unruly bastard" with a "wavering class standpoint" because his wife was a daughter of a rich peasant. The veteran reportedly was very worried about his future in the village.[73]

Qingpu veterans also expressed their frustration with corruption, the CCP, and rural poverty in poems and exposed it in meetings of their "representative committees" that were convened during the Hundred Flowers campaign. Chen Bolin and "several of his fellow veterans" composed this poem (which rhymes in Chinese):[74]

> News, news, it's really news
> The news comes out in Qiumaojin [a village in Qingpu] that
> The bandits and robbers are emerging in Qianjiajin [another village in Qingpu]
> The families of the corrupt and extravagant come out holding their dragon lanterns (*deng*)
> While the villagers beseech the People's Government to punish them (*chu fen*)
> But the People's Government does not hear their cries (*bu wen*)

Yang Caiyun and other villagers came up with these:

> The East in Red (*hong*)
> China has brought forth a Mao *Zelong*

The bamboo shoots are hollow (*kong*, to rhyme with *long*)
There are ten bins of rice, but nine are empty (*kong*)

Hailala, Hailala!
China has brought forth a giant monster (*yaoguai*)
You work hard and he eats up all your work points!

Chiang Kai-shek had no sympathy for the common folk
Eating three meals a day and dessert to boot
But that Mao Zedong, he's really wise (*zhen yingming*)
You have to get approval to eat the husk of rice

Similar scenes occurred in North China. In Henan Province, Longwan Township, for example, a veteran surnamed Wang "exposed the corruption of Niu Linsheng, the head of the district's militia department." Niu, with several of his men, immediately retaliated by fabricating charges against Wang. They then tied him up and pummeled him until blood poured out of his mouth and he became permanently disabled in his arm. Not content with this, Niu's militiamen then extorted a confession by cutting up the interior of Wang's mouth and placing thin tin foil inside it. His family was also made to pay. More than fifty militiamen raided his house and made off with his property. A local kangaroo "court" (comprising Niu and other district officials) sentenced him to two years in prison.[75]

Shanghai officials also retaliated against troublesome veterans. A report from 1955 noted that when veterans criticize "some unreasonable phenomenon in the factory," administrators think they are a "pain in the ass" and then falsely charge them with "violating labor discipline." Factory unions collaborated in the search for incriminating materials, arrests, and expulsions from the party. One union took pride in having veterans berated for their "mistakes," spreading the word on the factory floor that "the union really stuck it to the PLA."[76] A pharmaceutical firm's manager said at a public meeting, "On the battlefield they were heroes, but in the factory they're just stuffed bears" (*zhuang gouxiong*). These "mistaken views and attitudes" were reported to be "relatively common" in firms.[77] The view that discharged veterans had little clout was, in fact, confirmed by experience. A 1956 report in the Bureau of Civil Affair's bulletin *Minzheng jianbao* noted that some factory leaders "cannot accept" even "reasonable objections raised by veterans" and stood behind efforts of their personnel departments to get rid of them. And oust them they did. In one factory, four employees who "frequently complained" were transferred to perform menial labor in Wusong District, a semi-rural area on the outskirts of Shanghai.[78] "Very many" veterans were angered by this, according to the report (for more on the relationship between veterans and employers, see Chapter 4).

Transferring jobs, as it turned out, was one of the milder forms of nastiness that civilian leaders could inflict on veterans they considered too uppity. In 1955, a Shanghai veteran named Wu Hongji jumped into the Huangpu River and drowned, which prompted an investigation. According to the factory security officer interviewed by investigators, Wu jumped because he "had serious problems" and was "exposed during the *sufan* campaign." These claims notwithstanding, the investigators were unable to find any evidence of "serious" problems in Wu's dossier, only indications that his "social relationships were complicated." What precipitated the suicide, they found, was not his biography, but his *actions*: Wu had written a letter to the city government accusing a workshop director of "bureaucratism." When the factory got word of this, they launched a counteroffensive against him.[79] Harsh political language was also deployed against veterans. In a case that is further elaborated in the next chapter, one Shanghai veteran surnamed Zhang was labeled an "alien class element" (jieji yiyi fenzi) after he raised objections to factory management. But veterans knew this language too: the same Zhang called union members "the running dogs of capitalism" for refusing to promote him.[80]

The Shanghai area, to be sure, was not the only region where veterans "raised objections" to shady practices they witnessed among civilian officials. A joint investigation team from Tianjin's #1 Light Industry Bureau and Heilongjiang Province's Shuangyashan and Jixi Mining Bureaus in the mid-1950s found that "attacking and humiliating veterans" (*daji wuru*) was "quite serious" (*xiangdang yanzhong*) in these northern locales as well. The experience of Li Dequan was typical. After his demobilization, Li became a temporary worker in one of the Shuangyashan mines; he was also being considered for CCP membership. On one occasion, however, Li received work orders from two different bosses at the same time; one was a small-group leader, the other the district transportation director, a man surnamed Yan. Li decided to obey the former because he had "frequently complained" about Yan's work practices in the past. Yan decided to get revenge: he convened a meeting and publicly lambasted Li for "not following orders" and proposed that the Youth League punish him for his transgression. With Li's materials conveniently supplied by Yan, the League ousted him. According to the investigators, Yan had long-standing problems with veterans, not only Li, charging them with "palming off inferior products" like ugly theories (*gua yang tou, mai gou rou, chou lilun duo*) and "running off to the union and party branch all the time." Yan was not the only one making such comments. A pit foreman "frequently yelled and discriminated against veterans," telling them, "your commemoration badges are nothing compared to the counter-revolutionaries who were suppressed in 1951, and you don't have their spirit, either."[81]

To the extent that veterans were convinced that their contributions would be valued and their opinions respected, they were surely taken aback by the manner in which their assertions of status were often flatly rejected and how little consensus there was about their role in war and the revolution. While veterans pointed to military victory as the key to CCP power, other officials asserted that other forms of participation were equally important and "heroic," which significantly diluted veterans' claim to higher status. Absent a consensus about the meaning of victory and who was most responsible for it, veterans' claims to power and respect were primarily framed as *threats* to the legitimacy and authority of local power holders, who took advantage of other, more problematic, aspects of veterans' identity to push them down several notches.

VULNERABILITIES

Mobilizing the State

Scholars of law and society have often noted that laws and rights are rarely self-enforcing. Litigants, petitioners, and others who make political demands have better chances at success when they have resources (money, time, connections) and good organization than if they face the system standing alone. While Chinese veterans did not have "rights" in the Western liberal understanding of the concept, they were entitled to certain benefits, material and symbolic. They also expected to be treated as respected citizens whose opinions and criticisms mattered. Whistleblowing was but one manifestation of this sense of citizenship. At the same time, however, officials who did not share veterans' high opinions of themselves could counter-mobilize against these claims. Since veterans were often outsiders, particularly if they hailed from the countryside and had only recently demobilized to a city, it was far easier for local officials, who had superior knowledge of the political terrain, to mobilize the machinery of the state's coercive apparatus than it was for veterans to assert themselves against it. For instance, in Qingpu, a veteran told officials, "When we see something wrong (*budui de shiqing*) we say something about it, but then officials say we're 'arrogant,' 'hard to control,' and question our credentials. Now we're ignored, just like wild ducks" (as opposed to ducks raised for consumption).[82] Liu Haixian, a veteran in a village outside Beijing who was in charge of the militia, criticized another cadre's laziness. The latter organized members of his extended family and beat him up. Liu survived and sued, but the court ruled that, because they were cadres, they should simply avoid working in the same area.[83] In Shanghai, lineages were less important, but unions and party committees could play the same role in retaliation. A 1956 report noted that

> In state-owned firms leading cadres take revenge on veterans who dare to raise objections and criticisms. They do this by fabricating charges of "violating labor discipline" or some other offense and then reporting them to the police and judiciary. As a result there are many cases of mistaken arrests, verdicts, and other miscarriages of justice.[84]

When such cases as these happened, it appears that the state machinery that was set up to protect veterans rarely intervened in a timely fashion (although Intermediate Courts clearly helped them after the fact). Such cases came to light after dozens of complaints filtered up through the system (usually by way of family members, veteran committees, and the Bureau of Civil Affairs) and a large-scale investigation was finally mounted.

The relative ease with which union officials, factory managers, and rural political leaders were able to invoke the coercive machinery of the state against them highlights a significant vulnerability in veterans' political identity (courage, official sponsorship, knowledge of state language, etc.). Despite their common experience in the military, veterans—particularly those working in urban factories—suffered from internal divisions similar to any large social grouping. In English, the word *veteran* is used to indicate anyone who was discharged from the military. In China, however, the PLA's transition from a revolutionary fighting force to a more "professional" military after 1949 produced many different categories of veteran status: the term *fuyuan junren* was generally used to refer to PLA soldiers who participated in the wars against Japan, the Guomindang, and the United States and were demobilized in the mid-1950s; the terms *jianshi junren*, *zhuanye junren*, and *tuiwu junren* were generally applied to those who were drafted after the Korean War and who did a stint of three years in the PLA. This was not hard and fast; many officials remained confused about the difference well into the 1950s, and even a dictionary of military terminology cannot draw a sharp line between the three words. Nevertheless, several reports indicate a sort of "creaming effect" whereby *zhuanye, jianshi,* and *tuiwu junren*—those who did *not* participate in wars or combat—received more benefits and higher salaries than the *fuyuan junren*, who often did serve in this capacity. A report from the Shanghai's #1 Commerce Bureau noted that in some units *zhuanye junren* "received priority to live in apartments at a motel on Jiangsu Road, but *fuyuan junren* do not." During holiday festivities in some units, only the *zhuanye junren* were invited, but not the *fuyuan junren*; the latter were "very upset" by this, according to the report.[85] In a similar vein, a 1959 report from Shanghai warned officials to "prevent contradictions among workers and between *fuyuan junren* and *tuiwu junren* over salary."[86] The next chapter will explore this "contradiction" more deeply. Here it is sufficient to note that when some veterans blew the whistle against civilian officials, they could not count on a "united front" of organized "veterans" standing behind them, leaving them far more vulnerable. How this might have been prevented will be discussed in Chapter 5.

"Complicated" Histories

The cases described above illustrate the extent to which many veterans were vulnerable to predation by other officials on account of their precarious economic situation, political isolation, and the tactical deployment of impromptu and vague class labels such as "alien class element." Veterans, for their part, shared this language. Nevertheless, because most veterans remained out of power and had less "cultural capital" than others, they remained particularly vulnerable to political attack.

In making these class-based charges against the "flesh and blood" of the revolution, civilian officials capitalized upon a fundamental feature of the Communist Revolution: very few people, if any, were politically "pure" in the sense of having a perfect class background (poor peasants, worker, etc.) and an unblemished record of meritorious, selfless service to the cause; the revolution was full of Bernie LaPlantes (the Dustin Hoffman character in the film *Hero* noted earlier in the chapter), as it were. This was true of the early CCP, whose top leadership was dominated by urban cosmopolitans from elite families (Zhou Enlai and Liu Shaoqi, for instance) and its mid-level ranks during the war years, as well as the PLA. During its long road to power, the PLA could not afford to exclude everyone who did not have poor peasant background or a problematic personal history, such as membership in a bandit organization. During the Civil War, entire Nationalist units (many of whom fought very valiantly—and patriotically—against Japan) switched sides. These circumstances were quite complex, reflecting the chaos of war; shifting alliances between the CCP, Nationalists, warlords, and secret societies; and divided family alliances. Even death was complicated: as late as 1963 there were memorial sites that had Nationalist Party corpses mixed in with Communist Party martyrs.[87] As a result, the PLA that emerged from the civil war in 1949 was a predominantly rural force but also included people who had a variety of class and social backgrounds, and so did its veterans.

Complicated backgrounds were not easily massaged into the simple historical narrative of heroism and evil that characterized CCP propaganda, and veterans suffered as a result. The Provincial Civil Affairs gazetteer of Guangdong Province mentions veterans who suffered discrimination when they returned to villages "during the Land Reform campaign" on account of their bad family background.[88] Among 200 veterans who arrived in Shanghai in 1950–1951, roughly 27 had served with the Nationalists "for a long time"; some were officers with a "complicated" political history.[89] A 1952 analysis of the social and political background of 2,105 veterans in Shanghai showed that 70 percent were "volunteers," 6 percent left the Nationalist Army on their own accord and were absorbed into the PLA during the latter phases of the Civil War (known as *qiyi* soldiers), and almost one-quarter were pre-1949 POWs who were "reeducated."[90] As the PLA professionalized during the early to mid-1950s, the number of veterans with "problematic" political histories decreased. A 1956 analysis of 2,054 veterans identified only 109 (5 percent) with this problem, a figure that included those with "complicated social relations."[91] According to reports from the early years, *qiyi* veterans were quite cognizant of their "complicated" predicament, knew "it would be hard to find work," and feared that the government would "not care" about them.[92] But even these veterans were not as problematic as some of those who joined the PLA from urban areas after 1949, since they were more likely to have had extended contact with the Nationalists. According to the Minister of the Interior, these veterans were even more problematic than former POWs and Nationalist soldiers.[93] Which of these multiple identities were more salient in the crunch? Could someone who actually fought against Japan with the Nationalist Party (in other words, a "patriot") be recognized for this contribution? Could a veteran who fought against the United States in the Korean War but whose father or grandfather was a landlord be treated with respect? In the USSR, the answer to this was fairly clear. As noted by historian Mark von Hagen, in the 1936 Constitution, Soviet "citizenship" had superseded class as the primary way the state identified its population. Several years later a new law of universal conscription incorporated "nearly all national groups that had been excluded, and all social categories, even those which had been deprived of voting rights in previous legislation."[94] Mass war further reduced the significance of class status. By 1944, social origins were no longer the "dominant criteria of sociopolitical status"—bad class or family background was redeemed through wartime exploits, while non-combat service was marginalized.[95]

Until we have access to more archives (especially at the Center), it will be impossible to answer these questions in a conclusive manner, but the general pattern suggests that "civilian" party officials either flatly refused to recognize, or at least pretended to refuse to recognize when it served their interest, veterans' contributions (to fighting the Japanese or the United States), focusing instead on their anti-Communist history or (rarely existing) "class purity" as the most important method of evaluating political worthiness. In 1951, a report noted, veterans with "complicated" backgrounds languished without land, jobs, or housing for as long as a year; some lived in guesthouses and subsisted on welfare funds that were distributed to "ordinary" poor people,[96] and in villages some of these veterans were immediately placed under surveillance.[97] In 1952, the Shanghai Bureau of Civil Affairs noted that "it is impossible to solve" (*genben wufa jiejue*) employment problems facing those with "complicated histories" and that the government could not support them with aid indefinitely,[98] a problem that continued well into the mid- to late 1950s, as enterprise personnel directors, either by themselves or jointly with the local party committee, refused to hire veterans with complicated pasts. In contrast to depictions of urban life during the 1950s as "not particularly stressful,"[99] stress was endemic among these veterans, as were poverty (some had not worked for four years) and anger at local units for ignoring the "spirit" of State Council policies and directives from the Minister of the Interior that veterans' past problems should be "separated" from current ones and their own personal problems from those related to their families.[100] Veterans' suspicion of local officials' "willed ignorance" was, in fact, partially confirmed: investigations revealed that scores of documents from the Center to local officials were ignored or filed away, or else read, but not announced publicly.[101] By "blockading" this information, local officials gained an even stronger hand in their political battles with veterans.[102]

Recognizing the severity of this problem, the Shanghai Bureau of Civil Affairs analyzed 109 cases of veterans who were virtually unemployable because of "political problems." Among these, only 40 had themselves served with the Nationalists, while the rest were discriminated against because they had relatives or friends who were in Taiwan or Hong Kong, or they were arrested or executed as counterrevolutionaries; that the veteran had "come clean in the PLA" made little difference.[103] Civil Affairs officials had great difficulty placing veterans with complicated pasts or families;[104] close to 30 percent of veterans who had not found any employment after a year of searching—reducing them to welfare cases—were victimized by "political history problems and complicated social relations."[105] Gu Hua, for example, served in the PLA for 15 years and was discharged in 1955, but nine units in Hongkou District in Shanghai refused to hire him because his father was a "counterrevolutionary." One of these units was the District Government's educational section, whose staff likely included many educated people able to "imagine the nation" and produce patriotic education materials.[106]

Crime and suicide statistics reveal some of the personal repercussions from "problematic" social and political histories. In a 1957 investigation of 40 suicide cases occurring between 1955 and 1957, 12.5 percent were caused by stress and anxiety stemming from "political history problems,"[107] while some 25 percent of 135 criminal cases involving veterans in 1956 resulted from the politicized charge of "counterrevolution," the second-largest category after theft (36 percent).[108] The categories of "counterrevolution" and "problematic history" incorporated a wide range of experiences but mainly referred to veterans who were in the GMD at some point, had kin or friends in Hong Kong or Taiwan, had suspect class background (landlord, rich peasant), or whose father or brothers were in trouble with the government.[109]

Some cases flesh out the stories behind the statistics.[110] In Shanhe County, Shandong, Lu Yongwen was a veteran with a landlord background. After he was discharged, he returned to the county and sought permission to enter a mutual aid team. The county refused, and he threw himself into a well. In a Guizhou case (Songtao County), Wu Enyun joined the PLA while he was a student at Sichuan University. When he was discharged in the mid-1950s, Wu tried to resume his studies, but the university refused because his father was a "counterrevolutionary" who had been arrested (other relatives were also under investigation) and he had been in a Nationalist Party organization. Wu traveled to Beijing and lived in the guesthouse of the Ministry of Interior. From there he appealed to the Department of Higher Education, which sent a letter back to Sichuan inquiring about Wu's situation. The university explained its case, and the Education Department concurred with its decision. On January 5, 1956, Wu attempted suicide at Beijing's Worker's Cultural Palace, but this, too, failed. Another veteran, surnamed Zheng, was also a university student and served in the *Sanqingtuan*, a youth organization affiliated with the GMD, and then with a medical unit in the PLA but could not find work for more than a year. He wrote an angry and sarcastic letter to the State Council: "If I'm a counter-revolutionary, then I should be sent off to a reform-through-labor camp—at least that way I'd have work!"[111]

PLA Trash

Given the complex history of the Chinese Revolution and the need to remain on war footing in the early 1950s, the CCP may have been justified in limiting some former regime elements from gaining access to important jobs. It is not unusual. It took 30 years and the Spanish–American and Indian wars for former Union and Confederate soldiers to reconcile after the American Civil War. In Israel, between 1948 and 1963, Prime Minister David Ben-Gurion was very determined (more so than many in his party) to exclude from official commemorations those who died fighting for independence as part of the Etzel (Irgun) militia, the main rival to his Mapai (Labor) party in the pre-state period; militia veterans, widows, and bereaved parents were considered "politically worthy" of inclusion into the official "pantheon" only after Ben-Gurion's political star began to wane.[112] After the Spanish Civil War, the

Republican losers were subjected to harsh reprisals and discrimination by the victorious Nationalists, including a ban on memorial activities to remember their dead, a fate that was also suffered by the losers of the Finnish Civil War.[113] Even so, such veterans as Gu Hua served for a long time in the *victorious* PLA, but this did not immunize them from discrimination. But even less reasonable and far more indicative of the shaky foundations of social and political status grounded in military service was the discrimination veterans faced even when there was no evidence of participation in the Nationalist Army or political organizations.

Throughout the 1950s, a widely held perception in Chinese society and among civilian officials was that *all* veterans, despite the fact that most had a certificate of meritorious service, had some sort of "political problem"; otherwise, why would the PLA have demobilized them? Few appeared to understand that demobilization had to occur after the end of the Civil and Korean wars simply because there was no need for a large standing army. In my discussions with longtime Shanghai residents, some suggested that people at the time believed that the very fact that veterans survived the war was in itself "proof" of a problem—if they were "good," they surely would have died at the front. (Similarly, in Israel in the 1950s, Holocaust survivors sensed that people "questioned what immoral deeds they might have done in order to stay alive."[114]) The PLA, State Council, and CCP were aware of this sentiment since it appears in many reports, but there is no evidence that Chairman Mao or any other part of the state made any significant effort (through study sessions, campaigns, etc.) to dispel it; by 1955–1956, it had other priorities, such as rural collectivization, socialization of industries, and party rectification. Absent a sustained campaign, this idea surfaced in the early 1950s and did not go away. By discharging the soldiers, the PLA had "separated the bones from the meat," a union official claimed;[115] "If you were good, you would not have returned [from the PLA]," said another.[116] According to an investigation by the cadre section of a Shanghai firm, *all* veterans were said to have "physical or political history problems or else were purged by their units."[117] Another quoted a workshop director who said that veterans were "trash (*laji*) swept out by the military" or "inferior goods" (*ci huo*) because of all their baggage and ailments.[118] Others said, "Among veterans there isn't a good person, and there's no good person who's a veteran";[119] "only the bad ones leave the army; if you were good you wouldn't be here"; and "they wouldn't have been demobilized if the PLA wanted them."[120] Some were suspected of desertion.[121] The union chair at the Shenxin #1 Mill asked veterans, "How can it be that you don't have any problems if you've been discharged only after several years of service?"[122] In some cases, unions conducted unauthorized trials of veterans, which resulted in expulsion from the party.[123] Even as late as 1963, investigations revealed that some units were convinced that return-ing veterans were all either "sick, weak, or have problems."[124]

In villages, veterans encountered similar perceptions, but they appeared to be far less pervasive than in the cities, at least in the documentary record. For example, during local elections in the early 1950s, many veterans were on the candidate list. In many respects, their status and experiences made them ideal candidates. Nevertheless, village officials who rose to power through other means, sensing the arrival of a new political threat, "swiftboated" them by spreading rumors that they had been "purged" from the PLA and not hon-orably discharged (not unlike George Bush, Karl Rove, and Dick Cheney's treatment of veterans like John Kerry in the 2004 U.S. elections). Township and village cadres in Shandong, Henan, and Qingpu, for example, said, "The army didn't want him, so why should we give him a position?" and told vet-erans, "The only reason you're here is because you had trouble in the army," a charge veterans vigorously denied.[125] In other cases, village cadres resorted to violence to prevent veterans from assuming political posts. Not a few veterans were punched, kicked, and otherwise abused by village cadres.[126] Veterans' families were not immune to this view, either. Rather than welcom-ing them home with open arms after service, many military families were "afraid" of their return, considered it a "loss of face," and even suspected that they had "deserted."[127]

Unsurprisingly, many veterans were taken aback when encountering a wide-spread lack of appreciation (and understanding) of their wartime (and peace-time) service. A common metaphor (seen in documents from Hebei, Shanghai, and Shandong from the early 1950s to 1965) drawn from veterans' rural backgrounds compared their situation to "donkeys slaughtered after grinding the wheat."[128] In Qingpu, veterans complained they were like "a pair of socks, used when they're worn, tossed aside when they're not, just like the Guomin-dang."[129] Nostalgia for the camaraderie of military life (despite its rigors and discipline) quickly set in: documents suggest a widespread desire among vet-erans to return to the "warmth" of military service after their "cold" experience in civilian life.[130] Thinking back, they recalled their service as a time of great camaraderie and cried "in deep sorrow" about their present circumstances.[131] Some said, "In the army we were the most loved (*zui ke'ai*), but now we are the most pitiable (*zui kelian*)," and thought seriously about reenlisting.[132] In 1962, many veterans sought to reenlist, in part because of the impact of the disastrous Great Leap Forward on the countryside but also because of the cold reception they received.[133] Another veteran remarked (in 1963), "you're 'glorious' for three years, then eat crow for six—veterans suffer a lot."[134] Others said, "If I knew things would be like this, I would have died rather than become a vet-eran" and "I'll never allow my son to join the army."[135]

Disputing the Korean War

What might have improved this situation? First, we should consider the issue of a war's legitimacy. Wars that are seen as widely legitimate by a critical mass of citizens, but especially elites, will probably have a beneficent impact on the way veterans of that war are treated; it is less plausible that a war that is considered necessary, just, and legitimate will result in that war's soldiers' being maltreated and widely disrespected after their return. Switched around, the respect afforded to veterans can gauge the degree of legitimacy of a war (and by implication, the state's legitimacy). Second, if we take the case of Union and Confederate reconciliation after the American Civil War as a rough guide, a foreign conflict helps resolve, or softens, animosity between former combatants. During the 1880s and 1890s white veterans from the "blue and grey" reunited, as a sense of patriotism and citizenship based on camaraderie and respect for action, bravery, and common sacrifices—what O'Leary calls a "blood brotherhood"—overrode the residues of the past. Civilian "shirkers" and war profiteers were seen in a more negative light than former combatants.[136] If "nationalism" was pivotal during a hard-fought foreign war, the tensions of the civil war might have given way to a stronger sense of unity against the United States during the Korean War. This is the image the CCP projected to its own people and to the world during the campaign to "Resist America and Support North Korea" as well as in the war's aftermath, as the propagandists churned out film clips and commemorative volumes to solidify the "official" memory of the war in public consciousness. In the 1990s, when anonymous "new nationalists" printed a magazine cover with a "Korean War veteran" threatening the United States ("We have squared off before!"),[137] they were drawing from a deep well of officially controlled imagery of the war. Ironically, these media-savvy assertions of Chinese nationalism have coincided with a growing but (too) quiet debate within China about the sagacity of the war and its sacrifices, led, not coincidently, by its veterans.[138]

Thankfully, archival evidence—drawn from records detailing the unfolding of the "Resist America, Support Korea" campaign—allows us to move well beyond stock images and officially sanctioned memories toward something approaching a "vernacular" history of the war, or at least popular reactions to it. What did ordinary people think about the Korean War? If veterans were not given their due, was this partly because of the way people assessed the legitimacy of the war?

While not comprehensive—I would have liked to look at sources from at least another city—the evidence I do have at my disposal points to poorly implemented propaganda campaigns as well as widely shared skepticism, misunderstanding, and confusion about the war and its ultimate objectives.[139] In 1951, for example, there was a short-lived campaign to get Shanghai residents to sign "patriotic compacts" (*aiguo gongyue*) in support of the war, but reviews of these efforts noted that the campaign failed to materialize in 40–50 percent of firms; in an investigation of 950 work units, "empty and vague" compacts were found in 600 of them.[140] According to the Shanghai Textile Union, only 1,141 out of 14,003 "small groups" in factories under their jurisdiction (8 percent) signed these compacts.[141] When patriotic compacts were signed, it was often a *pro forma* affair. In one firm, for example, compacts were signed and then posted on a wall, but they were blown away by a strong wind. When investigators asked workers what the compacts were actually about, "no one could remember." In "very many firms," patriotic compacts simply became a method to discipline a fairly unruly workforce; patriotic compacts became "labor contracts": workers promised to avoid "dozing off," "eating whenever we feel like it," "working only when the manager passes by," "carelessly criticizing others," "arriving late, and leaving early and requesting a break instead of just stopping work." Workers "didn't see the meaning and the connection between themselves and the patriotic compacts."[142] Typical remarks included:

I'm old—let the young ones do it. I don't get why I should.

We're only doing this because the factory makes inferior cloth and we're going to be shut down. Let's hurry up and sign already!

What's a "compact"? I don't understand.

If you have a gong, bring it; if you have red cloth, put it up.

Signing a patriotic compact is like investigating a criminal. You go to a small room and Mr. Feng [a leader] reads a document line by line and then tells us to raise our hands in agreement. We all say "fine" (*hao*), but we really don't understand what the whole thing is about.

Workers were not the only ones who were confused. In a survey of 30 households on Caifu Lane in Shanghai's Laozha District, 23 had no idea what a "patriotic compact" was and why anyone should afford preferential treatment to military dependents and martyr families; 18 households did not understand why the CCP was attacking "counterrevolutionaries," either.[143]

Party officials who had hoped that the concept of "patriotism" could be taught through the concept of a signed "compact" were surely disappointed by the results of this campaign, which occurred in China's most modern city among workers who were at the "vanguard" of the revolution. The more serious propaganda effort—the campaign to "Resist America and Support Korea" (it also was called the campaign to "Resist America, Support Korea, Protect the Home, and Defend the Country")—yielded similar results: implementation was shoddy, and people's reactions were ambivalent. According to a draft of a summary report, the campaign unfolded reasonably well in "universities and hospitals" but "hardly anything was done in private firms; what is done stops at the cadre and activist level and doesn't go any further" (this sentence was crossed out and was not included in the final version).[144] In the industrial sector, it was mainly enforced in "large enterprises"; when it came to smaller units, many "thought that the campaign was already over." Workers and managers both thought the campaign diverted attention from production and was a waste of time. Some, however, were convinced by young workers "who had attended military cadre school" (*junshi ganxiao*) that "patriotism is a glorious thing."[145] An internal report from the Penglai District Party Committee found that its members "are too busy with work," "don't pay a lot of attention to spies and preserving secrets," "generally don't care about current affairs," "don't read newspapers or magazines," and "see propaganda work as a burden"; "very many" simply went through the motions, presenting it as nothing more than a "production drive," much like the "patriotic compact" campaign.[146]

As much as ex post facto investigations revealed "unbalanced development" in the campaign, this was probably no great surprise to party investigators; internal CCP documents often delved into its organizational weaknesses. On the other hand, party investigators were probably a bit more startled when they encountered local cadres and ordinary workers' reactions to the various protagonists in the war, namely, their own government, North Korea, the USSR, and the United States. In Laozha District, "very many (*xu duo*) people did not understand the political significance" and were confused by the campaign to support North Korea and go to war the United States. A woman surnamed Cao said, "I only understand resisting Japan, not resisting the U.S. and supporting Korea"; another said, "Why go to war with the United States?"[147] In Penglai District, cadres said that China should provide political support only to the North Koreans, but otherwise they should "liberate themselves." Many local cadres, despite the "Sino-Soviet Treaty of Peace, Security, and Friendship" signed in 1950, were suspicious of the USSR and wondered why China's foreign policy wasn't to "join the U.S.–British alliance" (NATO) instead of starting off fighting with the United States. Since Shanghai was an industrial center, the United States was sure to attack with the atomic bomb and the Marines.[148] Ordinary workers were similarly "confused," according to investigators, who summarized their views after extensive interviews:[149]

The United States is attacking North Korea, not us, so why go to war?

The Koreans helped the Japanese against us, so now that the United States is fighting North Korea we're getting our revenge. If the U.S. crosses the Yalu

River, we should help them. Why would the U.S. fight us then?

Penicillin is American, and even at its worst the U.S. isn't nearly as bad as the Japanese devils.

The U.S. is better than Japan; in the past they gave us flour and milk powder.

It's not worth helping those North Korean loafers (*lan ren*).

The USSR wants China to "carry the bridal carriage" [do the hard work, while the bride gets all the glory]; they want China to burn and they'll come in to reap the millet.

North Korea's in a war and wants us to fight but we shouldn't. What will we do if they decide to attack Shanghai? Their army is very tough.

West Korea, East Korea—I don't get the difference. (In Shanghainese, North Korea, or *chao xian*, would be pronounced as *chao xi*, which means "West Korea" in Mandarin.)

Where's North Korea?

Is Stalin the leader of North Korea?

We only understand the four words "Resist America, Support Korea"; if you asked us why, we'd have no idea. Whenever we hear reports it's in the east ear and out the west ear.

Does "Resist America, Support Korea" mean that we also oppose Japanese rearmament by the U.S.?

Today you tell us to "Resist America and Support Korea," tomorrow you say to "Suppress Counterrevolutionaries," then it's back to supporting fighters on the front line and then you tell us about peace talks. It's getting us all confused! [*sic*]

Local officials, of course, tried to "correct" these "incorrect" viewpoints. A speech by the vice-chairman of the Shanghai Branch of the All-China Textile Union to an audience of senior workers complained that even workers who attended large meetings and small group sessions and "recognize the innate character of paper tiger American imperialism" "still do not feel much hatred towards the United States" and "do not grasp the idea that 'America has always been our enemy.'" For workers, "imperialism" was more strongly associated with the cruelty of the Japanese during the war years, not with the United States.[150]

This skepticism was shared among a fairly large swath of the city's more educated classes, according to several investigation reports. For example, in 1950 the Shanghai Federation of Trade Unions convened a meeting of the "education workers [teachers] union" to hear their views on the war. Few appeared to accept the rationale for the war, and many were afraid of it. Lack of enthusiasm (*mabi*) was said to be "common." Some wondered: "We've already learned about social development; we know that imperialism will be defeated in the end and that the people will ultimately be victorious. What's the emergency now?"[151] Others panicked, fearing that "the atomic bomb would be dropped on them" and so "refused to utter a word." A few refused to wear red scarves or teach, fearing a Nationalist return to the mainland. One teacher explained: "When the GMD was here, we said 'The GMD is good.' Now the CCP is here and we say, 'The CCP is good, serve the people.' Now the GMD's returning. What should we do?"[152] A few teachers wondered why the CCP was helping North Korea instead of liberating Taiwan, and they queried local officials why "America" was now called "American imperialists"—in their view, America was just America. Rather than feeling any sort of antagonism toward the United States, most teachers, similar to their working-class counterparts, generally admired it: "What's wrong with America?" "We're not going to rise up." Despite numerous efforts to convince them otherwise, teachers, much like today's educated class, continued to admire the United States for its "material well-being and civilization" and therefore "ignored or downplayed the campaign."[153]

A report of a meeting with medical staff produced similar findings. Many medical professionals had studied in the United States and were far from enthusiastic about a major war against it. Many refused to serve on surgical teams; others commented that "medical equipment and drugs are from the U.S., as are objective textbooks" and shared the assessment that the war was happening only "because the USSR wants us to fight." "Illusions" about America's good qualities and "insufficient recognition of American aggression" were widespread, the report complained.[154] In light of Shanghai's history as a cosmopolitan city in the pre-1949 period and the popularity of Hollywood films throughout the 1930s and 1940s (despite the critiques leveled at them by prudish leftist intellectuals), these positive views of the United States should not be surprising.[155] Even after the Korean War, films that showed affluent and free Western living remained highly popular in Shanghai, despite repeated efforts by the propaganda authorities to convince people they were decadent.[156]

Peasants, more so than educated urbanites, faced the very real possibility of serving in the Korean War, and the burden of recruiting them for the cause fell upon the shoulders of rural officials. Did peasants and officials in rural areas respond to the call to arms with greater enthusiasm? A handwritten report on recruitment in Qingpu circa fall 1951 provides us with an insider's account of the draft process.[157] According to this report, very little went according to plan: local cadres "are very busy, don't know the policies, and don't know about the political status of new recruits, and neither did district-level officials; no one specialized in this matter."[158] As a result, recruitment efforts were improvised. To defeat other villages in a competition over which one could raise more soldiers, cadres in Chengxiang District took veterans, teenagers, people more than 40 years old, and villagers with various illnesses—knowing the whole time that they would eventually be rejected. If villagers refused to participate in this charade, they would be taken by force. Some cadres "faked leadership" to score political points: they went for their physicals—which encouraged others to follow suit—but then ran back to their villages. Others told the PLA lieutenant stationed there: "I've taken the lead, but I have to go back now—not enough people to work the land or take care of the village." Many of the peasants who followed the cadres to the recruiting station, however, did not leave.[159] In Puguang Township, cadres convened a meeting of young men and told them, "If you don't join the army, you'll be 'supporting America and resisting Korea.'" A peasant in the audience piped up: "I can also be 'supporting Korea and resisting America' by helping military dependents in their fields." The cadre responded: "If you don't go, you'll be responsible for helping 30 of them, all by yourself." The young man went to register feeling he had no choice in the matter. In Anzhuang Township in Zhujiajiao District, cadres told the assembled men, "Go register for a physical. I pledge to you that at most you'll end up here in Qingpu. Some could end up as clerks for the court; some might be in the local guard." Three men went to the district for their exam and were quizzed about their motivation, but all of them said, "We don't want to be in the PLA." Township officials who accompanied them said, "Fine. We guarantee you'll be able to guard in the court or the district—you absolutely will not have to go anywhere else." All three passed their physicals, but two immediately absconded. The one who reported for duty had second thoughts, and his family came to try to get him out, but they were eventually calmed down by a "veteran comrade." At the end of this process, owing to "poor vetting procedures" and the general reluctance to serve, Qingpu sent to the PLA one former GMD district chief, three sons of landlord families, 19 from a secret society, and 23 who were "GMD spies and bandits." Their problematic class backgrounds were discovered by the PLA; whether they went to the front is not clear.[160]

These reports were written in 1950–1951, so it is somewhat plausible that subsequent investigations (which I did not find in the archives) revealed a great deal more enthusiasm for the war in Korea. But I am skeptical of this scenario. "War fever" tends to wane, not rise, as conflicts drag on and as time passes; as early as late 1951, cadres in Qingpu thought that they did not need to contribute any more food for the war effort and wondered "why North Korea is still fighting."[161] This certainly would not be unusual: it was the case in Guangxi Province (one of China's most martial[162]) during the Sino-Japanese War; during WWI in Europe; during the "good war" of WWII, when the United States government mounted a desperate campaign to persuade the public to buy war bonds to rescue the Treasury (by using the imagery from the Marines raising the flag at Iwo Jima); and recently in the Iraq War. And, contemporary popular perceptions aside, the PLA's "victory" was not clear-cut at the time: there were many Chinese POWs. When it was over, veterans realized that time and peace were the enemies of memory. At a mass meeting in Shandong, cadres "investigated the lack of concern for veterans" and blamed "peacetime" for "forgetfulness" and "ingratitude" (*wangben*) toward the PLA.[163] In Shanghai, the Bureau of Civil Affairs' internally circulated bulletin noted "many people" who were not at all concerned about veterans "now that peace has arrived." In this take on veterans, the only reason to be concerned about soldiers and the military was because of wartime circumstances; if war was over, veterans, having done their part, could be ignored as life returned to normal. New cadres, in particular, were especially prone to "not understanding veterans' honor and hardships."[164]

More compelling evidence for the lack of enthusiasm for military service (and those who served) can be gleaned from intra-party reports from 1956, when the CCP attempted to enforce national registration for military service. On the surface, draft registration was conceptualized as a nation-building enterprise and couched in terms of civic republicanism—in documents, Chinese were called "citizens" rather than "the masses."[165] Draft registration was expected to apply to all 18–30-year-olds, but it mainly targeted young men in this age bracket.[166] But even during this period of state "centralization," nothing about getting peasants to register for the draft proved easy. Many cadres claimed that, having registered people for militia work, there was no need for registration for the PLA, that they were too busy with other tasks, and that since there was no war, there was no need for it in the first place. Some made big mistakes when conducting "education" about it—telling peasants that they would have to serve three years and that if they did not register, they would be considered "landlords, counterrevolutionaries, or rich peasants." Peasants, thinking that Chiang Kai-shek and the United States would retake the mainland, were extremely afraid of war and worried that registration was a trick to secure their enlistment, comparing it to the final stage of an engagement for marriage, a fish caught by a hook, ink on white paper, a rope around a cow's neck, and pulling someone's head by grabbing their ear. Some women locked their husbands in their homes, thinking that they would be forced to fight, or threatened to divorce them if they registered. But perhaps more significantly, the CCP was confronted with its own recent history dealing with the area's residents, who were described as "complicated" in the reports because of previous political affiliations and commercial backgrounds. Between 1950 and 1955, many families knew someone who had been targeted by one of the CCP's political campaigns (against former Nationalists, businessmen, landlords, etc.), which greatly complicated their efforts to assert a "shared" responsibility to protect and defend the state. According to the handwritten reports in Qingpu, anyone who had relatives suppressed by the CCP—this population was said to include many older people, merchants, fishermen, and boatmen—was extremely suspicious about the CCP's motives: having arrested or killed a relative, why would the party now want them to fight its wars? An elderly woman in Luwan Village told her son to avoid registering, "The fucking Guomindang has left and the cunning CCP has taken its place."[167] This issue also came up in a 1957 meeting of veteran representatives. A veteran surnamed Wei said,

> When the state wanted me, I was the most cherished (*zui ke'ai*), but now that the state no longer wants me, I'm just like trash (*laji*). So even though there is still imperialism in the world and even though they might attack us, if the government comes calling, I won't be going; I'll be watching from the side.

According to the transcriber of this report, Wei was particularly upset because he "harbored" his father, a former village head under the Nationalists, who was punished after he resisted the implementation of the unified purchasing system policy in the spring of 1955.[168] To be sure, peasants were not the only ones who felt that military service was an unwelcome prospect. Officials in Jiangsu Province also noted that "some students" objected to military service because it would "delay their studies and affect their futures."[169]

Given these views of military service, it should not be all that surprising that those who served in the PLA in war or in peacetime frequently could not reap many benefits from their experience. Rather than serving as a springboard for veterans to claim a positive patriotic identity and higher status and respect as citizens, the Korean War, as a confusing and complex event with multiple unpopular parties (North Korea and the USSR), did not yield significant dividends for many of its combatants. Even worse, the shame associated with becoming a POW "infected" even those veterans who returned in more normal circumstances. Calling a veteran a "POW" (*fulu*) was an epithet in Shanghai factories as late as 1956.[170] Moreover, thanks to the CCP's persecution of its perceived enemies in rural society, post–Korean War military service was also looked upon with suspicion. Those who did serve bore the brunt of these views. In Qingpu (1962), soldiers, military families, and martyr families complained of being "used during campaigns, and then forgotten" and "treated just like any other commune members."[171]

COMPARATIVE PERSPECTIVES

To what extent was the PRC veterans' sense of elevated status based on military service unique? Chinese history, including military history, is obviously different from the history of the United States, Russia, and Western Europe—there is nothing quite comparable to the influence of Confucianism in those societies, for example—but can we find similarities between PRC veterans' "frankness," "prideful arrogance," courage, and toughness among veterans in other societies? Have other societies responded more positively to returning veterans in terms of according them a basic form of respect and appreciation and civil exchanges as they navigated life in the post-war period?

Here the scholarly literature is unequivocal. In different times and places and under a variety of political and historical circumstances, veterans have been known for their strong sense of rights and status, and strong personalities—characteristics which often did not win them any popularity contests among civilians and politicians. Many post-war battles were about just how far governments and societies should accommodate veterans' claims to citizen status and patriotic identity on the basis of military contributions. As early as the Roman Empire, for instance, scholarly types—much like their Confucian-minded counterparts in China—often complained of veterans' "swaggering" and sense of themselves as beyond the law—a view, incidentally, that is not well supported by evidence that provides a better sense of everyday life, such as papyri.[172] In Britain during the 18th and early 19th centuries, Linda Colley argues, marginal groups could attain coveted British identity, and be empowered on this basis, by proving their patriotism through their contributions to the country's war effort.[173] In the United States after the Revolutionary War, Continental Army officers "who had risen in rank and gained experience organizing and commanding men showed less deference to local elites upon returning to civilian life."[174] After WWI, disabled soldiers demanded special treatment, but the British treasury was famously tightfisted;[175] German disabled veterans also had a strong sense of entitlement because of their sacrifices, and in the countryside traditional political and religious authorities complained that returning veterans "fancied themselves as 'barons,'" were unwilling to "fall in line," and resisted state controls and regulations governing the economy.[176] Much like the PRC, Nigerian veterans from WWI felt superior to their civilian peers (considered too "provincial") and were resented for it.[177] In Russia, Amir Weiner writes, the WWII experience "bred a new assertive citizen,"[178] and Catherine Merridale notes that after the war officers "were never at a loss for words" and "felt that they had a right, even an obligation, to put their views about the peace to the government" (many argued for liberalization; after seeing concentration camps, they sought to revise laws on political prisoners).[179]

During WWII, Indian soldiers of the British army in North Africa were said to have developed a "superiority complex; they think they are better than any British or Dominion troops . . . and will not meekly accept unemployment or return to the normal life of the Indian villager."[180] In the United States, many black veterans from both world wars felt a "new, potent sense of identity" and expected that state and society would reciprocate with more respect;[181] a similar feeling prevailed among American Indian veterans as well.[182]

Even as these U.S. veterans claimed the right to first-class citizenship, they also expressed not a small amount of anger at what they perceived to be civilian ingratitude, a feeling we have observed in China as well.[183] In the United States, these disputes cropped up early in its history. After the Revolution, "soldiers and officers alike began to feel increasingly isolated from civilians, and perceived that those who had stayed behind were making money from the war while they, the soldiers, risked their lives and exhausted their own wealth."[184] Alexander Hamilton, who served in combat in the Continental Army, railed against political opponents who spoke eloquently of the "venerable sacrifice made by American soldiers" during policy debates but who never served or fired a shot (e.g., James Madison).[185] Owing to the dominance of Jeffersonians' suspicions of standing armies, veterans of the Continental Army—many of them destitute—were virtually forgotten in popular culture and in law until they began to die off in the 1820s. According to John Resch, a major problem was that the early views of the war attributed success to the struggle of *American citizens* for independence (which included militias, merchants, politicians, farmers, etc., in equal measure) without singling out those who fought in a military capacity—all could claim, and did, that they were upholders of republican virtue, a problem we have seen in the Chinese case as well.[186] In revolutionary Massachusetts, for instance, "veterans' claims to moral superiority met with vilification. They received no special honors."[187] It took the election of a veteran (James Monroe) and the realization that a standing, well-trained army was important after military reversals in the War of 1812 to reverse this trend, but veterans were marked as a "special class" within American society only after the Civil War.[188] The situation was not much better in Western democracies that did not experience the bitter rivalry between Federalists and Jeffersonian Democrats. After WWI, Canadian veterans also felt that they had been forgotten after the war.[189] In post-WWI France, veterans were extremely angry about their treatment—Antoine Prost calls it "semi-revolutionary" for a while—but the anger was directed largely against "shirkers" and the "new rich" in particular,[190] a phenomenon that was also noted in the United States after the war.[191]

Veterans in China shared with many of their counterparts an often feisty and courageous political stance, as well as a penchant for direct, frank language. Trained with weapons and organization, they have often been a potent political force, striking fear into the hearts of civilians and politicians alike. Roman veterans petitioned the Senate and were suspicious of politicians.[192] Australian WWI veterans rioted and organized "secret armies" in the immediate post-war period,[193] and British veterans of that war mounted massive demonstrations at Memorial Day services in 1919.[194] "Rough honesty, realism and devotion" were said to describe the French WWI veteran,[195] and one of the more common character traits among Israelis—speaking *dugri*, "telling the truth to someone's face, without equivocation" in "unpolished, utilitarian, simple, and direct idiom"—has been said to derive from "speech under fire" in battle or briefings before it.[196] In the United States, veterans of the Union Army developed a very strong sense of "ownership" of the country because they believed (correctly) that they had saved the nation during the war; those who saw battle looked down upon those who did not and greatly resented the post-war power of rich and upper-class bondholders who opposed their pensions.[197] In the early 1930s, disgruntled WWI veterans, many of whom had a "new, potent sense of identity" after the war, mobilized *en masse* and in military formation for the Bonus March. The Federal Bureau of Investigation (FBI), much like the PRC authorities but with the political charges reversed, mobilized against them, accusing them of being "Communists" and compiling an extensive file on their "un-American" activities before they were eventually suppressed.[198] After WWII, veterans were said to be much franker than before the war: "they say what's on their mind, even if it is critical."[199] This sense of status did not affect only whites. Black WWI veterans who experienced a very different relationship between whites and blacks while abroad in France stimulated a broad rebellion against the status quo upon their return home.[200] Black WWII veterans played a similar role in the early stages of the Civil Rights Movement in the South, when the risk of retaliation was dangerously high. Medgar Evers "led a group of WWII veterans" to the county courthouse in Mississippi to vote in primary elections.[201] According to Jennifer Brooks, veterans in Georgia who developed a "sense of agency" from the war faced post-war challenges with a great deal of "confidence" and "determination," which encouraged others to speak up. Veteran activism led to record-breaking voter turnout in some places[202] and to direct confrontation with southern authorities in others. In March 1946, the United Negro Veterans and Women's Auxiliary in Atlanta organized roughly 200 people to demonstrate against police brutality, shouting "Square Deal for the Negro" as they marched on City Hall in a highly disciplined fashion.[203] In Columbia, Tennessee, "the presence of more than 150 Negro veterans" strengthened the local community's resolve to not be "pushed around" anymore—which then precipitated racial violence.[204] This strong sense of identity and frank political style also occurred in non-democratic societies. In Taiwan, mainland Nationalist veterans were known for their "straightforward manner"[205] and a heightened sense of status: they "perceived the title 'rongmin' [honored citizen] as a medal they carried with them" and therefore viewed themselves as a "group apart from civilians [Taiwanese]," who generally viewed them negatively. To counterbalance this view, evidence suggests that veterans tried to align their behavior with their title; one noted that the *rongmin* "brand of honor" was a "weight on my shoulders," and another refused to take a bribe in return for his support in a local election.[206] Similarly, after WWII in the USSR, veterans "assumed that they had earned special rights vis-à-vis the larger community they had defended"[207] and claimed a "moral right . . . to describe the history of the war as they had seen it"; responding to their critics was a "political right earned with blood."[208]

If Chinese veterans exhibited many similar personality traits as other veterans around the world, in what ways was their predicament quite different, and did this have any impact on their treatment after the war? In most of the cases mentioned above—but especially in cases when the ruling government has claimed victory in war and provided veterans with benefits and symbolic capital—there is little evidence of the utter contempt and hostility directed toward their counterparts in the PRC. Victorious veterans from the American, Spanish, and Finnish civil wars all had trouble readjusting to civilian life, but there is not much evidence that they were treated like the *losers* in these conflicts.

To help explain this, I suggest that we return to the arguments of this study: China was never a "nation-in-arms"; it did not have a state that institutionalized anything close to universal conscription or mobilized an army representative of all of its population; and its wars often had dubious legitimacy in the eyes of the public. As a result, what I have called a "martial" understanding of citizenship and patriotism remains fragile. If we look at many of the Western cases, veterans' sense of emboldened identity and citizenship took root because they had *allies in society*, especially among the upper classes who served in the military as well, or had friends and family who served in a mass-conscripted army. Veterans' ability to forge links to other groups in the post-war period was vital in shaping cultures and polities that had more support for demands for martial-based claims to citizenship (in terms of more respect, status, appreciation, and sympathy); even if many veterans were ostensibly very much part of the state, in the absence of any sort of consensus about "deservedness" or well-implemented counterveiling public policies, veterans, like other socially disadvantaged social groups, could not do it by themselves.[209] Most of the civic rituals associated with veterans in the West (Veterans Day, Memorial Day) were initiated by veterans, military families, and war widows (see Chapter 5), but these efforts were supported by cultural elites, charities, and businesses that valued their contribution and *sympathized* with their predicament. In Great Britain in the 19th century, for example, veterans' problems were exposed by new media technologies such as the telegraph and mass circulation newspapers, and the public sympathized with them because they were familiar with the work of Florence Nightingale and other charities; prior to this time, veterans from Britain's land armies were despised, much like soldiers who had very low status in the official Confucian hierarchy and later on during China's warlord period (1911–1927).[210] Demobilized writers and novelists in post-WWII Russia published diaries and stories in literary journals, books (*The Front, Greetings from the Front*), or plays. The heroes of a "barrage of popular novels" on the post-war countryside were "demobilized officers."[211] In his study of France, Eugen Weber argued that war and "something close to universal conscription" played an important role in promoting "national awareness" in the late 19th century,[212] while Prost notes that the National Union of Veterans was supported by the state, "men of good works," and business; the national veterans movement included peasants *and* small traders from cities.[213] When Nationalist veterans protested in Taiwan in the late 1980s, they "won the sympathy from the society at large" and several policies were changed.[214] In the United States, WWI veterans—who came from *all* social strata—were the "dominant object of commemoration," a multivalent symbol that received the support of businessmen, civil organizations, and politicians.[215] After WWII, African-American veterans teamed up with liberal groups and labor (all of whom had veterans among them) to press for changes in their status.[216]

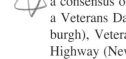

In China, by contrast, veterans had no allies in society, and there was never a consensus on how their contribution should be evaluated. The very idea of a Veterans Day, Veterans Stadium (in Philadelphia), Veterans Bridge (Pittsburgh), Veterans Park (Effingham County, Georgia), or Veterans Memorial Highway (New York) was not even on people's cognitive horizon, or on the state's, for that matter, rhetorical praise of veterans notwithstanding. In part, this is by design: despite its claims to "nationalism," the CCP has maintained its power largely by walling off groups from one another and fomenting conflicts among them (what Chen Yung-fa has called "controlled polarization"). It is also a reflection of the continued lack of respect and appreciation of military personnel by more educated elites, most of whom did not serve in the military and still look down upon those from rural areas. If we look at the composition of China's State Council in the 1950s (or Veterans Committees in the 1990s—see Chapter 8), veterans were scarcely represented on that body (many top leaders came from the machinery and petrochemical ministries); veterans were also a minority among Central Committee members, which were dominated by high school and college graduates until the Cultural Revolution.[217] Veterans' sense that "their" victory was lost to intellectuals, or to those who, in the words of the "Backward Person" cited above, "participated in the revolution later but who is blessed with a glib tongue," was not entirely off base, even if many Chinese intellectuals persist in seeing themselves as the primary victims of Maoist rule. Because intellectuals write many books about their victimization (but usually downplay their complicity and rarely mention their salaries, which far outstripped those of workers and peasants[218]) and the supposedly privileged veterans, workers, peasants, and others do not, it is no wonder that this perception is widely accepted in the West. If identity is seen as a two-way street—one's own sense of self has to be confirmed by others to be "real"—most veterans in China experienced a one-way road with multiple roadblocks and checkpoints: a strong sense of empowerment, courage, and entitlement that was rarely confirmed by those around them.

The forging of alliances between veterans and key groups in the society and state in many other countries, however, was not coincidental: there was a shared gender-based understanding of the meaning of war insofar as it affected the men who fought, which served as a post-war adhesive to political alliances as well as what Barbara Hobsen has called a "discursive resource" in strengthening veteran identity and citizenship claims. For Hobsen, discursive resources include "the cultural narratives and metaphors that social actors exploit in the public representations as well as the contesting ideological stances that they take on dominant themes and issues on the political agenda."[219] In many countries in the West, as well as in Russia, Japan, and South Korea, one "cultural narrative" related to military service was that it helped demonstrate worthiness as a man and exemplified several positive masculine virtues; this, in turn, sometimes translated into demands to be considered patriotic and for better treatment—"patriotic men" could not be easily dismissed and marginalized. The record of this linkage is extensive both in political theory—Machiavelli and Rousseau both made armed masculinity central to their conceptualization of civic republican-ism[220]—and in veteran politics and their relationship to state and society. In Australia, veteran identity after WWI explicitly drew upon the masculinity associated with the "bush worker" but was extended further by a decidedly masculine narrative surrounding the exploits of the ANZACs in Gallipoli.[221] In Germany, the *Kriegervereine*, the most important veterans association until the 1920s, literally means "Warrior Association."[222] Military service, particularly in combat, plays a significant role in the development of Israelis' sense of masculinity as well as strong ties of friendship among men, what Israelis call *re'ut*, a qualitatively different sense of "friendship" than that experienced by non-serving civilians.[223] In the major public schools in 18th-century Britain, education in "patriotic duty" (which was heavily influenced by the writings of Cicero and Homer and the example of Sparta) included a "lush appreciation of masculine heroism."[224] Years later, wounded British veterans of WWI felt that their manhood was strengthened by their tragedy and were often considered as "men among men" for having endured bodily harm.[225] In Spain, the Civil War was said to have destroyed Nationalist soldiers' "lean and manly figure" and "virility," so the only possible consolation could be "social recognition of their bravery and sacrifice."[226] According to George Mosse, fascism was highly gendered and militarized political ideology, based on the "myth of war experience" and "personified in ideals of male strength and beauty."[227]

This notion traveled far. Japanese disabled veterans during WWII were described as "manly war-wounded heroes."[228] According to Joshua Sanborn, Russian military authorities, particularly after the Russo-Japanese War and WWI, were critical in developing the notion that "masculinity" (based on the aesthetic ideal of ancient Greece) was an essential component of nationhood and citizenship; they harshly criticized intellectuals for their scorning of sports and physical fitness, since they would not be "capable of bearing arms to defend the national ideal."[229] In Korea, a country whose mainstream *yangban* literati elites were arguably more conservatively Confucian than China's (and had deeply negative associations with the military), the implementation of universal male conscription under General Park Chung-hee (in South Korea) led to a significant cultural change. Park's regime "managed to alter the negative social meaning of military service among elites (in contrast, among the less Confucianized members of society, "sex and violence could be a touchstone for manliness and a source of pride and enjoyment"[230]) and establish it as men's national duty"; a popular saying was "A man has to serve in the military to play a man's role," and a popular song during basic training and marches was "Real Men."[231] In Bolivia, where most conscripts come from the powerless sectors of society, soldiers are still able to "lay claim to militarized conceptions of masculinity to advance their own agendas. They advance a positive sense of subaltern masculinity tied to beliefs about bravery, competence, and patriotic duty . . . to earn respect from women and male peers . . . a counterpoint to the degradation experienced from more dominant males."[232] Similar to these marginalized Bolivians, for African-Americans in the United States, every war since the Civil War was seen as an opportunity to defend and prove their "manhood" against their detractors, and after wars veterans enjoyed a boost in status in their own communities, having proven themselves in this way.[233] While minorities were able to get special political leverage by their association with masculine ideals, whites also recognized that combat heightened masculinity and status among other men; as reported by Samuel Stouffer's research team after WWII—and sharply contrasting to the situation in China after the war—the "front line combat man" was at "the top" of the status hierarchy; he was "the only person who could not be asked, 'What are you doing for the war?' He had no need to justify himself. He had also proven his manhood by withstanding the severest kinds of stress."[234] This view was most certainly not new in the United States: Civil War veterans formed organizations that deliberately connected their masculinity and citizenship status,[235] while prominent individuals among them, such as Supreme Court Justice Oliver Wendell Holmes, in the most unlikely settings, such as at his 1895 Commencement Address at Harvard University, promoted an "ideology of manliness" (juxtaposed to the "comfort and greed of commercial culture").[236] In part, it was recognition of manliness on the battlefield, or "male warrior heroism," that helped (white) Northern and Southern veterans reconcile after the Civil War.[237] According to Andre Fleche, many white and black veterans "found that a common cause in ending the rebellion, a sense of shared experience and hardship as soldiers, and bravery on the battlefield proved more important than race in determining the worth of a fighting man. That sentiment persisted overwhelmingly among Union veterans into the late 19th and early 20th centuries."[238] To be sure, shared recognition of warrior masculinity is not entirely unproblematic: German POWs in the United States during WWII were widely admired for their muscular physique, tanned bodies, and soldiering skills; fraternization between these "bronzed" POWs (who "looked handsome in their soccer shirts") and American women was not uncommon and caused distress among American soldiers fighting against Germany.[239]

The cultural association between soldiering and masculinity (and between masculinity and claims to patriotism and higher political and social status) clearly helped veterans secure allies in many countries. It was not a historical coincidence that these "cognitive" and social connections were made, however. As we will see in Chapter 5, *veterans organizations* played a significant role in shaping the connection between military service, masculinity, and claims to citizenship status. In China, however, the military still has low status, veterans organizations do not exist, and the political and cultural elites have usually been civilians who emerged from the urban and educated classes (unlike General Park in South Korea). Even during the 1930s, when masculinity and military service appear to have been more closely linked in discourse, the Guomindang's objectives for military training in schools "focused as much on augmenting physical and disciplinary training as on cultivating young soldiers."[240] And despite a national military crisis, Chiang Kai-shek asserted that drills and the like would "temper the bodies and minds of the trainees and to mold their moral characters, [and] show the proper path of modern life," among other things.[241] Interestingly, the leaders of the party-led Scouting Movement, which is often associated with cultivating a martial version of masculinity, were mostly "major party politicos, ideologues and educators," who tended to stress proper etiquette and hygiene and provided their charges with "step-by-step instructions for decorous behavior in range of social contexts," such as formal banquets and how to deal with doormen.[242] The PRC leadership was not all that dissimilar in this respect; most of its top leaders were not military men. Even in more popular culture, China's "God of War," Guangong, was known in some areas as a patron of popular justice, wealth, courage, food protection, and community security, not masculinity per se.[243] As a result, when wars were over and other citizens questioned the extent to which they were worthy of high status, veterans in China could not claim this mantle, or "masculine cultural narrative," and others did not support them on this account.

In significant ways, this is not that surprising. In Chapter 1, I argued that martial citizenship and patriotism have tended to emerge during periods of *mass total warfare* and (almost) *universal conscription* not more limited conflicts or border wars; an intellectual such as Oliver Wendell Holmes most probably would not have spoken up in favor of masculine virtues if he had not served himself. In the modern period, China has not experienced warfare of this nature, so veteran identity has not received the "boost" that comes with a cultural narrative—usually promoted forcefully by elite veterans after war—equating masculinity with warfare. Chinese peasants, from among whom the PLA draws most of its manpower, also suffer from this lack of connection. They are far easier to dismiss because state elites do not admire them for "manly" service in the military.

NOTES

1. The soldiers who were paraded around during the Iwo Jima flag-raising bond drive did not cope very well with their fame. See James Bradley (with Ron Powers), *Flags of our Fathers*.

2. See Lynn White, *Policies of Chaos*; Andrew Walder, *Communist Neotraditionalism*; and Judith Stacey, *Patriarchy and Socialist Revolution in China*.

3. The term *civil religion* (which has a legacy running from Rousseau to Durkheim and Robert Bellah) is often associated with this effort.

4. SMA B168-1-655 (1960), 5.

5. Amir Weiner, *Making Sense of War,* Chapter 1.

6. Schneider and Ingram, *Deserving and Entitled: Social Construction and Public Policy*, 3.

7. Interestingly, there have been no large studies of Korean War veterans from the Korean perspective or of Japanese veterans in post-war Japan.

8. SMA B168-1-600 (1951), 108.

9. SMA B168-1-619 (1955), 48, 70.

10. SMA B168-1-632 (1957), 3.

11. SMA B168-1-633 (1957), 80; SMA B168-1-641 (1958), 14.

12. SA A1-2-516 (1957), 23; SA A20-1-411, 79.

13. QA 48-2-156, 22.

14. QA 48-2-61, 93.

15. QA 48-2-98 (1956), 66.

16. Elizabeth Perry and Li Xun, *Proletarian Power*, 44–45. They write that Wang "was not the obedient apparatchik—ready to champion whatever policies the party dictated—but a feisty individual willing to think and speak for himself." Among workers, he was "known for speaking his mind."

17. *Assembly* is based on a true story. It should also be noted that the film is based on a novel (*Guansi*) written by Yang Jingyuan, a veteran of China's war with Vietnam. Much of the film's depiction of veterans is accurately reflected in the archival documents from the 1950s and 1960s.

18. QA 48-2-109 (1957), 4.

19. QA 48-2-156, 19.

20. QA 48-2-109 (1957), 4; SA A1-2-516 (1957), 19.

21. In the Mencius example, people were inherently good because if they were walking by a well and heard a baby cry at the bottom of it, their first reaction would be to stop and try to help rather than just walk on.

22. SMA B168-1-619, 70.

23. SMA B168-1-517 (1956), 139.

24. Yu-Wen Fan, "Becoming a Civilian," 170, 168.

25. SMA B168-1-628, 31.

26. SMA B168-1-628 (1957), 73.

27. SMA B168-1-641, 13–14.

28. Yu-wen Fan, "Becoming a Civilian," 170.

29. QA 48-2-155 (1962), 24.

30. Guowuyuan jundui ganbu anzhi gongzuo xiaozu bangongshi (ed.), *Jundui ganbu zhuanye fuyuan gongzuo wenjian huibian* (*Jundui ganbu* hereafter), 160–61.

31. QA 48-1-35, 15.

32. QA 48-2-109 (1957), 4.

33. QA 48-2-141 (1957), 13.

34. Weiner, *Making Sense of War*, 49.

35. *Guangdong sheng zhi: minzheng zhi* (Guangzhou: Guangdong renmin chubanshe, 1993), 94; *Zhongjiang xian zhi* (Chengdu: Sichuan renmin chubanshe, 1994), 550.

36. SA A20-1-109, 4–5, 48.

37. SMA B168-1-632, 4.

38. *People's Daily*, April 25, 1955.

39. *People's Daily*, November 16, 1956.

40. QA 48-2-109 (1957), 14–15; QA 48-2-141 (1957), 15.

41. Weiner, *Making Sense of War*, 9, 70, 73. Also see Mark von Hagen, "The levee en masse from Russian Empire to Soviet Union,"187. Regular army troops were

given credit for victory after the battle of Stalingrad "at the expense of partisan and home guard units."

42. *People's Daily*, April 18, 1956.

43. *People's Daily*, August 6, 1956.

44. QA 48-1-26, 4.

45. SMA B168-1-633 (1957), 80.

46. QA 48-2-141 (1957), 15.

47. SMA C1-2-121, 49–50. Emphasis mine.

48. QA 48-2-141 (1957), 14.

49. SMA B168-1-628 (1957), 74.

50. SMA B168-1-628, 2.

51. SMA B168-1-628 (1957), 74.

52. SMA B168-1-632 (1957), 4.

53. They alone were given the title of "honored citizen" (*rongmin*). See Fan, "Becoming a Civilian," 24.

54. SMA B168-1-628, 159–61.

55. SA A1-2-516, 17.

56. *Jundui ganbu*, 158–59.

57. QA 48-1-35 (1956), 15; QA 48-2-61 (1954), 93.

58. SA A1-2-516, 18.

59. QA 48-2-156, 22; SMA B168-1-605 (1952), 79.

60. SMA B168-1-607 (1952), 71.

61. QA 48-2-109 (1957), 4; SA A1-2-516, 17; SMA B168-1-628, 21.

62. See *The Whistleblowers: Exposing Corruption in Government and Industry*, 5, 7.

63. MacFarquhar considers Peng the "chief critic" of the GLF. See *Origins of the Cultural Revolution, Vol. 3*, 15.

64. Jennifer Brooks, *Defining the Peace,* 7.

65. *People's Daily*, May 29, 1957.

66. SMA B1-2-1958 (1957), 25.

67. SMA B127-1-811, 8.

68. QA 48-2-7 (1955), 38.

69. QA 48-2-105, 140. Similar evidence can be found in accounts of the Marriage Law. See Diamant, *Revolutionizing the Family*, especially Chapter 2.

70. QA 48-2-71, 38.

71. QA 48-2-96 (1956), 59.

72. QA 48-2-71 (1955), 38.

73. QA 48-2-141 (1957), 15. Also see QA 48–35, 2, for exposing corruption in a private business.

74. QA 48-2-105 (1957), 135, 140.

75. DDA 11-7-89 (1954), 152.

76. SMA 168-1-628, 21.

77. SMA B168-1-628 (1956), 30.

78. *Minzheng jianbao*, December 21, 1956, 86.

79. Ibid.

80. SMA B168-1-628, 119-20.

81. SMA B168-1-628 (1957), 41.

82. QA 48-2-105 (1957), 135.

83. *People's Daily,* November 27, 1955.

84. SMA B168-1-630, 10.

85. SMA B123-3-1442, 6.

86. SMA B168-1-645 (1959), 67.

87. SMA B168-1-209 (1963), 29.

88. *Guangdong sheng zhi: minzheng zhi*, 93.

89. SMA B168-1-600, 108.

90. SMA B168-1-607, 53. I am not sure if this composition was typical, however.

91. SMA B168-1-630, 10.

92. SMA B168-1-600 (1951), 108.

93. *Minzheng jianbao*, May 24, 1956, 2.

94. von Hagen, "The levee en masse," 186.

95. Weiner, *Making Sense of War*, 8, 60, 68–69.

96. SMA B168-1-600 (1951), 115.

97. SMA B168-1-607 (1952), 49.

98. SMA B168-1-605, 79.

99. Barry Nauston, "Cities in the Chinese Economic System," 76.

100. *Minzheng jianbao*, November 7, 1956, 76; SMA B127-1-820 (1956), 28. According to one report, of 34 suicides among veterans in 1956, "most were because of political history problems" or being punished for "violating labor discipline." See SMA B168-1-628, 102. See also SMA B168-1-607, 49.

101. SMA B168-1-628, 3.

102. Kevin O'Brien and Li Lianjiang, "Suing the Local State," in Diamant, Lubman, and O'Brien (eds.), *Engaging the Law in China*.

103. SMA B168-1-630, 15.

104. SMA B168-1-611, 126.

105. SMA B168-1-630, 10, 15.

106. SMA B168-1-628 (1956), 30.

107. SMA B168-1-633 (1957), 78.

108. SMA B168-1-517 (1956), 139.

119. *Minzheng jianbao*, May 24, 1956, 2.

110. The following cases are in *Minzheng jianbao*, May 24, 1956, 26–27.

111. SMA B168-1-628, 31.

112. Udi Lebel, *Ha'derech el ha'patheon: Etzel, Lehi vi'gvulot ha'zikaron ha'yisraeli*, 118–27, 188–90, 261–64.

113. Paloma Aguilar, "Agents of Memory," 85, 91, 97. Mandy Hoogendoorn, "Remembering and Forgetting the Finnish Civil War," 37.

114. Isabel Kershner, "Israel's Unexpected Spinoff from a Holocaust Trial," *New York Times*, September 6, 2007.

115. SMA B168-1-628 (1956), 21.

116. SMA B168-1-607 (1952), 50.

117. SMA B123-3-1442 (1956), 6.

118. SMA B168-1-628, 47; B168-1-607, 50.

119. SMA B168-1-628, 91; SMA B168-1-517, 139. The word *trash* was also used in the countryside. See QA 48-2-105 (1957), 6.

120. SMA B168-1-607 (1952), 50; also SMA B168-1-628, 20; SMA B123-3-1442 (1956), 6.

121. SMA B168-1-607 (1952), 50.

122. SMA B168-1-628, 101.

123. *Minzheng jianbao*, November 7, 1956, 76.

124. SMA B168-1-666, 4.

125. DDA 11-7-89, 151; SA 1-2-516 (1957), 17; QA 48-2-105, 140.

126. DDA 11-7-96, 5.

127. SMA B168-1-607 (1952), 50.

128. SMA B168-1-600 (1951), 125; SMA B168-1-628 (11/1956), 159–62; SA A20-1-411 (1965), 80. In the Rongcheng County report, veterans explained some of their "bad behavior" by using this metaphor.

129. QA 48-2-105 (1957), 136.

130. SMA B168-1-628, 22; *Jundui ganbu*, 635; SA A20-1-109 (1952), 5.

131. SMA B168-1-630, 11; SMA A71-2-492 (1956), 4.

132. SMA B168-1-628, 22.

133. *Jundui ganbu*, 635.

134. SMA B168-1-666 (1963), 7–8.

135. SMA B168-1-619, 49.

136. O'Leary, "Blood Brotherhood"; Larry Logue, "Union Veterans," 424.

137. Gries, *China's New Nationalism*, 59.

138. John Pomfret, "Chinese Question Role in Korean War," *Washington Post Foreign Service*, October 29, 2000, A32.

139. John Gittings's analysis concurs with this assessment. See *The Role of the Chinese Army*, 91.

140. SMA C1-2-362, 29.

141. SMA A22-2-45, 149.

142. SMA C1-2-362, 30.

143. SMA A22-2-45, 98.

144. SMA C1-2-361 (1951), 31.

145. Ibid., 35.

146. SMA A22-2-45 (March 1951), 54.

147. SMA A22-2-45, 98.

148. SMA A22-2-25, 54–5.

149. SMA C1-2-361, 33; SMA A22-2-25, 55; SMA C1-2-121, 40; SMA A22-2-45, 147.

150. SMA C1-2-121, 40.

151. SMA C1-2-121 (1950), 22.

152. Ibid.

153. SMA C1-2-121, 31.

154. SMA C1-2-121 (1950), 1.

155. Hollywood films had a dominant market share in Shanghai (roughly 65 percent). Jishun Zhang, "Cultural Consumption and Popular Reception of the West in Shanghai, 1950–1966," 101.

156. Ibid., 120.

157. QA 48-2-31 (1951), 35–39.

158. Ibid., 39.

159. Ibid., 36.

160. Ibid., 38–39.

161. QA 2-2-60, 22.

162. See Diana Lary, "One Province's Experience of War: Guangxi, 1937–1945," 315.

163. SA A1-2-516 (1957), 19.

164. *Minzheng jianbao*, August 15, 1956, 55.

165. QA 2-2-75, 67–70.

166. QA 2-2-75 (1956), 94.

167. QA 2-2-75, 97–98; QA 2-2-75, 40–41; QA 2-2-75, 44.

168. QA 48-2-105 (1957), 135.

169. QA 2-2-75, 70.

170. SMA B168-1-628, 97–98.

171. QA 48-2-155 (1962), 24.

172. Richard Alston, *Soldier and Society in Roman Egypt,* 53–54.

173. See *Britons: Forging the Nation, 1701–1837.*

174. Susan Browne, "War-Making," 245.

175. Seth Koven, "Remembering and Dismemberment," 1192.

176. Deborah Cohen, *The War Come Home*, 163; Greg Eghigian, *Making Security Social: Disability, Insurance and the Birth of the Social Entitlement State in Germany*, 181; Benjamin Ziemann, *War Experiences in Rural Germany, 1914–1923*, 218, 250.

177. James Matthews, "Clock Towers for the Colonized," 268.

178. Weiner, *Making Sense of War*, 67.

179. Catherine Merridale, *Ivan's War*, 339.

180. B. Shiva Rao, "After the War in India," 172–73.

181. Donald Lisio, "United States: Bread and Butter Politics," 39; Samuel Stouffer et al., *The American Soldier: Combat and Its Aftermath*, vol. II, 308–09, 320; Jefferson, "Enabled Courage: Race, Disability and Black WWII Veterans," 1111.

182. American Indians fought valiantly in WWI and these sacrifices "went a long way toward convincing non-Indians that Native Americans were worthy of respect, equal rights and citizenship, and that they were capable of playing an important role in American society." In 1924, Congress passed the Snyder Act, which granted citizenship to all Indians, but enfranchisement varied widely among the states. After World War II, it was widely understood (in Congress and among whites) that "the war meant that Indians had won the right to be treated like all other Americans." See Jeré Franco, "Empowering the World War II Native American Veteran: Postwar Civil Rights," 32–33.

183. Mary Jessup, *The Public Reaction to the Returned Service Man after WWI*, 19; Desmond Morton and Glenn Wright, *Winning the Second Battle*, 120.

184. Browne, "War-Making," 240.

185. Joseph Ellis, *Founding Brothers: The Revolutionary Generation*, 61.

186. John Resch, *Suffering Soldiers: Revolutionary War Veterans, Moral Sentiment and Political Culture in the Early Republic*, 1. Herman Melville (in his *Israel Potter*) and other literary figures wrote eloquently about the gap between patriotic and public ingratitude in everyday life. See Edward Tang, "Writing the American Revolution: War Veterans in the Nineteenth-Century Cultural Memory," 63–80.

187. Browne, "War-Making," 244.

188. Logue, "Union Veterans," 411.

189. Canadian veterans from WWI also resented post-war criticisms by "slacker" civilians. See Morton and Wright, *Winning the Second Battle*, 65, 119.

190. Antoine Prost, *In the Wake of War: 'Les Anciens Combattants' and French Society*, Helen McPhail, trans., 33.

191. See Peter Karsten, *Soldiers and Society: The Effects of Military Service on American Life*, 257–58.

192. L. J. F. Keppie, *Colonisation and Veteran Settlement in Italy, 47–14 B.C.*, 122.

193. Stephen Garton, *The Cost of War: Australians Return*, 59–61.

194. Peter Leese, "Problems Returning Home: The British Psychological Casualties of the Great War," 1056.

195. Prost, *In the Wake of War*, 106–7.

196. Oz Almog, *The Sabra: The Creation of the New Jew*, 145. For a full exposition of *dugri*, see Tamar Katriel, *Talking Straight:* Dugri *Speech in Israeli Sabra Culture*.

197. Wallace Evan Davies, *Patriotism on Parade: The Story of Veterans' and Hereditary Organizations in America, 1793–1900*, 101, 160–61.

198. Lisio, "United States: Bread and Butter Politics," 39; van Ells, *To Hear Only Thunder Again*, 8; Paul Dickson and Thomas Allen, "Marching on History," 90.

199. University of Chicago Committee on Human Development, *The American Veteran Back Home*, 76.

200. Wray Johnson, "Black American Radicalism," 44.

201. John Dittmer, *Local People: The Struggle for Civil Rights in Mississippi*, 1, 5.

202. Brooks, *Defining the Peace*, 5, 14–15. Much of this activism was generated by the clash of rising expectations in the black community (largely generated by WWII) and limited opportunities for social mobility. See Sherie Mershon and Steven Schlossman, *Foxholes and Color Lines: Desegregating the U.S. Armed Forces*, 95.

203. National Archives, Record Group 160, Box 240, 291.2. Memos dated March 4, 1946.

204. The Social Science Institute at Fisk University, "A Monthly Summary of Events and Trends in Race Relations," 3, 8 (March 1946), 235–36. (National Ar-

chives, Record Group 160, Box 240, 291.2).

205. Fan, "Becoming a Civilian," 170.

206. Ibid., 156–57, 168, 183.

207. Mark Edele, "Soviet Veterans," 132.

208. Weiner, *Making Sense of War*, 57.

209. Schneider and Ingram, *Deserving and Entitled*, 2.

210. Diana Lary, *Warlord Soldiers: Chinese Common Soldiers, 1911–1937*; Peter Reese, *Homecoming Heroes: An Account of the Reassimilation of British Military Personnel into Civilian Life*, 44. Naval veterans, on the other hand, appeared to enjoy greater respect. That veterans were despised but also experienced a marked change in status should caution us to avoid assigning too much explanatory weight to "culture" writ large. Culture *can* change. For China, the relevant question seems to be why the official anti-military culture did not.

211. Weiner, *Making Sense of War*, 45, 49, 57.

212. Eugen Weber, *Peasants into Frenchmen*, 298.

213. Prost, *In the Wake of War*, 29, 34, 46–47.

214. Fan, "Becoming a Civilian," 99.

215. John Bodnar, *Remaking America: Public Memory, Commemoration, and Patriotism in the 20th Century*, 84.

216. Brooks, *Defining the Peace*, 7.

217. Victor Shih, Wei Shan, and Mingxing Lu, "The Central Committee Past and Present: A Method for Quantifying Elite Biographies," paper presented at the Workshop on Methods and Sources in Chinese Politics, University of Michigan–Ann Arbor, November 3–5, 2006, 27–28.

218. Good examples of this are Yue Daiyun and Carolyn Wakeman, *To the Storm: The Odysseus of a Revolutionary Chinese Woman*, and Heng Liang Heng and Judith Shapiro, *Son of the Revolution*. In the latter book, Liang's father is a journalist who resolutely supports and trusts the party to do no wrong, and his mother works for the Public Security Bureau until 1957. Liang describes her as working for the "police," without providing any details or acknowledging that the police in the early 1950s were responsible for a great deal of oppression.

219. Barbara Hobsen, "Women's Collective Agency, Power Resources, and the Framing of Citizenship Rights," 152.

220. See R. Claire Snyder, *Citizen-Soldiers and Manly Warriors: Military Service and Gender in the Civic Republic Tradition*. According to Snyder, Machiavelli "considered engagement in martial practices as constitutive of republican citizenship and thus as the foundation for a republic," and for Rousseau, "the practices of the civic militia form the centerpiece of the civil festival," which for him played "an important role in the creation of patriotism" (pp. 17, 52–53). These observations are not irrelevant to China. China is called a "republic." It also has militias and military-related civic rituals (see Chapter 5) and has been closer to civic republican ideals than liberal ones in terms of how it understands the relationship of state to society.

221. Garton, *The Cost of War*, 230–32.

222. Ziemann, *War Experiences in Rural Germany*, 241.

223. Eyal Ben-Ari, "Tests of Soldierhood, Trials of Manhood: Military Service and Male Ideals in Israel," 239–68; Danny Kaplan, *The Men We Loved: Male Friendship and Nationalism in Israeli Culture*, 14–25.

224. Colley, *Britons*, 167–68.

225. Cohen, *The War Come Home,* 130; Koven, "Remembering and Dismemberment," 1169.

226. Aguilar, "Agents of Memory," 88.

227. George Mosse, *The Fascist Revolution: Toward a General Theory of Fascism*, 30.

228. Lee Pennington, "Protecting the Wounded: Japanese Disabled Veterans on the Homefront, 1937–1945," paper presented at the Annual Meeting of the Association for Asian Studies, March 31–April 3, 2005.

229. Sanborn, *Drafting the Russian Nation,* 132–44.

230. Vladimir Tikhonov, "Masculinizing the Nation: Gender Ideologies in Traditional Korea and in the 1890s–1900s Korean Enlightenment Discourse," 1045. Interestingly, even late 19th- and early 20th-century nationalists, who made explicit the notion that Korea's weakness on the international stage could be attributed to weaker bodies and the absence of physical training, did not view the military as an outlet for better-trained, better-disciplined, and stronger bodies. Sports were generally considered the more appropriate settings for young men to prove their manliness (see p. 1058).

231. Seungsook Moon, *Militarized Modernity and Gendered Citizenship in South Korea*, 49, 52–53. According to Moon, educated elites were a "bastion of resistance" to military service and are more critical of military service than other social groups.

232. Leslie Gill, "Creating Citizens, Making Men: The Military and Masculinity in Bolivia," 527–28.

233. For the Civil War, see Donald R. Shaffer, *After the Glory,* 5–8, 143. For WWI, see Johnson, "Black American Radicalism," 33–34; for WWII, see Brooks, *Defining the Peace*, 3–4. Other marginalized groups in the United States shared this connection between masculinity, rights, and a stronger sense of national identity. For the case of American Jews, see Deborah Dash Moore, *GI Jews: How World War II Changed a Generation*, 9–10, 25–28.

234. Stouffer et al., *The American Soldier: Combat and Its Aftermath*, vol. II, 309.

235. O'Leary, *To Die For*, 55.

236. David Blight, *Race and Reunion: The Civil War in American Memory*, 209.

237. O'Leary, "Blood Brotherhood," 54.

238. Andre Fleche, "'Shoulder to Shoulder as Comrades Tried," 176. Fleche also notes that "white veterans, led by African-American military historians, spread the memory of black Civil War service through published memoirs and in the pages of the leading veterans' newspaper, the *National Tribune*" (p. 177).

239. Matthias Reiss, "Bronzed Bodies behind Barbed Wire," 481–84, 495–96.

240. Robert Culp, *Articulating Citizenship*, 200.

241. Ibid.

242. Ibid., 184–87.

243. Ralph Thaxton Jr., *Salt of the Earth: The Political Origins of Peasant Protest and Communist Revolution in China*, 19, 237–38.

4

The Job Front

For veterans returning from war or extended periods of military service, such issues as choosing where to live and receiving social confirmation of their often-empowered sense of identity and citizenship are critically important in shaping their sense of justice; the large-scale support of WWI veterans in Germany and Italy for right-wing parties that provided a "culture of appreciation" for their returning soldiers is testimony to the political repercussions of failing to satisfy this demand. A pat on the back, kind words of appreciation, and civic rituals can go a long way, but in the end, veterans, governments, and society all have to bow before the inevitable: taxes must be paid, food purchased, homes built, children raised, parents supported, and bosses satisfied. For most veterans, in the temporal space when war ends and civilian life begins, employment—getting hired, paid, and treated with decency—rapidly becomes the paramount concern; no number of Veteran Days or commemorative stadiums will ever alter this basic issue. While seemingly straightforward, few issues are as politically and morally complex. Should governments, having sent soldiers to war or service, mandate quotas for hiring or rehiring veterans? Should enterprises be allowed to fire them at will, depending on the vagaries of the labor market? Should skills learned in the military be considered for promotion? There are no clear answers to these questions: governments have adopted policies ranging from quotas (post-WWI Germany and Italy) to milder forms of affirmative action (contemporary United States) to mere "encouragement" (Great Britain after WWI) without conclusive proof that one method represents best practice. Whichever employment policy is adopted, veterans will always feel somewhat frustrated when they transition from a system where one can marshal non-technical skills such as courage and perseverance to one that demands constant production, labor discipline, and some mastery of process or technology. The question that I pose in this chapter, therefore, is not whether *all* veterans are satisfied—this will never happen—or whether government policies are well intentioned and implemented (see Chapter 5) but, rather, whether veterans in China had at least a sense that they were given a "fair shake" by employers during the hiring process and on the job.[1] This fair-shake standard does not require that the low-skilled veteran make more money than a highly skilled technician but that he be given opportunities to improve himself to earn promotion and be treated with decency on the shop floor or in the fields, even if this involves certain costs and sacrifices on the part of the employer and its non-veteran employees. To the extent that claims for martial citizenship were supported and patriotism manifested in "everyday" circumstances—hiring a veteran outsider might require denying a job to a local worker—the fair-shake standard strikes me as quite attainable, unlike a stricter, more mathematical measuring (e.g., the veteran should make x more money than a non-veteran).

The Chinese case provides us with a number of different ways of approaching this issue. From the perspective of the state, it is quite clear that significant efforts were made on behalf of veterans to meet this standard, and more. Hundreds of investigation reports, policy documents, regulations, and internal correspondence may not say all that much about positive results or even intentions—were the reports generated owing to respect or fear?—but they do indicate a reasonable investment of state energy and resources. To what extent did state policies make a difference in how veterans were treated throughout the employment process? For example, how did the sudden shift to urban modernization and industrialization following the adoption of the Soviet model of development in 1950 affect veterans' prospects of getting a fair shake? We can also consider veterans' biographical attributes. Since most of them were either peasants or came from the urban lower classes, providing them with a fair shake in urban employment could be more challenging than had veterans represented a cross-section of the general population, as was often the case in mass-conscripted armies. To what extent did veterans' high political status ameliorate disadvantaged social background in the workplace? From the perspective of factory management, what sort of "weight" was given to veterans' military accomplishments and experiences in light of other priorities, such as "increasing production" or fulfilling welfare-related demands? There has been very little systematic attention to large-scale demobilization in the social science literature, and even less to smaller-scale, more "conversational" interactions between veterans and co-workers and bosses, which makes it rather difficult to assess the Chinese case in comparative perspective, but the available literature does suggest some interesting patterns, which I will discuss later in this chapter.

This chapter, like the previous two, makes a dogged effort to follow in veterans' footsteps as they interacted with different parts of society and the state. I begin with the early stages of the employment process (how veterans got jobs, how they did not, and what sort of positions they had), their adjustment to those positions, and then how they were treated. I then turn to the different ways veterans expressed their discontent and the political and social resources they could draw upon when they felt that, state intentions and administrative regulations notwithstanding, they did not get a fair shake. Even though China does not have the sort of regulated market economy that would allow researchers to collect systematic data on how these decisions are made, the available data do suggest a very broad pattern of overt and covert discrimination against veterans from the get-go. In only a very limited sector of the economy—public security, and even there not at all times—were veterans' martial experiences appreciated and valued. For most managers, personnel directors, and party committees, veterans were, at best, a population that had to be tolerated, mostly out of fear.

GETTING HIRED (OR NOT)

As anyone who has ever sat on a hiring committee knows, decisions in such a sensitive matter as employment are rarely made in a completely "cold," rational process in which candidates' objective qualifications are totally walled off from institutional and national policies or candidates' demeanor, looks, mannerisms, ethnicity, and gender, and, in the case of more seasoned candidates, their reputation when they worked for a previous employer. This was certainly the case for veterans entering the civilian labor market in China. When evaluating veterans who came knocking at its door (either for the first time or after three years away from the enterprise), management opened it a tad, cast its eyes down, and saw dirty and tattered luggage, despite a plethora of "Glory!" stickers pasted on the exterior. Many immediately tried to slam the door shut and took veterans only when they had no other alternative.

Reports on serious difficulties in the hiring process came fast and furiously from all parts of the country in the early to mid-1950s and persisted well into the Cultural Revolution. Veterans, often unbeknownst to them, were already stigmatized by their association with the military and by the "prideful/arrogant" behavior many of them displayed after being told that they were heroes of the revolution or the Korean War. An early (1953) report on Qingdao in Shandong noted that among the 10,000 people who were provided "long-term employment," only eight were veterans. When Civil Affairs officials contacted employers, they simply replied, "We don't need anyone." As a result, for the first two quarters of 1953, 48 percent of returning veterans were jobless, "and still more were coming."[2] In the city of Linqing in Shandong, a report co-authored by a joint team from the Municipal Procurators Office and the Veterans Committee and published in 1955 in the *Shandong Administrative Bulletin* found that "not a few" work units used a variety of methods to avoid hiring veterans. When enterprises were looking for guards, they approached the local labor bureau with a key demand: "Just don't give us any veterans." When a power plant was looking to hire medical staff, the city health department provided them with the file of a veteran who had been a medic. "Right after they heard he was a veteran, they thought of all sorts of excuses and refused to hire him." According to the investigators, veterans were all tagged as having "problems," "hard to get along with," and "difficult to lead."[3]

Veterans' reputations preceded them in the Shanghai area as well; urban or rural locales did not differ significantly in their assessment of them. In a handwritten report in Qingpu, enterprise officials were accused of stereotyping all veterans from the "unhealthy work style of only very few" and "regarding them with hostility" (*choushi*) as a result. Civil Affairs officials noted an incident involving the director of a local cooking oil company who came to their offices looking for employees. "He walked in the door, opened his mouth, and the first thing he said was, 'We don't want veterans! We don't want any veterans!'" Government agencies shared this sentiment: when the county purchasing cooperative approached Civil Affairs to hire some temporary workers (in December 1954), the officials refused to even consider them because veterans "gave him a headache." When bureau officials pursued the matter and went to the cooperative's office, the director "shook his head, turned around, and ran off."[4] Health Department officials also resisted hiring veterans. Director Shen Boyun went to the Civil Affairs office himself in search of a good cook. When Civil Affairs officials asked whether he would hire a veteran, Shen "wrinkled his eyebrows, frowned, and asked 'Isn't there anyone else?'" The officials then reminded Shen of the State Council directives regarding preferential treatment for veterans in the hiring process, to no avail. Several days later, Shen called back, claiming, "We don't need a cook anymore."[5] In Longhua District in the Shanghai suburbs, Civil Affairs officials approached the local cooperative to "introduce" several veterans for employment, but the co-op's director of personnel said, "According to directives from higher authorities, anyone who hires a veteran will have committed a serious political error." When this incident was reported to the District Party Committee's Organization Department, which holds the fate of many a cadre in its hands, nothing was done about it.[6]

Enterprises in Shanghai and other provinces also tried to keep veterans at bay for as long as possible. "Very many factories and enterprises," an early 1950s Shanghai report noted, "say, 'Good people don't become veterans, and among veterans there are no good people,'" because of the "poor work attitude of some individuals."[7] Between June and August 1953, Shanghai absorbed 154 officers, among whom 13 were "outsiders" and were forced to return to the countryside. Of those who stayed, a report noted, quite a few were "difficult to place" because enterprises were "worried" about their attitude; supposedly, the officers overemphasized "personal interest" and "status." Civil Affairs officials informed them that they would not be able to get positions with that attitude.[8] In working-class Huangpu District, the Public Security Bureau (PSB) was seeking to hire 300 policemen (circa 1953). To help procure this number, the municipal Bureau of Civil Affairs (BCA) sent the PSB the files of 100 veterans the BCA personnel thought were eminently qualified for these positions (even though most veterans did not want to be policemen[9]), but not a single one of them was chosen. Even though the BCA's investigation concluded that personnel directors were very concerned about hiring veterans either because (1) they had a bad experience with a few of them, (2) veterans frequently "raised objections" to things, or (3) veterans were "difficult to lead,"[10] class, age, and political biases also played a role. As noted by Frederic Wakeman Jr., just prior to the Communist takeover, the Shanghai Public Security Bureau was staffed by "over 1,000 young students" who had been recruited for the job and trained in Jinan, and many police leaders and staffers were from the Shanghai underground or had served with the Nationalists and had since "reformed" themselves.[11]

Problems in the PSB extended to other places of employment. An investigation of Shanghai firms by the Shanghai Garrison and Civil Affairs in 1955 found "not a few" cases of "explicit" (*gongkai*) and "covert" (*bianxiang*) refusals to hire veterans. Sheng Mucai, the former party secretary of the #12 Textile Mill, told the investigators, "I'd rather employ ten unemployed workers; I don't want even one of them";[12] the personnel director of the Meichang factory in Shanghai's western suburbs told investigators that he "prefers to apply for 1,000 temporary workers than hire a single veteran," and when veterans were hired, they were treated so poorly that many missed the "warmth" of the army;[13] and the personnel director of the city's "Construction Committee" (*jianwei*) told subordinate units (in personnel departments), "According to the higher-ups, whoever hires a veteran will have committed a political error" (*fan cuowu de*).[14] In Fu'an County, Fujian Province, a veteran surnamed Chen was fired from a department store soon after being hired for not being "lively" (*huopo*), but management claimed he was fired because he had a "mental illness" and was not "clear headed." But as Chen was being dismissed, the store hired a large group of locals, among whom were several with "bad class" backgrounds, had family members under state "supervision," and had fewer qualifications than the dismissed veterans.[15] Such experiences as these led some veterans to comment: "Demobilized soldiers have become unemployed soldiers." Other veterans were out of work so long they would have died of starvation had it not been for state welfare payments.[16] Eight years later, in 1963, an investigation by the Shanghai Veteran Reception Office (formerly the Veterans Committee) found that views of veterans as hard-to-manage workers were still well entrenched. For instance, the office sent the files of 20 veterans to the Real Estate Bureau, which was hiring 300 people—but not a single one was chosen.[17]

Rehiring (*fuye*) could be just as problematic as the initial hiring. After 1949, the PLA recruited more intensively in cities, drawing mainly from the lower working classes such as peddlers, the unemployed, and temporary workers in factories. Some served in Korea, but others were drafted after the war and served a three-year tour of duty (unlike veterans from the pre-1949 period, who generally served longer). After their service, they expected to be welcomed back to their former positions. Not a few were disappointed to find that their old bosses were not keen on having them return. Jin Zhongnan, for instance, returned to his factory in 1954, but the management refused to hire him back. Jin filed a complaint with the Light Industry Bureau, but the director of personnel there refused to intervene. He got his old job back after filing a complaint with the city government. Similar incidents were reported at several factories operating under the jurisdiction of the East China Textile Management Bureau.[18] In Jixi in Heilongjiang Province, more than twenty miners could not get their jobs back after the Korean War. Apparently, a key official there—the director of the Salary Department—decided that the veterans joined the PLA "because of selfish reasons" (*zisi toujun*)—a claim of "impure motives" that was somewhat similar to one leveled at some American Civil War veterans who (successfully) demanded more generous pensions and a unique status in the polity.[19] When investigators balked at this reason, the salary director cited a single line from the "Labor Bureau Personnel Department Memorandum #121 Regarding Mobilized Workers' Re-Employment" to the effect that if the soldier "was mobilized by the unit to go to the army, he can be given his job back upon his return, but if he joins the army out of his own self-interest, in principle he should not get his job back." Since the veterans were not sent by the mine, the mine authorities had no obligation toward them.[20] This problem was apparently pervasive enough that in 1960 the Ministries of Interior and Labor issued a joint memo/investigation report chiding their subordinates for disregarding national regulations and preventing veterans from returning to their workplaces after service. The ministries did not focus on the sense of personal injustice felt by the veterans but the interests of the state: "It is not beneficial for recruiting."[21] The effectiveness of this directive is not clear, but there is some evidence that soldiers were still quite anxious about their job prospects. In 1963 in Beijing's Dongcheng District—five minutes away from CCP headquarters—many employers still managed to avoid hiring or rehiring vets by imposing "excessively high conditions" on them.[22] In 1966, soldiers wrote to their former employers well before their discharge dates to try to secure a guarantee they would be taken back,[23] but whatever guarantees or promises were made in 1966 were unlikely to be implemented because of the outbreak of the Cultural Revolution. In 1967, all veteran resettlement work effectively ceased, leaving them with little choice but to write petitions to higher authorities requesting intervention. This sort of activity was observed in Beijing, Shanghai, Tianjin, Wuhan, Nanjing, and Hebei provinces. One report noted, "Veterans returning to cities have a very difficult time finding jobs. Those without jobs have no chance of getting one, but there are even some work units that had already agreed to hire veterans which are now reneging and refusing to hire them."[24] The Liaoning Provincial gazetteer mentions veterans who returned home and found that they had no place to live and could not work and make a living, so they "went back to the army and asked them to solve their problems."[25]

Throughout the 1950s and 1960s, the determined reluctance, and often outright refusal, to hire veterans was no secret in China. During the mid-1950s, anyone who bothered to read *People's Daily* cover to cover would have been very aware of it. In a letter to the editor written by the Shanxi Veterans Committee, the Provincial Labor Bureau was singled out for consistently ignoring lists of veterans provided by the Bureau of Civil Affairs and the Committee when allocating labor to factories and government institutions, even after a 1955 "Decision" by the State Council urging hiring units to increase the employment of veterans in their ranks. A letter to the editor from Zhejiang attacked the Provincial Labor Bureau for raising unnecessary bureaucratic obstacles in the job search, even when firms decided to abide by the "affirmative action" clause in the State Council's "Decision." A company in the provincial capital of Hangzhou that manufactured electrical equipment for roads received approval to increase its workforce by 20 people and contacted the Municipal Veterans Committee, which chose 14 veterans and sent them to take physicals and an examination administered by the Commerce Department. They passed, and their files were sent to the Provincial Personnel Bureau. Twenty days later, however, there was still no response. After two further inquiries, the bureau responded that no workers would be allocated at all; the veterans' files were returned, unopened. Since the bureau had already agreed to the hiring, the Hangzhou Veterans Committee was suspicious, so they sent someone to investigate. At first, the company official, Huang Zhen-zhong, refused to even meet with the committee staffer, but after three more requests, a man surnamed Zhou came out and spoke with him. He said, "You guys do *fuyuan* veterans [mainly anti-Japanese, Civil, and Korean wars], we do *zhuanye* veterans [generally officers and soldiers who served in the PLA after 1953]," following the apparently widespread practice among personnel bureaus of not hiring anyone who was a sergeant or below, even though the overwhelming majority of veterans were within these ranks and the State Council never issued a policy document that differentiated between veterans in this way; the regulation was fabricated. But with this comment, the matter was concluded. "How is it that the Zhejiang Personnel Bureau can just ignore State Council regulations stipulating that 'resettling veterans is the glorious work of every level of government and the broad masses'?" the veterans wondered.[26] According to a report by the PLA's General Political Department and the State Council, veterans were not being hired so that firms could make room for private businessmen.[27]

As these letters to the editor more than hint at, there was a variety of reasons that would explain why veterans were generally undesirable hires, even if some employers were willing to avoid stereotyping all of them as poor workers who were "difficult to lead." In quite a few cases, state policies and bureaucratic arrangements worked at cross-purposes as far as veterans were concerned: they were supported by documents from the State Council but otherwise buffeted by other administrative decisions. Giving a "fair shake" to veterans was not easy, even if some employers were so inclined. From the early to mid-1950s, veteran job placement was one of the primary responsibilities of Civil Affairs offices, which set up "Labor Introduction Centers" that handled unemployed veterans as well as "ordinary" unemployed people. Veterans were often lost in the shuffle of people.[28] And even though Civil Affairs officials were supposed to "directly" find jobs for veterans, person-nel departments were ultimately responsible for staffing issues within enter-prises—a "contradiction" noticed very early on by the former bureaucracy. Even resourceful veterans who went from enterprise to enterprise and found someone to hire them sometimes lost their jobs because the Municipal Per-sonnel Bureau nixed their positions. "State planning," a Civil Affairs official ruefully noted, "makes the process very slow."[29] By the early 1960s, Civil Affairs officials were no longer responsible for placing veterans in enterprises (aside from those it ran itself); the responsibility was assigned to the mu-nicipal or county Veteran Reception Office, but even they could not "order" personnel departments to hire veterans.[30]

Larger structural changes in industry could also have a deleterious impact. Because of the "socialist transformation of industry" in the mid-1950s, private firms were not allowed to hire more workers (and capitalists were, in any case, not enthusiastic about hiring veterans[31]). Veterans, for their part, sensed where the winds were blowing and refused to be assigned to that sector.[32] According to a Shanghai report, 35 percent of resettled veterans were placed in the private sector in 1954, but only 20 percent got jobs there in 1955, with even more reductions expected in 1956.[33] In 1955, just as more veterans were coming to cities such as Shanghai, Beijing, and Tianjin, hiring restrictions were put in place in state-owned industries, the commercial sector, and all units directly administered by the central government; special permission was required to take on even one temporary worker.[34] Then, during an economic austerity and government retrenchment drive in 1957, the State Council made it very difficult for firms to add workers (unless they were veterans), so firms became very selective about whom they tried to bring on board and generally ignored the "veteran exception."[35]

Veterans were also easier to dismiss on non-policy-related accounts. While local officials could do little about the wording of State Council directives or campaigns, they had more leeway when choosing among the files that came their way from Labor, Civil Affairs, or Veterans committees. Although encouraged to give preferential treatment to veterans, there was little by way of actual incentives to adhere to the policy; "infractions" were never punished. Veterans' profiles, and the fact that many urban officials never experienced life in the military and had little to no sympathy for their predicament, made them highly vulnerable. Many veterans were also penalized by their age: having fought in wars since their late teens, many arrived on the workforce already in their mid- to late 20s, if not older. In 1955 in Linqing City, Shandong Province, a department store was looking for a cook, but when the Bureau of Civil Affairs sent over a veteran who was a cook in the PLA, the store sent him back, telling them over the phone that "we need a *young* cook, who has the future ahead of him."[36] A 1957 province-wide investigation (led by the Party Committee) noted that "some units . . . are only willing to hire young students, not veterans."[37] In Shanghai, when the personnel director of the Textile Bureau approached the city's Labor Bureau to apply for some apprentices, he specifically requested "young students" who had failed to move up the educational ladder, not veterans, claiming that his subordinate units had "weak leadership" and would not be able to manage them.[38] Older veterans (including officers) also suffered in the countryside. According to a report from 1963, these veterans "do not have the strength they did when they were younger . . . and because socialism is based on the principle of 'to each according to his work,' they cannot support themselves." Many of them requested transfers to urban factories, under the mistaken impression that their age would matter far less.[39]

In addition to age, employers could discriminate on the basis of skill level. Even though the state encouraged them to help veterans acquire skills on the job and appreciate their "good political qualities," employers found an easy way out of hiring them by stressing the extent to which they were "green" (*shengshu*) or "useless" in production (*buqi zuoyong*).[40] This was, to a limited extent, true and unsurprising, given that many veterans of the PLA came from rural areas. It was a problem Bureau of Civil Affairs officials recognized early on, noting in 1955 that skill level was a "very large obstacle" for many veterans in the city, particularly for newcomers.[41] At the same time, however, a significant percentage of veterans did have *some* skills. In an analysis of 2,812 veterans in Shanghai proper in 1960 (there were 3,527 veterans in the greater Shanghai area), with 96 percent of these drafted prior to 1956, a full 40 percent "had a definite skill," including metalworkers, mechanics, repairmen, wireless operators, woodworkers, cement specialists, and medics, among others.[42] This percentage decreased as one moved farther out in the countryside, however; among 426 veterans sent by the city of Shanghai to dredge part of Taihu Lake, 70 percent were from rural areas and 72 percent were classified as "unskilled." As hard as this work was, the veterans were pleased with it, since they thought that it brought them closer to gaining a valuable skill; their main fear was being forced to return to the countryside after the project was finished. The very thought of acquiring "some skill after 3–4 years in the army" and then becoming an ordinary peasant made them extremely anxious.[43] That roughly 30 percent did have a skill is indicative of the relatively high degree of industrialization in the Shanghai suburbs and the training some of them received in the military. The claim that veterans were "green," therefore, was an exaggeration (especially in Shanghai proper) that ignored critical differences between veterans—a new arrival from Shandong in 1950 was quite different from a veteran/migrant from Qingpu in 1955—as well as a reflection of many managers' view that veterans were a "burden" (*baofu*), not a population deserving of support.[44] The small number of veterans in Shanghai—in 1955 the city received only 5,000 out of roughly one million discharged that year (0.8 percent) amid an urban population of more than eight million—did little to change this assessment.[45]

Whether it was veterans' "bad attitude," age, or deficiency in skills, employers, at least when given the choice, rarely gave them the benefit of the doubt. In many reports, investigators amalgamated these issues into a more general complaint that employers were being unreasonably "nitpicky" (*tiaoti*) or "had too many demands" when going through files and were not giving any credence to military service when evaluating candidates, unless this service was offset by a bevy of other, more positive attributes. A report from 1952 chided labor officials for sending too few veterans to jobs (3–10 per day) and for demanding too many qualifications from them, such as a high skill level, education, and physical strength; one had to have all three of these, which substantially lowered veterans' chances to snag a good job. When enterprise officials were confronted by investigators, they blamed the Labor Bureau, claiming that they took whomever was given to them, but, in fact, the enterprise officials were making similar demands.[46] "Making excessive" or "unrealistic" demands was widespread and persisted throughout the 1950s and 1960s. Take the case of the Shanghai Factory #614, which received authorization from the Central Bank to hire 153 workers. When it made this authorization, the bank informed the National Veterans Committee, which in turn notified the Shanghai Veterans Committee, of 50 positions for which veterans were to receive priority. All had to meet the following conditions, however: "politically reliable, healthy, and junior high school education." The Veterans Committee sent 700 files of qualified veterans to the factory's personnel department, but the factory chose only six, after a month and a half of delays.[47] According to a 1954 investigation, "very many" (*xuduo*) enterprises informed labor officials that they wanted to hire only veterans who were members of the CCP or CYL. Since three-quarters of veterans were not party or youth league members around this time, this represented a "very large obstacle" to overcome.[48]

Similar problems were noted in firms and organizations in the publishing and cultural world. More than most, these institutions were staffed by the urban cultural elite, and their jobs probably involved publishing magazines, books, and films extolling the virtues of the PLA and CCP. When it came to actually hiring veterans, however, they were notably unenthusiastic. In December 1955, an investigation team found that publishing houses repeatedly failed to implement the 1955 State Council "Decision" regarding preferential treatment for veterans in employment. Here again, personnel directors appear to have been their primary nemesis. In 1955, Hu Zhangxian, a section chief of personnel in the Publishing Division (which was responsible for publishing houses), approached Zhu Chuanrong of the Bureau of Civil Affairs seeking 50 veterans, mainly to work as apprentice editors. The two agreed that they would consider veterans with high school education, "reliable" politics, "clean" political history, and relatively good physical condition. On May 25, Zhu sent more than 60 files for them to peruse. Sometime later, Hu called Zhu and told him that his superior in personnel, Gu Qiu, demanded that those selected also be CCP or CYL members, not "masses." If they could not satisfy these conditions, he would not even look at the files. Zhu from Civil Affairs called Hu Zhangxian, explaining that only 24 veterans of the 60 were CCP or CYL members, but most had the necessary educational credentials and had "undergone several years of revolutionary tempering." But the personnel director refused to reconsider. After another round of negotiating, they "reluctantly" agreed to take a look at the files. In the end, seven veterans were chosen as apprentices. Among those rejected were 2 CCP members and 15 CYL members who were teachers in the army or involved in the communication field.[49]

This sort of white-collar discrimination against veterans did not occur only in Shanghai. Take, for instance, the case of Zhou Xingkang, a veteran in Zhouning County in Fujian Province, who wanted a position at the county Tax Bureau. In a letter to the editor in *People's Daily*, he recounted the following:

> Tang Xixiong, the Bureau Director of the Tax Bureau, approached the Zhouning County Commerce Department requesting permission to hire a reporter. I called and began to tell him, "I am a 23-year-old veteran . . ." but when Bureau Director Tang heard those four words — I am a veteran — and without waiting for me to finish talking, he hung up on me. After that, Tang went to the Commerce Department to tell them that veterans could not be reporters — they "don't listen" (*jiao budong*) and "are hard to lead." When I asked him about this, he "compromised": "Veterans are OK, but they have to be 18 years old." I ask you: are there any veterans who are 18? Obviously, this Bureau Director is intentionally refusing to hire veterans. In my view, this sort of discrimination against veterans should be criticized.[50]

Despite large-scale national investigations into hiring discrimination in the mid-1950s and repeated admonishments to recognize the contributions of veterans, quite a few managers and personnel directors persisted in raising the employment bar extremely high. In 1964, for example, a dye factory insisted that they would not hire a single veteran who did not meet the following criteria: (1) good political history, (2) healthy, (3) completed their military service, and (4) were "young guys." The personnel director relented after considerable pressure, however, and hired 26 veterans. He confessed: "Those veterans we originally rejected as not meeting our conditions turned out to be very good."[51] Just how pervasive this sudden change of heart was is difficult to gauge — one would need access to factory personnel files to get a better sense of this — but reports from 1965 show that despite the militarization of society and the stress of "class status" in the run-up to the Cultural Revolution, many employers continued to have "excessively high demands" when hiring veterans, preferring those who were more educated, younger, healthier, and with uncomplicated pasts.[52]

Not only enterprises, but also cultural organizations and government institutions, had high expectations from their potential hires (despite the fact that firms in a socialist-planned economy are not driven by profit and competition). When entering the workforce, veterans had rather high expectations as well, as befitting people who, as we saw in the previous chapter, identified themselves as heroes of the revolution worthy of making certain claims on the government and society. In addition to expecting to be able to move to cities and be treated with respect, veterans expected that their high status would translate into reasonably good positions, ones that would take into consideration skills acquired in the military and allow them to "develop their talents" (*fahui nengli*) after their discharge. For them, their past mattered a great deal, but for employers the future was far more important. Perhaps this clash of expectations was inevitable. From as early as 1952, reports in Shanghai complained of veterans' excessive pickiness. Veterans were assigned a position in a factory, but when they arrived there they discovered that the job was beneath them and then immediately made their way back to the Bureau of Civil Affairs for re-placement. This happened often enough that the BCA convened special meetings where they chastised veterans for turning jobs down; veterans were told to avoid stressing "individual aspirations and interests" and consider "objective circumstances" when approaching employment problems.[53] In the same year, the bureau complained that demobilized officers "haggled over status and benefits" (*jijiao diwei daiyu*) but were "dazed and confused" when told that their expectations were much too high.[54] In 1957, a report by the Qingpu Veterans Committee included a confession by a somewhat frustrated junior Civil Affairs official in Baihe District: "When veterans came to the office with a problem I wasn't patient with them and didn't help them solve their problem. I just told them they were being too demanding."[55] As more attention focused on the role of the PLA in liberation during the early 1960s campaign to emulate Lei Feng (a soldier whose diary reflected selfless devotion to Chairman Mao and the CCP but who died in an accident), some veterans seemed to become even more demanding: if their contributions were so important, shouldn't the state and society reciprocate upon their discharge? In 1963, veterans who returned to Huangpu District in Shanghai made a habit of going around and asking people, "Which factory has the best conditions?"—a practice that earned them the ire of Civil Affairs officials, who deemed them "nitpicky during job assignment." Some veterans continued the 1950s practice of refusing the first job they were assigned, telling bureau officials that it was either "too far away," "required too much heavy labor," or "did not require skill." When they bit the proverbial bullet and finally went to work, many remained dissatisfied. Some "even took part in work slowdowns" to protest their situation.[56]

Even a cursory comparative glance around the world at veterans' employment problems reveals that Chinese veterans' experiences were not very unusual, despite China's very different historical trajectory. Veterans often have faced a very difficult labor market upon their return from war. In Nigeria after WWI, only a small percentage of veterans (far less than in China) could get jobs in government. The remainder had to "makeshift for themselves." "Ironically," Matthew notes, "most Nigerian veterans found that their military service had left them neither prepared for nor entitled to a wage-earning occupation," even as they felt "superior to their peers" when they returned home. A "certain amount" of civilian prejudice against the military, which was viewed as an oppressor of British imperial policy, partially accounts for this.[57] In Ghana after WWI, veterans expected "better jobs," war bonuses, gratuities, and pensions, but "on the whole, they were disappointed and disillusioned." Those veterans who managed better after the war tended to have good occupations *prior* to their enlistment, but "for most, war service merely heightened their frustrations by raising expectations that the post-war Gold Coast economy could not satisfy."[58] In the United States after WWI, employers, especially those in highly urbanized centers, were reluctant to fire workers who had taken veterans' places during the war, since in the meantime the former accumulated valued skills (and consequently earned more money than returning veterans). Like their employer counterparts in China, American managers complained that veterans were too slow and too picky (especially officers) and wanted too much money. When veterans begged and peddled odds and ends in their uniforms to gain sympathy, the U.S. government, like its Chinese counterpart, complained that uniforms were being misused.[59] (Canadian veterans, on the other hand, had an easier time, thanks to severe labor scarcity, but still earned less than civilians.[60]) On the whole, American WWII veterans, who shared with their WWI counterparts high expectations about post-war employment (fostered in part by posters that proclaimed that "a grateful nation would never forget" those who served and discharge officers who told them that "plenty of high paying jobs are awaiting him"[61]), fared better: the economy was humming, many veterans benefited from the GI Bill, and veterans' expectations for a rise in status were usually greeted sympathetically by elites ("Can we expect . . . that such a man should come home . . . to his place behind the cigar counter?"[62]). But even after this so-called good war, the "peace dividend" was unequally divided. African-American and Mexican-American veterans, like many of their Chinese and African counterparts, expected to see a rise in their economic status and better jobs because of their military service (in addition to more rights and privileges) but, because fewer of them had a high school education prior to their enlistment, did not benefit nearly as much as better educated white veterans,[63] a repeat of what had happened after WWI when there was no GI Bill.[64] Moreover, uneven implementation of the GI Bill's job training program in the Deep South (often due to racism) and Southwest left many African-American veterans at a disadvantage in the labor market;[65] very few were able to take advantage of its housing provisions, since the federal government agreed to guarantee loans only if banks agreed to lend the money.[66] Although veterans of WWII and the Korean War generally earned more than their non-veteran counterparts (particularly those from disadvantaged groups),[67] from the Vietnam War until today many American veterans have found themselves at a disadvantage in the labor market. The unemployment rate of young veterans under the age of 25 is higher than non-veterans (despite the GI Bill), a difference which disappears among older veterans. While the reasons for this are complex, veterans' high expectations clearly play a role. The notion that sacrifice should be repaid can lead to higher expectations and demands from employers, which the latter often cannot meet.[68]

These similarities, however, should not obscure important differences. First, the Chinese state took a far more active role in managing veteran employment issues than any Western country, as one might expect given the high degree of state intervention in the economy. As a result of this intervention, many veterans, like other urbanites, were eventually placed in jobs—though whether they were welcomed or found these positions remotely appropriate, satisfying, or commensurate with their high sense of status is a separate issue (after all, under central planning, most all jobs, not only those of veterans, were allocated by the state), particularly in the expanding sector of state-owned industries or in enterprises that employed veterans exclusively. In an eight-month period in 1955, for example, 61 percent of the 175 veterans absorbed by the city in that time frame were employed in either state-owned firms (36 percent) or joint state/private enterprises, but only 6 percent got government jobs and 10 percent landed positions in health and education.[69] In the late 1950s and early 1960s, veterans who did not return to agriculture were assigned positions by the central government. Veterans in China therefore were far more dependent on the state than in many other countries, and this dependence most likely prevented large-scale, veteran-led opposition to the CCP. Second, there is little evidence in the comparative cases of veterans' being forced to navigate the rough terrain between radical left egalitarianism and the state's embrace of the notions of martial citizenship and political worthiness based on military service in a patriotic cause. American and African veterans felt entitled to good jobs as a result of their service, but their governments did not condemn them for this by holding them up to an implausibly altruistic model. Martial-based claims to citizenship and patriotism were more acceptable, especially to elites, than in the Chinese case. Let us now see how these conflicts played out in the workplace after veterans joined the workforce.

OUT OF RANK

Adjustments to civilian life after years of military service are never easy. This has long been recognized by state leaders and lawmakers, who have provided veterans with land, laws, and pensions to ease this transition, as well as by popular media (in 1947 the Oscar for Best Picture went to *The Best Years of Our Lives,* a film depicting the troubled lives of four WWII veterans), psychiatrists, social workers, and soldiers' families. The type of war does not matter much: even after WWII many on the American home front worried that veterans were attracted to radical ideologies, were prone to outbursts of violence, and might even try to overthrow democracy.[70] Difficult transitions also explain why a not-insignificant number of veterans sometimes feel nostalgia for the comradeship of war and combat, sometimes years afterward—this was the case in the United States after WWII, in Australia after WWI, and in Britain after several of its numerous 19th- and 20th-century wars,[71] and we have already seen some of it in China as well. There are, of course, wide variations in the transition experience—returning to one's hometown will be different from returning to an unfamiliar place—but it is fairly safe to say that Chinese veterans' transition experience was bound to be discombobulating simply because they reentered a polity, economy, and society that were undergoing revolutionary change. For example, veterans who returned to the countryside after years of war were older and often weaker, but they found themselves having to make do in a rural economy in transition from household farming to collectivized agriculture where one's well-being depended on the amount of accumulated "work points" and having a good relationship with rural officials, most of whom were not veterans; in cities, rural veterans were placed in factories that had a pre-existing, non-veteran leadership structure, and their pay depended on the whims of unsympathetic managers as well as their skill level and seniority—none of which worked in their favor and could be easily manipulated to their disadvantage. Given these uncertainties, the general atmosphere among veterans was very tense: a 1956 meeting with recently discharged veterans found that "very many of them" were "worried" given the limited number of jobs "after years of economic retrenchments and reducing manpower." They were also "suspicious of government policy towards veterans," complained about the bad timing of their discharge, and were quite aware of the discrepancy between CCP propaganda—which they all acknowledged was done well—and implementation, which was far weaker.[72]

Unfortunately, there is not a great deal of evidence about this transition from the perspective of the individual veteran, but the available sources do identify two major causes of problems, at least in the initial stage of employment. The first was maintaining work discipline after leaving the ranks. Like WWI veterans in the United States who craved excitement in cities and higher wages after their demobilization,[73] some Chinese veterans, having lived through war and strict military organization, had a difficult time readjusting to yet another organization with rigid hierarchy, time management methods, and fixed routines—without any time to relax and get rid of "excess" energy. In the reports, chroniclers of veteran affairs tended to blame work-related problems on the entertainment attractions of the city, which "hick" veterans apparently could not resist.[74] Taking off from work early, not arriving on time, and tomfoolery on the job could all be attributed to the simple desire to relax and have a good time—not at all an unknown phenomenon among veterans returning from war.[75] Management, of course, was critical of veterans' wanderlust, and it most certainly was one of the reasons veterans were quickly tagged as "unruly" workers. Second, but equally problematic, was the sharp transition between military and civilian political economies. In the military, soldiers became accustomed to what was called the "free supply system" under "war communism"; they did not pay individually for food or other necessary products, and their pay was very egalitarian. In the PLA, officers did not wear rank and insignia, either. After discharge, reports noted, many veterans found it difficult to fend for themselves[76] and did not quite fathom post-1949 compensation methods. Veterans who had once prided themselves on bravery and courage and lived for years in an atmosphere of rough egalitarianism were not pleased that in civilian life their rank, and therefore well-being, depended upon their skill and seniority in the workforce and was determined by officials who not only did not have military experience but also were not keen to hire them in the first place.[77] This problem also affected veterans from the urban lower classes (such as peddlers) who never had a "rank" or "skill level" in the first place but, upon their discharge, had to fill out forms querying this. Some savvy peddlers lied effectively and ended up with very decent salaries that were not adjusted, despite coworkers' grumbling![78]

But putting wily peddlers aside, most evidence suggests that civilian administrators ranked veterans far lower on the skill and salary scales than what the latter perceived to be reasonable and fair, particularly given their wartime contributions or military service. Most investigations of veteran affairs from the mid-1950s backed up veterans on this account. Using the usual euphemism for "many," reports from 1957 noted that there were "not a few" problems in assigning veterans' salary and rank and that it was "relatively common" to assign them "inappropriately low rank," usually three to four levels below what an objective analysis would justify, but sometimes even nine levels too low. Only "some" of these salaries were adjusted after the investigation, however. Investigators noted that salary problems were "relatively complicated and involve many dimensions" but adopted a well-worn bureaucratic evasion stratagem: the issue "needs to be studied more in the absence of a unified policy."[79] The situation in rural areas did not appear to be much better. A 1957 Qingpu investigation of veterans in county cooperatives found many instances of veterans (mainly sergeants and corporals) who received salaries below the national standards set for their rank, and these were usually below what civilian officials received (more than 30 yuan a month). Because their salaries were not adjusted, "most comrades have enough to feed themselves, but have a lot of difficulty supporting their families." Sun An, a Qingpu investigator, stressed in his conclusion that veterans' status should be the same in the cooperative as it was in the army and that "from here on in, no veterans' salary should be lower than other cooperative members," but it is difficult to assess the extent to which this was enforced.[80]

The extent to which a "unified policy" would actually matter, though, is debatable. For a policy to be effective, it has to be seen as reasonably legitimate and taken seriously by administrators further down the chain of command, but investigators in Shanghai, and I suspect elsewhere as well, found that enterprise and work unit officials "commonly claim that they never received" documents from the State Council and the Shanghai Municipal Committee and were "too busy with production" to investigate what was happening with the veterans in their units.[81] Even by 1959, some units still knew absolutely nothing about resettlement or salary policy, and they did not even care to find out, investigators found to their dismay.[82] In 1960, a year after the State Council issued a "Notification regarding Salary and Benefit Adjustments for Veterans," a Labor and Interior Ministry report continued to notice widespread improvisation at the local level with regard to rank and salary issues and a general disregard for the State Council directives. The resulting disparities in wages bred resentment among veterans, who saw former comrades-in-arms making more money, but also between veterans and workers, skilled and unskilled.[83] A 1959 report cautioned officials to "prevent contradictions among workers and between veterans demobilized at different times (*fuyuan junren* and *tuiwu junren*) over salary."[84]

Given that many veterans were outsiders, had lower literacy rates, and entered the workforce after factories had already been established, perhaps it was inevitable that many found themselves at the low end of the salary scale. Most veterans were, in effect, the polar opposite of the pre-1949 labor aristocracy, which was dominated by senior skilled workers active in the Communist unions throughout the 1930s and 1940s. Their confidence and feistiness notwithstanding, veterans were often latecomers to villages, government offices, and factories and thus highly vulnerable; civilian managers were able to keep them that way by assigning them to jobs with lower salaries than other positions and then keeping them in those positions for years. Throughout the 1950s and 1960s, many veterans entered the ranks of the lumpenproletariat, consigned to apprenticeships (*xuetu*), temporary positions (*linshi gong*), or jobs with low status or opportunities for upward mobility. Sources indicate that many ordinary soldiers found positions in the "security field" as guards in factories or in militias.[85] Few were happy with these positions, despite their "expertise" in violence: "they say that if they're security guards for several years, it will be hard to transfer to any other job, so they're disgruntled."[86] Some workers mocked them by comparing them to dogs, a particularly nasty epithet in Chinese ("The veterans who guard the gates are guard dogs"; "Veterans' military insignia are their 'dog tags'").[87] Other veterans worked with animal hides or peeled off skin from dogs, cats, and snakes; were ditch diggers, ticket sellers, janitors, repairmen, or drivers; or served for years as apprentices to other workers. A factory-level report from a small leather enterprise, for instance, noted that its veterans were very dissatisfied with their positions, which not only were low-paying but also had low status; all were planning to write to the Bureau of Light Industry to request transfers to a large company, which they felt was a better "match" for their post-military status. In the meantime, they were generally apathetic: "They won't be party activists or backward elements . . . they don't talk much and have no ambition."[88] In Liantang Town in Qingpu County, veterans accused local officials of "violating State Council policies" because they were assigned "inappropriate" jobs (such as skinning animals, which left a terrible odor on their skin; the veterans were "very dissatisfied").[89] In other cases, veterans who acquired a skill in the army found that they were not able to use it after their service, which meant learning a new skill all over again as an apprentice at very low pay. In 1959, a Shanghai report noted veterans who joined the military with eight years' work experience and skill, "but when they come back the enterprise tries to force them to be apprentices again."[90] In 1960, the Ministry of Labor called attention to a case of 313 military drivers who were discharged but 150 of them ended up with limited pay and opportunity for advancement when they were assigned to apprenticeships or to odds-and-ends work in factories on a short-term basis.[91] Perhaps they were better off this way. According to a 1957 report, veterans feared driving in the city because "it's hard to avoid being sued."[92]

That reports indicating scattershot assignments as apprentices or temporary workers appeared in 1960—five years after a nationwide investigation campaign into veteran resettlement difficulties and State Council regulations stipulating (in watered-down form) affirmative action for veterans—is testimony to veterans' precarious employment status after their discharge and lack of political clout at the highest levels of government (see Chapter 5). Many of the early and mid-1950s investigations zeroed in on exactly this problem: employers in urban and rural areas had extremely wide latitude to place veterans in long-term, low-salaried, and insecure apprenticeship positions. In Qingpu, a county-level report noted that assigning veterans to be temporary workers—some had this status for more than two years—was "very inappropriate," in terms of both maintaining their officially high status and getting by on the low salaries attached to these positions.[93] Acknowledging "not a few problems," another Qingpu report (stamped "Secret") from 1956 complained that state institutions and enterprises not only refused to hire veterans, but they also kept them as temporary workers for "unreasonable lengths of time" and "in violation of State Council decisions."[94] A couple of examples from Qingpu illustrate this practice. Liu Kangmin served as a medic in the PLA from 1945 to 1953 and was discharged to the Health Department. In the subsequent four years, he was never assigned a formal status. He brought this to the attention of department officials on many occasions, to no avail; Liu was described as very anxious and depressed and had recently applied for a transfer to Fujian Province, where he grew up.[95] Policy knowledge was no panacea. Employment guidelines stipulated that veterans should be assigned "according to one's talents," but when veterans explicitly cited this principle and mentioned that it came from the State Council, they were generally ignored.[96] Not assigning jobs according to talents resulted in stressful situations. A Qingpu veteran was extremely worried that he would be held accountable for killing a patient in a hospital. A sanitation unit soldier in the army, he was assigned to work as a physician.[97]

Many veterans in Shanghai and its suburbs were also relegated to temporary worker status, sometimes for years. A 1957 report criticized employers for setting up unauthorized "trial periods" for jobs that somehow never ended as well as unions for refusing to allow veterans to join.[98] Apprentices who joined the PLA in the mid-1950s returned from the army after three years only to find out that their salary had remained exactly the same, while those who stayed earned more—a problem noted in Liaoning Province as well.[99] Veterans openly grumbled about the lack of reciprocity for service: "After three years, how can it be that your salary has not only not gone up, but declined?" "You're an apprentice for two years, serve in the army for three and then have to start your apprenticeship all over again from nothing!" "It's a big misfortune for the state when soldiers don't raise their skill level in the army, and a small misfortune for those whose salary has not gone up at all."[100]

When some veterans could not take it any longer and complained to factory or municipal authorities, they did not appear to fare very well. Zhang Shiya, for example, was discharged in 1952 and assigned to be an apprentice at the Hengxin Machine Tool factory in Shanghai. He was said to be a good worker and received several promotions, but his salary was still lower than younger coworkers. He complained to the factory union. When the union was unsympathetic, he screamed at them, calling them "the running dogs of the capitalists." After this incident, he became known as a troublemaker. The management and union decided to "get him out of the way" by gathering materials on him and having the police arrest him on charges of "undermining factory leadership and intentionally sabotaging the 'Resist America, Support Korea' campaign." Even though all of these charges were fabricated, the Changning District police arrested him without bothering to conduct an independent investigation. In the meantime, the Communist Youth League deemed him an "alien class element" and expelled him. The District Court, for its part, attempted to investigate but was stonewalled by factory leaders. Lacking any contrary evidence, the court sentenced him to six months in prison. Luckily, Zhang successfully appealed the verdict to the #2 Intermediate Court, which reduced his sentence to "criminal discipline" (*xingshi chufen*). The factory, however, continued to collect materials on him and sent a report to the Intermediate Court in the hope that they would not release him. This case was finally investigated by a joint team from the Bureau of Civil Affairs and the Procurator, which jointly determined that "retaliation" was the only reason Zhang had been arrested.[101]

As bad as this case sounds, it was not unusual. In 1955, in a print factory in Shanghai, two veterans received apprentice salaries, which put them both in difficult financial straits. The factory promised them that their salaries would be adjusted after six months but failed to follow through with this promise. The veterans then filed a complaint at the Bureau of Light Industry, but when the factory got wind of this, they put a disciplinary note in their personal dossiers.[102] A 1956 Commerce Department investigation report also found that when veterans "raise objections" to rank, salary, and other problems, officials accused them of being "backward," "individualists," and "status seekers,"[103] and an Interior Ministry report (1956) noted that unauthorized firings and expulsion of "problematic" veterans were "common" around the country.[104] At a food-processing factory in Beijing, for instance, an official surnamed Ma sent one of his subordinates to fetch the dossier of a veteran named Wang Duanjiang, who "had recently complained about his salary." To satisfy Ma, the official got the file and inserted a letter stating that Wang "opposed the leadership" and was "organizing a clique with the intention to strike." This had its intended effect, and Wang was expelled on these false charges.[105] In Fujian Province, veterans working at a native products factory were forced to sign a contract stating that "Party A [the veteran] forfeits his right to complain about anything in the factory."[106]

Life as a low-status but highly dependent temporary worker was surely full of stress and anxiety, particularly for veterans accustomed to military life or with families to support. When the Qingpu investigator argued that temporary work was the "least appropriate" for veterans, they probably had this in mind: demobilization was difficult, but temporary work made veterans even more vulnerable politically and economically. Cases we have seen thus far concerned well-established firms where veterans at least could be guaranteed that the factory would exist in the near future, but what if veterans were demobilized to build a factory from its foundations? Since China's industrial base expanded rapidly throughout the 1950s in both urban and rural areas, and veterans were seen as a source of cheap labor, this was not unusual. From these veterans' perspective, the future was as unsteady as the ground they prepared. An investigation of 259 veterans (10 CCP members and 172 in the CYL) at the Wujing Electric Power Plant in Shanghai gives us a very good sense of life "on the far edges" of the state's plan. Summarizing their situation as "complicated" and "grave," investigators found these veterans-turned-construction workers (including the "backbone" party members) very unhappy about this work, as the following comments reveal:

> Just what sort of "worker" are we considered? The poster on our dorms says "Construction Worker Dormitories."

> Construction work is very mobile. What will we do if we're sent to some other place after this?

> If we knew that we'll become regular workers of Wujing, today's bitterness will be worth it.

> Even if only a few of us are taken, there's no way that they'll want the rest of us. There are too many people.

> We came to learn a skill, not do menial labor.

According to the investigators' interviews, these veterans spent their days and free time mulling about the future, guessing what would happen to them and wondering "if there will be any surprises on the 8th" (their salary date). Rumors spread rapidly with this uncertainty: the latest was that "every veteran who had a skill prior to enlistment will make 42.40 yuan." They immediately started to grumble: "42.40 is too little," "It's not enough for a poor family to live on," "I won't be able to eat with that—I'll take my bedding and run away," "If the salary standard isn't clarified, we should all collectively refuse to accept any advance payment they give us!"[107]

An investigation report about the many veterans working in the Jinxing Pen factory added more flesh to these accounts of veterans' stress. Most all of these veterans, the report noted, had a very hard time getting by, largely because their "salaries are comparatively low" and "union and management don't care about them and find all sorts of excuses to not adjust their salaries." The report cited typical cases of how low salary and indifference affected veterans' lives. Take, for instance, the case of Jin Ronghua. Jin was heavily indebted because his mother had recently passed away. Because of this, he had no money to buy civilian clothes and came to the factory still wearing his uniform. Several workers ridiculed him on this account. Jin, however, did not hesitate to bring this treatment to the attention of the union and the factory director. The director bluntly told him, "The factory can't solve problems like this; go to Civil Affairs." After this, Jin contacted the leader of the factory's "veteran's small group" (*fuyuan junren xiaozu*), who took up the issue on his behalf. His appeal to the director, however, was also unsuccessful. "So Jin Ronghua doesn't have any clothes," he said. "Why don't you veterans contribute a little bit so he can get some? This isn't the factory's problem."[108]

This sort of discrimination was not only a Shanghai phenomenon. It was noticed in newer factories (such as Wujing Power), more established firms (Jinxing Pen), and factories in Shanghai's suburbs. In these factories, as in many other places, the salary spread could be quite wide, but how it became that way, and why certain veterans made more than others but all seemed to make less than other workers, was never explained. In a factory in Chuansha County with 235 workers, for example, there were 23 veterans among the contract workers. Most veterans made roughly 25 yuan a month, but salaries varied from 14 to 78 yuan for an apprentice. According to the investigation report, "they have already raised not a few complaints over their temporary worker status and low salary."[109] In a 1960 investigation of four factories in Nanhui County (also in the Shanghai suburbs), resentment was also found to run deep:

> Many veterans feel that they risked their life fighting the enemy, were not too late participating in the revolution and have made a definite contribution to it, yet when they return to their localities their salaries are lower than most everyone else's. Two veterans make 35 yuan a month, but have four children and their wives don't work. It's very tough for them, but they can't raise the salary issue given the political atmosphere.[110]

At one of the factories, there were 14 veterans (four were defined as *fuyuan junren* and nine as *tuiwu junren*) who were "introduced" to the factory via the Bureau of Civil Affairs in 1958 or 1959. With the exception of two *fuyuan*, all of them were temporary workers with "relatively low salaries." At another factory, a state-owned dye operation, the veterans were assigned by the Industry Ministry in 1958. None of the veterans had come skilled at dying clothes, so all were assigned to be apprentices, with salaries starting at 20 yuan. In 1959, after the veterans posted big-character posters at the county seat and "making a big stink," management, with the approval of the county government, raised their salaries a bit—workers who made 20 yuan now made 30; those who earned 32 got bumped up to 35—but the gap between veterans and senior workers was still quite wide. At another Nanhui firm, the veterans said:

> We participated in the revolution but we are still temporary workers with low salaries; the *shehui qingnian* in the factory [youth, generally from lower class backgrounds, who did not move up the educational ladder] also make 32 yuan a month, and now make 35.[111]

These sorts of complaints generally fell on deaf ears, however. Evidence from the PRC's Commerce Department suggests that widespread discrimination and ostracism in factories were intentional and tactically deployed "to force veterans to leave" on their own accord, since this was much simpler than firing them. At a metalwork firm in Fushan (Liaoning Province) with 46 veterans, seven had been subjected to "administration discipline" or criminal prosecution in a two-year period; the veterans said, "Here you get punished for every single mistake." In Hepu County, Guangdong Province, a government department took in one veteran as an operator. To make his life so miserable that he would request a transfer, officials demanded that he wash the clothes of all his fellow workers as well as carry water for their showers. When he objected, his boss said, "We'll get you arrested if you don't do it—veterans are no big deal (*mei you shenma liaobuqi*)." In Fu'an County, Fujian, officials tried to accomplish the same objective by placing a veteran in a "trial period" for more than a year and sending him on numerous tasks, sometimes at the same time. If he complained, they would fire him for "opposing the leadership." This discretion was also applied to salaries: if veterans could be kept at low salaries, they might either complain or try to transfer—in both cases management would have an excuse to fire them. This may have been the calculation in a case in Beizhan County, Liaoning Province, when officials sent a Muslim veteran to work at a slaughterhouse for pigs.[112]

Frozen salaries, to be sure, were not a problem that affected only veterans; many workers did not see any significant rise in their salaries from the late 1950s until the Cultural Revolution. Still, a salary freeze had particularly adverse economic consequences on veterans. Aside from the obvious discrepancy between their "revolutionary status" and their comparative poverty, the millions who were discharged in 1955 or 1956 would have had only two or three years to gain a foothold in a firm before the freeze, while those beginning their three year military service in 1955 would have been discharged just as the freeze took hold, having missed three years of promotion possibilities. Perhaps unsurprisingly, salary problems were frequently raised in veterans' correspondence with the Veteran Reception Office in 1963 (68 percent). Prominent issues raised in these letters included:

- A lack of consideration existed for whether a person served his mandatory service or did extra time—everyone received the same.
- Apprentices who completed two years were told to work yet another two years.
- Salary was not based on the skills they learned in the army.
- Those who served after graduating from technical school were not given a salary in accordance with their education level.
- Rural veterans, including officers, didn't have the strength they had when they were younger and didn't have good agricultural skills, but "because socialism is based on the idea of 'to each according to his work,' cannot support themselves."[113]

A common denominator running throughout many of these letters was the "discounting" of veterans' time in the military, whether at war or in regular service, and the problems that absence from civilian life created upon their return. For many work units, time essentially stopped when workers became soldiers but started again only after they returned.

MISSING YEARS

To the extent that military service was valued in China, it would not be unreasonable to expect that time and accomplishments in service, or at least some portion of them, would be included in establishing veterans' post-demobilization salary. Officially, the central government produced a lot of paperwork stipulating that time spent in the army (*junling*) and one's rank in it "should" be included in the calculation of "work years" (*gongling*);[114] its intentions, at least on paper, appeared to be fair. But to what extent was this enforced at the local levels? Less officially, to the extent that non-inclusion of military years in the calculation of salary was widespread, could we consider this a violation of a "fair-shake" standard? A strong case can be made for this, given that most veterans came from the countryside and the urban lower classes, so ignoring time and rank when it came time to determine their salaries would have a particularly deleterious impact. The fair-shake imperative would require at least reasonable consideration of their years in the military.

Throughout the 1950s and 1960s, in addition to numerous complaints about work units refusing to hire veterans, hiring them only as a last resort, and then assigning many of them to low-skilled and highly vulnerable positions in the workforce, veterans took issue with many employers' refusal to include years spent in the army and their rank upon discharge in the calculation of their wages. Let's first take a look at a government institution where one might expect rather sympathetic treatment: a rural hospital. Since China experienced a peasant revolution, perhaps rural locales would identify more closely with veterans; in addition, if nationalism and patriotism were more common among educated classes, we should expect physicians and other personnel in this field to at least *try* to give veterans a fair shake after demobilization by making their salaries somewhat comparable to local staff. In Qingpu, however, this was not the case. Administrators at the Red Cross Hospital effectively nullified the three years it took for a veteran surnamed Zhang (who served from 1945 to 1952) to rise from pharmaceutical technician (*jiyuan*) to pharmacist (*siyao*) at sergeant rank by giving him a position as a technician at a salary that was 10 yuan lower than his military pay. Told he would have to spend several more years regaining his pharmacist status, Zhang complained, "Why should I have to do technician's work again?"—but it did not help.[115] Similar complaints were "common" in medical facilities in the county, according to another investigation report. Local favoritism was blamed for this. When promotions were awarded and salary scales assigned, 80–90 percent of the local staff received promotions of two to three levels, but only a small minority of veterans did. Veterans were incensed, claiming that Health Department leaders "do not treat us equally and fairly" (*yishi tongren*); they also heard that in "neighboring counties" veterans who deserved a certain rank received it, so "why is it that in Qingpu no one got an appropriate rank?" Another veteran at the Red Cross Hospital served in the PLA for 10 years but found himself working in the lowest-paying positions. There were "not a few [i.e., many] similar cases in the Health Department," the investigation concluded.[116]

These complaints echoed those in other areas. In Liaoning, veterans in a number of work units were unable to obtain insurance because years in the military were not considered "work years"—a problem that *People's Daily* claimed was "rectified" after investigation.[117] At the Shuangyashan mine in Heilongjiang Province, an investigation revealed that "the absolute majority of veterans do not get their years of service included in their seniority status, nor do they received labor insurance."[118] In Shanghai, the Bureau of Civil Affairs bulletin *Minzheng jianbao* noted that same year that "in setting veterans' salary level it is relatively common" for units to ignore their military rank altogether, so their current civilian status is lower than their rank in the army.[119] Among the findings of a large-scale investigation into veteran salary and resettlement issues (circulated among the relevant government agencies) was that work units "don't take military experience and rank into account when assigning wage levels" and that it was "relatively common" to give them "inappropriately low rank."[120] Low assignments, unsurprisingly, generated numerous complaints, which led to countercriticism of veterans as "arrogant" and "difficult" for having such high and mighty opinions of themselves.[121]

This problem continued well into the 1960s, *People's Daily*'s claims of "rectification" notwithstanding. Perhaps owing to numerous complaints, in 1959 the State Council and Ministry of Labor mounted a large-scale investigation—involving almost 40 work units in Hubei and Hunan provinces—into the implementation of "Labor Ministry Directive #103," which directed units to improve veterans' salary and benefits, which were said to have been "obviously on the low side" (*xianran piandi*) until that point. Ignoring veterans' time and rank and military service by assigning them to long-term apprenticeships was wrong, the State Council argued, because veterans, unlike regular youth who were learning a skill on the job, were older and had more family responsibilities; moreover, they also "have made some contributions to the state, so the state should take care of them." The problem, of course, was that the slice of "the state" that mattered most, as far as veterans were concerned, was not the State Council or even the provincial government but, rather, lower-level officials who had more discretion over setting salaries and rank. National-level investigators found a number of different practices, even between two provinces. In Wuhan, the capital of Hubei, for instance, officials simplified salary matters by ignoring all biographical differences between veterans (such as between veterans who came from the countryside and city, and between those who were employed prior to enlistment and those who were not). They simply raised all *fuyuan* veterans (those who were recruited during the wars) to Level 2 workers and all *tuiwu* veterans (generally those in the military after 1953) to Level 1 workers. When it came to the directive mandating the inclusion of military years into "work years," the Hunan and Hubei investigations revealed very weak implementation. In some cases, this was a moot issue, since "not a few" employers refused to rehire veterans after their service, but even when they were rehired and "despite clear regulations" in previous years, "some units still do not follow the policy." In some cases, employers counted half a year for every year in the army; in others, years in the army were not treated as "consecutive work years," which meant that they did not count toward seniority; and in others they were not included at all. "Further reiteration of this regulation" was necessary, the report concluded,[122] but even in 1959 an investigation found that salary regulations "stopped at the level of the responsible bureau or company and are not implemented in the factory."[123] Judging by the types of complaints received by Shanghai's Veteran Reception Office in 1963, it is not at all clear that whatever reiterations took place in the interim years made a difference. One complaint was that "salaries are determined by the apprenticeship period, not the length of military service."[124]

A PLACE TO LIVE

Let's now briefly consider a somewhat less stringent "test" of the fair-shake standard—the housing allocation process. If we give employers the benefit of the doubt with regard to a critical resource such as good employment—for instance, if they rapidly promoted veterans to more senior status, budgets would be strained and other workers could become very jealous—the allocation of housing establishes a somewhat easier "threshold" of compliance. True, in large cities that witnessed the influx of millions during the 1950s, good housing was a scarce commodity, but it involved fewer long-term costs and potential interpersonal problems than providing lifetime employment to an individual whose personality was a bit off-putting. Did veterans fare better trying to find a place to live than a place to work? Since China did not experience widespread homelessness during this period, it is clear that veterans found places to live. Its record in this respect is better than the United States in the late 20th and early 21st centuries, a period generally coinciding, and not coincidentally I think, with the end of conscription. In the United States, veteran homelessness, particularly among minorities and those with service-related disabilities and lower incomes, is far too common (affecting half a million people) in a wealthy society, in large part because government programs have been "remarkably limited and inconsistent with our nation's history and rhetoric."[125] My focus here is on the more qualitative, interactive, and interpersonal dimensions of the question "How did they fare?" How were veterans *treated* by officials when dealing with this issue?

According to a key 1955 State Council document, veterans were supposed to receive "priority" (*youxian*) in the housing allocation process. If they were too poor to afford rent, local governments were expected to provide them with "appropriate assistance" as well as "mobilize the masses" to help them repair dilapidated units.[126] Assessing the extent to which these regulations were implemented on a nationwide scale would require a fairly massive research effort, but there is enough material from Shanghai, Qingpu, and elsewhere to suggest that these regulations often proved to be toothless, much like other State Council regulations regarding "preferential treatment" in job allocation were routinely flouted. There is no question about the extent of the housing crunch, however. Reports from the early 1950s gave a clear sense of this by using strong language to describe the situation, noting that "solutions *must immediately* be found" instead of the more common "*should be* found." Like previous waves of migrants, many veterans came to Shanghai because their homes were destroyed by war or natural disasters; others were already living in Shanghai with their families but only had one bed for everyone in the family. Shanghai's Real Estate Bureau officials, however, allocated veterans only "30 units a month," which was not nearly enough for them and certainly not enough if they had families outside the city who wanted to move in; in a *People's Daily* article, "some veterans" complained, "We engaged in battles all over the country and braved untold dangers for the revolution and the country, but now that it's peacetime the CCP no longer wants us to be 'Buddhist monk soldiers' (*heshang bing*; i.e., celibate), but you are now asking us to become 'Buddhist monk workers'? Give us housing for our families!"[127] *People's Daily*, however, toned down this problem. According to a detailed investigation of Shanghai's western suburbs, "very many veterans" (not "some" in the newspaper version) had housing problems: "They have been in the army for many years; their families have grown, and some have no place to sleep after their return. If they want to marry, even less can be done to help them (*geng mei you banfa*)." Investigators ran interference with the Real Estate Bureau on three separate occasions, without success.[128]

Factory officials, for their part, also do not seem to have been spurred to energetic action because of sympathy for the veterans' predicament. An investigation of a textile mill in Shanghai revealed several examples. A veteran surnamed Liao, for instance, was about to get his apartment—his name was already on the union's blackboard—but the deputy factory director, Shen Shengbai, saw it and told union officials to "wipe it off, wipe it off—he doesn't qualify for it." Liao's name was then replaced by that of another worker, Jiang Xiangbao. Liao asked Shen Shengbai why his name was removed. Shen said, "You don't have enough tenure at the factory," to which Liao replied, "It *is* enough, *if* you count the years I was in the army." Shen did not want to get into a debate about this, so he simply retorted, "Jiang Xiangbao works better than you," and that was that. Shen Shengbai, together with the former factory director, Xu Quanfu, was also said to have denied a larger housing unit for veteran Wang Deyi, who was getting married. According to the investigation, Shen told Zhu Jincai, the official responsible for these matters, "Tell them to go to Hebei [Province] and find a thatched hut there." Unaware of this, Wang Deyi asked for a bedroom, but Shen said, "OK, but give him a single bed." Wang was said to be very unhappy about this but had little choice but to return to his fiancée's village in the countryside to marry. As of late 1956, he was still living with relatives in the countryside. By denying him proper housing, Shen had effectively ended his job at the factory and probably his coveted urban residence. Investigators concluded that key officials at the factory "were insufficiently aware of the great political significance of resettling veterans" and therefore "did not study the relevant policy documents."[129] In other factories, however, top factory officials appeared to be more sympathetic—they actually informed veterans that they had priority for housing—but lower-level officials "did not implement the instructions."

Noting that "mistaken viewpoints and attitudes about veterans were relatively common," investigators also found cases of unions refusing to give a loan to a veteran who arrived at the factory in winter with only one layer of clothes and to another who was so poor he had no money to buy clothes for his newborn baby, who was "always wrapped up in a sheet."[130]

In other cases, investigations found that housing was allocated, but it was in such a state of disrepair that it was practically uninhabitable. Ironically, given that the CCP emerged victorious in the revolution, even "elements under state supervision" were said to have had their housing problems solved by 1956, while veterans still had many difficulties. A veteran surnamed Zhou, for example, was assigned a room in a dormitory with a leaky roof, which flooded every time it rained. When he became ill with tuberculosis, he began to spit blood and was unable to sleep because of the dripping water and a persistent cough. Seeking a drier place to live, he put in a request for a worker's apartment on three occasions but heard nothing back. Desperate, he borrowed 400 yuan—roughly a year's salary at the time—to buy a single room, but he was mired in debt and unable to repay the loan. Thinking back "very fondly" on their army days, Zhou and other veterans "cried in deep sorrow" (*yinlei*).[131] Even as late as 1959–1960, some veterans were said to have adopted "guerrilla tactics" to solve their housing problems—they lived "in the east one day, the west the next"—which made it difficult to arrive to work on time, made them more likely to receive disciplinary notes, and further bolstered their reputation for unreliability.[132] In a national-level report of the Labor Ministry in 1960, work units were charged with not caring about veterans' living situations. Owing to their low status in the workforce, some returning veterans (drafted in 1956) were placed in damp dorms full of mosquitoes and ate in unsanitary kitchens that caused illnesses that were then not treated well. As a result, "very many" veterans complained that "things that should be criticized don't get criticized, and people who should be 'educated' don't get educated."[133]

In the countryside, housing issues tended to be somewhat less problematic—housing was generally simpler, and space was less contested. Still, housing problems did surface in meetings with veterans. In 1957, for example, Qingpu veterans complained that they were forced to live in dormitories upon their return to the countryside and that local officials did not do nearly enough to help them secure a home (which undoubtedly affected their marriage prospects). A veteran said, "Township and village cadres are not concerned with veterans. When I returned to the village I had no place to live, but the township didn't do anything to help me; when I had no food to eat, village officials did nothing to help me."[134] The extent to which this sentiment was widespread is difficult to assess, however. For reasons that are not clear, investigation reports rarely commented on rural housing issues, and gazetteers provide only gross numbers of housing units, without any mention of political conflict surrounding the allocation process.

VETERANS' VOICES

How did veterans respond to frequent and widespread discrimination as well as to a distinct sense among many of them that, propaganda notwithstanding, they had been left behind by the revolution in which they were key players, and were any of these responses effective? The sources reveal several different methods for "getting justice and getting even" (using Sally Engle Merry's terminology[135]), ranging from writing letters to newspapers and public officials to more dangerous forms of collective action, such as posting big-character posters, strikes, work slowdowns, and violence, especially during the Cultural Revolution. That veterans were willing to take these risks should come as no surprise: many had a strong sense of worthiness and identity (as seen in Chapter 3) as well as a certain amount of personal courage and feistiness. Although some collective action theorists consider "personality" to be a "hoary micro issue," its importance cannot be underestimated in cases of collective action in high-risk environments.[136]

Letters to the press and other government agencies were one of the most common forms of communication between veterans and those institutions they considered to be on their side—Civil Affairs Bureaus, provincial governments, People's Congresses, and especially the central government in Beijing. Their ambitions often stifled by local authorities, veterans, rather naïvely, appeared to believe that if only higher authorities were aware of their problems, they could be solved lickity split. The timing of the publication of letters in the press, however, was shaped more by national-level events than demands from below: the more revealing and critical letters appeared mainly between 1955 and 1957, which coincided with massive demobilization, the "Hundred Flowers Campaign" (which encouraged people to express grievances against the party), and the promulgation of several State Council policy decisions that were followed by a nationwide investigation into veteran affairs, but they tailed off toward the end of the 1950s as the leadership turned to other matters. Despite this sporadic attention, veterans pressed their cases. For instance, in 1955, Wang Jiemin in Dawu County, Hubei Province, was accused of maltreating veterans in a letter written by two members of the county Veterans Committee in the August 21 issue of *People's Daily*. In the October 16 issue that same year, Jiang Weidi, the deputy director of the Discipline Inspection Committee of Xiaogan District (one level below

Dawu County), informed the paper that Wang Jiemin was given a "warning" and might be demoted in rank.[137] In 1956, a seven-year skilled veteran from Anxi county in Fujian wrote to *People's Daily* in a section called "Veterans' Voices" (*fuyuan junren de husheng*) with a piece entitled "How Long Can One Be a Temporary Worker?" in which he bemoaned the fact that he and fellow veterans had been temporary workers for more than a year, with no end in sight: "I don't get it. What sort of conditions does one have to meet to be a permanent worker?" he wondered.[138] In 1957, Shi Feng, a county chief in Shanxi, issued an apology after an investigation singled out his county for expelling veterans from jobs and cutting off their salaries (but whether or not the veterans actually got their positions back is not known).[139]

In addition to writing to authorities, veterans also wrote to each other to "buck themselves up" in light of a great deal of adversity. Like many veterans at other times and in other parts of the world who develop strong feelings of camaraderie because of their experiences, veterans in China, despite a weak communication infrastructure, managed to maintain ties with one another by writing letters, some of which were published in *People's Daily*. One letter, signed off by "Your comrades-in-arms," was addressed to a Korean War veteran who encountered "very many difficulties" after his discharge. To raise his spirits, his fellow soldiers reminded him of how they had improvised during the Korean War and managed to get by on very little.[140] When *People's Daily* published a letter like this, it served multiple purposes. On the one hand, it sent a message to society that the government cares about veterans. On the other, the message to veterans was that they could not count on the government for everything and would also have to figure out a way to get by in civilian life. Finally, it conveniently shifted the blame to local officials rather than the national government, which cared enough about them to publish the letter.

Since letters to the editor in major national newspapers were a hit-but-mostly-miss affair (like the United States), veterans also wrote to other venues. Quite a few took advantage of municipal-, county-, and national-level "Letters and Visit Offices" (*renmin laixin laifang*) as well as specific bureaucracies (such as the Bureau of Civil Affairs) to complain about job placement, salary issues, job transfers, abusive bosses, and health and marriage problems;[141] a 1957 document from the State Council's Personnel Bureau, for instance, mentions receiving "very many letters and visits from work units and veterans" related to salary and pension issues.[142] A 1956 letter from a "representative" of the Tianjin Regional (in Hebei Province) Veterans Committee to Liu Shaoqi, then-chairman of the National People's Congress (and concurrently the chair of the National Veteran's Committee), provides a good sense of many veterans' sentiments at the time:[143]

Dear Liu Shaoqi, Committee Chairman:

We obeyed our superiors' orders and left the army to work in various localities. We thought this was glorious work. Even though the nature of it was different, it was for the socialist construction of our country. Of course we had no objections to it. But after we started work we saw that the determination of our rank violated cadre policy—our past work for the revolution was completely tossed aside, as if we were greenhorns. Then the local authorities decided that they didn't like us, so when we were assigned jobs, our rank was reduced by two or three levels. . . . We think this is illogical and unreasonable: a cadre who was in the revolution for 12 years is not the same as some young office worker who's been on the job for a year or two. All of us veterans say: "People like us can only look forward to next year, since that's the only way we'll be popular" [a war was expected to break out]. We request that the National People's Congress investigate veterans' job assignments and that the conclusions be published in the newspaper.

According to our understanding, in the last three years not even a single veteran demobilized to various localities has been promoted. We say to each other: "This is just like the way white people treat black people in the United States!"

. . . We don't think we're stupid (*chunchong*); we gave the party a great deal: the victory in the Anti-Japanese War, the war against the Guomindang, and the Korean War. How is it that the National People's Congress doesn't know about these problems? We request that you intervene on our behalf by asking the Center not to adopt a policy of "slaughtering the mule after he's finished grinding the wheat."

Despite both the volume and the level of articulation in some of these letters (which were surely exceptional), there is little evidence that they succeeded in changing the fortunes of many veterans, for reasons we will see more clearly in the next chapter. Evidence from inner-party and public documents on the internal operations of Letters and Visits Offices reveals why this was the case. A 1952 report penned by officials in the East China Military–Political Committee on this subject complained that "some leading cadres" didn't pay them serious attention, let them pile up (*jiya*), procrastinated, and delayed dealing with them. Others "don't investigate," which often led to "rash handling" or "pushing off responsibility to someone else." A few even took personal revenge on individual letter writers. Officials worried that actions such as these "seriously undermine the trust between the government and the people." In Shanghai, officials pointed to "serious deficiencies" in this work as well. In some work units, no one was even tasked to this job and no records were kept, but even when someone was assigned, "different people do the job" and "they just go through the motions." The Letters and Visits Office was described as existing in "name only," since quite a few cadres believed that letters "are just a big headache for the government."[144]

The maturation of the regime between 1952 and the latter half of the decade did little to change the grim picture of this institution. Even when officials actually read a letter and processed it, it usually just ended where it began. Take, for instance, the history of two letters (written by veterans requesting employment in Dongyang County, Zhejiang Province) as reported in a short investigation piece in *People's Daily* by Wang Shineng in 1955–1956:[145]

Letter 1:

July 1	Letter sent from Dongyang to State Council.
July 7	Letter received by State Council, sent to Ministry of Interior.
July 13	Letter received by Ministry of Interior.
July 23	Ministry of Interior sends it back to Dongyang County for "handling."

Letter 2:

January 1	Veteran writes letter to CCP General Office in Beijing accusing the county of negligence in its handling of veteran resettlement issues. General Office sends letter to Ministry of Interior.
February 22	Interior Ministry's "Preferential Treatment Bureau" (*youfu ju*) sends it to Zhejiang Provincial Government.
March	Zhejiang Provincial Committee sends letter to the Provincial Bureau of Civil Affairs.
April	Provincial Bureau of Civil Affairs sends letter back to Dongyang County government.

After these road trips, both letters ended up at the exact same place they started and in the hands of the very same officials who were held responsible for the problems cited in the letters in the first place. The potential for abuse was vast, and internal government documents suggest that it was not uncommon. An investigation by the Shandong Provincial Procurator's Office in 1955 found that in many units, "letters and visits work" was not considered important (70 percent of the letters complained about cadres' attitude and violations of party discipline) and thus was handed over to officials who were considered "relatively weak" and unable to get things done. As in the early 1950s, job turnover was very high. County officials just said "forget it" (*suanle ba*), claiming that they were too busy. Quite a few letters were lost and long delays were common. For example, in one letter a veteran surnamed

Zheng accused the Shijia township chief of misreporting the harvest, as well as subjecting him to blows and criticisms. Because the letter was never handled, Zheng wrote to the county government nine times, went there on four occasions, and later made his way to the provincial government. Because of the interminable delays, veterans' fellow villagers were very upset: "The government is so shady and irresponsible. What sort of people are these? What is this?" As it turned out, the county government had forwarded 50 letters to the district-level authorities who were responsible for the goings-on in Shijia Township, but in the course of an entire year, not a single letter was unsealed. Desperate peasants could be found crying in government offices and refusing to leave until their problems were handled and "skipping" the district level to lodge their complaints at the county or provincial level and even in Beijing.[146]

Brushed off by letter handlers and many officials throughout the PRC's gargantuan and convoluted bureaucracy, veterans found other means of protesting their employment situation. Much like today, when unemployed workers stage protests to garner official attention to their problems, veterans in the 1950s and 1960s were involved in a number of "incidents" such as petitioning, "work slowdowns," and wholesale destruction of factory property during the Cultural Revolution. Some of these protests proved to be a far more effective political resource than penning letters about their particular problem, although there has not yet been a more comprehensive solution to veterans' employment problems. Research by Elizabeth J. Perry has already shown that temporary and contract workers were at the forefront of the 1957 "Strike Wave" in Shanghai,[147] and we have seen that veterans were generally relegated to these positions; hence, it is quite possible that veterans participated in these strikes. In Guangdong Province, the Civil Affairs gazetteer mentions cases of veterans' "collective petitioning" in the 1950s in response to difficulties securing jobs, financial difficulties, inability to do agricultural labor, and "contradictions" between them and local cadres.[148] In Shandong, a provincial-level investigation that same year noted cases of veterans petitioning, which were caused mainly by "problems that have not been solved for a very long time" and "discrimination, abuse, and revenge" on the part of local cadres. The Provincial Party Committee ordered local officials to avoid arresting petitioners, with the exception of those "involved in criminal activities," and instead work to improve "letters and visits work" at the local levels to prevent petitioning events from reaching the provincial capital in the first place.[149] But veterans did not necessarily wait for official approval to stage protests, as was the case in 1956–1957 when workers joined other groups to "bloom and contend" as Mao exhorted them to during the Hundred Flowers Campaign. In Shandong, the provincial report noted that many petitioning incidents "had already occurred in the province," prior to 1957.[150] In early 1956, veterans at a key state industry, the Jiangnan Shipyards in Shanghai, were involved in a work slowdown that succeeded in catching the eye of municipal officials, who imposed a solution that met some of their demands. Thankfully, municipal officials produced a detailed record of this incident, opening for us a very wide window on veterans' employment problems as well as their sense of identity in the years after their discharge.

THE JIANGNAN SHIPYARD INCIDENT[151]

The 1956 dispute at the Jiangnan Shipyards shows how many of the adverse circumstances that confronted veterans could produce a critical mass that was willing to take political action against the state. As a key state military installation, the Jiangnan Shipyard was a major employer of veterans.[152] Altogether, there were 544 veterans working at the shipyard, including close to 200 who had arrived in 1955. Every one of them was designated as an "apprentice" and then assigned to various workshops. The "incident" at the shipyard began with a small argument but, like many small arguments that hide larger issues, quickly escalated. In the latter half of 1955, the shipyard was forced to cut back production, owing to a shortage of raw materials, so its veteran apprentices were organized for study sessions. This was something the veterans had eagerly anticipated, since only through improving their technical skills would they have any chance of promotion and higher salaries. On February 22, 1956, during one of the study sessions, an argument broke out between a veteran who was apprenticing in the steel workshop and his master, a man named Lu Ermin. Both were angry. The next day, another skilled worker/master, Lu Bixian, told the assembled veterans, "Now we have work to do in the workshops, so we'll be stopping classes." This immediately raised the veterans' suspicions, since this decision came down only one day after the argument between their fellow veteran and Lu Ermin. Some raised the possibility that they were being collectively punished for the argument. Anxious, but determined to continue class, the veterans said, "If class is cancelled, we'll go to the classroom and just wait." Their teacher, Lu Ermin, sensed danger in the air and told them he could not be responsible for the consequences of their actions.

The next morning, more than twenty veterans in one workshop refused to go to a small group meeting and, instead, went to class to wait for it to start. Sitting there together with nothing to do, the veterans began to vent their grievances and decided to go directly to the management to force them to address their problems. At this point, workshop leaders panicked and refused to meet with them; even worse, they reported to their bosses that the veterans were "stirring up a strike for 64 yuan." The following day, this strike spread to even more workshops: veterans left their posts and gathered in the classroom to voice their complaints. On the afternoon of the 26th, the factory's deputy director and an official from the Municipal Military Liaison Office went to meet with the veterans. Upon arrival, they were besieged by even more complaints. Finally, on the 27th, the factory organized a meeting to discuss their grievances; more than 120 veterans attended. In the meeting, the management committed itself to solving veterans' "concrete problems." After this, the veterans returned to their workshops.

The Shanghai government, alarmed by both the size and the sudden onset of this "incident," dispatched an investigation team to the shipyard. Not surprisingly, given what we have seen thus far, veterans' salary was a key issue and cause for grievance; in fact, the 1956 "strike" was only one of several that occurred at the shipyard between 1949 and 1955. According to the investigation, many veterans who had snagged positions in the shipyards had immediately brought their rural relatives into the city and faced higher expenses at a very low salary. Some had large wedding expenses. In addition, the shipyard veterans, much like those at the Wujing Power Plant, had heard rumors that the State Council had issued a directive stipulating that "all factory apprentices should earn 64 yuan" and were therefore very upset that the shipyard was not implementing this regulation. Apparently, they were also under the mistaken impression that the salary adjustment of 1955 — which raised their salary from 38 yuan to 49 yuan — was caused by a previous disturbance they initiated. Topping this off, in 1955, two veterans who were sergeants in the PLA came to the shipyard and received the "rumored" 64 yuan, precisely the sum stipulated in the State Council Regulation. Many of the striking veterans were of the same rank. This is why factory officials claimed that the strike was for 64 yuan.[153]

The second cause of the shipyard disturbance was also widespread among other urban veterans we have seen. Even though a large percentage of them were assigned employment, their job assignments in factories did not take into account their individual circumstances and qualifications, such as skill, heath, or disability. Management simply took the list of veterans, read off names, and assigned them to the different workshops. Those who had learned a skill in the army (radio operators, technicians, repairmen) and those who were "sick and weak" were upset at the lack of consideration for their individual circumstances. When factory management and unions failed to respond to other individual and family-related problems — housing for their family, wives in the countryside who wanted to come to Shanghai, work safety issues — veterans came to feel they had no recourse but to take riskier political action.[154]

Finally, the report indicated that veterans themselves shared some of the blame. Like many of the veterans we observed in Chapter 2, shipyard veterans were convinced that, having succeeded in war and ushering in the revolution, they were tried-and-true patriots. Others, having endured far less in their eyes, were not as deserving of high status. According to the investigation, shipyard veterans refused to acknowledge their factory mentors as their political equals and showed their disrespect in many ways. Some talked back and shouted in class; many arrived late. When asked for a reason for their tardiness, the veterans replied, "What qualifications do you have to control us?" "Why are *you* so arrogant and proud? When we were in the army you weren't even born!" Their teachers took umbrage and complained publicly that veterans were "old, uncultured, stupid, and can't learn anything." Aware of their power over them in the workplace, skilled workers mocked them: "You all had level eight in the army and had a gun, but here you are level one and will never make grade eight."[155]

At least at the Jiangnan Shipyard, these views were not as bluntly expressed by management, but the investigation revealed that the shipyard management did not give high priority to helping veterans adjust to civilian life, particularly the nitty-gritty issues such as housing, family, and salary. The shipyard's party committee and leading officials (like those in other factories[156]) "don't know anything about veterans' situation and problems, rarely convene meetings with them, and do not pass on city government directives . . . they believe that if they step in to solve one person's problem someone else will object, so they prefer to not solve anyone's." Absent party committee intervention, lower-level factory management and veterans' old nemesis, personnel departments, felt they had a free hand to treat veterans as they saw fit. It was the shipyard's personnel department that refused to post in workshops a rather discriminatory citywide directive stating that the increase in apprentice's salary from 37 *yuan* to 49 *yuan* was *only* for middle school graduates (which most rural veterans were not), claiming that "there was no need; whoever wants to create a disturbance, let them go ahead." It was also the personnel department that routinely denied veterans' requests for more food or housing (according to veterans, food was so meager they had to buy gruel on the street from vendors). A typical response to these requests was, "If you are not happy with the factory's policies, go ahead and leave; the factory will be just fine with or without you."[157] The report concluded by emphasizing the need for more transparency in the factory and the need to trust that workers would act responsibly with information. Had management let workers know about regulations and decisions (especially about salary), the entire incident would probably have been prevented. One veteran, Wang Guihua of the steel workshop, confirmed this view:

I'll tell you what's on our minds: Who doesn't like more money? When we hear that veterans with the same rank [in the army] get different salaries we naturally get upset. Still, when talking to management no one dares to openly explain our concerns, so people then fault the management and complaints about cadres grow. If we had meetings where such issues were discussed openly, this whole thing would not have happened.[158]

There is little evidence, however, that management adopted policies that allowed veterans access to state directives about key issues that affected many veterans' lives. Despite the assurances of *People's Daily* that veterans' salary and rank problems were basically solved after they were "discovered" in the mid-1950s investigations,[159] veterans continued to press for higher salaries and converting temporary and apprenticeship positions into permanent positions throughout the late 1950s and early 1960s, usually in the form of big-character posters and work slowdowns.[160] Most of these efforts, however, were fragmented and solutions were stopgap measures. For some, relief came only during the Cultural Revolution, when ambitious veterans such as Wang Hongwen and Geng Jinzhang, leaders of the General Workers Headquarters in Shanghai, mounted a successful attack against the municipal leadership, which was composed of non-veteran officials active in underground CCP unions in the 1930s and 1940s. As among non-veteran contract and temporary workers, long-standing demands for permanent employment, job training classes, and salary hikes poured forth,[161] leading to countercharges that veterans were not really interested in revolution per se, just practical issues like money and self-interest (i.e., "economism"). There is some indication that veterans did benefit from the political upheaval and the attacks on the civilian-dominated CCP: an August 1967 municipal directive from the newly installed "Shanghai Revolutionary Committee" stipulated that "creating permanent jobs for apprentices and veterans" would henceforth be done on a "routine" basis.[162]

But discontent still simmered. Even as Red Guards were parading around the country wearing military fatigues pretending that they were the little soldiers of Chairman Mao, veterans still faced many of the discriminatory employment policies they had dealt with in the past, only now without the assistance of Civil Affairs, which was embroiled in the Cultural Revolution. Only officers with the rank of lieutenant colonel and above were placed in government jobs and enterprises; those below this rank were sent back to wherever they came from, with the exception of those who were sent to work on various "National Defense Construction" projects in border provinces. Some were dispatched to secure harbors, train stations, and underground passages in streets. Facing difficult employment prospects, some military units, with the support of regional PLA commanders, refused to demobilize (in Guangdong). In the early 1970s on Hainan Island, veterans who had been sent to work on large construction projects were told that they would have to remain there unless they were evaluated as top workers. Upset at this prospect, some 6,000 veterans, organized in 70 separate units, took off and formed autonomous, self-regulating communities in the mountain region. Hippie-style, they lived off the land and were generally free from higher-level political controls; the police were aware of this but turned a blind eye; many policemen had themselves been veterans, as we have seen. According to reports, other persecuted individuals joined these veteran groups, which worried Public Security officials in the area.[163]

Most veterans, however, did not have access to the sorts of tropical fruits that grew on Hainan or the advantage of the island's distance from urban centers, where the police were located in far greater numbers. Discrimination continued unabated. According to ROC intelligence reports on Fujian Province (where they had particularly good access, owing to the province's proximity to Taiwan), in May 1972 in Nan'an County, Fujian, a group of ten veterans burned communal granaries and stole weapons from the local militia; in Shunde County, Guangdong, disgruntled veterans burned down part of their factory in the middle of the night because of a dispute with fellow (non-veteran) workers. At the Shunde factory, there were more than 1,000 workers but only ten veterans, and all ten were said to have been unhappy with their salaries and had a difficult time adjusting to the work environment after their military service.[164]

In addition to the usual, more everyday forms of discrimination, veterans faced yet another, more political one during the Cultural Revolution. As the PLA was drawn into factional struggles during the Cultural Revolution and was involved in both "supporting the left" in its early stages and then suppressing it later on, PLA veterans could not but be "tainted" by association with unpopular policies. Veterans were aware of this. In Jiangxi Province, the PLA's support of the left was so unpopular that veterans who were being discharged were warned by their units that locals might "take revenge" upon them if they encountered them on the road back home.[165]

Whatever prestige may have accrued for the PLA in the previous years of intensive propaganda (beginning in 1963–1964) seemed to be lost during these years of intra-party and civil–military conflict. For most veterans, however, the transition between pre–Cultural Revolution political dynamics and the Cultural Revolution was not very sharp. Very few enjoyed a "trickle down" effect from efforts to raise the status of the PLA in the 1960s, but this was not very different from their failure to claim a political or economic dividend from the PLA's successes in the wars against Japan, the Kuomintang, or the United States during the 1950s. The vulnerability of claims to higher political and social status on the basis of military service, even during the Cultural Revolution when the PLA was a dominant political force, contrasts sharply with the experience of workers during this period. To the extent that veterans enjoyed a boost in status, it was only thanks to their post-1949 class identity as "workers," long the heroic class in Marxist political theory and among Marxist- and Christian-inspired theorists of more symbolic forms of "self-sacrificial" violence (such as promoting a cult of "proletarian martyrs") in the course of political struggle;[166] veterans as such are entirely absent from the corpus of Marxist political theory as historical "actors" in their own right. Backed by strong organizations, many workers secured better benefits and felt that their status had improved. Miners at the Anyuan coal mine in Jiangxi, an important site in the Red Guard's "revolutionary tourism" of the period, commented that during that period, unlike today, they were proud to be workers and felt appreciated. A key indicator of this rise in status was the simple fact of women's agreeing to marry them.[167] Ironically, this sort of class-based "revolutionary citizenship" did not extend to veterans, even though they represented the institution that was, by any objective account, most responsible for the Communist victory. In the next chapter I take a look at the organizations in the state that were supposed to prevent this outcome, why they failed, and what sorts of political and social arrangements seem most conducive to promoting veterans' interests, rights, and identity as valued citizens in society.

NOTES

1. Even though "fair shake" is usually used informally in the sense of an "equitable bargain or opportunity," the term does appear on the mission statement of the U.S. Equal Opportunity Employment Commission's website. "Everyone should get a fair shake, and EEOC works to make it happen."
2. SA A20-1-109, 4.
3. *Shandong xingzheng gongbao*, March 24, 1955, 12.
4. QA 48-2-71 (1955), 35.
5. Ibid., 38.
6. SMA B168-1-615 (1954), 52.
7. Ibid., 53.
8. SMA B168-1-3 (1953), 10.
9. SMA A71-2-492 (1957), 10.
10. SMA B168-1-615 (1954), 52; SMA B168-1-619 (1955), 49.
11. Frederic Wakeman Jr., "'Cleanup': The New Order in Shanghai," 24, 38.
12. SMA B168-1-628, 101. The same phenomenon was noted in Liaoning Province as well. The Provincial Civil Affairs gazetteer mentions units that hired people "from society" instead of veterans. See *Liaoning sheng zhi: minzheng zhi* (Shenyang: Liaoning kexue jishu chubanshe, 1996), 106.

13. SMA A71-2-492 (1956), 12.

14. SMA B2-2-23 (1955), 19.

15. SMA B98-1-98 (1956), 14.

16. SMA B168-1-619 (1955), 49.

17. SMA B127-1-358 (1963), 36.

18. SMA B168-1-615 (1954), 53.

19. Larry Logue, "Union Veterans," 433.

20. SMA B168-1-628, 41–42.

21. SMA B127-1-1036 (1960), 18.

22. DDA 11-7-399 (1963), 29.

23. SMA B168-2-132, 5.

24. SMA B168-3-131 (November 1967), 22.

25. *Liaoning sheng zhi; minzheng zhi*, 112.

26. "Bixu jiuzheng paichi fuyuan junren de cuowu zuofa," *People's Daily*, August 3, 1955. Since this letter was printed in the paper, the Zhejiang Personnel Bureau responded two months later with a six-line response that admitted no error but promised to do a better job in hiring veterans. See "Piping jianyi de fanying," *People's Daily*, October 10, 1955. According to a report by the PLA's General Political Department, there were personnel departments that were unwilling to accept a single veteran (*yi lü buxu xishou fuyuan junren*). They either said that "they never received orders" or said "OK" but then raised the qualification level, knowing veterans could not pass. See SMA B2-2-50, 2.

27. SMA B2-2-50 (1956), 2.

28. SMA B168-1-605 (1952), 78.

29. SMA B168-1-611 (1953), 124.

30. SMA B127-1-869 (1965), 10.

31. SMA B168-1-607 (1952), 71; SMA B168-1-615 (1954), 52.

32. SMA B168-1-619 (1955), 52.

33. SMA B168-1-623 (1955), 30.

34. SMA B168-1-619, 52. According to one 1955 report, administrative units were expected to reduce staff by 40–50 percent. See SMA B168-1-623, 30.

35. SMA B168-1-641 (1958), 15.

36. *Shandong xingzheng gongbao*, March 24, 1955, 12.

37. SA A1-2-516 (1957), 21.

38. SMA B168-1-619 (1955), 49.

39. SMA B127-1-358 (1963), 38.

40. SMA B168-1-628 (1957), 74; SMA B168-1-633 (1957), 80; QA 48-2-141 (1957), 13.

41. SMA B168-1-619 (1955), 52.

42. SMA B168-1-649, (1960), 20.

43. Ibid., 21.

44. SMA B168-1-645 (1959), 70; SMA B168-1-628 (1956), 74.

45. SMA B168-1-623, 30.

46. SMA B168-1-605 (1952), 78.

47. SMA B168-1-619, 53.

48. SMA B168-1-615, 53. According to a survey of 2,105 veterans in Shanghai in 1952, 8.5 percent were CCP members and 16.2 percent were in the CYL. See SMA B168-1-607, 53. In later years, many more veterans were CCP or CYL members. In 1957, they constituted roughly 42 percent, and according to a survey of 3,610 veterans in Shanghai in 1960, 60.7 percent were in the CYL and 22 percent were in the party. See SMA B1-2-1958, 24; B121-1-838, 59.

49. SMA B168-1-628, 43–44.

50. "Qunzhong husheng," *People's Daily*, October 19, 1956.

51. SMA B168-1-666 (1964), 5.

52. SMA B121-1-869 (1965), 10.

53. SMA B168-1-611 (1953), 122–23.

54. SMA B168-1-3 (1953), 10.

55. QA 48-2-141 (1957), 13.

56. SMA B168-1-666, 7–9.

57. James Matthews, "Clock Towers for the Colonized," 264–65, 268–69.

58. Adrienne Israel, "Ex-Servicemen at the Crossroads," 361–62.

59. Mary Frost Jessup, *The Public Reaction to the Returned Serviceman after World War I*, 10, 16–18, 21, 32.

60. Desmond Morton and Glenn Wright, *Winning the Second Battle,* 80.

61. University of Chicago Committee on Human Development, *The American Veteran Back Home*, 98, 149, 163; "Extracts from Letter by a Veterans Employment Representative," May 28, 1945. National Archives, RG 160, Box 241, 292.

62. See Alfred Shuetz, "The Homecomer," 375.

63. Jennifer Brooks, *Defining the Peace*, 17; Henry Ramos, *The American G.I. Forum,* 2–4.

64. Jessup, *Public Reaction*, 38.

65. David Onkst, "First a Negro . . . Incidentally a Veteran."

66. Florence Roisman, "National Ingratitude," 149–56.

67. David R. Segal, *Recruiting for Uncle Sam,* 89.

68. John Spano, "Johnny Got His Gun, but Now He Can't Find a Job," *Los Angeles Times*, May 21, 2006, B3.

69. SMA B168-1-623 (1955), 30.

70. In the U.S. case, both Union Army veterans and veterans of WWII were suspected of violent and criminal tendencies, moral depravity, and anti-democratic impulses because of their service in the military. See David Gerber, "Heroes and Misfits," 547; Also see the cartoons by Bill Mauldin in his *Back Home*, 54, 155. For the Civil War, see Logue, "Union Veterans," 413.

71. van Ells, *To Hear Only Thunder Again*, 58–63; Garton, *The Cost of War: Australians Return*, 222–23; Reese, *Homecoming Heroes,* 142–43.

72. SMA B168-1-633 (1957), 85.

73. Jessup, *Public Reaction*, 8–9.

74. SMA B168-1-600 (1951), 110. Veterans also wandered around the city while they waited for a job. Described as "very anxious" during this period, district officials complained that veterans were "spreading backward talk" and engaging in illicit sexual relations. See SMA B2-2-23 (1955), 128.

75. Morton and Wright, *Winning the Second Battle*, 117.

76. SMA B168-1-607 (1952), 49.

77. *Minzheng jianbao*, December 21, 1956, 87; SMA B1-2-1958 (1957), 21.

78. SMA B168-1-645 (1959), 24.

79. SMA B168-1-633 (1957), 79; SMA B168-1-628, 88. A 1957 report noted large discrepancies in the same work unit between firms under one ministerial authority (*xitong*) and between different firms and *xitongs*. See SMA B168-1-633 (1957), 81.

80. QA 48-2-96 (1957), 51–52.

81. SMA B168-1-628, 89.

82. SMA B168-1-645, 22.

83. SMA B127-1-1036, 18.

84. SMA B168-1-645 (1959), 67.

85. SMA B1-2-1958 (1957), 28.

86. SMA B123-3-1442 (1956), 5.

87. SMA B168-1-633 (1957), 97.

88. SMA B163-2-494 (1957), 81–82.

89. QA 48-2-109, 78–79.

90. SMA B168-1-645 (1959), 68.

91. SMA B121-1-838, 24.

92. SMA B168-1-633, 89.

93. QA 48-2-96, 50.

94. QA 48-2-98, 67.

95. QA 48-2-141 (1957), 14.

96. QA 48-2-71 (1955) 37.

97. QA 48-2-105 (1957), 136–37.

98. SMA B1-2-1958, 29.

99. SMA B1681-645 (1959), 22; *People's Daily*, November 29, 1955.

100. SMA B168-1-645, 24.

101. SMA B168-1-628, 119–20.

102. SMA B168-1-628 (1956), 30.

103. SMA B123-3-1442, 6.

104. SMA B127-1-820 (1956), 24–25. For Qingpu, see QA 48-2-98 (1956), 67.

105. SMA B98-1-98, 14.

106. Ibid.

107. SMA B168-1-645, 24.

108. See SMA B168-1-628 (1956), 45–46; SMA B168-1-517, 139.

109. SMA B168-1-645 (1959), 65.

110. SMA B168-1-649 (1960), 31.

111. SMA B168-1-649, 30–31.

112. SMA B98-1-98 (1955), 14–15.

113. SMA B127-1-358 (1963), 37.

114. This meant that if a veteran was an apprentice in 1950, joined the military for five years, and then returned to the factory, his salary should be based on five "work years."

115. QA 48-2-98 (1956), 67.

116. QA 48-2-141 (1957), 14.

117. *People's Daily*, November 29, 1956.

118. SMA B168-1-628, 42

119. *Minzheng jianbao*, November 19, 1956, 81.

120. SMA B168-1-633, 79.

121. SMA B123-3-1442 (1956), 5.

122. SMA B127-1-1036 (1960), 16–18. This was also noted in Liaoning Province. The Civil Affairs gazetteer notes that "some units refuse to take veterans back after their service even though they came from there. They are treated the same as ordinary idle labor (*xiansan laodong li*)." If rehired, their salaries were lower than they should have been. See *Liaoning sheng zhi: minzheng zhi*, 110.

123. SMA B168-1-645, 31.

124. SMA B127-1-358 (1963), 37.

125. Roisman, "National Ingratitude," 105–8.

126. See SMA B127-1-811, 5.

127. *People's Daily*, May 5, 1957.

128. SMA A71-2-492 (1957), 10.

129. SMA B168-1-628, 3.

130. SMA B168-1-628 (1956), 21; SMA B168-1-628, 3; SMA A71-2-492, 20.

131. SMA B168-1-630 (1956), 11.

132. SMA B168-1-645 (1959), 31.

133. SMA B121-1-838, 25.

134. QA 48-2-105 (1957), 140.

135. See Sally Engle Merry, *Getting Justice and Getting Even: Legal Consciousness among Working-Class Americans*.

136. See Ron Aminzade, Jack Goldstone, and Elizabeth Perry, "Leadership Dynamics and Dynamics of Contention," 225.

137. See "Renzhen jiancha anzhi fuyuan junren de gongzuo," *People's Daily*, August 21, 1955; "Piping de fanying," *People's Daily*, October 16, 1955.

138. Li Shumin, "Linshi gong, heshile?" *People's Daily*, July 4, 1956.

139. "Dui piping de fanying," *People's Daily*, January 28, 1957.

140. "Fuyuan junren yao hao hao anpai shenghuo," *People's Daily*, May 9, 1955.

141. SMA B168-1-619, 70.

142. SMA B168-1-632, 98.

143. The letter can be found in SMA B168-1-628, 162.

144. SMA B127-1-21 (1952), 3, 7

145. "Jianshao chuli renmin laixin de cengci," *People's Daily*, September 6, 1956.

146. *Shandong xingzheng gongbao*, December 1955, 19.

147. Elizabeth Perry, "The Shanghai Strike Wave of 1957," 1–27.

148. *Guangdong sheng zhi: minzheng zhi*, 94. Petitioning was also noted in the Liaoning Civil Affairs gazetteer. See *Liaoning sheng zhi: minzheng zhi*, 106.

149. SA A1-2-516 (1957), 26.

150. Ibid.

151. See "Jiangnan zaochuan chang fuyuan junren naoshi shijian jiancha baogao," SMA B168-1-628, 140–56.

152. For a detailed history and exposition of labor–management relations at the Jiangnan Shipyard during the 20th century, see Mark W. Frazier, *The Making of the Chinese Industrial Workplace: State, Revolution and Labor Management.*

153. "Jiangnan," 143.

154. Ibid., 144.

155. Ibid., 145.

156. According to a 1956 report, "very many work units do not even know how many veterans they have." Veterans complained that the factory had never convened a meeting of its veterans, even on Army Day (August 1). See SMA A71-2-492 (1956), 20.

157. "Jiangnan," 148.

158. Ibid., 154.

159. *People's Daily*, November 29, 1956.

160. SMA B168-1-666 (1963), 9.

161. SMA B168-3-131 (1967), 11; SMA B112-5-256 (1968), 6. On the wave of economism during the Cultural Revolution in Shanghai, see Perry and Li, *Proletarian Power*, Chapter 4.

162. SMA B227-1-1, 4; SMA B82-2-1137 (1969), 6.

163. These reports were gathered by ROC intelligence agencies. See Zhou Zi-qiang (ed.), *Gongfei junshi wenti lunji*, 209–10.

164. Ibid., 210.

165. ROC National Security Agency, Intelligence Analysis Board, "Dui gong-fei muqian xinbing zhengji ji laobing tuiwu qingkuang zhi fenxi," (1968), Call #590.83/7231, n.p.

166. See Jesse Goldhammer, *The Headless Republic: Sacrificial Violence in Modern French Thought*, 112–14.

167. Elizabeth Perry, "Anyuan: Mining China's Revolutionary Tradition," Harvard University, December 1, 2006.

5

Stuck in the State's Cement and Falling through Its Cracks: Veterans in Policy and Bureaucracy

Support for claims to higher status, respect, and support on the basis of military service does not happen in a coincidental manner or in a vacuum, even if this service is deemed highly patriotic; there is little that naturally predisposes people to respect veterans (or appreciate the sacrifices of soldiers' families), let alone consider them worthy of receiving exclusive benefits. There is also nothing natural in politicians or civilian leaders actually fulfilling promises made to soldiers in the sometimes pell-mell rush to war, or even during peacetime when state priorities shift to other matters. And there is no guarantee that state programs designed to boost citizens' appreciation for martial qualities or the legitimacy of a given war, as we have already seen in the previous chapter, will be successful, even if implemented.

But even as the outcomes of veteran policies will always depend on a host of other factors, the very idea of a "veteran policy" has remained fairly constant over time and place. Given the centrality of war in human civilization, and especially since the advent of the citizen–soldier after the French Revolution, no government has permitted itself to adopt an entirely hands-off approach to the problems and challenges facing demobilized soldiers. Given veterans' experience with the trauma of war, skill with weaponry, and exposure to the power of organized collectives, politicians often have been wary of returned warriors even as they have expressed gratitude for their service. Whether policies have been designed to reward, rehabilitate, co-opt, disarm, or disperse, veterans—as a direct result of their experiences—have been forced to deal with such policies from the state or a leader (such as Caesar or Augustus) in one way or another. Unlike other social groups such as women, workers, the poor, and ethnic minorities, who often have to clamor and mobilize significant resources to get official attention, veterans, magnet-like, invite attention. In the United

States, various programs for veterans and war widows have been in place since the early years of the republic and have expanded after every major war, well before other groups (such as workers, the poor, and the "ordinary" elderly) began to receive some form of assistance from the government.

Despite sustained attention to veterans in the form of policies, laws, and regulations, political history is replete with examples of governments that got it generally right vis-à-vis veterans (that is, veterans returned home and were able to become productive members of society, form families, and enjoy a measure of respect) as well as those whose policies toward veterans proved disastrously wrong, with the fallout reverberating around the globe. For example, in post-WWI Germany, the drafters of the Weimar Constitution mistakenly prohibited the awarding of military medals and decorations. It was also a mistake to refuse to build a monument to the war dead[1] and force disabled veterans to apply for their benefits through the very same unpopular bureaucracy that served more ordinary welfare cases, since it left veterans with the sense that their sacrifices were unappreciated (especially as many other groups claimed to have been victimized by the war). Partly as a result of this, many veterans participated in the *Freikorps* and other reactionary political parties that, at least rhetorically, recognized their past. Along similar lines, in 1930 it was a mistake to cut back pension rates, raise eligibility requirements, and tighten administrative procedures in an attempt to balance the budget when revenues declined after the Depression.[2] Bad law, to be sure, was not solely a German phenomenon. In the United States, the first Pension Act of 1819 was known for its "ambiguous provisions": Congress did not even define the composition of the Continental Army or the precise meaning of "reduced circumstances" and "in need of assistance from his country." This produced a "flood" of petitions from veterans, who devised all sorts of means to prove their neediness, in addition to hundreds of imposters, deserters, and even men who had hired substitutes. Fraud rocked the program from the beginning and continued for two years as various middlemen stepped in to "assist" the elderly veterans in filling out the forms in the proper way (for a cut of the pension). Citizens endured the sad spectacle of aged Revolutionary War veterans marching to courts in their old uniforms, accompanied by martial music; the resulting scandal made American citizens and public officials very wary of welfare programs for the next 40 years, when the Civil War dramatically changed the political and social landscape of the country.[3] After toppling Saddam Hussein, it was a blunder to dismantle the Iraqi Army without making any provisions for its veterans, many of whom later joined the insurgency against the American occupation.

But governments can also get it right, particularly if they have the desire and wherewithal to learn from past mistakes.[4] As noted in Chapter 2, the

Canadian government learned from its post-WWI errors and introduced much-improved legislation during WWII. The GI Bill in the United States, particularly its education provisions (but housing far less so), has been given credit not only for smoothing over what might have been a difficult readjustment period but also for building the foundations for a strong middle class, civic activism, and decades of economic growth. Long-term beneficiaries, Suzanne Mettler found, "gained an especially strong sense that government had made a difference in their lives, and they were more likely . . . to feel that it was their responsibility to give something back to American society."[5] (Even today, members of the American Veterans of Foreign Wars outvote their fellow citizens by almost a 2:1 ratio; some 91 percent vote in presidential races.[6]) The GI Bill was a product of political learning: politicians did not relish the thought of witnessing veterans from yet another successful war building "Hoovervilles" in downtown Washington, as was the case during the 1932 Bonus March. Germany also learned from its interwar errors. In post-WWII West Germany, the government, mindful of the legacy of failures of the Weimar Constitution, unanimously passed the Federal War Victims Benefit Law. Buoyed by a strong economy (after 1953) as well as the Cold War atmosphere that "at least blurred the old promilitary/antimilitary dichotomy that had divided German society since the foundation of the German Empire," veterans from WWII have been very quiet politically, supportive of democracy, and generally operating within the confines of veterans organizations and political parties.[7]

While these are better-known examples of policy successes and failures, they still highlight the political significance of getting policy right or, if budgets are strained, at least making a determined effort to pay veterans "emotional compensation" in forms of civic rituals, medals, and parades. This is not easy: wars produce very many victims and heroes. Who is the most deserving of financial compensation from government entitlement programs? Whichever way governments decide these matters will roil some who may feel just as entitled and, in democracies, vote. As with any entitlement program, people are bound to dispute the worthiness or "deservedness" of the recipients;[8] after any successful venture, many will claim credit for having sacrificed for it and demand rewards for their efforts.[9]

To the extent that such a societal consensus can be achieved—and we have already seen in the last chapter how elusive this can be when wars are contested and political legitimacy is weak—governments have to figure out how to best implement policies. This brings matters regarding veterans' treatment by state officials and fellow citizens into the realm of administration and public policy. For instance, should benefits for veterans be administered through local governments or branches of the central bureaucracy? Should benefits be grounded in statutes or administrative regulations? Should courts have jurisdiction over veterans' claims? Even in the best of circumstances, decisions about entitlements, whether focusing on the basic issue of worthiness or the means to move monies from one place to another, will rarely be optimal, particularly since veterans, more than other groups, can bring to bear the emotive power of wartime sacrifice, of having a "moral right" to benefits as their "just reward" for service, an "obligation" and not a "gratuity," as American Revolutionary and Civil War veterans and Australian WWI and Soviet WWII veterans all put it, with much success.[10]

Assuming that central state leaders were serious, if not necessarily unselfish, in their effort to integrate, mollify, honor, or defuse veterans, what sorts of "variables" (as social scientists like to put it) would best achieve their goal? Scholars of public policy and law have long recognized the difficulties in implementing central government programs (which, in the Chinese case, would be State Council directives, bolstered by Civil Affairs and Propaganda bureaucracies) aimed at raising veterans' social, political, and employment status. In the early 1970s, for instance, several studies on policy implementation in the United States arrived at pessimistic conclusions about the ability of the federal government to "get its way," since most all programs could be "vetoed" at some point on their way to the local level.[11] This pessimism was also echoed in law-centered studies of the Supreme Court's impact on social change.[12] Several subsequent studies, however, including some in the China field, noted that implementation success or failure can vary quite widely across programs (changing racial attitudes or preference for male children is different from enforcing accounting changes in firms, for example) as well as political entities;[13] local officials in China often have the discretion to cherry-pick which laws or regulations they enforce more seriously than others, depending on their popularity among villagers.[14] Here is not the place to review this vast literature, but it is worthwhile to take a moment to point to several factors that seem to be the *most conducive* to effective policy implementation, as summarized by Paul Sabatier and others.[15] These points can serve as a loose frame of reference for the rest of the chapter:

- Clear and consistent objectives. The law should not be ambiguous and "implementing officials" should all be aware of what the final goal is.
- The "target group" of the policy should be *positively constructed*. People should associate the group with positive images such as "deserving," public-spirited, and honest.
- Adequate "causal theory." Officials must understand how A (the policy) will lead to B (the result). If the goal is "racial equality" and the policy is "school integration," the superintendent of the school system

must be able to construct a causal narrative as to why and how A will lead to B.

- The implementation process, or "implementation structure," should "enhance compliance by implementing officials and target groups." Local officials need incentives to comply and sanctions if they do not. To this we might add "the certainty of detection" as a reasonably good predictor of compliance. The knowledge that one will likely be caught enhances compliance, even if the sanctions are not particularly severe.[16]

- Committed and skillful implementing officials. Since local discretion is "unavoidable," national policies and law will be difficult to enforce unless people at the bottom, or "street-level bureaucrats," have sufficient resources, are competent, and have "bought into" the program.

- Consistent support of executives and interest groups. Because implementation often takes a long time, groups that support the policy (assuming that the political system allows such groups to form) and political elites cannot allow their attention to wane. Every law and policy requires *allies in society and in the state*; if not, the chances of successful implementation decline significantly.

- Changes in the socioeconomic conditions do not undermine political support or the causal theory behind the program. For instance, it will be more difficult to enforce anti-poverty programs during a time of rising wages and a booming stock market than during a depression.

If we can consider policies designed to improve the status of veterans an "entitlement program" and we subsequently discover quite a few problems in it, the issue of policy or regulatory effectiveness springs to mind as one plausible cause. In other words, is it possible to attribute the weakness of veterans in politics and society to an underlying problem of *poor or inadequate policies and administration*? Since it was not always the case that veterans in the West had political clout but, rather, gained power and respect in a gradual fashion—one need only compare the subsistence rights of Revolutionary War veterans to those enjoyed by veterans of the second Iraq War—it is possible that better policies could have made a big difference.

At first glance, this possibility would seem rather unlikely. Veterans in China appear to have reaped the benefits of sustained state attention, political support at the highest levels, very positive social construction in official documents, bureaucratic attention (two sections of all bureaus of Civil Affairs dealt with veterans), and an economy that did not value competition and profit, thereby eliminating one of the main rationales for Western employers to avoid hiring veterans. Moreover, during the 1950s and 1960s there were obvious examples of policy successes; implementation was never smooth, but the central state, to its credit, was able to accomplish a great deal in society, including eliminating many communicable diseases, vastly improving dismal infant and maternal mortality rates, extending life expectancy, industrializing on a very large scale, and improving the status of women through implementation of a new Marriage Law in 1950. This is exactly what makes the problems with veterans all the more puzzling from an administrative perspective: how is it possible that the PRC met these formidable challenges but at the same time frequently failed to improve the social status of its own veterans and successfully implement equitable pay policies or "preferential treatment" in hiring, let alone prevent several thousand suicides among them, as we will see in the next chapter?

As it turns out, policy- and administration-related problems were close to the core of veterans' difficult predicament, as we will see in this chapter. To gain a far better sense of why this was the case, we have to adopt two perspectives: (1) a worm's-eye view of what happened in the administrative "trenches" and district offices of the state (for example, what happened *inside* bureaus of Civil Affairs and how "preferential treatment" regulations were actually worded)[17] and (2) a more panoramic, bird's-eye view of veteran administration in comparative perspective. If we can roughly identify different outcomes in veterans' status, it behooves us to take a look at the more successful cases to see what made a significant difference. To briefly preview the main argument, China stands out as one of the only countries in the world—including regimes that are structurally similar to it, such as the Soviet Union, Vietnam, pre-democratic Taiwan, and other authoritarian states—that experienced major wars but never established a nationwide or provincial-level veterans organization, either independent, linked to, or fully integrated into the state. Strikingly, China does have nationwide organizations—for youth (the Communist Youth League), the disabled (China Disabled Persons Federation), women (the Women's Federation), labor (the Federation of Trade Unions), and overseas Chinese—just not for veterans, the "flesh and blood" of the revolution. The veterans committees that did exist were short-lived and were most always limited to veterans' *representatives*, duly vetted by the party.

THE ORIGINS OF THE CRACK:
VETERANS IN BUREAUS OF CIVIL AFFAIRS

One of the central tenets of theories of modernization is that as societies industrialize, urbanize, and become more bureaucratically and socially "complex," functional roles within society and government will become more specialized and less diffuse: specialist agencies and individuals, rather than an all-powerful village chief, for example, will handle matters under their assigned jurisdiction. This was a vision of "modern" government that successive Chinese regimes (as well as modernizing states in Japan, Thailand, Turkey, and others) aspired to, if not always achieved; both the Nationalist government and the Communists built extensive, specialist bureaucracies with administrative jurisdiction over different sorts of industries, populations, and legal matters (multiple levels of appellate courts, types of police forces, etc.). For reasons that are still obscure, this modernizing wave bypassed Civil Affairs: few bureaucracies anywhere accumulated as many diverse, seemingly disconnected, roles as it did. (Even in the 21st century, Civil Affairs has retained jurisdiction over many of the same affairs it handled back in the early 1950s.) Equally problematic, veterans were touted (by the media and in political campaigns) as charismatic exemplars of wartime heroism, sacrifice, and devotion to the revolutionary cause. But, as Max Weber noted, the imperatives of bureaucracy (organization, routine, and classification) tend to be antithetical to those of charisma: how can a war hero remain a hero in the eyes of others if he or she is required to fill out forms and apply for financial aid and a job that carries low status?

As a bureaucracy that was not involved in deciding or implementing key economic and political decisions (such as Energy, Finance, Industry or the State Planning Commission[18]), Civil Affairs has not been the subject of intensive study by Western analysts. Few bureaucracies, however, were as involved in more mundane and unspectacular bureaucratic interactions with millions of ordinary people than Civil Affairs. The category of "civil" (*min*) 民/ was interpreted diffusely: in addition to its overall responsibility for "ordinary" veterans, disabled revolutionary veterans, "revolutionary martyrs" (*lieshu*), and military dependents (*junshu*), Civil Affairs was responsible for, or involved in, a bizarre array of other activities whose only common denominator was that they were not considered "political" (*zheng*) or "legal" (*fa*). 政 . 法 These included resettling refugees; distributing welfare to the urban and rural poor; registering marriages and divorces (and mediating conflicts among feuding couples!); running orphanages, mental hospitals, senior homes, and village elections; rehabilitating opium addicts and prostitutes; providing relief to victims of natural disasters; supervising religious organizations and ethnic minority affairs; and even naming districts.[19] Within the overall jurisdiction of taking care of military-related personnel, however, there were two distinct sub-bureaucracies: *disabled* veterans, along with *lieshu* (martyr) and *junshu* (military) families, were assigned to the "Preferential Treatment" division (*youfu chu*), which dealt mainly in the distribution of economic assistance, while "ordinary" veterans were handed over to the "Resettlement" (*anzhi*) sub-bureaucracy. In terms of personnel, Civil Affairs clerks, some of whom were veterans, tended to have primary to middle school education, unlike more elite ministries that were dominated by technocrats and educated elites.[20] More problematically, within the PRC's administrative flow chart, Civil Affairs offices were nested *in* local governments and subordinate to the party committee or party secretary and were not vested with any authority to "order" the placement of a veteran in a job or release a veteran who was falsely accused and found himself in court.

Situating PLA veterans (and their dependents) in the same bureaucracy that handled other urban poor—as "welfare" cases—did not bode well for their status in society or for their sense that their martial contributions would be appreciated by other state officials as bona fide contributions. Administrative problems in Civil Affairs offices were noted early on. As in many welfare systems, early PRC efforts to saves the lives of the urban poor by distributing free rice or by granting small sums of money were riddled with mismanagement and fraud. In Qingpu, veterans bitterly complained that Civil Affairs officials helped out only those who made a big stink (*naode xiong jiejue le, bunao de bu jiejue le*) rather than "honest people" who merited assistance, frequently ignored State Council directives, and did not even look at their personal dossiers when assigning them to jobs, rendering moot any mention of particularly meritorious service.[21] In Beijing, Civil Affairs officials, many of them new to their jobs, were criticized for giving away excessive amounts of aid, using their personal discretion to "take revenge" upon certain people, being easily swayed by tales of woe, or acting far too "bureaucratically," that is, not handling welfare distribution on a case-by-case basis but, instead, according to simplistic rules of thumb.[22] This was said to be the case even among Civil Affairs cadres who had been at their positions for several years: "Some cadres have worked for two years and still don't know anything about welfare policy." Even after high-level officials explained what the policy was, many low-level administrators "just didn't get it." When dealing with needy veterans, Civil Affairs officials were said to avoid differentiating between new recruits and veteran soldiers or between currently mobilized soldiers and veteran revolutionaries—everyone got the same amount.[23]

The extent of waste was such that work teams would be sent into urban neighborhoods to figure out how people were using their aid and how welfare rolls might be reduced. Reports indicated that these officials often acted quite harshly with all aid recipients, asking personal questions and requiring them to fill out extensive forms. In some areas, interviews succeeded in reducing the welfare roll by some 65 percent; on the other hand, PLA veterans and family members of mobilized soldiers (*junshu*) felt that they were unfairly investigated. (For more on the interactions between the state and *junshu*, see

Chapter 7.) Some thought that the price for receiving state assistance was too high. One family member of a veteran said, "It would be easier if we took down our honorary plaque (*guangrong pai*); that way we wouldn't have to deal with all this hassle."[24] Other reports complained that officials "investigate only to investigate" and did not bother to conduct "education" among those they were investigating.[25]

In other cases, however, the source of veterans' problems was not extensive state surveillance but just the opposite: getting lost in the shuffle between their military units and home. In Qingpu, a 1952 report complained that no one—not bureau officials or anyone representing the party committee—was on hand when officers returned to their communities; there were no parties for "returning heroes," no receptions, flowers, music, or the like. At the county seat, they were given minimal amounts of food and had to spend their own money to buy more.[26] A report by the East China Veterans Committee noted that in northern Anhui Province, veterans who returned from war were also ignored by district bureaucrats: they were not provided with housing; physicians and nurses at the district outpatient clinic refused to see them; and when everyone else was receiving "financial aid and agricultural tools," veterans were bypassed. The internally circulated report called this "incorrect" and called upon all government agencies to give them "the same treatment" (not better) that "the masses" got.[27]

Assessing responsibility for such problems as these is not easy. If we assume the best of local officials, that is, that they actually wanted to help veterans, it would not be unreasonable to suggest that the main cause was bureaucratic. Each of the items and services mentioned above was under the jurisdiction of separate agencies: Civil Affairs controlled welfare, not housing, and it did not have a stash of hoes and sickles. Given that veterans officially "belonged" to Civil Affairs, perhaps other officials simply were hoping that discharged veterans would go there to procure everything they needed. For their part, however, Civil Affairs officials were entirely dependent on other agencies' resources to assist veterans. Recognizing this fundamental weakness (also noted in American federal and municipal bureaucracies[28]), in 1960 the "Preferential Treatment" Division (*chu*) of the Shanghai Bureau of Civil Affairs noted, "The only way we can fulfill our duty is to rely upon the cooperation and concerted efforts of the relevant departments,"[29] but these often were not forthcoming. In 1963, an Interior Ministry clarification of aid eligibility approved emergency financial assistance for direct relatives of revolutionary martyrs and soldiers' families "when their work unit's aid is insufficient," but it drew the line at providing aid to veterans, who, as "employees," had to go through their work units for assistance. The only exception was for disabled revolutionary soldiers who had to support large families with many small children and were having an "especially hard time getting by."[30] Whether factory or county officials ever received or read these documents cannot be assumed—but from what we have seen thus far, veterans often were *not* seen as *full-fledged* employees who were worthy of receiving many benefits. In practice, this meant that enterprise leaders, township officials, and others perceived Civil Affairs (or Veterans Committees), and not themselves, as veterans' primary caretakers. Sensing this bureaucratic no-man's land, veterans were irate. A two-page, handwritten investigation of veterans in a leather factory found that they were "especially upset" with district-level Civil Affairs, who they believed assigned them to the leather factory "just to get us out of their office." Veterans said, "They told us, 'Give it a try!' so we did, but now we can't transfer back. They promised us a transfer, but broke the promise." The discrepancy between their experience and newspaper stories also irked them. "In the paper they always write that 'Veteran resettlement is going very well,' but that's false (*jia de*)! Bad news isn't published!" Another veteran said, "Capitalists are better off—if I had money I'd become one too." Yet another quipped, "I'm a free man" (*ziyouzhe*), since neither the factory nor Civil Affairs was concerned about him.[31]

In theory at least, Civil Affair's dependence on external organizations to fulfill their organizational mission should not have been an insurmountable problem. As we have seen in previous chapters, Civil Affairs officials often served as members of the interagency teams that investigated problems in veteran employment and in hiring discrimination, as well as with health care and suicide (see Chapter 6). But these interagency task forces were more the exception than the rule, since most of them were mandated by the State Council with specific instructions about their membership. In the ebb and flow of routine administration, coordination between Civil Affairs and its more powerful counterparts was never very good. In addition to its own problem of "just getting veterans out the door" when they appealed for help, internal Civil Affairs evaluations noted that both the "vertical" ties between district- and municipal-level officials and "horizontal" ones between Civil Affairs and its counterparts in Labor, Personnel, and Industry were problematic to the extent that there was virtually no bureau-initiated follow-through when a veteran was dispatched to a job. "Officials finish their job and then just relax" was a common complaint in internal reports and in veterans' public statements.[32]

Similar problems with Civil Affairs administration and intra-governmental cooperation were noted in rural areas. Even after seven years and multiple demobilizations—by 1956 there were roughly 50 veterans in every township—some counties did not even have a single Civil Affairs official whose task was to handle veteran resettlement, which can largely be explained by the vast scope of the Civil Affairs' administrative portfolio and the low priority assigned to this issue. When officials were assigned to this job, it was rarely full-time; turnover was quite high. Equally problematic, national-level reports indicated that Civil Affairs officials at the county level rarely "made the rounds" to subordinate administrative units at the township or village levels or to factories or government offices. The State Council mandated that "one or two Civil Affairs cadres must routinely go to the village" to investigate veterans' situations and "suggested" that one member of the township party committee or personnel department, preferably a veteran, be assigned to resettlement work; as things stood in 1956, most large organizations had only established *welfare* committees that distributed aid to military and martyr families.[33] But even if these policies were implemented—the word *suggest* probably did not instill much fear or provide an incentive for compliance—it would not have been enough. If even ten veterans in a township had problems, one part-time official could not have accomplished much.

The bureau's weak position vis-à-vis other organizations, as well as the perception among many party officials that veterans still "belonged" to it even after they became "employees," was confirmed in an August 1, 1955, investigation of veteran problems in Shanghai's Changshu District. This date was not coincidental: August 1 was "Army Day," the one day of the year when state and society were expected to reflect upon the military's contribution to "liberation." Led by Civil Affairs officials, the Changshu officials descended upon a factory to check up on its veterans. Cao Hongfa, the factory's party secretary, however, had other things on his mind. "We're too busy with the socialist transformation of industry," he said; veterans' problems were "trivial issues, Civil Affairs' matters." When the team returned to their offices, they wrote up a report and sent copies of it to other government agencies as well as to the factory director, but to no effect: "Nothing has been done and the situation is still very serious. During the investigation we spoke to him, but he doesn't show much concern about the problems."[34] In Qingpu, veterans also found themselves in bureaucratic no-man's land and complained, "There is not a single level of government that is concerned with veterans. If there's a problem, local officials say 'Go to Civil Affairs.' We go, but Civil Affairs says, 'Go to the township.' At the township they tell us to go to Civil Affairs again."[37] Perhaps in recognition of Civil Affairs' low status and lack of clout vis-à-vis hiring units and rural political leaders, in 1957 the State Council decided that, henceforth, personnel departments would handle the resettlement of sergeants, officers at the rank of lieutenant and above, skilled soldiers, and "soldiers who came from cities,"[36] a policy that clearly discriminated against the majority of veterans and divided veterans who shared similar interests—a very useful divide-and-rule strategy. As it was, veterans who were demobilized in different periods (1952–1955; 1955–1957; 1958–1962; 1962–1965) were subject to different salary policies, which, unsurprisingly, led to no small amount of frustration among them, particularly those veterans who actually fought (discharged between 1952 and 1957), whose salaries were lower than those discharged after 1958 but who had not fought.[37]

Even though Civil Affairs officials did not appear to have much sway with factories, unions, or rural political authorities, many veterans were still under the impression that a good word or letter from a Civil Affairs official, even a lowly section chief, could open the door to decent and better paying employment. But like many citizens who have to deal with street-level bureaucracies, red tape and unreturned letters were more common than forceful and effective interventions. In Qingpu, a letter from a veteran to the Resettlement Section chief complained that "other veterans" received work but that several letters that he wrote were never answered, causing him to feel "very worried." Another letter, also addressed to the section chief, was more direct:

> After we had a meeting of several veterans at the township, several of us decided to call you. We were all very worried and anxious at the time, so we really blew our tops when we spoke to you. The reasons we are so anxious are the following:
>
> 1) Even though we returned to the village with medical problems, and told our superiors about this, we were not assigned easier work.
> 2) We came back to the village to build our socialism, but because people in some areas despise us, no one is helping us [with our work]. Veterans have difficulties at home because of illnesses, and have a hard time with agricultural labor, so we have a hard time getting by.
> 3) We don't like the way the government is functioning. Higher-level party organizations talk very seriously about policy, but policies are not enforced; party members are the same: they don't go to meetings and don't implement party policies.

These veterans then called upon the section chief to help them get an education and apologized for calling him in a burst of anger. Before closing the letter with a note of gratitude to Chairman Mao, they also wondered if the section chief would "write a letter of introduction" if the veterans managed to find a job through their own efforts, and they expressed hope that he would help solve their problems. They added that it would be great if he would come see them, and if he didn't want to post a letter back, could "you just give it to the Chairman of the Township Peasant Association to pass on to us?" Similar themes emerged in another two-page letter requesting a job transfer: the section chief had not yet responded to previous letters; the veteran, owing to illness, "could not undertake hard physical labor," which depressed his income in the "to each according to his work" system. He concluded, "Please respond to my request very soon; I'm willing to go anywhere."[38] Responses to these sorts of complaints were unlikely to be positive, if only because Civil Affairs could not simply hand over jobs to veterans in organizations that were not directly under its jurisdiction, even if it wanted to.

Despite their pessimistic tone (befitting the genre), these letters do hint at another ally in veterans' quests for appropriate jobs and respect: the veterans in Qingpu met at a township Veterans Committee meeting. This was not an unusual occurrence in the 1950s. Veterans' party-vetted "representatives" led these committees, which were authorized at the township, district, county, provincial, and national levels, in a structure parallel to many other party and government organizations.[39] "Ordinary" veterans sometimes joined in as well. In factories, veterans might be allowed to organize a veterans' "small group" (*xiaozu*). At the national level, these meetings were somewhat of a big deal: the 1957 "All-China Veterans Work Meeting" was addressed by Marshal Peng Dehuai, and Premier Zhou Enlai popped in to schmooze with the attendees; in the audience were 16 provincial party secretaries (roughly half), 15 political commissars of military regions, and 28 officials from Civil Affairs and conscription offices.[40] More locally, veterans committees could have some impact; their members were active, writing to the media and doing the sort of "follow-up" work after resettlement that Civil Affairs officials neglected. Equally important, veterans committees succeeded in co-opting a certain number of veterans (and thus weakening their solidarity) and gave many the impression that veterans were a critical and highly valued regime constituency. At the same time, however, veterans committees existed in bureaucratic no-man's land and could not serve as a base for protecting or enhancing veterans' interests and status.[41] Like Civil Affairs, they had no supervisory authority over any other organization: their role was limited to "investigation," "summarizing resettlement work," hearing veterans' complaints, and conducting "political education" among them[42] and therefore were easily ignored at no cost; even their name was bureaucratically odd. Whereas other social groups had "federations" or "leagues," many of which have remained intact until today, only veterans had a "committee," which, between 1959 and 1963, depending on the area, morphed into the "Veteran Reception Office." In the 1970s, the reception office was turned into a "Veteran Resettlement Work Leading Small Group" (*fuyuan tuiwu junren anzhi gongzuo lingdao xiaozu*), which, at least in Songjiang County, was but one portfolio among many handled by a single deputy county chief (who was usually not a veteran).[43] In some respects, the very existence of veterans committees was counterproductive, since it made it easier for other officials to slough off their veteran problems. In 1951 in Shanghai, some district officials said, "The veterans committee handles veterans' problems, not us," when confronted by complaints about veteran poverty and jobs.[44] In 1956, the Civil Affairs internal bulletin noted that meetings of the veterans' representative committee were no longer occurring on a regular basis (at the very same time that society was absorbing millions of veterans) and that Civil Affairs officials did not attend them; cooperation was induced from above, usually during an investigation, and ended when it was over.[45] In 1960, the Shanghai Civil Affairs Bureau's "10-Year Work Summary" was frank in its assessment of its work methods: "We still make a big noise, do a big campaign, but have many shortcomings in work that requires careful attention to details and follow-up."[46] Of course, this problem was not unique to Civil Affairs; the CCP's "campaign-mode" of policy implementation was applied to many policy areas and could be quite successful. But when it came to handling veterans, welfare, job assignments, dealing with letters, and the like, making a lot of noise once or twice a year while not responding to "routine" matters did not serve the best interests of many veterans, especially those who were less skilled, of low rank, and from the countryside.

BUREAUCRATIC BIG NOISE: THE CIVIL RELIGION OF VETERANS AND MILITARY FAMILIES

Use of the term *civil religion* to understand political and social dynamics in a rigorously secular, atheist state such as the PRC may seem inappropriate at first glance. The PRC, after all, claimed legitimacy largely on the basis of its wartime nationalist credentials, land reform, and political and military achievements in the pre-1949 period. The role of religion (or "ritual" or "ceremony" in a narrower sense), whether organized or practiced privately, was negligible in political affairs throughout the 1950s.[47] The CCP also drew from the deep anti-traditionalist, iconoclastic legacy of May 4th (1919) radicalism among intellectuals and rejected the notion that religion—as an element within "tradition"—could provide any meaning for its citizens. In this respect, the CCP was not very different from the Soviet Union or other political movements that saw themselves as holding up the banner of modernism against a tradition that was deemed backward, stale, enervating, and irrelevant.

This being the case, how might we rethink the role of "religion" in these sorts of states? Here the history of Zionism in Israel—yes, Israel—is instructive. Like the Communist Party in China, most of the early labor Zionists (who immigrated to Palestine in the late 19th and early 20th centuries) rejected many elements of "traditional" life in the *gola*, the diaspora. In particular, many Zionists rejected the centrality of religion and religious ritual in everyday life. Religious devotion, they felt, produced a people who were far too "bookish," physically weak, effeminate, and prone to accommodation over resistance, a critique similar to that of 19th-century intellectual reformers in China who wanted to elevate people's appreciation of "martial values." If Jews wanted a homeland, the early Zionists argued, they needed to "seize the moment" and begin to remake themselves as a people; the discourse surrounding the creation of a "new Jew" was not very dissimilar from the post-1949 birth of a "New China."[48] In practice, this meant working the land rather than studying religious texts; it meant creating "facts on the ground" in Israel through conquest and settlement rather than waiting for divine intervention; it meant creating a republican ethos whereby the ultimate goal of individual self-fulfillment was to serve the larger community, whether this was the agricultural settlement (the *kibbutz*) or the state. And, like Mao's early essay on the need for physical education and his pre-Cultural Revolution criticism of education to strengthen the nation, early Zionists called for the creation of a new "active" Jewish body, one that would be stronger and more suitable for battle.[49]

However, despite this ideological rejection of "tradition" among Zionist leaders and intellectuals, Zionist leaders, following Jean-Jacques Rousseau's notion that civic festivals play an important role in the creation of patriotism, made sure to insert key elements of Jewish religious traditions into many of the political rituals of the avowedly secular state that was established in 1948.[50] Religious pilgrimages were replaced by pilgrimages to the grave sites of Zionist leaders or sites of famous battles; Memorial Day for Israel's fallen soldiers began with the lighting of large torches, much like Jews greet the Sabbath and other holidays by lighting candles; the concept of "martyr" was redefined so as to focus on individuals who gave their lives for the state instead of for religion. In the Israeli case, Zionist leaders found that many elements of religion could be grafted onto the secular state and in this way "tie" tradition to modernity in such a way that it had real meaning for ordinary citizens. Military threats and wars, to be sure, strengthened this connection, but this was not entirely different from China's siege mentality during the 1950s and 1960s, especially during the Korean War, the Quemoy and Matsu crises (1954–1955; 1958–1959), and the buildup of American forces in Vietnam in the early 1960s.

Commemorative civil religion, however, was never an entirely statist enterprise. Even though the state ceremony for fallen soldiers and victims of terror is still a very impressive affair,[51] families and communities also take part. At a 2007 ceremony at a synagogue in the Tel Aviv suburb of Kfar Sava, local children (ages 8–17) sang songs about dead soldiers and the sad necessity of war ("My Younger Brother Yehuda" and "I Have No Other Country" by Ehud Manor), read poetry lamenting death in war ("The Last War" by Haim Hefer), and recited an excerpt from a speech from David Ben-Gurion and a eulogy for Jonathan Netanyahu, an officer killed while trying to rescue hostages in Uganda in 1976. Some adults went to the podium to read psalms in order to explain to the audience what constitutes a just war.[52] The public is engaged in other ways as well. Even though Israel has many private television and radio stations, on Memorial Day all programming is dedicated to the stories of fallen soldiers and terrorist victims; the state channel broadcasts the name, rank, and date of death of every single soldier and terrorist victim from the late 1940s until the current date. Newspapers still carry accounts of military heroism and the price families pay when sons and husbands (and occasionally daughters) lose their lives in war. (On Independence Day, papers provide readers with a free flag.[53]) Other businesses do their share. In cafés, one can even pour sugar from packets with the pictures and short biographies of famous Zionists and military heroes![54] Of course, this does not suggest that Israelis agree that all wars were necessary and even legitimate—on the contrary, there is vigorous debate about each—but that there is a significant threshold of understanding for suffering, a sense of common history, and recognition of the importance of sacrifice and military service, even if the politics are disputed and people serve in the army because it is legally required. Since most Jewish Israelis serve in the military and know someone who died in war, the civil rituals on Memorial Day and Independence Day are meaningful both at the private level and in strengthening the connection between the individual, community, and state. At the same time, successful civic rituals can backfire. When the hoopla of Memorial Day is over and war widows and disabled veterans face bureaucratic problems, they grow annoyed at the gap between lofty rhetoric and bureaucratic red tape.[55]

When looking closely at PRC politics during the Maoist period, it is fairly easy to see how the state attempted to make similar use of traditional rituals to boost patriotism and an appreciation of military service. The government organized students to make pilgrimages to the grave sites or memorials of various "martyrs" of the revolution. During Spring Festival, students young and old were recruited to help the family members of revolutionary martyrs, military families, and disabled veterans clean their homes and do the laundry; the latter, in turn, were expected to convey their appreciation of the party to the students. While in their homes, the students hung honorary plaques and certificates on the entrances and walls. During Army Day, groups of veterans were mobilized through the Veterans Committees and instructed to convey their revolutionary experiences to a new generation; at least during these "big noise" days, cooperation between agencies went somewhat smoothly.

Viewed from the perspective of the mid-1960s, when Red Guards paraded around in military uniforms and sought to emulate the People's Liberation Army, it would seem that these campaigns were at least moderately successful in elevating the political and social status of those who served in the armed forces.

Archival sources, however, tell a somewhat different story. As befitting the general chaos that seemed to prevail at many state institutions, one theme that recurs quite often in the documents is the sheer absence of order in many of these bureaucracy-led ceremonies. Because Civil Affairs officials were spread out thinly to address all of their responsibilities and could not rely on assistance from veterans organizations in civil society (such as the American Legion, Grand Army of the Republic, or Yad Labanim in Israel), they were often found rushing around hither and thither between offices, unable to plan well for anything. Meetings that did take place were often said to last far too long and did not accomplish anything. Sometimes loudspeakers did not function properly, and veterans could not make themselves understood to the audience because of unfamiliar dialects. Other reports pointed out that Civil Affairs officials had a "bad attitude" toward veterans and military and martyr families. Combined with the "shallowness" of political education (which reflected the larger failure of the ideology to "activate preexisting cultural understandings which are themselves compelling"[56]), infrequent meetings, and weak coordination among bureaucracies, these rituals became entirely pro forma affairs devoid of meaning to participant and officials alike; the military dependents committee in Dongcheng District in Beijing called these affairs *mafan* (a bother) that they would rather do without,[57] and ordinary people compared them to a wind that blows in and then disappears, leaving no trace.[58]

Children were another logistical problem, particularly at screenings of patriotic films. During these screenings, military and martyr families in a particular neighborhood were invited to the theater to enjoy themselves, while simultaneously absorbing the political significance of their own sacrifices for the state. In theory, this plan was easy to execute, since the state controlled access to theaters, distribution of tickets, and the like. But behind the scenes the situation was a bit more chaotic. In Dongcheng District during Mid-Autumn Festival (also known as Full Moon Festival), many women came to the theater with their children but were denied entrance because of a "government regulation" prohibiting children's attendance, particularly those under six. Repeated efforts to persuade the martyr and veteran wives to leave their children at home failed, and loud arguments broke out by the theater ticket booths, disrupting the entire event. Unable to attend the film, the women returned home fuming and with the impression that the same state that sought to increase "patriotic education" was either incompetent or uninterested in accommodating the basic needs of patriotic exemplars.[59]

CIVIL AFFAIRS IN COMPARATIVE PERSPECTIVE

Has bureaucratic handling of veterans *ever* been good? Sadly, the history of demobilization reveals that many of the bureaucratic snafus encountered by returning veterans in China were all too common, even in states with a reputation for the cultivation and greater appreciation of martial values. In Australia, for example, veterans who returned from WWI were often frustrated by bureaucratic delays in getting payments processed and their pensions.[60] In Great Britain after that war, Peter Leese and Seth Koven both note the "clumsy, insensitive and uncooperative attitude of state welfare agencies" and "rough treatment" of healthy and disabled veterans. The same state that so enthusiastically called soldiers to war now had "an overriding concern to limit the state's financial commitments." Finding this treatment unacceptable, in the summer and fall of 1919, veterans marched and demonstrated around the country. The Ministry of Pensions report from that year could have been written in China circa 1958 since it attributed the main causes of discontent to the lack of interdepartmental cooperation, the unhelpful attitude of staff, and the narrow interpretation of government guidelines; officials' attitude was to "get rid" of the applicant rather than examine the case and offer appropriate government resources.[61] In inter-war Germany, scholars have noted that a major source of veterans' discontent was their negative interactions with the bureaucracies that were supposed to help them. Bureaucratic "impersonality" and complexity effectively reduced veterans to the status of "anxious supplicant," since the eligibility process was "often arduous and humiliating." Like their Chinese counterparts, German veterans resented being placed in the same bureaucracy as "ordinary" welfare cases, such as victims of accidents and the ordinary poor.[62] Deborah Cohen's findings also resonate for the Chinese case. The Weimar state, like the PRC, monopolized benevolence by placing all private charities, which they incorrectly suspected of massive fraud, under the umbrella of the state. This had the effect of raising veterans' expectations about their benefits and the overall smoothness of the bureaucratic process. These expectations were quickly dashed when the veterans were forced to deal with bureaucrats, whom they found to be intractable, inconsiderate, and overly prying. German WWI veterans came to believe that bureaucrats were more interested in protecting the government coffers from fraud than assisting them. Over time, veterans' dissatisfaction with public assistance increased even as it expanded in scope and size; German benefits were far superior to those of their British counterparts.[63] Upon their assumption of power, the Nazis made only "limited" material improvements but did provide what James Diehl calls psychological "perks,"[64] which proved to be a critical facet of veterans' attraction to right-wing politics.

Seen in this light, the PRC's Civil Affairs bureaucracy was not exceptional, which strongly suggests that the problem was not "Chinese" or cultural, but more structural in nature. Veterans appear to have a very difficult time when placed in a dependent relationship in veterans bureaucracies that are "stuffed" into larger, more diffuse ones, where they are forced to compete with other "worthy" populations for resources and attention. This dependence is particularly problematic when "their" bureaucracy lacks clout vis-à-vis other power holders in the state and society. That said, we should not overemphasize "structure" at the expense of "agency"—it was not inevitable that PRC veterans encountered some of the bureaucratic problems that they did. North Vietnam, for example, shared many features of the PRC, including a rural-based Communist revolution, Confucian heritage, and an agrarian economy, but there the state, "faced with the prospect of inattentiveness . . . created a new senior position in the local administration, the social policy officer," who reported directly to one of the deputy presidents of the commune's People's Committee" and had "exclusive responsibility" for assisting the so-called "policy families"—those who had a family member serving in the military or had been disabled or killed.[65] Despite the prevalence of state rhetoric about the sacrifices and contributions of veterans and martyrs in China, no such senior, specialized position was ever created in China's local administrative apparatus.

THE NARROW REALM OF THE "POLITICAL"

As suggested above, structural explanations can only go so far. Bureaucracies, after all, are ubiquitous, as are the frustrations dealing with them, but there are wide discrepancies in how veterans are treated and the clout they have in politics and society. To deepen our understanding of the *modus operandi* of the Chinese state, we also need to examine the various *ideas* circulating in Civil Affairs offices about "veteran work," "welfare," and "caring" for the military-affiliated populations. What did its officials think about their work? If we can get a reasonably good sense of this, it would be easier to account for the lack of "routine" interventions on veterans' behalf as well as the often halfhearted efforts to serve as their advocates within the state apparatus.

In the archival sources from Beijing, Shanghai, Qingpu, and elsewhere, one issue consistently stands out amid the clutter of bureaucratic jargon. For most Civil Affairs officials, helping veterans and other military families was rarely, if ever, conceptualized in *political terms* (unlike in democracies, where veteran issues are "political" because veterans vote). In the PRC, a problem or issue that was defined as political (*zhengzhi*) in nature was, by definition, high-priority, fear-inducing, and potentially face-giving. Deciding policy issues, war, capturing "counterrevolutionaries," mass campaigns, and production drives would be included in this category: the stakes were high and outcomes easy to measure and grasp in terms of their political significance. As far as most Civil Affairs officials were concerned, however, the issues that they handled—distributing aid, placing people in jobs, running senior homes, and the like—were, again by definition, "social" or "civil" and therefore a great distance away from the "front lines" of revolution, modernization, or industrialization. Cadres who staffed labor and personnel bureaucracies shared this notion of "civil affairs" work, as did leaders of villages, townships, and factories. Efforts to forge a conceptual linkage between the civil/social and the political, which might have induced greater compliance and initiative, floundered during the rush from one political campaign to the next.

This problem surfaced in the earliest reports from Civil Affairs offices, first as a way to explain why *other* government officials were treating veterans poorly and then to account for their own administrative shortcomings. In a report concerning Civil Affairs work from January to August 1951, its officials complained that "some cadres" at the district levels did not appreciate the "relationship between veteran work and caring for martyr and military families to national defense and reconstruction of the economy"; it was on account of this that the district officials persistently emphasized that "there's too much to do, and not enough cadres."[66] In 1956, Civil Affairs officials who investigated veteran resettlement work in Shanghai's Changning District noticed that little had changed in five years, despite the Korean War and the return of many veterans to China. Not only was no "political education" being conducted with veterans newly hired in factories, but "some units do not seriously enforce State Council policies" because the leading cadres at the factory did not consider giving jobs to veterans as their "political duty" (*zhengzhi renwu*). Civil Affairs complaints, therefore, generally fell on deaf ears.[67] In a 1957 speech, General Fu Qiutao, head of the National Veterans Committee (who in this capacity had access to many provincial-level reports), told his audience, "Some units do not see veteran resettlement as politically significant, but rather as an additional burden, and therefore do not have enough revolutionary feelings (*geming ganqing*) towards them."[68] As General Fu surely realized, this was an understatement, since many local investigation reports that were sent to higher levels carefully documented the extent to which unions, factory managers, and others ignored national-level policies;

for instance, rather than conduct a "welcome ceremony" as stipulated in State Council documents, at the #3 Textile Mill in Shanghai, Lu Yuexian, the union chair, said, "I've never spoken to a veteran. The union cadres may say good things or bad, but since management and the party committee haven't issued any instructions, there's not much we can do." Unable to anchor complaints in official guidelines, the fifteen veterans who were interviewed all said, "If there's a problem, there's nowhere to go; if you raise a problem, there's never a solution."[69] Even by 1963, hundreds of documents, a military crisis (Taiwan Straits, 1958), and a successfully prosecuted war (against India) later, a report by the Veteran Reception Office noted that "some basic-level units do not implement the Municipal Party Committee's policies vis-à-vis resettlement, as they do not consider it their 'political duty.'"[70]

This rather narrow conception of political responsibility was also noticed by Civil Affairs and veterans committee officials in Qingpu. In rural areas, the "political realm" encompassed big, transformative events such as land reform and collectivization; veteran administration paled in comparison. Citing "not a few problems" among veterans in the county, in 1957 the local veterans committee convened a meeting of township chiefs and other officials to see if anything could be done to improve the situation. Upon arrival, however, the attendees quickly revealed that they did not quite grasp why anyone would even convene a special meeting on veterans. The head of the Tax Bureau said, "I don't have any veterans, so why come?" The chief of Xicen Township said, "We're busy with our central tasks. Why are we having this meeting? All we have to do is send some of the more difficult veterans to the Civil Affairs office and that's that; you're making a mountain out of a molehill."[71]

From the Xicen chief's position, sending "difficult" veterans to Civil Affairs made sense, but then again, he did not have access to internal Civil Affairs documents showing that his own view toward veterans' work was, in fact, widely shared there. A recurring theme in these reports was that Civil Affairs officials thought of their own jobs as insufficiently political and revolutionary, with precious little room for advancement. In 1954, Civil Affairs officials considered their work as "having no future" and a "burden"; their "client" populations were all "difficult to deal with" (*nan chan*) and "gave them a headache." The section chief of Gaoqiao District's "Preferential Treatment" Section considered his job to be mainly one of routine processing (*shiwu gongzuo*), devoid of any political import.[72] A year later, these complaints resurfaced in a speech by the deputy bureau director in Shanghai, who noted that many Civil Affairs workers were basically clueless about national policies and how to enforce them (*quefa jiben banfa*) and did not devote time to studying the documents that came their way. Civil Affairs work methods were described as frequently chaotic (*mangmu xing*).[73] After the establishment of communes during the Great Leap Forward, Civil Affairs officials considered this the end of their jobs because communes would take care of veterans, military dependents, and martyr families; they had to be reminded that those without much labor power would still suffer. Nevertheless, investigations found that Civil Affairs officials spent only 25 percent of their budget in Shanghai and only 15 percent in Guangxi, Yunnan, and Ningxia. Unsurprisingly, given the functional diffuseness of Civil Affairs offices and the social crises engendered by the Great Leap Forward, some cadres were completely ignoring veterans and the other "elite" populations and devoting all of their time to disaster relief and welfare.[74]

It is difficult to evaluate the effectiveness of these speeches and meetings — it probably was not very realistic to expect people to be convinced that "burying corpses is also revolutionary"[75] — but persistent complaints that Civil Affairs work lacked "glory," had "no future," and dealt only with "odds and ends," and that its officials feared they would "lose face" and remain bachelors as long as they stayed in the bureau suggest that these exhortations could not really compensate for a more deeply entrenched perception that "welfare work" was apolitical and thus less important than other positions.[76] In 1965, morale, or, to use more modern lingo, "job satisfaction," in the Civil Affairs bureaucracy appeared to have hit a low point. According to one report, new Civil Affairs employees "bawled when they found out that they were assigned to the job," "don't get what it is that the bureau does," "don't know who it is that they're working for" (this may not have been explained to them), "seek immediate transfers when criticized for anything," and had poor working relationships with their superiors, which also caused frequent attempts to transfer positions.[77] If they were assigned to a suburb of Shanghai, they would be "very upset" and then try to wheel and deal to get out of it. The report's explanation for these problems was on the money — Civil Affairs was not really involved in "class warfare" (courts and the police were "at the front" of this war) and it was not "revolutionary work."[78] Hong Tianshou, the director of Shanghai's Bureau of Civil Affairs, complained in 1965 about the lack of *espirit de corps* among his officials, but given the constraints of a bureaucratic structure and the difficulty awarding individual incentives, there was very little he could do about it. Not a few considered Civil Affairs work to be "wasting their talent" (*dacai xiaoyong*) in work that was "trivial and trifling" (*suosui*).[79]

Lower-level officials who bore the brunt of these criticisms, however, were unlikely to evaluate their problems in highly ideological terms. For them, it simply boiled down to their lack of political clout, reflected in staffing, meetings with higher officials, and other bureaucratic problems. After a 1964 meeting that was intended to "revolutionize" Civil Affairs work, the director of Civil Affairs in Chuansha County was frustrated: "At this meeting you've all talked about 'revolutionizing,' but I still don't get exactly how to do this. We're six officials. One gets sick and two others are doing something else important, leaving us with three for the county. You all say the 'human element' (*ren de yinsu*) is the most important, so if a human is taken away, the element is, too."[80] According to a vice-mayor, many suburban Civil Affairs officials complained that county authorities did not provide them with enough administrative support but then criticized them for doing a poor job, which led to even more resentment of their work.[81] This was not only a Shanghai phenomenon: district-level reports from Beijing tell a very similar story.[82]

Civil Affairs' charges—veterans, the disabled, poor, mentally ill, seniors, and refugees (among others)—most surely sensed that officials in the organization that was expected to help them were less than enthusiastic about their jobs and had few incentives to help them in routine times; short-lived major investigations, however, were another matter. This helps explain the wide discrepancy in how Civil Affairs officials are portrayed in investigation reports (sometimes positively) and by those summarizing events in non-investigation years.

MAKING SENSE OF POLICY

Despite numerous complaints about Civil Affairs officials' low morale, rude behavior, and incompetence, it would still be a bit too easy and flippant, albeit not unusual among many politicians, to place blame purely on "bureaucrats." Civil Affairs officials operated within a larger political context not only in terms of the ideas about what counted as "political" or "revolutionary" but also in terms of their place in the flow of people and documents originating elsewhere in the political system. Civil Affairs, like most bureaucracies, was *reactionary* in a literal understanding of the word: it reacted to directives from the State Council and the PLA and received veterans and military dependents after their discharge, but it appeared to have little clout in the formulation of key policies or the determination of how many veterans it would be responsible for. Inasmuch as successful policy implementation is dependent on the coherence of documents, a "clean" paper flow, and a shared language between officials, we have to consider the sorts of "inputs" that Civil Affairs officials had to deal with.

The first bit of exculpatory evidence comes from the PLA, or, to be more precise, the long-term near-absence of sustained and clear communication between discharge officials in the military and local Civil Affairs officials. In the early 1950s, the PLA was largely responsible for inflating veterans' expectations of a "soft landing" in cities after their discharge by telling them that they would "immediately" (*mashang*) be given a job upon their arrival, apparently without consulting harried Civil Affairs or municipal officials. When they arrived to find that the local employment situation was difficult, they were perplexed and angry, since they assumed a tidy, military-style hierarchy where subordinate units (cities) followed orders from the Center.[83] This disconnect persisted well into the latter part of the 1950s. Municipal officials, while acknowledging their "support" for the PLA, lambasted "some military units" for their logistical sloppiness and for making promises that could not be kept. Based on what veterans told Civil Affairs officials, PLA officers, for reasons that are not yet clear, told demobilizing soldiers to "go to a good place" (*youli de difang*) and "there's work just waiting for you," without accounting for their native place or even warning them of possible difficulties. Civil affairs officials complained, "These PLA units just acceded to the veterans' demands," and did not do enough to teach them to follow civilians' orders after discharge; apparently, veterans "repeatedly refused to be assigned to certain areas and jobs," making Civil Affairs officials' work that much more difficult.[84]

Documentation was also problematic. Prior to 1949, there were military units that did not issue official documentation when their soldiers were discharged and others that were renamed, renumbered, and amalgamated in the chaos of war, but after the establishment of the state, paperwork was necessary to claim benefits, which placed those who were poor and not highly literate in a difficult situation.[85] Not knowing what to do with these veterans and suspecting fraud, the National Veterans Committee chairman instructed the PLA to avoid reissuing official documents "because too much time has lapsed" and asked that Civil Affairs officials "find an appropriate solution" to their difficulties. This, of course, increased the burden on low-level officials, who now had to read letters and hear oral histories about each veteran's often highly complicated service record.[86] The passage of time did not enhance administrative legibility. In 1957 and 1959, Civil Affairs clerks complained that the PLA did not send veterans' paperwork on time or sent it in error; some documents lacked official seals, while others had "conclusions" about an individual's political history that proved to be inaccurate after investigation—but it was left to the "worried and anxious" veteran to fix these problems through correspondence while waiting for a job and subsisting on welfare funds. These complaints were confirmed by General Fu Qiutao, who also complained about "rash" discharges: "Some military units do not educate the soldiers, and do not contact the locality beforehand."[87] But even when Civil Affairs officials were completely out of the employment loop, they still had to deal with the messy aftermath. Many of these Center-allocated veterans hailed from faraway provinces (mainly in the Southwest or Northeast), had no family locally, were given low apprenticeship salaries, and encountered language and housing problems, all of which required official attention. Not a few wanted to go home. Civil Affairs officials recommended that the Center relocate people to the same region from which they came and establish "a special coordinating authority to handle all the issues surrounding veterans." They also wanted the PLA to remain in contact with veterans after their discharge, but I have not seen evidence that any of these recommendations were carried out.[88] Veterans wrote to the Ministry of Defense about these problems, but they were "turned over to Civil Affairs, who could not do anything about it" (*wufa chuli*).[89] Even by 1960, there was still a weak connection between the PLA and Civil Affairs.[90]

This story of bureaucratic bungling and lost, missing, or incorrect paperwork would certainly sound familiar to veterans with low socioeconomic status elsewhere; it is not an outcome easily explained by China's authoritarian state structure. Take the United States, for example. After the Pension Act was passed in 1819, the difficulty of procuring official paperwork, the requirement to prove "need," and the lack of experience handling large numbers of petitions contributed to massive problems in administration. Tensions rose "between veterans and their neighbors over alleged cheating," as the former claimed that the pension was their "just reward" but were denigrated by others as "greedy frauds."[91] It was even more difficult for African-American veterans and war widows to procure pensions after the Civil War. Because pension regulations stipulated that all veterans prove their worthiness (which involved filling out forms, getting testimony from witnesses, furnishing vital dates, traveling to a surgical board to evaluate disability, and "proving that they were the same person who had served in the Union Army"), African-American applicants encountered many difficulties. Owing to slavery, many lacked birth certificates, could not legally marry, were illiterate, and joined the army under their masters' surnames but changed them after the war, which made it far more difficult for processing clerks to establish the truth.[92] The main issue here, at least as I see it, is a conflict between bureaucracy, which tends to insist on forms and proper signatures, and societies where many types of events and interactions are not typically recorded on paper. Even now, some 140 years after the Civil War, American veterans sometimes have to struggle long and hard to obtain promised benefits because of bureaucratic hurdles (see Chapter 9).

That said, what could have made a significant difference? What might have reduced confusion or made it easier for Civil Affairs officials to do their jobs well? Chinese veteran administration officials certainly could have benefited from extremely clear wording, if not in law per se then in bureaucratic regulations and State Council policy documents, guidelines, and "Decisions." The second major piece of exculpatory evidence to countermand the charge of Civil Affairs' incompetence can be found here: many key documents were vague and abstract. Although this was often intended to allow local flexibility in policy implementation, the language provided enough leeway, or escape clauses, to avoid enforcement all together. For instance, in 1952, the Shanghai government stated, "In hiring, veterans *should* get preference over ordinary unemployed workers."[93] When the State Council Secretariat issued directives to enterprises and other institutions regarding the hiring of veterans and the provision of public housing, the operative term was always the normative *should* rather than the more law-laden and perhaps fear-inducing term *must*, leaving localities a great deal of latitude and a ready excuse for not hiring them.[94] *Should* was also used to encourage local governments to include veterans as "basic-level cadres"[95] to encourage salary departments to adjust veterans' salaries[96] as well as to induce local governments to fulfill their responsibilities vis-à-vis their housing, repairs, rental assistance, provision of public housing, and other, more "mundane" benefits they were supposed to receive.[97] An even more watered-down term—*may (keyi)*—was used in a 1957 policy document referring to stipends for veterans attending vocational schools[98] and in 1960 directives (along with several *shoulds*) regarding veterans qualifying for the same insurance and welfare benefits as other workers,[99] salary, and the calculation of time spent in the army.[100] All of these phrasings gave little sense of how important these issues were to the Center, most certainly did not generate fear for noncompliance, and, most problematically of all, erroneously assumed a shared view of veterans' basic entitlement to these benefits. *Should* and *may* belong in the realm of moral or ethical exhortations, not state policies and regulations; *absolutely must* probably would have been more effective, but it was rarely used. However, if there was a stronger societal consensus (or pressure) that veterans were a worthy and deserving population to begin with, *absolutely must* would not have been necessary and *should* could have sufficed.

Veterans were well aware of the soft core in State Council documents; we have already seen veterans, as early as 1956, commenting on the wide discrepancy between propaganda and shoddy, scattershot implementation, signs of a weak state apparatus. Their assessment was on the mark. As noted by MacFarquhar and Schoenhals, after 1958 Zhou Enlai and his State Council "played second fiddle to the Central Committee Secretariat in the overall running of the country."[101] For some, the only solution to their difficulties was in the formation of a veterans organization. During the Hundred Flowers Movement in early 1957, for example, Huang Bi, a veteran working in the Guizhou Provincial Forestry Bureau, in cooperation with an unemployed veteran and two others from different units, formed an organization called the "China Veterans Association." This group demanded "organizational independence" and "parallel" status with the CCP. According to the press report (uncovered by Gordon White), the veterans held secret meetings "during which members complained that veterans were dregs who were not receiving adequate attention from the party and government" and tried to recruit veterans in Shanghai, Beijing, and Sichuan. In May 1957, the China Veterans Association, taking advantage of a scheduled meeting of "veteran representatives," threatened a street demonstration if their demands were not met. Huang's critique went well beyond bread-and-butter issues, however. Belying the image of veterans as arch conservatives, in June he argued that French-style democracy (not American) could be adopted in China. In 1957, the CCP counterattacked: Huang was declared a rightist and the veterans association was disbanded as "reactionary."[102]

Efforts to form veterans organizations to fill the void left by the absence of any form of effective interest group representation did not end in 1957. Absent any other effective way to convey their grievances to those at the Center, veterans tried—like other disgruntled groups—another tactic when the Cultural Revolution broke out. On December 21, 1966, at 3:30 p.m., more than 80 veterans, with others waiting outside, met at CCP Headquarters (the compound is known as *Zhongnanhai*) with the official who signed off on many of these ineffective State Council directives, Premier Zhou Enlai.

VETERANS IN ZHONGNANHAI: 中南海
THE AUDIENCE WITH PREMIER ZHOU ENLAI[103]

The premier had hemorrhoids, so he preferred to stand, but he was not pleased to be meeting with so many people at the same time; it "did not follow regulations," and it was "difficult to talk." Still, he was willing to make this one exception for the veterans, most of whom came from Jiangsu and Fujian provinces and the city of Nanjing, where problems were said to be "serious"; a second meeting under those conditions would not be acceptable, however.

This was not the first time Zhou was dealing with veterans' issues during the Cultural Revolution. Just one month earlier, in November 1966, dozens of veterans pressed for a meeting with him, but since he was "busy," or at least claimed to be, the tête-à-tête never took place. Miffed, several veterans managed to barge into (*chongjin*) Zhongnanhai, where they requested an audience with other top CCP leaders. Roughly 10 of Zhou's deputies and other officials, including marshals Chen Yi (foreign minister), Ye Jianying (vice chairman of the Military Affairs Commission), and Xie Fuzhi (minister of public security), did meet with them. When the veterans finally met Zhou, he was still upset at their earlier maneuver: "It doesn't matter if it is several people or several hundred," he admonished them, "and it doesn't matter which gate you come in from, you can't just break into Zhongnanhai. After all, this is Chairman's Mao's place, and he said that no one can just come in here." Veterans, he emphasized, were very different from students who could leave their campuses and travel about the country to "make revolution": "You can't just leave your jobs; do you see me leaving my position?" Still, to reassure the veterans of the sincerity of his concern, he identified himself as one of them: "You're veterans and I'm also a veteran—I've fought in wars!" He also expressed awareness of their problems, noting that when he met with the Capital Red Guards, a student umbrella organization, "some others gave me notes describing veterans' problems, including persecutions, beatings, and unemployment."

But when it came to the veterans' central demand, which for them was the only solution to these problems—the establishment of an "independent, national veterans' organization"—Zhou was less accommodating. Citing a policy that he had articulated at the Capital Red Guard meeting, Zhou reiterated that veterans could establish only a "liaison organization" (*lianluo jigou*) but otherwise would have to participate in the Cultural Revolution in their work units, such as schools, factories, and enterprises; "veteran" status could not be the basis of self-organization. Some of the attending veterans were skeptical about the authenticity of this order, however, and asked Zhou if this policy, which was part of a three-part decision regarding veterans in the Cultural Revolution (known as "The Three Directives"), was personally approved by Chairman Mao and Vice Chairman Lin Biao and whether it would be possible for Lin to come out personally to prove that it was authentic. Zhou assured them that it was: "Chairman Mao approved it himself; it's not fake. Who would dare issue orders under his name without his approval?" Since veterans had already taken some controversial actions during the mass movement, Zhou then read "The Three Directives" aloud, one by one, so it would be crystal clear what they could and could not do during the Cultural Revolution:

1) Veterans are not allowed to establish a "Red Army" [*Hongwei jun*, on the model of student Red Guards] or any other named independent organization. Veterans are allowed only to participate in their work units.
2) Veterans are not allowed to break into PLA installations and other related military units, and veterans cannot establish contact with them or distribute leaflets and handbills.
3) All veterans must preserve and carry on the glorious tradition of the PLA, help the military prepare for war, and protect the Great Proletarian Cultural Revolution.

These three directives, Zhou stressed (using the clear phrasing that was absent from his State Council documents), were "absolutely correct" and must be "completely supported." He then warned them, "If you are suspicious of them, then you are suspicious of Mao Zedong Thought" itself.

Zhou, a master of diplomacy and duplicity, then shifted to a more accommodating tactic, describing why a "veterans liaison office" (VLO) was a good idea and how it would be formed. For Zhou, the VLO had two advantages. First, because veterans are dispersed, a VLO that had a national register of veterans would make it easier for veterans to locate one another. Second, it would make it "easier for the government to mobilize you in case of a war, when you would be needed." To facilitate the operation of this organization, Civil Affairs and local garrison cadres would handle most of the work; "when necessary," it would accept "one or two" veterans in order "to provide veterans' perspective." This non-veteran veterans organization would then "help the relevant government departments solve your employment problems, so that you'll be able to make a living." A veterans organization of precisely this type "may" be established, he allowed, but it should not be too large, so as to avoid problems typical of bureaucratic organizations. In the meantime, however, Zhou instructed the veterans to avoid using the word *veteran* in any of their organizations, creating organizations "based on veteran status," or telling other organizations that "only veterans are revolutionary." If veterans wanted to take a leading role in the Cultural Revolution, they could do so only in other organizations or by struggling against leading cadres and revisionism "to make sure the country does not change color."

Zhou's solution, attending veterans realized, was an empty shell and a very far cry from their demand: a "national, independent veterans' organization." Not only did he continue to use the softer concepts of *should* and *may*, but he also included the phrase *when necessary*, which would allow Civil Affairs and military officials in a VLO to easily exclude veterans. Even if they participated, they would not have a dominant role. More transparently, Zhou argued that a VLO would only "help" other government departments; like previous incarnations of this arrangement (veterans committees and reception offices), the liaison office would exist in a bureaucratic no-man's land, having no authority, or budget, to change any individual's situation. Its close connection to Civil Affairs and its all-too-familiar bureaucracy did not bode well, either.

As it turned out, Zhou's proposal was unenforceable. Civil Affairs offices could not function very well during the chaos of the Cultural Revolution in mid-1967. This had the effect of stranding thousands of veterans who either returned from service or took advantage of the administrative breakdown to leave the countryside and look for work in the city;[104] those who depended on "temporary financial assistance" had to find other means of making ends meet.[105] Unsurprisingly, veterans pressed back, complaining about persistent discrimination against them and their family members as well as their "fear of losing jobs." A national veterans organization, they insisted, "will help those who don't have work, find work" as well as "protect the fatherland and the Great Proletarian Cultural Revolution." Zhou replied that such an organization would be "inappropriate" but that "we will help you find solutions to your legitimate problems." Given that the State Council oversaw veterans affairs since 1949, this was probably little solace. The veterans were ushered out, empty-handed, with the exception of the few official "representatives" who received travel money back home; the rest had to pay their own way.

The fate of veterans organizations during the latter phases of the Cultural Revolution was not much better. Even though Zhou denied calling these organizations "illegal" or ordering their immediate dispersal (instead, he asked the veterans "to consider dispersing or not," which was a clear signal to disperse), more radical leaders did not hesitate to brand them as such, or even as "counterrevolutionary" during 1967 and 1968, and to order the PLA to suppress them wherever they existed. Despite their grievances, which were shared among many on the "left," evidence suggests that most veterans were not sympathetic to Mao's call to "bombard the headquarters" and were aligned with the established party-state, or "royalists" as the radicals put it, in much the same way that many veterans on Taiwan were resolutely supportive of the Guomindang when the United States transferred its recognition to the mainland in 1978, thereby challenging the legitimacy of the state.[106] There were significant exceptions to this pattern, however; apparently one-third of (mostly urban) veterans were aligned with rebel organizations because of long-standing grievances about their job prospects, forced resettlement in the countryside, and a broad "hostility to cadres in general."[107] The "Red Flag Army" (*hongqi jun*) in Hunan, for example, operated under the umbrella of *Shengwulian* (Provincial Proletarian Revolutionary Alliance Committee), a large "rebel" organization of the political "have-nots." Its leader, Jonathan Unger notes, "had been denied a proper civilian position for having held a Guomindang membership card before 1949."[108] Other veteran–rebel organizations were active in Guangdong and Guangxi ("August 1st Combat Corps"), Shanghai ("First Column Headquarters of the Red Banner Army"), Guizhou ("Red Guard Army"), Jiangsu, Hebei, and Sichuan.[109] Even after these organizations were disbanded, sporadic protests continued. In 1975 in Guangdong, veterans protested "discrimination in wage and bonus policies" but after a crackdown "issued a statement pledging to comply with party policy and end all wage protests."[110] Although most "conservative" counterrevolutionary veterans were officially "rehabilitated" between 1978 and 1980,[111] the rebels might have endured a more bitter fate. To this day, however, veterans have not been permitted to establish a national, let alone "independent," organization.

THE BUMPY PATH TOWARD RESPECT AND RIGHTS: VETERANS ORGANIZATIONS AND CIVIL SOCIETY IN COMPARATIVE PERSPECTIVE

Were Chinese veterans during the Hundred Flowers Movement and Cultural Revolution onto something when they demanded a national, independent veterans organization? Is there a relationship, either causal or correlative, between the formation of a veterans organization and veterans' status or, more broadly, their claims to martial-based citizenship? Moving from our close encounter with Zhou Enlai in Zhongnanhai in 1966 to a bird's-eye view of the larger world, the answer is a qualified "yes." As early as the Roman Empire, veterans have come to understand that political organization and unity, not necessarily independence or regime type, are key in securing rights;[112] these are the main areas where China failed its veterans most egregiously.

Let us first take a look at democracies after major wars, since these would seem to be more promising political environments for veterans organizations than authoritarian states. Although all democracies have praised veterans after their return from battle (much as the propaganda authorities did in China), veterans organizations have not always fared well. Great Britain and Canada on the one hand, and the United States, New Zealand, and Australia on the other, are good cases in point. During the course of WWI in Britain, at least four different veterans organizations were created, including the National Association of Discharged Sailors and Soldiers (formed in 1916 and connected to the Trade Union and Labor Party), the National Federation of Discharged and Demobilized Sailors and Soldiers (1917, affiliated with the Liberal Party), Comrades of the Great War (1917, led by a Conservative Member of Parliament [M.P.]), and the National Union of Ex-Servicemen (1919, closely affiliated with the left). In 1921, these groups merged into an umbrella organization and were renamed the "British Legion" (now called the Royal British Legion).[113] In Canada, there was no significant veterans organization prior to 1914, but, like the British case, massive casualties in a war that touched the lives of all social classes immediately prompted veterans to create several organizations: the Royal Canadian Legion, for example, was founded in 1925, and ANAVETS, the Army, Navy and Air Force Veterans in Canada Association, was incorporated by a special act of parliament in 1917. These organizations understood quite well that "entitlement would be established only by organization."[114]

Despite veterans' right to vote, both of these organizations proved no match for many officials in the U.K. and Canadian governments, whose post-war priorities quickly shifted elsewhere. According to Reese, General Douglas Haig, the leader of the British Legion, was a veteran but also a member of the upper classes and made the mistake of being "too dignified" and sticking to "high ideals" when dealing with tight-fisted officials, especially from the Treasury. Because the fair-minded British Legion refused to "indulge in knockabout tactics" or "rock the domestic boat," the state was able to "virtually ignore" its members when making key decisions on the state budget; British veterans received less than their counterparts in other European countries or Canada, Australia, New Zealand, and South Africa. Like their Chinese counterparts, quite a few had to sell matches and boot-laces on the street just to get by. Luckily for the British government, the vast majority of veterans were "stoic and uncomplaining," taking their sacrifices for granted.[115] Post-war Canadian veterans organizations were similarly in-effectual, despite several battles with the government, largely because they suffered from disunity and lack of serious commitment. After the war, many veterans shunned veterans organizations and Armistice Day ceremonies and "claimed neither pensions nor benefits."[116]

Veterans organizations in Australia, New Zealand, and the United States, on the other hand, have fared far better in securing their members both rights and respect. In post-WWI Australia, veterans had a very high rate of enrollment in the Australian Returned Servicemen's League (one-third of all veterans, a higher rate than any other country), and the organization engendered "intense member support" and a highly masculine "front-line pride and ethos."[117] Not only did veterans organizations play a "crucial role in cementing the Anzac legend as a national narrative"—in memorials, sol-diers were acknowledged for "founding the nation"[118]—but they also proved to be a highly successful pressure group for their members. According to a comprehensive political history of the Returned Servicemen's League (RSL), the organization was far more successful than its British counterpart. Thanks in part to its "direct access to the Commonwealth government," the RSL was "completely successful" on many important issues as well as a "very definite factor in decision-making on all matters of repatriation."[119] In addition to access, the RSL and the New Zealand veterans organizations were noted for *not* being particularly fair-minded and polite when dealing with the state. Peter Reese describes the former's tactics as "muscular" and the latter's as "feisty."[120] Because of this, Australia probably provides the sharpest contrast to China: its soldiers generally came from the countryside but, unlike China, were respected for this fact; veterans were seen as a repository of masculine virtue, a cultural understanding that was lacking in the PRC; they fought in battles that were widely perceived as legitimate and heroic; they had an organization that was allowed to participate in politics (unlike China); and they refused to be bullied by civilians after their return.

The experience of veterans organizations in the United States reinforces these points. Until the Civil War, veterans, owing to their relatively small numbers, did not have a great deal of political clout, and their best-known—and infamous—organization was restricted to officers and their descendants (the Society of the Cincinnati, whose president was George Washington, was viewed by New Englanders as the first step toward a new aristocracy[121]). After the Civil War, however, few organizations in American politics had more influence than that of Union Army veterans, known as the "Grand Army of the Republic" (GAR), whose membership grew from 30,000 in 1878 to 409,000 by 1890. The GAR, according to Elizabeth O'Leary, attracted large numbers of veterans who were "drawn to an organization whose massed presence assured respect when individual veterans could become objects of scorn and pity."[122] In 1888, a GAR member, Benjamin Harrison, was elected president over Grover Cleveland (despite losing the popular vote), who had hired a substitute during the war, frequently vetoed private pension bills for individual veterans, and was agreeable to returning Confederate flags to the southern states.[123] Largely because of its electoral clout and successful lobbying of Congress, by 1893 military pensions absorbed one federal dollar out of every three; by 1907, the Federal Dependent Pension Act (1890) cost the government more than one billion dollars.[124] By 1910, pensions for veterans and widows represented 25–30 percent of average national earnings.[125]

This influence moved well beyond budgetary matters. Far more than the federal government, the GAR and its auxiliary Women's Relief Corps (WRC) profoundly shaped the larger culture surrounding military service and the meaning of citizenship and patriotism. This was not unusual; in Germany in the late 19th and early 20th centuries, important national monuments were financed by associations of war veterans.[126] Memorial Day in the United States originated with the Women's Relief Corps, as did the placement of flags in classrooms and the recitation of the Pledge of Allegiance; during the 1880s and 1890s members of the GAR visited classrooms, and spectacles of military power "dominated public ceremonies." The GAR and WRC also promoted martial conceptions of citizenship and patriotism, stressing themes of self-reliance, individual duty to the nation, sacrifice, and masculine courage.[127] American participation in World War I swelled the number of veterans and led to the creation of the American Legion, the Disabled American Veterans of the World War (founded by a self-help organization in Ohio and a group of disabled veterans from the University of Cincinnati, who, without the draft, probably would not have gone to war[128]), and the Veterans of Foreign Wars (1919). Like its counterpart in Germany after that war,[129] local branches of the Veterans of Foreign Wars brought veterans together for "good times," social support, camaraderie, grassroots activism in support of veteran causes, and sharing memories and army jargon with other veterans, all of which "contributed greatly to the solidarity of the veterans' 'in-group' feeling, and to the prestige that their status as veterans brought."[130] In addition to having created a national holiday that commemorates their service and sacrifices (Veterans Day can be traced to the efforts of Raymond Weeks, a World War II veteran, in Birmingham, Alabama, in 1947), in towns across America veterans often lead Independence Day parades, initiate local memorials, are active in community service, and, with the support of their local VFW and American Legion chapters, support organizations that promote patriotism, such as the Boy Scouts (which was created by a veteran) and Boys' State and Boys' Nation events.

Veterans organizations also mounted wide-scale collective action, such as the 1932 Bonus Army's "occupation" of a district in Washington, D.C. (black and white veterans marched and lived in integrated camps), and were intensely involved in the legislative arena. The American Legion, despite its conservative reputation, supported legislation that granted citizenship to Japanese, Indian, and other minority veterans, and it was the legion that drafted the 1944 GI Bill, arguably the greatest expansion of veteran rights in American history and, by many accounts, the foundation of the post-war middle class.[131] Politicians passed the GI Bill into law as a measure of gratitude and "genuine concern" for the veterans but also because "policy makers hoped to avoid a repeat of such events [the Bonus Army] by ensuring from the start that veterans of World War II would receive better treatment."[132] Passing the GI Bill, however, was not enough: the law had to be "taught" to have an impact. Prior to discharge, the government itself "indoctrinated" the soldiers "with the knowledge of their rights"; afterwards, "veterans' organizations were a clearinghouse for information relating to these benefits and explicitly 'stood for' the protection and extenuation of these rights."[133] For most white veterans, but particularly those who were better educated or advantaged in some other way, the promise of the GI Bill was fulfilled, and veterans repaid the nation through very high rates of participation in civic organizations, but many minorities (such as Mexican-Americans, Indians, and African-Americans) continued to experience everyday discrimination and difficulty taking advantage of their legal rights. Even these problems, however, were largely addressed through the formation (or reinvigoration) of feisty and politically well-connected, minority-led veterans organizations (such as the American GI Forum, formed in 1948, which served Mexican-American veterans).[134]

The contrasts between the more aggressive veterans organizations in the United States and Australia and the more accommodating ones in the United Kingdom and Canada demonstrate that it is not enough to have an interest group to protect and advance veterans' rights and status; once established, veterans organizations have to fight hard for a long time, since the tendency among most politicians and the public is to forget the past and move on to the future. That said, democracy, at least on the surface, seems to provide veterans with more political openings to press their case: they are allowed to organize, they have the freedom of speech, and they vote. While not guaranteeing respect or even the provision of any benefits, the relatively open "political opportunity structure" certainly reduces the risks when engaging in collective action, which, as the history of the GI Bill, shows, can be quite decisive. On the other hand, this same political opportunity structure makes it relatively easy for *veterans' opponents* to organize: there have always been critics of veterans' benefits (including Franklin D. Roosevelt), accusing veterans of using their service to "extort" funds from the public coffers. On balance, however, it would seem that the Chinese veterans who had an audience with Zhou Enlai were at least partially on the mark. Can China's persistent veteran problems be attributed largely to its repressive political system? Looking at how veterans have fared in different sorts of authoritarian regimes, which China is often described as, suggests otherwise.

Let's look briefly at several examples of these regimes, ranging from "soft" authoritarianism to harder versions of it in interwar Italy, Spain under Franco, Taiwan under Chiang Kai-shek, the Soviet Union, and Russia after the fall of Communism. War, lost and won, was critical in the formation of all these regimes, so the treatment and reintegration of veterans was an unavoidable issue both in policy and in society at large. Although different in some respects—Franco and the Bolsheviks won wars, while all the others were on the losing sides—they all share something that China lacks to this day: powerful and significant veterans *organizations.* Even though war makes states (and also veterans and widows),[135] the opportunities for most all rank-and-file veterans to "make the state" in China were therefore more limited.[136] In Italy, for example, the "Fighting Fascists" was a "polyglot" group that included war veterans, university students, futurists, and nationalists, but veterans were allowed their own representation and identity, quite unlike Zhou Enlai's order to leave veteran identity at the door after joining a work unit. The planning committee for the first anniversary of Mussolini's 1922 "March on Rome" included representatives from "The National Association of War Wounded" and the "National Association of Combatants." In the town of Perugia, the local commission was composed of the town mayor, a general, two lawyers, the secretary of the Fascist Party, two representatives of the local War

Veterans Association, as well as a countess who was the president of the National Association of War Mothers and Widows. Unlike the iconoclastic CCP, which often bungled commemorative activities, Fascists, like Zionists in Israel, proved more adept at fusing religious symbols in ceremonies to commemorate veterans and martyrs.[137] Similar to Italy, authoritarian Spain also allowed its veterans to form their own organizations. Less than a year into the Civil War, disabled Republican veterans created the "League of the Wounded and Disabled of the War in Spain" (1937). In the context of this organization, they "campaigned for the state to provide special schools, as well as artificial limbs, for disabled veterans." Without large state subsidies, the league developed its own sources of income; members paid dues, and they placed emotive advertisements in newspapers to "raise money from the general public." Disabled Nationalists, for their part, fearing that they would receive little sympathy and society "might come to hate them" as time moved on, created their own organization, which they called the "Honorable Corps" (1938). After the war, many of the non-wounded Nationalist veterans created their own organization: the "Brotherhood of Provisional Subalterns" (1958) was known to be politically conservative, but they were involved in creating "special memorials" to their "own fallen."[138]

We can see comparable organizations in more Leninist-oriented, "harder" authoritarian regimes. The Soviet Union, the political and economic model for China for most of the 1950s, created a Potemkin-style "Soviet Committee of War Veterans" (SKVV) in 1956, but it was "quickly appropriated by veterans' activists who refused to believe that this was not the long awaited lobbying organization";[139] most of its leaders had been officers in the Civil War and WWII. Having experienced total war in a mass conscription army (unlike China), veterans were in a far better position to use the SKVV as a their lobbying arm; over the years it became the primary, and increasingly powerful, forum for veterans to sustain their identity and solidarity as an "entitlement group" (most veterans, unlike their Chinese counterparts, were able to stay in touch with almost all of their comrades "for the rest of their lives"[140]) as well as a platform for advocating for the bread-and-butter welfare issues that concerned most veterans. The SKVV, however, was not the only veterans organization in the former USSR. Local "Committees of Wounded Soldiers" had existed since the Civil War, as well as a "Union of Frontline Soldiers" and regional "Friendship Societies," all organizations which provided the mid-1950s SKVV with many activists and delegates, known as "double veterans."[141] In post-Communist (but still quite authoritarian) Russia, disabled veterans from the failed war in Afghanistan did not benefit from the halo of victory after the "Great Patriotic War," as WWII is known. Moreover, many were discharged just as the Soviet Union was breaking apart, leaving them with the same rights as their WWII counterparts but without the benefits. Most veterans were "on the edge of poverty" and faced a great deal of bureaucratic "insensitivity." But, unlike the PRC, Russian veterans were allowed to form an association, and Boris Yeltsin established a fund with more than a billion tax-free rubles for their activities. The association promptly linked up with similar groups in Ukraine and Uzbekistan; Western veterans organizations also offered their assistance. As a result of these multilateral contacts between veterans organizations, Russian veterans of the war in Afghanistan received so many wheelchairs that they had to give some to the WWII veterans as well as to the "ordinary" disabled. In the long term, Ethel Dunn predicts, their best hope is with "the economic strength of their veteran organizations."[142]

Veterans of the North Vietnamese Army and the Vietcong also appear to have more clout than their counterparts in China, a reflection of the greater legitimacy of their long anti-colonial wars against France and the United States. In Vietnam, there are disillusioned veterans, such as Bao Ninh, who are able to write and publish biting novels about their wartime and post-war experiences. (Ha Jin's *War Trash*, a comparable book on the Korean War, is available in China, but only in English.) Veterans in Vietnam also organize more legitimately. According to a report by David Ignatius, "The closest thing to an organized opposition party here is a group of veterans that calls itself the 'Old Resistance Fighters Club.' Their hero is General Vo Nguyen Giap, the great strategist of Vietnam's victories against the French and Americans."[143]

With the exception of their very difficult marital situation (described in Chapter 6), veterans also fared better in Taiwan. The Guomindang, a party that shares its Leninist orientation with the PRC and the USSR, took a different path from the CCP by creating a separate government agency for veterans (the *Fudao weiyuanhui*, or Veterans Affairs Commission) that had sub-cabinet level status in the Executive Yuan, publishing a veteran newspaper to maintain a sense of camaraderie (*Cheng gong zhi lu*—the Road to Success) and a separate system of veterans hospitals—claiming that these arrangements for veterans were "unprecedented" in Chinese history.[144] Unlike the PRC, whose veterans committees do not appear to have benefited from much international support, Taiwan's *Fudaohui* maintains relations with the American Veterans of Foreign Wars, the American Legion, and AMVETS; the Australian RSL; the European Veterans Association; and many others.[145] With the help of $42 million provided by the U.S. government in 1954 (which was in a separate and independent budget[146]), able leadership by Chiang Ching-kuo (Chiang Kai-shek's son) from 1956 to 1965, single-party dominance, and advice from a management consulting firm, the ROC's Veterans' Administration was generally successful in providing employment in public works projects, "veterans farms," and the private sector, as well as reasonably good medical care to most of the veterans on the island. Very many of these veterans, unlike their counterparts on the mainland, were not released into society at large, since local women "were unlikely to look upon [the veterans] as good marriage prospects—at least not in any large numbers" [owing to language barriers, poverty, and the fact that they came from the mainland].[147] Veterans—many of whom were bachelors—were also allowed to set up their own "lineage groups," complete with shrines and genealogies, from the beginning of the 1960s.[148] To be sure, resettlement of veterans on Taiwan was not bureaucratically unproblematic: there were registration problems, insufficient education about benefits, and problems getting assistance, particularly among those who chose to received a lump sum payment rather than live in a state-funded institution—so-called "independent veterans."[149] In the second half of the 1980s, after martial law was lifted, some 15,000 of these veterans organized a "Self Salvation Association," which mounted several protests against the government and did not suffer state repression. In 1986, 264 signed a petition to Chiang Ching-kuo, in 1987 some raised ROC flags and pictures of Chiang Kai-shek, and in November 1987, more than 1,000 gathered at the Executive Yuan to file a petition, where the leaders "knelt down in front of Chiang Kai-shek's picture, crying for help from his spirit."[150]

South Korea and Japan, despite sharing the legacy of Confucianism, also had different institutional arrangements for its veterans. Like Taiwan, South Korea's veteran agency is housed in a *separate* ministry (the Ministry of Patriots and Veterans). It also maintains close contact with the U.S. Veterans Administration and veterans organizations in civil society. South Korea, unlike the PRC, has a "Korean War Day," which the veteran agency helps organize. The establishment of the Ministry of Patriots and Veterans as a separate agency probably was not a coincidence. Unlike the PRC, whose top leaders have never been military generals, in South Korea, General Park Chung-hee was the driving force behind this more beneficial arrangement for veterans.[151] In post-war Japan there were numerous veterans organizations (some were organized by former commanding officers, and others were organized by enlisted men or NCOs from the same unit): the Kita Pagoda Society (whose members served in Burma), the League for the Protection of Livelihood of Repatriates from Soviet-Occupied Areas, the Locust Society, the Dandelion Society, the Japan Great Leap Society, and the Japan Cherry Friendship Society, among others. Few of these organizations focused on politics (occupation authority investigators were worried about veterans' becoming enamored with Communism or right-wing parties) but, rather, were involved with youth education, helping war orphans, providing mutual aid, providing information (in the newspapers they published), and a sense of friendship and camaraderie. Many were also very committed to providing welfare assistance to the families of dead soldiers, ranking this as their most important "demand" vis-à-vis the government, just above job opportunities (24 to 20 percent, in a newspaper's survey of 3,000 veterans).[152]

VETERANS' ALLIES

Money, as Ethel Dunn notes, is definitely important, but it is not enough; well-funded organizations, public and private, do not always get what they want. More so than money, what has been absolutely critical to the promotion of veterans' status and rights is the extent to which veterans, working in the context of organizations (independent of the state or not), have been able to forge short- and long-term alliances with other sectors in society. By themselves, and in certain political circumstances (such as post-Civil War America), veterans organizations can be reasonably successful, but the cultivation of a culture, laws, and institutions that work to veterans' benefit requires the opening of a broader front involving a wider variety of groups. The PRC, unlike democracies and most all of its authoritarian family members, has not allowed this to happen and, instead, continues to use a governing strategy of "controlled polarization" masked by nationalistic and patriotic rhetoric. Even more indicative of veterans' low status in the PRC is that there are very few signs that non-veteran groups in China are even interested in their situation.

Assuming once again our birds'-eye view of veterans' status around the globe, the extent to which other groups in society support them immediately stands out as a Himalayan-like topographical landmark to China's plateau. In Australia, for example, veterans organizations were strong, feisty, and had great access, but they were also assisted by newspaper reporters and war historians, who became boosters of the ANZAC legend through such publications as *Smith's Weekly* and *The Bulletin*, the most important veterans newspaper in the interwar years, as well as one of the most widely read accounts of the war in the late 1930s, Raymond Lording's *There and Back: The Story of an Australian Soldier*.[153] In the United Kingdom, the social and political status of its land army was quite low until the Crimean War, when "embedded" journalists, aided by new technology like the telegraph and photography, helped shift the cultural tide through sympathetic reporting and criticism of the government for apathy toward returned soldiers. They were not alone: charity organizations and the prominence of Florence Nightingale also helped generate support for veterans prior to the formation of the Royal British Legion.[154] After WWII in the Soviet Union, an even greater variety of cultural elites—many of them veterans—supported their claims to status

through the publication of novels, plays, diaries, stories in literary journals
("The Front," "Greetings from the Front"), and plays; many of the heroes of
a "barrage of popular novels" on the post-war countryside were "demobilized
officers."[155] In post–Civil War Finland, the victorious Whites benefited from
a vast network of official organizations, but since state bureaucracies were
not very attuned to veterans' emotional problems, "members of civil society
stepped in" where "there was a call for more sensitivity." Spin-offs of official organizations proliferated to lend a hand to those with problems.[156]
In Canada after WWI, veterans did not enjoy much assistance from weak
veterans organizations, but other groups in society pitched in. Their pension
demands had the support of "leading figures in Toronto society"; upon their
return they were greeted by the Red Cross and later assisted by the Knights of
Columbus, the YMCA, and the Women's Christian Temperance Movement;
businessmen and professors were involved in the official Canadian Pension
and Claims Board. Toronto was not the only city to help out absent a strong
national response: Winnipeg's mayor created the local veterans organization
and, together with other city elites, conducted "vigorous fundraising."[157] In
France, Antoine Prost notes that the National Union of Veterans was supported by the state, "men of good works," and business; the national veterans
movement included peasants *and* small traders from cities.[158] Despite harsh
criticism of the officer corps in Germany after WWII, public opinion surveys
in the late 1940s and early 1950s found that many sympathized with the plight
of former soldiers (who were allowed to organize), in part because, with near-
universal conscription, "everyone had either served or had a father, brother,
or husband in uniform."[159] In Taiwan, veterans from the mainland benefited
from activities sponsored by local native-place associations (*tongxianghui*),
which veterans could also join.[160]

The contemporary United States, with its many holidays, highways, stadiums, and bridges commemorating veterans, as well as a hospital system
and cabinet department devoted to them, is probably the tallest peak around
when observing the supportive role of civic organizations, but it was not always this way. For the first 40 years of America's existence, ordinary Revolutionary War veterans were as neglected as many of their counterparts in
China, but popular writers came to their aid.[161] Subsequent veterans were
the beneficiaries of the activities of a wider circle of groups as the mass
nature of war and the draft touched more people. After the Civil War, many
businessmen promoted the activities of the Grand Army of the Republic
(with reduced railroad fare), as did other organizations such as churches
and women's groups.[162] After WWI, veterans once again were helped by
the Red Cross, churches, and university faculty.[163] During the interwar
period, veterans received the support of businessmen, civic organizations,

and politicians; the promotion of patriotism itself was a collaborative effort involving veterans and the business and professional classes.[164] When these veterans marched on Washington to protest legislation that would require an extensive wait to receive promised bonuses, they were assisted by many sympathetic citizens: a novelist visited their shantytown to express support; railway workers helped with transportation; ordinary and wealthy Washingtonians provided food and tents; and the police chief solicited food from local merchants, paying $773 from his own pocket. Unlike the situation in China, the WWI veterans' cause was viewed as legitimate in the eyes of many: the government's repression of the veterans was widely condemned—both the Army and Douglas MacArthur were booed—and this smoothed the path toward even greater veteran benefits in the GI Bill.[165]

The critical role of civil society in supporting former soldiers' claims for martial citizenship and patriotic status can be seen by looking not only at contrasting cases to China but also at cases where the weakness of civil society had a similar impact on the status of veterans. Japan after WWII and Weimar Germany are good examples. In the former case, disabled World War II veterans were treated quite poorly by society.[166] In part, this was because they represented defeat. However, John Dower also calls attention to cultural and social factors: Japan was a society without "a strong tradition of responsibility toward strangers, or of unrequited philanthropy or tolerance of sympathy towards those who suffered misfortune."[167] In Weimar Germany, civil society was weak to begin with, but the government's monopolization of charity resulted in ordinary citizens' becoming disengaged from veterans and their problems. (Many veterans were accused of being "greedy" when they appealed for more state assistance.) As noted by Deborah Cohen, veterans soon turned their wrath against German society for failing to appreciate their sacrifice, a form of "emotional compensation" that was more important to them than pensions and welfare. Moreover, whenever veterans bumped into bureaucratic problems and insensitivities, they quickly blamed the government (which, like the PRCs, often bragged about how well veterans were cared for) as well. In contrast, British WWI veterans enjoyed little state support and generally held their government in disdain, but they did receive a great deal of assistance from civil society and charity. More important than money, many British veterans had the sense that their military experiences were appreciated by society and that their fellow citizens honored them.[168]

Of course, one could easily object to these comparisons, on two grounds. First, as I suggested in the introduction, did German and Japanese citizens not appreciate their veterans simply because they *lost* their respective wars and fought for illegitimate and discredited regimes? Second, is it fair to compare China, a largely rural, pre-capitalist country, with more industrialized and urbanized counterparts? I am, overall, sympathetic to this critique of Cohen's argument—it is hard to separate loss in war from its legitimacy in the eyes of the public and the support of civil society. As a thought experiment, we might ask ourselves: would civic institutions in Great Britain have been as generous if they had lost the war? I have my doubts about this. A Japan/Germany comparison would seem to make more sense in this respect, since both countries lost. PRC veterans, however, should not really "belong" to this category: they did not represent defeat, but "glorious victory." However, in significant (and ironic) ways, they were treated not radically different from German and Japanese veterans, who lived in countries with a larger middle class and more mature capitalist economies. Because respect for military service does not require democracy or capitalism, one common denominator when looking at the trio of the PRC, Weimar Germany, and Japan is the underlying weakness of civil society in the context of an overbearing state, whose promises to veterans are difficult to enforce through often-insensitive bureaucratic mechanisms or, in the Chinese case, through bureaucratic regulation occasionally bolstered by campaigns. One key difference is that Japan and Germany *allowed* the formation of veterans and widows organizations, which proved effective in lobbying for changes and working for greater follow-through in policy implementation, but this has not happened to any significant degree in China. Without organizations or support in civil society, veterans continue to be ignored by society, even if the state is forced to pay them more heed because of their protests, which we will see a lot more of in Chapter 8.

But is there something deeper, perhaps, that explains why other members of Chinese society seem quite impervious to their veterans' status, why China still lacks veterans organizations or federations and why China has a weak foundation of republican patriotism? I argue the China (unlike Germany, Japan, Russia, the United States, Australia, or France) never fought a war that had either widespread consensus or a military based something close to universal conscription—a "national army," not a party-army. Absent such conscription in peacetime (as in South Korea, Taiwan, and Singapore) or war, most urban workers, intellectuals, and businessmen did not serve, so PLA veterans were easily "forgettable" without their own organization to fight a battle for memory (what some theorists of nationalism and commemoration have called "memory work") and for the patriotic status of military service. In other words, even as state policy stressed the idea that welfare could never be an entirely state-run service and that "society" or "the masses" had to be involved as well,[169] there was never a social consensus about the legitimacy of veterans' claim to status or their worthiness as beneficiaries for state entitlement programs; the argument that "revolutionary humanitarianism" required "service to the proletariat" was certainly no help to veterans, whose needs were quite different from those of workers.[170] In the West, Russia, and Japan, veterans and others associated with the military (not professors, lawyers, and businessmen) have taken the lead in pressing for a version of citizenship and patriotism that stresses *sacrifice* and *action* as opposed to words that do not involve costs[171] as well as pushing for civic activities and holidays that promote "love of country," such as placing flags in schools and public buildings, reciting the Pledge of Allegiance in schools, the establishment of national holidays, the singing of the National Anthem at sporting events, building war memorials, organizing parades and fireworks, and committing themselves to social and political activism.[172] Veterans have also been known to take the lead in contesting official versions of wartime conduct, the meaning of sacrifice, and the behavior of politicians. In the United States, WWI veterans in the town of Orange, Massachusetts, commissioned (along with other civic groups) a decidedly anti-war memorial, and they were supported by the American Legion (44 percent of its membership believed that WWI was a mistake);[173] Joseph Heller's *Catch 22* is another example of veterans' capacity for irreverent wit and biting criticism. In Japan, Kazuo Hara's documentary *The Emperor's Naked Army* (1987) was a blunt indictment of Japan's wartime behavior and the role of Emperor Hirohito. Not coincidentally, it "starred" a rather off-kilter veteran, Kenzo Okuzaki, whose dogged quest to find out the truth about illegal executions (officers killed privates and then ate them) was the basis of the movie, which "marked a breech in representations of wartime Japan."[174]

Absent a more integrated military (or other sorts of shared experiences between classes), veterans organizations, and what Charles Epp has called a "support structure" in civil society, genuine respect for military service and support for veterans' claims for citizenship and patriotic status on that basis were very limited in China, no matter how much money was spent, or how many investigations were launched, or how many committees met on veterans' behalf in Beijing.[175] Given that China is not a democracy and does not allow independent organizations, a more effective strategy could have been a Soviet- or Fascist-like incorporation of a veterans organization into the state. As things stood in 1966, however, many ordinary veterans had the worst of many worlds: a culture that did not appreciate the masculine dimensions of military service, a state where institutions did not count nearly as much as officials' personal discretion, a bureaucracy that did not absorb the most talented elites in the country and that had difficulty enforcing veterans' claims vis-à-vis other organizations, and a national leadership whose policies did not match its flowery rhetoric about veterans' contributions to the state.

Viewed from the perspective of the conditions for "effective implementation" mentioned earlier in this chapter, this outcome is not very surprising. Successful implementation requires that "the law should not be ambiguous and implementing officials should all be aware what the final goal is," but State Council documents were generally dripping with ambiguities; it also requires that the "implementation structure" should "enhance compliance by implementing officials and target groups," but there appear to have been no significant sanctions for those who violated State Council policies or rewards for those who did;[176] target groups should be "positively constructed," but in China many officials disagreed that veterans deserved higher status and disputed the "causal theory" behind entitlement programs; the condition of "committed and skillful implementing officials" was also quite weak, as the more prestigious ministries absorbed the most talented manpower; and finally, and probably most critically, scholars have called attention to the need for "consistent support of executives and interest groups." This, too, was sorely lacking in the PRC. In the next chapter we will look at veterans' suicides, which were, in significant ways, a predictable result of their problems finding their place in the sun within the state and their precarious position in society.

NOTES

1. James Diehl, *The Thanks of the Fatherland: German Veterans after the Second World War*, 18.

2. James Diehl, "Victors or Victims? Disabled Veterans in the Third Reich," 705–6; David Crew, *Germans on Welfare: From Weimar to Hitler*, 83–85; Greg Eghigian, "The Politics of Victimization," 382–83.

3. John Resch, *Suffering Soldiers,* 89, 119, 125. On debates on the "deservedness" of Revolutionary War veterans and the pension scandal, see Laura Jensen, "Constructing and Entitling America's Original Veterans," 35–62.

4. On the important role of "policy legacies," see Peter Hall, "Policy Paradigms, Social Learning and the State: The Case of Economic Policymaking in Britain," 275–96.

5. Suzanne Mettler, *Soldiers to Citizens*, 116. However, as noted elsewhere, the GI Bill had more limited impact on poor minorities.

6. Jeff Zeleny, "Clinton and McCain Differ on Iraq at Veterans' Meeting," *New York Times*, August 21, 2007. The rate is based on a survey released by the VFW's internal magazine.

7. Diehl, *Thanks of the Fatherland*, 237; Lockenour, *Soldiers as Citizens*, 19–20.

8. Anne Schneider and Helen Ingram (eds.), "Introduction," in *Deserving and Entitled: Social Constructions and Public Policy,* 2.

9. During WWII, many Americans claimed to be making some sort of sacrifice for victory, and engaged in pitched public battles over who was sacrificing more, but

they were at least able to agree, unlike the Chinese, that the "boys at the front" had made the most significant ones. Leff notes that "claimed sacrifices and contributions could be parlayed into political advantage or into efforts to shift war burdens onto others." See Mark H. Leff, "The Politics of Sacrifice on the American Home Front in World War II," 1296–98.

10. Garton, *The Cost of War: Australians Return*, 235; Resch, *Suffering Soldiers*, 85; O'Leary, *To Die For*, 45–46; Mark Edele, "A 'Generation of Victors'? Soviet Second World War Veterans from Demobilization to Organization, 1941–1956," (Ph.D. dissertation, Department of History, University of Chicago, 2004), 552–54. Some polls in the United States show that large majorities consider veteran benefits to be an entitlement (78 percent) and that veterans should benefit from hiring preferences (69 percent). The first poll was conducted by the Kaiser Family Foundation (1,309 respondents, 1997) and the latter by K Associates (309 respondents, 1996). See http://poll.orspub.com.

11. See, for instance, Jeffrey Pressman and Aaron Wildavsky, *Implementation*; Eugene Bardach, *The Implementation Game*.

12. Gerald Rosenberg, *Hollow Hope: Can Courts Bring About Social Change?* and Stuart Scheingold, *The Politics of Rights: Lawyers, Public Policy and Political Change*. For a more optimistic account, see Michael McCann, *Rights at Work: Pay Equity Reform and the Politics of Legal Mobilization*.

13. Donald van Meter and Carl Von Horn, "The Policy Implementation Process: A Conceptual Framework," 445–88.

14. See Kevin O'Brien and Lianjiang Li, "Selective Policy Implementation in Rural China," 167–86.

15. See his "Top-Down and Bottom-Up Approaches to Implementation Research: A Critical Analysis and Suggested Synthesis," 23–24.

16. John Braithwaite and Toni Makkai, "Testing an Expected Utility Model of Corporate Deterrence," 7–40.

17. For the conceptualization of different layers of the state, see Joel Migdal, "The State in Society," 16.

18. Kenneth Lieberthal and Michel Oksenberg, *Policy Making in China: Leaders, Structures and Processes*, Chapter 2.

19. For an elaboration of Civil Affairs' role in marriage and divorce, see Neil J. Diamant, "Making Love 'Legible' in China," 447–80. For a comparison to the Social Security Administration in the United States when it was required to add needy disabled, blind, and aged persons to its traditional clientele of retirees and the resulting problems, see Martha Derthick, *Agency under Stress*, Chapter 2.

20. Interview with Bureau of Civil Affairs Director, Qingpu County, February 1994.

21. QA 48-2-105, 136.

22. *Minzheng jianbao*, August 8, 1956, 51.

23. DDA 11-7-201 (1953), 3.

24. DDA 11-7-201, 2.

25. *Minzheng jianbao*, November 7, 1956, 3; and September 28, 1956, 3.

26. QA 48-2-37 (1952), 1.

27. SMA B168-1-600 (1951), 126.

28. Derthick, *Agency under Stress*, 184.

29. SMA B168-1-655, 6.

30. SMA B168-1-664, 28–29.

31. SMA B163-2-492 (1957), 82.

32. DDA 11-7-116, 5; SMA B168-1-607 (1952), 70.

33. *Minzheng jianbao*, August 15, 1956, 56–57.

34. SMA B168-1-628, 47.

35. QA 48-2-105 (1957), 136.

36. SMA B1-2-1958, 21.

37. SMA B123-6-1374 (1965), 15–18.

38. Letters from Qingpu veterans to Civil Affairs, no reference number, in author's collection.

39. SMA B168-1-619 (1954), 10.

40. SMA B1-2-1958, 20.

41. Ezra Vogel notes that even in the 1960s, when the official status of the PLA rose, veterans were still trying to build a "base of support" by appealing to veterans discharged in previous years. See *Canton under Communism*, 312.

42. SMA B127-1-811 (1954), 6.

43. See *Songjiang xian zhi* (Shanghai: Renmin chubanshe, 1991), 284. It is difficult to track the exact dates of these transformations. For example, the Jing'an District gazetteer (Shanghai) claims to have established its reception office in 1963 (several years after some rural counties) and its "leading small group" in 1978, more than five years after those in other places. See *Jing'an qu zhi* (Shanghai: Shanghai shehui kexue yuan, 1996), 792.

44. SMA B168-1-600 (1951), 111.

45. *Minzheng jianbao*, August 15, 1956, 56.

46. SMA B168-1-655, 6.

47. For one particularly compelling account of PRC semi-religious rituals, see Richard Madsen, *Morality and Power in a Chinese Village*.

48. For an interesting discussion on the Zionist concept of time, see Eyal Chowers, "Time in Zionism: The Life and Afterlife of a Temporal Revolution," 652–85.

49. On this ethos, see Oz Almog, *The Sabra*; George Mosse, "Max Nordau: Liberalism and the New Jew," 161–75.

50. Rousseau asks, "By what means are we to move men's hearts and bring them to love their fatherland and its laws? Dare I say? Through the games they play as children, through institutions that, though superficial man would deem them pointless, develop habits that abide and attachments that nothing can dissolve." See *The Government of Poland*, 4.

51. Even "alternative" Memorial Day ceremonies "emanate from the same ethos that begot the conventions" and "recapture the same myths, while adjusting their style or political content." See Lily Galili, "They Want to Distance Themselves, but Can't," *Haaretz*, April 23, 2007.

52. Personal observation, April 19, 2007.

53. Yonatan Lees, "Rikud, k'tiva u'makhela," *Haaretz*, April 22, 2007.

54. I collected packets with Max Nordau ("journalist and physician, Herzl's right-hand man"), Josef Trumpeldor ("veteran of the Russian army, lost his right arm during the Russo-Japanese War, died defending Tel Hai"), and Orde Wingate ("veteran of the British army, loved the Bible, Israel and supported Zionism . . .").

55. Lea Shamgar-Handelman, *Israeli War Widows: Beyond the Glory of Heroism*, 32–48; and Shamgar-Handelman, "Administering to War Widows in Israel: The Birth of a Social Category," 35–43.

56. Eyal Ben-Ari, "Tests of Soldierhood, Trials of Manhood," 262.

57. DDA 11-7-25 (1950), 11; DDA 11-7-89 (1954), 91; DDA 11-7-47, 132; DDA 11-7-380 (1963), 97–98. In organizing these events, Civil Affairs was supposed to rely on the assistance of the leaders of state-organized military and martyr family committees, but reports indicated that there was infrequent contact between leaders of these committees and "rank-and-file" members. See DDA 11-7-380 (1963), 95.

58. DDA 11-7-321(1956), 11.

59. DDA 11-7-47, 132.

60. Garton, *Cost of War*, 235.

61. Peter Leese, "Problems Returning Home," 1056–57; Seth Koven, "Remembering and Dismemberment," 1201.

62. Diehl, "Victors or Victims," 719.

63. Deborah Cohen, *The War Come Home*, 62, 102, 164–68; Eghigian, "The Politics of Victimization," 378.

64. Diehl, "Victors or Victims," 723.

65. Shaun Malarney, "`The Fatherland Remembers Your Sacrifice," 53.

66. SMA B168-1-600 (1951), 111.

67. *Minzheng jianbao*, November 7, 1956, 76.

68. SMA B1-2-1958, 24. Emphasis mine.

69. SMA B168-1-628 (1956), 2.

70. SMA B127-1-358, 36.

71. QA 48-2-109 (1957), 4–5.

72. SMA B168-1-617, 16.

73. SMA B168-1-619, 29–30.

74. SMA B168-1-651 (1960), 2–3; Thaxton, *Catastrophe and Contention*, 310.

75. SMA B168-1-64 (1965), 27.

76. SMA B168-1-226 (1965), 21.

77. To be sure, this was not a problem unique to Civil Affairs in China. For American bureaucracies, see James Q. Wilson, *Bureaucracy: What Government Agencies Do and Why They Do It,* 174–75.

78. SMA B168-1-64 (1965), 27–28.

79. SMA B168-1-582, 2–4. This was not different from a decade earlier, when Civil Affairs officials called their work "drudgery." See SMA B168-1-619 (1955), 30.

80. SMA B168-1-582 (1964), 214.

81. Ibid., 170.

82. In 1964, it was noted that the clerks "are working for 8–9 years and still don't know the policy, objective or what they are supposed to be doing, nor do they understand its significance," See DDA 11-7-399, 107.

83. SMA B168-1-607 (1952), 49.

84. SMA B1-2-1958, 55.

85. This confusion can clearly be seen in the film *Assembly*. Captain Gu Zidi is the sole survivor of a unit whose number was changed and reassigned to a different regiment. It takes more than seven years to set the record straight.

86. SMA B1-2-1958, 30.

87. Ibid., 55.

88. SMA B168-1-633 (1957), 81–82; SMA B168-1-645, 21.

89. SMA B168-1-633 (1957), 81.

90. SMA B168-1-645, 21.

91. Resch, *Suffering Soldiers*, 143.

92. Donald Shaffer, "'I Do Not Suppose That Uncle Sam Looks at the Skin,'" 132–36; O'Leary, *To Die For*, 47.

93. SMA B168-1-605, 81.

94. SMA B127-1-811 (1955), 4; SMA B168-1-645 (1959), 41.

95. SMA B1-2-1958 (1957), 29.

96. SMA B168-1-632 (1957), 129.

97. SMA B127-1-811 (1955), 5.

98. SMA B168-1-632, 131.

99. SMA B127-1-1036 (1960), 48.

100. SMA B127-1-1036, 18.

101. MacFarquhar and Schoenhals, *Mao's Last Revolution*, 156.

102. Cited in Gordon White, "The Politics of Demobilized Soldiers," 205–6.

103. This account is based on a transcript of Zhou's meeting with veteran representatives in SMA B168-3-131, 3–6. All quotes in the text below are from these pages.

104. B168-3-131 (1967), 22.

105. See, for example, *Qingyuan xian zhi*, 734, for Guangdong Province. The Langxi County gazetteer (Anhui Province) mentions that "during the Cultural Revolution, there was a large group (*dapi*) of previously resettled veterans who entered the city looking for work, which made resettlement work chaotic." See *Langxi xian zhi* (Beijing: Fangzhi chubanshe, 1998), 684.

106. See, for example, the case of the "Veteran Army" (*rongfujun*) in Heilongjiang, as reported in *People's Daily* (January 26 and February 15, 1967) and in the journal *Hongqi*, February 3, 1967 (p. 17), and March 3, 1967 (p. 38). For Taiwan, see Yu-Wen Fan, "Becoming a Civilian," 151–52. According to Fan, veterans made many financial contributions to the government during this period.

107. According to Gordon White's analysis of veterans' activities during the Cultural Revolution, 77 percent of veterans joined the conservative faction. See "The Politics of Demobilized Soldiers," 207, 211. He argues that this pattern of political response demonstrates that CCP policies toward veterans were generally more successful than not ("success outweighed failure"). By incorporating "a majority of demobilized and transferred soldiers from both phases of demobilization" into the state structure, the CCP managed to hold onto their loyalty during the Cultural Revolution (p. 212). As we have seen in Chapter 2, however, in very many areas only a minority of veterans were incorporated into the state structure in rural areas. There is also a question with regard to labels. That most

veterans were "conservative" does not necessarily mean that they supported the CCP as such. It could mean that they *did not support* the effort to destroy it *completely.*

108. Jonathan Unger, "Whither China? Yang Xiguang, Red Capitalists, and the Social Turmoil of the Cultural Revolution," 23.

109. White, "Politics of Demobilized Soldiers," 208; Vogel, *Canton under Communism,* 342; Hong Yung Lee, *The Politics of the Chinese Cultural Revolution,* 233. Veterans were also involved in the radical "Committee to Criticize Tao Zhu" in Beijing (p. 129). According to Lee, 40 percent of the 160,000 members of the August 1st Combat Corps in Guangdong were veterans.

110. See CIA, "Staff Notes: Chinese Affairs," February 18, 1975, p. 5. Accessed electronically in the National Archives, College Park, MD.

111. *Rongfujun* was rehabilitated in 1978, but it probably took longer elsewhere. The Jing County gazetteer (Anhui) notes that between 1978 and 1980, thirty-nine "veterans, disabled soldiers and martyr families who were wrongly accused during the Cultural Revolution had their verdicts reversed and their reputations and benefits restored." See *Jing xian zhi* (Beijing: Fangzhi chubanshe, 1996), 601.

112. Richard Alston, *Soldier and Society in Roman Egypt,* 158.

113. Reese, *Homecoming Heroes,* 110.

114. Desmond Morton and Glenn Wright, *Winning the Second Battle,* 13, 64.

115. Reese, *Homecoming Heroes,* 99, 106, 166–67, 143.

116. Morton and Wright, *Winning the Second Battle,* 119, 178.

117. G. L. Kristianson, *The Politics of Patriotism: The Pressure Group Activities of the Returned Servicemen's League,* 189, 212.

118. Stephen Garton, "Longing for War: Nostalgia and Australian Returned Soldiers after the First World War," 224–29; Michael Keren, "Commemoration and National Identity: A Comparison between the Making of the Anzac and Palmach Legends," 17–18.

119. Kristianson, *Politics of Patriotism,* 146, 188–89, 198.

120. See *Homecoming Heroes,* 137, 168.

121. Browne, "War-Making and U.S. State Formation," 244.

122. O'Leary, *To Die For,* 37.

123. Larry M. Logue, "Union Veterans and Their Government," 425–26; Theda Skocpol, *Protecting Soldiers and Mothers,* 126–27.

124. Stuart McConnell, "Who Joined the Grand Army?" 140.

125. O'Leary, *To Die For,* 47.

126. George Mosse, *The Nationalization of the Masses: Political Symbolism and Mass Movements in Germany from the Napoleonic Wars through the Third Reich,* 62, 69–70; Benjamin Ziemann, *War Experiences in Rural Germany,* 254.

127. O'Leary, *To Die For,* 91, 97, 151–52, 179, 182.

128. See Fleischer and Zames, *The Disability Rights Movement,* 171.

129. Ziemann, *War Experiences,* 247.

130. University of Chicago Committee on Human Development, *The American Veteran Back Home,* 200. For WWI, see Wallace Davies, *Patriotism on Parade,* 119.

131. Mettler, *Soldiers to Citizens,* 20–21.

132. Ibid., 17.

133. University of Chicago Committee on Human Development, *The American Veteran Back Home*, 209.

134. On the American GI Forum, see Carl Allsup, *The American G.I. Forum: Origins and Evolution*.

135. For the connection between war making and state making in Europe, see Charles Tilly, *Coercion, Capital, and European States, AD 990–1992*, Chapter 3.

136. I am grateful to Andrew Rudalevige for this formulation.

137. Mabel Berezin, *Making the Fascist Self*, 75–76, 83–84.

138. Paloma Aguilar, "Agents of Memory: Spanish Civil War Veterans and Disabled Soldiers," 86–90, 96, 101.

139. Mark Edele, "Soviet Veterans," 112.

140. Catherine Merridale, *Ivan's War*, 357.

141. Edele, "A 'Generation of Victors'?" 500–505, 517–18.

142. Ethel Dunn, "Disabled Russian War Veterans: Surviving the Collapse of the Soviet Union," 253–68.

143. See David Ignatius, "Vietnamese Begin to Question If War Was Worth Sacrifices: Popular New Book Is Soldier's Angry Tale," *Washington Post*, November 12, 1991.

144. Fan, "Becoming a Civilian," 45. In addition to hospitals, the Veterans Administration signed contracts with county authorities so that veterans *and their families* could go to public health clinics for basic care. Veterans' families on the mainland had no such rights (p. 48).

145. The entrance room and lobby of the *Fudaohui* are full of plaques, flags, and letters from veterans organizations around the world. Personal observation. For the full list of cooperative agreements, see http://www.vac.gov.tw.

146. Fan, "Becoming a Civilian," 51.

147. See Fred W. Riggs, *The Consulting Firm, the U.S. Aid Agency and the Chinese Veterans Program* (Syracuse: Inter-University Case Study Program, 1970). When the American consulting firm arrived on Taiwan in 1955 to assess the program already in place, they found many of the same problems as Civil Affairs on the mainland: the top leaders, up until the arrival of Chiang Ching-kuo, often held concurrent jobs and had not even wanted to be working with veterans in the first place (pp. 11–12, 27). Its effectiveness improved toward the end of the 1950s and early 1960s, however. Throughout this period, American advisors worked closely with the Veterans Administration. The transition to private employment was also facilitated by American funds, which provided the veterans with an initial subsidy. By early 1959, close to 3,000 veterans had obtained private employment, and 2,447 were given job training (p. 46). Reports from the late 1990s suggest that the Veterans Administration is still helpful in locating jobs for veterans. Among the 38 percent of veterans who participated in VA-sponsored job training programs, 54.2 percent considered it "very helpful" and 28 percent somewhat helpful. Only 9 percent believed it was not helpful. See Xingzheng yuan guojun tuichu yi guanbing fudao weiyuanhui tongji chu (ed.), *Zhonghua minguo 90 nian Tai-Min diqu rongmin jiuye zhuangkuang diaocha baogao* (Taibei, 2002), 4.

148. Fan, "Becoming a Civilian," 49.

149. Ibid., 92.

150. Ibid., 94–95.

151. Interview with Gil Hyun Lee, Manager–Counselor, Ministry of Patriots and Veterans, Pittsburgh, PA, November 10, 2007.

152. National Archives, RG 331, Box 2275U, "Fukuin Gunjun Dantai" folder; RG 331, Box 05897. The survey was conducted by the *Hokkoku Mainichi* (Kanazawa), April 6, 1946.

153. Garton, "Longing for War," 228–29. In the PRC, unlike the ROC, there was no veteran newspaper from the 1950s to the 1970s, but one has been published in the reform period.

154. Leese, "Problems Returning Home," 1057; Reese, *Homecoming Heroes*, 44.

155. Amir Weiner, *Making Sense of War*, 45, 49, 57.

156. Mandy Hoogendoorn, "Remembering and Forgetting the Finnish Civil War," 41.

157. Morton and Wright, *Winning the Second Battle*, 46, 62–63.

158. Antoine Prost, *In the Wake of War,* 29, 34, 46–47.

169. Lockenour, *Soldiers as Citizens*, 27.

160. Fan, "Becoming a Civilian," 158.

161. Resch, *Suffering Soldiers*, 85.

162. O'Leary, *To Die For*, 41.

163. Mary Frost Jessup, *The Public Reaction to the Returned Service Man after World War I*, 8, 13, 36.

164. John Bodnar, *Remaking America*, 84. 86. Emphasis mine.

165. Paul Dickson and Thomas Allen, "Marching on History," 84, 88, 90, 92. The veterans succeeded. In 1936 Congress passed the "Cash Now Bonus Act," which provided an average of $580 per man. Two billion dollars were distributed to three million veterans.

166. Ziemann refers to the "everyday contempt shown towards disabled survivors." See *War Experiences in Rural Germany*, 252.

167. John Dower, *Embracing Defeat: Japan in the Wake of World War II*, 61.

168. Cohen, *The War Come Home*, 4, 7–9, 63, 93, 96.

169. SMA B1-2-1958 (1957), 21; *Minzheng jianbao*, October 11, 1956, 67.

170. DDA 11-7-399 (1964), 64.

171. Prost writes of French WWI veterans: "It is impossible to overstate the veterans' hatred for the patriotism of the home front. They detested the middle-aged men who demanded offensives and paid for them light-heartedly with the lives of others—their own lives" (*In the Wake of War*, p. 81). *All Quiet on the Western Front* conveys the same feelings among German troops.

172. See Mona Siegel, "History Is the Opposite of Forgetting: The Limits of Memory and the Lessons of History in Interwar France," 784–87; Prost, *In the Wake of War*, 53–54.

173. David Glassberg and J. Michael Moore, "Patriotism in Orange," 160–90.

174. I am grateful to Professor Dennis Washburn of Dartmouth College for this reference. See Jeffrey Ruoff and Kenneth Ruoff, "The Memory of War: Notes on The Emperors' Naked Army Marches On," in the DVD version of the movie.

175. Charles Epp, *The Rights Revolution: Lawyers, Activists, and Supreme Courts in Comparative Perspective*.

176. As noted by Xiaobo Lü, decrees and announcements in China often are regarded as "ad hoc, less stringent, and replaceable," and *policies* in documents or circulars "can be easily bent to suit the needs of the people who are to execute them rather than statutory regulations, containing rules and procedures." See *Cadres and Corruption*, 164, 172.

6

Vulnerable Heroes: Veterans' Health, Family, and Sexuality in Chinese Politics

It was the middle of the night, but the PLA veteran, a former officer, could not fall asleep. He was, by most all accounts, a bona fide war hero (mainly in battles in China's Northeast), decorated and praised for his courage, poise, and clear thinking under fire; he was wounded in battle in 1938. After a mediocre career in the 1950s, he rose rapidly in the party in the early 1960s. But wounds, recurring illnesses, and years of artillery fire had wreaked havoc on his sleeping patterns; in peacetime, sleep was fitful because it was *too* quiet for comfort. Years on the battlefield also took a toll on his health. Those around him reported that he had been ill for many years, was in constant pain (he could work for only one or two half-hour periods a day and rarely attended meetings), and sometimes behaved erratically, all of which limited his ability to build bridges to other party leaders; most of his close contacts were in the PLA, not the "civilian wing" of the party. Like many other veterans we have seen, the officer often found himself politically isolated and thus politically vulnerable in the no-holds-barred world of Chinese politics. Still suffering from serious health problems, the veteran, together with his family, died during the Cultural Revolution in circumstances that can only be described as highly murky. His reputation has still not been rehabilitated by the party he helped bring to power.

For those familiar with the Chinese political scene, the above story should have a somewhat familiar ring to it. Subtract my literary license, and the veteran officer in question is none other than Marshal Lin Biao, Mao Zedong's minister of defense and heir apparent until 1971, when he and his family, sensing that walls were crumbling on them, perished in a plane crash while attempting to flee China. What might be a bit more surprising to students of Chinese politics is the causal weight I have placed on Lin's *medical condi-*

tion: his erratic behavior at home and work habits (according to one source, he was better able to relax amid the sounds of a motorcycle—placed *in* his home—at full throttle, surrounded by fumes from diesel fuel), his frequent illness, his difficulty managing relationships (including with his wife), and ultimately his fatal political weakness strike me as symptomatic of post-traumatic stress disorder (PTSD) combined with more run-of-the-mill ailments of the body that have affected veterans throughout history.[1] Boasting a military record second to none (and superior to those of Deng Xiaoping and Zhou Enlai, who successfully straddled the civilian–military divide), Lin's case, I suggest in this chapter, can best be understood as simply the most famous, but not atypical, instance of how wartime experiences affected the bodies, minds, and families of thousands of more ordinary veterans and led to their difficulty taking their civilian opponents "to the mat" in many political wrestling matches. If Marshal Lin had a hard time managing his political career and his family affairs (his wife, Ye Qun, was said to have been able to easily manipulate him[2]), consider the predicament of less well-placed veterans.[3]

Lin Biao's sudden demise was a shock to the political system—even Mao was not quite himself after it—but it should not have been at all surprising to any official who had access to reports on PLA veterans in the 17 years prior to the beginning of the Cultural Revolution. Unnatural deaths among veterans (and their family members, we will see in the next chapter) were one of those inconvenient facts that were known at the top but kept well hidden from the youth who imitated soldiers' marches, battle tactics, and uniforms during this period. They had been a long-standing feature of political life since the earliest years of the PRC. In 1952, An Fuhan, a veteran from the old revolutionary base area in Shanxi Province, took his life when he returned home and found that his wife had remarried, both of his parents had died, and "no one came by to console him"; another veteran from Shanxi attempted suicide in Beijing's Zhongshan's Park after he could not get settled into a job, was poor, and "had an illness that was not being cured." A passerby, however, noticed his body and notified the authorities, who brought him to the hospital, where he recovered and was released.[4] A decade later, and in wealthier areas of the country, reports called attention to veterans' medical vulnerability: in Qingpu, there was Han Enyou, 66, a disabled veteran who suffered from chronic high blood pressure and committed suicide; Li Hailin, whose marriage was poor, was frequently sick, and "could not afford medicine"; and Hu Jinfa, a 28-year-old veteran from Songjiang County who was frequently ill, resulting in his wife's petitioning for divorce.[5] Lin Biao may have been one of the most prominent veterans for whom medical problems impacted his political and personal fate, but he certainly was not the only one in China; a 1956 estimate noted that nationwide there were roughly half a million veterans who were chronically ill, "old and weak," and with Level 3 (the least injured on a scale of 1–3) disabilities.[6] To the extent that we seek to understand the sources of veterans' problems in "political wrestling" in China, perhaps we need look no further than their bodies: pain, illness, and sexual and family-related problems were all handicaps that many of their younger, civilian rivals did not have.

Whether the victim was Lin Biao, Hu Jinfa, or Han Enyou, the political tale of war-related disability and vulnerability is an old one that refuses to fade away, even now. For instance, Sophocles' story of Philoctetes is about the son of the King of Poeas, a famed archer and a warrior who was bitten by a water viper on the way to the Trojan War. The odor from his festering wound was so offensive to his comrades that he was marooned on the island of Lemnos.[7] The disabled Philoctetes, however, had something that was indispensable to the war effort, which had been going on without him for ten years. Cassandra, the seer, told the Greeks that the war could not be won without the bow of Heracles, which was in Philoctetes' possession after he inherited it from his warrior father. The Greeks, forced to eat crow, sent Neoptolemus and Odysseus to Lemnos to ask Philoctetes to rejoin them. The wounded warrior was initially too proud to accept their apology: "What things you've done to me, how you've cheated me! Are you not ashamed to look at me here at your feet, a suppliant to you, yourself shameful?" Eventually, there was a *deus ex machina* (a sudden, unexpected story contrivance) that relieved him of the burden of this decision; the Greeks regained the bow and eventually went on to win the war.[8]

Like Sophocles, spinners of political fables in 20th-century China and the United States recognized the power of narratives involving heroic wounded soldiers whose sacrifices and sufferings are redeemed. Despite the Korean War and rising international tensions, disabled soldiers were almost invisible in Chinese films during the 1950s and early 1960s—CCP cultural elites insisted on showing images of a "healthy, strong nation"[9]—but in the years prior to the Cultural Revolution and during it, Chinese by the millions read Mao's essay about the non-mythological Dr. Norman Bethune ("In Memory of Norman Bethune"), a Canadian physician who tended to wounded PLA soldiers in the late 1930s (and who died from septicemia after cutting himself during surgery). The constant repetition of this story (together with many works of art) has created the impression that wounded PLA veterans received proper care; it has also forever sealed Canada's reputation as a "friend of China." Like the soldiers he treated, Bethune was a complicated figure—he had a fondness for women and drinking—but the narrative spun around his exploits was a simplified tale of heroism, selflessness, and martyrdom. More recently in the United States, the story arc of Private Jessica Lynch, who was said to have been wounded in Falluja, Iraq, while valiantly repulsing her attackers, served, at least for a while, to convince Americans of the valor attached to being wounded in combat and the legitimacy of the cause. However, like the mythological Philoctetes, many elements of the Jessica Lynch story were also fiction. She was awarded a medal for heroic action largely as a result of pressure from politicians on the Pentagon (through their congressional liaisons), against the recommendation of officers who examined her case and found that she had never fired her weapon.[10]

Wounds tended, disabilities surmounted, and physical hardships overcome in the line of duty are convenient tropes for spinmeisters in the political world and storytellers in literary circles. However, these kinds of representations or (to use the more fashionable term) *discourses* about suffering, care, and redemption tell fewer significant truths about the impact of war on the body than more "everyday" interactions, or lack thereof, between flesh-and-blood individuals who returned from war and the state officials and members of society who were entreated to hold them in high esteem; most veterans, after all, did not live on islands like Philoctetes on Lemnos or benefit from interviews with celebrity journalists like Jessica Lynch. While we recognize that wounded and sick veterans are inescapably embedded in particular cultures, histories, and political systems, it is also important to look at this relationship from the perspective of veterans' bodies: chronic pain, disorienting medications, and the time required to navigate bureaucracies and clinics could easily limit their ability to get along and get ahead. Good health is a *resource*, an important part of an individual's social and political "capital," much like time, social connections, and financial resources. Lin Biao's dependence on his politically ambitious wife, erratic behavior, isolation, lack of sleep, and the ease with which he was manipulated by others might just demonstrate the inherent limitations of engaging in politics while distracted by more corporeal problems. How society treats those with these sorts of problems can also serve as a gauge of the extent to which government and society give meaningful patriotic credit and citizenship status (that is, not limited to official praise or policies) to those who served in the military as well as accommodate their obvious needs. Health care, like good health, is a scarce resource that involves significant costs (medicine, hospital beds, sick leave) and is bureaucratically complex and fraught with tension since the determination of disability is "inescapably subjective."[11] Moreover, it involves many educated personnel (doctors, nurses, and personnel officials)—in short, those who, at least according to scholarly accounts, were most exposed to patriotic sentiments. If the PLA was an esteemed institution, if ordinary people bought into the CCP's thousand-told narrative of victory, and if pride in nation was manifested in the resurgence of national power, it would not be unreasonable to expect that those victors whose bodies were scarred and marked by war would be treated well and with a good dose of sympathy and concern for their welfare. These criteria should apply with extra force to educated elites in the health field, whose position gave them tremendous powers to heal, cure, and reduce suffering. They can also apply to other sectors of society: Were women willing to marry disabled soldiers? Were employers willing to take into consideration chronic pain when assigning jobs? Were Civil Affairs officials sympathetic when approached by a veteran with personal problems?

Tracking down the interactions between veterans with disabilities or family- and sex-related problems and other members of Chinese society is not easy. Despite the overwhelming importance of warfare in the history of modern China, few have studied what actually happened to those who experienced war firsthand after their discharge. This neglect has more to do with academic bias against military topics and an unfortunate propensity in China studies to follow whatever topic, methodology, or theory is in vogue in our disciplines (political economy, democratization, cultural studies, etc.) than a scholarly consensus that military or civil–military relations are unimportant politically, culturally, or sociologically. As a result, we now face the rather odd predicament of knowing more about disability as a biologically rooted, quasi-ethnic identity (thanks to research by Matthew Kohrman on disability in China and Karen Nakamura's study of deafness in Japan, for instance) than the political and social experiences of millions of Chinese, Japanese, and Koreans who returned from war in the 1940s and 1950s with missing body parts, chronic pain, and scarred minds.[12] That many would also have serious psychological problems should not be particularly surprising. According to psychiatrist Jonathan Shay, veterans' ability to recover from combat trauma often hinges on *staying together* with other veterans, but in China policy focused on returning them to their native place (see Chapter 2), even if this meant separating them from their comrades-in-arms.[13]

In Asia, the neglect of research on war-related disabilities is more understandable. Unlike the United States, which did not experience war on its territory, Asian countries suffered enormous devastation. After WWII, it was far easier, and maybe even necessary, to look toward the future than to dwell on the messy consequences of the past. Chinese leaders repeatedly referred to "new China" after 1949, and Japan's national narrative focused on its "economic miracle" by the late 1950s; Westerners duly chronicled the revolutionary changes in China, and studies of the sources of economic growth in Japan became a cottage industry. But perhaps there was something else at work: a keen awareness that despite state policies, disabled and ill veterans were not treated well and that this poor treatment reflected poorly on their societies and governments. In China, at least, archival research suggests that this often was the case: many disabled veterans found themselves exposed and vulnerable to several lines of attacks against their status. Officials and ordinary people were dubious about the value of their war-weakened bodies to the state and virulently contested their claims of worthiness for status and certain benefits. As these attacks took place, many veterans were unable to find the support they needed in bureaucracy, the media, veterans organizations, law, civil society, or family—all "institutions" that historically served to shore up veterans' status in the face of adversity. In extreme cases, veterans by the thousands committed suicide, but in others they muddled through, often depressed, angry, and in pain.

HEALTH, MARRIAGE, AND SUICIDES:
SOME NUMBERS AND PATTERNS

More than a century ago, Emile Durkheim published *Le Suicide* (1902), a landmark study in sociology that attempted to use suicide rates among disparate groups to demonstrate a more general theory of social cohesion, or the "integration" of society. For Durkheim, suicide rates could be used to study how "macro" causes, such as dislocation caused by urbanization and industrialization, shape individual-level behavior; the more dislocation, he suggested, the higher suicide rates would be in a given group. Suicide was a "social fact" that could be studied separately from the individual acts that constituted the total rate.

It was Durkheim's good fortune, at least as a researcher, to have had access to fairly good data on suicide rates for the time, something that has eluded students of Chinese society until very recently. What we have instead are snippets of information from speeches and investigative reports, an unsystematic collection of statistical data, scattered numbers, and individual cases which need to be stitched together to get a more general sense of its causes. In contrast to U.S. data vacuumed up by public health officials in the Department of Veterans Affairs that showed a statistically significant correlation between combat trauma and propensity to suicide,[14] the scattershot information from China does not allow us to conduct statistical regression to determine what sort of veteran was more likely to commit suicide than others or a more Durkheimian analysis of how veterans' suicides compared to those of other groups.

Even with these caveats, however, it is possible to observe several general trends. Chinese veterans' suicides occurred throughout the 1950s and 1960s in numbers large enough (and in some areas, with increasing frequency over the years[15]) to warrant investigations at the county, provincial, and national levels. Very little was done to prevent suicide, aside from ex post facto analyses whose conclusions were not implemented; most suicides were not caused by the macro-variables identified by Durkheim. For instance, for Durkheim, moving to a city could cause anomie, but in China, as we have seen, this was a more celebratory event. There were, of course, other "macro" causes at work. These included widespread discrimination against disabled people due to the pervasive notion that in the "new," "strong," and "reconstructing" China, a person identified as "weak" or suffering from various maladies and ailments, even though he may have had a heroic past on the battlefield, was less valuable than someone who was young, healthy, and strong. This notion was reinforced by the Marxist emphasis on the importance of "production," which made it difficult for ill veterans to prove their worth through continued sacrifice, as well as grinding poverty that sometimes resulted in Darwinian-like struggles for survival that placed even the heroic weak at a disadvantage.[16] It is also possible that some veterans committed suicide as a dramatic form of political protest—a last-ditch effort to call attention to their plight and to make a statement about the ways in which the revolution had gone astray (see Chapter 8 for suicide in the reform period). There is ample evidence about this use of suicide (and suicide attempts) among other groups in China (but particularly women),[17] but assessing motives without more detailed documentation is somewhat hazardous.

The historical circumstances of the Chinese revolution almost guaranteed that there would be hundreds of thousands of heroic but unhealthy veterans. Generally speaking, since the emergence of cities and metropolitan lifestyles, most people who have served in the military have come from the lower socioeconomic strata, especially among enlisted men, and *rural areas* in particular (in many cases, of course, *rural* and *poor* overlapped). As noted by historian Azar Gat, such military authorities as Vegetius, as well as Machiavelli, considered cities the least desirable recruiting ground compared to the countryside, with its stock of "sturdy farmers, accustomed to hard physical labor."[18] This was true of the Continental Army during the American Revolutionary War,[19] the German army in the 20th century,[20] the British Army until World War I (during which time its best troops came from farms in the rural dominions of New Zealand, Australia, and Canada),[21] and Russia until the Bolshevik victory over the Whites.[22] In those countries, however, the mass nature of total war and near-universal conscription in the 19th and 20th centuries led to a gradual broadening of the social classes that were drafted into military service; writers, poets, businessmen, clerks, laborers, and government officials were all thrown into the mix.[23] There was a relatively high degree of literacy among ordinary soldiers. China was notably different in this respect. Owing to the rural-to-urban dynamic of the revolution and the absence of conscription, the majority of soldiers (and thus veterans) were peasants who hailed from some of the poorest provinces in the country (mainly the northern provinces of Anhui, Shaanxi, Henan, Shanxi, Shandong, and Hebei), where health conditions were poor. Not unlike the United States during the Civil War, when "the frequent transfer of units to areas of unwholesome conditions, or simply of different climate increased the vulnerability of men,"[24] years of fighting without proper medical facilities or trained physicians (there were not enough Norman Bethunes to go around) exacerbated this problem. PLA veterans' health status could also be compared to that of Mexican-Americans drafted into the U.S. Army during WWII. Like the PLA rank and file, these soldiers usually came from impoverished areas and returned to small towns with "great health needs" but lacked adequate heath care.[25]

Most all archival reports concerning PLA veterans chronicle their health-related problems, particularly chronic diseases, post-traumatic stress disorder (then diagnosed as "insanity"), depression, and a host of unexplained maladies. A 1951 report from Shanghai classified only 228 out of 406 veterans as "not having illness" (56 percent); close to 100 of them suffered from either respiratory or digestive ailments; and 16 suffered from psychiatric disorders.[26] A 1952 report on 2,105 Shanghai veterans noted that "most" were "not healthy." Chronic illnesses were common (818 veterans, or 38.8 percent), and some suffered from STDs (89 veterans, or 4.2 percent) and mental illness (32 veterans, or 1.5 percent); only 893 of the 2,105 veterans (42 percent) were said to be in good health.[27] A 1956 analysis of the 3,134 disabled veterans residing in Shanghai found that slightly more than half (54 percent) were officers (whose rank allowed them to move to Shanghai) and that 70 percent were disabled at Level 3.[28] In Shandong circa 1951, 20 percent of all veterans were diagnosed as disabled (roughly 100,000 people), and 98 percent were living in villages;[29] among the 550,000 residing there in 1956, 60,000 had chronic diseases (11 percent); and in 1960, the figure stood at 52,000.[30] In Liaoning Province, a recently published Civil Affairs gazetteer notes that many Korean War veterans who returned to their villages were sick or had been wounded and often lacked land, housing, and family.[31] In the entire Northeast region, a 1952 report noted that 3,000 veterans had already returned home, found a place to live, and got land "but could not work because of chronic illness, and 60 had already died." Reports coming in from Beijing, Shanxi, and Hebei also noted dozens of veterans suffering from various lung diseases, mental illness, and pain from old wounds who died without having received medical care; they were among hundreds who were waiting to be admitted to hospitals.[32] To relieve some of this pressure, rural officials wrote letters of introduction for veterans and family members of revolutionary martyrs for hospitals in Beijing, but because many city hospitals had no free beds (according to the

Ministry of Health), some patients died while seeking medical attention.[33] In Qingpu circa 1957, 8.2 percent of veterans had officially recognized disabilities, mainly severed limbs and facial injuries,[34] a category that did not include those with chronic or recurring illnesses (as noted in a report from 1961): tuberculosis, leprosy, leukemia, gastric ulcers, chronic bronchitis, schistosomiasis, hepatitis, inflammation of old wounds, arthritis, and partial paralysis of one or more limbs.[35]

A random sampling from county gazetteers provides similar numbers regarding the extent of disabilities and illness among returned veterans. In Wuqing County in southeast Hebei, 24 percent of veterans had disabilities.[36] The Yutian County gazetteer does not provide the percentage of veterans with disabilities but does note that 51.3 percent of those with disabilities were "war-related";[37] the Yi County gazetteer (also in Hebei) mentions that, in 1954, some 45 percent of veterans had some sort of recurring illness or disability;[38] while the Wu'an gazetteer simply states, "Resettlement work commenced in 1950s; among the resettled veterans, most were wounded or ill."[39] Further confirmation of the sorry condition of PLA veterans can be found by looking at their counterparts on Taiwan, who shared similar conditions on the battlefield. In 1954, the government designated roughly 70,000 veterans as "combat ineffective" because of psychiatric problems (1,000 cases), tuberculosis (15,000), leprosy (800), blindness (300), and amputations (150), and "many others suffering from various chronic disabilities."[40]

Pain, illness, and disease were not the only sources of post-war challenges to veterans' bodies. Marriage and reproduction—critical to a young man's sense of place, status, and identity in most societies—were also difficult, particularly in the context of the 1950s, when the PRC liberalized laws governing divorce. Many veterans had been away at war during those years when, in more normal circumstances, they (and their parents and relatives) would be actively searching for spouses. Unsurprisingly, many veterans were bachelors and, thus, anxious about their prospects for marriage and family. Some rushed into marriage with the very first woman they met, but others may have given up because of their health problems;[41] likewise, in the USSR after WWII, veterans who were over the age of 30 were anxious to be rapidly demobilized: "In five, ten years a man loses his chances with the female sex. The season for that [having children] doesn't go on after age thirty-five to forty, it's no secret to anyone."[42] In Shandong, among 550,000 veterans in the early 1950s, roughly 25 percent were unmarried at the time of their discharge because of lengthy military service.[43] In 1954, after more veterans were discharged, the provincial government found that 65 percent of them were not married.[44] In Fan County, Henan Province, 64 percent of veterans were bachelors when they returned from war.[45] Some veterans lost their entire families in the war and had little choice but to move to villages where they were strangers or became adopted sons of poor families, typically a low-status position in the family and community.[46]

Given that in poor communities women were often in relatively short "supply" (mainly due to female infanticide)[47] and, after 1950, eager to divorce using the provisions of the 1950 Marriage Law, bachelor veterans—particularly if they were older, chronically ill, or disabled—faced obstacles that many ordinary men did not. Take, for instance, Xu Family Village in Shandong. According to the minutes of a meeting of county-level officials, 25 out of 32 young village women divorced in 1952 and moved to cities;[48] those who remained in the village probably had considerable leverage when choosing a spouse and probably would be somewhat hesitant to marry a 26-year-old veteran missing a leg. Indicative of this are the sporadic calls for the Women's Federation, village officials, and fellow peasants to help in "matchmaking" veterans (the disabled in particular) with local women.[49] In Dongzhi County, Anhui Province, for instance, 28 percent of the veterans absorbed between 1949 and 1958 (327 of 1,168) received some assistance finding a spouse,[50] and in Ningyang in Hebei, 38 percent received help.[51] Widows appear to have been especially attractive candidates for marriage to the severely disabled.[52] Shanghai was not immune to these difficulties: a 1949 handwritten report called the marriage situation of disabled soldiers (especially Level 2 and above) "relatively complicated"—only two were able to marry, and others "frequently approached the government for help."[53] Civil Affairs publications, gazetteers, and archival sources from the city and countryside also hint that not everything was hunky-dory in these relationships: several mention the government's role in "solving veterans' marriage problems" (in Ningyang County, Hebei, 20 percent of returning veterans received help resolving marriage disputes, in Pingding County, in Shanxi, the government claimed to have "helped over 300 veterans" by mediating interpersonal conflicts (15 percent), and in Jiangsu Province a report noted that there were women who married veterans and later sued for divorce because of the veterans' "physical problems"[54]), but a search of Women's Federation records in Qingpu and Shanghai did not turn up a single investigation of veterans' marriage or family problems—this was probably considered a "military matter."

Suicide data substantiate the extent to which health- and family-related problems took a toll on veterans. Officially (although never published in gazetteers), roughly 4,000 PLA veterans took their own lives between 1953 and 1957, a figure which probably underestimates the extent of the phenomenon; the PRC during the early 1950s did not have a national system for reporting such deaths as these.[55] Among the causes of these deaths (accomplished by hanging, jumping into a well or river, ingesting poison, jumping off buildings, or gunshots[56]), chronic pain, disability, poverty, abuse, ridicule, and marital and family problems figured prominently, even more so than the politically oriented causes (bad class status) mentioned in Chapter 3. These suicides were not simply a product of the initial, more chaotic phase of demobilization; they persisted into the 1960s, some 15 years after the state had established functioning bureaucracies devoted to veteran resettlement and health care. The earliest indications that some veterans resorted to suicide emerged in 1951 in an analysis of 34 suicide attempts in Shanghai that resulted in more than 10 dead veterans; of the 34, seven were caused by poverty, five because of "marriage problems or adultery," and five had "psychiatric disorders and were ridiculed."[57] In 1952, General Fu Qiutao rattled off regional figures: in the Southeast, 19 suicides; in the North and the Northeast, more than 60 each; and in a several-month period in Sichuan, 33 veterans committed suicide, mainly due to "marriage problems, poverty, and a feeling of hopelessness and depression because of incurable illness."[58] A 1953 report from Shandong, noting "not a few problems" dealing with the disabled veterans and revolutionary martyr families, admitted that suicides had occurred because "their problems were not solved" (these may have been a form of political protest).[59] In the mid-1950s, similar causes were at work in Shanghai and Beijing. An investigation of 43 suicide attempts between 1954 and 1956 (in which 11 died) revealed that 30 percent were caused by "marriage problems and unrequited love" and 21 percent by "mental illness and chronic disease."[60] In 1955, for example, a Shanghai report noted a case of an out-of-town veteran who came to the city with mental illness, but he deteriorated because he was the butt of constant ridicule. When he was "locked up in a bathroom, he screamed that he was going to commit suicide."[61] In 1957, noting "not a few" cases of veteran suicides and expulsions from the party, the Shanghai Bureau of Civil Affairs compiled the following list of causes for 40 of the suicide attempts (12 dead):[62]

Financial difficulties	7
Marriage problems	8
Adultery-induced panic	3
Beaten up, took revenge	5
Inappropriate jobs	7
Political history	5
Other	5

This pattern held in the early 1960s in Shanghai as well. In an analysis of 12 veteran suicides between 1960 and 1962, the main causes were marriage difficulties, "inappropriate flirting" (*luan tan lian'ai*), chronic illness, and sex scandals. These causes, however, were not always easily distinguishable; one suicide could easily fit two or even three categories. For instance, a veteran committed suicide because his boss ridiculed him as a result of his wife's having an affair, but she was having the affair because "he has been sick for a long time."[63]

Rural suicides displayed a similar dynamic. In an analysis of 24 veteran suicides that occurred between January and June 1954, 18 had been caused by either "marriage problems" or "family disputes," three because of poverty, and one because the veteran was depressed owing to age and illness (the other two causes were unrelated to health or poverty). Although this suicide rate was lower than the previous years, during which time 89 veterans committed suicide, the report acknowledged that veteran resettlement work was "woefully inadequate" (*hen bu gou*).[64] A 1955 report compiled by Shandong's Provincial Party Committee (which I was not allowed to read in full) focused specifically on the problem of recurring suicides among rural veterans.[65] A 1957 investigation of veterans in Shandong did not cite any numbers but called attention to "serious" problems of veterans "committing suicide, causing disturbances and fleeing the province,"[66] and in 1960 (during the Great Leap Forward) seriously disabled veterans left villages to seek help at county governments and the provincial capital because their problems were not being addressed locally—"a bad influence on the reputation of the party and government."[67] This particular report did not cite precise causes, but others did. Qingpu County suicides resulted from "chronic illnesses," "marriage disputes," "political history problems," and "unsubstantiated accusations against them."[68] In a 1959 meeting of senior Civil Affairs officials from six northern provinces and Beijing, the deputy minister of the interior told his audience, "The problem of medication for veterans with chronic illness is an old one that has not been completely resolved; among veterans who committed suicide in the last several years, a considerable proportion of them were caused by chronic illnesses that were not treated in a timely fashion." Bumbling administration was partially to blame: with the establishment of communes during the Great Leap Forward, no one was sure who was responsible for paying disabled veterans' medical expenses.[69]

Other officials, however, mentioned more proximate causes. A 1962 study of Letters and Visits work in the Provincial Department of Civil Affairs found that 82 percent of 3,066 letters and 2,135 visits were by disabled veterans and martyr and military families. In these letters, disabled veterans accused local cadres of lowering their disability level, beating them up, cancelling their benefits, and denying them financial assistance, and they also complained about their poverty and problems in securing medicine.[70] A rare breakdown of veterans' letters in a county gazetteer (in Shandong) provides us with a sense of both the type and scale of problems faced by the disabled and other veterans and their families. In Haiyang County, officials were kept quite busy, as Table 6.1 demonstrates.

Table 6.1. Petitioning in Haiyang County, Shandong, 1953–1965

Year	Letters	Visits	Content of Letters and Petitions
1953	___	16	Finding work, medicine, marriage problems
1956	344	603	Financial difficulties, marriage conflicts, medicine
1957	341	959	Burial of martyrs, reporting on local cadres, evaluation of disability level, locating the whereabouts of soldiers
1958	615	1,670	Disabled soldiers reporting on local cadres, requesting a change in class status, financial difficulties
1959	522	210	Aid recipients requesting emergency funds for medicine and food, evaluation of disability level, locating soldiers
1960	449	720	Pension requests, evaluation of disability level, finding work, migration problems
1961	481	990	Requests for financial aid to buy medicine, finding work, disability-level problems
1963	650	1,280	Requests for financial aid to buy medicine, reporting on local cadres
1964	656	1,274	Requests for pensions
1965	361	863	Veterans seeking work

Source: *Haiyang xian zhi* (Haiyang, 1987), 649.

Although the gazetteer does not mention this, there are some indications that many of these "reports on local cadres" were substantiated upon further investigation: provincial-level officials tersely confirmed cases of "beating up, taking revenge upon, and causing the suicides of disabled veterans and members of military and martyr families."[71] Still, those who wrote letters rarely saw remedial action. According to the summary of the Letters and Visits work report, "some counties and cities pay no attention to this job; they shove letters they've received in the drawer, and this isn't revealed until an investigation takes place; other letters were placed in the bottom of the closet."[72] As a result, some disabled veterans decided to take more aggressive action. A 1956 analysis of "disturbances" (*naoshi*) among veterans found that one major cause was "disabled soldiers disagreeing with their level of disability and demanding a reevaluation."[73]

Some abbreviated case histories from the Shanghai countryside (circa 1963) put a little more meat on these overly bureaucratic analyses. A veteran surnamed Yu, from Chongming Island, hung himself at the age of 27 because "his wife looks down upon him; before the suicide there was a big fight, and the party secretary often criticizes him." Another Mr. Yu, from Fengtai County, was "depressed because of chronic illness that was not improving"; Mr. Ai, 26, from Jinshan County, was a worker who suffered from bad migraines; Ouyang Yingyan shot himself when his work unit tried on numerous occasions to send his wife back to his hometown in Hunan, but she refused to go.[74] These sorts of cases, which probably continued into the Cultural Revolution years, do not appear to have prodded significant improvements in how veterans' family and medical problems were handled; it was not coincidental, or necessarily unjustified, that in 1965 Chairman Mao famously criticized the Ministry of Health for the lack of decent health care in the countryside.[75] A 1963 report by the Shanghai Party Committee complained that neither the Bureau of Civil Affairs nor the Labor Bureau conducted follow-up investigations after assigning veterans to jobs—"if they did, some of the suicide cases could have been prevented"—but this, as we saw in the previous chapter, was never really in the political deck of cards.[76] Problems related to veterans' poverty and medical issues were not handled well, either. If veterans had hoped that their suicides would provide a jolt to the system and lead to better care, they were mistaken: "Even suicides are not given a lot of attention and investigation; no one thinks about concrete ways they could have been prevented," the report concluded.[77]

NO DIRECT DEPOSIT: POLICY-RELATED VULNERABILITIES

As the reports above hint at, some veterans turned to suicide with a keen sense of isolation and abandonment, of having served the revolution which placed them in a job but then forced them to fend for themselves as they tried to cope with medical, family, and financial challenges. To be sure, this assessment did not hold for all disabled veterans; those in the higher ranks of the PLA probably had less to complain about and fewer committed suicide. The suicide data in China indicate that veterans committing suicide were usually in their late 20s, which would preclude a very high rank. Even though those veterans who committed suicide did not succeed in getting the CCP to heed the "message" they may have been sending about medical neglect, in hindsight their desperate acts do tell us about their primary administrative cause: an excessive degree of local discretion (involving officials in unions, villages, bureaucracies, and various committees) over the allocation of official status and distribution of benefits. Disabled veterans, so to speak, never had "direct deposit" into their bank accounts from the Center; all funds were distributed by district (in cities) or county (in rural areas) governments. Absent a direct, secure link to the Center, local cadres who either disliked them or contested the legitimacy of their worthiness and entitlement were able to cause veterans no small amount of hardship. Disability provided an easy pretext for this, since (1) there was money involved and (2) the precise origins of the disability and degrees of suffering, need, and pain could be subject to different interpretations and political narratives.

Local discretion in policy implementation was nothing new for the CCP. Under the rubric of the "mass line," it was long-standing policy to take into consideration people's opinions when dealing with numerous issues, ranging from whom to execute (landlords, capitalists, corrupt officials) to more mundane economic issues, such as evaluating salaries. Veterans, who had their share of detractors, could easily become vulnerable to negative assessments of their worthiness. For instance, Ma Yuanchun, a chronically ill veteran in Qingpu, had his factory salary lowered during a "salary reevaluation" in November 1954. Making roughly 36 yuan a month with a wife and three children, Ma, like many veterans with illnesses, had a hard time making ends meet. He received two additional stipends totaling 25 yuan during the 1955 Spring Festival, but he was still having problems. He requested an additional stipend, "but the masses did not agree" to his request. In a fit of anger, Ma jumped into a nearby river in an apparent suicide attempt but was pulled out by several eyewitnesses.[78] The evaluation of disability level, a critical assessment because the amount of a disabled veterans' monthly stipend depended on just how "officially" disabled he was, also involved input from a wide range of people. In the early years of the PRC, disability levels were apparently established by a committee comprising officials from health departments, Civil Affairs, and disabled veterans,[79] but this proved to be problematic: veterans were pleased if they were diagnosed with serious problems (which meant more money) but raised a ruckus if their degree of disability was lowered. This was not uncommon: in Chahe'er Province (now Inner Mongolia), among 64 disabled veterans who showed up one year for a reevaluation, 17 (or 25 percent) had their level lowered, one was raised a level, and 44 remained the same.[80] To rectify this, a larger committee (roughly 12 people) was established, comprising county- and district-level Civil Affairs officials, veterans representatives, physicians, and local cadres. According to one report, this method resulted in fewer problems and was praised by veterans, but just how frequently these committees met has been difficult to assess.[81] Later in the decade, evaluation of disability was complicated by political campaigns, which kept officials too busy to get involved with this issue. In 1957, a Shanghai investigation noted that reevaluations were "very complicated" and could only be done if the disabled applied for assistance; otherwise, no proactive measures would be taken.[82]

Without more information about Ma Yuanchun and the deliberations surrounding his request for financial aid, it would be premature to conclude that the "masses" did not appreciate him—perhaps Ma wasted his money chugging local wine?—but the case does hint that present-day assessments of worthiness could interfere with the credibility gained from a "glorious" past. But what would happen if even the past was murky and officials had a hard time assessing the extent of disability and how this corresponded with policy and budget expenditures? The complexity of war and China's long revolution (which involved multiple periods, actors, turnabouts, and shifting alliances) made this even more difficult. A "Question and Answer" guidebook (published by the Ministry of the Interior for the internal use of its officials) concerning disability and pensions makes this clear. Let's briefly take a look at a sample of questions and answers, not so much to discern policy outcomes (we cannot be sure if anyone read the guidebook) but, rather, to get a sense of the sort of complicated questions about disability status that were lingering in the air:[83]

Q: Who is a "revolutionary disabled soldier"?

A: Members of the PLA and Chinese Volunteer Army (who fought in Korea) and security cadres who became disabled because they participated in war or because of selfless action (*yingong*).

Q: Who are "revolutionary disabled personnel"?

A: With the exception of those in the military, those who left their jobs and participated in revolutionary work and belong to either democratic parties, government institutions, or mass organizations who were injured or became disabled because of the struggle against enemies or because of selfless action.

Q: How should we differentiate between disability documents?

A: There are five types: (1) proof of being a "disabled revolutionary soldier"; (2) a "disabled revolutionary soldier who receives preferential treatment"; (3) proof of being a "disabled revolutionary personnel"; (4) "disabled revolutionary personnel who receives preferential treatment"; (5) disabled militia and public works workers.

Q: What does "disabled in public service" (*yin gong zhi can*) mean?

A: An injury that did not result from a mistake or not being careful. It does not include accidents during routine activities (not in war). It is given to those who tried mightily to fix something or rescue someone and were injured because they bravely took action.

Q: What about those in the GMD who fought against the Japanese and were disabled? How should they be handled?

A: After the Marco Polo Bridge Incident (September 18, 1937), those who fought for the GMD against the Japanese and were injured and have proof that they have severed their connection with Chiang Kai-shek and have public testimony by the local masses can get "disabled revolutionary soldier" status. Ordinary people must get approval of the County, but those with more complicated histories must apply to the provincial level and above. Only those at Level 2 disability (out of three) and worse can get pensions.

> Q: What about someone in the army who was slightly injured in war and did not get documentation, but after discharge the old injury flares up and now he meets the disability threshold?
> A: He needs authorization of his army unit and at least two people who were in the unit with him. If they do provide authorization, his work unit should investigate and give their opinion to the district government.

As we can see in this virtual conversation, many kinds of questions were "pose-able" to those claiming disabled veteran status from the PLA as well as those from other institutions: What motivated them? Whose side were they on? Who witnessed their actions? Moreover, the answers assume a simplicity that is generally lacking in wartime (What if "the local masses" had conflicting opinions? What if they had certain biases?) and unlimited financial and health-related resources: it was up to the veteran—even if he was in chronic pain—to locate his army unit, contact eyewitnesses, and prod the government to conduct its own "investigation" (which could be overturned by the district). The questions also do not address possible biases on the part of elite physicians, who could have easily used their power of diagnosis to repudiate veterans' claim to status. For instance, in the United States after WWII, many (white) Veterans Administration physicians questioned and rejected claims by African-American veterans, claiming that they were injuries that occurred prior to military service and that the disabled were "fakers."[84] Equally problematic, the CCP, given the length of the revolution and the number of people who "participated," "struggled," or "fought" in one capacity or another, was forced to be quite promiscuous in its designation of "disabled" status, which, like the frequent use of the term *glorious*, diluted veterans' contributions in the eyes of many, including officials responsible for taking care of them.

This complexity did not end after 1949. Although disabled veterans officially belonged to the "red" classes, they still could be caught in the net of political campaigns or prosecuted for such crimes as theft, solicitation, or adultery, a trio of crimes directly related to their relative poverty and complicated family situation. The early 1960s was an interesting period in this respect. At the same time that the PLA was represented as the epitome of all that was good, true, and pure about the revolution, its disabled soldiers who served in official capacities in villages and cities faced a particularly acrimonious political environment. During the "4 Clean-ups" campaign in 1964 (mainly targeting corruption), hundreds of officials, including PLA disabled veterans, were charged with corruption and other abuses of power; some lost their political rights in the process. These prosecutions, which often originated in local rivalries between lineages and different leadership styles, further complicated the lives of veterans and administrators: What should be done about those official, hard-to-get documents and disability payments? Should present-day "crime" (becoming a "capitalist roader") take precedence over losing a limb during a war? In other words, should class identity trump martial status? A flurry of questions and letters from the provinces to the Center in the mid-1960s attested to this confusion. According to the Ministry of Interior and the Public Security Bureau, disabled veterans who were the "worst offenders" or accused of "counterrevolution" should lose everything—including payments, certificates of merit, and stipends. Ordinary criminals, they instructed, must also turn in their documents but should have them returned when their sentence was complete. This leniency was not granted to the more serious offenders who completed their sentences: until their "bad element hat" was officially removed, their documents would be placed "with the local archives" and their payments placed on hold. Officials in Shanghai and Shanxi were confused, however. Who was responsible for reporting the disabled veterans' situation to the higher authorities? Was this a matter for Public Security or the courts? Who had the authority to cancel payments? Shanxi officials asked if they had to take back the disability documents on a permanent basis or only temporarily and if the pension had to be stopped "completely" because of the loss of political rights. The response from the Center was straightforward: "If their hats are removed, their documents should be restored to them and their payments resumed." Using the vague word *keyi* ("may"), local authorities were authorized to distribute financial aid "in accordance to their level of disability and financial difficulties," but this was not mandated.[85]

This sort of treatment and denial of political status may have been the proverbial straw that broke the camel's back for some disabled veterans in terms of how they assessed the legitimacy of the CCP and its policies in the year prior to the Cultural Revolution. In Shandong, a significant number of disillusioned disabled veterans threw in the revolutionary towel (perhaps also a confirmation of the idea that people's willingness to obey law is related to how they are treated by state and legal authorities[86]). A 1965 investigation of 256 households that had members designated as martyrs or disabled soldiers or had sons currently serving in the PLA (representing 16 percent of the population) in Laoshan Commune, Rongcheng County, found that disabled veterans were involved in profiteering, smuggling, tax evasion, and different forms of collusion with various "class enemies" such as landlords and other "bad elements," all behaviors which had a "very bad influence" on the masses.[87] Even though the investigation lauded the impact of the story of Norman Bethune's heroism in China, many veterans were more concerned about day-to-day matters. In a June 1965 meeting of 30 families of disabled veterans, 19 were designated "backward" (*luohou*) by Civil Affairs. Among these were several who had traveled to Beijing to submit petitions on three separate occasions and were well known for their willingness to complain to the county government. All ignored party policies. One veteran refused to join a cooperative and worked by himself; another stole state property; a Mr. Xu frequently left the area; and a Mr. Ye "frequently met with bad people, and told others that he's not satisfied with the party or socialism," in part because it "prevented his wife from progressing and caused his family to split up on two occasions." A veteran surnamed Miao expected to be treated well by local authorities upon his return to the village but was disappointed. He lashed out at them: "When I was in the army, you were still a baby! Who do you think you are now?" To higher authorities in the party, he said, "When I was out conquering the country, you were here enjoying yourself!" Of the party generally, Miao and others repeated the analogy we have seen as early as 1952: disabled veterans were like "donkeys slaughtered after having ground the wheat." These accusations were not entirely unfounded. In their self-criticism, local officials, like those in the early and mid-1950s, admitted that they did not interact much with veterans, thought they were pains in the neck, and did not cultivate them for good jobs and positions.[88] It is not clear what these particular veterans did during the Cultural Revolution, but it would seem that veterans like them were involved in the angry meeting with Zhou Enlai in mid-1966. One can only wonder what they thought about the young, mostly urban Red Guards parading through streets in military uniforms.

Shifting policies regarding class status and what constituted "corruption" or "crime" were not the only political storms that disabled veterans had to weather. Even when the Center did not unleash a political campaign, disabled veterans, as well as those with chronic illnesses, could still find themselves in the middle of a formidable bureaucratic maze, particularly if they lacked documentation or had to consult physicians, gather testimonies, request leave from work, and the like. In Qingpu, for example, a female veteran surnamed Ye had tuberculosis, but her work unit did not allow her to visit a physician and sent her home instead; another veteran's wife had schistosomiasis and required hospitalization. Physicians told her that without urgent medical care her situation would deteriorate but refused to admit her because she could not pay. Concerned about his wife, the veteran was said to have been very distracted at work.[89] At the heart of this problem was concern over money, coupled with a lack of sympathy for veterans or their families. Even though the PLA gave veterans with chronic illnesses money for medicine, reports (as late as 1964[90]) indicate that it was not enough to cover the costs of long-term care and medication. To cover the extra costs, the disabled had to request supplemental funds from local Civil Affairs offices, but even these officials admitted that their assistance was insufficient and that veterans and their families suffered a great deal of hardship and mental anguish as a result.[91] Discussions between Civil Affairs and the Health Department, which controlled medicine and medical care, came to naught.[92] This was also nothing new: even in the mid-1950s, there was little agreement over who should take care of disabled veterans, even though all assumed that veterans would have to pay something. In 1952, for instance, General Fu Qiutao lambasted the medical establishment, complaining that "even though the Center has already decided that veterans with chronic illnesses can go to nearby hospitals and have their expenses paid by the hospitals, which will then be reimbursed by the Ministry of Health," there are "some hospitals that falsely claim that 'we never received any directive from the Ministry of Health' to deny medicines and refuse admission to hospitals." This problem was said to be "relatively common" in the Northeast, and if it was not resolved quickly, it could have severe implications for veteran resettlement generally.[93] A 1951 report from Chahe'er Province confirms regional difficulties. There, Civil Affairs officials were charged with both ignoring disabled veterans and, when dealing with them, treating them harshly. (They thought the disabled were "bothersome.") When those officials were upbraided for this, they tried to please their superiors by paying personal visits to disabled veterans' homes, but it was too late: veterans told them, "Get out the house! Don't treat us so hypocritically (*xuwei*)—ignoring us, then coming to our house, and then ignoring us again."[94]

But four years later the problem was no closer to being solved. In 1955 the State Council issued a provisional document that placed a heavy burden on disabled veterans: hospitalization required the approval of city- or county-level health department officials; if the chronically ill could not get work, they could request an investigation which would then go to the county government for approval; there was no financial assistance to pay for medicine for the "ordinary chronically ill veteran" (he should "rest at home and ask a local doctor to come"), but "those few" who needed help could seek assistance from the government ("district level and above") for a discount; veterans had to pay for transportation and food, but work units had to pay for hospital fees if they were admitted; those with "light mental illness" should remain at home; and any sort of temporary aid to relieve extreme poverty had to be approved by the county.[95] Even though these guidelines were highly restrictive, their very existence seemed to create the impression that the government would eventually pay for something. At least in Qingpu, some village and township officials ignored the plight of poor veterans for this reason. Wu A'xiao, for example, was a disabled veteran with a wife and two children. His wife became ill in 1955 and could no longer work, and Wu's disability made it difficult for him to collect enough work points. When he approached village officials for financial aid, they refused on the grounds that he was already receiving a pension; they also refused to give him a break on the price of grain. According to the report, Wu was extremely angry about this (perhaps because most of the village officials had not served in the military and were not disabled), refused to work in the fields, and put in numerous requests for a transfer to a wage-earning position outside the village.[96] Sick children could push veterans into poverty. Another Qingpu veteran told officials at a 1957 meeting of veteran representatives, "My kid got sick and we had to spend over 40 yuan. I went to Civil Affairs to request emergency funds but they refused, even though other people got some. It's not right."[97] These Qingpu cases were not unusual. In a 1956 report by the Ministry of Interior, General Fu Qiutao noted that all over China, disabled soldiers (including the chronically ill) generally had lower incomes than others because they could not work as hard and that, when sick, they "frequently (*shichang*) experienced difficulties obtaining medical care and medicines."[98] In 1957, Fu added "serious mental illnesses that cause hardship for their families" and "many family members to take care of" as two more of the "many causes" of veterans' difficulties in civilian life.[99] A 1962 investigation of Civil Affairs work between 1958 and 1961 in the Shanghai area, including its rural counties, noted that disabled veterans also earned less than military dependent families. For instance, a veteran was married with three children, but because he could not work and his wife did not earn much, their household income was 307 "labor days," which converted into a per-person average monthly income of 3.1 yuan, which was 56 percent lower than the "average" peasant household. After receiving state aid, their income still did not exceed 4.01 yuan, which was still 42.8 percent lower than the average.[100] If disabled veterans managed to reach the "average peasant" income standard, medical expenses could lower their real income significantly, making them even more dependent on the goodwill of others and probably less respected in the community because of this.

A synopsis of a 1951 meeting between disabled veterans and district-level officials provides us with a good sense of just how dependent disabled veterans could be on the goodwill of low-level officials and how they tried to find allies in other parts of the state structure to solve financial and family-related problems. During this meeting, several disabled veterans from Qingpu and the surrounding counties stood up and vented their anger at the lack of responsiveness to their difficult situations, in the hope that officials would intervene on their behalf. A veteran surnamed Gao complained that he never received aid and could not work his land because his father was old and that he was over the age of 30 and still unmarried; he also lacked fertilizer and did not own his home. "Don't district officials, Civil Affairs cadres, and the

PLA Political Instructor know my family situation, and that I participated in the revolution?" he asked. One veteran complained that he did not receive any land during land reform. Another said,

> I participated in the revolution since 1937. There were six in my family—my father and mother, wife, and my son and daughter. When I returned, my father and mother both died, and so did my daughter. My wife left with my son. There's no one left. I have requested that the government help return my son to me, but they refused.

Yu Aiqing then got up and told the audience,

> After I participated in the revolution, I returned to find that my wife married another man; she gave my son away to someone else; now there's no one at home. I have six *mu* of land, but village officials only provide assistance cultivating three *mu*.

District officials jotted down these comments and then sent them along to the Qingpu County chief along with a cover letter summarizing some of the complaints: "Local cadres do not show enough concern for them, they are assigned impractical jobs [given their health], and are dissatisfied with a host of other things." According to the district, "not all of these complaints are correct," but the county chief should still try harder to improve veteran administration.[101]

It is difficult to assess with certainty how much improved in the next six years or so, but judging by the complaints of disabled veterans at a 1957 meeting, some problems remained quite intractable. At that meeting Su Baosheng stood up and said, "I was demobilized in Subei and came to Qingpu to work in transportation. Even though I'm injured, I've never received my disability pension. I've gone to Civil Affairs, but nothing has been solved." A Mr. Gao complained about an "inappropriate" job assignment: "I was wounded in my head by an enemy plane in Korea so I don't have the strength to work in agriculture, but the government wants me to do just this. I can't do it and want to be transferred to a paper-producing factory, but nothing has been done." For a veteran surnamed Chen, jobs and medicine were the critical problems: "Civil Affairs does not take into consideration anyone's unique situation. My hip's bad, and I have trachoma, but I can't get medical care. I requested to change jobs and they refused. The director of the Conscription Bureau even said that they 'wouldn't bother about me' (*bu yao guan wo*). Is this the right way to treat veterans?"[102]

Given the problems we have seen in Qingpu in the mid- and late 1950s, it is clear that there were still many unresolved issues. What the district failed to realize, however, was that even if a county leader did his utmost for veterans, he would still be highly constrained by the vagaries of the past, the complexity of the political economy surrounding medical care, the discretion of village and township officials below him, and veterans' own present-day behavior. Without powerful allies in or outside the state or their own organization, disabled veterans were quite vulnerable to attack, as the following case shows.

LIU JUNMIN AND THE STRANGE CASE OF THE
10-YEAR REVOKED PENSION

In August 1965, Yishui County's (Shandong Province) Bureau of Civil Affairs issued a report to provincial authorities vouching for the full restoration, with back pay, of the pension provided to a 47-year-old disabled veteran named Liu Junmin, who, despite being wounded in 1942, had had his pension revoked since the end of 1955. The Yishui letter was the culmination of a two-year investigation surrounding the circumstances of his injury and the cancellation of his pension. It also included a healthy dose of self-criticism. "Our bureau," it noted, "has direct responsibility for Liu's case." Insufficient awareness of the importance of handling letters, lack of implementation of party policies, sloppy investigation, and "a bias toward oral testimony" were all cited as the main causes for the 10-year pension hiatus. Yishui promised provincial authorities that they would investigate "Letters and Visits work during the past several years" as well as veteran resettlement and preferential treatment work "in the entire county."[103]

In all likelihood Yishui officials were not overly enthusiastic about admitting to these administrative deficiencies, but their hand was forced by several other investigations into Liu's case. According to a comprehensive investigation by an ad hoc team of six officials (from the provincial, district, and county governments) that lasted six days, Liu Junmin's case began back in 1944, when he was in a security detachment attached to *The Masses Daily* (*Dazhong ribao*), the newspaper of the provincial CCP. While pulling guard duty in the town of Beiguan, Liu was "shot by a special agent," which caused numerous wounds to his torso and leg. In September 1946, Liu returned home and was elected a member of his village party committee during Land Reform. The village was evacuated during a Nationalist offensive in 1947, but he returned in the spring of 1948. In August of that same year, he was "introduced" to the party by a fellow villager—Ma Jie—and some new cadres who had arrived from south-central Shandong. In 1951, he was given a certificate confirming "Level 2 disability." By the end of that year, Liu was the secretary of the village's party branch. In 1953, however, he was expelled from the party, and in 1955 he lost his disability payment.

This rapid turn of Liu's political fortunes resulted from the testimony of a fellow veteran in his unit, Yang Changxue. Yang charged that Liu's injury was not the product of being "beaten by a special agent" but, rather, was a "self-inflicted wound" designed to remove himself from harm's way; Liu, he charged, "betrayed the revolution." As "proof," Yang told village party members that Liu's wound was "top-down, on a slant, and began in the interior part of the leg"; this would not have been possible if someone standing in front of him attacked him. Moreover, Yang claimed that hospital physicians also thought it was self-inflicted, since they "did not give him any medicine or a splint for his leg, and allowed maggots to fester in the wound." Ma Jie, the village cadre, piped up: "If he was treated unjustly, why didn't he say anything for 10 years? His uncle told him to say something, but he didn't."[104] Faced with these two accounts—a war injury caused at night with no eyewitnesses and a self-inflicted wound—the special investigation team now faced the task of disproving one of the versions.

As it turned out, this proved easy to do. After two days they were able to ascertain that there was no proof that the wound's origin was on the inside of the leg or that it was self-inflicted. Three other members of his security unit testified that "no one at *The Masses Daily* said anything about a self-inflicted wound; everyone said a special agent did it." As early as September 1963, even Yang Changxue (who lodged the accusation) said that he "never heard of any leader disagreeing with the agent story" but decided that Liu's injury was fake "on the basis of the sound of the gun" and the position of Liu's body vis-à-vis the shell casing, which the investigation team re-created to show that the wound could only have come from the outside. The allegation about the hospital's denial of care did not stand up to scrutiny, either. The other "proof"—that Liu's decade-long wait for justice was in itself evidence of his guilt—was also challenged. Liu claimed that he did, in fact, report the case to the county-level Bureau of Civil Affairs and "talked to the township chief Wang Gui and others," who all confirmed that it was very difficult for Liu to pursue his case because he had a hard time walking and "needs money and free time." The outcome of the investigation was now clear: Liu was framed by Yang Changxue. But why?

Under pressure from investigators, Yang Changxue admitted to fabricating the story because of a personal vendetta against Liu. Access to medicine and illness, however, were at its messy core. According to Yang's 1965 confession, back in the early 1950s he had gone to Liu's village when the latter was the party secretary in order to procure medicine for his son, who was very sick. Liu was hanging out in the local pharmacy when Yang came in. Yang asked that Liu cover the cost of the medicine as a personal favor, but Liu, for reasons that were not addressed in the report, did not intervene on his behalf (*mei you biaoshi taidu*). Even though the pharmacy agreed to give him credit for the cost of the medicine, Yang was incensed: "We were once together in the army, and now it's as if he doesn't even know me." The medicine did not help, however, and Yang's son died. Distraught, he vowed to Liu: "Your leg will be my retribution! Your disability's fake! Just wait until the CCP has a rectification campaign!"[105]

In pursuing his grief-induced vendetta against Liu, Yang Changxue found an ally in Liu's non-veteran political rival in the village, Ma Jie. It was Yang who told Ma Jie during the 1955 rectification campaign that Liu's injury was "fake" and Ma who passed on this nugget to the leader of the outside work team running the campaign, who then moved to get Liu expelled from the party by sending off the materials about Liu's "betrayal of the revolution" to the County Party Committee. Why did Ma react in this way? According to the testimony by the former township chief, there were two factions in the village: Ma Jie's faction was on the ropes; Liu's was in ascendancy. Ma, however, was politically ambitious—"he really wanted to be an official"—but his background was somewhat problematic: he had been a bandit during the war. When this piece of information regarding Ma was exposed, Liu and others had requested that Ma be expelled from the party. Higher levels of the party, however, did not approve this decision. When village officials deliberated whether to restore Ma's status, Liu had been among those who decided against it. Since that time, Liu told investigators, "He has a grudge against me." Thus, when Ma was told about Liu's "self-inflicted injury," he quickly gave the information to the work team and met with Yang Changxue on three separate occasions; he also went to three others who provided corroborating testimony against Liu, just so they would all be on the same page. In sum, the investigator concluded, "It was all Yang Changxue's personal revenge and Ma Jie's ability to take advantage of the situation to cause him harm. Wu Chuantong, a township leader, was used by Ma, as were the others. Liu has his faults, but his main weakness was letting others take advantage of him." In 1955, at a meeting with 200 people led by the district's party secretary (whom the investigators blamed for allowing the likes of Ma Jie into the party), Liu was expelled from the CCP. To kill two birds with one stone and to prevent Liu from "creating pressure," they also decided to discontinue his disability payments; the paperwork for this was wrapped up in 1955 and authorized by the regional party committee (which received concurring reports from provincial and regional Civil Affairs), even though they did not have this authority, according to the regulations. The provincial government never authorized revoking his pension or his "revolutionary disabled soldier" status.[106]

Not long after his pension was cancelled, Liu paid a visit to the Civil Affairs office to request that it be reinstated. When they said that it was now out of their hands, Liu "did not object." It was only in 1963, when an old acquaintance (and former editor at the *The Masses Daily*) named Huang Fengxian brought Liu back to the county to request that his payments be reinstated, that the case was reopened. Still, their letter to Shandong Province cast doubt on Liu's veracity: "Why did he not complain if something was wrong?" On the other hand, the county did note that "all the evidence is unreliable." Until the matter was resolved, however, "Liu should not get his payments reinstated."[107]

Liu's saving grace was that, unlike most soldiers organized in battalions and brigades, he happened to serve in a security detachment to the Shandong's most important newspaper, *The Masses Daily*, whose highly literate officials stepped in to prod other agencies to reopen the case. From 1963 to 1965, two editors at *The Masses Daily*, Huang Fengxian and Zhu Min, repeatedly intervened on Liu's behalf. Huang and Zhu jointly wrote a letter to the Bureau of Civil Affairs in December 1963 with a blow-by-blow account of Liu's version of events; after writing to provincial Civil Affairs and not receiving a response, Huang accompanied Liu to their office to talk with them face-to-face; he also gave Liu money for medicine. Another newspaperman called Yishui County Civil Affairs in an effort to figure out what went wrong; the director's response was "We had testimonies from two people" and "Liu didn't get along with other cadres." A year passed and the matter was still unresolved, so they wrote yet another letter to provincial Civil Affairs in April 1964. Zhu Min procured a letter about proper administrative procedure from the newspaper's party committee and sent it to the provincial party committee. "According to the [unspecified] regulations," it noted, "disability status and pension are generally not revoked as a disciplinary measure, and only sometimes for criminal offenses." Because Liu was never prosecuted for a criminal offense, "his pension should not have been revoked." They found other officials who were able to locate members of Liu's former unit who were able to confirm that the wound was not self-inflicted. In 1965, with the matter still unresolved, Zhu Min wrote to the district-level Letters and Visits Office to request a special investigation and sent an eight-page report to the Shandong Party Committee. These efforts did the trick. A special investigation team finally was formed, the witnesses were located, and the truth was uncovered. Justice, however, probably did not last too long. A year after his pension was restored, the Cultural Revolution broke out, and Civil Affairs bureaus, which handed out the money, were pulled into the turmoil.

Liu Junmin's case, even though it has a less-than-tragic ending, is still sobering. It was resolved only after two years of active and persistent intervention by a large newspaper. Had Liu not managed to reconnect with his former wartime unit, the injustice of 1955 would not have been corrected; by himself, he was no match for the non-veteran politicians in the village or the various levels of government who weighed in on the case. Alone, he could not go back to the complicated past, find all of its actors, and correct a distortion of his personal history. Even though the press eventually came to his rescue, his alliance with *The Masses Daily* was personal and ad hoc, with little room for future shared battles. There was no general commitment on the part of the press, or other educated elites, for that matter, to advocate for veterans as a distinct group, and the post-1949 policies of returning veterans to their villages and not creating a veterans organization only made this less likely. This is not all that surprising when we think about the strong peasant base of the PLA (Liu was from a poor peasant background) and the absence of universal conscription, which could have provided a stronger basis for solidarity, or at least sympathy, after the war was over. We have observed some of this in the comparative cases and will see even more at the end of this chapter when I take a brief look at disabled veterans in Israel. Absent this sort of cross-class alliance, older and disabled veterans like Liu could not fight the good fight when challenged. Liu, however, was not the only victim in this story. Even though the investigation pinned the blame on Yang Changxue, who framed Liu, it is important to remember that Yang lost his son because he could not get timely medical care and took out his rage and frustration on Liu. What seems clear from this case is that for those in predicaments similar to Liu (or worse) and who were contemplating suicide, the state was not a protector, ally, or place of refuge.

VULNERABLE FAMILIES

"Veterans have not a few problems in their marriage and family life," noted a 1955 State Council document on veteran resettlement, using its usual choice of adjectival euphemism.[108] It is difficult to assess the extent to which ministers and their deputies were surprised by this—in the previous six years they had been receiving numerous reports about this issue—but if they had bothered to study even a little bit about the impact of war on family and marriage life in addition to highfalutin Marxist–Leninist theory, they would have found that this problem was entirely predictable. Veterans rarely return home the same as when they departed, and it is often left to families to deal with the consequences. In the U.S. case, John Resch notes that veterans from all wars have experienced some degree of alienation and have been difficult to get along with;[109] after World War II, a study of post-war readjustment by the University of Chicago's Committee on Human Development noted that "most returning servicemen appeared to feel a need for the company of other veterans," much to the chagrin of their spouses who wanted them to stay home. Despite sociologists who openly wondered whether returning veterans would "turn into Storm Troopers who will destroy democracy,"[110] upon their return most veterans became better known for their restlessness and adventuresome spirit; their successful readjustment (into small communities) largely depended on their "ability to find a job that [they] liked and keep it."[111] Hollywood may have sealed this image in the minds of many post-war Americans in the Oscar award–winning film *The Best Years of Our Lives* (1947), in which all of the characters, but particularly Homer, the disabled veteran, have a difficult time adjusting to the routines of family life. Homer's wife, Wilma, eventually turns him around by being patient, calm, understanding, and appropriately feminine by the standards of the late 1940s.[112] Of course, American veterans were not the only ones who had a difficult time adjusting to family routines: WWI veterans in Great Britain also acquired a reputation for misbehavior, drinking, and carousing.[113] The British disabled also caused much concern; there were even proposals to "procure wives" for them in order to give them back their "manliness."[114]

Complicated returns to family life were a product of not only shifting identities, new experiences, and expectations among veterans; time did not freeze while they were away: spouses might fall in love with someone else (in the "Dear John letter" romantic scenario) or find a man on whom they could depend for resources to get by (in the more pragmatic version of this story that we saw some of in the letters from the Qingpu veterans above and which has been noted in many other contexts).[115] Some women might get used to calling the shots themselves and resist sharing authority after the soldiers' return. After protracted wars, the shortage of men of marriageable age can complicate relations between women and lead to unorthodox family and sexual arrangements (high rates of illegitimacy, prostitution).[116] For these reasons, post-war marriages and relationships have been known for tenuousness and fragility. In Vietnam after the "American War," many people divorced or lost their girlfriends when the war was over, having spent too many years apart;[117] in post-war Japan, some soldiers who were declared dead but remained alive came home to find their wives remarried to a brother or close friend;[118] after WWI in Canada, divorce laws made it difficult to divorce, which only helped encourage bigamy and desertion among returning veterans—"marriage breakdown" was an all-too-familiar experience in "many families";[119] and in the contemporary United States, not a few veterans of the war in Iraq have experienced family-related difficulties (including spousal infidelity and financial problems) in addition to a sense of isolation, an increased tendency to sexual abuse, and suicide.[120] To the extent that we want to explain post-war suicides in China and the high percentage of marriage- and family-related causes among them, we need to get some sense of why veterans—many of whom were bachelors upon their return—were vulnerable in this respect. If suicides might have been prevented by a strong sense of family support, why was this lacking in many cases?

Much like their counterparts around the globe, PRC veterans' marriage and family situations hardly matched the stereotypical image of the stable, patriarchal "Asian" family. Marriage-, sex-, and family-related problems, which sometimes led to criminal prosecution or social ostracism, were noticed early on in the city and countryside and continued well into the 1950s and 1960s. A 1952 report by the Shanghai Veterans Committee found that some veterans, like their counterparts in Japan mentioned above, returned home to find their spouses living in common-law marriages with other men. For example, a veteran in Shanghai's working-class Yulin District found his wife in an "ambiguous" relationship with a worker in a private firm. Wang flew into a rage and demanded the worker's address so that he could smite him on the spot. Somehow, word of this threat reached the ears of someone in the district government, who found the worker and invited him in for a "talk" in which he was roundly criticized. His wife also got a talking-to: she was told that her husband was a "glorious veteran," so the two should find a way to get along. According to the report—in which this case was presented as a "model" for other institutions—the two then lived happily ever after, much like Homer and Wilma in *The Best Years of Our Lives*.[121]

We should be skeptical of this sort of narrative. Problems such as these could not be kept secret, and it was a serious "loss of face" to be forced to wrest a wife from the arms of another man (even when the mythological Helen of Troy did not keep the faith by having an affair with the Trojan prince Paris, her husband, the King of Sparta, also became a loser!); it might also be dangerous from a political and legal standpoint. According to a report on suicides from 1956, 4 out of 18 suicides "in the last several years" were because veterans were "ridiculed because of marriage problems or because of fear of punishment because they themselves had illicit sexual relations";[122] in another report from that year, 13 out of 43 suicides, also "in the last several years," were because of "marriage and unrequited love."[123] Moreover, contrary to the hopes of their critics, not all veterans were so determined to stay in a monogamous marriage; some bachelors and married veterans had a hard time keeping away from local prostitutes or could not resist leaving work to flirt with neighborhood women,[124] both activities which left them vulnerable to arrest and dismissal from their jobs (a problem also noted among mainland veterans living in Taiwan[125]). In the 1956 investigation of crimes committed by veterans (mentioned in Chapter 4), investigators found that 20 percent were due to rape, adultery, or prostitution,[126] a statistic that led the Civil Affairs bulletin, *Minzheng jianbao*, to note that "most veterans have relatively pressing demands with regard to marriage problems."[127] Other crimes were more serious but also attributable to their sense of vulnerability in their relationships. Some veterans murdered their wives because they suspected them of having affairs.[128] In other cases, however, veterans were on the other side of the courtroom. Some married veterans discovered during the course of their service that local cadres were having their way with their wives (a phenomenon I will address in greater depth in the next chapter). In Jintang County in Sichuan, 5 out of 17 veterans who had wives back in the village had their marriages violated by local officials; in Huiyang County in Guangdong, there were 42 veterans with pending marriage cases at court; two involved suicide, seven were murder cases, and many of the others focused on cadres accused of ruining their marriages.[129] These were not isolated incidents. A national-level report on veterans also noted cases of veterans who filed charges after enduring ridicule by cadres who had raped or seduced their wives.[130]

Veterans in Qingpu County were also embroiled in sex- and marriage-related conflicts and shenanigans, some of which seemed to stem from jealousy over others' access to sex. The case of Tao Baoqing, discussed at length in Chapter 3 as an example of whistleblowing on sexual improprieties (Tao made life difficult for a female cadre with a lover from another village), might also be understood as a case of sexual frustration—the woman's lover, after all, was from another village.[131] A 1956 investigation noted other sorts of cases. One veteran, who worked as a security guard, had two goals: to get married and to become an official. When he found himself smitten with a woman who did not return his affection, he (for reasons that are unclear) "pretended to be insane, hitting and yelling at people." This went on for days, despite numerous attempts to get him to stop. Finally, they sent him to Shanghai, where he was committed to a mental institution affiliated with the Public Security Bureau.[132] These Qingpu reports were echoed farther north in Shandong. A report on veterans proudly noted that "over 22,000 veterans received help getting married" but also that "over 1,931 cases involving marriage disputes, ostracism (*paichi*), and abuse" were handled by the authorities.[133]

Even though the Shandong report did not mention how many disputes were *not* handled, the brief reference to "ostracism" in the context of marriage and family is intriguing, particularly in light of some comparative evidence on post-war family situations. Although there is a fair amount of literature attesting to the discrimination faced by African-American veterans who fought for the Union during the Civil War, evidence does suggest that in the context of their own families, those veterans *gained* a great deal of status and respect ("face"); they were sought after as prospective husbands. As suggested by Donald Shaffer, "While veterans fought a losing battle to retain their political rights in the wake of Reconstruction, the gains that they and other African-Americans in the South made in terms of marriage and family law remained largely intact despite the rise of Jim Crow."[134] Although we would need far more microscopic studies of Chinese veterans' status within their families to make this sort of statement, there is some evidence suggesting that PLA veterans, and the rural disabled in particular, did not enjoy this sort of post-war boost in status because of the policy of forcing most veterans back to the countryside. For instance, a 1956 report on the national status of veterans instructed officials involved in veteran administration: "We need to do more education in military families to get some of them to stop thinking that their sons or husbands are 'good-for-nothings' (*mei you chuxi*) because they returned to the countryside."[135] In Chuansha County near Shanghai, a veteran surnamed Zhu returned from the army in 1959 after three years of service. His father was very disappointed, telling him, "You've served three years, and now have a skill, but there's no future in the countryside." To compel him to leave, he refused to feed him, but Zhu threatened to jump in a river and commit suicide and his father relented.[136] In Shandong, another investigation report found, families "resented those veterans who were not able to work because of sickness and disability and just sat around and ate."[137]

Nowhere did ostracism, resentment, and family problems intersect more problematically, and, on occasion, tragically, than in instances of veterans with some form of mental illness. Post-traumatic stress disorder (PTSD), though never diagnosed as such at the time (in WWI it was usually called "shell shock" and during WWII either "combat fatigue" or "war neurosis") surely affected hundreds of thousands of veterans of PLA combat operations, if evidence of comparative cases can serve as a rough estimate of this.[138] In the United States, David Gerber notes that 500,000 WWII veterans suffered from some form of mental illness,[139] and the National Center for Post-Traumatic Stress Disorder estimates that 1 out of 20 WWII veterans suffered from such symptoms as bad dreams, irritability, and flashbacks. The National Vietnam Veterans Readjustment Survey (conducted between 1986 and 1988) found that 15.2 percent of all male veterans were diagnosed with PTSD, and almost half of them had been arrested or jailed at least once, a reflection of the more difficult background of these recruits. A 2003 study published in the *New England Journal of Medicine* found that one of six soldiers returning from the war in Iraq (not the 1991 Persian Gulf War) suffered from PTSD.[140] Care for those with PTSD has always been challenging. In Russia, Ethel Dunn notes that the most severely disabled from WWII were "kept out of sight" and probably lived together on an island near St. Petersburg.[141] In Japan, WWII veterans with PTSD were shunned by their communities,[142] and in Mozambique, after its long and violent civil war ended in 1992, veterans who were considered traumatized by their experiences had to undergo a "healing" process that involved the administration of specific medicines and a cleansing ritual next to a river (which would wash away some of their problems).[143] In China, there has been little published research on this topic, owing to its political sensitivities (mentally ill veterans do not fit into the heroic narrative of the CCP's victorious wars), the weakness of psychiatry as an autonomous medical profession, and the lack of state resources committed to this problem, but it was an issue that could not be completely ignored.

At least officially, the most serious cases of mental illness would be treated in hospitals, while "light" cases would be treated at home. In practice, however, the line between serious and light was blurry, and because care was not cheap or necessarily good—reports indicated that veterans with mental illness were beaten[144]—many veterans with PTSD remained at home. In Shanghai, a 1956 report on veterans with long-term illness identified 24 who had mental disorders, 30 with tuberculosis, and 23 others with heart, stomach, circulatory, and other ailments. Officials admitted that "even though we have done some work to take care of their employment and medical issues, their problems are not taken seriously enough." As a result, the burden fell primarily on their families, who were said to be "dissatisfied" with the government on account of this. Some mothers said, "My son was fine when he left, but he's changed and become mentally ill and now no one cares"; others complained, "When they wanted people [for the PLA] they were very good about approaching you, but now when they're sick they push them on the family." Lacking money for food and medicine, desperate families "frequently" went to government offices and "raised a ruckus, demanding a solution for their problems." Most of these demands went unheeded. As a result of Civil Affairs' investigation, only two veterans were transferred to Beijing hospitals, but the officials encouraged veterans and their families to focus on the bright side: "Our government is better than previous ones, which left people like this to die."[145] This was only partly true. Though not left to die, Civil Affairs data from that same year indicated that 9 out of 43 veteran suicides were caused by either "mental illness" or "other forms of disease that caused abnormal behavior."[146]

If access to mental health care was difficult in one of China's most modern cities, in poorer areas of the countryside it was far worse. In a meeting of Shandong county chiefs in 1952, the gathered officials reported on veteran suicides in Jiaohe County because they returned to the village and found that "they had no land or housing" as well as problems with mentally ill veterans; "These veterans are all scattered around now, and it creates a great burden on their families," they pointed out.[147] Several years later, families still bore the brunt of care. In 1954 Shandong officials "diagnosed" 720 veterans with mental disorders in the province, among whom 242 were "very serious." Since Shandong had only limited facilities, "most all" of these veterans remained at home, where parents and relatives struggled to feed and take care of them. In some cases, families pooled resources and hired others to help, but in the most serious cases, the report noted, "even three hired people are not enough to care for them." Some mentally ill veterans were beaten to death. "A very bad influence on the people," the report concluded.[148] This situation may have improved later in the decade, but since reports and investigations consistently pay short shrift to the mentally ill and focus instead on employment issues, this issue is difficult to evaluate with any degree of certainty.

VULNERABLE BODIES ON THE JOB

job discrimination

Illness and disability produce certain vulnerabilities even in the best of circumstances, and vulnerabilities, in turn, create dependencies on those individuals or institutions that have power to provide good health or decrease pain, offer assistance around the household, or provide money to buy food and medicine. If workplace relations in China have already been characterized as "principled particularism" (in which a worker is dependent on the goodwill of a supervisor as well as adherence to political ideas),[149] those who were chronically ill or disabled experienced yet another layer of workplace dependency: they might have to take off work to get to the hospital; they might need a less strenuous job; or they may need certain workplace accommodations. Helping chronically ill veterans in the workplace is not easy anywhere—veterans after the American Civil War were handicapped by "wounds or chronic illnesses" and faced job competition "from men with several years' head start"[150]—and this is why it serves as a good measure of society's willingness to value martial contributions and expend valued resources to accommodate them in a reasonable way.

In China, employers were not unaware of the costs they would incur by hiring disabled or chronically ill veterans. Rather than taking them on because it was the "right thing to do," or to express gratitude for a well-fought battle (against the Japanese or Americans, for example), many employers did their best to avoid them altogether. As we have seen in the chapter on veteran employment, for many years factory personnel directors and managers had enough discretionary power to turn them away. As employment practices go, this was not unusual—unlike Weimar Germany, neither the United States nor England enforced quotas for hiring disabled veterans after WWI and WWII—but China's ample labor supply made these decisions much easier. Reports indicate that one of the reasons many work units refused to hire veterans was their perception that *all* veterans had some sort of medical problem. In the mining districts of Shuangyashan and Jixi in Heilongjiang Province in China's far northeast, for example, "very many" veterans managed to secure jobs only by pretending that they were *not* veterans, just ordinary peasants. When investigators interviewed 28 of these veterans, 25 of them "did not reveal that they were veterans" during the job registration process and initial trial period on the job; in a sample of 12 veterans' photos, 11 had taken off their fatigues to disguise their true identities. They did this after learning from other veterans' experiences. Zheng Jinfa, for example, was a veteran and CCP member who wore his uniform for his photograph and was immediately turned down. He came again without his uniform, claimed he was a "peasant," and passed the first stage, but was then sent for a physical. The doctor, however, discovered that, like many other veterans, Zheng had a respiratory illness and flunked him, not believing his claim that the problem was only an ulcer. Still determined to get the job, he tried a different physician. He passed only by covering his mouth with his hand whenever he had to cough. Still, of the 72 veterans introduced by the county Bureau of Civil Affairs, only nine were hired.[151]

Employers made similar efforts in the Shanghai area. Disabled veterans who left their villages because of political discrimination or difficulties working the land or earning enough work points (both prior to and after collectivization[152]) found little help upon their arrival in Shanghai. As early as 1949, city employers tried to avoid hiring them on the grounds that they were difficult to control, were too proud of their accomplishments, and would "harm efficiency."[153] A 1956 investigation of veteran–migrants to the city found a great deal of dissatisfaction among them. "Local government doesn't help," they complained. Still, none considered returning to the countryside: "Even if I lose my party membership I still won't go back to the village," one disabled veteran said.[154] Factory-level investigations substantiated these complaints. In the spring of 1955, the China Record Factory was preparing to hire 200 workers. Someone "mentioned hiring veterans," but the leading cadres at the firm said, "They've all been disabled fighting wars. But some might have some skills—those guys we can assign to do cleanup."[155] For the Shanghai Ocean Shipping Bureau (*haiyun ju*), age was associated with physical strength, so even if veterans were not actually ill, their bodies might still be too weak. When veterans arrived at the bureau with their letter of introduction in 1958, they were told that they had to "lift 200 *jin*" (roughly 220 pounds or 100 kilograms) to get the job. "As soon as they heard this, they left."[156] In 1963, the same bureau took in 54 veterans but then immediately assigned all of them to be boatswains, "even though some of them can't handle the physical labor."[157] Not surprisingly, in Qingpu, 50 percent of letters the Bureau of Civil Affairs received from veterans in the late 1950s were job-related. Of those, half were written by the disabled or sick veterans appealing for employment assistance or transfer to a more appropriate job.[158]

Ill veterans who passed through this hoop and found positions in government or factories did not necessarily fare very well, however. Poor health could enhance political and job-related vulnerability. In 1951 in Shandong, a report noted that when some disabled veterans and martyr families complained about their treatment to village cadres, the latter immediately took revenge by denying them the right to participate in village meetings.[159] In Qingpu, Ling Lin-sheng returned to the county in 1953 as a disabled veteran and was appointed secretary of a township's youth league and militia. He was reported to be very effective at his job but was frequently ill. This led to arguments between him and the township's non-veteran party secretary, Tao Genfu. Using Ling's re-curring illness as an excuse, Tao forced him out of power, sending him back to his village to work in agriculture. Two village officials, however, opposed this move, but Tao falsely told the two that Ling was to return "by order of the district party secretary." They eventually relented and Ling returned home.[160] In 1963, the Shanghai Bureau of Civil Affairs still noted many intractable problems in the treatment of disabled veterans in rural areas: "Some commune and brigade leaders show little concern for the placement of veterans who are older, weaker, disabled, or sick and do not have much labor power; this is reflected in their difficulties with medical care, housing, and financial difficulties."[161] In 1965, at the height of pro-PLA propaganda, a joint report by the Shanghai Garrison, Civil Affairs, and the Labor Bureau found that veterans who returned to villages "with illnesses" and had problems with medicine, work, and finances were "not provided with timely assistance."[162]

The situation in Shanghai was not much better. The cases of Shi Maoru, who was hired by the Jinxing Pen factory in 1954; Chen Youxian (Tianfu Manufacturing); and Shao Ran, who worked at the Jiangnan Shipyard, are good cases in point. After being hired, Shi Maoru was forced to go on sick leave on several occasions due to a recurring illness. Citing his frequent sick days, the factory refused to make him a permanent worker. His salary was particularly low: after a factory-wide salary adjustment in 1956, other than Shi's (who earned 21 yuan a month), the lowest salary was 40 yuan. When he approached management for a raise, the personnel director took out a pen produced by the factory and quizzed Shi with all sorts of technical questions. When Shi could not answer, the director told him, "See. This is why I can't give you a raise."[163] Chen Youxian, a CCP member, also fell victim to his health but in a more severe way. Introduced to the factory in 1951 by the Labor Bureau, Chen had Level 3 disability because of a respiratory illness which caused him to fall asleep on the job. He also had to request several leaves of absence. The factory, however, considered his behavior as a manifestation of "poor labor discipline." When Chen was in the hospital, the party branch, without notifying Chen, convened a meeting and announced that he was being expelled from the CCP. Even after this came to light and his status was restored, Chen never received an apology.[164] Shao Ran also suffered because of health-related difficulties stemming from his service (in the Korean War). Similar to many veterans we have seen, Shao frequently experienced flare-ups of his old wounds. On one occasion, an infection caused a fever and a temperature of 40° Celsius (roughly 104° Fahrenheit). He requested that the shipyard's personnel department arrange for a vehicle to send him to the hospital, but its director, Qu Mengzhang, refused on the grounds that Shao's injury "was not a work accident," so it was not the shipyard's responsibility to help him. When his fever flared again, Shao asked Qu for a letter of introduction to the Shanghai Military Medical University Hospital, but he again refused; an appeal to another official was also unsuccessful. Thanks to help from some other workers "angered at this injustice," Shao found a car that did not belong to his work unit and made it to the hospital. But his problems did not end there. Because of his absence, the factory docked 50 percent of his monthly salary. When he complained about this to the Salary Department, they accused him of "economism" (or looking at issues only through the narrow lens of money) and refused to correct their error. "There are not many cases like this in every work unit," the report noted, "but if they were all collected together, it would be not a few."[165]

Whatever the actual numbers, there is evidence suggesting that even "not a few" cases were sufficient to create a very strong association between the concepts "veteran" and "poor health." In 1963, and even during the Cultural Revolution, this linkage was alive and well. "Some cadres," a Civil Affairs report complained in 1963, "think that veterans are sick, weak, and have problems."[166] According to Republic of China intelligence reports on Fujian Province in the early 1970s, employers who had only reluctantly taken on veterans prior to the Cultural Revolution (and paid them low salaries) now absolutely refused to hire them, "especially those who were disabled or ill." Some returned to their villages because of the daily discrimination they faced.[167]

DEATH AND CLOSE CALLS

Most veterans, of course, did not die as a result of discrimination or family- or health-related problems. Suicide, by its very nature, is an extreme act, even among distressed populations. It is, however, the proverbial canary in the mine, a phenomenon that can render visible more widespread problems in a group hidden by everyday struggles to survive and manage during or after a trauma. Take the case of British veterans of the Falklands War. Although known in society for their "stiff upper lip," there are some indications that more soldiers died of suicide than from the war itself, largely as a result of PTSD. While this is a minority of the soldiers who fought, the "social fact" of the suicides is indicative of a larger failure of both the society and the state to deal with the long-term repercussions of war-related trauma, enhanced by the macho self-image of elite units who fought.[168] Most governments also appear to be aware that suicides are indicative of larger problems, despite their infrequency. At least in the case of veterans, the PRC government took these more seriously than the abnormal deaths of landlords, former GMD officials, and other enemies of the regime, and the U.S. Congress, for its part, worried about rising suicide rates among veterans after wars in Afghanistan and Iraq, introduced a bill (the "Joshua Omvig Veterans Suicide Prevention Act," or H.R. 327) that "directs the Secretary of Veterans Affairs to develop a comprehensive program designed to reduce the incidence of suicide among veterans."

Chinese statistics about veterans' suicides, with their rather odd phrasings (such as 43 veterans "died in the last several years") cannot be relied upon to measure overall frequency—even in the United States, with its sophisticated statistical bureaucracies, it is not clear how many veterans died of post-war suicides after each conflict—but some of the case histories can provide us with a deeper understanding of the circumstances swirling around those who died, or tried to, even if they cannot be generalized in a scientific sense. Below are some examples of marriage- and health-related suicides from the 1950s.

MARRIAGE- AND SEX-RELATED SUICIDES: WU QINGYUN, LI RUFA, AND WANG YUEQING

Wu Qingyun was a veteran who returned to Wenjiang County in Sichuan Province. Said to be a good worker, Wu was participating in a mutual aid team in 1951. Because of poor health, however, Wu was a frequent visitor to the inpatient ward of the county hospital. It was there that he met a widow "from a poor peasant family," fell in love, and decided to get married. When he returned to his village and announced his intentions, however, the village chief objected, calling him a "degenerate" (*fuhua*), and threatened him with unspecified sanctions. Soon after, he hung himself. Farther east, in Yichun County, Jiangxi Province, veteran Li Rufa met a village woman named

Zhong Guiying and petitioned to get married. Officials at the district government, however, refused to register the marriage because Zhong's late father had been a landlord. Li was also harshly criticized for his choice. When he returned to the village, the township cadres convened a meeting of his fellow veterans and initiated a struggle session against him. Feeling hopeless because of his failed marriage efforts and pitted against his fellow veterans, Li threw himself into a river and drowned.[169]

Shanghai was also the scene of these sorts of suicides. Veteran Wang Yueqing returned to Shanghai in 1951, but because the district government was not able to secure a job for him, he found himself wandering around the district with nothing to do. After a while, the district arranged for temporary work on the "Patriotic Hygiene" public health campaign. During this campaign, he met a housewife who had also been mobilized for it and had an affair with her. This indiscretion was exposed, and Wang found himself in the Laozha District Police Station. He was released, the report noted, "but he still could not solve his marriage problems." Sometime later he was given an introduction to a private firm, where he acquired a reputation of a braggart by "exaggerating his personal contributions to the country." When one lie was exposed—he told management that he had joined the PLA when he was 9 years old—he "lost face, and felt as if he had no future." On August 7, 1952, he drank poison. Fortunately, he was discovered and sent to the emergency room before he died and was saved. According to the official report, Wang tried to commit suicide because he "found his personal problems burdensome, is vain, and likes face."[170]

HEALTH-CARE-RELATED SUICIDES: QIU GUANGMING AND JIN RONGHUA

Qiu Guangming worked in the dye department of an underwear factory. Suffering from chronic stomach ulcers, he found his assigned work too strenuous. Frequent requests to see a physician were turned down except on one occasion, but even then he was not provided with insurance money. Reported to be "very dissatisfied" by this treatment, Qiu complained to the factory, which finally relented and allowed him to see a doctor. He went to the hospital for treatment, but the factory had already called the hospital in advance, informing them that Qiu's problems were not medical but, rather, "political" in nature (without providing specifics). When Qiu heard about this in the hospital, he flew into a rage, ran up to the roof, and yelled that he was going to jump off. According to the report, he was "seen and pulled off the roof," but it does not indicate whether his problem was solved.[171]

Jin Ronghua, who also worked in Shanghai (at the Jinxing Pen Factory), encountered similar apathy toward his medical problems. Much like Shao Ran, Jin suffered from a frequent relapse of a war-related disease and needed a "letter of introduction" to a hospital. He managed to procure the letter, but when he went to the emergency room, the personnel refused to treat him, even as he was writhing in pain on its floor. Apparently, they had tried calling the factory's "insurance section" on three occasions, but when they did not get a return phone call, they sent him back to the factory's infirmary. Before he left, however, the physicians provided him with free advice: Jin should ask his sister or aunt to come to the factory to help him out. When he approached Huang Chuanwen, the head of the insurance section, with this idea, Huang yelled at him, "Don't you know our factory is in the middle of production competition? I have work to do." Because Jin's injury continued to flare up and he frequently had to take off from work because of pain, management deducted the time from his salary; on occasion, the deduction totaled 40 percent of his monthly salary. Facing this cash shortfall, Jin went to the union and told the union personnel that he was a revolutionary disabled veteran and "according to central state regulations, I'm entitled to 100 percent labor insurance coverage." But the union ignored him. Its chair, Xie Yimin, was surprised that Jin was not satisfied with the symbols of high status and also wanted more substantial benefits: "You're a war hero and a labor model and you still want 100 percent insurance coverage?" A co-worker, Zhu Yongyi also complained about Jin's demand: "Do you think you get full insurance just because you have two red certificates [one for being a veteran, the other for being disabled]?" Jin then contacted the two organizations that were expected to help enforce central state regulations: Civil Affairs and the Veterans Committee. Both called the chairman of the factory union about Jin, urging him to implement the regulation guaranteeing 100 percent coverage for disabled veterans. In a response that complicates the notion that China had a "command economy" during these years and that the CCP was a highly disciplined organization, the chairman refused, telling both organizations, "Government institutions can't order our factory around" (*zhengfu jiguan bu neng lingdao women gongchang*). Sometime later, Jin overdosed on drugs in a suicide attempt, which failed because he did not consume a sufficient dosage. According to the investigation, management was unmoved. Factory officials claimed that Jin attempted suicide because of "heartbreak" (*shilian*) and his only goal was to try to scare people.[172]

In fact, this may have been the case; it is entirely possible that Jin, like many veterans, did have problems with marriage and women that did not figure into this report. Nevertheless, it was a blatant effort by factory officials to shift responsibility for the suicide attempt away from their neglect of Jin's poor health and disregard for health care "rights" that were merely embedded in State Council policies. While the precise circumstances surrounding Jin's overdose (or Qiu Guangming's rooftop stand) may have been unique, I would venture that even a short perusal of documents in other archives would reveal roughly similar circumstances: poor health, institutional failure, social apathy, and uneven enforcement of central state directives. Still, the question remains: was this "perfect storm" of individual circumstances, state incapacity, and a lack of cultural or political appreciation for veterans worse in China than in many other countries, and if it was, why? Research on disabled veterans in countries as different as Namibia and the United Kingdom has also noted their marginality, particularly if their disability is severe.[173] On Taiwan, unemployed veterans tend to be older, holding lower rank, and in poor health as well.[174] To get an even sharper perspective on this, let's briefly turn to a country where, for many reasons, disabled veterans faced a far more hospitable environment than their Chinese counterparts—Israel—and see how they have fared over time.

THE STRUGGLE FOR RIGHTS AND ENFORCEMENT OF RIGHTS AMONG DISABLED VETERANS IN ISRAEL

If there is any country in the world where disabled veterans should have had a much easier time reintegrating into society and acquiring rights and respect, surely Israel would be a prime candidate. Since its founding one year prior to the PRC's (1948), Israel's military, the Israel Defense Forces (IDF), has fought six wars against states and conducted numerous military operations against Palestinian organizations and uprisings,[175] ensuring that service-related disability would always be politically salient; there has been no "peacetime lull." Israel, unlike China, is a very small country, both in terms of size and population. Governing Israel is challenging, but not quite on the same scale as China. Israel has always had compulsory and near-universal military service for most Jewish men and women[176] as well as conscription for men from the minority Druze community. Between 1948 and 1973, Israel, for better or worse, has been a militarized society: unlike China's State Council, many cabinet ministers were former generals; Israel's first prime minister, David Ben-Gurion, viewed the IDF as the heart of nation-building efforts; IDF officers—pilots in particular—enjoyed very high prestige; and Israeli culture was suffused with images of heroic, self-sacrificing, and courageous "fighters" not unlike Lei Feng in the early 1960s.[177] The Israeli landscape is full of memorials to fallen soldiers of its many wars; until 1957, the dead of the 1948 war were represented in no fewer than 121 monuments.[178] Surveys reveal that disabled veterans, particularly if they were wounded in combat, have benefited from these attitudes.[179] Israel, unlike China, has had a statute, based on pre-state programs, governing disability rights that have awarded disabled veterans generous, expanding, and generally non-means-based benefits linked to civil service salaries and degrees of injury. In contrast to China's diffuse and overstretched Civil Affairs bureaucracy, David Ben-Gurion placed the Ministry of Defense—the most prestigious ministry in the state— in complete charge of implementing these benefits. As a result, the IDF's disabled, unlike those born with disabilities or injured in car accidents, do not have to deal with the regular welfare bureaucracies. Israeli disabled veterans, also quite unlike their PRC counterparts, have a representative organization, the Zahal (IDF) Disabled Veterans Organization (ZDVO hereafter), which is recognized in law as the "official" body representing the military disabled. In terms of its budget, Israel spends more on disabled veterans pensions than any other industrialized country (in 1994, 0.4 percent of the gross domestic product).[180] Politically, Israel is a vibrant democracy with a free press. As a "best-case scenario" for disabled veterans' rights, Israel can tell us two important things. First, it allows us to eliminate, or at least reduce, the weight of key variables as the most critical to an explanation. For instance, if Israeli disabled veterans also encountered very serious problems (even if not on the scale of China), we can rule out the size of population or territory as the most critical variable; since Israel is a democracy, perhaps China's problems should not be attributable primarily to its regime type. Second, by looking at the story behind the expansion of rights and generous benefits for Israeli disabled veterans, we can also tease out the conditions for proper veteran disability care that may have been lacking in the Chinese case.

Contrary to my own expectations, even a rather cursory glance at the mainstream Israeli press (*Ma'ariv*, *Yediot Achronot*) reveals that, despite their many advantages, disabled Israeli war veterans were not handed rights or benefits on a silver platter, and the state's protective umbrella was not necessarily wide enough, either. Disabled veterans, either as individuals or through the ZDVO, had to fight (usually against officials in the Finance Ministry[181]) for most of the necessary adaptations for their everyday needs as well as for preservation of memory. In March 1960, for example, disabled veterans (at the time there were 6,000 of them) were described as "furious" at the state, and the Ministry of Finance in particular, because of the nitpicking negotiations over their benefits (involving tax breaks, medicine, disability levels, unemployment issues) which led many disabled to feel that they were being treated like supplicants to be pitied, or just another interest group. "It's not how much you give," one correspondent summarized, "it's how you give it and how the state returns the debt it owes you."[182]

This complaint, however, was partially disingenuous, since Israeli disabled veterans were not beyond combining high-minded appeals to their status with concrete discussions over meat and potatoes. In December of that year, the "Organization of Disabled Veterans from the War of Independence" (the predecessor of the ZDVO) complained about "insulting treatment" on the part of the Ministry of Defense and threatened to initiate a sit-in strike at the ministry if various income tax deductions were not resolved and their compensation scale was not adjusted "to level 15 on the Civil Service salary scale"; the statute governing their compensation stipulated that it be set at level 10, but this level "no longer exists."[183] In 1965, the same organization initiated a "public struggle" to improve upon their rights, which they claimed had lost much of their value during the previous decade. Claiming that their struggle "will affect military morale," organization leaders sent a letter to the minister of defense demanding an upgrade to their benefits, since those who were non-disabled enjoyed a significant boost in their standard of living. When time passed and no answer was received, the organization contacted the media, which published their letter to the minister of defense. Two days later, there was some action: an interagency meeting was convened between representatives of the Finance, Defense, and Labor ministries. When an interim report from this meeting was brought before a crowd at the disabled organization's headquarters, a wave of protest erupted, in part because two days earlier, some veterans, in a matter unrelated to the legislation, had "broken into the Finance Ministry" but were also given the bureaucratic run-around. After this heated meeting, the deputy minister of defense, Shimon Peres, called the chairman and other officials of the organization and they worked out an agreement whereby monthly payments would be made to disabled who had "19 percent disability" (the organization initially demanded 24 percent) as well as increased payments for the unemployed and those who had extremely serious disabilities (such as paralysis and blindness).[184]

This national-level action was not the only one prior to 1967, when the Six Day War began and a new generation of disabled veterans was created. In January 1966, the disabled veterans organization was "preparing for a struggle" against Israel's two primary transportation cooperatives, "Dan" and "Egged," on grounds already familiar to us from Chapter 4: job discrimination. According to the news account, many disabled veterans began to work at these co-ops after their release from the hospital in 1950, but usually as "hired" workers (repairman, ticket punchers, etc.). Because many disabled veterans could not drive, they could not become full members of the cooperative, since the co-ops' charter stipulated that all members must have a driver's license. Frequent attempts to find a compromise solution failed, including a back-channel intervention by former Defense Minister Shimon Peres, which prompted threats of collective action: "The public should know that disability is not a crime that should be punished. Our comrades at the cooperatives are not alone. We will all come together to demand our rights, if necessary.[185]

This call for solidarity proved prescient. Six months later, the Six Day War broke out. The decisive victory in the war did not always translate into a smooth transition to civilian life, however. The years immediately following the war witnessed a flurry of small skirmishes and larger battles between disabled veterans and the state, public agencies, and individual employers.[186] Between 1967 and 1968, the key law governing disability benefits was revised and expanded, thanks largely to activism by the disabled themselves, their allies in the media, and strong public opinion in their favor, the latter of which provided a great deal of leverage in negotiations between the various ministries involved.[187] For instance, in the summer of 1968, 200 disabled veterans planned to protest outside several movie theaters in a town near the northern city of Haifa, claiming that the owner of the theaters was not doing enough to employ disabled veterans, as was required by law.[188] In March 1969, a well-organized task force of 500 disabled veterans "conquered" the Postal Service Building "without encountering much resistance"; the Post Office, which was also in charge of installing landlines in the pre-cell-phone era, had refused to implement various tax breaks and, gallingly, "did not respond to their correspondence"; this conflict apparently had been brewing since 1958. Even though the disabled entered clerks' offices, "no one even thought about calling in the police" (they invited them for drinks instead).[189] The media was sympathetic to the veterans and railed against "government and public agencies" for their "apathy and lack of sensitivity" in dealing with the disabled, a charge that was echoed by many disabled in a 1971 Ministry of Defense survey of this population.[190] Eli Landau, the military correspondent of the mass circulation daily *Ma'ariv*, wrote, "The shameful sight of an Israeli government minister being forced to 'receive' hundreds of disabled veterans 'attacking' him could have been prevented if it were not for their blatant disregard and neglect of this painful problem which is shared by thousands of families in Israel." The disabled's fight against the Post Office was successful.[191]

In other cases, disabled veterans, like their PLA counterparts, wrote to the press. In 1968, a man with the initials M.S. penned the following letter to *Ma'ariv*:[192]

Disabled veterans encounter problems that have nothing to do with their physical condition. From experience I know that many problems are not resolved. For example, every factory is supposed to allocate 5 percent of their positions for the disabled, but this is not enforced. Many of my disabled friends are unemployed. Education grants from the Ministry of Defense are insufficient, but when I asked the clerks how I could manage with such a paltry sum, they said, "We know it's hard, but that's all the law allows." Employees of the Civil Service get telephones at half-price, but the disabled person has to pay full price, even though he needs to make emergency calls on occasion.

. . . Again, my point is to spur those involved in these matters to take action. If there is a government agency handling these issues, please do something!

Veterans also took legal action to contest the state's determination of their disability level or to obtain "disabled veteran" status, problems we have also seen in China, albeit in Letters and Visits Offices or the Civil Affairs bureaucracy. On the whole, Israeli disabled veterans, despite living in a democracy and a generally supportive social atmosphere, were not very aware of their rights; an unpublished study of disabled veterans (1971) found that 54 percent were either unclear, or knew nothing, about their rights (of 45 specific rights, only three were clearly identified by 75 percent of respondents), a legal deficit that the large majority of veterans (77 percent) blamed on the Ministry of Defense's "not doing enough to let us know about our rights."[193] Those who were more aware of their rights, and had the wherewithal and resources for a lawyer, did take the Rehabilitation Department and other agencies to court. In *Arye Dayan v. State of Israel*, the plaintiff was injured in his spine in 1964 and recognized as 20 percent disabled. In the 1980s, however, his condition deteriorated, and he had several operations. A medical board then established his degree of disability at 44 percent "permanently." He appealed this decision at the District Court in Haifa, which decided to send his medical records back to the medical board.[194] Israel's Supreme Court (convening as a Court of Appeals) heard a case involving a soldier who developed diabetes several years after shell shock during a battle in the Yom Kippur War; his initial claim for compensation was denied because the law stipulated that the statute of limitations for claims was three years, so the plaintiff was too late. This decision was overturned at the district level, but the Ministry of Defense appealed the decision at the Supreme Court. The court ruled against the ministry and ordered it to pay 2,000 new Israeli shekels (NIS).[195] These cases are not unusual: according to the late Judge Sara Sirota, a former vice president of Tel Aviv District Court, courts tend to be quite sympathetic to claims by disabled veterans, even those whose circumstances are somewhat murky; when they err, it usually benefits the veterans and not the bureaucracy.[196]

Despite ongoing wars and conflicts, protests involving disabled veterans continued unabated in Israel. In 1984, the ZDVO threatened to "blockade the Rehabilitation Department offices" if the government did not rescind what they claimed were "sharp cuts" in their rights that resulted from a fiscal austerity program.[197] In 1985, a group of 500 disabled veterans, including amputees and soldiers whose entire bodies were burned inside tanks, camped outside the Ministry of Defense to demand that the minister, Yitzhak Rabin, intervene on their behalf with the prime minister and finance minister because their pensions were not keeping up with double- and triple-digit inflation. (A placard read: "Rabin: in '67 we went into battle with you; in '85 you're abandoning your fighters.") If their demands were not met, "thousands of disabled veterans would stage a protest outside the Finance Ministry and Prime Minister's Office."[198] In 1986, the ZDVO took out a half-page ad in *Ma'ariv* in response to the state's effort to tax their benefits. The appeal was very emotional, evoking themes of debt, sacrifice, and pain:

> Government Ministers, from where did you derive the courage and gall to tax bereavement, orphans, widows, and disabilities?
>
> Have you lost your sense of humanity, feeling, and shame?
>
> How can you not see that we have already paid the government with our blood in all of Israel's wars?
>
> How can you not understand that we paid this tax with our bodies, our eyes, limbs, and ugly and painful scars or sense of taste?
>
> We've been through the hell of defending the Golan Heights and Sinai, the Chinese Farm [in Sinai, during the Yom Kippur War], and Ammunition Hill [in Jerusalem in the Six Day War]. Those wars were imposed on us by our enemies; our government should not impose upon us another war.[199]

But protests continued. In 1987, amputees staged a protest in the middle of Tel Aviv because the government disallowed exchanging their vehicles for new ones after several years of use. Echoing a phrase heard among veterans in China ("slaughtering the mule after he ground the wheat"), one of the protesters said, "The war's over, and the grunt's work is done, so now he can go. That's what's happening now: we did what we did, paid the price, but no one remembers us for it."[200]

Despite their flair for aggressive tactics, as well as highly emotional and dramatic gestures and language, disabled veterans did not face their problems alone, even when the ZDVO did not directly advocate on their behalf. After the Six Day War, employees of the Nature Authority contributed the proceeds from one day of work to the disabled; a "spontaneous volunteer organization" with 600 members was created by Pinchas Yom-tov to help them "reenter civilian life";[201] and volunteers from WIZO (the Womens International Zionist Organization) stepped in to help disabled soldiers' families adjust to the difficulties after returning from the hospital and rehabilitation clinics.[202] In 1977, the Supreme Court implored the legislature to revise the disability law (in force since 1959) so that disabled veterans would have an easier time ob-

taining the benefits to which they were entitled; many of the disabled encountered health-related problems many years after their service, which was well
past the statute of limitation for making claims.[203] Private foundations both
inside and outside Israel have also helped pay for big-ticket items such as new
medical facilities.[204] Disabled veterans have also had many allies in the media, exposing problems with buildings that lack access for the disabled, very
serious difficulties getting good care for those suffering from extreme forms
of PTSD, insensitive bureaucrats, employment discrimination ("The names
of factories in the North that refuse to employ disabled veterans [from the Six
Day War] will be published"), or physicians who did not have good bedside
manners.[205] In Israel, problems with disabled veterans (and those disabled by
terrorist attacks) remain acute, but they are generally exposed and stay fairly
high on the public agenda. Unlike many would-be critics of the government
in the United States, Israelis do not fear being labeled as "unpatriotic" if they
speak out on these matters.

So what have we learned from this brief survey? Let's first look at some of
the important similarities between the two cases. In both Israel and China, it is
clear that bureaucracy, no matter where, does not appear to be well equipped
to deal with emotionally fraught issues such as loss and disability and, as a
result, will always draw the ire of the disabled. We have also learned that in
both cases employers usually draw the most "red cards" for not accommodating veterans after their injuries; in Israel, however, this is more understandable because they operate under the constraints of a market economy driven
by competition and profit, which was not the case in China. Furthermore, in
both cases, disability was a "contested concept"—there were arguments over
who was disabled, the "degree" of disability, and just how long one can claim
benefits and status as a result of war-related injuries. It was also the case that
disabled veterans in both countries used similar rhetorical strategies to frame
their claims, using such phrases as "debts owed," "sacrifices made," and the
"moral responsibility" of the state to take care of them after their injuries.
Finally, in both cases, accessing rights and benefits was not easy; there were,
in effect, battles after the wars in terms of making sure that politicians lived
up to their promises and patriotic rhetoric.

By looking at the differences, however, we can see just how far China
has to go in terms of providing disabled veterans with a sense of social and
political appreciation. In Israel, disabled veterans benefited from a law and
institutions that were able to overrule or critique bureaucratic practices, but
Chinese disabled veterans do not have recourse to the law; its veterans almost
certainly would benefit from a statute where their rights are clearly spelled
out. A free press can also make a positive and significant difference in exposing problems, shaming employers and bureaucrats, and spurring politicians to

take necessary remedial action. Unlike Chinese veterans, the Israeli disabled also had a very feisty and aggressive organization, which we have seen is critical in securing rights and benefits. (This was also the case among some African-American disabled veterans after WWII, who formed their own organizations in response to discrimination.)[206] Their allies at home and abroad have eased the burden on state coffers to some extent. It is also apparent that there were key differences in the extent of public support for their cause. Israeli disabled veterans did complain about bureaucratic apathy and some public indifference, but there is little evidence of the nastiness and derision in everyday interactions between the disabled and other citizens of the sort we have seen between Chinese and their disabled veterans.

These differences, I suggest, can be traced to several root causes, some shallow and others deep. Among the former I could include the difference in political systems. Democracy, law, and freedom of the press and association do matter, even if they cannot be said to be indispensable, since many veterans in the USSR appear to have had an easier time than their counterparts in the PRC. The root that lies deeper under the surface, however, is the nature of military service and the legitimacy of the wars that produced so many disabled soldiers. In Israel there is near-universal conscription, which has led to a higher degree of respect and sympathy for those wounded in action; it is not a coincidence that disabled veterans have allies in many places in society. In Israel, the wars have had a clear foreign enemy and were generally seen as necessary and legitimate (until 1982), and this perception rubbed off on the status of disabled veterans. In China, I argue, the military was too narrow in terms of its social composition and its wars were more complicated and less legitimate, which had a negative impact on the status of disabled veterans.

NOTES

1. PTSD, or anything equivalent to this ("shell shock," "battle fatigue"), does not appear in a county-level census of patients in mental hospitals. See QA 48-2-300. The USSR also did not recognize PTSD, and veterans suffering from it were unlikely to get treatment. See Merridale, *Ivan's War*, 364–65. The DSM-III-R symptoms that would seem to apply to Lin include difficulty concentrating, detachment and estrangement from others, sense of a foreshortened future, difficulty falling or staying asleep, and diminished interest in significant activities, as well as chronic health problems stemming from chronic mobilization of the body for danger. See Shay, *Achilles in Vietnam*, 166–69.

2. Frederick Teiwes and Warren Sun, *The Tragedy of Lin Biao*, 12.

3. For Lin's sleep-related disorders and poor health, see Qiu Jin, *The Culture of Power: The Lin Biao Incident in the Cultural Revolution*, 145–47. Jin writes that

Lin's poor health made him "more vulnerable and submissive." MacFarquhar and Schoenhals note the connection between Lin's health and political isolation but seem to question whether Lin was actually ill: "Lin's long years of *apparent illness* meant that he had no constituency outside of the PLA. And he would almost certainly have had to rely upon his clique of senior generals in the center and PLA first secretaries in the Provinces." See MacFarquhar and Schoenhals, *Mao's Last Revolution*, 23, 300–301; emphasis mine). Teiwes and Sun also note Lin's detached and introverted manners but cast less doubt on the authenticity of his health problems: "Clearly poor health was a major factor." However, they also suggest that Lin may have used ill health as an excuse to get out of meetings. See *Tragedy of Lin Biao,* 10, 78, 89.

4. *Jundui ganbu*, 159–60.

5. SMA B168-1-209 (1963), 24.

6. *Minzheng jianbao*, August 15, 1956, 56.

7. Homer, *The Iliad*, Robert Fagles, trans. (New York: Viking, 1990), 122. For a book-length study on *The Iliad* through the prism of combat trauma, see Jonathan Shay, *Achilles in Vietnam.*

8. Sophocles, *Philoctetes,* Carl Phillips, trans., 73.

9. On the gradual inclusion of disabled people in PRC films, see Sarah Dauncey, "Screening Disability in the PRC," 481–506.

10. Lieutenant General Michael DeLong, deputy commander of the United States Central Command, complained that "politicians from her home state, West Virginia, wanted the military to award her the Medal of Honor" and that the "politicians said that a medal would be good for women in the military." DeLong was responding to politicians' efforts to pin the blame for the Jessica Lynch myth on the Pentagon, which he calls "utter hypocrisy." See "Politics during Wartime," *New York Times*, April 27, 2007. I have not seen a rebuttal of this version of events.

11. Derthick, *Agency under Stress*, 37.

12. See Matthew Kohrman, *Bodies of Difference: Experiences of Disability and Institutional Advocacy in the Making of Modern China*; Karen Nakamura, *Deaf in Japan: Signing and the Politics of Identity.*

13. Shay, *Achilles in Vietnam*, 187–88.

14. Tim Bullman and Han Kang, "The Risk of Suicide among Wounded Vietnam Veterans," 662–67.

15. DDA 11-7-306 (1959), 72.

16. This idea was not new—eugenics and Social Darwinism were extremely influential in China prior to 1949, and sports and physical education were heavily promoted as remedies to China's weakness vis-à-vis the West. See Andrew Morris, *Marrow of the Nation: A History of Sport and Physical Culture in Republican China.* For the importance of physical prowess as an important criterion for political and social status in rural China, see Chan, Madsen, and Unger, *Chen Village under Mao and Deng*, 29.

17. See Diamant, *Revolutionizing the Family*, Chapter 3; Lee and Kleinman, "Suicide as Resistance in Chinese Society," 289–311.

18. Gat, "The Democratic Peace Theory Reframed: The Impact of Modernity," 91.

19. Gary B. Nash, *The Unknown American Revolution*, 216–17. This included immigrants, who composed a significant portion of the Continental Army.

20. Gat, "Democratic Peace," 91.

21. Alan Skelly, *The Victorian Army at Home*, 297–98; John Keegan writes that the primary motive for enlisting in the British Expeditionary Force in 1916 was usually "simple poverty." See *The Face of Battle*, 216. On troop quality, see Gat, "Democratic Peace," 91.

22. John Keep, *Soldiers of the Czar: Army and Society in Russia, 1492–1874*, 147.

23. Between 1940 and 1973, a period that combined the draft and selective service in the United States, "those entering the military tended to come from low- and high-status families without discrimination." See Neil Fligstein, "Who Served in the Military, 1940–1973," 298.

24. Gerald Linderman, *Embattled Courage: The Experience of Combat in the American Civil War*, 115–16.

25. Henry Ramos, *The American G.I. Forum*, 3–4; according to Carl Allsup, Mexican-Americans had the highest incidence of illness and disease because of poverty and discrimination. See *The American G.I. Forum: Origins and Evolution*, 57–58.

26. SMA B168-1-600, 113.

27. SMA B168-1-607, 54.

28. Among the officers were 2 brigadier generals, 60 colonels, 250 battalion commanders, 554 first lieutenants, and 625 second lieutenants. The rest (1,293) were classified as "soldiers." See SMA B168-1-632 (1956), 80.

29. SA A20-1-029 (1951), 17.

30. SA A1-2-516 (1957), 19; SA A20-1-295 (1960), 43.

31. *Liaoning sheng zhi: minzheng zhi*, 104.

32. *Jundui ganbu*, 161–62.

33. SMA B242-1-574 (1953), 2–3. Rural officials were admonished on account of this.

34. QA 48-2-141 (1957), 12.

35. QA 48-2-146.

36. *Wuqiang xian zhi* (Beijing: Fangzhi chubanshe, 1996), 416.

37. *Yutian xian zhi* (Beijing: Zhongguo dabaike quanshu chubanshe, 1993), 371.

38. *Yi xian zhi* (Beijing: Zhongyang bianyi chubanshe, 2000), 360–61.

39. *Wu'an xian zhi* (Beijing: Zhongguo guangbo dianshe chubanshe, 1990), 698.

40. Fred Riggs, *The Consulting Firm*, 4–5; Yu-Wen Fan notes that the percentage of veterans with mental illness was far higher than average. See "Becoming a Civilian," 130, ft. 35.

41. Cited in Gittings, *The Role of the Chinese Army*, 98; in the film *Assembly*, Captain Gu Zidi, a former officer, loses part of his eyesight. After the war, he resigns himself to bachelorhood.

42. Merridale, *Ivan's War*, 355.

43. SA A1-2-516 (1957), 19.

44. SA A20-1-109 (1954), 47. In Tai'an county, 1,025 out of 1,636 veterans were not married (63 percent); after several years, 426 got married and 129 were engaged, which still left 28 percent unmarried, assuming all the engagements resulted in marriage. See SA A1-2-516 (1957), 19.

45. *Fan xian zhi*, (Henan renmin chubanshe, 1993), 514. Guomindang veterans on Taiwan experienced similar problems. ROC statistics indicate that 21.2 percent of veterans were bachelors. See Yang Ruizong, "Taiwan diqu yu dalu diqu tuiwu junren anzhi zhidu bijiao yanjiu," (Ph.D. diss., National Taiwan University, East Asian Studies, 1998), 85; Yu-Wen Fan, "Becoming a Civilian," 110–16, 125–27, 136–38.

46. *Wuqiang xian zhi*, 416. Wuba County, located on the Hebei-Shandong border, also took in homeless veterans. See *Wuba xian zhi* (Beijing: Fangzhi chubanshe, 1998), 581.

47. According to the gazetteer of Huangling County in Shaanxi Province, in 1956 for every 100 women there were 118 men, and in 1960, 144 men. See *Huangling xian zhi* (Xian: Ditu chubanshe, 1995), 85. In Anhui, for every 100 women (in 1953), there were 110 men. See *Anhui sheng zhi: renkou zhi* (Hefei: Anhui renmin chubanshe, 1995), 163.

48. SPA A20-1-41, 69.

49. SA A20-1-81 (1953), 18.

50. *Donzhi xian zhi* (Hefei: Anhui renmin chubanshe, 1991), 538.

51. *Ningyang xian zhi* (Beijing: Zhongguo shuji chubanshe, 1994), 258.

52. SA A101-1-607, 7; SA A20-1-109 (1954), 47.

53. SMA B168-1-596 (1949), 63.

54. Luo Pingfei, *Anzhi guanli*, 63; *Ningyang xian zhi*, 258; *Jieshou xian zhi* (Hefei: Huangshan, 1995), 352; *Pingding xian zhi* (Beijing: Shehui kexue chubanshe, 1992), 394; *Minzheng jianbao*, August 15, 1956, 56; Diamant, "Making Love 'Legible' in China," 73.

55. This was reported by General Fu Qiutao in SMA B1-2-1958 (1957), 30.

56. For this list, see the 1963 report in SMA B168-1-209, 24.

57. SMA B168-1-517, 139.

58. *Jundui ganbu*, 159.

59. SA A20-1-81, 62.

60. SMA B168-1-628 (1957), 72–73; *Minzheng jianbao*, August 15, 1956, 56.

61. SMA B168-1-619, 30.

62. SMA B168-1-633, 78.

63. SMA B168-1-209, 21.

64. SA A20-1-109 (1954), 48.

65. SA A20-1-133 (1955); for 1957, see SA A1-2-422.

66. SA A1-2-516, 17.

67. SA A20-1-295, 103.

68. QA 48-2-98, 112.

69. DDA 11-7-306 (1959), 3.

70. SA A20-1-332 (1963), 81–82. A 1960 report on letters and visits in Shandong noted that 90 percent of letters from Civil Affairs' revolutionary clientele came

from Level 3 disabled veterans, who also accounted for 83.57 percent of visits to the provincial capital (they often came with their families). See SA A20-1-295, 91. In the United States, administrative decisions regarding disability were also "highly susceptible to changes in the political context," but citizens had far better access to several levels of appeals if benefits that flowed from disability were cancelled. See Derthick, *Agency under Stress*, 44.

71. SA A20-1-332, 1.
72. SA A20-1-332 (1963), 83–84.
73. SMA B1-2-1958, 31.
74. SMA B168-1-209, 24.
75. See Stuart Schram, *The Political Thought of Mao Tse-tung*, 152–60.
76. SMA B168-1-209, 21.
77. Ibid., 21.
78. QA 48-2-96, 58.
79. QA 48-2-30 (1951), 122.
80. Ibid., 125.
81. "Geming canfei junren canfei dengji jianping gongzuo," QA, in author's collection.
82. SMA B168-1-632 (1956), 83.
83. SMA B1-2-1959, 32–33.
84. Robert Jefferson, "Enabled Courage," 1105, 1115.
85. SMA B168-1-671 (1965), 24, 18.
86. Tom Tyler, *Why People Obey the Law*, 82.
87. SA A20-1-411 (1965), 62, 79–80.
88. Ibid., 79–80.
89. QA 48-2-96 (1956), 51.
90. SMA B168-1-582 (1964), 201. Some complained, "The government sees people dying but doesn't come to their rescue"; "The Health Department doesn't do anything about leprosy; Civil Affairs only cares about expenditures, nothing else. Where are we supposed to go [for care]?"
91. QA 48-2-141 (1957), 14.
92. SMA B127-1-358 (1963), 39.
93. *Jundui ganbu*, 162.
94. QA 48-2-30, 124. On one occasion, local officials called for all Level 3 disabled veterans to gather at the county for a reassessment of the disability level. However, when they finally arrived—no doubt a difficult journey for many—they found that no one had prepared a place to stay or even food for them. After some time, the county chief found out about this and made the necessary arrangements, but the disabled were not mollified.
95. SMA B127-1-811 (1954), 6.
96. QA 48-2-141 (1957), 14.
97. QA 48-2-105, 136, 140.
98. *Minzheng jianbao*, August 15, 1956, 56; for Qingpu, see QA 48-2-96, 8.
99. SMA A54-2-49 (1957), 34.
100. SMA B168-1-565 (1962), 11–12.

101. QA 48-2-30 (1951), unpaginated.

102. QA 48-2-105 (1957), 134–35, 139.

103. "Guanyu huifu Liu Junmin tongzhi canfei fuxu wenti de baogao," SA A20-1-432, 2.

104. "Dui Liu Junmin tongzhi shangcan wenti de diaocha baogao," 4.

105. "Dui Liu Junmin tongzhi," SA A20-1-432, 7.

106. "Yishui xian minzhengju, "Guanyu dui Liu Junmin canfei wenti," SA A20-1-432, 24.

107. Ibid., 28.

108. *Jundui ganbu*, 325.

109. John Resch, *Suffering Soldiers*, 62.

110. Cited in David Gerber, "Heroes and Misfits," 548.

111. See Robert Havighurst et al., *The American Veteran Back Home: A Study of Veteran Readjustment*, 72, 78, 90.

112. Gerber, "Heroes and Misfits," 550.

113. Deborah Cohen, *The War Come Home*, 145.

114. This proposal came to naught. See Seth Koven, "Remembering and Dismemberment," 1189.

115. For Australian veterans who were cuckolded by their wives while they were away at war, see Stephen Garton, *The Cost of War: Australians Return*, 235. For fragility of American wartime marriages, see Susan Hartmann, *The Home Front and Beyond: American Women in the 1940s*. For Germany during WWI, see Benjamin Ziemann, *War Experiences in Rural Germany*, 121, 164.

116. For post-war West Germany, see Elisabeth Heineman, "The Hour of the Woman," 374, 380.

117. Karen Gottschang Turner (with Phan Thanh Hao), *Even the Women Must Fight: Memories of War from North Vietnam*, 152. This theme can also be found in novels. In Bao Ninh's *The Sorrow of War*, the protagonist returns from war a broken man and loses his girlfriend.

118. Dower, *Embracing Defeat*, 60.

119. Morton and Wright, *Winning the Second Battle,* 118.

120. Deborah Sontag, "Injured in Iraq, a Soldier Is Shattered at Home," *New York Times*, April 5, 2007. Monica Davey, "For Soldiers Back from Iraq, Basic Training in Resuming Life," *New York Times*, May 31, 2004.

121. SMA B168-1-607, 73.

122. SMA B168-1-628, 22.

123. Ibid., 72.

124. SMA B168-1-619, 70. German chaplains leveled similar complaints against rural veterans after WWI: "Many married men have also gone wild." See Ziemann, *War Experiences in Rural Germany*, 219.

125. Fan, "Becoming a Civilian," 119–20. Officials complained that veterans "courted women recklessly," which, of course, included falling for women working in "teahouses" (*chashi*), a popular type of brothel in the 1950s, 1960s, and 1970s.

126. SMA B168-1-628, 90.

127. *Minzheng jianbao*, December 21, 1956, 87.

128. *Jundui ganbu,* 160.

129. *Zhu-Mao*, 45.

130. SMA B1-2-1958, 31.

131. QA 48-2-98 (1956), 68.

132. QA 48-2-96, 60–61.

133. SA A1-2-516 (1957), 19.

134. See *After the Glory: The Struggles of Black Civil War Veterans*, 97.

135. SMA B1-2-1958, 28.

136. SMA B168-1-645, 41.

137. SA A20-1-109 (1955) 48.

138. Exposure to combat significantly increases the risk of PTSD as well as chronic diseases and early death. See Lee, Vaillant, Torrey, and Elder, "A 50-Year Prospective Study of the Psychological Sequelae of World War II Combat," 516–22.

139. Gerber, "Heroes and Misfits," 549.

140. Jack Epstein and Johnny Miller, "U.S. Wars and Post-Traumatic Stress Disorder," *San Francisco Chronicle*, June 22, 2005.

141. Ethel Dunn, "Disabled Russian War Veterans," 253.

142. Dower, *Embracing Defeat*, 61.

143. See Paulo Granjo, "The Homecomer: Postwar Cleansing Rituals in Mozambique," 387. As noted by Jonathan Shay, cleansing and purification rituals for veterans have a long history, such as in the Book of Numbers in the Old Testament (31:19ff) and in the medieval Christian Church. See *Odysseus in America,* 152.

144. SMA B168-1-226 (1965), 21.

145. SMA B168-1-630, 22.

146. SMA B168-1-628, 72.

147. SA A20-1-41, 69.

148. SA A20-1-109, 48.

149. Andrew Walder, *Communist Neotraditionalism.*

150. Stuart McConnell, "Who Joined the Grand Army?", 139.

151. SMA B168-1-628, 40.

152. *Minzheng jianbao*, October 11, 1956, 67; QA 48-2-27 (1956), 48.

153. SMA B168-1-596, 55.

154. SMA B168-1-633 (1957), 101.

155. SMA B168-1-628, 74.

156. SMA B168-1-645 (1959), 30.

157. SMA B127-1-358 (1963), 37.

158. QA 48-1-40, 18.

159. SA A20-1-29 (1951), 58.

160. QA 48-2-98 (1956), 68.

161. "1963 nian yilai jieshou anzhi fuyuan," SMA B168-1-666 (1964), 4, 9. There were also more serious cases. Jin Maogen, a veteran of the Korean War in Songjiang County, was falsely accused of theft. He was beaten with the butt of a gun, tied up and hung upside down on an electric pole, and spent three months in jail. He filed multiple charges against the officials responsible, which, after an extensive

investigation, were proven to be "basically true." However, only one person was expelled from the party; the others received warnings or made public confessions. See SMA B123-5-1314 (1963), 24–25.

162. SMA B127-1-869, 10.

163. SMA B168-1-628 (1956), 45–46; SMA B168-1-517, 139.

164. SMA B168-1-628 (1956), 120.

165. Ibid., 74, 102; *Minzheng jianbao*, November 19, 1956, 81; SMA B168-1-517 (1951), 139.

166. SMA B168-1-666, 4, 9.

167. Zhou Ziqiang (ed.), *Gongfei junshi wenti lunji*, Bureau of Investigation–Ministry of Justice Archives (Xindian. Taiwan), #590.8/3882, 209.

168. "Falkland Veterans Claim Suicide Toll," *BBC News*, January 13, 2002.

169. *Jundui ganbu*, 160.

170. SMA B168-1-607 (1952), 58–59, 73.

171. SMA B168-1-628 (1956), 22.

172. Ibid., 121; SMA B168-1-628 (1956), 46.

173. On Namibia, see Rosemary Preston, "Integrating Fighters after War," 468; according to Deborah Cohen in *The War Come Home*, the slightly disabled benefited the most in post-war WWI Britain; by the mid-1920s, the severely disabled were "forgotten men" (pp. 109, 147).

174. *Zhonghua minguo 90 nian Tai-Min diqu rongmin jiuye*, 2, 5–6.

175. These include the War of Independence (1948), the Sinai Campaign (1956), the Six Day War (1967), the War of Attrition (1969–1971), the Yom Kippur War (1973), and the first Lebanon War (1982–1985). Every war added to the number of disabled veterans. For instance, 2,300 were added immediately after the Six Day War and the War of Attrition (mostly amputees of arms and legs). See Ze'ev Schiff, "2,300 nechim me'az sheshet hayamim," *Ma'ariv*, January 27, 1971. According to one report from 1989, 2,000 disabled veterans are added to the state's roster per year as a result of ongoing conflicts. See Shmuel Tal, "2,000 nechei Zahal nosafim midai shana," *Hadashot*, May 16, 1989.

176. Exemptions were generally limited to the ultra-orthodox. Arab men have not been eligible for the conscription owing to questions about their loyalty to the state, which from the beginning was defined as Jewish.

177. On these aspects of Israeli "militarism," see Uri Ben-Eliezer, *The Making of Israel Militarism*. Even today, the military is viewed very positively. In a 2001 survey of accountability and trust in different state institutions, the highest-ranked institutions were the Secret Services (73 percent approval), Israel Defense Forces (71 percent), universities (68 percent), and the judiciary (65 percent). Political parties came in dead last (38 percent). See Eran Vigoda and Fani Yovel, *Bitsua Hamigzar hatziburi biYisrael*, 31.

178. Yoram Bilu and Eliezer Witztum, "War-Related Loss and Suffering in Israeli Society," 10.

179. Shlomo Kravetz, Shlomo Katz, and David Albez, "Attitudes toward Israeli War Veterans with Disabilities," 377.

180. John Gal and Michael Bar, "The Needed and the Needy," 580–86.

181. Gal and Bar, "The Needed," 589.

182. Ze'ev Schiff, "Nechei Zahal zo'emim," *Ma'ariv*, April 12, 1960.

183. S. Ben-Haim, "Nechei milchama ma'ayemim," *Ma'ariv*, November 14, 1960.

184. Eli Landau, "Nechei milchemet hashichrur," *Ma'ariv*, April 19, 1965.

185. Eli Landau, "Nechei hamilchama mamshichim lihilachem," *Ma'ariv*, January 17, 1966.

186. This does not suggest that *all* disabled veterans were dissatisfied. An unpublished study commissioned by the Ministry of Defense in 1971 found that "only" 40 percent of the disabled were dissatisfied to some extent with the compensation they received from the state, and 75 percent were generally satisfied with officials (private and public agency employers were not mentioned). Ze'ev Ben-Sira, "Pe'ulat hashikum shel ma'arechet ha'bitachon" (Jerusalem: Institute of Applied Social Research, 1971), IDF Archives 2384/1996-51, 204. The number of dissatisfied surely increased after the Yom Kippur War in 1973, which vastly increased the number of disabled veterans.

187. Eli Landau, "Nechei Zahal lo gamru lihilachem," *Ma'ariv*, January 9, 1968.

188. "Bi'motzash—dorshim avoda," *Ma'ariv*, July 23, 1968.

189. Tzvi Lavie, "Nechai Zahal 'kavshu' et misrad ha'doar," *Ma'ariv*, March 6, 1969.

190 . Disabled veterans complained that Rehabilitation officials (like their Civil Affairs counterparts) helped them with jobs and then "forgot about them," did not give enough individual attention, acted as if they were "giving money from their pockets," did not care enough ("some officials have been there for far too long"), were not flexible enough, pushed them from office to office, and took too long to return letters. See Ben-Sira, "Pe'ulat hashikum," 204–7.

191. See "Histararut hanechim hitzleecha," *Ma'ariv*, April 6, 1969.

192. "Hatipul binechei Zahal adayin lakui," *Ma'ariv*, July 2, 1968.

193. Ben-Sira, "Pe'ulat hashikum," 101, 204. The disabled were aware of their right to assistance with employment, exemption from television and radio tax, and right to coupons for the IDF supermarket. More important rights (medical, education, housing) were much less known.

194. Dayan v. State of Israel, Tel Aviv, 901/91 (Israel Bar Association records).

195. State of Israel v. Avraham Caspi, 455/85.

196. Interview with the late Judge Sirota (conducted at her home in Mishmar Ha-Sheva, Israel, in Hebrew), April 21, 2007. One finds similar sympathy in higher-level appeals in the United States. See Derthick, *Agency under Stress*, 40–41.

197. "Nechei Zahal: Nachsome hayom misradai agaf hashikum," *Ma'ariv*, August 26, 1984.

198. "Nechei Zahal: Rabin, ata notesh et lochamaicha," *Ma'ariv*, December 31, 1985.

199. See *Ma'ariv*, December 17, 1986.

200. "Protzot nisrafot, mafginim k'tuai raglaim," *Ma'ariv*, March 26, 1987.

201. *Ma'ariv*, July 7, 1969; Yishayahu Avi'am, "Yesh Ezrachim she echpat lehem," *Ma'ariv*, January 14, 1968.

202. Ephrat Arad, "Tipul nashi binechei Zahal," *Ma'ariv*, March 2, 1971.

203. "Beit Mishpat Ha'elion kore litaken et chok hanechim," *Ma'ariv*, September 29, 1977.

204. "Taram reva million lirot," *Ma'ariv*, November 21, 1968; "Press Release," U.S. Information Service, American Embassy, July 4, 1974. *Ma'ariv* Archives, Tel Aviv; "Merkaz hadash lishikum," *Yediot Achronot*, May 21, 1984.

205. Amiram Cohen, "Nichnas 97, yatza 21," *Al-Hamishmar*, May 19, 1989; Alex Fishman, "G. shav misadeh hakrav," *Al-Hamishmar*, November 26, 1985; Yosef Micha'eli, "Nechim hazkukim litna'ai diur," *Ma'ariv*, July 17, 1974.

206. Jefferson, "Enabled Courage," 1102–3.

7

Between Glory and Welfare:
Military Families, the State, and Community

THE FLESH OF THE REVOLUTION (ARIES)

In and around Shanghai, the city well known for its leftist radicalism in the years prior to the Cultural Revolution, a flurry of confidential investigation reports threatened to tar its well-deserved revolutionary reputation. Officials reading these reports in the mid-1960s (when the PLA and its soldiers were being touted as the institutional and personal models for revolutionary virtue) were probably shaking their heads at the more literal, risqué twist on the so-called "flesh-and-blood" relationship (*xuerou guanxi*) that was said to exist between those who served in the military and the party-state: cadres and others were having sexual affairs with the fiancées and wives of PLA soldiers. In a report furnished by the Bureau of Civil Affairs to the Shanghai Party Committee, this phenomenon—known as "ruining a soldier marriage"—was deemed "quite serious" (*xiangdang yanzhong*), affecting soldiers in urban and rural areas.[1] In 1963 alone, the report found, some 253 cases had been "discovered" in the greater Shanghai area, including 193 in the suburbs and 60 in the city proper. Most of the perpetrators held positions of authority; in the suburbs, 57.4 percent of them were cadres at the township (or "commune"), village ("production brigade"), or sub-village ("production team") levels; Communist Party and Communist Youth League members figured prominently (39 percent) in the overall statistics, although blame was also appropriately apportioned to "bad elements, hooligans, and hoodlums" (*afei*).[2]

Ruining soldiers' marriages was not simply the result of a few bad characters with inappropriate sexual appetites, however; there were larger, or what social scientists like to call "structural," causes at work as well. According to the report, military families' poverty, which should have been alleviated by

government programs and community-based assistance, combined with officials' access to resources, created the opportunity for sexual mischief. Local
officials "got close" to PLA wives by expressing "concern about them," and
this quickly developed into an exchange of food and fun (like local opera)
for sex. That the women already were married to soldiers defending national
sovereignty made little difference. In the Jiangnan shipyards in Shanghai, a
CCP member surnamed Ye was having sex with a Mrs. Yang, whose husband
was in the army. To encourage Yang to divorce her husband, he invoked
the high probability of defeat if China were to be attacked: "Do you want to
become a counterrevolutionary when Chiang Kai-shek attacks the mainland
and returns here? You'll be a widow if you're married to a soldier." Divorces
and pregnancies were not unusual—54 babies were born from these Shanghai relationships, with another 30 expected in 1965—and 32 soldiers were
divorced, in addition to 32 who had their engagements broken because of
adulterous sex.[3]

Peasants were aware of this problem; secrets are hard to keep in villages.
The praise heaped on the PLA by state propagandists for defending China
against external enemies could not counter the real, literally tangible, domestic threats faced by PLA soldiers. Some youth were warned, "If you're
married, you'd better not join the army." Soldiers who got wind of these
problems requested leave to "visit relatives" but were mainly interested in
making sure that village officials had not already gotten to their fiancées and
wives. Unsurprisingly, municipal officials were concerned because recruiting
and morale were adversely affected, but their capacity to prevent such alliances was limited. When confronted, local officials claimed that they were
not responsible ("If the soldiers don't lodge a complaint, there's nothing we
can do about it"), blamed the soldiers' wives, or argued that sex between PLA
wives and villagers was "just an ordinary sex problem" (*yiban nannü guanxi
wenti*) which did not merit further attention. The evidence is mixed on the issue of whether this lax attitude spread to upper echelons of the party. Courts
and party organizations rendered 146 verdicts on these cases, with close to
half (43 percent) of the perpetrators ordered to undergo "criticism and education," while the rest were punished more seriously (28 percent received
criminal sentences, ranging from one to five years and up). Such cases might
represent a fraction of what actually occurred in villages. Because leveling
an accusation against a party official was (and remains) no small matter, and
sex-related offenses could be particularly embarrassing or shameful, "lump-
ing it" was probably common.[4]

But however many officials' heads were shaking, fingers wagging, and
pens scrawling, there is little evidence that the situation improved much
between 1964 and 1966, the peak years of pre–Cultural Revolution milita-

rization. A nationally circulated "Situation Report" authored by the Political Bureau of the Guangzhou Military Region in March 1966[5] noted that 16 cases of adultery had occurred "only recently"; six were classified as involving "seduction/rape," while eight were said to have been consensual: the soldiers' wives had "low political consciousness and were attracted to material possessions."[6] This phenomenon was not limited to South China: Shandong, Shanxi, and other northern provinces (all of which had a stronger military heritage than those of the South) reported similar problems. In Shandong, for example, a soldier's wife surnamed Wen was raped by the village accountant, a Mr. Wang. Wen reported Wang to the county Public Security Bureau, but because "they did not handle the case expeditiously," the still-horny accountant "snuck into her bed again." Fighting Wang off, Wen grabbed his leg and held on tightly as he dragged himself from the cooking area toward the door, but he escaped by bashing her finger. Word of this incident leaked out. From his military base, Wen's husband dashed off a letter to provincial-level public security officials, who dispatched an investigation team. Upon arriving in the village, however, they found that Wang already had been tipped off and escaped. But his disappearing act did not last long. Soon enough, he was back in the village, where he once again confronted Wen, saying, "I'm back. Let's see what you can do about it!"[7]

Guangdong's report seems to have had some impact, at least at the level of pushing paper around. In the Cultural Revolution's first summer of 1966, the Supreme Court and Ministry of the Interior issued a directive to their subordinate units to look into the problem of "ruining soldiers' marriages" more seriously, since many soldiers were "unsatisfied" with the situation. In response to this directive, the Shanghai High Court and Bureau of Civil Affairs convened a joint meeting, which was also attended by officers from the Shanghai Garrison.[8]

Despite the urgent tone in the correspondence leading to this meeting, garrison officials were already well aware of this problem—they had sponsored a large-scale investigation of 28 work units in Nanhui County only two years earlier and reported on the situation in 1965. That earlier investigation found that of those 28 units, 23 (82 percent) had soldiers whose wives or fiancées were involved with other men, with 61 cases in total. Garrison officers fingered civilian party officials as the primary perpetrators (a bit more than 50 percent of cases) but also blamed courts for not taking the issue seriously; the verdicts were "too lenient" (*pian kuan*), they complained, and "many objections" were raised to them. One example they provided involved yet another lustful township accountant, a Mr. Su, who was having affairs with two PLA wives (separately or in a ménage à trois is not clear). Local officials were aware of Su's indiscretions but decided to look the other way. The case came to light only when one of the soldiers' wives "drowned her baby in the toilet of a bathroom at the commune seat when a meeting was going on."[9]

The other agencies in attendance also arrived well prepared to the meeting. The Shanghai High Court supplied a detailed investigation of 71 cases undertaken by the Songjiang County Court between 1964 and 1965. In Songjiang County, cadres' trousers often were off for the wrong reasons; they constituted 77 percent of all perpetrators.[10] In one township, there were 11 cases every year; every single defendant was an official, including the party secretary and his deputy. Given their own involvement, these cadres were in no position to reprimand officials lower down the hierarchy for the same offense. The impact on soldiers was unmistakable. Some heard about their wives and immediately went AWOL; some "immediately fainted on their bed and did not get up for several days." Soldiers circulated in the village to encourage the fathers of draft-age boys to question recruiting cadres "whether you've got your eyes on my daughter-in-law again" (*nimen shi bu shi you kanzhong le wo de xifer*).[11] In that politically hot summer of 1966, the contrast in images could not have been starker: while Mao was pinning a badge on Song Binbin's (a female Red Guard) fatigues in Tiananmen Square and youthful Red Guards were parading around as Chairman Mao's "little soldiers," *real* soldiers were going AWOL, their families were up in arms about cadre abuses, PLA wives were being raped and aborting babies, and the Shanghai Supreme Court complained of a "very dim (*danbo*) conception of national defense and supporting military families."[12]

Was this phenomenon new, or was it a temporary reflection of the relaxation of political controls after the chaos of the Great Leap Forward? Although the temporal and spatial distribution of "ruining soldiers' marriages" is difficult to assess quantitatively, archival reports unequivocally demonstrate that it occurred in many areas of the country and well prior to the mid-1960s. In 1959, an investigation of six counties in the Shanghai area also noted that violations of soldiers' marriages "happened frequently" (*pinduo fasheng*) and were a "big problem." In Chuansha County, a soldier's wife had an affair with a village cadre that resulted in the birth of a baby, who was already three months old at the time of the investigation. The village official was sentenced to a year, which the soldier considered far too short a period. "Old veterans" in the county came to his assistance—several of them went to Civil Affairs to lodge a petition for a harsher sentence —but the prevailing view was to consider these problems under the rubric of "ordinary marriage conflicts."[13] In 1955 in Qingpu's Baihe District, there were at least four cases of local cadres violating soldiers' marriages, all of which were "not handled seriously,"[14] and a report from Lufeng County in Yunnan Province that year found that wives of PLA soldiers, fearing for their safety, "don't dare go out at night or go to meetings."[15] An investigation of 16 townships in 12 counties in Henan Province turned up four cases of PLA wives' "secretly remarrying," 8 cases of rape, 32 instances of adultery, and 3 cases of instigating a divorce. One PLA wife was subjected to a serial rape involving four men, but their leader was only reprimanded for four days at the district government. Emboldened by kid-glove treatment, when he returned to his village, he raped two more PLA wives in quick succession. The husbands filed charges, but "until today they have not been handled."[16] In a single administrative region (*zhuanqu*) in Jiangxi Province in the mid-1950s, there were more than 1,100 cases, including 330 that resulted in pregnancies. Township and village authorities were also mentioned as the primary suspects (with 149 of them involved in these cases).[17] In Hubei, a soldier filed charges against a village cadre at the district government for having an affair with his wife but was told, "This is a problem left over from the old society. We don't have the authority to deal with it." Finding this explanation unacceptable, the soldier phoned the county court, but they, too, saw no grounds for legal action: "Your wife is having an affair because you've been away for so long. All we can do is tell the district government to educate him. We can't prosecute a peasant because of something like this."[18] Lacking legal recourse, soldiers tried other ways to get justice. Some wrote letters home ridiculing their spouses (which sometimes prompted the latter to seek divorce) or to the National People's Congress; others traveled to Beijing seeking audiences with CCP leaders, a pattern we have seen in other chapters.[19]

Cases such as these demand further exploration because they are puzzling; they were not supposed to happen. To the extent that the state succeeded in cultivating respect for the military, soldiers' family members should have been well treated (or at least not be egregiously *mis*treated), particularly in the years prior to the Cultural Revolution (1964–1966). These years, after all, witnessed repeated campaigns about the revolutionary virtues of the PLA and military service, the importance of good class status, and international crises (with the USSR and the United States), which elevated the political salience of the military. Rural politicians and villagers were "supposed to provide [military dependents] with special consideration and benefits" (not in exchange for sex).[20] The Center, to its credit, allocated funds to military families, set up a bureaucracy to assist them, and invested in them symbolic resources such as honorary certificates and state holidays. So how did it happen that some military wives who were on the receiving end of state welfare distributions remained so poor that they prostituted themselves for food? Why did local officials think that military wives were fair game when their husbands were serving in the army? Why were many military dependents vulnerable to "seduction" by local officials, many of whom apparently felt little apprehension about villagers' reaction to their sexual predations?

Aside from the puzzling nature of this sexual dimension of "civil–military relations," examining the interactions between military families, state officials, and ordinary people is also important in terms of the themes and argument of this study. Chronologically, this chapter gives us a "preview" of what happened in some soldiers' families before they became "veterans." If we can see what sorts of problems their families faced while they were away, we can trace yet another source of their post-discharge anger, vulnerabilities, and depression and at least try to imagine the family conversations that must have taken place after their return. Methodologically, when we temporarily shift the spotlight away from veterans to families of soldiers whose service was still in progress, we might add to, or subtract from, the causal weight of some of the explanations offered thus far. For example, if one reason many veterans were not treated well was because they were a political threat to officials who rose to their positions from non-PLA backgrounds, military dependents (or *junshu*) were significantly *less* threatening, either because they were women or too old to compete for power. If many veterans were mistreated because they demanded too many prized resources from the economy (respectable jobs, positions in government), *junshu* demands were generally less difficult to accommodate—a 50-year-old woman was never considered a viable substitute for a 23-year-old male worker, who might have something to fear from a 26-year-old veteran. If many veterans were mistreated because their post-service status was complicated by social and political problems, we can gain a more "pristine" view of how civilians felt about the military by looking at military families whose sons were still serving and had yet to undergo post-discharge dislocation. If veterans were not respected because the patriotic status of their pre-1949 military service (and therefore the legitimacy of the honors afforded to them) was contested, in the case of military families, we are looking at people whose sons were serving during periods of international crisis, not in wars fought years ago when China was still divided. By looking at military families, we can also "turn up" the sympathy factor: if veterans failed to gain social support in part because they were young, single males (factors that are considered threatening to stability in many societies), the *junshu* population had many women (mothers and wives) who were vulnerable owing to age, health problems, financial difficulties, or living in a village without their husbands. In this chapter, then, I am plucking out some of the more problematic aspects of civil–military relations and enhancing the potential for better treatment and positive interactions with state officials and ordinary people on grounds of sympathy. This, in effect, significantly lowers the bar for gauging the extent to which military service was valued, respected, and appreciated and whether patriotism played a meaningful role in shaping behavior. With veterans, I set the bar moderately high, since reasonably good treatment required real sacrifice and a willingness to overlook or tolerate some problematic aspects of their experiences. If state officials and ordinary citizens demonstrated little pity, sympathy, or respect even for poor families with members serving in the PLA, my arguments about the low status of the military and the brittle nature of the state's legitimacy will be significantly strengthened.

The archival evidence presented in this chapter largely supports these claims. In urban and rural areas, and in clear contradiction to the "cult of the red martyr" that was elaborately developed in the 1950s and 1960s,[21] there is little evidence of appreciation for PLA victories on the battlefield; its successes were not a wellspring of legitimacy the CCP could draw upon to convince citizens and low-level officials to respect military families or those of revolutionary martyrs (*lieshu*). On the other hand, there is evidence that pity (more than sympathy) for these families could, in some circumstances, legitimize the provisions of different forms of economic assistance, especially in rural areas. Economic assistance based upon pity, however, could not substitute for respect and honor in terms of providing *junshu* or *lieshu* with a sense that their sacrifices were appreciated by the state and their communities, and it could not generate the sort of seriousness and determination to get things right on the part of the officials placed in direct charge of aid distribution. Many policies for providing economic assistance to *junshu* and *lieshu* were implemented poorly or only partially, were too stingy, or did not work well. In many instances, they backfired by increasing the amount of "friction" between military families and the state and members of society (many of whom remained as divided about their political and individual worthiness as they were about veterans' contributions) and by creating dangerous dependencies on those in charge of aid programs. Economic assistance programs and state propaganda efforts also generated a high sense of status among some *junshu* and *lieshu*, but this was not reciprocated by those around them, so resentment and jealously ran high. The combination of pity-based aid, economic vulnerability, and the very limited appreciation for the role of the military in society and national affairs constituted the framework within which soldiers' marriages were violated as well as for the hundreds of letters sent by military families to their sons in the army asking them to come home immediately or get an early discharge. Suicide also occurred in worrisome numbers, as noted in the previous chapter.

This chapter consists of four sections. In the first, I eavesdrop on the interactions between *junshu* (as well as family members of revolutionary martyrs[22]) and Civil Affairs clerks, local administrative cadres, and hospital staff and employers, all of whom were the gatekeepers for the essential services they required and benefits to which they were entitled. I then examine the economic assistance programs that were designed to boost their status and make sure that they would not become impoverished because their sons were in the army (or because their husbands had died during the revolution). After this, I turn to the content of the interactions between military dependents and martyr families and ordinary citizens. The chapter will conclude by looking at some of the ways military families responded to the way they were treated by officials and citizens.

JUNSHU CONFRONT THE STATE

Just who, precisely, was a "military family"? Given the complicated history of the PLA and multiple and shifting alliances between the CCP and GMD, deciphering the importance and meaning of the first part of the term, *jun* (military), was no simple matter. Yet another layer of complexity was unavoidable in the second part of the term — *shu* ("family member" or "dependent"). Just who counted as a dependent or family member? A soldier's parents and spouse would seem obvious enough, but what about more distant relatives such as aunts and uncles (who may have raised the soldier), or stepfathers and stepmothers, let alone more ambiguous relations such as ex-wives or fiancées? In a society emerging from years of chaotic domestic and foreign wars that sometimes took place simultaneously, and in a state that had never developed a reliable national system for keeping track of births, deaths, divorces, marriages, or remarriages (especially in the countryside), defining the boundaries of the *jun* and *shu* categories was complex, even under the best of circumstances.[23] In 1950, for example, a report pointed to the "complicated environment" for the provision of assistance to military and martyr families. In the case of martyr families, many soldiers' corpses had been haphazardly buried in fields (and then swept away by storms and typhoons) and their names, ranks, and native places were unknown. Among, *junshu*, some fearing the return of the Nationalists, were afraid of jotting their names down because "their status will get them into trouble."[24] As if these factors weren't complicating enough, when the state spread the word that material and symbolic benefits could be gained through the acquisition of *junshu* (and *lieshu*) status but did not assign skilled personnel to make these decisions about entitlements (as we have seen in Chapter 5, Civil Affairs was a backwater bureaucracy), the situation was ripe for problems.

Most of the early accounts of this sorting-through process emphasize confusion, administrative bungling, and no small amount of entrepreneurship as state officials tried, often without much success, to place people with convoluted, hard-to-trace histories into their appropriate social and political boxes. In an investigation of "Preferential Treatment" work in Shanghai's working-class Penglai District (circa 1953), researchers were immediately struck by the complicated class and social backgrounds of military and martyr families, even those who were selected as leaders of nascent "Martyr and Military Family" committees. A survey of 28 of these local (but unsalaried) activists found that their ranks included two capitalists, seven small-time merchants, three medium-scale businessmen, a landlord, a GMD official, and "four people who have been arrested and served sentences"; 64 percent of the *junshu* leaders had been affiliated in some way with the Nationalist Party, while "very few were working people." (These impure committees were disbanded in late 1954.) But after registering their occupations, Civil Affairs clerks still had a hard time getting to the bottom of *junshu*'s and *lieshu*'s circumstances. In Shanghai, clerks came under criticism for registering peasant women from Jiangsu Province as *Shanghai junshu* because they had sons temporarily based in the city and despite the fact that "their land and home are in the countryside." Some distant relatives were also allowed to register as *junshu*, as were those who merely pretended (*maochong*) to have a family connection to a soldier. "Not a few" uncles successfully pretended to be fathers, aunts pretended to be wives, nieces and nephews pretended to be sons and daughters, and stepfathers and stepmothers pretended to be biological fathers and mothers who falsely claimed to have had a role in raising the soldiers. In another case, a stepfather and the soldier's aunt pretended to be a married couple.[25]

According to some accounts, having a smooth tongue served as a respectable replacement for accurate documentation: *junshu* who managed to present their circumstances to the district government with poise managed to get their problems solved, "while those who don't go running off to the district, or cannot speak well, encounter many delays or do not get their problems solved at all." The investigation found that "upper-class elements" (*shang ceng fenzi*) and those with "complicated political histories and impure class status" did better than the ostensibly favored working classes for this reason.[26] In the #12 Street Office (*banshiqu*), the three households that received the most benefits from the state "had various positions in the GMD." Jealous of these benefits, poorer residents complained that jobs and free tuition were given to the *junshu* because they "yelled about their problems: If it hadn't been for the army, those families would starve," they noted. In contrast, a Mr. Sun, a *junshu* from far more modest circumstances and with three children at home, could not make ends meet even though he was assigned a job (but the salary was too low). The main reason cited in Sun's case was his inability to speak well and reluctance to pay multiple visits to the district demanding assistance.

In other instances, officials cited concern with face: "Some are poor, but fear losing face, so they don't ask for help."[27] Neighbors said, "If you're honest, you're screwed; those who are tricky and raise hell can easily cheat and deceive."[28] Even though this sort of complaint reeks of CCP propaganda—the urban poor being taken advantage of by the Nationalist upper class—there was something to it. A report from the Dongcheng District Archive noted that many people from bad class background received assistance because Civil Affairs cadres' understanding of "class" (i.e., good class "workers," "bad class" capitalists) was muddled and they took pity (*lianmin*) on them because they were poor.[29] Reports from 1954 in Beijing found that even less well-off and "good-class" aid recipients were requesting aid but then using it to make usurious loans.[30]

In part, this reliance on persuasive rhetoric was unavoidable given the complex history of the Communist Revolution and its wars (Mao and Zhou Enlai, after all, had also worked closely with Nationalist officials in the 1920s) and the difficulty of establishing a neat, tidy, and reliable paper trail for everyone who claimed *junshu* or *lieshu* status. It was, however, facilitated by both the weak investigative capacities of the Civil Affairs bureaucracy and the reluctance of many officials to leave their offices to investigate residents who otherwise posed no immediate threat to anyone. A repeated refrain of reports throughout the 1950s was the lack of *diaocha yanjiu* (investigation and research) when it came to deciding who deserved what and how much. A 1950 report on work among *junshu* noted that newly hired Civil Affairs cadres gave money when asked, did not investigate, and registered whoever wanted to register because they "do not understand revolutionary policy" and "consider their job to be a big hassle."[31] (This, however, did not stop them from fraudulently issuing *junshu* papers to their own relatives.)[32] According to a 1953 letter from the Interior Ministry to the Shanghai Bureau of Civil Affairs (citing a report in the internally circulated CCP newsletter *Internal Reference*), there were roughly 30,000 military and martyr families living in Shanghai, but "not a few" barely had anything to eat, and some 8,000 were waiting for work; the "main cause" for this problem was that city- and district-level officials and Civil Affairs clerks "never once undertook any sort of thorough investigation of their conditions, and as a result they have no understanding of their needs."[33] One year later a Penglai District investigation confirmed this, noting that cadres in charge of distributing aid to *junshu* lacked both training and skill and tended to "sit in their office and rely on the *junshu* group leaders to handle problems,"[34] even though these groups did not function very well and had little clout in local politics.[35]

Comparable problems surfaced in Beijing. According to a 1955 report, city officials still did not have an accurate count of the number of *junshu* or *lieshu* in the city but were able to determine that there were roughly 1,000 "fake" or "ghost" military and martyr families. Some of these errors were caused by aid applicants providing false testimony and others by Civil Affairs clerks or district officials who did not look too deeply into individual circumstances and mistakenly provided aid to *junshu* whose soldier was no longer living in the area or had fled to Hong Kong. In the Beijing suburbs, some districts allocated funds to townships only on the basis of oral claims: "The more they ask for, the more they get; the less they ask for, the less they get; if they don't ask, they don't get." This lack of supervision provided ample incentives to misreport the number of *junshu* and *lieshu* and was said to have led to embezzlement, underutilized funds, and corruption.[36]

Given the millions of people who were related to PLA soldiers over the years and the number of agencies involved in distributing aid (Civil Affairs, local governments, and residence committees), it is very difficult to assess with any precision exactly how much money was awarded, who benefited the most, and how much remained in the bank in these early years. For instance, one 1953 investigation report found that Civil Affairs clerks would see a *junshu* with a stall and quickly conclude, without any further investigation, that he or she "had income" and would then reduce or cut that person's aid; in Zhabei District, "quite a few" (*xiangdang duo*) *junshu* remained at home with pain because they did not have enough money to see a doctor, even though they received some aid; a woman surnamed Lu, whose son had served in the PLA since 1944 and was a battalion commander in Korea, was found begging for food near a creek but received no assistance because it was assumed that, as the mother of an officer, she was doing well. "Randomly setting standards" according to the "subjective opinions of the clerks" was not an uncommon problem[37] (easily recognizable to scholars of "street-level" bureaucracy[38]). The one aspect of "preferential treatment work" that seemed to become less random over the years, however, was defining the scope of entitlement. By the mid-1950s, cases of "fake" *junshu* appear far less frequently in the sources.

From the perspective of *junshu* requesting a few yuan from Civil Affairs, however, the more problematic aspect of dealing with this slice of the state was not always in the amount of aid they received or whether former Nationalist officers received it (although few believed that there was "distributive justice" if state aid meant only that they would remain poor, just not hungry). More troublesome to *junshu* was the often-wide discrepancy between Civil Affairs clerks' attitudes and comments toward them and their high status in state propaganda. *Junshu*, like veterans, expected to be appreciated for their sacrifices, but for Civil Affairs officials, the more salient dimensions of their identity were poverty, gender, vulnerability, lack of education, and dependency (whereas for veterans it was usually their "prideful arrogance" coupled with their willingness to "blow the whistle" on corruption), *not* what their son was doing in North Korea or elsewhere in the PLA. In other words, *junshu* mostly were pitied, not respected, by Civil Affairs officials, who came to see their work more in terms of handing out charity rather than helping out the families of venerable PLA soldiers.[39] Several *junshu*—much like Civil War widows and military families in the United States[40]—noticed the inherent contradiction in their status and the fact that they needed charity in the first place, which was humiliating: "Some object to the word 'relief rice' (*jiuji mi*); they say there's a contradiction between the words 'relief' and 'glorious' (*guangrong*); it gives society a bad impression about us." A Mrs. Chuan from Hongkou District said, "My son's fighting for the country. How is it that I've become a relief recipient?" A Mrs. Tai in Changshu District remarked, "We get to wear a great big beautiful hat during New Year's, and that's that."[41] For many Civil Affairs clerks, however, there was no contradiction at all, since few drew a conceptual line between their everyday experiences doling out money, arranging jobs, and figuring out if an aid recipient deserved five or nine yuan, and the larger issue of military morale, national defense, or the prestige of the PLA in society at large. As noted in Chapter 5, Civil Affairs officials often were criticized for ignoring the political and humanitarian aspects of their work. In a 1953 report, investigators noted that the problem "is not that we lack resources, but that the work is not seen as politically important, especially during the last year (1952–1953)," the height of the Korean War.[42] A decade later, in a summary of Civil Affairs work between 1958 and 1961, officials were similarly criticized for handing out money without a sense of respect for the people to whom they were giving it.[43] This was not only a Shanghai problem; in Shandong, a 1953 provincial report noted that, even during the Korean War, very little "patriotic education" about the importance of military and martyr families was conducted, with the exception of holidays.[44]

Numerous accounts of the day-to-day interactions and conversations between *junshu*, *lieshu*, and Civil Affairs officials reveal this clash of incompatible conceptual understandings of identity, entitlement, sacrifice, and the role of the government and the military in society. Behind their backs, *junshu* and *lieshu* were called "nags" (*nancan*).[45] In Songshan District in Shanghai, a clerk told a *junshu* who requested a job, "You old ladies are only good for cleaning up bathrooms"; to another he said, "There's work if you want, but let's see if you can leave the house." Some officials banged on the table with their fists and yelled at them, which led some *junshu* to write to their sons on the front, "A 'glorious mother' (*guangrong mama*) can't even get enough relief rice to fill her stomach. Where's all the 'glory'?"[46] Some *junshu*, after making their way to the district government, filling out forms, and dealing with the officials, said, "Next time I'd rather die of hunger than go to the district again." Others, the report noted, were asked by officials, "Do we look like a barbershop?" (barbershops in Shanghai tended to employ people from poor areas of Jiangsu Province), or they were told, "Don't come again," "Your son volunteered for the army" [so why do you deserve aid], or "There must be something wrong with your politics if you want emergency relief"—just like "an ordinary person on welfare." These sorts of remarks led some *junshu* and *lieshu* to say, "A hungry person needs to eat, but if a person throws food on the ground and wants me to eat it from there, I'd rather die of starvation."[47] According to a Beijing report in 1963, many (*daliang*) *lieshu* and *junshu*, disgusted by this treatment at the local level, went to Beijing to try to solve their problems. When some of them "caused a ruckus," it was said to have had "a very bad political influence." To solve this problem, Beijing called upon local officials to avoid using "harsh" work methods, such as uttering two or three words and telling them "to leave."[48]

Even during the height of "patriotic sentiments" during the Korean War, military and martyr families found little comfort in their dealings with the state. Soldiers' children who tried to get into schools were rebuffed because the Education Bureau appealed to schools to open their doors to "children of workers and peasants" but forgot to mention "soldiers' kids." Comments regarding the "ferocity" of cadres were said be "widespread" (*pubian*).[49] Two years after the war, according to a 1955 report, "very many" (*hen duo*) *junshu* and *lieshu* explicitly compared their interactions with the state to "petitioning the *yamen* (government)" in traditional times: "You have to pass through three 'gates': first getting through the door, then sitting on the cold wood bench, and lastly being reprimanded by the official."[50] This assessment, largely because it was widespread, clearly worried state investigators, who realized that giving out money without respect and fair treatment was not going to cut the mustard: "The key in determining the success of preferential treatment work is the attitude of the cadres," investigators warned. "If these problems are not immediately rectified, they will cause serious political damage."[51] In 1956, however, the internal bulletin of the Shanghai Civil Affairs Bureau was still reporting that cadres were "rigid" and "cold" and that they "escaped from their offices before the storm came," i.e., when *junshu* and *lieshu* came for help. In a meeting with fellow *junshu*, Li Baiyun said, "I really don't want to go to the district government and see their cold faces again."[52]

Most surely contributing to this sense of injustice was the aid distribution process itself during the mid-1950s to 1960s. Whereas in the early years of the PRC many reports complained about emergency relief that was handed out without sufficient attention to the actual needs of families, later on in the decade the process became more decentralized (which weakened the role of district governments and Civil Affairs) and multilayered, affecting particularly those who were very poor and needed a steady monthly stipend (*dingqi dingliang*), a population that often included elderly mothers of martyrs whose husbands had died and whose other children could not help or military families with many children to feed. According to Civil Affairs guidelines, to get a monthly stipend, a completed application had to be submitted to the Residence Committee and the small group leader of the "Martyr and Military Families" organization for discussion and approval. If the stipend was approved, the Residence Committee would draft a letter to the "Lane and Alley Office" (*jiedao*) or, in rural areas, the township, which would then give its thumbs up or down. To make sure that no money was wasted, a review would take place every six months, during which time receipts would have to be produced. This review could lead to a reduction, an increase, or forfeiture of aid. For "emergency relief," the process was a bit simpler but still depended on the discretion of local officials: if the sum was less than 20 yuan, the Lane and Alley Office could approve; if it was greater, the district had to authorize. They would do this upon receiving a positive evaluation by the "street office" (*banshiqu*), the administrative body standing above the Lane and Alley Office and under the district (or the township in the countryside). While these measures were probably cost-effective for the state, military and martyr families were not pleased. They worried that Residence Committee officials "don't know what to do" and feared they "would be treated just like everyone else."[53] Evidence suggests that the process did deter some from requesting state aid, even if they really needed it.[54] Equally important, this bureaucratic process was at odds with the highfalutin rhetorical flourishes lavished upon their offspring's glorious service that were bestowed annually during Spring Festival and Army Day as well as during periods of international tensions (1950–1953, 1957, 1962, 1965). Moreover, it probably convinced some to take an easier route to secure aid, like sleeping with an official.[55]

Junshu and *lieshu*, however, were not the only dissatisfied parties in their encounters with Civil Affairs officials. They considered these officials disrespectful, but Civil Affairs workers griped that *junshu* and *lieshu* were "arrogant," taking far too much credit for revolutionary and wartime successes than they were worthy of. As early as 1950, internal Civil Affairs reports commented on *junshu*'s and *lieshu*'s sense that "they have rendered a great service to the country (*gongchen sixiang*)," a sentiment that was said to be "especially common among elderly *junshu*" and was said to be directly responsible for the "excessive demands" that they were placing on the government (for housing and monthly food allotments).[56] In a 1955 summary of four years of Civil Affairs work, criticism was meted out to officials who failed to see any connection between their work and the "glory of the PLA" as well as to *junshu* who were *too proud* of this glory. This excessive pride was manifested in their sense that they had "done enough for the revolution," their unwillingness to work where they were told to, and some violations of labor discipline and law. They should not allow "past glory to turn into a burden" on society and the state, officials admonished.[57] The precise laws that were allegedly violated were not specified in this particular report, but the investigation of Penglai District indicated that they were mainly minor ones, and the charge of "prideful arrogance" was a bit overstated; one of these arrogant *junshus* liked to gamble and was told to stop by the Residence Committee, but she retorted, "I'm a *junshu* with two sons in the army; it's not a big deal; if there's a problem, I'll take responsibility."[58] In Qingpu County, military and martyr families were also criticized for similar attitudes (displayed in comments such as "The revolution was successful, now it's time to enjoy life in comfort"), unduly relying on state aid, and cooperating with "illegal businessmen" to steal state grain and manipulate the market to make money.[59]

Similar problems, but without the shady businessmen, were also noted in Shandong during these years[60] and continued into the early and mid-1960s. Some *junshu* in Shanghai's Luwan District (which was deemed to be a model area) were criticized for having "excessively high and even unreasonable demands," such as requesting aid even though they did not need it, being dissatisfied with their work and requesting transfers too frequently, and refusing employment "if it was too far, had poor conditions, or the salary was too low" (called the "three won't goes").[61] In an investigation of Beijing's Dongcheng District's military and martyr families (1963), researchers also found cases of women who complained about insufficient state aid even though they were getting some and who invoked their status if their children got into trouble with the law. One martyr's son was arrested for illegal business transactions, but instead of trusting the authorities, his mother "frequently came to the police station and raised a racket." When the police pointed out that her son was doing illegal business, she immediately denied it but then added, "I'm a *lieshu*, what can you do to me?"[62] While this was used as an example of "conceit," her comments might simply have been a reflection of the fact that she was old and had already lost a family member for the revolution or war.

A disinterested observer walking around a city would likely find more *junshu* and *lieshu* in the hallways and examination rooms of hospitals than in police stations yelling at policemen, owing to their age, poverty, and stressful life experiences. Hospitals, like Civil Affairs offices, certainly had their share of interactions with the *junshu* and *lieshu* populations, albeit not quite of the same intensity level; the "Preferential Treatment" offices of Bureaus of Civil

Affairs dealt exclusively with the "worthy poor," whereas hospitals would always see a more mixed population. What experiences did family members of mobilized soldiers and martyrs have when seeking medical care? Were they treated with respect because of current or past sacrifices, or did those other, less attractive parts of their identity hold sway?

The bulk of the evidence strongly suggests that hospital personnel, particularly those in cities, did not afford *junshu* and *lieshu* high status on account of their contributions to the state or society. This may have been because hospital personnel simply did not agree with the underlying premise that these were worthwhile and legitimate contributions (as we have seen in Chapter 3, many did not want to go to war with the United States) or because they were simply frustrated dealing with relatively demanding older people with problems. There were good reasons to be frustrated. In 1950, the government allowed ill *junshu* and *lieshu* to see a doctor at a public or private hospital for free (though they had to pay for food) "with district government approval" and to stay in the hospital with the approval of district authorities and the Health Bureau "after investigation of the circumstances"[63] but did not provide sufficient funding to the hospital to cover their expenses—what in the United States is often called an "unfunded mandate." By 1953, hospitals in some counties in the northern provinces that were home to many military and martyr families (Shandong, Shanxi, Shaanxi) were operating in the red because of excessive use of their facilities by direct relatives of soldiers and martyrs as well by distant relations who officially did not belong in the *junshu* and *lieshu* categories.[64] Only four years after the revolution, and well before the massive discharge of PLA soldiers in the mid-1950s, there was already a move to limit the provision of free inpatient health care and medicine to those who could demonstrate—and get approval for—destitution and urgent need; those who could pay at least something should do so.[65]

It is unlikely, however, that poor and often ill-educated martyr and military families were aware of the details of these restrictive regulations. Many were caught unprepared when they came for medical care and were not treated as well as they expected, given their needs and status. A special investigation team in Shanghai in 1953 had to listen to many tales of medically induced grief. Military and martyr families, they noted, "often have to run around from institution to institution to save a bit of money" and often could not get the care they needed because of poverty, even during the Korean War. Li Wenzhen, for example, was a soldier's mother who was very sick and required hospitalization. She went to Zhongshan Hospital, but administrators there, fearing she could not pay her bill, demanded that she prepay for their services. She could not afford this, so she approached a friend in the Public Security Bureau, who gave her some money. By then it was too late, and she died. Some *junshu* wondered, "Isn't the Health Department for *junshu*, too?"[66] In Zhabei District, a working-class area of Shanghai that suffered a great deal during the Anti-Japanese War, investigators found that "quite a few" military and martyr families did not have money to see a doctor or were not allowed to take off from work, so they "endure all the pain they can at home"; there were "very many situations like this," they added. The Zhabei *junshu* and *lieshu* interviewed by investigators said that city hospital workers "think that giving medical treatment to them is a big hassle, and that they've come only to scrounge for extra benefits (*kaiyou*) at the state's expense." Investigators generally concurred with this perspective: "Not only do *lieshu* and *junshu* not receive 'preferential treatment'; on the contrary, the medical staff hates them (*yan e*), and they know it." In conversations among themselves, *junshu* warned each other, "When you go to a city hospital, don't mention you're a *junshu*; if you do, you'll be screwed." They cited the case of a *lieshu* acquaintance who arrived at the #4 Hospital in an ambulance hailed by a policeman. She was very ill and about to die, but "when the hospital heard she had *junshu* status, they refused to admit her, and could not be persuaded otherwise; they also demanded reimbursement for the ambulance." Ruefully, the investigators noted that there were cases like this in Laozha, Yangpu, and Bamiao districts, "mainly because the medical staff's attitude is especially bad. Unless their views on this population change and they learn that respecting and cherishing military families, martyr families, and disabled soldiers is part of the general mood of the new society we are initiating, the regulations will all be moot."[67] This assessment was on the mark. According to two 1954 reports, those who had chronic illnesses and did not require emergency care generally remained at home because they were poor,[68] and many hospital staffs still had a "bad attitude" toward them and refused to admit them, even in emergency cases.[69]

According to interviews with *lieshu* and *junshu* prior to, during, and after the Korean War, urban employers' views generally marched in step with those of hospital staff, and often for the same reasons: age, gender, poverty, illiteracy, and a lack of appreciation for past and present sacrifices. While many *junshu* and *lieshu* were able to secure employment as bicycle parking lot attendants, hot-water distributors, and tea shop workers, when it came to better-paid and "face-giving" work, they were generally shut out. This forced the Bureau of Civil Affairs (reluctantly, since "the Party Committee is responsible for production, not us") to establish its own small-scale industries, which were, according to many reports, mismanaged and chaotic and lacked basic materials throughout the 1950s and 1960s.[70] These low-status, low-pay positions might have worked out quite well if it were not for other state officials praising *junshu* and *lieshu* for their "glorious" contributions to the revolution and victory, which, unsurprisingly, raised their expectations about their status in society. But when they approached factories with this sense of status and found that other considerations were more important, many were bitterly disappointed. According to the 1953 investigation, many *junshu* and *lieshu* were obsessed with finding employment, since they wanted to avoid the stigma associated with "relief rice" and be able to support themselves. Employers, however, wanted nothing to do with them and conveyed as much to Civil Affairs and Labor Bureau officials. Many were deemed "difficult to control" or "too old" at 35 or 40 years of age (50 was out of the question).[71] In Zhujiajiao District in Qingpu, Civil Affairs officials noted in 1951 that *junshu* "frequently come to the government for work, but we cannot help them."[72] In Yangpu District in Shanghai, factory directors and unions either "failed to see the connection between the war effort and preferential treatment work" or "hadn't done anything related to the war effort" and, as a result, "did not enforce employment policies vis-à-vis military and martyr families or disabled soldiers." (Most all had never read the main directives from the Center.) All were concerned that their skill level and degree of literacy were insufficient and were "unwilling to hire them." The main exception appeared to have been cotton mills, which generally relied upon a low-skilled female workforce, but even there they were taken on as temporary workers. Some *lieshu* and *junshu* told their interviewers that they secured temporary positions only by *not* disclosing their "high" status to their employers, much like some of their veteran counterparts did when seeking employment. These positions, by definition, were insecure. For instance, Zhang Linbin's older brother was serving on the front lines in Korea and she "had nothing to live on and was all alone in the world." When her three-month contract in the #9 Cotton Mill was over, she was released, an action the investigation team called "absolutely not fair and unreasonable."[73]

In other cases, bureaucratic obstacles proved insurmountable. As the CCP gained control over the labor market, jobs were difficult to procure without official approval, usually in the form of a letter of introduction. One *junshu*, surnamed Chen, told investigators that he tried to find work on three separate occasions. On the first occasion, he found a position with the help of a friend, but when he went to the factory, he was told that he needed a letter of introduction from the district. Chen went there, but the clerk "forgot about it" and the job was filled by someone else. On the second occasion, Chen heard from a friend that the Public Security Bureau was looking for policemen, so he went to register. The PSB, however, soon informed him that they were supposed to help only veterans find jobs, not military families. On the third try, Chen went with a friend who knew someone else at a factory that was looking for a guard for the dormitory gate. Union and management agreed to hire him, provided that he supply a letter from the district. At the district office, officials told him to hold on—they needed to find the telephone number of the factory and its director of personnel. When the call was patched through, district officials asked, "Do you really want to hire someone who's over 50? If the Labor Bureau objects, it will be on your head." With that, the third employment opportunity evaporated.[74] As was the case with veterans, there was little Civil Affairs officials could do about problems like this, since, as noted in Chapter 5, they were not empowered to order any organization to hire anyone. Even if officials battled other units on the *junshu*'s behalf, administrative arrangements made the prospects for victory slim, particularly in the absence of a strong lobbying organization. In the PRC's administrative environment, factories simply did not see themselves as responsible for soldiers or their families—this was the province of Civil Affairs. Like many veterans, *junshu* and *lieshu* also fell between the cracks when it came to respectable employment opportunities in cities.[75]

To what extent did rural *junshu* and *lieshu* experience these difficulties dealing with officials? If at least some of their problems in cities can be chalked up to their deficient "social capital" in an industrializing and modernizing economy (which, in turn, can be attributed to the lower-class makeup of the PLA), in rural areas there were more possibilities for positive interactions: the PLA drafted many peasants, the revolution was based there, and stratification based on such qualities as higher education and technical skills were less acute in the rural economy. Evidence from archives in Shandong, Beijing, Shanghai, and Qingpu, however, reveal a similar pattern: *junshu* and *lieshu* were provided some financial assistance, but this was infrequently paired with respect for their families' contributions or sacrifices. Signs of conflict between local cadres and *junshu* were noticed very early in the 1950s, even in North China during the Korean War and immediately after it. Provincial-level reports from Shandong in 1953 noted the absence of any effort to enhance patriotic education or respect for martyr families during the war[76] as well as a "a lack of sense of responsibility toward both veterans and *lieshu* and *junshu*," which the authors attributed to a "weak sense of national defense" and "the lull of peace during the last several years."[77] The "lull of peace" was also blamed for problems between civilian cadres and military personnel at a 1954 meeting summarizing four years of work among the "preferential treatment" population in the province. Officials waxed nostalgic: "During the meeting we reminisced about the relationship between the party and the army during the war with Japan and how close it was and why is it that the relationship between the party and veterans and *lieshu* and *junshu* isn't the way it was before,"[78] ignoring the fact that in CCP base areas there were also incidents of township cadres embezzling funds intended for *junshu*.[79] In Shandong's neighboring province of Henan, a 1954 investigation of thirty counties that otherwise played up the positive impact of a campaign to encourage support and respect for the military (*yongjun, youshu*) also hinted that not all had been well in the past: "We raised the social and political status of *lieshu* and *junshu*" and "enhanced the unity of local cadres with *lieshu* and *junshu*." In Chengguan District, Zhenping County, they noted, "there were some *junshu* who, when encountering a cadre, did not speak to them."[80] Moving south to Qingpu during the Korean War, a *junshu* surnamed Heng "made trouble" (*daoluan*) at a meeting of the Peasant Association in Shengang Township, "mainly because she had a poor relationship with the village's cadres," whom she called "selfish" for not helping her with planting and bringing in the harvest. Because of this, Heng was often at the township government requesting "relief rice." Some help was provided by a veteran, who went to Heng's village and "taught the village chief that *junshu* should be honored," but the situation was still tense.[81] In 1956 in the Shanghai suburbs, a report found that local cadres neglected *junshu* after their sons' enlistment. This led some mothers and fathers to rue their decision to allow their sons to join the army. Lu Haimei, for example, told cadres who interviewed her, "Before my son joined the army, township cadres came by every day to see me and talk, but now that he's in it, not one person has stepped through my doorway." She was resigned to "bitterness for the next three years" when her son would return home: "Only then will I be able to manage."[82]

During the early 1960s, state efforts to prod local officials and their communities to be more involved in the minutiae of administration of aid for *junshu* and *lieshu* did not succeed very well; cadres preferred to deal with this population in broad strokes. This was fairly easy to do: counties exercised very little supervision over "preferential treatment work" and were rarely held accountable by their superiors at the municipality level.[83] In 1962, both rural cadres and Civil Affairs officials adopted a policy of willed ignorance, or "don't hear, don't ask" (*bu wen, bu wen*), regarding the financial circumstances of military dependents or martyr families, rarely stopping by to see how they were faring. They also did not try to "educate" peasants about why *junshu* and *lieshu* were worthy of respect in the first place. In some reports, officials again blamed "the long-term peaceful environment" for these problems.[84] Other reports suggested other causes. In Qingpu, some rural officials had stopped providing any assistance to *junshu*, *lieshu*, and disabled veterans since 1960 because "there was no specific regulation about this" in the Center's guidelines for establishing communes; "preferential treatment" for medical problems was not enforced from 1960 to 1963 as well.[85] Indicative of just how little the Center knew about the situation of veterans and *lieshu*/*junshu* at the local level, this neglect occurred at the same time that the 60 Articles on Agriculture (intended to revive the rural economy after the Great Leap Forward) called upon local congresses to include veterans and *lieshu* in order to "prevent ideological backsliding"![86] Moreover, as in the 1950s, village and township cadres, who were ostensibly part of "the state," still considered the job of taking care of military and martyr families to be "a state issue that had nothing to do with them" (*zhengfu de shi, yuji wuguan*). Absent any sort of political education about *why* it was important to support military and martyr families, the mere provision of aid generated resentment. Some local officials were said to be "fed up with" (*yanfan*) *junshu* and *lieshu* and discriminated against them not very subtly. After dealing with officials, some mothers of soldiers and martyrs went home and "cried looking at their photographs."[87]

This acidic reaction to military and martyr dependents cannot be blamed on the more commercial, non-militaristic values that often are said to characterize the Shanghai area. In 1963, at the same time the Shanghai suburbs and Qingpu reports were compiled, officials in Beijing pointed to comparable political views, only in more dire economic circumstances. Unlike the wealthier Shanghai region (where there were also fewer military personnel), some military dependents in the Beijing area had no money to buy food and were forced to give their sons and daughters to other families to raise. (However they felt personally, the authors of this report seemed more concerned with the impact of this poverty on the state: "It's not beneficial for the stability of the army or future recruitment efforts.") In the North as well, officials blamed "the long period of peace" as well as the conviction of many lower-level officials that all problems related to martyrs and military dependents should be handled "by the state" (*guojia*), not them. As a result of this conception, "not a few" rural officials in the Beijing area did not undertake any effort to provide for them using community labor contributions. Some objected to the very principle of providing *gratis* work points to military dependents and martyr families, since it constituted a "transfer without compensation and not in accordance with guidelines for the allocation of manpower." Still others disagreed with the state's rationale for providing aid in the first place. China, like most states, provided benefits even to those who were drafted (for instance, the GI Bill included all military veterans who served more than six months, regardless of how they entered the service), but in rural China, officials were perplexed as to why families of those who were drafted should receive the same benefits and respect as those who had volunteered, and as a result, very little, if anything, was provided.[88] In Chapter 4, however, we have seen local officials use exactly the *opposite* principle to discriminate against veterans: it was *your* choice to join the army, so why should the state support you? In either case, there is little evidence suggesting many positive interactions between local officials and military dependents, even when the circumstances would seem to most merit this—during the Korean War and the rural crisis of the early 1960s. Whether owing to long-term peace, disagreement over who owed them, or the legitimacy of the causes which military and martyr families represented, local officials were content to provide some material aid, but this was not matched with a sense of gratitude or appreciation for their contributions to war or revolution.

LAND AND MONEY

The debates over exactly who was responsible for "taking care of" (*zhaogu*) military dependents that erupted with full force during the economic crisis of the 1960s (in the aftermath of the Great Leap Forward) were not new; it was long-standing state policy that since military dependents (and family members of revolutionary martyrs) were making sacrifices for the good of the whole political community, the responsibility for ensuring their livelihood should be a shared one. As noted in an instructional Q&A for rural officials in 1956, in response to the question "Why should a rural cooperative provide preferential treatment for *junshu* and veterans?" the answer provided was "Because their beloved relatives have contributed to the People's Army, or they have served in the People's Army, they have made a very large contribution to the state and the people. Therefore, the entire country has the responsibility to be concerned about their production and livelihood, and so of course should the cooperative."[89] Even though local officials frequently disputed this conception of civil–military relations and the worthiness of those awarded "preferential treatment," there was little they could do to prevent the Center from at least trying to foist most of the expense and responsibility for various heroes of the revolution onto them. Of these efforts, probably none was as difficult as the "substitute tilling" (*daigeng*) program, which had its origins in some revolutionary base areas prior to 1949 but was then enforced on a far wider scale after 1949. The core of the program was that other villagers, recognizing the contributions of the military and those who died for the CCP, would help PLA and martyr families through the sacrifice of their labor, especially during the agricultural busy seasons. Depending on their needs, *junshu* or *lieshu* could get "partial *daigeng*" (part of their land would be tilled by others) or "full *daigeng*"; in Zhujiajiao in Qingpu circa 1951, 58 out of 89 families received the partial version.[90] For a number of reasons, however, the *daigeng* assistance program ended abruptly in 1955.

The demise of *daigeng* in all of its incarnations was quite predictable in light of the problems we already have seen in veterans' social and political status. Even though instructional Q&As and other policy documents spoke of the contributions of the "People's Army" (instead of the People's *Liberation* Army), the complexity and length of the revolution meant that many individuals (in both rural and urban areas) could plausibly claim a reward for contributing something to its outcome. When *daigeng* was enforced as an entitlement program for *junshu* (and martyr families), rural officials quickly took advantage of it under the presumption that they, too, had made legitimate sacrifices and now deserved help. In the investigation of 80 townships in Henan Province, *daigeng* was faulted both for its chaos—there was no plan in place for who would do what and when—and for its inflated list of beneficiaries. Martyr families and *junshu* received some *daigeng*, but township and village officials were its primary beneficiaries. In 1953 in one township, for example, the three top officials had used 210 peasants to work their land as well as to sew and mend their clothes. The party secretary sent other villagers to his own mutual aid team but recorded their work as his own, while the head of the Finance and Grain Committee left his mutual aid team because he found it very convenient to dispatch workers to his land as a *daigeng* beneficiary. Because peasants also had their own land to worry about, their burden increased significantly.[91] In Shandong, an analysis of 43 townships noted an "unequal and unbalanced distribution of burden in the allocation of *daigeng* labor."[92] While this report did not mention officials who received it inappropriately, others did. In one village all of the officials received *daigeng*, but they completely ignored the officially entitled families; some *lieshu* said, "The dead are treated better than the living; those who are close are treated differently than those distant."[93] This and other investigations also focused on hundreds who exempted themselves from working on *junshu* and *lieshu* land; these included township government officials, CCP members, local representatives, and militia officials.[94] All of this was justifiable in the CCP's grand narrative of its revolutionary success.

Adding to the overly broad conception of worthiness seemed to be a genuine confusion over who was officially entitled to *daigeng*. For example, in the Beijing suburbs in the early 1940s, where major battles took place during WWII and the Civil War, local cadres awarded *lieshu* status to three households of soldiers who died from illness as well as to the family of a village chief appointed by the Japanese military who was killed when he and fellow villagers fled a bombing raid. In Beijing's Xidan District, on the other hand, a woman lost her son to illness during his service, but Civil Affairs officials did not grant her *junshu* or *lieshu* status, yet two households of students who went down south as part of a work team had been receiving aid as *junshu* since 1949. This confusion resulted in "not a few deviations" in *daigeng* assignments. In Hou Township, there were six households of *lieshu* and *junshu* that deserved *daigeng* but received none at all and some *junshu* whose land "should have been completely tilled [but] was tilled only partially." In some cases, *daigeng* was assigned only on the basis of the number of working people in the family and not whether they had any particular difficulties.[95]

Similar problems were noted in eastern China. In 1953 in Zhujiajiao District in Qingpu County, family members of officials at regular state bureaucracies (known as *gongshu*), heads of township-level peasant associations, and local militia leaders, in addition to *junshu*, had their land tilled by other peasants.[96] Lacking the resources to investigate the landholdings, capital, and the family situation of every officially entitled household, local officials tended to send peasants to each and every *junshu* family, even if they were managing without it. Since there were only so many people who could be spread out over the *junshu, lieshu, gongshu*, and cadre populations, families that did not require much help (such as *gongshu* and cadres) found themselves with extra labor power, while those that were in more dire need did not receive enough help. When it was at the complete discretion of local officials, *daigeng* was said to be "too wide and too narrow" (that is, distributed to too many people, but in insufficient amounts).[97] Some resented providing assistance to *junshu* with money in the bank but who still requested *daigeng*. As noted in a handwritten report from Qingpu's Baihe District, peasants said, "*Junshu* are living alright and they still get *daigeng*; a couple more years like this they'll become landlords!"[98] Others in Baihe pleaded, "It'll kill us if we have to do it every year" and "Can we not do it this year?"[99] Some, however, were as confused by the category of *junshu* as their rural counterparts in the Beijing suburbs: "What sort of *junshu* are you? You can't be a *junshu* when your son's in Qingpu; only when he's in North Korea can you be one." Such comments as these prompted the author of the report to claim that *junshu's* political status was low and had not risen as a result of the Korean War.[100]

What made *daigeng* even more unpopular than its unclear scope and boundaries were the seemingly haphazard methods through which it was implemented. Considering *daigeng* a "big headache" and probably worried about its degree of legitimacy, local officials improvised. Some handed over produce rather than workers, so land lay fallow; some rotated workers on a given field, and others were dispatched to work for a certain period of time with a "preferential treatment" household.[101] In 1951, it appears that in most cases a particular individual or peasant household was responsible for helping military and martyr families,[102] but a 1952 investigation in Qingpu found that 70 percent of *junshu* and *lieshu* were assigned a peasant or team that would assist them, and the other 30 percent had workers with more short-term assignments;[103] by 1953, responsibility was more diluted: "not a few peasants" became de facto temporary workers for them.[104] While this would seem a more promising solution (from the perspective of *junshu* and *lieshu*), other reports noted many gaps. County and district officials found that some township and village cadres "neglect *daigeng*" or "don't pay much attention to it" because they do not consider it their "central task."[105] Some fulfilled their duty on paper by tasking someone else to the job, but that someone was a former landlord who had no firsthand experience tilling the land (until 1949 they had hired help) or a "little girl," which, of course, left the purported recipients in exactly the same place they had been before, or worse (when their income was so low they could not afford the land tax).[106] In other cases, adequate labor was assigned in the springtime, but no fertilizer was provided, and other villagers did not help with pest control after planting; local government payments to *junshu* were often late, so they could not pay the workers who helped them.[107] According to correspondence between Zhujiajiao District and Qingpu County, these and other problems resulted in "some military and martyr families with nothing to eat, and others on the verge of having nothing to eat, eating perhaps one meal a day."[108] There were, however, some officials who ate a bit more than their rightful share. Some reports noted such shenanigans as corruption, stealing funds intended for martyr families, sending off false reports to party superiors about the amount of land that was tilled for military families, issuing fake receipts, and forging the signatures of *junshu* and *lieshu* for having received assistance when they had not.[109]

To explain these problems with the *daigeng* program, authors of annual summary reports on Civil Affairs work, as well as more thorough investigations, fingered lax supervision by county- and district-level authorities. This, in turn, was often attributed to a more general confusion about the program's political importance to civil–military relations. In the Shanghai suburbs, Civil Affairs officials complained in 1954 that "some peasants do not see *daigeng* either as a national policy or their individual duty."[110] During that year in Baihe District in Qingpu, officials noted that because "not much propaganda was conducted regarding *daigeng* policy and its political significance," both cadres and ordinary peasants were "confused" about what to do and why they were doing it.[111]

But this was only partly true. Officials and peasants were called "confused" because their understanding of the program did not agree with its original goals and rationale. Even though methods still varied widely among townships, in many places *daigeng* was understood as part and parcel of the CCP's *land revolution* that pitted the poor against rich peasants and landlords, not as a form of recognition for the contributions of the PLA or the sacrifices of its dependents.[112] As early as 1951, village officials provided *daigeng* to military dependents because "everyone *fanshen*'ed (literally "turned over," or received land during land reform), so everyone should participate," without mentioning the PLA.[113] In Baihe, *daigeng* was less of an opportunity for the community to pitch in to help *junshu* than a chance to force rich peasants and former landlords to do their fair share through the contribution of money that paid for extra labor. For example, two elderly *junshu* in Nanyao Village collectively held eight *mu* of land that was supposed to be included in the *daigeng* program. During the spring planting season, village officials neglected to mobilize the villagers to help them. Come summer, they had little growing on their land. Upset, they made their way to the township government, complaining that, while other villagers had already completed much of their work, their land was not even plowed, so it was too late to harvest anything for the fall. Rather than mobilize other villagers, the village cadres "sent three households of landlords and rich peasants to do *daigeng*." A township Civil Affairs Committee member objected to this method, but the village chief retorted, "There's no other way. So what if it violates *daigeng* policy?"[114] A year later (1955), Baihe District continued to report that rich peasants continued to shoulder a disproportionate share of the *daigeng* burden, which prompted officials to complain that peasants "still do not understand that *daigeng* is a glorious duty for all, and that everyone should contribute."[115] Those *junshu* who received *daigeng* were the secondhand beneficiaries of the revolution that mattered more to peasants—getting land—rather than a population that was worthy of support because of military contributions and sacrifices; many veterans, after all, were not even there when land reform took place. Participation in land reform also provided the cushion of legitimacy for civilian and militia officials who claimed status and benefits such as *daigeng* and who disputed the entitlements granted to veterans and their family members.

HANDOUTS

Even though the village official cited above belittled his deviation from state policy, reports from Shanghai and other regions made it amply clear that *daigeng* was not a sustainable policy, especially in peacetime. Moreover, gradual collectivization of the rural economy meant that responsibility for taking care of *junshu* land (and land of martyr families) would have to shift to the larger community, since land titles belonged to the state and farming was no longer based on the household unit. *Daigeng* was officially cancelled in 1955 and replaced by a new national program called "Preferential Treatment Labor Days" (*youdai laodongri*). According to this plan, villagers would contribute a day or several days of labor to a collective pool, and rural cadres would then divide these pooled days by the number of needy military and martyr families and disabled veterans in the community. Officials would then convert this number into a monetary figure by calculating the value of labor days in "work points," which would be added to their own separate income from their work in a mutual aid team or cooperative. Should this prove inadequate—according to state policy *junshu* were not supposed to make "less than the average peasant" and martyr families were to make "a little more than the average"—supplemental state funds would kick in. Civil Affairs, at their discretion or by order of the township government, could authorize either a temporary supplement or a fixed monthly stipend, again depending on need. If there was no need, *junshu* would get nothing except for symbolic rewards such as plaques, certificates, or, in some cases, a *bian* (a horizontal picture inscribed with a note of thanks or good wishes).

From the moment it was handed down until at least the mid-1960s, this scheme rarely worked as intended. To the consternation of the numerous investigation teams that looked into the implementation of "Preferential Treatment Labor Days," village and township officials routinely flouted one of its main provisions—that "labor days" be allocated on the basis of demonstrated need—and instead provided roughly equal amounts of labor days or funds to all military dependents and martyr families in their jurisdictions. This practice, critiqued as either inappropriate "egalitarianism" (*pingjunzhuyi*) or "universalized special treatment" (*pubian youdai*), was noticed early on. In 1955, an investigation of the registration of *junshu* and martyr families in the Beijing suburbs found that there were townships that practiced "excessive egalitarianism" (*yanzhong pingjunzhuyi*) when distributing assistance. In Laojuntang Township in Nanyuan District, investigators complained that "all eight *junshu*, regardless of their economic situation, received 37.5 yuan in aid."[116] In 1960 in the Shanghai suburbs, a large-scale investigation classified counties according to the level of enforcement: some completely ignored "Preferential Treatment Labor Days," while others implemented it "partially," in an "unbalanced way," or without sufficient attention to "details." Among these omitted details was whether families actually needed help. In Nanhui County, Nicheng Township (by then called "commune"), there were 18 *junshu* and martyr families with a fairly wide variety of family circumstances, but "all of them received some work points—the most was 300, the least 200."[117] Two years and much paperwork later, an investigation of "preferential treatment work" in the suburbs found that "in the city's rural suburbs, most governments do not question people whether they have any problems or whether their difficulties are large or small; when distributing 'preferential labor days,' they have the tendency of being excessively egalitarian, giving small amounts to too many people."[118] According to 1962 statistics on 82 villages in eight counties that were compiled by Civil Affairs, 67 villages

(82.5 percent) gave some labor days to every single *junshu* and martyr family. According to the bureau's calculation, 60 percent of these families should not have received any aid because their standard of living was "average"; roughly 25 percent deserved a little but got too much.[119] In Qingpu County, reports from 1962 to 1965 also indicate that "universal special treatment" and "egalitarianism" were common, even though only 14 percent of *junshu* and martyr families in some villages were officially entitled; in Baihe District, officials said that "they have done it for many years; the custom (*xiguan*) is universal distribution."[120] Farther north in Shandong, a 1962 report found that, generally speaking, local governments were too tightfisted with the amount of money distributed to *junshu* and too generous with martyr families and Level 2 disabled veterans given their respective needs, but the overall tendency was to give everybody something (*yilü youdai*).[121]

From late 1963 until the Cultural Revolution, years of effort to eliminate these egalitarian practices yielded some, but very strange, fruit. At the same time that the cult of Mao and the PLA were reaching their pre–Cultural Revolution zenith and thousands of peasants were being drafted to prepare China for a possible war with the USSR or the United States, there was a parallel campaign to severely curtail the provision of benefits to military dependents whose income did not justify assistance. In a process that was bound to be very problematic since "need" is difficult to determine, researchers fanned out to the countryside to determine how much they made, their sources of income, their daily and monthly expenses, and, Goldilocks-like, whether or not they were receiving just enough, too much, or too little supplemental aid (more on these results later). In Qingpu, village officials were frustrated and flabbergasted and refused to believe that this was the Center's policy, figuring it to be a scheme hatched by county Civil Affairs.[122] Charged with recruiting young men, these officials were convinced that few would join the PLA if their families did not receive some aid, even if they did not need it according to the state's standards. Many local officials were "very worried" about conversations they would have with potential soldiers' parents should they inform them that their government refused to give them money; as it was, it took much effort, cajoling, and flattery (*xuyuan*) to get them to enlist. In their words, it was "not reasonable not to provide universal special treatment"; "It could not be stopped," they warned. Faced with this resistance, the county lowered its demands for drastic cutbacks,[123] but as late as 1965, local governments, following directives from the Center, were still insisting on inserting some sort of means test into the allocation of work points. A backlash soon followed. In Qingpu, aid recipients were said to be upset and confused by the very prospect of war and by the efforts of the township (commune) government to discontinue "special treatment"; some *junshu* immediately took off to the county to complain, claiming that "it was not 'glorious' not to receive aid."[124] Despite hearing complaints earlier in the decade that the PLA soldiers were no better than "mercenaries" (*guyong bing*) because their fathers would not send them unless they received benefits,[125] village officials—following most all international and historical precedents—still argued that the state owed something to those who served.[126] The Center, however, following long-standing historical precedent, blamed local officials for the problems in implementation.[127]

How effective this resistance was is not clear—the Cultural Revolution broke out a year later, and most records from that period are not open—but the curtailment of aid in the mid-1960s may have been an important factor leading some *junshu* into the open arms and beds of local officials, who were in a position to provide them with the sorts of benefits they thought they were entitled to by virtue of their sons' military service. This assessment is supported by examining the motives for the "egalitarian" distribution of benefits. The fact that rural officials were avid fans of the practice does not necessarily indicate that they appreciated the PLA, or soldiers, for that matter. By most accounts, they supported "egalitarianism" because it was *administratively convenient* (just figuring out "average" income in a village was a real hassle for them, not to mention the precise circumstances of each family), because it smoothed interpersonal relations by "giving face" to all (it also would be a hassle if *junshu* recipients and non-recipients started fighting amongst themselves), and because it made it easier to get young men to serve.[128] While seemingly admirable, egalitarianism detached from a sincere interest in how *junshu* were faring proved problematic. Many reports noted that distributing community resources broadly, while administratively convenient, had only a very limited economic impact on those families whose needs were more acute and pushed poorer *junshu* (and martyr families) to higher-level governments for supplemental resources.[129] When this happened in increasingly large numbers in the mid-1950s and early 1960s during collectivization (many mutual aid teams were reluctant to admit them because they were older or female or would admit them only if they had enough resources of their own to invest[130]) and after the Great Leap Forward, *junshu* (and martyr families) were criticized for becoming overly "dependent" (*yilü sixiang*) on government aid to support their livelihood as well as for their unwillingness to toil hard in the fields to support themselves. This was noted in urban districts in the mid-1950s[131] and in Qingpu in the early 1960s.[132] At the same time, the rather indiscriminate distribution of aid in the absence of broad agreement over the worthiness of its beneficiaries triggered resentment among those who did not have *junshu* or martyr family status. By the mid-1960s, not only were many *junshu* vulnerable socially and economically, but their frequent visits with government offices to request aid also provided ample opportunity for powerful local officials to assess their needs, chat them up, and "seduce" them with promises of more aid and good jobs in exchange for sex — a "sexual opportunity structure," so to speak.

INEQUALITIES

Even though official policy stated that military families' standard of living should "not be below" that of the average peasants, and martyr families' should be "a little higher," evidence shows that these standards were not maintained. Overly broad but insufficient distribution of work points was only one cause of this problem. In many instances, local officials who were supposed to help them did the opposite; the aid that should have supplemented community support did not kick in or did not match the income lost from having a son in the army or a husband killed as a "revolutionary martyr."

It was not long after the regime was established that high-level officials were made aware of inadequate or nonexistent "preferential treatment" for *junshu* and *lieshu*. According to a 1951 investigation of "preferential treatment work" in Shandong, only "some areas" and "a minority of work units" actually enforced regulations that *junshu* and *lieshu* "had priority for preferential treatment." In some cases, regulations were entirely ignored; for instance, when fertilizer and livestock were distributed throughout the village, *junshu* and *lieshu* "received nothing at all," apparently because officials feared that they would never get anything back. To this litany of complaints investigators added even more flagrant abuses: "Village and township cadres with impure class status" refused to allow them to participate in peasant association meetings and "humiliated, hit, and screamed at them, sometimes to the point of murder"; there were roughly 30 cases like this in three areas, including the beating of a soldier's wife who was pregnant. In one county there were 500 people who lost sons during the Anti-Japanese War who still had not received any pension as well as thousands of *junshu* and *lieshu* who were scrounging for food in drought-stricken areas.[133] In Henan during 1951, most all assistance to military families was suspended due to natural disasters, but even the usual Spring Festival activities were said to be perfunctory and "cold."[134]

If it was not drought that contributed to the suspension of benefits, political campaigns could get in the way. At the same time that the PRC was prosecuting the Korean War and mounting a campaign to support military families, CCP leaders simultaneously embarked on two massive efforts to attack former regime officials and supporters, as well as corruption in its own ranks, in the "Five Antis" and "Three Antis" campaigns, respectively. Fear of committing a serious political mistake in the appropriation of funds resulted in administrative paralysis. An investigation of Yulin District in Shanghai found that there was "no routine administration of benefits because of the Three and Five Antis campaigns," which led to a great deal of dissatisfaction among the families of soldiers fighting in Korea.[135] Other reports from 1953 noted that officials thought it was much better to be "strict than loose," a policy an investigation team called "divorced from reality" and "completely wrong," given the dire condition of *junshu* and *lieshu*. In all of Zhabei District, one of Shanghai's most populated, only 61 *lieshu* and *junshu* households received monthly stipends (out of roughly 850 such households,[136] or 8 percent), and fewer than 1 percent of households received 120–200 *jin* of rice (1 *jin* is roughly half a kilogram); most received 60–70 *jin*, which investigation officials deemed a "half-starved standard for distributing aid" and which was in violation of municipal regulations that had been sent out in August 1951. What happened was simple but not unusual: a Civil Affairs clerk stuffed the regulation away, so other clerks knew nothing about it. When *junshu* and *lieshu* found out about it from their colleagues in other districts, they gathered in the district Civil Affairs office "demanding to get aid according to the city's standard."[137] More money was distributed, but it was still insufficient. In 1955, some *junshu* and *lieshu,* the "flesh and blood of the revolution," continued to embody this metaphor by selling their blood to hospitals to make ends meet in Bamiao District.[138]

Statistical data from later in the 1950s and early 1960s demonstrate the long-term trend of relative poverty among *junshu* and *lieshu,* even after the chaos of the early 1950s subsided. In a handwritten 1958 study of Civil Affairs work in Nanhui County in the Shanghai suburbs, only 14 percent of 1,393 military dependents and martyr households lived above the standard of living of ordinary peasants, while 55 percent were at the same level and 31 percent were worse off; these findings prompted officials to begin a campaign to remind peasants about the sacrifices others had made for the revolution.[139] According to the Civil Affairs gazetteer of Anhui Province, 21.9 percent of *lieshu* and *junshu* households were poorer than the average peasant, 73.8 percent were considered at the average level, and only 4.3 percent were above average.[140] In Shandong in 1958, Civil Affairs officials from around the province met to discuss a draft proposal from the Center that would have disqualified *junshu*, soldiers missing in action (MIAs), and veterans from receiving state aid but allowed it to be distributed to martyr families and disabled veterans. Shandong officials suggested revisions that would allow families of MIA soldiers to receive aid because "like martyr families, they have lost their main source of support and have many difficulties," but they concurred that "*junshu* and old, sick and weak veterans should no longer receive aid from Civil Affairs and should rely instead on the welfare provisions

given to others in society who have problems."[141] Like many directives in
the PRC, this document should be read as a better gauge of intention than
outcome. Documents from 1960 show that aid continued to be distributed to
martyrs, veterans, *junshu*, and the disabled; 10 percent of martyr families and
1.3 percent of disabled veterans and poor veterans received a fixed monthly
stipend. Still, Civil Affairs officials acknowledged both that "reliance on
the collective's labor days"—which supposedly obviated the need for state-
administered funds—did not help many military and martyr families and that
funds they continued to disburse were insufficient for families who tilled poor
land, lived in poor villages or drought areas, or had few working adults in
relation to their overall family size.[142]

In contrast, officials in the Shanghai area put a more positive spin on the
ever-lower number of aid recipients. In 1956 in Xuhui District, 5 percent of
junshu (27 of 488 households) received a fixed monthly stipend that averaged
5.7 yuan a month. This could not go far; the monthly living expense for an
average family of four was estimated to be 36 yuan.[143] In 1960, 1.5 percent
of military and martyr families received a fixed stipend, compared to 7.5
percent in 1953, a reduction which officials attributed to "their lives improving year by year."[144] In the suburbs, where there were many complaints that
"special treatment" was distributed too broadly, there were also quite a few
who received nothing at all. According to a 1959 statistical table, 65 percent
of 21,331 *junshu* and martyr households in 11 Shanghai suburban counties
did not receive "Preferential Treatment Labor Days,"[145] and according to a
1961 survey of five villages in Chongming, Jiading, and Qingpu counties, 57
percent of 90 military and martyr families did not receive state aid, but even
the assistance provided to the 51 recipient families was deemed by officials
to be inappropriately high.[146]

Lurking in the shadows of these figures, averages, and assessments of
what constituted "appropriate aid" was the crotchety proverb that wealth
and poverty are all relative. In theory, military families who benefited
from "egalitarianism" should have been quite pleased with receiving
something—if absolute sums were the only thing that mattered. But when
aid was not linked to respect, money meant less. For families that received
nothing, the lack of assistance was consequential, even if they were not
deemed sufficiently poor to receive a fixed monthly stipend. Being defined
as "average," and thus not qualified for state aid, was grating because the
state defined their sons' contribution as "glorious"; military service was
deemed to be worthy of the people's and state's support. (In contrast, after
the massive mobilization of Russians in WWI, the Duma's bill on aid to
families was based on the notion that assistance was a *legal right* due to all
soldiers in return for their sacrifices on behalf of the state—an entitlement

rather than assistance benevolently extended.)[147] Moreover, military families compared their glorious sacrifice to families who did *not* have sons in the service and what their income *might have been* had their sons not joined the PLA. According to a 1963 investigation of military families in Beijing's Dongcheng District, family income could be adversely affected once a working-class son entered the army. In a survey of 433 *junshu* households in one residential area, close to one-third of families witnessed a drop in income. Of these, 30 percent saw their family income fall by a third, but sometimes it might be cut in half. Officials noted that it was difficult to entice families to join the PLA because of financial problems incurred as a result of service. "Even though they feel they have been hit hard," this drop was not low enough to qualify them for state assistance.[148] In 1964 in Liantang Township (Commune) in Qingpu, officials promoted the slogans "Military Service Is the Most Glorious" and "Not Receiving Preferential Labor Days Is Also Glorious," but *junshu* families still believed that they should receive aid "even if they did not need it." Poorer families who saw their income drop when their sons left (but who may have been "average" from the perspective of a visiting investigator) accused the government of tricking them into encouraging their sons to join. "We would have had more if our son was home," they complained.[149]

GETTING ALONG

To the extent that the sense of injustice was confined to interactions with officials or money-related matters, perhaps it would have been tolerable; in Great Britain after WWI, as we have already seen, most military personnel detested bureaucrats and politicians but did not feel that their sacrifices had been in vain because they sensed that society supported them. In China, this was not the case. Despite valorization by the state propaganda, military dependents represented "victories" that had questionable legitimacy among ordinary people. Moreover, *junshu* (as well as their older counterparts, *lieshu*) mainly came from the lower classes of peasants and workers and therefore had little cultural capital, or "face." As a result, military dependents and martyr families generally did not receive the "thanks of the nation" they believed they deserved. At best, they were pitied; at worst, they were despised for being a burden on society and for receiving benefits and status many believed were undeserved.

Reports on tensions between *junshu, lieshu,* and ordinary people surfaced in the earliest reports circulating in the new state and tended to center on the mismatch between their sense of entitlement and society's unwillingness to accept their status as such. In 1950, Civil Affairs officials in Shanghai noted in one of their first summary reports that workers, like union officials and employers, did not want to accept military dependents into their factories despite their obvious poverty, preferring instead to bring in "regular" unemployed people. In one case, hundreds of *junshu* congregated around a factory official and screamed at him when he informed them that they could not work there; "They are not reasonable," he complained.[150] According to archival sources in Beijing, martyr families also suffered discrimination in society and in the job search because "their misfortune was seen as a social stigma."[151] In the absence of good jobs, and placed in the position of supplicants to an often-malfunctioning bureaucracy, *junshu* sometimes had to depend on charity. In February 1952, *Internal Reference* informed cadres that "some seriously ill *junshu* and *lieshu* had to resort to asking people for donations or sold off their furniture to pay for medicine; some are so poor they have written letters to their children at the front lines in North Korea requesting money."[152] While some people were willing to contribute money for the war, providing charity to *junshu* was a different matter. In Qingpu, a 1953 report did not give high praise to the popular view of *junshu*, noting only that "their status has been raised a little" during the war. Local residents said, "Who told their sons to go to the army? Why should we have to pay?"[153] In a 1955 report summing up five years of work, Civil Affairs officials in Shanghai blamed these negative assessments of *junshu* and *lieshu* on their "prideful arrogance" as well as people not quite understanding the "blood-and flesh-relationship between the army and the people."[154] In Qingpu, officials warned them that their behavior was getting on people's nerves. In a meeting in Shiniu Village, a *junshu* surnamed Chen confessed, "We *junshu* shouldn't act like 'Lady *Junshus*'; we should help other people" (*woni junshu bu neng zuo junshu tai tai*).[155] Farther north in Henan Province in 1955, some *junshu* and *lieshu* were said to have a "poor relationship" with ordinary villagers, and this partially accounted for their reluctance to enter mutual aid teams where they would be dependent on others' assessment of their work as well as peasants' refusal to accept them into their teams.[156]

During the early 1960s the state made another effort to raise the status of the PLA, military families, and martyr families among ordinary people but found that attitudes toward them had not improved and may even have hardened. Some people felt no need to help them because they believed state propaganda that they were cared for, but those who did help acted on the basis of pity, not an appreciation for the military. In a three-year summary of Civil Affairs work (1958–1961), officials commented on public sentiment:

> People say, "In any case the government guarantees their livelihood [so there's no point in our helping them out]." If they give them a bit of assistance, it's out of pity for old people, and helping them is a good deed. They have only a very

fuzzy understanding of the slogan "Supporting the Army and Helping Military Families Is Everyone's Responsibility" (*yongjun youshu renren you zi*) and the more political dimension of supporting military families.[157]

The failure of the state to cultivate a sense of respect for military families in society was, as previously noted, sometimes explained by the "long peace" that prevailed on the mainland since 1949, but never in terms of the PLA's or CCP's lack of legitimacy in many areas. In 1962, however, Shanghai officials conducted an investigation of elderly and widowed mothers of martyrs living in Luwan District, a population that symbolized the Communist Revolution in a broader sense, since some martyrs died during war and others while performing different revolutionary tasks. According to the investigation, these *lieshu* were managing financially, but ordinary citizens did not respect them, and "some even experienced discrimination and chilly treatment." Many *lieshu* had problems associated with aging: they fell down stairs, burned food, had trouble walking to markets to shop, and fell down at home because of poor eyesight. Even though they received aid, "their practical problems go unanswered because people ignore them." Owing to these difficulties and the lack of public support, the burden of helping them was mainly shouldered by their families, and the younger women in particular, who came to resent them for their problems. Neighbors frequently made disparaging remarks about them: "All she does is eat and sleep, eat and sleep; one can die of boredom from them"; "They eat our food and exploit the government—they should die already!" One elderly woman was called "Madame Rich" by her niece, and another woman, who apparently made many trips to the local government requesting food items, was called a "Glorious Mother" to her face but "Martyr King" (*liewang*) and "Madame Martyr" (*lie taitai*) behind her back.[158]

As a result of being "jibed, taunted, and ridiculed" by their neighbors, these *lieshu* were said to have shed their designated role in politics. Expected to remain true to their sons' or husbands' cause and remind people of the glory of the military and party, they refused to hang up ribbons and plaques that signified their "glory," fearing that "people will look down on them after they find out that their son was sacrificed." Others cried, "If my son didn't die, I would not have ended up like this."[159]

OPTING OUT

If crying had been the only response of martyr mothers to their sense of social ingratitude, and if military families' difficulties with other people and administrators were confined to grumbling and making half-hearted apologies for their "arrogance," it is doubtful state officials would write so much about them and investigate their situations so thoroughly. The reason *junshu* and *lieshu* garnered so much attention was because of what they symbolized (the notion of a "good death" for the revolution and the prestige of the CCP and PLA) and what they *did* in response to their sense of unappreciated sacrifices. From the mid-1950s until 1965, evidence suggests that martyr and military families, but especially the latter, took an active role in trying to secure promised benefits, and when these did not materialize in ways that satisfied them, they attempted to secure their sons' early discharge from the army. According to an investigation in Qingpu, "the absolute majority" (*jueda duoshu*) of *junshu* and *lieshu* "do not know anything" about the war in Vietnam, were afraid of a relative's dying, and "particularly do not understand why sons have to go to the army because 'war is unavoidable.'" Some were so afraid of a "glorious" sacrifice that they could not sleep or eat and lacked energy to go to work.[160] Some were in even more desperate straits. Like their veteran counterparts, some *junshu* and *lieshu* committed suicide. Since these activities could not be kept entirely secret (jumping in a well in a village, for example), military and civilian officials became highly concerned about PLA readiness and morale in the event of a conflict—concerns which later proved justified during the PRC's misadventure in Vietnam in 1979. These officials left behind a paper trail that is reasonably easy to follow in the 1950s but unmistakably clear in the 1960s.

The Communist victory and the end of the Korean War appear to have been the catalyst for the initial wave of letters to sons in the PLA. Communist Party propaganda relentlessly promoted the ideas that the CCP was victorious in its wars against the Japanese, the Nationalists, and the Americans during the Korean War. Living in a population that was already war weary, many *junshu* understood these victories to mean that wars were over, the army would demobilize, and their sons would return. In early 1953 in Qingpu, for instance, *junshu* spoke of "peace" because "the revolution was successful" and demanded to know why their sons and husbands were not home yet.[161] During that year in Penglai District in Shanghai, *junshu* confronted officials, asking them, "The campaign to 'Resist America and Support Korea' has been victorious, so why isn't my son home yet?" Some did more than ask. To the consternation of officials (who intercepted these letters before they reached the front), some *junshu* "wrote letters to their sons instructing them to come home."[162] Others merely threatened to write: "If the government continues to deny me aid, I'll write my son in the army and tell him to come home!" one father warned.[163]

These demands intensified in the 1960s. The economic crises engendered by the failure of the Great Leap Forward played a role, but the lack of respect and gratitude also figured prominently. For instance, in 1962, a Civil Affairs report noted instances of military and martyr families writing their sons in the army asking them to come home "because they are not respected, are depressed, and their economic difficulties are not resolved."[164] In 1963, an Interior Ministry report noted that in some areas there were "very many *lieshu*, *junshu*, and disabled veterans who complained that they had not received enough work points" and, because of this, wrote letters to the army requesting the early release of their sons.[165] According to documentation that was provided to the Shanghai Bureau of Civil Affairs by a PLA unit in 1963, two companies in a battalion that included 17 soldiers from the Shanghai suburbs "continuously received letters or telegrams from their families asking them to come home; in one company they received three telegrams in a single day, and all said, 'Mom's critically ill; hope you can return quickly.'" The unit, worried about the rising pile of telegrams, dispatched someone to see if this was indeed the case. Their investigation revealed that all the mothers were healthy but that they were suffering financially, owing to inadequate aid. They had decided to write only when "they could no longer contain their anger."[166] These letters were not without consequence: in Qingpu, "problems with financial assistance" led to soldiers who secured leave from the army but "did not return for a long time."[167]

Reports such as these led higher-level officials to severely cut back on all "preferential treatment aid" other than to the neediest families, which essentially transformed preferential aid into welfare. In Qingpu, a report from October 1965 indicated that this effort provoked fierce resistance. One *junshu*, Chen Silin, was a party branch secretary charged with enforcing this policy but was bitter about the notion of serving the country for free. Chen went to the township (commune) government to complain, saying, "If I don't get anything, I'll die with my eyes wide open!" (a reference to either those who died of starvation or being very angry). He then took four other *junshu* families who were being cut from the rolls and went to the county party committee to complain that the commune was not being fair (*gongdao*). Eventually, he appeared to calm down and spoke at a meeting of military martyr families in which he expressed support for the policy, but after the meeting he told other families that he would not allow his sons to be drafted. "To escape the storm" of recruitment, he and some others "sent their sons of military age to Sheshan Commune in nearby Songjiang County to work as unskilled labor." This had a "very bad influence on recruitment work," the report noted dimly.[168]

Anti-war sentiment further complicated recruitment efforts. Unlike the gung ho activists who came into communities spreading war propaganda, many *junshu* were worried about their sons and preferred that they return home. One said, "It's best not to go to war and let my son come home alive and well."[169] Others looked at their sons' photographs and cried or made their way to army bases to implore them to get out before the war began.[170] Although propaganda and "civil religion"–type activities during the early 1960s and Cultural Revolution were supposed to rectify this, problems remained. In rural Shandong (circa 1960), memorial parks, statues, halls, and grave sites were widely neglected and, in some cases, used for other purposes, such as raising pigs; some martyr graves had washed away or were destroyed during construction projects because they "were mistaken for ancient relics." Even in counties that provided many PLA soldiers, there were few commemorative activities. (In the United States, veterans and widow organizations usually tend to these tasks.)[171] Elsewhere, memorial sites were used for offices, warehouses, and even entertainment centers.[172] In May 1966, in what strikes me as a telling image about the course of the Chinese Revolution, Civil Affairs offices in Shanghai received irate letters from martyr families when they organized a pilgrimage to the Hongqiao Martyr Shrine and the assembled *lieshu* noticed that "everything was misplaced and disorganized, and there were even some so-called Guomindang martyrs there mixed in with the rest."[173] One can only wonder what martyr families were thinking when, 30 years later (1994), the Yuhuatai Martyrs' Cemetery in Nanjing was leased for a dog show.[174]

Tears flowed, letters were posted, and army bases were visited in the Beijing area during these years as well. In a 1962 report, Beijing Civil Affairs officials noted that some martyr and military families were frequent visitors to government offices to request more assistance and that "some had even written to the army or asked the government's permission to let their son out early."[175] The reasons for these requests emerge more clearly in a 1963 handwritten report about military families in Beijing's Dongcheng District. When he was interviewed by officials, one soldier's father "cried for over an hour, requesting that his son return home." This father, a driver, was particularly distraught because his wife had died and he was raising three children without enough time or money (he was in debt); he also had a very hard time with tasks that his wife had fulfilled, like sewing and looking after the children when he was at work. According to the report, his son had written home 60 times during the year "because he was very worried about his family (*dian ji*)." But letters also flowed in the other direction. Some *junshu* in Dongcheng were extremely distraught that their sons were in the army and "frequently wrote them pleading with them to come home early." One *junshu* had 11 people in her family with a total income of 170 yuan. Even though her family's income was deemed to be "not lower than ordinary urbanites'," the report noted, "She repeatedly requested that the officials [who interviewed her] promise that they would intervene to get her son out early." Another *junshu* wrote her son, "Your father's gravely ill, please come home quickly," even though her husband had already recovered from his illness. She also tried, without success, to get neighborhood and Civil Affairs officials to provide her with false documentation to this effect. Other worried families gathered *en masse* (parents, uncles, aunts) and made their way to remote army bases to see their soldier, but military bases had great difficulty accommodating all of them.[176]

Although I have not been able to gain access to archives in far poorer regions, it would stand to reason that there was even less enthusiasm for military service in these areas because of the uncompensated burdens that fell on military families and the dearth of public support. Some evidence for this comes from reports and investigations of *junshu* and *lieshu* who committed suicide, a phenomenon that can be documented in detail in the early and mid-1950s and probably persisted into the 1960s. For instance, a 1953 report from Shandong mentioned suicides "among some military and martyr families" because of financial problems that "were not solved."[177] A 1955 report on PLA wives' suicides in Shanxi, Zhejiang, and Jiangsu provinces divulged widespread abuse and neglect. In Shangzhang Village in Zhejiang Province, for example, a soldier's wife surnamed Zhou had six people in her household and they were entirely dependent on agricultural income. But because Zhou's parents were shopkeepers, she had difficulty farming; moreover, she was often ill with tuberculosis. According to the investigation, Zhou's family had been hungry for more than a year, despite government welfare payments and her inclusion in the *daigeng* (substitute tilling) program. To get by, Zhou stole rice and other food from her mutual aid team, angering other peasants; officials harshly reprimanded her. When her children went outside, they were ridiculed by other children. In 1955, she threw herself into a river and died.[178] In Henan Province in 1954, suicides resulted from the violations of soldier's marriages that began this chapter. One PLA wife was raped by a township-level cadre and committed suicide by hanging after no one was charged or apprehended; another *junshu* died after self-inducing an abortion after a rape. After her daughter-in-law's death, the soldier's mother "died of anger" (*qisi*).[179] How it was possible to assess that someone died of anger without an autopsy is not clear, but the report was probably not far off the mark.

In this chapter we have seen that many military families, as well as those designated as "family members of revolutionary martyrs," often shared veterans' perceptions that their sacrifices were unappreciated by both officials and ordinary citizens and that there was little sense of a nation "united in gratitude," to use Melissa Stockdale's phrase. While the state promoted veterans' virtues to the public and to its own rank-and-file cadres, there is little evidence that they were seen in this light. Even though funds were provided by the Center, they were often inadequate. Moreover, money, which the state often represented as a form of "distributive justice" or "doing right" by way of *junshu* and *lieshu*,[180] could not substitute for the harsh or indifferent attitudes and bureaucratic processes that accompanied its provision. For many, "preferential treatment aid" became a form of welfare, and its recipients experienced the sort of dependency, pity, and derision that welfare inspired among the general public and the low-level officials distributing it. For others, state aid and propaganda created a sense of entitlement, or what state officials called "prideful arrogance," a complaint that we have also seen in accounts of healthy and disabled veterans.[181] Whether the public pitied or hated them, military dependents and martyr families were unlikely to receive the respect they thought they earned absent a more general consensus in the state and society that they were worthy of their status and that the causes and institutions they represented were highly legitimate. If there had been a greater consensus about the legitimacy of the CCP, the very meaning of the revolution and wars, and the role of the PLA in society and the wars fought over the years, officials probably would have tempered their remarks and ordinary people would have lent them more assistance, not only out of pity. Raping vulnerable women, violating soldiers' marriages, and issuing highly critical comments toward women who have lost husbands and sons do not strike me as meeting even a low threshold of respect for martial-based contributions to the state, state propaganda about the glorious role of the PLA and the CCP in Chinese history notwithstanding.

Although these findings might seem counterintuitive, some of the evidence from other chapters suggest that they are not all that surprising. In Chapters 2 and 5, we noted that veterans' rise in status—in terms of both their identity and concrete benefits—has generally been associated with the formation of strong and feisty interest groups, fraternal organizations, and ties with other supportive segments of civil society and parts of the state. In China, military dependents and family members of revolutionary martyrs had "representatives" and "committees" (much like veterans), but these were weak, did not have a committed membership, met only infrequently, and could not serve as a counterweight to their detractors. Where military families and widows have had more influence in society has usually been in the context of organizations that successfully linked such concepts as family, sacrifice, and citizenship to nationalism and patriotism. In Japan after WWII, for example, some war widows joined women's political groups "in an effort to define their own interests" when these did not dovetail with the state's; the Japan Association of War Bereaved Families (which was led by fathers of dead soldiers) has been a very successful (and politically conservative) pressure group that "was able to compete equally with other interest groups for state support."[182] In the United States after WWI, such organizations as the American War Mothers

Organizations

and the Gold Star Mothers argued that their service to the nation as mothers of the war dead "entitled them to a special claim on the nation." (The former favored universal military service.) The "Gold Star pilgrimage" to European battlefields from 1931 to 1933 "affirmed for its participants and the larger society that those who died for their country in Europe had fought for a noble cause."[183] In Israel, after the Yom Kippur War, war widows gained more clout (and rights) when they organized a "Widows Organization" annexed to Yad Labanim, the umbrella organization of families who lost a son in war but which was dominated by soldiers' parents, whose interests often diverged from the spouses; in 1991 they broke of completely.[184] The Daughters of the American Revolution, the largest hereditary patriotic organization in the United States, has been at the forefront of efforts to promote patriotic education (through the schools, parades, and other civic rituals) as well as support for veterans and the military.[185] After September 11, 2001, many widows of firefighters and other victims banded together to make sure that the Bush administration investigated the causes of the 9/11 terrorist attacks and that the memory of their loved ones would be properly commemorated.[186] Given that the PRC has consistently refused to allow the establishment of veterans or military families and martyr organizations similar to those in the United States, Russia, Japan, and other countries, it should not be all that surprising that the status of military personnel frequently is fragile and that patriotism and nationalism are rather hollow sentiments in China.

If my argument is correct that the state, despite many propaganda campaigns and claims of victorious and legitimate wars, failed to convince people that veterans' and soldiers' families were deserving of respect, what would happen to veterans if the state prosecuted a war in which there was no victory and the PLA was delegitimized? How would veterans fare if campaigns, which at least tried to convince the public that they were worthy of support, were stopped, and if many jobs in the state sector that some were able to obtain were lost to industrial restructuring and the introduction of market forces? How would veterans respond to continued affronts to their sense of status and rights? I take these issues up in the next chapter, which deals with veterans in the post-Mao period. Much like its predecessor, the post-Mao era was also ushered in with war, only this time against its Asian neighbor, Vietnam.

NOTES

1. SMA B168-1-223 (1964), 13.
2. Ibid.
3. Ibid., 14.

4. Ibid., 13–14.

5. SMA B168-1-132, 24–25.

6. Ibid., 24.

7. Ibid. In Yuanping County in Shanxi Province, a soldier's wife was raped and gave birth to the rapist's child. The distraught husband sought a divorce and filed a complaint against the responsible official. In other cases, the community conspired against soldiers. In Shandong, villagers sent "poison letters" about their wives and fiancées "to instigate conflict between the two" or stole letters posted by the soldiers "which led the relationship to deteriorate" (pp. 24–25).

8. Ibid., 28.

9. Ibid., 29–30. In contrast, Friedman, Pickowicz, and Selden argue in *Revolution, Resistance and Reform* that "infidelity to soldiers was treated harshly" (p. 183).

10. Twenty-four were cadres at the sub-village level, 11 were village cadres, and 4 were township-level officials. Only one had bad class status.

11. Ibid., 34.

12. Ibid., 38.

13. SMA B168-1-645 (1959), 41–42.

14. QA 48-2-73 (1955), 45.

15. Chuxiong Prefectural Archives (CXA) 16-B1-12, 58.

16. DDA 11-7-89 (1954), 52.

17. CXA 11-77-14B-1, 22.

18. Ibid.

19. DDA 11-7-405 (1963), 21.

20. Victor Nee, "Between Center and Locality," 241.

21. Chang-tai Hung, "Cult of the Red Martyr," 282. He calls it "a core element in the CCP's political culture in the 1950s."

22. In reports, these two populations were often difficult to disentangle. Some referred only to *junshu*, others to *liejunshu* (family members of soldiers and martyrs) or only to *lieshu*. In my translations, I remained faithful to the original wordings.

23. For similar problems identifying pension beneficiaries in the United States after the Civil War (especially among African-Americans, who usually lacked formal documents), see Megan McClintock, "Civil War Pensions and the Reconstruction of Union Families," 472–74; Richard Reid, "Government Policy, Prejudice, and the Experience of Black Civil War Soldiers and Their Families," 376, 389–91. Because so many people could not furnish proof of their relationship to the soldier, bureaucrats became tolerant of pension claims that did not meet the official standard.

24. SMA B168-1-596, 85–86.

25. SMA B168-1-616 (1954), 42–44. In a 1950 summary report, roughly 50 percent of "preferential treatment aid" was distributed to those associated with the GMD. See SMA B168-1-596, 51.

26. SMA B168-1-616 (1954), 43.

27. SMA B168-1-600 (1950), 77.

28. SMA B168-1-616 (1954), 43.

29. DDA 11-7-74, 26–27.

30. SMA B168-1-617, 13.

31. SMA B168-1-596 (1950), 57.

32. SMA B168-1-616 (1954), 9.

33. SMA B168-1-609 (1953), 4–5.

34. SMA B168-1-616 (1954), 46.

35. SMA B1-2-850 (1953), 13.

36. DDA 11-7-? (1955), 116–17, 119, (final digits omitted in original).

37. SMA B168-1-609 (1953), 22.

38. As noted by Michael Lipsky, "street-level bureaucrats have considerable discretion in determining the nature, amount, and quality of benefits and sanctions provided by their agencies." See *Street-Level Bureaucracy: Dilemmas of the Individual in Public Service*, 13.

39. SMA B168-1-609 (1953), 22.

40. Megan McClintock, "Binding Up the Nation's Wounds: Nationalism, Civil War Pensions, and American Families, 1861–1890," (Ph.D. dissertation, Department of History, Rutgers University, 1994), 191.

41. SMA B168-1-609, 14, 16.

42. Ibid., 16.

43. SMA B168-1-565, 7.

44. SA A20-1-81, 18.

45. SMA B168-1-617 (1954), 16.

46. SMA B168-1-609 (1953), 5. This certainly was not unique to China. As noted by Martha Derthick in her study of the Social Security Administration in the United States, tensions between administrators and clients "were endemic to a means-tested program." See *Agency under Stress*, 186.

47. SMA B168-1-609 (1953), 17, 22.

48. DDA 11-7-405 (1963), 20–22. There is some historical precedent for this kind of protest. During the Qing dynasty, a Chinese Catholic priest recorded the following in his diary on May 31, 1748: "The widowed wives of soldiers fallen in the [Jinchuan] war, who had not received the stipend owed to them, all came in mourning to the prefectural offices, complaining loudly with reproaches and insults of the injustices they had borne. The officials consoled them so they would not arouse tumult and sedition in the city." I thank Robert Entenmann and Elizabeth Perry for this reference.

49. SMA B168-1-609, 22.

50. SMA B168-1-619 (1955), 8.

51. SMA B168-1-609 (1953), 24.

52. *Minzheng jianbao*, October 11, 1956, 69.

53. *Minzheng jianbao*, October 22, 1956, 74.

54. *Minzheng jianbao*, October 11, 1956, 68.

55. SMA B168-1-632 (1957), 79.

56. SMA B168-1-596, 56.

57. SMA B168-1-616 (1955), 9.

58. SMA B168-1-616 (1954), 45.

59. The phrase was *geming yijing chenggong, laozi keyi xiangfu*. See QA 48-2-53 (1953), 31, 36.

60. SA A20-1-109 (1954), 68.
61. DDA 11-7-421 (1962), 18.
62. DDA 11-7-400 (1963), 4.
63. SMA B168-1-598 (1950), 31.
64. SMA B242-1-573 (1953), 85; SMA B242-1-574 (1953), 94–95.
65. SMA B242-1-573 (1953), 85.
66. SMA B168-1-609 (1953), 15.
67. Ibid., 22.
68. SMA B168-1-616 (1954), 6.
69. SMA B168-1-617 (1954), 16.
70. SMA B168-1-596 (1950), 58; SA A20-1-109 (1954), 68; SMA B168-1-559 (1959), 8; SMA B168-1-619, 33.
71. SMA B168-1-609, 13; B168-1-596, 54.
72. QA 48-2-46, unpaginated.
73. SMA B168-1-609, 20.
74. Ibid., 13.
75. DDA 11-7-400 (1963), 6.
76. SA A20-1-81, 18.
77. Ibid., 62.
78. SA A20-1-109, 67.
79. Chen Yung-fa, *Making Revolution*, 316.
80. DDA 11-7-89 (1954), 144.
81. QA 48-2-46 (1952), n.p.
82. SMA B168-1-623 (1956), 51.
83. SMA B168-1-651, 20–21; QA 48-2-168 (1963), 43.
84. SMA B168-1-570 (1962), 48.
85. QA 48-2-145 (1961), 18; QA 48-2-168 (1963), 70.
86. Cited in MacFarquhar, *Origins of the Cultural Revolution, Vol. 3*, 288.
87. SMA B168-1-571 (1962), 169.
88. DDA 11-7-364, 46.
89. SMA B168-1-622 (1956), 87.
90. QA 48-2-46 (1951), unpaginated.
91. DDA 11-7-89 (1954), 150.
92. SA A20-1-81 (1953), 18.
93. SA A20-1-29 (1951), 58.
94. Ibid.; SA A20-1-81 (1953), 18.
95. DDA 11-7-? (1955), 118–19 (final digits omitted in original copy).
96. QA 48-1-19, 4.
97. QA 48-1-15, 4.
98. QA 48-2-64 (1954), 30.
99. QA 48-2-46 (1952), 34.
100. Ibid., 76.
101. QA 48-2-46 (1951), 33.
102. QA 48-1-13, 9.
103. QA 48-1-15, 2.

104. QA 48-1-19, 4.

105. QA 48-1-15, 4; QA 48-2-56 (1953), 38.

106. QA 48-2-46 (1952), 76; QA 48-2-64, 28; QA 48-2-46 (1951), unpaginated; QA 48-2-73 (1955), 45.

107. SA A20-1-81 (1953), 18; QA 48-2-73 (1955), 45.

108. QA 48-2-56 (1953), 39.

109. QA 48-1-13 (1951), 11; QA 48-2-73 (1955), 45.

110. SMA B168-1-616 (1954), 10.

111. QA 48-2-64, 28.

112. Ibid.

113. QA 48-2-27 (1951), 9.

114. QA 48-2-64 (1954), 28–29.

115. QA 48-2-73 (1955), 44–45.

116. DDA 11-7-? (1955), 119 (final digits omitted in original copy).

117. SMA B168-1-651 (1960), 19–20.

118. SMA B168-1-570, 12; SMA B168-1-565 (1962), 9.

119. SMA B168-1-570 (1962), 46–47.

120. QA 48-2-168 (1963), 43; QA 48-2-168, 28; QA 48-2-190 (1964), 6; QA 48-2-211 (1965), 72.

121. SA A20-1-332 (1962), 43, 46. However, in 1960 "in some areas," *junshu*, Level 3 disabled veterans, and old and sick veterans received no aid whatsoever. This was said to have been rectified in 1961.

122. Here there are similarities to the implementation of Supplemental Security Income (SSI) in the United States. According to Derthick, central-level officials "failed to foresee how field staffs would respond and what the consequences of their attempts to respond would be." See Derthick, *Agency under Stress*, 60.

123. QA 48-2-168 (1963), 43.

124. QA 48-2-211 (1965), 72, 74.

125. SMA B168-1-664 (1963), 19; SMA B168-1-565 (1962), 11.

126. QA 48-2-211, 67–68.

127. See Patricia Thornton, *Disciplining the State: Virtue, Violence and State-Making in Modern China*, 44, 93, 129, 131.

128. SMA B168-1-651 (1960), 21.

129. SA A20-1-109 (1954), 67; SA A20-1-81 (1953), 62; SA A20-1-332 (1962), 46; SMA B168-1-664 (1963), 18.

130. DDA 11-7-89 (1955), 147; SA A20-1-109 (1954), 68. In three districts in the Shanghai area circa 1954, 32 percent of military and martyr families were in mutual aid teams. See SMA B168-1-616, 5.

131. SMA B168-1-625 (1956), 41. For more evidence on the vulnerability of *junshu* and *lieshu*, see Friedman, Pickowicz, and Selden, *Revolution, Resistance and Reform in Rural China*, 19, 82.

132. QA 48-2-168, 43. This was also a source of friction between veterans and the state on Taiwan. The Veterans Administration worried that "idle *rongmin* [veterans] seeking assistance again and again" would "foster a psychology of dependence on the state." See Yu-Wen Fan, "Becoming a Civilian," 84.

133. SA A20-1-29 (1951), 58–59.

134. DDA 11-7-89, 145.

135. SMA B1-2-850 (1953), 12.

136. I have not found Zhabei District figures for 1953, but a 1956 document places the *lieshu* and *junshu* population at 1,000 households (5,000 people). See SMA B168-1-556, 11.

137. SMA B168-1-609 (1953), 21. This was not the only time this happened. In 1960, investigators found Interior Ministry documents locked in a drawer of the Jing'an District section chief's desk. He took them out "only when he had to issue a report." See SMA B168-1-651, 13.

138. *Minzheng jianbao*, November 19, 1956, 80.

139. SMA B168-1-644 (1960), 5, 10.

140. *Anhui sheng zhi: minzheng zhi*, 101.

141. SA A20-1-225 (1958), 43.

142. SA A20-1-295 (1960), 9.

143. SMA B168-1-625 (1956), 39. For the calculation of living expenses in 1956, see SMA B168-1-632, 83.

144. SMA B168-1-655 (1960), 2.

145. SMA B168-1-650, 31.

146. SMA B168-1-565, 9.

147. See Melissa Stockdale, "United in Gratitude: Honoring Soldiers and Defining the Nation in Russia's Great War," 461. Stockdale cites the work of Emily Pyle, "Village Social Relations and the Reception of Soldier's Family Aid Policy" (Ph.D. dissertation, University of Chicago, 1997). According to Stockdale, this legislation "created an obligation of the state to its defenders that had not previously existed in imperial Russia . . . what was being created was clearly a right of citizenship: *the universality of the military obligation required from the state a similarly universal and equal provision of aid to the family of the mobilized soldiers*." Emphasis mine.

148. DDA 11-7-400, 3–4.

149. QA 48-2-190 (1964), 8–9.

150. SMA B168-1-596, 59–61.

151. See Hung, "Cult of the Red Martyr," 291.

152. SMA B168-1-609, 4; also see Hung, "Cult of the Red Martyr," 291–92.

153. QA 48-2-53, unpaginated.

154. SMA B168-1-616, 9.

155. QA 48-1-13 (1951), 11.

156. DDA 11-7-89 (1955), 147.

157. SMA B168-1-565, 13; Also SMA B168-1-571, 169.

158. SMA B168-1-565, 8–9.

159. Ibid., 9.

160. QA 48-1-211 (1965), 35.

161. QA 48-2-53 (1953), 31.

162. B168-1-616 (1954), 46.

163. Ibid., 45.

164. SMA B168-1-571 (1962), 169.

165. SMA B168-1-664 (1963), 2.

166. Ibid., 19.

167. QA 48-2-145 (1961), 18.

168. QA 48-2-211 (1965), 74–76.

169. Ibid.

170. QA 48-2-211 (1965), 64; QA 48-2-211 (1965), 35.

171. SA A20-1-295, 76.

172. Hung, "Cult of the Red Martyr," 303.

173. SMA B168-2-131, 41.

174. Hung, "Cult of the Red Martyr," 303.

175. DDA 11-7-364 (1962), 46.

176. DDA 11-7-400, 7, 4.

177. SA A20-1-81, 62.

178. DDA 11-7-? (1955), 128–29.

179. DDA 11-7-89, 52.

180. In reports, most of the "good news" section was full of numbers and figures, generally of amounts allocated (not necessarily funds spent or received).

181. A strong sense of entitlement was also noted among military dependents in Russia during WWII. Some took part in wartime subsistence riots. See Stockdale, "United in Gratitude," 463.

182. Franziska Seraphim, *War Memory and Social Politics in Japan, 1945–2005*, 12, 74, 84.

183. G. Kurt Piehler, "The War Dead and the Gold Star: American Commemoration of the First World War," 177–78.

184. Shamgar-Handelman, *Israeli War Widows: Beyond the Glory of Heroism*, 23–26. They also received significant support from the media.

185. On the Daughters of the American Revolution (DAR), see Barbara Truesdell, "Exalting U.S. Ness: Patriotic Rituals of the Daughters of the American Revolution," 273–89.

186. See Andrew Jacobs, "Trade Center Widows Lobby for Independent Inquiry," *New York Times*, June 12, 2002.

8

Salt in the Wounds: Veterans in the Reform Era, 1978–2007

In the summer of 2004, I boarded a flight to Shanghai, where I would be staying a couple of days before traveling to my main destination—the city of Jinan, home of the Shandong Provincial Archives. Until then, my research had been based in the Beijing and Shanghai areas, so I was interested in both increasing the geographical diversity of the study and including more materials from a province that had a CCP "base area" during World War II and which supplied the PLA with many recruits (and thus veterans) throughout the history of the People's Republic. I thought that I had prepared the groundwork in advance. In the spring, Foreign Affairs officials at the Shanghai Academy of Social Sciences (SASS) had contacted their counterparts in Shandong and at the Provincial Archives, and they consented to my visit. For this reason, I was a bit unprepared for the telephone call to my hotel room the evening of my arrival. After an awkward hesitation, SASS officials regretfully informed me that they had just received an urgent call from the Shandong Provincial Archives requesting that I not show up. Their materials about veterans were "scattered and could not be organized in time."

A bit miffed that I received this update only *after* arriving in China, I (perhaps foolishly) decided to go, anyway. My plan was to go to the archive (in the Provincial CCP compound) every morning for at least a week and request materials that were officially declared "open" until someone either took pity on me or refused to let me in. After an uncomfortable reception, materials began to trickle in: a government bulletin from 1957; a case of a disabled soldier trying to get benefits (see Chapter 6); and reports of veterans moving out of the province and the "substitute cultivation" program, most of which I was not allowed to photocopy. After several days of watching me struggle through some of the materials, archive officials seemed to warm up. Some came down to chat, take photographs, or ask questions about my salary. After a week, a mid-level official came down to apologize for the meager pickings and cold reception. They had no choice: the archive director had been ordered to limit my access to materials about veterans. He also explained the reason: between the spring and summer of 2004, veteran protests had erupted all over Shandong. My research subject had become too "hot" politically, and higher-level officials did not want to be held responsible for any materials exposing their problems.

Having read accounts of Shandong veterans in the 1950s and 1960s from some other sources, I was not all that surprised by this bit of information, and the more I thought about it, the more I realized that the circumstances surrounding veterans in the reform period were eerily parallel to those in the earlier period. Like the early 1950s, the reform period was ushered in on the heels of little-understood, ungainly named foreign wars ("Resist America, Support Korea" in 1950, then the "Counterattack in Self-Defense on the China–Vietnam Border" in 1979) and after years of domestic political strife (the Civil War between 1945 and 1949 and then the Cultural Revolution). As in the earlier period, veterans were disgorged into an economy undergoing rapid, unpredictable transformation and into a political system that rested on crumbling foundations in terms of legitimacy and which did not allow the formation of veterans organizations. As was the case in the early 1950s, urban intellectuals joined the CCP in droves and quickly occupied its top ranks over the next two decades, replacing "good-class" but less educated officials who rose to power during the Cultural Revolution; by the end of the 20th century, "technocrats" educated in engineering at Qinghua University in Beijing dominated the CCP.[1] And like the 1950s and 1960s, when Chinese were "asked" to sign "patriotic compacts" and listen to propaganda about the wartime heroism of the PLA and CCP, in the reform period state propaganda and cultural ministries have praised veterans' "glorious" contributions, invested millions in "patriotic education," sponsored the publication of "nationalist" authors' creeds against the United States or Japan, and sometimes bused students to protest sites. Unsurprisingly, these activities, as well as the occasional outbursts of Chinese soccer fans and fanciful statements by some intellectuals about China's becoming the world's "benevolent leader," have produced a cottage industry of foreign scholarship on the "rise of Chinese nationalism" in the reform era—not unlike some scholarship on the rise of the CCP and the "patriotic" surge during the Korean War.[2] In their explanation of why access to materials on veterans would be restricted, Shandong officials confirmed what earlier generations of provincial officials have known since 1949: veterans and their problems are a source of fear and migraine-size headaches, even as they are effusively praised. Veterans have organized to try to protect their status and interests and to survive in the new "socialist market economy," and they have been at the core of numerous, ongoing protests throughout the reform period. China's inability to accommodate veterans' sense of elevated status (and desire for respect and appreciation) based on their military experiences, I suggest, has had wide-ranging repercussions on the stability of the state.

Despite the prevalence, ferocity, and political significance of veteran protests, scholars of China in the reform period have not paid nearly enough attention to their dynamics and causes.[3] This relative neglect is particularly odd given the gargantuan scale of demobilization of the reform-era PLA and the aftershocks it has sent throughout the polity, but it is hardly surprising; the study of demobilization, like that of other military-related topics, has not received its due share of scholarly attention in other fields, either (for reasons discussed in Chapter 1). Yitzhak Shichor placed the number of demobilized soldiers at roughly 750,000 between 1982 and 1984[4] and estimated a more recent count at 1.7 million between 1985 and 2005, noting "ample evidence of dissatisfaction" among them,[5] but piecing together fragmentary data from the Chinese press between 1982 and 2001 suggests larger numbers. In 1983, for example, Xinhua News Agency reported that "in recent years" Civil Affairs departments around the country had made arrangements for "the placement of more than six million demobilized military service personnel," among whom "most . . . are former peasants."[6] I have not seen this number repeated elsewhere, but even if it was exaggerated, the true total was surely higher than 2.5 million. As early as 1984, the CCP Central Committee had authorized the demobilization of one million PLA personnel in the next "2 or 3 years";[7] half of these were resettled in only three provinces: Jiangsu, Hebei, and Hunan.[8] Among the million veterans were roughly 500,000 officers (100,000 officers were discharged in 1985 alone); most were about 40 years old and had senior middle school education.[9] A decade later, Willy Wo-lap Lam, a Hong Kong reporter with excellent contacts in Beijing, filed a story noting that "at a secret enlarged meeting of the Central Military Commission on December 18 and 19, the top brass also agreed to implement the long-stalled decision to demobilize up to half a million soldiers,"[10] but in 1995—the same year that the state mounted a massive propaganda campaign to commemorate "China's victory" in the Anti-Japanese War—Xinhua reported that "in China an average of 600,000 soldiers are demobilized every year, and need to be resettled by local governments."[11] This higher number was confirmed in January 2001, when Xinhua reported that 2.02 million soldiers had retired "between 1998 and 2000,"[12] almost double the Kivlehan-Wise figure for the entire two decades of the reform era; this number is also supported by other reports noting "several hundred thousand service members" leaving the PLA in the winter of 2001.[13] Even if these numbers merely suggest a range of more than three million, they are still impressive enough to merit an entire book, not merely one chapter or article; if history (or the war in Iraq) is any guide, these veterans did not, and could not, quietly dissolve or "melt" into the population after their discharge. How did they react to their discharge in the reform period? How similar is veteran activism in the reform period to the decades that preceded it? What explains the widespread dissatisfaction among them, and what has been done to ameliorate their conditions?

This chapter takes our account of veterans up to the present. Its central finding is that veterans' status remains as problematic as, if not more than, it was in the 1950s and 1960s, even though so much has changed in China since 1978. In areas that matter to them most—where they can live, their conditions of employment, marriage, and "everyday" treatment by officials and civilians—veterans, usually justifiably, have found a great deal to complain about, even in this purportedly "nationalistic" era. Veterans still do not have a national organization or a statute remotely comparable to the "GI Bill" in the United States. There is little evidence that the PRC government has sought to learn from more successful foreign examples in veteran administration and demobilizations, in stark contrast to their enthusiasm for learning about Western and Asian businesses, stock markets, pension programs, legislatures, police work, sciences, and other fields. Even worse, from the veterans' perspective, there is scant evidence of public sympathy among elites, a sentiment that one might expect to emerge in the context of an army (or any other social experience) that brought together, in large numbers for an extensive period, members of all social classes.[14] "Controlled polarization" of the population, long a staple of CCP rule, remains strongly in place.

LOSERS

Veterans demobilized after the end of the Cultural Revolution (1976) and the war against Vietnam (1979) faced challenges as daunting as their early 1950s counterparts. Like civilians, many had been victimized during the Cultural Revolution or neglected owing to the breakdown of the Civil Affairs Resettlement Division. In other cases, Red Guards and others ransacked Civil Affairs offices and destroyed personal dossiers, leaving veterans (and martyr families) hard-pressed to prove they were not counterrevolutionaries but actually deserved "preferential treatment."[15] Owing to Mao's use of the PLA to "support the left" in the Cultural Revolution's most radical phases, and then to restore order by force during the campaign to "Cleanse the Class Ranks" in 1968 (a politicization that had not been initiated by the PLA[16]), veterans from that period could not even hope to symbolize a cause that was widely seen as right and just. The highly public and political roles of the PLA in what amounted to a civil war resulted in a blow to its remaining prestige. As early as the mid-1970s, Deng Xiaoping, China's future "paramount leader," allegedly criticized the PLA as bloated (the PLA grew by more than 85 percent between the mid-1960s and the mid-1970s[17]), inefficient, factionalized, and wasteful and later did his best to reassert total civilian control over it, considering it a conservative, anti-reform group determined to protect narrow interests.[18] Adding insult to injury, the 29-day border war against Vietnam, a country that had benefited from China's support since the early 1950s during its anti-imperialist wars against France and United States, ended poorly from a military perspective[19] and, given its short duration, was not accompanied by a mass campaign to educate the public. (PLA morale, unsurprisingly, given what we have seen about the treatment of veterans, was said to have been problematic during the war.[20]) Although the PRC claimed victory (as did Vietnam), it is doubtful that many Chinese, veterans included, took pride in the war's results, let alone understood why Chinese would want to kill Vietnamese (just like many were confused about why they would kill Americans in Korea after the United States was allied with China during WWII).[21] In any event, most were preoccupied with trying to restore their lives after the chaos of the Cultural Revolution.[22] Even worse, in the list of the "Four Modernizations" that ushered in the reform period, the military figured last (after agriculture, industry and science, and technology), signaling that the Center had more important priorities than the care of PLA personnel. As we have seen, even in the pre-reform period, this was never really considered prestigious "political work."

It did not take long for veterans to voice their discontent in posters in the 1979 Democracy Wall Movement and in more dramatic protests, most of which were documented by European, Japanese, and Hong Kong journalists as well as in relatively obscure PRC news outlets (whose reports were collected by the Nationalists' intelligence agencies and later placed in its archive[23]). On May 8, 1979, for instance, a reporter from Agence France-Presse (AFP) encountered 15 veterans (aged 36–40) staging a quiet, month-long protest outside the PLA's "Civil Division." (In the evenings they slept on the street, and they ate food left on the tables at a state-run mess hall for the indigent.) According to the report, the veterans had served between three and four years and were discharged between 1964 and 1965. They were sent to the countryside and had made their way to Beijing to secure non-agricultural employment. But work was not their only problem. The veterans were all bachelors and feared for their marriage prospects, given their age and skill level. Some had married prior to the Cultural Revolution, but their wives, having expected that their service would lead to higher status, divorced them when they were forced to return to the countryside; they "refused to accept that their husbands had even lower social status than before their military service." During their month-long protest, the veterans had written signs, which they showed to the reporter. The sign of the 40-year-old veteran read "Why join the army if veterans are unemployed after their discharge?" Other signs lamented "No one cares about us; we just wander around on the streets. We're very worried" and "Who will investigate veterans' problems?"[24]

This was not the only sign of veteran discontent in the city. At the Beijing train station, French reporters noticed quite a few big-character posters that veterans had put up. One of these took comic book form, picturing an official talking to a veteran who asked for work. The official's "bubble" said, "Getting you a job is absolutely impossible." Another poster-writer complained, "We wanted to return to our original units, but the leaders forced us to go to the countryside, but in the countryside we were considered criminals."[25] Japanese journalists wandering around the city also noticed "very many" big-character posters written by veterans who had been expelled from their work units after being accused of "taking the capitalist road" during the Cultural Revolution, leaving them in dire poverty. Many had fought against Japan and in the Korean War and were recognized for meritorious service. One poster said "This January Chairman Hua Guofeng instructed the PLA's General Political Department to investigate this matter, but nothing has been done, so our reputations are still tarnished."[26] Two years later, veterans were still protesting the injustices of the Cultural Revolution. In 1981, a reporter from Hong Kong got word of fifty veterans who were staging a quiet protest outside the Ministry of Defense in Beijing to demand the reversal of Cultural Revolution "verdicts" against them and the restoration of their reputations. Most of the veterans were 30–40 years old, but some were closer to 50. On their placards they jotted down their native place and that they had been "suppressed by Jiang Qing and Lin Biao's clique from 1969 to 1975." Like their predecessors in the late 1970s, these veterans also were noted for their orderliness: they were sitting on the ground, wearing straw hats. Public Security allowed them to remain there for two days before dispersing them.[27]

Compared to events in other parts of the country, these Beijing-area demonstrations were tame. Farther away from Beijing, where political controls were looser, veterans' discontent took more violent forms. By some accounts, three Southwest provinces witnessed a large share of these protests, perhaps because many veterans were dispatched there after the war with Vietnam. *Research (Yanjiu zazhi)*, an internally circulated journal, noted that during December 1979, there were six to seven incidents of veteran petitioning (*shangfang*) in the provincial capitals of Chengdu (Sichuan Province), Guiyang (Guizhou), and Kunming (Yunnan), but far more in the country-side. According to Guiyang officials, there were no fewer than 40 separate "incidents" involving veterans, including the posting of big-character posters, small- and large-scale petitioning, and more dramatic protests. Although concentrated in the Southwest, officials suggested that veteran protests were breaking out all over the country and blamed them on the long-standing policy of *yuan ji an zhi*, or refusing to allow veterans to settle in cities after their service (examined in Chapter 2), and the lack of public support for them. As a result, they noted, "Young people do not want to serve, and sol-diers are isolated in society. In the street, people call them 'Big Soldier' (*da bing*), not 'comrade.'"[28]

Reports published in the Hong Kong press provide us with a better look at veterans' discontent in the Southwest as well as the dangers posed to the state when such veterans were able to liaise with each other and other disaffected groups. In 1981, a report pointed to a large-scale outbreak of violence in the three Southwest provinces. These violent incidents brought together roughly 1,000 veterans and youth from minority communities, many of whom suf-fered from desperate poverty and Han discrimination and violence during the Cultural Revolution. Pushed to the edge, the veterans and minorities reportedly destroyed grain storage facilities, as well as trucks and boats that transported grain, before local officials called in reinforcements to suppress them. This was followed by a large manhunt in the railway stations and roads in Sichuan. Railroad workers, generally a good source of information since they travel a lot and hear officials talking, had their theory of what was behind these incidents: "The CCP has sent very many veterans to the Southwest, but because a lot of them don't have any work, they are extremely dissatis-fied and frequently create disturbances (*nao shi*), for many different reasons. CCP cadres have been killed and wounded. On this occasion, they united with minorities, who also can't find jobs, and they have very many problems getting by."[29]

The credibility of this Hong Kong–based report on organized veterans in the Southwest is strengthened by internally circulated reports indicating com-parable developments in other provinces in the same time period. On Hainan Island, several thousand veterans who worked on a farm subordinate to the military district "rebelled" when they read a 1982 State Council document calling for the introduction of a fiscal responsibility system. They allegedly attacked the county party committee, shouted slogans, and denounced the state's "capitalist and revisionist policies" in graffiti.[30] In Shandong, railway stations were also at the center of the action. According to the May 1981 is-sue of *Jiaodong tielu* (Transportation and Railways), during March of that year close to 10,000 veterans had returned to the province after their military service. Dissatisfied because "their post-service positions are worse than the ones they had before joining the PLA and there is very little work for them," veterans organized to find other ways to survive or take revenge; the journal reported 132 "criminal incidents" involving veterans. Railway stations in Jinan and Qingdao were attacked—veterans stole switching lights, signs, and other equipment, which they probably tried to sell on the black market.[31] In Qingdao, ports were raided. They were an especially tempting target since luxury items from abroad moved through them, and port equipment was far more sophisticated than railway station equipment. According to Qingdao's *Gangkou kuaixun* (Port Bulletin), forty veterans were arrested in the spring of 1981 for stealing television sets from a Japanese commercial liner. They also stole materials from a shipyard and ship repair factory and destroyed motors and other expensive equipment. Port officials were worried because the veterans were organized (and probably armed), led by a discharged lieutenant and a staff sergeant.[32]

It is difficult to ascertain how exactly the veterans organized; a good guess would be that they served in the same unit in the army and corresponded after their discharge. However they accomplished this, it was not new; as early as 1951, veterans were capable of staging dramatic forms of collective action, and they continued to organize during the Cultural Revolution. And this organization was not only aimed at the theft or destruction of state property. Discharged in very large numbers to villages whose leaders were not necessarily happy to see them return (and who were often successful using their position to make decent money while veterans were in the army), veterans banded together to protect their interests and status. In a 1980 report in a Hong Kong newspaper, veterans were said to have been engaged in "protests and disturbances" but also formed veterans organizations to fight for reasonable treatment by local authorities. In Zhejiang Province, for example, veterans who returned to villages organized (in December 1980) the "Zhejiang Province United Veterans Federation"; in Xing'an County in Guangxi Province, veterans organized the "Xing'an County Veterans Action Committee," with separate departments (mimicking CCP organization) for organization, propaganda, communication, and security; and in Kunming, veterans formed the "Yunnan Province, Kunming City Action Committee General Headquarters" and the "Negotiating Team of the Disabled Veterans Fighting for Employment Rights." Although based in Kunming, both groups dispatched members to scout out other veterans to boost their organizational strength. According to the analysis in the newspaper, many veterans were in dire straits: some had committed suicide because of depression and their inability to find jobs, especially those that came close to matching their expectations of post-service upward social mobility. The simultaneity of the end of the Cultural Revolution and the initiation of reform-era policies worked to their disadvantage. Because of the Cultural Revolution, veterans had many political enemies in their villages and "could not return" (*huibuqu*), but owing to the "Household Responsibility System," which placed the burden of agricultural production on the household rather than the collective and added to the surplus of agricultural labor, many veterans could not find jobs; even at this early date in the history of the post-1978 demobilization, reports noted some 400,000 veterans who did not have appropriate jobs and had a very hard time surviving.[33]

As this report hints, disabled veterans faced even more challenges than healthy and relatively young veterans (unlike those over the age of 40). Again, this was not new, but the post-reform drive to get rich quickly and the lack of a safety net left many disabled veterans behind and feeling quite vulnerable. In an article in the *Guiyang wanbao* (Guiyang Evening News), a reporter interviewed a public security official regarding a street protest involving 13 disabled veterans and family members (including children) that had taken place on June 13, 1981. Although the official claimed that the disabled veterans—all of whom lived in Provincial Disabled Veterans Homes—were "well cared for" and people "highly respect them," he also admitted that the June 13 protest was not the first time they had protested; it had happened on "many occasions." In most of the incidents, the disabled were protesting ("unreasonably," according to the official) state policies that did not allow the disabled to marry while living at the home, denied urban residence to their family members, and banned their relatives from living with them at the Disabled Veteran Home, even temporarily. Some of the protests got out of hand: the disabled veterans "pulled, grabbed, and yelled at cadres and said irresponsible things." Sometimes they stopped the flow of traffic. In deference to their physical condition, the police classified these protests as conflicts "among the people" and tried to handle them without using force. Those veterans who "hit, captured, and detained policemen," as well as those who "climbed on police cars and refused to get down," however, were forcibly returned to the home, and the protest leaders were arrested.[34]

This sort of protest appears to have been quite widespread in the early to mid-1980s. Some of the strongest evidence about their scope, frequency, and internal dynamics during this period emerged in various media outlets in Hong Kong, whose reporters and residents were permitted to visit their relatives, many of whom lived in nearby Guangdong Province. In 1981, for example, Hong Kong resident Xiang Mulin returned to the city of Zhanjiang to visit his relatives. By chance, one of them was a Vietnam War veteran who was quite knowledgeable about veteran issues and organization, and over the next several months, Xiang wrote up a series of essays on veterans in the province (originally published in *Ming Bao*); these, in turn, were picked up by Nationalist intelligence agents in Hong Kong.[35] Xiang's relative, who had been unemployed since the end of the war, confirmed the broad outline sketched out above. Between 1980 and 1981, he noted, veteran protests had occurred in Fujian, Anhui, Zhejiang, Shandong, Guizhou, Guangxi, and Jiangsu provinces.[36] Veterans had also mounted collective hunger strikes, paraded down streets, and sabotaged state property; not a few tried to commit suicide. Like the multi-provincial protests in the early 1950s and during the Cultural Revolution, Xiang's relative claimed that many of these protests involved "veterans from different areas of the country who had secretly organized." The causes he cited have a déjà vu quality to them. Many protested because they were unable to secure employment after their discharge, and the disabled among them took to the streets because they "could no longer work in agriculture after their return to the village but had not been assigned to any other job, so they are very unhappy."[37]

Xiang Mulin's relative, however, was in a position to provide far more detailed information to his inquiring visitor. Not far from Zhanjiang was Wuchuan County, which had "not a few veterans," probably a result of the fact that the Guangzhou (Canton) Military Region was assigned a key role in the campaign against Vietnam.[38] Only recently, these veterans, as well as others from nearby counties, had established a veterans organization—the "Grieving Hearts Army" (*Xinsang jun*). Its demands, organization, and activities posed a serious threat to the local political establishment, which retaliated very harshly against it.

THE GRIEVING HEARTS ARMY

Although it came to be known as the Grieving Hearts Army (GHA) and its leaders claimed that it was Wuchuan County's veterans organization, the GHA had other names during its brief history. At different stages it was called the "Guangdong Province Veterans Auxiliary Division" and simply the "Veterans Committee." At the peak of its activities, it was said to have had roughly 6,000 members, although this number is impossible to verify. According to Xiang's relative, most veterans in the GHA were peasants who, prior to joining the PLA, lived in areas afflicted by natural disasters in Wuchuan County. Their motivation to join the PLA had been to make more money, get a state-assigned job when they got out, and "forever leave the bitter sea" of the disaster-afflicted countryside. In the middle stage of the Cultural Revolution, when the PLA temporarily gained clout vis-à-vis the civilian wing of the party and Civil Affairs did not function very well, it did get easier for veterans to secure urban employment, or at least not remain in the countryside. In Wuchuan County, "most" of those discharged prior to 1975 were able to move to cities. Some had been sent to Guangzhou and Zhanjiang to work. Because of this, their fellow villagers thought that military service was the way to go.[39]

After the end of the Cultural Revolution and the fall of the so-called "Gang of Four" in 1976, however, the government once again made it more difficult for veterans to secure urban employment and residency rights. This caused great distress among the Wuchuan County veterans. This sense of injustice was felt even more acutely in the early 1980s. Between 1978 and 1981 the young Wuchuan men who did not serve in the army had been able to make good money and build new homes; in contrast, the veterans had received 200–300 renminbi (RMB) in demobilization money, but their families (*jun-shu*) were still hard up because they were short a young man's labor power. Relative poverty and the post-reform policy of ignoring class labels also made it difficult to marry. When young women no longer applied any sort of political criteria for deciding whom to marry, they (and their families) stressed marriage prospects' individual income and their families' resources. The returning veterans, like those before them in the 1950s, struggled to find wives. Even those who had girlfriends or were married before the war might find themselves in a tough predicament upon their return; in one company deployed to Vietnam, twelve men "had gotten divorced or lost their girlfriends before their deployment" because the women were afraid of "being widowed or living with a disabled veteran for the rest of their lives."[40] According to Xiang's relative, "Many veterans felt that they had lost the best years of their lives, and felt cheated and swindled by the government and society. That's why they said their hearts are now grieving (*xin dou sangle*)."[41]

In this state of mind, veterans in the county sought out their comrades-in-arms and in 1980 organized a "Veterans Committee." Their first plan was to organize a petition drive to prod the government to fulfill its promises about their jobs. After presenting several of these to the county government, they realized the government was not going to come to their assistance, and they would not "receive the sympathy or support of the masses" for their demands. It was at this juncture that the veterans decided to use more drastic measures to pressure the government to answer their demands. Meeting secretly, they organized the "Grieving Hearts Army" and established its "command center" in Tangwei Commune. After several hundred of them staged a loud protest at the county seat, the county government dispatched three officers from the People's Armed Police, an auxiliary paramilitary force, to GHA headquarters to arrest its commanders. The veterans anticipated this move: when the PAP officers arrived, they found that the GHA leaders had already organized the villagers (who may have come from the minority Hakka ethnicity), who then pummeled them before they could beat a hasty retreat. The conflict between the GHA and local authorities quickly escalated after this.

The establishment of the GHA and its bold actions evidently struck a chord. Veterans from Wuchuan and the surrounding counties got together in a restaurant some of them had opened up. Using Tangwei as their headquarters and the restaurant as a meeting place, they began writing big-character posters in their collective name, demanding that local authorities do something to solve their employment problems. These big-character posters also accused political leaders of "cheating them" because they had joined the PLA to fight in Vietnam only after being promised jobs (verbally) after their return (*dawan Yuenan huilai jiu anpai gongzuo*).[42] In July 1980, when their demands still were not met, several thousand angry veterans (Xiang's relative claimed 3,000), following an "Order of Battle" they had agreed upon in advance, marched to the small town of Meilu (40,000 residents), where the Wuchuan county government was located.

A melee ensued. GHA members easily overcame the surprised and outnumbered guards protecting the government compound. Once inside, the GHA burned documents and archival materials and then broke into a meeting commemorating the "60th Anniversary of the Establishment of the CCP"; GHA leaders knew in advance that the meeting was taking place and that they could snare all the important officials at the same time. After securing the room, the veterans tied up and held hostage the party secretary, the head of the county government, and others. Local police quickly arrived at the scene, but they were clobbered; 30 people were injured before reinforcements managed to get to the town. During the next two days (July 2–4), the GHA broke into the county Public Security Bureau's offices and its jail and freed five members who had been arrested. According to Xiang's investigation, Meilu factories stopped production, its stores closed, and town residents "did not dare to go outside, saying it was just like the armed struggle during the Cultural Revolution." With the situation growing from bad to worse (from the perspective of the CCP), on July 4 the Guangdong Provincial Party Committee ordered the group suppressed and its leaders arrested, using "political" means.[43]

With the backing of provincial authorities, the area's CCP quickly mobilized against the GHA. On July 5, Huang Mingde, the Zhanjiang District deputy party secretary, went to Wuchuan County and organized an all-county broadcast in which he announced that the GHA incident in Meilu town was "counter-revolutionary," a harsh, sometimes death-dealing verdict that was fresh in the memories of those who had experienced the recently concluded Cultural Revolution. Huang also demanded that the leaders of the GHA voluntarily surrender. This was then followed by a large-scale "Three Rectifies" (*san zhengdun*) campaign. Feeling they had nowhere to turn, GHA leaders gradually turned themselves in. After the suppression, the Public Security Bureau searched their headquarters. There they claimed to have found the GHA's attack plans, which they used to write up a 10,000-character charge sheet against them. Their crimes included inciting an armed uprising, disturbing the peace, staging illegal protests, fleeing abroad, entering into restricted areas, and the like.[44] After the arrests, all veterans in the western part of the province were gathered together for "study sessions" so that they could "learn from this experience."

When Xiang Mulin returned home from visiting his relatives in Guangdong, he published his account in the Hong Kong press. Perhaps because news of the war in Vietnam was still fresh and the "Grieving Hearts Army" name was a public relations dream, his account was popular. In the preface to its sequel, Xiang wrote that "readers wanted to know more about what happened, and about the leaders and how they were treated after their arrest." Spurred on by this interest, Xiang returned to the scene of the crime. He soon saw evidence of the provincial counterattack: the verdicts of the Zhanjiang District Intermediate Court. The leader of the GHA, Ling Jian, 32 years old, was sentenced to life in prison and the loss of his political rights until his death; Liao Zhi, 28, who served as the head of the GHA's "Political Department," received 12 years in prison and lost his political rights for five years. Ten other GHA leaders received between 1 and 15 years. The trial had taken place in Wuchuan County, and the verdict was upheld by the Zhenjiang District Intermediate Court and then by Guangdong Province's High Court.[45]

After jotting down the verdict, Xiang copied down the details of the state's case against them. According to the official notice, Ling and Liao began their activities by "petitioning the county on many occasions." Later, they organized a "Veterans Committee" with more than 40 people, all of whom were "demanding work." These activities transpired at the township (commune) and county levels. After the establishment of the Veterans Committee, Ling Jian was appointed as the organization's "Commanding Officer" and Liao Zhi the director of its Political Department. Having formed this illegal organization, the court claimed, Ling and Liao, along with other members of the Veterans Committee, descended into crime. Some "resisted taxes," while others stole peasants' livestock and sold it, which led to their arrest. (They were later freed in the attack on the jail.) In June 1980, they escalated their illegal activities by meeting in Weilan Village in Meilu town, where they established a "Veterans' Steering Division" (*fudao chu*), with Ling at its leader.

The court also claimed that the GHA had made extensive preparations to "seize power from the CCP." As proof, they pointed out that the GHA "had a chop, a flag, and signboards."[46] This was unlikely, however. The veterans were radicalized because promises were broken and they were not treated respectfully after their return. Their job situation was clearly important, but more crucial was the county government's refusal to accept their petitions in a satisfactory manner.[47]

STAYING THE COURSE

Even though protests involving veterans were not new in the PRC, their scale in the reform period appears to have dwarfed those in the pre–Cultural Revolution period. Undoubtedly, the widespread disillusionment with the party after the Cultural Revolution, the inconclusive war with Vietnam, and the administrative reorganization in the early 1980s provided both the incentive and the "political opportunity structure" for veterans to vent their grievances in greater numbers. Despite these protests, the reform-era PRC government has not only failed to introduce significant ameliorative measures based on a serious evaluation of best practices elsewhere in the world, but it has also remained wedded to many of the policies and administrative practices that have long been recognized as highly problematic and were openly detested and contested by veterans as early as 1950. The state has maintained many restrictions on veterans' residential opportunities, it has not legislated a "Veterans Law" or established a "Veterans' Administration" (or allowed a national-, provincial-, or county-level veteran fraternal organization), and it has been unable to square highfalutin propaganda about veterans' sacrifices and contributions with the harsh realities they faced in everyday life.

As noted in Chapter 2, the policy of returning veterans to their hometowns was generally problematic. Not only were rural areas poorer to begin with, but the countryside was also systemically deprived of resources and investment after the CCP's takeover, when priority was placed on urban development. Having been the force that united China in terms of administration and sovereignty, many veterans were baffled and upset by a policy that denied them the possibility of living where they wanted to after their demobilization. Despite two brief relaxations of this policy in some areas—one in the late 1950s and the other during the high tide of PLA influence during the Cultural Revolution (1969–1971)—*yuan ji an zhi* was quickly resurrected by civilian CCP leaders in the waning years of the Cultural Revolution and was not significantly modified during the reform period. In a 10-day meeting of the State Council in 1980 whose proceedings reached Nationalist intelligence, officials noted that "very many problems" with veterans had "piled up" during the Cultural Revolution, largely owing to the lack of enforcement of the standard resettlement policy and the subsequent migration of veterans to large- and medium-sized cities. Because of the "excessive burden" the veterans placed on cities, the State Council noted that it was of utmost importance to "continue to resolutely uphold the policy of sending veterans back to wherever they came from" and that the "focal point" of veteran resettlement would still be "the countryside." Aware of the problems this would cause, the State Council called for "strengthening 'political thought work' among veterans, and raising their level of political consciousness" so that they would peaceably settle down to a life of agricultural labor and lend their efforts to the modernization of agriculture. It also urged that rural veterans who were "homeless" upon their return be assisted by the (now rapidly disintegrating) "collective," in addition to relying on their own efforts to break out of poverty. According to the State Council's calculations, successful reintegration of veterans in the countryside would alleviate pressure on urban employers, many of whom—including units under the direct administration of the State Council itself—were still refusing to hire them.[48]

This reinforcement of *yuan ji an zhi* was passed down to the provinces, whose officials again were forced to reconcile central mandates with local difficulties. In a March 1981 meeting of Xinjiang officials devoted to the issue of veteran resettlement, leaders "urged all localities to implement the principle of 'returning to where one came from' in resettling demobilized and retired servicemen so that everybody will be pleased wherever he will be assigned." Not all was going smoothly, however. Officials urged that "housing construction for retired military cadres [not enlisted men] must be expedited, and that matters concerning medical care and their families and children's settlement must be properly taken care of."[49] In Guangdong Province, at a gathering of "heroes among retired and demobilized soldiers"—the very first that had taken place in the province since 1949—Liu Tianfu emphasized that the government "at all levels must specifically strengthen work regarding the education and settlement of retired and demobilized soldiers." *Yuan ji an zhi* was encountering problems. Local officials, who had never appreciated returning veterans, were again instructed to "show warm concern" and "parental love and fraternal affection" for the returning soldiers.[50]

Evidence from randomly selected county gazetteers published in the mid-1980s to the mid-1990s confirms the extent to which military service was not easily convertible into urban residence rights. In Jingde County in Anhui, almost 80 percent of 1,052 returning veterans (between 1976 and 1987) were resettled in agriculture; only a few received positions as cadres: six at the township/town level (0.5 percent) and 88 at the village level (8 percent).[51]

In Taihe County in that province, between 1979 and 1985, an average of 83 percent of veterans were sent back to the countryside—the highest proportion was in 1980 (93 percent) and the lowest in 1984 (77 percent).[52] According to the Taihu gazetteer, "all" veterans who were recruited from the countryside had to resume agricultural labor "between 1958 and 1985," with the exception of those wounded in battle in the war against Vietnam.[53] In Fufeng County in Shaanxi Province in the Northwest, an average of 88 percent of veterans returned to the countryside between 1978 and 1988,[54] and in Puning County in southern Guangdong (29,712 veterans), with the exception of those with highly needed skills, "the absolute majority" were forced back to rural areas between 1950 and 1988.[55] While these gazetteers are quite open about these numbers, they provide little sense of how returning veterans felt about this policy, which, for many, was a betrayal of promises made to them prior to their service. The protests in the Southwest and elsewhere in the country, however, do suggest that veterans in the reform period were as angry at the *yuan ji an zhi* policy as their 1950s and 1960s comrades-in-arms, if not more so. After all, unlike the earlier period, when a minority of urban youth moved to the countryside, the reform period witnessed the return migration of rusticated urbanites to the city. Although there is no direct evidence of this, one could easily imagine that veterans sensed the injustice in these policies: young urbanites, most of whom were better off than veterans, gained the freedom to earn even more privileges, while rural veterans remained tied to the land, at least according to the "principle" of the policy as articulated by the State Council.

That veterans did not gain any more residential rights than they had in earlier periods should come as no surprise. Now, as before, they were largely beholden to officials from the State Council, few of whom had military or rural background (and, after the Cultural Revolution, probably had less-than-positive memories of the PLA), and to the same low-prestige bureaucracy that did not serve veterans particularly effectively in the past—Civil Affairs (which, after 1978, gained ministerial status). From the beginning of the reform era, most all policies regarding veterans' resettlement were hashed out in various inter-ministerial "Working Groups" in the State Council; veterans, lacking their own mass organization like the Women's Federation or the General Federation of Trade Unions, were completely shut out of this process except insofar as leading non-veteran officials claimed to speak on their behalf. According to a report from 1986, for example, an enlarged meeting of the Central Military Commission in 1975 presided over by Deng Xiaoping decided that "the army should be reorganized." Once this decision was taken, the job moved over to the State Council, which, in turn, established a "Working Group for the Resettlement of Demobilized Soldiers" in

1980. This Working Group was not led by a senior statesman, a member of the Politburo's Standing Committee, or a respected PLA general, but by Jiao Shanmin, who also served as one of several deputy ministers in the Ministry of Labor and Personnel.[56] In 1991, veteran issues were still handled by a "Working Group" under the State Council, this time led by Minister of Personnel Zhao Dongwan, who had previously been a deputy minister in one of the machine-building ministries.[57] Even though Zhao appears to have been a capable official, he served in a ministry that had come under harsh criticism in the pre-reform years for discrimination against veterans, and there is little evidence suggesting that he was knowledgeable about veterans' issues before taking up his post.[58] In other years, members of the veteran policy "Working Group" included Fan Baojun from Civil Affairs in Tianjin; Han Jianxu, formerly a female cotton worker (!) from Qingdao; and Mou Xinsheng, whose background was in security, customs, and narcotics control. Others were officers: Yu Yongbo served in the PLA (from 1947) and later became the director of the PLA's General Political Department, and Song Defu, who headed the Working Group in the mid- to late 1990s, served mainly in the political department in the air force, the most elite branch of the military. Song was later appointed minister of personnel and then party secretary of Fujian Province.[59]

As was the case in the 1950s and 1960s, it was highly unlikely that the newly christened Ministry of Civil Affairs (MCA) would be able to serve as veterans' advocate vis-à-vis the Ministry of Personnel or the State Councils' decade-old "Working Group." Still saddled with the same portfolio as in the 1950s (such as running village elections, supervision of religious organizations, marriage registration, disaster relief, and orphanages), the MCA was also charged with helping veterans (especially those at the lower ranks) locate jobs at their home locales. In an interview with Xinhua in 1985, Minister Cui Naifu spoke of his ministry's good intentions: "Civil Affairs departments at all levels will make every effort to help the army reform its structure, streamline and reorganize itself, and earnestly carry out the work of resettling and re-employing demobilized and retired Army cadres and soldiers. . . . Civil Affairs departments and cadres at all levels resolutely support the brilliant policy decision of the Chinese government."[60] As well-intentioned as Cui may have been, his ministry was swimming upstream, just as it was in earlier years; many government institutions and factories were reluctant to take on new staff and could not easily be forced to hire veterans. Since veteran administration was just one part of a gargantuan ministry (in terms of assigned tasks) that was subservient to the State Council, the MCA could not argue on behalf of veterans while at the same time promoting the overall policy of "economic reform."

The ambiguous and light hand of the Working Groups and the Ministry of Civil Affairs can clearly be seen in the torrential downpour of orders, circulars, and regulations issued by the State Council. In 1985, for example, the General Office of the CCP Central Committee, the State Council, and the Central Military Commission issued a "Notice" regarding the resettlement of veterans that did nothing more than "urge all localities in the country to do a good job resettling demobilized cadres [which does not include ordinary soldiers] from the Armed Forces." This "Notice" was accompanied by yet another "Opinion" (without referring to any of the other "Opinions" issued in the 1950s and 1960s) regarding the "Proper Resettlement of Demobilized Military Cadres," authored by five seemingly powerful institutions: the State Council's Working Group on Veterans, the CCP's Organization Department, the PLA's General Political Department, the Ministry of Labor and Personnel, and the Ministry of Finance. As usual, veterans themselves were not represented. But even more problematic was the document's language, a problem we have seen in Chapter 5 as well. The "Notice" stated that "all the recipient units and departments must consider the needs of the general situation and warmly welcome these demobilized cadres from the Armed Forces," leaving it up to middle management to figure out what the "general needs" were and whether they were obligated to help veterans beyond a "warm welcome." Subsequent clauses were no less vague and provided numerous ways for local officials to avoid accountability: *in principle*, cadres *should be* resettled and assigned to work at the basic-level units of all trades and professions; cadres *should be* placed *according to the needs of local construction* . . . as well as their qualifications and their jobs in the military. Neither the "Notice" nor the "Opinion" gave any indication that local officials would be evaluated on the basis of veteran resettlement issues, even though these veterans were more than likely to have been officers.[61] Two years later (1987), the Ministry of Civil Affairs proudly announced that it also was issuing new and separate regulations regarding the resettlement of non-cadre PLA veterans. The vice minister, Fan Baojun, inaccurately announced that "in the past 29 years we have *always* used temporary provisions for ex-servicemen" [in 1955 the State Council issued an authoritative "Decision" on veterans], but since the situation had changed, new regulations were necessary. The core of the "new" regulation was quite old, however: "The new regulation stipulated that in principle ex-servicemen should go back to their hometowns after leaving the army." Overlooking the fact that no empire or state had ever banned most all veterans from moving to cities or towns, Fan said that since "80 percent of soldiers come from the countryside, it is impossible to allow all of them and their families to settle in cities and towns."[62]

The state's urban bias can also be seen in another document, the Revised Military Service Regulation (1999). Continuing policies that were adopted in the 1950s that differentiated between veterans on the basis of time served, year recruited, and rank attained (*fuyuan junren, zhuanye junren, tuiwu junren*), the 1999 regulation categorized active-duty soldiers into "conscripts" and those in the "volunteer system," mainly noncommissioned officers who began their service after their conscription period was over. Rather than provide benefits and rights to "veterans" as a generic category, the regulation stipulated that the conscripts would be entitled to "proper settlement in accordance with the rules of the state," without defining what "proper" meant. But when it came to whether or not veterans would be able to live in a city, the regulation was specific: if the NCO had come from a rural area and was an "intermediate sergeant [or petty officer] with ten years active duty" and requested an urban residence permit, he would be entitled to one. Unlike these NCOs, who would be in their 30s upon discharge and thus presumably healthy and fit, older NCO veterans ("those with more than 30 years of service or over 55 years old") saw their rights to an urban residence permit curtailed, perhaps because city officials feared they would be a burden on local resources (even as cities had grown far wealthier than rural areas). According to the regulation, older NCOs "*may be* given transfer settlement with the consent of the officer himself *if the locality has the need*," a highly unlikely prospect for an older rural veteran.[63]

This reliance on localities was also evident in yet another circular in 2003. According to the text, the State Council and Central Military Commission "asked local governments to spare no effort to help ex-soldiers who left the service this year to find jobs, and protect their rights; governments at all levels should get local government departments, institutions, state-owned companies, and private firms to employ them." If veterans who read up to this point were unimpressed with the language (*ask, should, as possible*), they would have probably thrown up their hands when reading on. Following its usual *modus operandi*, the Center, rather than providing funds for veterans, "urged local governments to raise funds to help ex-servicemen who are willing to start their own businesses or find jobs through their own efforts."[64] Given the flexibility the Center gave local authorities, veterans remained highly dependent on the goodwill and resources of provinces, towns, counties, and townships. For veterans demobilized to the poorer Southwest (like many Vietnam veterans) or interior provinces, decentralization did not bode well. In 1994, an official in Sichuan told a Hong Kong reporter from the *South China Morning Post* that "at least 5 million demobilized soldiers and disabled soldiers were living in poor conditions because financial allowances had been kept at such low levels for years. We can't increase the amount for each grade [of disability] very much every year because our provincial government does not have enough funding," he explained, also noting that "other provinces suffered from a similar problem."[65] Subsidies for conscripts were also recognized as inadequate.[66]

This miserly approach to handing over money, however, did not apply to propaganda, which gushed generously from the mouths of high-level officials into radio outlets and the mass media. The content was also quite different: as much as the language in circulars and regulations hemmed and hawed about the state's and society's obligations to veterans, official speeches in the press and elsewhere were effusive and ornate, but still generally disconnected from the everyday reality most veterans faced. In 1981, for example, Ren Zhongyi, the first secretary of the Guangdong CCP Committee, called veterans a "positive force in developing the Four Modernizations" a year after he suppressed the Grieving Hearts Army.[67] A decade later, Song Ping, a member of the Politburo, called the PLA "a great school" that had trained veterans extremely well and praised them for having "contributed their youth to national defense building."[68] Not to be outdone, two years later, Jiang Zemin, the CCP general secretary, used the same language found in documents from the 1950s and 1960s: it is "very glorious work to render services" to old Red Army veterans, he told his audience of veterans, whom he urged to "maintain the sterling qualities of Red Army veterans forever, and to give play to their own role in carrying forward the fine tradition of our party and army."[69] A bit later in the decade, young people were urged to learn from PLA veterans. In 1995, Zhang Zhen, vice chairman of the Military Commission, urged university students who had concluded a visit to former CCP base areas (as part of the 50th-anniversary commemorations of "China's victory" in the Anti-Japanese War) to "learn from the revolutionary veterans and martyrs in the Anti-Japanese War and take up their historical responsibility to today's modernization drive."[70]

Despite the high praise heaped on veterans in political speeches, a close reading of some of these political texts reveals that the state's megaphone was cracking and that the leadership was having a difficult time aligning its praise with what it knew to be happening in the provinces. In 1981, Liu Tianfu, the Guangdong provincial governor, "demanded that party committees and government at all levels include this work in their important daily agenda," which they apparently did not.[71] At a provincial work meeting on the placement of veterans in Zhejiang in 1990, Li Zimin, secretary of the Provincial Party Committee, admitted that local governments, much like those 40 years prior, were not in accord with the Center when it came to "warmly welcoming" returning veterans and that there was a gap between state rhetoric and everyday realities:

All departments should understand [the] difficulties and practical problems confronted by demobilized Army cadres when they settle down in a locality. It is
necessary to show concern for their work and life and do everything possible to
solve practical problems for them that they will more quickly adapt themselves
to their new jobs and contribute more to the cause of the party.[72]

Using very similar language, PLA leaders also combined high praise for aging Red Army veterans with concern over their treatment in various localities.
Speaking at military festivities during Spring Festival in 1999, the officials
called the veterans a "precious asset to the Party." Because of this, showing
concern for them was a "political responsibility we should not evade." Government officials, they urged, "must have compassion for the veteran cadres
. . . and do everything possible to help them solve their problems so that the
vast number of them can enjoy healthy and peaceful lives in their remaining
years."[73] In 2004, a commentary in *Liberation Daily* (the PLA newspaper)
struggled to muster praise for local governments' handling of veteran affairs:
"Local governments at all levels . . . have made increasingly greater efforts to
ensure that the work of settling demobilized soldiers is carried out as planned,
and have protected the rights and interests of demobilized soldiers in a comparatively satisfactory fashion."[74]

CONFLAGRATIONS AT THE HEART OF THE REVOLUTION

Given that veterans of the Anti-Japanese, Civil, and Korean wars were used
as powerful symbols of the state's legitimacy and power, it was understandable that references to their problems in newspapers and political speeches
would remain abbreviated and oblique. Those able to publish outside the
mainland, however, were far less constrained in their reporting of veterans'
difficulties, many of which bubbled to the surface in the very same areas that
were used to educate students and others about patriotism—the poor-but-he-
roic "base areas" of the pre-1949 CCP. As was the case in the early 1980s,
veterans mounted dramatic, sometimes violent, protests in the early 1990s
as well. Poverty, broken promises, and the gap between official rhetoric and
rituals (such as the hoopla during Spring Festival) and everyday experiences
appear to have been at the heart of these protests. Lo Ping, a Hong Kong
reporter for *Cheng Ming*, traveled to China's revolutionary Northwest and
witnessed several "disturbances" involving veterans of the 8th Route Army.
Apparently, beginning in February 1990—in the midst of the crackdown on
the Tiananmen protesters—these protests reportedly erupted in the Jinggang
Mountains (on the Jiangxi/Hunan border), Guizhou Province, and in Yanan,
the CCP's WWII headquarters, where Lo claimed that they were particularly

violent. In Guizhou, for instance, dozens of veterans petitioned the authorities "by prostrating themselves in front of the county party committee for 56 hours," apparently with several thousand onlookers, and in Ningxia Province, "hundreds" of Anti-Japanese War veterans and more recently demobilized veterans "smashed state-owned shops and banks," targets which surely were not randomly chosen. In Yanan, after staging several protest rallies, poor Red Army and 8th Route Army veterans burned flags of the Communist Party, broke into the county party committee, and occupied the county's broadcasting station. Although little bloodshed was reported in that incident, in the western part of the county, fifteen 8th Route Army veterans were said to have "scuffled with police while they staged a demonstration and injured two policemen." Elsewhere in Yanan, approximately 100 disabled "bare-backed veterans held a demonstration calling for the Communist Party to give them food." Reminiscent of the protests in the 1950s that called attention to the gap between the rhetoric of heroism and poverty, the early 1990s Northwest veteran protesters also challenged the state and society to "put their money where their mouth is." According to Lo's account, the veterans announced that "they want food, not 'isms'" and asked, "Why are liberated areas so poor?"[75]

Veterans from the 1930s and 1940s were not the only ones creating disturbances in the early 1990s. Reports also surfaced that Vietnam War and other recently discharged soldiers and veterans protested in several other provinces, notably in Anhui, Hebei, and Shanxi. Anhui was the site of an incident similar to those we have already seen in Shandong and the Northeast in the early 1980s, when disgruntled veterans took up arms against the CCP. According to the *Cheng Ming* report, two soldiers who served as special-class scouts in the war against Vietnam were "so discontented with the local government over salary issues" that they vandalized the Public Security Bureau and railroad station and stole weapons and ammunition from the depot of the Peoples' Armed Police on twenty separate occasions. Thus armed, the veterans blew up "the local armed forces oil depot." They remained on the lam until June 1990.[76]

These dramatic events involving heroes of the revolution struck a nerve in China's leadership, perhaps because they occurred so soon after the controversial suppression of the Tiananmen protests—a move that was not popular with many ranking PLA officers—and at the same time that the state was busy resurrecting Lei Feng (the dead PLA soldier from the 1960s) as a role model for the country's wayward youth. Jiang Zemin, who had only recently been appointed to the top leadership post in a highly questionable succession process, and others in the Central Committee were worried these incidents could spread to other areas, and they immediately ordered local authorities and the military to "never increase the conflict and never use force" as well as to "solve the practical difficulties for comrades in old liberated areas as soon as possible while increasing ideological work." The Central Military Commission then transferred 20,000 cotton-padded quilts and 20,000 sets of military quilts and uniforms "from various localities" and arranged a transfer of seven million yuan that suddenly became available. To prevent the reoccurrence of these problems, the Center established yet another "fact-finding group" to investigate veteran problems around the country.[77]

A year later, in 1991, even larger protests in Shaanxi, Guizhou, and Jiangxi revealed the extent to which these measures were half-hearted and ineffective. The timing was not coincidental. Much like the "Grieving Hearts Army" that raided the Meilu government in 1981 on the 60th anniversary of the establishment of the CCP, veterans in some of the revolutionary base areas staged protests during the celebrations of the CCP's 70th anniversary. By undermining this political ritual, they tried to call attention to the gap between the party's promises and policies and the lack of effective follow-through and stuck a knife in the heart of the party's claim to legitimacy on the basis of how it treated the purported patriotic heroes of the revolution. In these protests (unlike those in Wuchuan) military veterans were joined by elderly CCP officials from the area, which both underscored the extent of the problems and made it far more difficult for the local authorities to suppress them. Their demands, however, closely resembled those of veteran protesters in the 1950s, Cultural Revolution, and early 1980s.

Citing a special report entitled "Where Are the Problems?" for the Xinhua News Agency's *Internal Reference*, feelings of "alienation" from the party were quite widespread among military and party veterans in the old headquarters in Yanan but were particularly acute among veterans who sought to join the party soon after the Anti-Japanese War broke out in 1937, "patriots" by most all measures. Admitted to the party mainly in 1938, *Internal Reference* noted that now, 13 years after the reforms and more than 40 years after the peasant-based revolution, most of the veterans were hard-pressed. Even though they, like other poor people, were granted relief money and supplies, local governments skimmed off a significant portion of these funds. In one case, for example, the PLA General Political Department and the Ministry of Civil Affairs allocated 200,000 yuan to "Yanan's old liberated areas" with the "request" that each veteran Red Army soldier or party member receive 100 yuan (approximately US$12) from the fund. Instead, each veteran received only 15 yuan—the rest was appropriated by officials between Beijing and the villages where they lived. Relief grain was also misdirected. The Center requested that each veteran who joined the party in 1938 receive 20 *jin* of flour, 10 *jin* of rice, 5 *jin* of pork, and 2 *jin* of white sugar, but each veteran received less than half of this amount, and "large quantities of white sugar were put on sale" in free markets at high prices. Many officials got in on the act. A Civil Affairs official in one district embezzled 700 *jin* of pork, and the deputy head of the Yanan Prefectural Propaganda Department (who was overseeing "patriotic education") and the deputy chief of the District Bureau for Veteran Cadres' Affairs siphoned off more than 1,500 *jin* of rice.[78]

Upset by their poverty and CCP corruption, the "1938 veterans" chose the symbolic date of May 1 to stage their protest. Apparently upset because the county did not accept a collective petition they had written up, the 1938 Group smashed the offices of the county's "Leading Office for Celebrating the 70th Anniversary of the Founding of the Party," injuring its deputy secretary. Public Security Bureaus at the district and county levels quickly mobilized, dispatching more than 200 policemen who immediately encircled the veterans. These police were withdrawn after they received an urgent dispatch from the Provincial Party Committee, which apparently feared scenes of mass arrests and bloodshed. The veterans' age, and the symbolic investment in them over the years, probably also contributed to restraint.[79]

In the absence of state repression, the 1938 Group quickly tried to gather more support from the larger veteran community, yet another theme we have seen in this study. Another group was formed, comprising veterans who joined the party in 1945, and they tried to "establish ties" with the 1938 Group. Veterans from other prefectures in Shaanxi tried to join in as well. After some time, these groups amalgamated into the "Leading Group for Claiming Justice" (which was reportedly led by the platoon leader of Marshal Zhu De's personal guards). The "Claiming Justice Group" soon penned an open letter to party committees at the district, city, and provincial levels with the following demands, many of which will sound familiar from protests and whistleblowing cases from the 1950s and 1960s. Though not mentioning the word "democracy," the veterans were clearly interested in establishing the principles of representation, transparency and accountability, which democracy, at its heart, purports to offer.

- Establish a prefecture-wide fraternal association for veteran party members, Red Army soldiers, and cadres.
- Establish a financial inspection group for veteran administration that would "check the financial relief expenditure accounts" over the last decade and "publish the results."
- Request that the Provincial Party Committee sack 35 prefectural, city, and county CCP cadres "specifically named by the fraternal association for being greedy and corrupt."
- On the eve of July 1 [the founding date of the CCP], a delegation of 10 veterans elected by the fraternal association will go to Beijing "to report to the central authorities on the actual conditions" of the veterans.

- On July 1, the veterans will stage a large protest march "across the prefecture."[80]

On receiving word of the veterans' protests, organization, and collective letter, the Central Committee immediately dispatched leaders of the Civil Affairs Ministry and the PLA's General Political Department to Yanan. The situation was getting dangerous: some university students from Beijing, Shanghai, Tianjin, Xian, and Lanzhou were heading toward the former base areas, probably as part of the commemoration activities planned for that year. When the central authorities were alerted to this, they ordered policemen to stop the students at the railway stations in Xi'an and other areas. Many students bypassed the dragnet, however, by getting out of the trains before their final stop and then making the rest of the way by tractor or long-distance truck. Locals offered to guide them to Yanan; when this became too dangerous during the day, they moved by night. According to local officials, the youth were confused by what they heard from different people: "They did not know whom they should listen to—a veteran party member with 40 years of party membership, or a young county party committee secretary less than 40 years old."

While the state mobilized to prevent an alliance between students and the veterans, the "Claiming Justice" veterans kept busy. According to *Internal Reference*, many veterans, in preparation for the large march they expected to conduct on July 1, "retrieved from museums red flags and party flags they had donated earlier," while others made new red-tasseled spears for the march. They were quite bitter, expressing sentiments very similar to veterans from the 1950s (they were "like donkeys slaughtered after grinding the wheat"): "All that blood we shed has been wasted, and our comrades-in-arms have died in vain!"; "We have been had by the Communist Party; it has cheated us. For what purpose did we join the party and the revolution? Now there is no justice in the Communist Party." What seemed to concern central leaders more than these sentiments, however, was the possibility that the Yanan veterans would manage to form an alliance with veterans in other provinces—serious problems were brewing in Hubei (in Hongan County, another "old liberated area"), Jiangxi, and Guizhou. Li Xiannian (chair of the Chinese People's Political Consultative Conference at the time, but also a "party elder" with clout) issued stern warnings to county-level authorities using words not found in the vague circulars and told them to take preventative measures. Adding some carrots to the stick, Li also instructed various departments in the State Council to send large quantities of wood, steel, and concrete to Hongan for construction projects that would employ veterans.[81]

These measures did the trick, at least temporarily, but the central government was sufficiently worried to convene yet another large meeting about

veterans' issues that year. Without the presence of any organization representing the veterans themselves, high-level officials from the Ministry of
Public Security, Ministry of State Security, PLA, Civil Affairs, Propaganda,
the Central Committee, Women's Federation, and Federation of Trade Unions came to hear a report by the Shaanxi Provincial Government and "study
solutions." The solutions they proposed, however, were sobering, perhaps not
surprising given the presence of two security ministries in the tense context of
post-1989 China. On the positive side, the CCP Central Committee, already
bruised by the reaction to the suppression of the 1989 protesters, decided that
"There is to be no brute force . . . authorities must exhaust all kinds of ways
and methods to properly conduct ideological struggle." Moreover, to figure
out what went wrong, or at least to pacify the veterans, "leading authorities"
at all levels of government, the party, and the PLA were ordered to send
small units to the revolutionary base areas "to conduct work household by
household, and individual by individual" (even though these officials were
often blamed by veterans for their problems). More ominously, however, the
officials also claimed that "There is an issue of class struggle here." It was entirely possible that "a small number of bad elements and hostile forces inside
and outside the country" were taking advantage of problems in the old revolutionary base areas in order to damage the CCP. To prevent further problems, a
gentle crackdown was warranted, lest other veterans be emboldened; if "party
discipline" could not bring the veteran leaders to heel, then the police should
arrest them. As for the veterans' demand to attend the celebrations in Beijing
for the 70th Anniversary of the Founding of the CCP, the Center met them an
eighth of the way: certain "delegates" from Yanan could attend, but not any
veteran associated with their "fraternal association," which was branded an
"illegal organization." Harsh words were also meted out to the students who
tried to lend assistance. In no mood to tolerate more challenges from students
after the Tiananmen debacle, the leadership authorized the public security
organs to show "no mercy" for student leaders "responsible for agitation and
creating trouble."[82]

The successful crushing of yet another incipient movement by veterans to
create an organization to represent their rights and interests (and to help the
party fight corruption in its midst) did not prevent smaller-scale incidents
from erupting, however. These cases were more tolerable to the state because
they were more isolated and did not involve organization, cross-provincial alliances, or cross-class ties, but they were no less tragic from veterans' points
of view. They were also similar to pre-reform events. In 1991, for example,
five 70-year-old veterans who had fought in the war against Japan and had
then defended Yanan against the Nationalists at the beginning of the Civil
War committed suicide. Prior to their suicides, they had complained to the

Yanan municipal authorities about local officials who mistreated veterans and ordinary people. Whistleblowing led to retaliation by local authorities, which the veterans detailed in a letter to the Central Committee. The Center, following the usual *modus operandi* for handling such letters, simply sent it back to the Shaanxi Provincial Committee for handling, but nothing happened. On May 2, 1991, the veterans took the weapons with which they had battled the Japanese and Nationalists and, together with some 40 relatives, headed out to the Yanan Municipal Government to protest. For reasons that are not clear, the protest escalated: the veterans smashed their rifles and spears and publicly burned their party membership cards and individual citations, much like the American "Vietnam Veterans against the War" (VVAW) did in the early 1970s to protest the U.S. government's prosecution of the war. Then, without warning, they marched to a cliff and hurled themselves off it. According to the report, word of this collective suicide spread in Shaanxi, but the CCP Central Committee Secretariat ordered the Propaganda Department to ban media coverage to the wider public.[83] To be sure, not all protests in the early 1990s were so dramatic, but in the tension-fraught atmosphere after the suppression of the Tiananmen protests, the growing scale of mobilization led to concerns that they would be used by "politically hostile" organizations and governments. In 1992, for example, local governments were told to "keep a close watch" over an organization called the "National Alliance of Demobilized Servicemen in Rural Areas," which had a membership of "several tens of thousands," including those who served in the People's Armed Police. (Anyone who had served in the PLA and had been forced to return to the countryside after 1949 was eligible for membership.) Aside from these numbers, the party also was very worried about intelligence reports suggesting that veterans organizations were linking up to regular army units, perhaps in an effort to recruit more members. "This could be a very dangerous thing," noted the report in the Hong Kong press. Members of the organization had systematic military training, were "quite combative," and could be easily mobilized. Even worse, the PLA might not be able to suppress them. In a confrontation, the veterans would invoke "the similarities between the two sides."[84]

STANDING ON SHAKY GROUND

Throwing oneself off a cliff was surely not a typical veteran response to frustrations over poverty and a sense of injustice and powerlessness, but the geologic metaphor it suggests is rather appropriate. In the reform period, particularly in the latter half of the 1990s as industrial reform deepened, many veterans felt the ground shake underneath them, and the future did not seem to go anywhere but down. During this period, many state-owned factories, where the lucky veterans managed to secure some form of employment, went belly up or were effectively privatized. Making matters worse, many employers in the reform era, including the private and state sectors, preferred to avoid hiring veterans. Reform-era policies allowed many employers to shed veterans they did not want in the first place or simply not take them on. Vague exhortations in "circulars" were easy to ignore, and the Center did not have great success in enforcing preferential treatment policies for veterans, even during the heyday of "centralization" in the 1950s. While the overall picture has not been encouraging, some veterans have managed to find their place in the rural economy. Thanks to the growth of rural industries (Township and Village Enterprises, or TVEs), one of the most dynamic sectors in the Chinese economy,[85] many veterans who were forced to return to the countryside have gained non-agricultural employment even as they had to remain in the countryside.

   Signs of strain on veteran employment in industries appeared in the mid-1980s but intensified in the mid-1990s and at the turn of the new century. Despite the passage of roughly four decades, the sense of déjà vu is inescapable: officers receive inadequate compensation when transferring from the PLA to the civilian sector, and low-ranking veterans encounter difficulties securing employment after discharge. In 1985, for example, the State Council and Central Military Commission issued a "Notice" not all that different from notices issued in the 1950s and 1960s, stating that "all officers whose demobilization[s] were approved after July 1, 1985, are to be fixed [assigned] according to the civilian posts commensurate with their original ones in the Army." The reasons for reiterating this policy were also familiar. Officers at the battalion and regimental levels had been assigned to civilian jobs but were given lower positions, and thus less money, than before. The "Notice" stipulated that such officers "*should be* given appropriate preferential treatment" but also included the all-too-common escape clause: "The specific methods are to be determined by the provinces, municipalities, and autonomous regions in accordance with the actual conditions."[86] In 1985, Xinhua reported that demobilization and the transfer to civilian jobs proceeded "more quickly and efficiently than in many previous years," but this probably came at the expense of many veterans. According to the report, many areas were making it more difficult to secure employment by "giving priority and special treatment to personnel who have earned second-class merit or high honors in the Army," a policy that probably (if based on the record from the 1950s and 1960s) led to no small amount of résumé inflation and document forging among officers on the verge of discharge.[87] Lower-ranking rural veterans may have had an easier experience in this respect—many of them did not anticipate a tenured sinecure and could more easily fit into a riskier sector of the economy. In 1986, it was estimated that only 25 percent of veterans took up farming upon their return to the countryside, many of them finding employment in TVEs and other tertiary industries. That year Civil Affairs, based on a survey of six provinces, estimated that 55 percent of rural veterans were employed in TVEs,[88] but in some areas it might have been higher: in Suizhou, Hubei Province, 66 percent of veterans were said to be working in small-scale industries and trades.[89] In 1992, in Anhui Province, veterans were said to constitute one-third of the personnel in the tertiary industry in the province;[90] its provincial-level gazetteer also indicates large numbers of veterans going into TVEs.[91] In the Shanghai area, TVEs saved most all veterans from agricultural employment: in Chuansha County, 84 percent of veterans were employed in TVEs between 1986 and 1990, and a Civil Affairs official in Qingpu District in Shanghai (formerly Qingpu County) reported that 100 percent of its veterans were employed in these firms since the 1990s.[92] While we certainly should not take Xinhua's statistics or its claim that veterans played a "backbone role in promoting technology and development" at face value, we should at least consider the possibility that veterans, a population known for risk-taking and hard work and in possession of some skills learned in the army, were a very important force behind the explosive growth of the Chinese rural economy; even in a conservative village in Hebei Province, there was a veteran who emerged as a model entrepreneur.[93] This would not be unprecedented: post-war American veterans also played a vital role in reinvigorating the American economy in the 1950s, for many of the same reasons. Unfortunately, TVEs were not the only growth sector of the economy. The CCP's weak basis of legitimacy, the events of 1989, and the growth of social unrest expanded the public security forces as well (People's Armed Police, anti-riot squads, and urban "patrol police"), which also absorbed mostly lower-ranking veterans (we know almost nothing about how veterans view this position; was it seen as a blow to their status or the opposite?).[94] From 1989 to 2000, the People's Armed Police doubled in size to roughly 1.3 million men, "boosted by demobilized soldiers from China's regular armed forces."[95] According to Yitzhak Shichor, the number of veterans who were employed by security units calls into question whether a military-to-civilian manpower conversion has even taken place in the reform era.[96]

The growth of township and village enterprises that could absorb veterans, however, was the mirror image of many other sectors of the reform economy, particularly in the 1990s. Under pressure to become more efficient and streamlined, the state bureaucracy and state-owned industries were reluctant to hire more personnel. For the millions of veterans being demobilized, the timing could not have been worse. In 1990, the Ministry of Civil Affairs, facing the discharge of 600,000 soldiers, stated that resettlement "is facing more difficulties than last year," largely because the government "has to find jobs in state institutions for at least 40,000 veterans" (only 6.6 percent of the total, not including officers), but these jobs were in short supply. "Few enterprises or units," the ministry claimed, "have job openings due to the austerity program, while the total number of demobilized soldiers this year remains as large as last year's." But the problem was not only job slots. Like previous generations of veterans in China and elsewhere, 1990s veterans also expected better treatment and a rise in status and standard of living because of their military service, but to most these were not forthcoming. To forestall unrest in an already tumultuous year for the leadership, the State Council increased the wage quota in state-run enterprises in order "to cover the veterans employed this year," but this had less bearing on those who were not hired in the first place for lack of space.[97] Similar problems were also noted in 1991. In addition to the austerity issue, veterans were said to face another obstacle—a test they would be given by their employers. According to Personnel Ministry officials, "the bulk" of demobilized officers needed "at least six months" of professional training programs to prepare them for the test, but little indication is given of whether these courses were being provided or if the officers passed them.[98] In 1994, an article in *Liberation Daily* hinted at this problem in the senior ranks. In 1993, it noted, "Due to the large number of demobilized officers or for other reasons, a small number of localities did not implement the policy of arranging jobs for demobilized regimental officers [mainly lieutenant colonels, colonels, and major generals]." This problem, of course, was said to have been solved immediately after General Secretary Jiang Zemin learned of this situation.[99]

Veteran unemployment problems also were exacerbated in the mid-1990s as a result of a shift in PLA recruiting policy. For reasons that are not clear, in the early 1990s the PLA recruited heavily from cities; perhaps this was to avoid even larger-scale unemployment problems in rural areas after veterans' discharge. A 1993 report noted that the 500,000 soldiers who were being demobilized that year (roughly the same number as in 1992) placed a "strain" on China's labor market largely because "half of the men were drafted from urban areas" and therefore "expected to be assigned jobs" in the state sector, which could not absorb them all. The state, however, was at a loss about how to proceed. An official told reporters from the *China Daily* that they were "making every effort" to help veterans and were even considering a somewhat ironic proposal that would require 150,000 *foreign-funded* and non-state bodies to hire them. New labor regulations, however, strengthened the position of employers. Veterans who signed on with state-owned companies would become contract workers (as many were in the past) and would have at least one year to "get familiar with their jobs." With the sharpness of an infant's gums, the state told work units that they "should give them professional training" and "should not fire them" during this period.[100]

How much of this helped or harmed veterans' situations cannot be determined without more research, but some evidence suggests that employers often felt they had free reign to ignore the Center. In 1995, the "Office of the Leading Group for the Placement of Demobilized Army Officers" issued a document indicating that problems were quite serious. All employment units were again reminded to "not make up excuses to reject the placement tasks assigned by local government," and those higher-level departments in charge of hiring "must not go against the policy on the placement of retired soldiers." Those who refuse, they warned with the usual admonishment, "should be called to account or punished," although there is little indication that this ever happened. In the past several years, they noted (with words readily recognizable to veterans from 1956):

> Some units and departments made up various excuses to reject the placement of retired soldiers, or refused placement in a disguised form [such as mandating tests, or telling veterans there was no money or space] so that the placement progressed in a slow fashion and retired soldiers became unemployed for a long time.[101]

But even as local authorities often did their best to avoid hiring veterans, PLA officers who took the time to read *Liberation Daily* prior to their discharge might have come away with somewhat different expectations. In a 1995 commentary entitled "Bon Voyage, Comrades-in-Arms," local authorities were said to have done "meticulous and conscientious work" in advance of the demobilization and that "your fellow countrymen are waiting for you, and local governments will accord you a warm welcome." Still, the commentary also hinted at future challenges: "You should first and foremost rely on, control, and manage yourselves."[102]

Officers, of course, were not the only ones affected by non-compliance. The 1998 Military Service Law and the 1999 Revised Military Service Regulation cut the mandatory service for conscripts to two years, which meant that the annual turnover rate for conscripts was 50 percent. Because this happened during a time of rising unemployment and cutbacks, the job prospects for low-ranking veterans were dim, especially in cities and areas without successful or sufficiently large TVEs. The result, as Kivelehan-Wise rightly notes, has been a "stressed resettlement program with the potential to be a source of significant discontent among the PLA enlisted corps and the communities tasked with resettling them." Problems included, but were not limited to, work units' violating policy by refusing to provide jobs for veterans who had been assigned to them, long wait periods for jobs, and living allowances that were not issued while they were waiting for jobs. *Junshu* (military dependents), for their part, complained that they were not being granted the "preferential treatment" to which they were entitled, also a problem that we have seen on many occasions in the past.[103]

To their credit, national-level officials recognized this problem. But, as in many other areas of governance (such as environmental and consumer protection, enforcement of building safety codes, protection of intellectual property, taxation, and sex selection of babies), the Center's enforcement capacity was limited, and veteran resettlement never seemed to rise to the level where it garnered sustained, top-level attention, except when protests threatened CCP power and social stability. Veterans were aware of this problem; even in the mid-1950s, they complained that the CCP was far better at propaganda than enforcement. It is unlikely that many would be impressed with the flurry of employment-related regulations that drifted down from the Center between 1999 and 2004. In 1999, for example, the State Council and Central Military Commission issued a circular which called on "*all* agencies, enterprises and institutions" to partake in resettlement work. No unit was allowed to refuse local governments in resettlement matters.[104] But refuse they did. In Gansu Province, 21 veterans filed a complaint with the Labor Dispute Commission because the Lanzhou City Tap Water Company, a state-owned firm, did not fulfill work agreements and "left them poor and unemployed." According to the Hong Kong report, the veterans claimed that they had each paid a 10,000-yuan "training fee" to the company but were still not receiving salaries (or housing or benefits) "after waiting between one and three years." Criticized by the Civil Affairs Bureau, the company noted that they "usually have to wait for someone to retire" before they could fill a new vacancy and that "there is only so much our company can do in this difficult period of state-owned enterprises' restructuring."[105] Because such cases as these were quite common, in 2001 the Center responded by issuing its "Interim Procedures for the Resettlement of Military Cadres to Be Transferred to Civilian Work," which encouraged PLA veterans to find jobs on their own, even though prospects were acknowledged to be slim; in Jilin Province, for example, organizational reform at the city, county, and township levels "streamlined office workers by 20 percent," and officials noted that "the situation of this year's resettlement work is not optimistic." What would happen to veterans who remained unemployed for a long time was unclear, but provincial officials prepared for the worst "in light of the possibility that some local governments may turn their backs" on the veteran officers. "We will certainly encounter many problems in our work," officials predicted.[106] At the Shandong Archives, a fellow researcher—a veteran who was collecting documents to support his own petition against the government—took me aside to tell me that in 1996 and 1997 veterans gathered at Tiananmen Square in a very disciplined protest and that "employment problems" were the key issue affecting most all of them, including the officers.

The Jilin official's prediction proved correct, and in 2004 the General Office of the State Council issued another job-related policy, its "Opinion on Policies That Support Demobilized Veterans in Urban Areas to Find Jobs by Themselves." It is unclear how many veterans actually read this policy—in the United States, veterans *organizations* helped veterans better understand their rights and how to take advantage of the GI Bill—but to the extent that they did, many probably walked away in dismay. According to this Opinion, urban veterans who wanted to find a job by themselves "in the area in which his or her permanent residence is registered" would be issued a certificate by the Ministry of Civil Affairs after signing an agreement with its local branches. Having this certificate, according to the Opinion, would provide preferential treatment in a number of areas, ranging from employment to schooling. The precise wording, however, made it amply clear that veterans who had real experience in the job market had little to no input in the drafting of the Opinion. For example, work units "*should* give priority to hiring demobilized soldiers . . . *if* applicants have equal qualifications"; when veterans applied for loans and were short of working capital, the commercial bank "*should* give priority to their applications"; *if* a veteran in an urban area took the national entrance exam to colleges and universities—a fairly remote prospect for most veterans—they would get ten extra points; those who opened a business would be exempt from taxes for the first three years.[107]

On the face of it, these measures were progressive, but the Opinion never explained why these benefits were awarded to only urbanites, why veterans needed to stay in their hometowns to enjoy the benefits when some areas suffered from very high employment, or why "equality" in qualifications was the point at which preferential policies would kick in when many veterans came to the job market with some disadvantages. At least in these respects, the Opinion was not very different from the GI Bill in terms of the opportunities it opened for poorer and less educated whites, blacks, and other minorities (especially the latter): veterans were not entitled to loans from the federal government but, rather, loan guarantees *if* loan officers at banks decided that a veteran had sufficient collateral; veterans were entitled to tuition and a living stipend at institutions of higher education or in job training programs, but for those with very minimal education, this threshold was too high. Those who were best positioned to take advantage of the GI Bill were those who represented, in at least some respects, the more privileged segments of the population.[108] That said, the GI Bill's language did not exclude minorities in the same way that the 2004 Opinion excluded peasants, whose support brought the CCP to power and fought its wars. Moreover, the GI Bill, unlike the ever-changing, "interim" administrative regulations in China, was a widely recognized and publicized "national law," a status that has not been granted to PRC veterans in their quests for the enforcement of rights.[109]

TWENTY-FIRST CENTURY PRAIRIE FIRES

Veterans' problematic status has forced many of them into a highly confrontational stance vis-à-vis the state even in the new century, making China one of the only "modern" states that has experienced large-scale veteran protests in peacetime. Unlike protests in the early 1980s which coupled economic grievances with demands for political rehabilitation after the Cultural Revolution, veterans' political activism in the twenty-first century appears to center around bread-and-butter issues regarding employment, wages, and job status and is fueled by their anger at rampant corruption and ethical lapses in the CCP. Despite a rising tide of veteran activism—manifested mainly in crime, petitioning, and protests—the PRC has refused to adopt measures that, in other political contexts, have significantly reduced levels of discontent. Scholars at China's universities and research institutions, for their part, have also avoided the study of veterans for political and personal reasons—the chances for publication would be quite low—but, from what I can gather, few would be inclined to study veterans' predicaments, anyway. There is a great deal of scholarship on "regular" unemployment, for example, but, with rare exceptions, the impact of this on demobilization—and vice versa—is hardly mentioned, in contrast to Western research on demobilization and employment.[110] As of 2007, the PRC does not seem any closer than in 1957 or 1987 to legislating a Veterans' Law, allowing the formation of national- or even provincial-level veterans organizations or federations. Absent these or other dramatic measures, it is not clear how the PRC will be able to come to grips with its "veteran problem." For now, repression, buyouts, and "controlled polarization," rather than more meaningful reform, appear to be the main counter-veteran tactics.[111] There is logic to this approach, particularly if we consider preservation of power, not justice, nationalism, patriotism, or genuine concern over the welfare of citizens, as the core preoccupation of China's leadership.

More frequently than more media-savvy democracy activists, "nationalist" students, or intellectuals, veterans—whether out of economic desperation or a sense of justice denied or prolonged—have been willing to "go to the mat" against many levels of state authority, provoking repressive countermeasures. As was the case with 1950s veterans who drew the attention of the Public Security Bureau because of crimes related to their poverty, some of their 21st-century counterparts have also turned to crime to make ends meet when all other options have seemed to fail. In Changde City in central Hunan Province, for example, several veterans attempted to rob the local Agricultural Bank of China and in the process shot and killed three security guards, two bank employees, and a taxi driver and ran over a child as they attempted to flee. This wasn't their first heist: they were also suspected of twelve bank robberies in Hunan and Hubei provinces and Chongqing City in Sichuan Province. According to a report from Agence France-Presse (the PRC media did not discuss their backgrounds), the veterans had recently been demobilized and struggled to find jobs they felt were commensurate with their status: "They can't do any high-ranking jobs, but they're too proud to do any menial labor." Excessive pride—long a civilian complaint about veterans—was only one part of the problem, however. The discharge of 500,000 soldiers a year since 1997 forced hundreds of thousands of veterans on a labor market that already had too many people fighting for reasonably good positions. According to a bank employee (who learned about the robbers' background from a police investigator with a loose tongue), demobilization problems explained their crimes: "They are unemployed soldiers. They weren't properly assigned to civilian jobs, so they turned to crime." This Hunan gang was not an aberration; according to Frank Lu, a Hong Kong–based human-rights activist, quite a few veterans were getting involved in crime, including the organized variety. According to Lu, veterans, because they "are bolder and more physically fit than most people," were prime targets for recruitment into the Triads (a mafia-like organization). Veterans from China crossed the border into Hong Kong, committed a crime for the Triads, and then crossed back into the PRC.[112] Reports from 2001 suggest that Lu's assessment was on the mark; China's veteran problem had entered the global economy. In another crime-related event unreported by the PRC media, a Chinese crime syndicate in Sydney, Australia, was frequently using PLA veterans as "hired muscle" to win a gang war for control of the country's heroin trade. According to a report in the *Daily Telegraph*, the veterans were being used to invoke fear in the local Chinese community and rival drug-importing gangs. They had managed to enter Australia after receiving business visas (which were probably arranged by the gangs). Political tremors followed—the premier of New South Wales, Bob Carr, accused immigration officials of "not being tough enough on people applying for entry into Australia."[113]

The involvement of some veterans in criminal activities most certainly does not help their "cause" with the Chinese public. Even when there was no evidence of veteran involvement, some people pointed to them as possible suspects. After four buildings were exploded in one night in Shijiazhuang, the capital of Hebei Province, the police nabbed a man named Jin Ruchao, a 41-year-old deaf-mute, near the border with Vietnam. These weren't the first explosions in the city: in September 2000, five bombs went off on buses and near shopping malls, injuring 28 people. Many Shijiazhuang residents and "participants in China's lively Internet chat rooms" were understandably skeptical. How could one person carry so many explosives? The police did not provide any information on Jin's motives, so residents and a city official pointed the finger at those who clearly had motivation to cause damage to the state and urban denizens: laid-off workers; organized crime gangs linked to the city's former mayor, who was awaiting trial for massive graft; and "disgruntled ex-soldiers made jobless by the recent downsizing of military personnel."[114]

If veterans were primarily involved in crime, PRC leaders would probably have breathed a heavy sigh of relief. Criminals, after all, tend to operate as individuals or in small groups and are more easily contained and stigmatized by the police (especially in an authoritarian state) than larger numbers of people engaging in officially sanctioned acts of defiance and resistance. Over the last decade, substantial evidence demonstrates that PLA veterans have played a leadership role in thousands of social protests, displaying a now-familiar boldness and a wide array of organizational, mobilizational, and rhetorical skills, including the well-worn tactic of invoking the state's own rhetoric and policies to close the gap between central state regulations and less-than-favorable local circumstances. This also is not new; we have seen it in veterans' interactions with state officials in the 1950s and 1960s as well. For example, Li Lianjiang has found that "PLA veterans are more likely to defy local officials than are villagers who had never joined the army" (by a factor of 2.76),[115] and his joint research with Kevin O'Brien identified veterans who "found themselves locked out of the village leadership when they returned home" as the leaders of several peasant protests. Their survey of 1,600 villagers in four counties in three provinces (Fujian, Jiangsu, and Jiangxi) between 1999 and 2001 also showed that "men and army veterans were considerably overrepresented among rightful resisters," that is, among those who invoked state law, policies, and rhetoric to combat non-compliance at the local level. This finding was further supported by surveys in 2003 and 2004–2005.[116] Their description of the mentality of these veteran–activists dovetails seamlessly with the findings of this study, and remind us of the many similarities between the pre-reform and reform periods.

Like demobilized soldiers in many villages, they believe they are more capable than the current power holders, they tend to look down on village cadres who have never left the village, and they feel they know more about the outside world and have received superior political and ideological training than the current leaders. Yet they are frustrated; each of the four veteran-activists is a Party member but none serve on the village Party committee. They consider themselves to be more politically sophisticated and capable than ordinary villagers, yet their political status is hardly higher. . . . They do not, as far as can be ascertained, enjoy the confidence of the current village leaders, who seem to believe that the veterans would never have become Party members if they had not served in the army. The veterans, for their part, have decided that lodging complaints against Wang [the village chief] provides their best chance to win a place in the village leadership and to improve village governance. They appear to be acting partly out of ambition, combined with a measure of public-spiritedness and moral righteousness derived from strongly held beliefs about how villages should be run and how cadres should behave.[117]

Similar findings were also reported in the outbreak of protests against excessive taxation in Hunan, Shanxi, and Sichuan provinces. According to Bernstein and Lü, "many or perhaps even most" of the peasant leaders in these protests were from the "relatively well-educated village-level elite such as PLA veterans," thanks to the organizational and communication skills they learned in the army. In a tax protest in Shanxi, they note, "several hundred peasants confronted local authorities led by a PLA veteran," and in the massive 1993 protests in Renshou County, Sichuan, many of the key leaders were veterans as well. In Hunan, one of the "peasant heroes" was also a veteran "who became a teacher at a local school." In their analysis, Bernstein and Lü suggest reasons for discontent similar to those we have seen thus far: many were "disgruntled at having had to return to their home villages upon demobilization" and they "did not have positions commensurate with their background and experience."[118] Although less well documented, there are some signs that veterans have led protests in urban factories. In one case, a county government in Hainan Province sought to sell the Changjiang Sugar Factory to a private enterprise, a move which would have resulted in the layoff of 200 workers from the factory. Neither the county nor the factory offered workers a lump-sum compensation for their years employed in the factory. In Feng Chen's account, "sixty workers, all demobilized soldiers in the factory, gathered to discuss measures to defend workers' interests and prepared a collective petition to the county government."[119] This sort of activity probably was not unusual. The website of the Heilongjiang provincial government refers to an "important meeting" in 2005 to discuss veterans' collective petitioning, and the website of the Ministry of Civil Affairs refers to 26,000 veteran petitions in 2000, a 16.3 percent decrease from 1999.[120]

Beyond their involvement in gangs and the protests of other social groups, it was probably veterans' willingness to gather *en masse* and across provincial lines that made the knees of the engineers currently running the CCP wobble. In April 2002, a group of approximately 20,000 veterans—most of them retired officers—descended upon Beijing in order to file a collective petition to the Ministry of Civil Affairs for better treatment after their demobilization. Around their necks, many had hung placards with the words "I am a veteran" on their fronts and "I want to eat" on their backs. The veterans made two, by now familiar, demands: to be provided with jobs with decent salaries as they were promised and to establish a national veteran association. According to one source, the government, pursuing its usual course of unfunded mandates, issued orders to local governments to pay the veterans "no less than what they had been paid in the army, regardless of whether they had received a job" but flatly refused their demand to organize. The Center then arrested the leaders of the petition movement, fearing that it could quickly lead to larger protests. This protest was ignored by the PRC media and did not receive any international attention.[121]

This repression, however, did little to quell veterans' mass activism in the first decade of the century. In January 2005, 70–80 veterans of the Vietnam War reportedly protested in Shaanxi Province, demanding government assistance with employment and daily living expenses.[122] Several months later, the first large-scale veteran protest in China finally hit the international press. In April 2005, close to 2,000 veterans—most had been second lieutenants to majors, but there were also colonels—gathered in Beijing, where they staged a sit-in protest outside the headquarters of the PLA's General Political Department to demand pension increases. Wearing their old uniforms (an old tactic), the veterans, who had come from twenty different, mostly northern, provinces, did not shout slogans but unrolled banners that read "We want equality, reason, and justice." Benjamin Kam Lim, the reporter on the scene, explained that "Millions of low-ranking PLA officers and rank-and-file soldiers who were given jobs at state-owned industries after retirement feel that their pay and new status fail to live up to their contributions to the country. Many have lost their jobs because state firms are losing money." Even though the protests were entirely peaceful, the CCP was worried; it did not know how the veterans had managed to organize such a large protest across provincial lines. Another cause for concern, although probably unwarranted, was that the veterans would form an ad hoc alliance with the urban protesters against Japanese history textbooks that either downplayed or ignored its wartime behavior in China. After 36 hours, the police moved in. The veterans were forced onto buses or trains and sent back to wherever they came from—the coercive version of the *yuan ji an zhi* policy that has been practiced since the earliest years of the state.[123]

But veterans returned to the capital to press their cause. Like those who protested on commemorative dates in the past (usually the date of the founding of the CCP), on August 1, 2005 (Army Day), hundreds of veterans once again gathered in the capital, at the same locale as the April protests—the General Political Department of the PLA. This protest, which was reportedly dignified and quiet, began at 7:30 a.m., when the office was not yet open, and continued through the early hours of the afternoon before the police took them away. The demands were similar: in the absence of adequate pensions or reasonable-paying jobs, the veterans were hard-pressed. The story of the father of one of these veteran protesters, Gan Guozhong, sums up many of the issues discussed in this and other chapters. A Korean War veteran, Gan had recently died from a bone disease but had spent the last six months of his life bedridden at home because he could not afford medical treatment. Despite his war service and battlefield injuries, "the government did not cover more than 60,000 yuan in medical expenses over the past decade," so his family continued to shoulder the debt. He was assigned to a job in a state-owned factory in 1976 (when the political conditions were more favorable to veterans), but the company went bankrupt in 1993 and he lost his pension and medical benefits. After seven years, he managed to get his pension resumed but not his medical coverage. He spent the next years petitioning the central government, which followed its usual practice of forwarding the letters to the local government, which did nothing. His son, who was also a veteran, had come to Beijing to protest. He explained,

> They once fought for the nation, risking their necks. Now they are old and society has changed a lot, but they haven't gotten love or care from society or the government. My father left the world with regrets.[124]

As suggested by the Gans' case, this kind of bureaucratic runaround most surely took a toll on veterans' family members as well, particularly if they depended on the veteran's pension. Some evidence suggests that problems related to pensions, the Cultural Revolution, political rivalries, and unclear laws and jurisdictions continued well into the reform period. In the late 1990s, for example, a *New York Times* reporter found a 78-year-old woman named Dong Xiulan in the vicinity of the State Council's Letters and Visits Office. She had come to Beijing in 1983 and had been living under a bridge because local officials refused to help her secure her husband's pension. Dong claimed that her husband, a PLA soldier during the war against Japan, "had not been awarded his proper pension when he was discharged in the 1950s." During the Cultural Revolution, her husband was declared a "capitalist roader" and beaten to death, leaving behind his wife and their three children. Holding a stack of old papers from his service and letters from state authorities, Dong said, "I'm

not asking for another life in return for the life of my husband. I'm just asking for the compensation my husband was entitled to. My husband fought
for the revolution for many years, but now nobody has any sympathy for my
misfortune." She managed to get by in Beijing by eating discarded food and
begging.[125] Whether she eventually received compensation is not known.

 In the absence of meaningful political change or policy innovation, veteran
protests have persisted into 2006 and 2007. According to the Demobilized
Military Cadre Resettlement Office, 70–80 percent of China's large-scale
protests were led by veterans. This number appears to be confirmed by
General Guo Boxiong, a vice chairman of the Central Military Commission,
who noted in speech that many veterans were filing petitions in Beijing and
protests were occurring in most every part of the country. In Hainan and
Hunan provinces, veteran-led demonstrations almost developed into revolts.
Guo complained, "The Central Committee has had to spend a fortune to settle
them."[126] Several large-scale protests in 2007 illustrate Guo's predicament.
In September, roughly 2,000 veterans in three separate cities (Baotu in Inner Mongolia, Wuhan in Hubei Province, and Baoji in Shaanxi Province)
protested against their poor living conditions in training centers run by the
Ministry of Railroads. According to reports—all denied by local authorities—the veterans, who had been together in the army but were separated
after their discharge, had been sent for two years of study but found that the
training centers had run-down dormitories, had expensive but poor food, and
lacked study materials; the veterans were also charged one yuan every time
they charged their mobile phones because their rooms did not have power
sockets. The protests, which were coordinated, were somewhat violent: the
veterans smashed classrooms and windows and overturned their instructors'
cars before the police moved in. Their classes were immediately suspended,
and one suspects that they were forced to return to their hometowns.[127] Less
than one week later, veterans from all over Shandong Province once again
gathered outside the Provincial CCP in Jinan to protest, and 300 veterans protested outside the city government's offices in the city of Tai'an. According
to a report in *The Economist*, however, Shandong had already seen quite a bit
of veterans' protest that year. In mid-July, about 2,000 of them had gathered
in the city of Yantai to demand that its People's Congress do a better job "supervising the government" (a demand we also saw in the 1950s) as well as to
demand better jobs. But more than accountability and jobs was at stake: the
veterans had been "taught idealism in the army," but after completing their
service they were sent back to their villages, where there was "next to nothing
to do" and corruption was not uncommon. Little of this mattered to the Yantai
authorities. After turning down the veterans' demands, they ordered the police to "step up surveillance" of their homes and day-to-day whereabouts.[128]

What the PRC government seems not to understand, or perhaps understands quite well but deliberately ignores, is that veterans were protesting not only over money and conditions but also for respectful treatment from state officials and their fellow citizens—a recognition of their claim to martial citizenship and patriotic status. While the state could provide more money or at least order local governments to disburse funds, it could not command local officials and ordinary citizens to respect veterans. This could come only through a broader consensus about the role of veterans in the revolution and state, the legitimacy of the CCP's wars, the meaning of the revolution, and the core identity of the nation and state, and these are still sorely lacking in the PRC. But we should not be surprised by this. As we have seen in other chapters, veterans and their organizations, together with widows and other family members of those most directly affected by war, have been at the forefront of efforts to supply states and societies with a "political narrative" about the meaning of war and sacrifice as well as the civic rituals related to patriotism and republican citizenship. In China, these were mostly top-down efforts manufactured by urban state intellectuals and were therefore not very successful. By failing to provide a wider channel for veterans, war widows, and military families to express themselves, the PRC has stunted patriotism, nationalism, and respect and appreciation for the military.

NOTES

1. For the rise of technocrats, see Cheng Li, *China's Leaders: The New Generation.*

2. For this evidence of "mass nationalism" in the early stages of the reform period, see Harry Harding, *China's Second Revolution: Reform after Mao*, 245. For the late 1990s, see Gries, *China's New Nationalism.*

3. Veterans have been mentioned in essays and books by Kevin O'Brien, Li Lianjiang, Thomas Bernstein, Lü Xiaobo, and June Dreyer, but there has been little extended research on them. Linda Wong, in *Marginalization and Social Welfare in China*, includes eight pages on veterans, but it is based entirely on official sources (statistical yearbooks, Civil Affairs journals).

4. See "Demobilization: The Dialectics of PLA Troop Reduction," 343.

5. See Maryanne Kivlehan-Wise, "Demobilization and Resettlement: The Challenge of Downsizing the People's Liberation Army," 255.

6. "Several Million Demobilized Soldiers Resettled," in Foreign Broadcast Information Service (FBIS hereafter), April 11, 1983, K1. In 1987 officials noted that 80 percent of soldiers come from the countryside. See FBIS-CHI-87-250, December 30, 1987, 19.

7. "Notice on Resettlement of Demobilized Armymen," FBIS, September 10, 1985, K16.

8. Xinhua, "Demobilization: A Boost for the Rural Economy," FBIS, July 30, 1985, K4.

9. See report by Liu Dizhong in the *China Daily*, July 7, 1985 (in FBIS, July 8, 1985, K3–4).

10. See his "CMC Orders Major PLA Shuffle, Demobilization," FBIS-CHI-94-009, January 13, 1994, 30.

11. "Jiang, Li Peng Attend Meeting of Ex-Servicemen," FBIS-CHI-95-241, December 15, 1995, 27.

12. "PRC Civil Affairs Minister Visits Army Headquarters," FBIS-CHI-2001-0119, January 19, 2001.

13. "PLA Holds Meeting on Arrangements for Retiring Soldiers," FBIS-CHI-2001-1108, November 8, 2001.

14. This is not only the case for veterans. As noted by Elizabeth Perry (citing Zhao Yuezhi's *Communication in China: Political Economy, Power and Conflict* [2008]), there seems to be little sympathy for migrant workers, even when they are beaten by the police. Sun Zhigang, a university student who was mistaken for a migrant laborer, was beaten to death by the police while in custody. When this case was exposed, intellectuals generated an uproar—but only because he was a university student. If Sun had been a genuine migrant worker, his death at the hands of the police would not have created the same public outcry.

15. *Anhui sheng zhi: minzheng zhi*, 123.

16. Ellis Joffe, "The Chinese Army after the Cultural Revolution: The Effects of Intervention," 452.

17. Shichor, "Demobilization," 339.

18. Joseph Fewsmith, "China's Defense Budget," 203; Harding, *China's Second Revolution*, 215–16.

19. See Gerald Segal, *Defending China*; Steven J. Hood, *Dragons Entangled: Indochina and the China–Vietnam War*. According to Sijin Cheng, the PLA's credentials were "badly damaged and its failings laid bare for the world to see." See his "The Challenge of Conscription in an Era of Social Change," 236. For a more positive assessment, see Xiaoming Zhang, "China's 1979 War with Vietnam: A Reassessment," 851–74.

20. Xiaobing Li, *A History of the Modern Chinese Army*, 258.

21. According to an interview by Howard French with several veterans, materials about the war were removed from libraries, and a "compendium about the 1980s so complete as to have the lyrics of the decade's most popular songs said nothing of the conflict." Asked what the war was about, veteran Long Chaogang said, "I don't know." Another noted, "We were sacrificed for politics, and it's not just me who feels this way—lots of comrades do, and we communicate our thoughts via the Internet." See Howard French, "Was the War Pointless? China Shows How to Bury It," *New York Times*, March 1, 2005. I am grateful to Yinan He for bringing this article to my attention.

22. Xiaoming Zhang, in contrast, makes the case that the war was accompanied by a surge in patriotic emotions. He writes (p. 855) that "there was a public outpouring of anger against Vietnam" because Vietnam was ungrateful for China's aid since

the early 1950s but backs this up with a single citation from a book published in the PRC (*A 40-Year Development of the China–Vietnam Relationship*). See "China's 1979 War."

23. These reports were in original form. The intelligence agencies made it a point to note "original document" on the sources, apparently believing that the best way to win the propaganda war against the Communists would be to use more objective sources. See *Gongjun futui zhuanye zhenxiang* (*GFZZ* hereafter) (Taipei: Ministry of Defense, 1984), Ministry of Justice–Bureau of Investigation Archives (Xindian).

24. *GFZZ*, 165–67; Also see Dreyer, "Demobilization of PLA Servicemen," 305.

25. *GFZZ*, 167 (based on AFP, May 14, 1979).

26. *GFZZ*, 167 (based on Kyodo News Service and reported by UPI, September 1, 1979).

27. *GFZZ*, 177–78 (based on *Ming Bao* (HK), July 4–5, 3rd edition, 1981).

28. *GFZZ*, 170–71.

29. *GFZZ*, 172 (based on *Xianggang shibao*, May 11, 1981).

30. Cited in Dreyer, "Demobilization of PLA Servicemen," 308.

31. *GFZZ*, 172–73.

32. *GFZZ*, 173 (based on *Gangkou kuaixun*, May 1981).

33. *GFZZ*, 173–74 (based on a report by Yang Junshi in *Xianggang shibao*, June 2, 1981). This situation would be even more acute if the veterans were bachelors. According to the Liaoning Province gazetteer (Civil Affairs), among veteran–bachelors, "not having a home to return to is relatively prominent." See *Liaoning sheng zhi: minzheng zhi*, 114.

34. *GFZZ*, 175–77 (based on *Guiyang Wanbao*, June 16, 1981).

35. These reports first appeared in *Ming Bao* (September 12, 1981) but were later republished under the title "Zheng Wu" (The Whistle of Struggle), no. 50 (Baijia Publishing). They were republished in *GFZZ*, 178–86. These reports also caught the eye of Western intelligence agencies. See FBIS-CHI, December 14, 1981, W/1.

36. The Civil Affairs gazetteer of Anhui Province also called attention to veterans' frequent visits to the provincial capital in 1979 for employment-related problems. See *Anhui sheng zhi: minzheng zhi*, 142.

37. *GFZZ*, 179.

38. Zhang, "China's 1979 War," 857.

39. *GFZZ*, 181.

40. Li, *History of the Modern Chinese Army*, 257–58.

41. *GFZZ*, 181. This phenomenon has also been noted by Dreyer. See "Demobilization of PLA Servicemen," 307. In Hebei Province, Friedman, Pickowicz, and Selden note that in the reform period, "military families fell behind. Young soldiers could not build a cash nest egg to win a proper bride." See *Revolution, Resistance and Reform*, 247.

42. Local officials were hard-pressed to find recruits because of the timeline imposed by Beijing. China amassed roughly 320,000 troops on the border within four to five months (fall 1978 to January 1979), and as a result many were unprepared for battle.

43. *GFZZ*, 182.

44. *GFZZ,* 181–82.

45. *GFZZ,* 183–84.

46. *GFZZ,* 185.

47. Semi-fictional accounts provide a vivid sense of veterans' frustration in the early reform period. For one particularly poignant story, see Mo Yan, *The Garlic Ballads.* The main character, Gao Ma, is a veteran who is very upset about corruption and is knowledgeable about national laws. Not coincidently, Mo Yan was born in the countryside and served for a long time in the PLA.

48. *GFZZ,* 60–62 (based on "1981 Annual Intelligence Report," published by *Zhonggong yanjiu zazhi shilun*).

49. "Xinjiang Meeting Discusses Veteran Resettlement," FBIS-CHI, March 10, 1981, T6.

50. "Ren Zhongyi Attends Guangdong Veteran's Congress," FBIS-CHI, July 31, 1981, P1.

51. *Jingde xian zhi* (Hefei: Huangshan, 1982), 174.

52. *Taihe xian zhi* (Hefei: Huangshan, 1993), 269.

53. *Taihu xian zhi* (Hefei: Huangshan, 1995), 503.

54. *Fufeng xian zhi* (Xi'an: Shaanxi renmin chubanshe, 1993), 586.

55. *Puning xian zhi* (Guangzhou: Guangdong renmin chubanshe, 1995), 465.

56. "Training of Demobilized Soldiers Viewed," FBIS-CHI, January 31, 1986, K1.

57. "Peking Appoints Five Younger Ministers," *New York Times*, September 7, 1985.

58. On his role as minister of personnel, see Gordon White, "The Politics of Economic Reform in Chinese Industry," 365–89.

59. Fan Baojun was born in 1940 and joined the CCP in 1965. He was the director of the Tianjin Municipal Civil Affairs Bureau and in 1987 was appointed vice minister of Civil Affairs. In 2000, he became the vice chairman of the China International Committee for Natural Disasters. See www.chinavitae.com/biography (a well-respected Hong Kong–based website for information about CCP officials). Other information about Working Group personnel can also be found on this site.

60. "1 Billion Yuan allocated to PLA Resettlement," FBIS-CHI, June 24, 1985, K9.

61. "Notice on Resettlement," FBIS-CHI, September 10, 1985, K16.

62. "Ministry's New Regulations for Ex-Servicemen," FBIS-CHI-87-250, December 30, 1987, 19.

63. "New Revised Military Service Regulations," FBIS-CHI-1999-0728, July 11, 1999. Emphasis mine.

64. "PRC State Council, CMC Urge Local Governments to Find Jobs for Ex-Soldiers," FBIS-CHI-2003-1223, December 23, 2003.

65. Irene So, "Millions of War Veterans Living in Poverty in Sichuan," in FBIS-CHI-94-173, September 7, 1994.

66. See, for instance, "PRC's Retired Compulsory Servicemen's Subsidies to Increase," FBIS-CHI-97-289, October 17, 1997.

67. "Ren Zhongyi Attends Guangdong Veterans Congress," FBIS-CHI, July 31, 1981, P1.

68. "Li Peng, Song Ping Meet Delegates," FBIS-CHI-91-206, October 24, 1991.

69. "Jiang Receives Delegates to Meeting on Veteran Cadres," FBIS-CHI-93-184, September 24, 1993.

70. "Young People Urged to Learn from Army Veterans," FBIS-CHI-95-151, August 1, 1995.

71. "Ren Zhongyi Attends Guangdong Veteran's Congress," FBIS-CHI, July 31, 1981, P1.

72. "Leaders on Placement of Demobilized Army Cadres," FBIS-CHI-90-109, June 6, 1990, 54.

73. "PLA Leaders Visit Military Retirees during Holidays," FBIS-CHI-1999-0217, February 12, 1999.

74. "JFJB Commentator on Promoting Reform of Settlement of Demobilized Soldiers," FBIS-CHI-2004-0224, March 2, 2004.

75. "PLA's Internal Discontent, Problems Viewed," FBIS-CHI-90-154, August 9, 1990, 33.

76. Ibid.

77. Ibid.

78. "Army Veterans Reportedly Protest Oppressive Rule" (citing *Cheng Ming* and *Internal Reference*), FBIS-CHI- 91-131, July 9, 1991, 31.

79. Ibid.

80. Ibid.

81. Ibid., 32.

82. Ibid., 32–33.

83. Ibid., 33.

84. "CPC Takes Strict Precautions against Non-Governmental Groups," CIA-RDP96-00792R000200480002-2, 15–18. National Archives, College Park, MD.

85. On TVEs, see Jean Oi, *Rural China Takes Off: The Institutional Foundations of Economic Reform*; Susan Whiting, *Power and Wealth in Rural China: The Political Economy of Institutional Change*.

86. "Demobilized Officers to Be Paid Increased Salary," FBIS-CHI, December 18, 1985, W4.

87. "Official on Resettled Cadres," FBIS-CHI, July 8, 1985, K5.

88. "Demobilized Soldiers Help Rural Development," FBIS-CHI, October 20, 1986, K17.

89. "Demobilized Soldiers Vital Force in Rural Areas," FBIS-CHI, July 30, 1985, K4.

90. "Ex-Servicemen Help Develop Tertiary Industry," FBIS-CHI-92-222, November 17, 1992, 20.

91. *Anhui sheng zhi: minzheng zhi*, 147. Between 1986 and 1989, 4,482 veterans returned to Anhui. Of these, 1,442 were in TVEs. Only 69 veterans (1.5 percent) were given positions at the township-level government and higher. Village government was more promising, but only 419 became village cadres (9 percent).

92. *Chuansha xian xuzhi* (Shanghai: Shanghai shehui kexue yuan, 2004), 578; telephone interview with the Director of the Resettlement Section of Qingpu Civil Affairs, June 2007. In Baoshan County, all veterans were employed in TVEs

in 1985. See *Baoshan xian zhi* (Shanghai: Shanghai shehui kexue yuan, 1992), 685.

93. Friedman, Pickowicz, and Selden, *Revolution, Resistance and Reform*, 256–57.

94. Shichor, "Demobilization," 354.

95. "Clashes Highlight China's Problems with Paramilitary Police," FBIS-CHI-2000-1219, December 21, 2000.

96. Shichor, "Demobilization," 355.

97. "Demobilized Servicemen Guaranteed Jobs," FBIS-CHI 90-072-S, April 13, 1990, 42. The title of this is misleading. According to the policy, jobs were "guaranteed" only to urban veterans and to "rural volunteers who have served in the armed forces for at least 13 years."

98. "Resettlement of Former Military Personnel Urged," FBIS-CHI-91-054, March 20, 1991, 27.

99. "Article Views Placement of Demobilized Officers," FBIS-CHI-94-090, 19.

100. "Over 500,000 Demobilized Soldiers Seek Employment," FBIS-CHI-93-23, December 15, 1993, 31–32. Emphasis mine.

101. "Enforcement of Veteran Placement Policy Stressed," FBIS-CHI 95-233, December 5, 1995, 39.

102. See FBIS-CHI-95-238, December 12, 1995, 13.

103. Kivlehan-Wise, "Demobilization and Resettlement," 261.

104. Ibid., 265. Emphasis mine.

105. Staff reporter, "Former Soldiers Fight for Jobs, Homes and Benefits," *South China Morning Post*, September 8, 2001, 7. I thank Bill Hurst for this reference.

106. "PRC Provincial Leaders on Resettlement," FBIS-CHI-2001-0529, May 29, 2001.

107. "PRC State Council 'Opinion' of Preferential Policy for Urban Demobilized Soldiers," FBIS-CHI-2004-0224, April 9, 2004. Emphases mine.

108. Roisman, "National Ingratitude," 149–56.

109. At least some security intellectuals see this status as problematic. See Mo Ji-long, "Cong falü shang jinyibu guifan zhuanye junren anzhi gongzuo," *Guofang zazhi* (June 15, 1999), in Taiwan Ministry of Defense (ed.), *Gongjun youshi ziliao huibian: Gongjun junzhuan anzhi zhuanji*, vol. 2 (2000), 127–28. This is a collection of original articles published on veteran issues in the PRC, primarily from national security, civil affairs, and international relations journals, and compiled into one volume.

110. Shichor, "Demobilization," 350.

111. In Shanghai in 1994 and 1995, the city government also established a fund and a foundation to support military families and the PLA (*yongjun youshu jijin hui*), but it is not clear how this money (reportedly 80 million yuan) is dispersed or who controls it. See *Shanghai renmin zhengfu zhi* (Shanghai: Shanghai shehui kexue yuan, 2004), 661.

112. "Men Who Killed 7 in Botched PRC Robbery Ex-Soldiers," FBIS-CHI-2000-0910, September 12, 2000.

113. "Chinese Gang Hires Former PLA Troops," FBIS-CHI-2001-0816, August 17, 2001.

114. "PRC Citizens Express Doubts regarding Investigation of Shijiazhuang Bombing," FBIS-CHI-2001-0324, March 26, 2001.

115. Li Lianjiang, "Political Trust in Rural China," 244.

116. O'Brien and Li, *Rightful Resistance in Rural China*, 88, 89, note 20, 136.

117. O'Brien and Li, "The Politics of Lodging Complaints in Rural China," 768–69.

118. Thomas P. Bernstein and Xiaobo Lü, *Taxation with Representation in Contemporary Rural China*, 148. Yu Jianrong of the Chinese Academy of Social Sciences reports similar findings. See his "Organized Struggles of the Peasants and Political Risks Involved: An Investigation in County H of Hunan Province," *Zhanlue yu guanli*, May 1, 2003, 1–16.

119. Feng Chen, "Industrial Restructuring and Workers' Resistance in China," 243.

120. See Heilongjiang Provincial Government, "Zhongyao huiyi, 4/2005," at www.hlj.gov.cn. For the Civil Affairs report, see "2000 nian minzheng shiye fazhan tongji kuaibao," at www.mca.gov.cn.

121. Personal correspondence with a scholar in Beijing.

122. "Laoshan fuyuan junren xiang zhengfu jiti qingyuan," *Radio Free Asia*, January 27, 2005.

123. See Benjamin Kam Lim, "2000 Retired Servicemen Stage Protests in Beijing," *The Seattle Times*, April 16, 2005 (4th edition); this was also reported by *Radio Free Asia* (April 13).

124. Personal correspondence from William Hurst.

125. Erik Eckholm, "Beijing Journal: Please, Mr. Bureaucrat, Hear my 20-year-old Plea," *New York Times*, December 7, 1998.

126. Guo was quoted in an article about *Trend Magazine* in *The Epoch Times* (see Xin Fei, "Potential Military Turmoil Afflicts Hu Jintao," January 29, 2007). While this source is somewhat dubious, the evidence does square with other reports in the same period.

127. These riots did come to the attention of the international press. See, among others, Christopher Bodeen, "Thousands of Demobilized Soldiers Riot in China over Job Retraining," *Associated Press Worldstream*, September 11, 2007.

128. "Beware of Demob," *Economist.com* (November 8, 2007).

9

Conclusion:
Walter Reed, Iraq, and China

In early 2007, just as I was drafting the chapter on Chinese veterans'
medical and family difficulties, reporters Dana Priest and Anne Hull of the
Washington Post broke a story that exposed numerous cases of inadequate
care of disabled Iraq and Afghanistan war veterans at the outpatient clinic
at Walter Reed Army Medical Center, one of the premier military medical
facilities in the United States. Unlike many of the cases I had been reading
and writing about in China, Walter Reed was not located in some remote,
poor rural county but in the capital of the wealthiest country on the planet;
its proximity to the White House and Congress made it an ideal location for
politicians of all stripes to demonstrate their "concern for the troops" by drop-
ping in to visit the wounded. The hospital's elite reputation, prime location,
and the extent of official attention made Priest and Hull's findings all the
more shocking to Americans: rooms with mouse droppings and upside-down
cockroaches, crowded rooms, moldy carpets, walls and peeling wallpaper,
long waits for benefits, and the lack of proper bedside manner on the part
of some hospital staff. In scenes somewhat reminiscent of China half a century ago, Priest and Hull found that "disengaged clerks, unqualified platoon
sergeants and overworked case managers fumble with simple needs: feeding
soldiers' families who are close to poverty, replacing a uniform ripped off by
medics in the desert sand or helping a brain-damaged soldier remember his
next appointment." American veterans, much like their Chinese counterparts,
could not be blamed for expecting better treatment given official rhetoric (and
bumper stickers) about "supporting the troops." As noted by Marine Sargeant
Ryan Groves, 26, an amputee, "We've done our duty. We fought the war. We
came home wounded. Fine. But whoever the people are back here who are
supposed to give us the easy transition should be doing it. We don't know

what to do. The people who are supposed to know don't have the answers. It's a nonstop process of stalling."[1]

Priest and Hull's article proved timely. Working independently of the *Washington Post* reporters, in February 2007 Bob Woodruff from ABC News broadcast a prime-time, very well-publicized expose of American veterans who also were shortchanged upon their return from battle. That Woodruff pursued this story was, however, quite coincidental. Seriously wounded himself while reporting on the war, he was immediately returned to the United States for treatment, his celebrity status and deep pockets (an angle that was largely ignored in the report) ensuring that he received the best of everything during his long rehabilitation. To his credit (and as a stark reminder of the power of empathy stemming from similar experiences), Woodruff came to realize that not all people wounded in war were equal. After his recovery, he prepared his own account of the wide discrepancies in health care, following soldiers from the relatively well-equipped hospital in urban areas to their hometowns, where treatment facilities were either non-existent or very far away. (After this report, Woodruff began an "unofficial second career" as spokesman and fundraiser for wounded soldiers.[2]) Paperwork and guidelines for treatment and disability checks often were delayed, which substantially increased the burdens on soldiers' families, many of whom were not well-off to begin with and some of whom lacked even basic health insurance or access to Veterans Administration (VA) hospitals—a scenario that is also quite familiar from the Chinese case.

This double punch from the *Washington Post* and ABC News led to a storm of media reporting on the problems facing American veterans (with the exception of the "hawkish" *Wall Street Journal*'s editorial page, which ignored the story for three weeks, and the conservative *Weekly Standard*, which devoted two sentences to it). In early March 2007, for example, the front page of *Newsweek* promised to tell readers "Why We're Failing Our Wounded," who were "shattered in body and mind." (This headline was placed next to a photograph of an obviously upset and angry female veteran who was a double amputee.) Editors at the *New York Times* assigned more reporters to the "vet beat," which included problems at Walter Reed and regional Veterans Administration facilities and veterans returning with life-altering medical problems, particularly head wounds.[3] Between March and May 2007, the media attention was unrelenting and led to the issuance of an official apology from President Bush (who promised to "fix the problem")[4] and the establishment of a blue-ribbon commission, the "President's Commission on Care for Returning Wounded Warriors," led by former Senator Bob Dole and former Secretary of Health and Human Services Donna Shalala, who were tasked with figuring out a comprehensive solution to the problems facing veterans upon their return from war. On March 7, Dole and Shalala vowed "to conduct a comprehensive and vigorous investigation, possibly leading to recommendations that could change the system for decades."[5] During April and May, the commission—whose members included some wounded veterans and their family members—heard an earful of complaints about veterans' difficult transition to civilian life. As reported by Robert Pear in the *New York Times*, "wounded soldiers and veterans poured out their frustrations with the military health care system on Saturday, telling a presidential commission that they often had difficulty getting care because military doctors were overwhelmed by the needs of service members injured in Iraq. Speaking from experience, the soldiers and veterans described the military health care system as a labyrinth, said their families had been swamped with paperwork and complained that some care providers lacked compassion." For veterans of the Vietnam War, whose travails in the VA medical system and in American society were graphically portrayed by Ron Kovic in *Born on the Fourth of July* (starring Tom Cruise and directed by Oliver Stone—a veteran—in the 1989 film), there was a *déjà vu* quality about this. Richard F. Weidman, the director of government relations for the Vietnam Veterans of America, noted, "What happened at Walter Reed was not an aberration." It resulted from a policy of "taking care of our soldiers on the cheap."[6] Several months after the Dole–Shalala commission (and others) was formed, little seems to have changed in the care of wounded soldiers.[7]

Weidman's sentiments were certainly understandable; the perception that the government went to war in Iraq with very ambitious goals "on the cheap" (insufficient manpower, protective equipment, and planning, and poor execution) was widely shared in America. Lack of funds, however, was not the only or the most serious problem. Most press accounts, as well as the testimony of wounded veterans, pointed to a bungling bureaucracy as a major cause of veterans' frustrations—also a sentiment very familiar to PRC veterans, as we saw in Chapter 5. According to *Newsweek*, the bureaucracy was "cluttered with red tape," forcing veterans to wait "weeks or months for mental health care and other appointments," while families slid into debt as case managers studied disability claims.[8] This assessment was confirmed by academic research; Linda Bilmes found that, on average, veterans had to wait roughly six months for a claim to be processed, but if the disability claim was denied by the Pentagon, it took roughly 22 months for the appeal to move through its various stages.[9] Other accounts were more sympathetic to the bureaucracy, noting the very high (but probably underreported) incidence of mental health problems affecting the veteran population—close to 36 percent of disabled soldiers and 50 percent of National Guard members reported suffering from some form of psychiatric disorder, especially post-traumatic stress disorder

(PTSD)—as well as the large numbers of veterans returning from war; thanks to improvements in emergency medicine, soldiers who would have died of injuries in previous wars now managed to survive, but with many physical problems.[10] Still other reports pointed to informational and legal deficits. As was the case in China, many American veterans were never informed about their rights and after their injuries were in no position to make sense of the myriad of laws and regulations affecting their care. Politics also entered into some analyses. In one telling, the Bush administration, in its rush to war, did not prepare the groundwork for returning veterans and, once it realized that the war lacked public support, tried to hide its true costs in lives, limbs, and minds from the public. Rather than appoint an experienced manager to lead the Veterans Administration, President Bush appointed Jim Nicholson, a Vietnam veteran and Bush supporter who brought little previous experience to the job of managing a 235,000-person bureaucracy while working for the Republican National Committee, in real estate, and as ambassador to the Vatican.[11] Clustering around some combination of veterans' high expectations for good treatment, bureaucratic bungling, legal problems, and politics, few accounts fingered funding per se as the most significant problem; the problem was moving money and services from point A to B to C—a problem certainly familiar to PRC veterans in cities and the countryside.

As disheartening as these accounts were, they also revealed some of the strengths of the American system and, by the same token, the precise weaknesses of the PRC. Initially, the problems *were* revealed, reports were widely disseminated, and the two-star general in charge of Walter Reed was fired. Public opinion seemed to have made a difference; in the United States, citizens did not question whether veterans deserved benefits (as often was the case in China) and lined up with them and against the state. In addition, American veterans have, at least to some extent, benefited from organizations in civil society that have helped their cause. American veterans, wounded and otherwise, are less "isolated" in society than their PRC counterparts. Wounded Afghanistan and Iraq War veterans have received the support (including lobbying and investigations) of such veterans organizations as Disabled American Veterans, Veterans for America, Iraq and Afghanistan Veterans of America (founded in 2004), Homes for Our Troops, the Wounded Warriors Project, and Veterans of Foreign Wars and such funds as the Intrepid Heroes Fund and the Fisher House Foundation. Several large foundations (Ford, Mott, Robert Wood Johnson, and Kellogg, among others) have contributed funds to help veterans reintegrate into civilian life.[12] Some lawyers have also stepped up to the plate. After the reports about Walter Reed and VA hospitals hit the front pages, three large law firms teamed up with Disabled American Veterans (the country's largest organization of disabled veterans) to help Walter Reed patients navigate veteran-related laws regarding their benefits, free of charge.[13] Finally, in the United States the multi-party system provides the opportunity for the opposition to make political cal hay out of mismanagement of veterans' problems, and this can work to the veterans' benefit. Particularly in the United States, where everybody pays at least lip service to supporting the troops, the scandal at Walter Reed provided a juicy target for Democrats to question the competence and patriotic credentials of the Republicans. In China, of course, the one-party system does not allow veterans to be anyone's "cause" against the state.

Even though it might appear that American Iraq and Afghanistan war veterans will benefit from the involvement of civil society and a free press and democracy, the findings of this book suggest that their longer-term prospects might be somewhat similar to their Chinese counterparts, and for similar reasons. The same American media that exposed the shabby treatment of wounded veterans at Walter Reed and at other facilities, and wrote impassioned editorials, soon moved on to other "hot" issues (i.e., the shenanigans of Britney Spears and Lindsay Lohan).[14] (This view dovetails with academic analysts of the media as well, who call it a "collective tuning out."[15]) Iraq War veterans will also suffer because many Americans view the war as illegitimate, and a failure to boot, with none of the "glory" associated with WWII. I anticipate that even those who were very pro-war (and ran for election deploying flags galore and criticizing war detractors) will wash their hands of the Iraq debacle in the years to come. In this respect, the post-war Iraq situation will likely be similar to its Vietnam counterpart as far as veterans are concerned. It's also a situation familiar to veterans in the PRC—many of the conflicts they were involved in were not recognized as legitimate exercises in political power, and this reflected back on how they were treated. Since the "default" mentality of many societies is to quickly forget wars and their consequences—the creation of lasting memories requires hard work and is an uphill battle usually fought by veterans and families of dead soldiers—I expect Iraq War veterans to end up bitter and angry.

But if the media and politicians often are unreliable allies, could not veterans rely on the assistance of organizations in civil society, particularly veterans organizations? As we have seen in this study, veterans organizations—to the extent that they were feisty, represented a cross-section of the overall population, and formed alliances with other groups in society—have made a significant difference to veterans' post-war prospects. Here again, American veterans will probably be disappointed. Veterans can, and do, organize, but it is highly unlikely that their cause will gain much traction among elites in either academia or business. Academia in the United States—like its counterparts in the PRC—has never taken much interest in veterans or the military; university presidents and deans are unlikely to launch a large-scale public effort on veterans' behalf, despite reports of rising homelessness and other serious problems among Iraq War veterans.[16] Businesses profit by selling American flags and other patriotic paraphernalia on July 4, but it is unlikely that they will get involved in veterans' affairs. News accounts suggest that it is mostly veterans and those with close affiliations with the military who take care of and protect other veterans, again showing the connection between shared experiences, empathy, and support. For example, Steve Robinson of Veterans for America, a "fixer" for many veterans' problems vis-à-vis the Veterans Administration and Department of Defense, is a veteran-turned-activist;[17] Paul Rieckhoff, a graduate of Amherst College, founded Iraq and Afghanistan Veterans of America after serving in Iraq in 2004; James Wright, the president of Dartmouth College, who has made many visits to wounded veterans at Walter Reed and other facilities and initiated a college counseling project for seriously injured veterans, served in the Marines in his youth.[18] The United States is also very similar to China in the dilution of the concept of "patriotic sacrifice." If United States citizens have not even been asked to sacrifice in a "global war on terror" and for a war to uphold "civilization," but its president claims that paying taxes is sufficient wartime sacrifice; praises an indicted, wealthy political aide ("Scooter" Libby) for "sacrificing much in the service to this country"; and argues that Americans are sacrificing their "peace of mind" when watching carnage on television,[19] how will veterans ever be able to assert unique claims to patriotic sacrifice years after their return? Many PRC veterans faced similar challenges to their status by civilians who claimed to have made some sort of sacrifice (whether in the context of a militia, union, or party organization) and some sort of contribution to the success of the revolution, even though few could claim to have served for a decade and endured massive enemy fire, months-long hunger, and debilitating illnesses.[20]

This rough comparison between the United States and China, as well as between China and other countries in other chapters, suggests that the circumstances under which veterans will be treated well or poorly, or receive "patriotic credit" and martial citizenship for their service, are quite complex. As I noted in the introduction, there have been no systematic efforts to compare state expenditures on veterans cross-nationally and temporally, and there have been no comparative attitudinal surveys about veterans past or present, so the best I can do (at least without a very large research budget) is to tally up a rough "scorecard" based on the available historical evidence, much of which was presented in the preceding chapters. Let's summarize these circumstances:

- Wars that are widely perceived as necessary and legitimate will bolster the support networks in society for returning veterans and will increase the chances that veterans get reasonable credit for the outcome. The contrasting experiences of American veterans of WWI and Vietnam on the one hand, and of WWII on the other, are a good example of this. The positive assessment of disabled veterans in Israel (chapter 6) also demonstrates this point.

- Wars that are successful, or at least widely perceived as such, will enhance the "patriotic credit" veterans receive and the chances of positive interactions with fellow citizens afterwards. Japanese and German veterans of WWII, for example, could hardly have demanded such credit given their loss, and many German veterans of WWI and Soviet veterans of the war in Afghanistan had comparable problems in the interwar period (see chapter 3).

- Total wars and near-universal conscription will produce a more heterogeneous and stronger veteran community in the post-war period, as well as a public that is more attune to veterans' problems, than limited or border wars that do not require the full mobilization of society and involve mostly lower- and lower-middle-class military personnel. Here we can point to the powerful veterans organizations established after the Civil War in the United States, most combatant countries after WWI, Japanese veterans after the Sino-Japanese and Russo-Japanese wars, and the United States after WWII.

- Veterans fare better if they can stay together after a war, organize (either autonomously or semi-autonomously), and have strong member support. The relatively high status of veterans in the early Roman Empire has been attributed to all of these factors. The importance of "staying together" was highly visible in the relative quiet among veterans who lived on "veteran farms" in Taiwan and in extensive psychiatric research on U.S. combat veterans. The critical role of organization played out in the contrasting experiences of Canadian veterans after WWI, who did not organize well, and their counterparts in Australia, who did (see chapter 5). Even rural German veterans, who did not benefit from the halo of victory after WWI, could find some comfort and camaraderie in veterans organizations and local watering holes.

- Veterans will face significant challenges to claiming patriotic credit if the wars in which they fought *also involved* militias or partisans and the political leadership does not apportion patriotic credit between them. The case of Revolutionary War veterans in the United States is an example of the former, while the post-WWII Ukraine in the USSR is an example of veterans successfully asserting leadership vis-à-vis partisans (see chapter 3).

- Veterans will do better if they are not grouped with the "ordinary" poor and disabled in public policy and administration. A differentiated "Veterans Administration" (United States), "Ministry of Patriots and Veterans" (South Korea), or "Rehabilitation Division" (in Israel's high-status Ministry of Defense) helps to consolidate veterans' claims for benefits and raise their profile in state and society (chapter 5).

- Veterans will benefit to the extent that they are the beneficiaries of high-level political patronage. This seems more likely to occur if political leaders were themselves in the military or were directly indebted to veterans for gaining power. The status of veterans in the early years of the Roman Empire seems to be a good example of this (see chapter 2), as are the support of President Monroe for the 1819 Pension Act and the expansion of benefits under President Harrison after the U.S. Civil War (chapter 5).

- Veterans will tend to fare better to the extent that there is a cultural association between military service and valued masculine values. Veterans in Bolivia, Australia, Russia, the United States, England, Spain, Germany, and South Korea, among others, have used masculinity as a "discursive resource" in their claims to higher status (see chapter 3).

- There is *no* direct connection between democracy and ample veteran benefits and positive treatment. American and British WWI veterans received far less than their counterparts in Nazi Germany and Fascist Italy; Vietnam War veterans were not treated particularly well after their return. Having the vote *can* make a difference, but only when there are large numbers of veterans (for instance, the Grand Army of the Republic after the U.S. Civil War). That said, democracy will benefit veterans if the press is sufficiently concerned about veterans' welfare and can expose problems with benefits, poor treatment, and health care. We have seen this in the Walter Reed scandal and in Israel (chapter 6), Great Britain, and Australia (chapter 5).

While these nine bullet points are separated for clarity of presentation, it is important to point out that they are not disconnected *causally*, and I do not assign them equal causal *weight*. For instance, veterans organizations that had significant cross-class membership were able to strengthen the cultural nexus between wartime service and masculinity; veterans had more electoral clout, and stronger political patronage, after a war in a democracy in which there was a large-scale draft or when the politician himself led troops into combat. In terms of explanatory weight, I would argue that mass warfare and near-universal conscription, legitimacy, and feisty veterans organizations are the most critical factors (in that order), without which veterans will have only a remote chance of securing benefits and positive treatment from society at large. The first item on this list—mass war and conscription—can be a force bringing about changes in the latter two, as well as other items on my scorecard.

The case of Iraq might serve as a good case in point. The rush to a dubious war; veterans' relative isolation in society; the disengagement of intellectuals, business elites, and celebrities from the war; and the dilution of the concept of sacrifice can all, in my view, be traced to a decades-long separation between the military and civilian society since the end of the draft and Selective Service. Since few children of America's political elite serve in the military, is it all that surprising that the decision-making regarding the war in the executive branch and legislative levels was undertaken with such rashness? Politicians with military background, after all, are fairly scarce these days, and this is reflected in the shortage of people who can speak truth to military and political power. Because patriotic credit is often attached to combat service, it is also not surprising that many politicians were often cowed and defensive when administration officials (most of whom lacked military experience themselves) accused them of "unpatriotic" behavior if they questioned the war or President Bush's decisions and that the most vocal critics of the Iraq War in Congress, and the first to reply very aggressively when charged with "undermining the troops," often were veterans, who knew first-hand what war was like (for instance, Representative John Murtha and Senators Chuck Hagel and Max Cleland). As noted by the political reporter Matt Bai, "in contrast to the insecurities of the many boomer politicians who avoided service in Vietnam or marched against it, the Senate's former soldiers exude a confidence that goes beyond military matters."[21] In contrast, Israelis, who serve in the military, are far less awed by "the state" and do not reify "the government" in any way or cower if accused of "sticking a knife in the back of the nation"; protests by reservists, as noted in Chapters 3 and 6, are common. The same timidity applies to non-political American elites. Absent a draft that threatened the conscription of their sons and daughters, American business leaders, university presidents and deans, and editors of major newspapers were far too willing to give the administration the benefit of the doubt and avoided asking sharp questions in veteran-style blunt language, lest they, too, be accused of "not supporting the troops," "disrespecting the presidency," or demonstrating other forms of "unpatriotic" behavior. Had more people served and sacrificed, these sorts of attacks could have been easily repelled.

The lack of conscription will surely affect the ability of veterans to use the war as a rhetorical and organizational resource for future political battles. As noted by Kevin Baker, absent mass participation, shared experiences, and sacrifices during the course of military service (or in other forums), the war "cannot be passed off as an heroic endeavor."[22] Veterans organizations will not benefit from substantial cross-class membership, which, comparatively, has been a crucial asset to securing equitable treatment. Post-discharge benefits will also be affected. It is probably not a coincidence that veterans-turned-politicians (James Webb and Chuck Hagel) were the driving force behind an effort to legislate a new and improved GI Bill for veterans of the Iraq and Afghanistan wars.[23] (Similarly, on Taiwan, a law that provided pensions to servicemen who retired before June 30, 1970, was proposed by legislators with a military background; before that date, servicemen's salaries were "much lower than those of government employees."[24])

These "distilled" points culled from the comparative literature and more current examples are, I believe, highly instructive for the Chinese case. If I am right in attributing many veterans' problems to such factors as the nature of warfare and the place of the military in society, legitimacy, and organizations (rather than money per se), it also means that many of the problems that veterans faced in China should not strike us as particularly unusual. What *is* somewhat strange given all of this comparative research on poorly treated veterans is that Chinese veterans, or least the large majority of them, were ever perceived as part of the elite and accruing very significant benefits from their status, particularly given their rural background, health, the complex circumstances of the CCP's rise to power, its controversial wars, and the party's policy of isolating groups from one another. In part, this positive perception could be attributed to the high profile of PLA generals at certain periods, the position of some of them on the Standing Committee of the Political Bureau and Military Affairs Commission, and the fact that a portion of them (but only a minority) received political positions. More important than these, however, has been the one area where the PRC *has* shown strength—its Oz-like ability, thanks to its monopolization of education and the media as well as its success in recruiting highly educated people into the CCP's Propaganda Department (in the Maoist period, this bureaucracy had more intellectuals than any other state organ[25]), to create certain *perceptions* about its power, or what Joel Migdal has called an "aura of invincibility."[26] This was certainly not new—creating impressive form, even when the substance was weak, has long been a staple of Chinese statecraft—but the CCP has been able to take impression management to new heights. As astutely noted by Chang-tai Hung, the focus on imagery reflected the CCP's realization that "seizing power was more than a political and military campaign; *perhaps even more important was the aesthetic battle over the control of colors, signs, symbols, and visual vocabulary.*"[27] From generating misperceptions of "rising patriotism" among its citizens (not coincidentally, after a "patriotic education" campaign in the early 1990s) to its capacity for making enforceable international deals and treaties, the CCP has been notably successful in convincing many observers that what is legislated in Beijing matters a great deal[28] and that "the center" (unlike the local state) is a coherent and even virtuous entity.[29] Since the reform period, this perception has been relatively easy to maintain since few foreign scholars in international relations (where claims of rising nationalism and patriotism tend to be the most pronounced) use archival materials.[30]

In this study, I have tried to play the role of Toto, Dorothy's feisty little pooch, to the CCP's Wizard of Oz by pulling back, ever so slightly, the official curtain and bringing to light sources that reveal what happened to veterans in everyday life as they interacted with bosses, workers, other peasants, and officials at all levels of government (what Migdal calls "the trenches," "dispersed field offices," "the agency's central offices," and "the commanding heights"[31]) rather than as subjects of propaganda. Absent a free press, oral history projects, independent research organizations, large-scale surveys, and the personal memoirs that scholars have used to examine veterans' status in other areas of the world, I found archives to be the best available place to examine veterans' and military families' interactions with all levels of state and different communities and how they viewed their place in each. This was interesting in its own right—to date, veterans have not really had a voice in our understanding of Chinese politics—and as a window to examine, from the bottom up, patriotism and nationalism, citizenship, civil–military relations, and the legitimacy of the state; veterans and those associated with the military, after all, were an important part of the state's legitimizing universes with regard to all of these concepts. If the PLA was a highly respected institution, why were so many veterans treated so poorly, even if some of them were allocated jobs? Why were military (and martyr) families subject to derision? If nationalism and patriotism were important sentiments after 1949, why would veterans, whom the state claimed symbolized state power and newfound sovereignty, suffer widespread, flagrant, and openly acknowledged discrimination? If the CCP and its wars were indeed so legitimate, why would PLA veterans not enjoy a significant boost in status?

The argument that best explains most of the new archival evidence (no explanation can resolve everything) broadly focuses on the history of the CCP revolution and its wars. Given that the Communist Revolution was based primarily in the countryside, that most of its veterans had rural backgrounds, and that the CCP was a movement and party *with an army* rather than a modern state *leading* or *creating* a "nation-in-arms," it is not very surprising to find that many veterans in cities suffered discrimination. That veterans' welfare did not strike a sympathetic chord in the CCP elite seems plausible given that the latter were better educated, were strongly oriented toward cosmopolitan cities, and generally refrained from military service even as they wrote articles in support of a strong state and army;[32] it also conforms to international patterns when there is a large degree of separation between the military and society. The disputes surrounding veterans' own claims for martial citizenship and patriotic status also make sense when considering the length and complexity of the Communist Revolution. What was essentially a military success won on battlefields was (re)defined by non-veteran political elites as a much broader-based victory that included, in equal measure, intellectuals, enlightened businesspeople, minorities, workers, unions, women, guerrillas, activists, militiamen, and others, who then carved up glory like a melon and challenged veterans' claims to this status and their "negotiating" power in society.

The complexity of the revolution and wars did not help veterans' claims to status and power. As argued by Michael Dutton, CCP politics were centrally animated by defining "friends" and "enemies,"[33] but the list of each could be quite long and was often interchangeable: rich and middle peasants could be allies or enemies; Nationalist soldiers were "friends" during the first and second "United Fronts" (1923–1927, 1938–1945) but became enemies in a fight to the death in the Civil War; Lin Biao was a war hero and the heir apparent, then a traitor; the USSR and Vietnam were friends, then enemies; PLA veterans secured "victory" in Korea but were potential enemies because their parents had bad class background; people were urged to respect Marshal Peng Dehuai, but during the Cultural Revolution even veterans who fought under him were instructed to smudge black ink on his image on their official certificates of meritorious service.[34] All of these shifts in elite politics rendered veterans highly vulnerable to political attacks and made their claims to patriotic worthiness easily contestable. In these respects at least, PRC veterans' situations were somewhat more complicated than those of many of their counterparts around the world, where 20th-century wars were shorter, fought by more centralized states with a higher degree of "infrastructural power," with better integrated armies (thanks to conscription), against an easily identifiable, less shifting enemy. After World War II, ordinary American and Russian citizens and low-level officials could not plausibly claim the same degree of sacrifice, commitment, worthiness, and heroism as the front-line combat soldier, which *was* the case in urban and rural China, thanks to the more protracted and complex nature of its wars.[35] If the CCP revolution and wars were a novel, keeping track of its characters' vices, motives, and multiple alliances would be a formidable task; if they were a theatrical production, there would be too many characters on the stage claiming the spotlight at the same time. In the post-WWII American version of this novel or theatrical production, the narrative line would be tighter and "cleaner" because veterans' heroism would be placed at the center (with workers, women, and others in important, but still secondary, roles), and the spotlight would be far less scattershot in its signaling of patriotic credit for victory. While academics generally tend to dismiss the virtues of simplicity, it surely would have made it easier for veterans, as well as military and martyr families, to assert themselves politically had the narrative of the CCP's eventual victory included far fewer "glorious" actors, acts, and political sets.

What might have simplified the story and made veterans more palatable to both the public and scores of CCP officials would have been a stronger sense of nationalism and patriotism, particularly in a country that at least claims to appreciate the consequences of the CCP's military victory: enhanced national power, sovereignty, and social stability. In many other countries, veterans had more opportunities to benefit from their service because their organizations claimed, often successfully, that they embodied a heroic, masculine ideal of republican citizenship, which dovetailed with a sense of national identity based on these ideas. Although some contested the extent to which veterans were entitled to particular benefits, there has been little conflict over the more basic claim that veterans are worthy of public support for their sacrifices and commitment. That this has not been forthcoming in China—it still strikes urban Chinese as entirely understandable and reasonable that veterans should not be allowed to live among them—suggests to me that nationalism and patriotism are rather shallow and cheap sentiments of the bumper sticker and American flag lapel variety, and, notwithstanding all the hoopla surrounding this topic, the world should not have to worry too much about the threat it poses to the rest of the world. In China, some city folk occasionally will protest against Japan and vilify its wartime behavior but not boycott its products;[36] businesses host large groups of Japanese as sex tourists; national and city icons like the Forbidden City and the Beijing National Opera House are reconstructed or named for foreign companies (American Express and Dannon, respectively); the government does little to protect its workers from the predations of factory owners from Taiwan and Japan; it was Chairman Mao who denied Chinese citizens the right to sue Japan when it renounced war reparations in Article 5 of the 1972 "Joint Statement" normalizing relations (which Japanese courts now use to deny claims by sex slaves and forced laborers[37]); and the brain drain to the United States and other countries did not slow down after the United States bombed the Chinese Embassy in Sarajevo. If nationalism is so important, why has it largely bypassed many of the veterans who brought the CCP to power, fought its wars, built factories, toiled in industries in remote regions (including oil), rescued villagers from floods, and protected the borders the state sees as so critical to its self-identity?[38] This disparaging attitude can also be found among some Western international relations scholars who see China as a rising threat on account of its "surplus males." In a much-ballyhooed article in *International Security*, Valerie Hudsen and Andrea Den Boer worry about the growth of the People's Armed Policc (PAP), fearing that this force, designed to contain domestic unrest, could be turned outward. Calling the new members of the PAP "dregs" who pose a threat to the peace because they lack families ("bare branches"), Hudson and Den Boer do not give any patriotic credit to the *veterans* who have been assigned to the PAP because of limited job opportunities and discrimination against them in the civilian sector, hardly strong indication of rising patriotism.[39] But even if one does not see a connection between veteran status and patriotism, would there be much to fear from rising *economic* patriotism? Here again, we should apply a behavioral test: if more contemporary nationalism is based on pride in China's rising GDP, why are the ordinary workers, migrants, and others who built the modern cities and produce the goods not given credit or recognition, let alone respect, in everyday interactions with officials and more privileged citizens?

In light of China's history, the fragility of nationalism and patriotism is not very surprising. These concepts, as well as "community" and "citizenship," are essentially foreign, transplanted to China from Western Europe, often via Japan, not very long ago. The European (and Russian, Japanese, Turkish, Israeli, Singaporean, Korean, and American) experiences of state- and nation-building, of which nationalism and patriotism were an inseparable part, were strikingly different than in China, however. In those countries, mass wars with mass conscription (which sometimes coincided with industrialization) or a national draft, the military, generals, and veterans and widows organizations played more critical roles in forging patriotism and nationalism (often through the creation and support of patriotic civic rituals) as well as respect, support, and appreciation for military service. Because these concepts were not "natural" anywhere—even in the more "martial" Great Britain, patriotism had to be learned and people "needed to see some advantage" learning it[40]—it often fell to the military and military-affiliated personnel to develop them, and it was during mass war (or conscription) when people from all walks of life had no choice but to meet each other for the first time under conditions more likely to forge a sense of unity or, at least, more understanding. In South Korea, for instance, a 1985 survey on military service and socialization of young men found that "a majority of male college students, who have been generally more critical of military service than other social groups, accepted martial duty and reported that they learned patriotism, endurance, and masculinity through military service";[41] more than 20 years later, and long after South Korea became a democracy, 85 percent of South Koreans told Gallop Korea pollsters that they intend to fulfill their military service requirements; among Koreans more than 50 years old, 82.5 percent value military service.[42] Similar findings about the role of the military in nation-building have been found in Singapore (which also drafts most young men) as well.[43] China, to be sure, had military engagements but never had a "national army" to speak of (or, for that matter, national, or *non-party*, education); the PLA belongs to the CCP, whose legitimacy was always questionable, and its military manpower policies were always tinged with class politics. (In the USSR, WWII diminished the importance of class background—even former kulaks joined the war effort.[44]) Perhaps the reason Chinese veterans ran into trouble when demanding that "the nation" repay its debt to them for their patriotic contributions—a frequent rhetorical strategy in veteran politics—was because there was never an agreed-upon understanding of the "nation" or "patriotism" in the first place. Instead, there were "people," "networks," "families," "lineages," "villages," and "officials" and the like, upon whom educated political elites occasionally, and usually opportunistically to guarantee their own status and power, superimposed patriotic rhetoric and assertions of collective identity.[45] Surely it is not a coincidence that "patriotism" suddenly resurfaced as a legitimating ideology after the Cultural Revolution and that the party began its "patriotic education campaign" in 1994 after the debacle of Tiananmen Square in 1989, rising inequality, and political corruption. For the most part, however, the pursuit of power and money crowds out most all other "isms" and ethical concerns. Economic neoliberalism and republican forms of patriotism and citizenship do not coexist very easily. In most cases, I would argue, the former weakens the latter.

In this respect, it might be argued that one of the main problems with Chinese politics is that it was poorly militarized before 1949 (warlordism) and *insufficiently* and *superficially* militarized after 1949 (with the exception of the latter years of the Cultural Revolution). True, Chinese politics was infused with military terms (*front*, production *brigades*, *campaigns*, etc.) and PLA marshals had high status for a time (but this did not help many of them during the Cultural Revolution) and were strongly represented in the Military Affairs Commission. At the same time, the most experienced military personnel did not have enough clout to stop reckless schemes such as the Great Leap Forward or the Cultural Revolution (including the rise to power of radical leftist intellectuals and propaganda specialists such as Chen Boda, Yao Wenyuan, or the likes of Kang Sheng) and at the local level could not stop the predations of local officials with background in the militia;[46] on the whole, military officials tended to be more practical, less prone to romantic visions of politics (more Hamilton than Jefferson), and less ideological than intellectuals, who generally did not suffer the consequences of policies they advocated and supported, particularly when it came to violence and war.[47] Mao, for his part, was militarized along the model of *guerrilla warfare*. In a somewhat similar vein, the reckless Iraq War was also opposed by most of the Pentagon brass (who support civilian control over the military almost to

a fault) but pushed through by civilian "defense intellectuals" (Paul Wolfow-
itz, Douglas Feith, Richard Perle) who lacked military background, let alone
experience in war.[48]

Conceived in this way, perhaps an early tragic moment in modern Chinese
politics was the death of Yuan Shikai in 1916, a non-ideological national
leader and state builder who also had extensive military background,[49] not
unlike Park Chung-hee in South Korea (who instituted conscription that finally forced educated Koreans to serve and played the most important role in
creating the Ministry of Patriots and Veterans in 1961), George Washington,
Alexander Hamilton, James Monroe, Kemal Ataturk, Harry Truman, Napoleon, Josef Pilsudsky in Poland, Karl Mannerheim (Finland), Yamagata Ari-
tomo (Japan), or the generals under Czar Alexander II who instituted a universal draft.[50] Due to the long-term problem of weak infrastructural power,
the years of political chaos that followed the collapse of the imperial state,
and the inability of the CCP or Nationalists to consolidate a state capable of
"drafting the nation" in wartime, China did not experience the dramatic surge
in state- and nation-building and citizenship expansion that characterized
other states during mass-mobilized wars (including the United States, which
was more known for its aversion to a strong central government). In these
respects, China was similar to Latin America, where limited war-making
also resulted in weak but despotic political centers, shallow nationalism, and
a highly fragmented political community.[51] As noted by Patricia Thornton,
rather than the mobilization of troops, the Chinese process of state-making
has "long been shaped by the recurring need to define and redefine the center
as a moral agent—in fact, *the* moral agent—in modern Chinese history,"[52]
which has merely draped itself with what Waldron calls the "appurtenances
of nationhood on the Western model" (national flags, anthems, patriotic
holidays).[53] This helps explain both the hollow quality of many central state
laws and regulations (which were, and continue to be, regularly flouted,
even when they were addressed at problems as serious as corruption) and
China's lack of welfare and medical institutions to care for the majority of its
population and elite sympathy for them. In Great Britain, France, Germany,
the United States, and Japan—all models for Chinese elites at one point or
another—welfare provisions were greatly expanded during long mass wars,
often at the behest of the military—conscripted citizens needed to be healthy
to fight in these wars and, having fought for the nation, could not be easily
ignored afterward. In China, however, the status of the military remains low
despite nearly a century of attempts to raise its status. Male peasants get little credit for joining the PLA in large numbers, and military service, a very
important avenue for social mobility for poor men in many countries, has far
more limited possibilities in China.

The low status of the military might also affect China's relationship with Taiwan. If the two sides of the bloody U.S. Civil War were able to reconcile because of a shared appreciation of martial/masculine qualities (courage under fire; fighting for a cause, even a mistaken one), perhaps the still-unresolved conflict over Taiwan also can be explained in terms of a more general failure to recognize the patriotic status of wartime military service. According to one account, the newfound recognition of the contributions of Chiang Kai-shek and his generals to the war effort against Japan derived largely from "the attempt by Beijing to lure Taiwan into an agreement of unification" and the sudden need for a new legitimating ideology (patriot-ism) after the collapse of Marxist–Leninist–Maoist ideology after the Cul-tural Revolution,[54] hardly sincere recognitions of military service. Given all of these differences, one wonders whether it is even appropriate to call China a "modern nation-state" with all that this implies about notions of patriotism, citizenship, and forms of state power. Perhaps older terms such as *realm, ritual, subjects,* and *empire*—which implicitly recognize very large zones of local autonomy, ideological flexibility, and despotism (in the sense of very limited input into decision making)—are more relevant to understanding contemporary (not "modern") Chinese politics?

If this assessment is largely correct, the future prospects for citizenship and patriotism in China (and the United States, I fear) are bleak and precari-ous. Unlike the Cultural Revolution generation that experienced life in the countryside, the reform-era generation will produce leaders who have little connection with or knowledge of the countryside; one can live a lifetime in Shanghai and never meet a peasant in his or her home. Chinese will have no common experiences to speak of, and "citizenship," to the extent that it exists, will largely consist of difficult-to-enforce rights on paper rather than more respectful views and actions toward others, particularly the less fortunate. Nationalism, for that matter, will largely remain in the realm of imagination, with few implications for the generation of meaningful, action-oriented "fel-low feeling," which should be at the heart of this concept (such as making the nation "strong" by providing better health care in rural areas or helping the veterans who helped defeat the United States in the Korean War secure their pensions). The very fact that the CCP feels compelled to mount extensive "patriotic education" campaigns is, in my view, testimony to the unbearable lightness of this concept in the population.[55]

In many respects, it would be easy to "blame" the CCP for the poor treat-ment of veterans and the fragility of patriotism in China. The CCP, after all, has denied a voice (either personal or organizational[56]) to the populations that have been most noted for their patriotic credentials as well as for their sacrifices for the state—veterans, military families, and widows. From the perspective of the more fundamental goal of the CCP, that is, preservation of its power, however, there can be no blame because its goal has been achieved. Despite all the terrible calamities that occurred on its watch, the CCP still has power, and this, more than any imported foreign concept or political principle, is the coin and language of the realm. To keep power over the long term, the CCP has been willing to sacrifice many, even its most patriotic, supporters. Many veterans sensed, quite accurately, that they were like "donkeys slaughtered after grinding the wheat." This was an appropriate metaphor for their status in a radically pragmatic regime beholden to no political principle or moral or ethical stance. Little change is upon the horizon: the CCP is not considering any version of the "GI Bill of Rights" or any form of national or provincial veterans organization. Hypocritically, the propaganda machinery continues to blare—in 2007, large billboards in Qingpu's main thoroughfare carried the same slogans about "the people's support of the military" as during the 1950s—reminding veterans of the large gap between rhetoric and everyday realities.

NOTES

1. Dana Priest and Anne Hull, "Soldiers Face Neglect, Frustration at Army's Top Medical Facility," *Washington Post*, February 18, 2007, A1.

2. Jacques Steinberg, "Recovering from Injury, Returning to TV, Speaking for the Wounded," *New York Times*, October 25, 2007.

3. Paul Giblin and Randal Archibold, "Veteran Director in Arizona Steps Down after Violations," March 28, 2007; Deborah Sontag and Lizette Alvarez, "For War's Gravely Injured, A Challenge to Find Care," March 12, 2007.

4. Peter Baker, "At Walter Reed, Bush Issues an Apology," *Washington Post*, March 31, 2007.

5. William Branigin, "Dole, Shalala Promise Full Investigation into Military Care," *Washington Post*, March 7, 2007.

6. Robert Pear, "President's Military Medical Care Panel Hears Frustrations of Soldiers Wounded in Iraq," *New York Times*, April 15, 2007.

7. See Hope Yen, "Report Says Veterans' Care Woes Remain," *Boston Globe*, September 26, 2007.

8. Dan Ephron and Sarah Childress, "Forgotten Heroes," *Newsweek*, March 5, 2007, 31.

9. See "Soldiers Returning from Iraq and Afghanistan: The Long-Term Costs of Providing Veterans Medical Care and Disability Benefits," KSG [Kennedy School of Government] Faculty Research Working Paper Series RWP07-001, January 2007.

10. Sontag and Alvarez, "For War's Gravely Injured." According to their account, the *Washington Post* revelations and "Bob Woodruff's reporting on ABC about traumatic brain injury" led to greater cooperation between the military and the

civilian sector, which until then had been kept at arm's length. For the National Guard figure, see Ann Tyson, "Pentagon Report Criticizes Troops' Mental Health Care," *Washington Post*, June 16, 2007.

11. Steve Robinson of Veterans for America, an advocacy group, levels this charge. See "Forgotten Heroes," 37. Nicholson's official biography is on the Department of Veterans Affairs website (www.va.gov). Nicholson resigned from the VA in July 2007, citing personal reasons.

12. Susan Berresford, "Easing Veterans' Transition to Civilian Life," *The Chronicle of Philanthropy*, November 15, 2007.

13. Hope Yen, "Vet Group, Lawyers Team to Help Soldiers," *Associated Press*, June 6, 2007.

14. See Francis Clines, "Editorial Observer," *New York Times*, June 18, 2007.

15. Susan Carruthers, "No One's Looking: The Disappearing Audience for War," 73.

16. Erik Eckholm, "Surge Seen in Number of Homeless Veterans," *New York Times*, November 8, 2007.

17. See Joshua Hersh, "The Fixer," *The New Republic*, May 21, 2007, 37–41.

18. Tamar Lewin, "The Few, the Proud, the Dartmouth-Bound," *New York Times*, May 23, 2007.

19. See Theda Skocpol, "Will 9/11 and the War on Terror Revitalize American Civic Democracy?" 538; Thomas Friedman, "Don't Ask, Don't Know, Don't Get," *New York Times*, March 7, 2007. Bush praised Libby for his sacrifices after he was indicted and resigned in October 2005. See *New York Times*, June 2, 2007.

20. When Huang Ju, an engineer who became party secretary of Shanghai and a member of the Political Bureau's Standing Committee, died, the CCP obituary called him a "long-tested and faithful Communist fighter." See "Leaders Pay Their Last Respects to Huang," *China Daily*, June 6, 2007.

21. Matt Bai, "The McCain Doctrines," *New York Times Magazine*, May 18, 2008, 42.

22 Kevin Baker, "Stabbed in the Back!", *Harper's,* June 2006, 42.

23. See "A Post-Iraq G.I. Bill," *New York Times*, November 9, 2007.

24. Yu-Wen Fan, "Becoming a Civilian," 102.

25. Hong Yung Lee, *The Politics of the Chinese Cultural Revolution*, 128.

26. This was seen early on in the PRC. One of the first major military spectacles of the PRC—the march of the PLA into Beijing on February 3, 1949—was staged to give the impression that the CCP was welcomed by the population. See Chang-tai Hung, "Mao's Parades," 412; Migdal, "The State in Society," 14.

27. Chang-tai Hung, "Oil Paintings and Politics: Weaving a Heroic Tale of the Chinese Communist Revolution," 784. Emphasis mine.

28. For instance, it takes credit for the reform policies and solving the famine of the early 1960s, among other things. For a magisterial account of the reforms in the Yangzi Delta from a non-central-state perspective, see Lynn T. White III, *Unstately Power*, 2 vols. In North China, "Citizens credited themselves, not the government, for rising standards of living, even while cursing the authorities as obstacles to that rise." See Friedman, Pickowicz, and Selden, *Revolution, Resistance and Reform*, 275.

29. For an elaboration of this point for the Qing, Republican, and Communist periods, see Patricia Thornton, *Disciplining the State.*

30. For a very polite critique of theorists who slight questions of implementation (and the data necessary to look at this issue), see Andrew Mertha, *The Politics of Piracy: Intellectual Property in Contemporary China.*

31. Migdal, "The State in Society," 16.

32. See Arthur Waldron, "Looking Backward," 257.

33. Michael Dutton, *Policing Chinese Politics: A History.*

34. QA 48-2-227 (September 1968), 43.

35. As noted by Catherine Merridale in her account of the Red Army in WWII, "no one felt prouder, or more entitled to claim ownership of this victory, than the soldiers themselves." See *Ivan's War,* 337.

36. There is little evidence that "rising" patriotism influences consumer choices. See Alfred Hille, "Patriotism Plays Little Role in Brand Choices," *Media* (H.K.), December 12, 2003, 10; Andrew Jacobs, "Despite Boycott Threat, a French Retailer's Aisles Are Far from Empty in China," *New York Times*, May 2, 2008.

37. Norimitsu Onishi, "Japan Rules against Sex Slaves and Laborers," *New York Times*, April 28, 2007, A5.

38. See Gittings, *The Role of the Chinese Army*, 178, 183.

39. See "A Surplus of Men, A Deficit of Peace: Security and Sex Ratios in Asia's Largest States," *International Security*, 26, 4 (Spring 2002), 30.

40. Ibid., 295.

41. Seungsook Moon, *Militarized Modernity,* 55.

42. Gil Hyun Lee, "Patriotism in Korea: Results from an Annual Survey," presentation at the symposium on "The United States and the Koreas: A Critical Relationship," November 10, 2007.

43. According to one small survey of military service and nation-building (thirty-three reservists), 76 percent answered in the affirmative to the question whether "national service in Singapore helps to forge stronger ties and links between different racial groups who coexist in Singapore." According to the study, "conscript service appears to help in creating a common shared experience among youth." See Elizabeth Nair, "Nation-Building through Conscription Service in Singapore," 106.

44. Merridale, *Ivan's War,* 166. For this reason, class warfare similar to the Cultural Revolution would probably have been impossible *after* WWII in the USSR. The same logic would apply to post-war Vietnam as well.

45. For a similarly skeptical view of intellectual elites at the end of the Qing dynasty and early Republican period (in the context of the Beijing University), see Timothy Weston, *The Power of Position: Beijing University, Intellectuals and Chinese Political Culture, 1898–1929.*

46. Mao's reliance on radical intellectuals and propagandists is well documented. See MacFarquhar, *Origins, Vol. 3,* 39–40. Ralph Thaxton's study of Da Fo village also notes the extent to which local officials, most of whom emerged from a violent wartime militia, systematically sidelined returning Korean War veterans. Unlike the former militia members, the PLA veterans "shared patriotic goals learned in the army, by and large agreed on the importance of *not using coercion to effect popular*

compliance, and formed a cohesive political reference group within the village." See *Catastrophe and Contention*, 82. Emphasis mine.

47. Modern-day "nationalists" who would push for attacking Taiwan if it declares independence would not be on the front lines and, given China's poor history with veterans' administration, would probably not advocate on veterans' behalf after the war. Advocating violence with someone else's blood does not a "nationalist" make.

48. A recent study has shown that in the United States, the propensity to initiate armed conflict *decreases* the *higher* the proportion of veterans in the cabinet and Congress. See Chistopher Gelpi and Peter Feaver, "Speak Softly and Carry a Big Stick? Veterans in the Political Elite and the American Use of Force," 788.

49. Yuan, with the assistance of German advisors, was largely responsible for building up China's infantry after the Sino-Japanese War and the Boxer Uprising. He also substantially increased the number of military academies, including the famous Baoding Academy. See Hans van de Ven, "War in the Making of Modern China," 739.

50. Some would argue that Chairman Mao was such an individual. Although Mao officially "led" the military, he was not a military man at heart but a romantic revolutionary and Leninist politician. Deng Xiaoping was also not a military man but, rather, "Mao Zedong's loyal lieutenant and essentially his operational executive at the front-line, who was *nominally* (from January 1938) the Political Commissar of the Eight Route Army's 129th Division, the main CCP military force in the base area and border region." See David S. G. Goodman, *Social and Political Change in Revolutionary China*, 14. Emphasis mine.

51. Centeno, *Blood and Debt*.

52. Thornton, *Disciplining the State*, 2.

53. Waldron, "China's New Remembering," 978.

54. Parks Coble, "China's 'New Remembering,'" 402.

55. For a similarly bleak view of citizenship in China, see Thornton, *Disciplining the State*, 20. She calls attention to a "pathological" public sphere and a "vacuum of both moral and authority and power."

56. As one international relations expert and party member in Shanghai told me, "Veterans are not heard from."

Appendix A

A Brief Survey of
Archival Materials in China

Having advocated archival research as an effective way to lift the curtains that often hide many aspects of Chinese politics, it is worth saying a few words about archives and the sort of materials they house. Given that access to archives is not always smooth sailing and researchers' resources (such as time and money) are usually limited, what sorts of documents are worth pursuing with dogged determination, and which can be given up with little loss of sleep or increased blood pressure? The rules of thumb I have used most frequently in requesting materials (for this study and my earlier work on the 1950 Marriage Law) are (1) the less censored, the better; (2) the more local, the better; and (3) get everything with the words *diaocha* or *jiancha* (investigation) in it.[1] Since these rules of thumb can encompass a fairly wide range of documents, what can researchers expect to find in archives, and why are these materials more useful than other sources? Below is a brief survey.

MINUTES OF MEETINGS

Minutes can be a very useful source, since, unlike more official sources such as newspapers, they are mostly unedited and uncensored and thus bring to light information "direct from the horse's mouth." I am not sure at what level of government it was mandatory to have a secretary jot down notes, but the practice was fairly widespread. I have read minutes of work teams implementing the Marriage Law, judges' deliberations, Civil Affairs officers learning about the marriage registration process, meetings of county officials, and officials' comments on proposed policies. Like reading recordings of Kissinger's phone calls to foreign leaders (see *The Kissinger Transcripts*), minutes provide a generally unvarnished representation of how the state works in the "trenches" and at the intermediate levels, such as district offices. At the same time, reading minutes can be very labor-intensive, particularly for those not accustomed to reading handwritten Chinese with various shortcuts for characters. Unless you have a lot of time, these materials should be photocopied.

INVESTIGATION REPORTS

Of all sources I have used in this study, these have probably been the most valuable. First, many satisfy my "local" rule because investigations occur at all levels of the party/state apparatus. Trade unions, factory party committees, courts, hospitals, and military units were all ordered, at one point or another, to investigate something. When the State Council ordered an investigation (on veterans in 1956–1957, for example), investigation teams were formed throughout the country, which means that archives in Shanghai, Yunnan, and Guangdong will have important materials on the same problem. (Of course, the quality of investigation, and the extent of follow-up, will vary widely.) This facilitated interesting comparisons between locales. These materials can be printed or handwritten, depending on the "authors" and resources at their disposal. Second, investigations were quite common and generally conducted in a reasonably objective manner by external work teams. To our benefit, the PRC was obsessed with research. Although their findings are never couched in terms other than Marxist or Maoist, the verbatim quotes from officials and ordinary people provide a very candid and frank look at the interface between state and society. Third, because investigation reports were never intended for outside eyes, they are not heavily censored (if at all); many are stamped "secret" or "top-secret." Even better, one can sometimes read multiple drafts of the same report to see exactly what parts were excised as it went up the bureaucratic ladder.

At the same time, investigation reports need to be handled a bit gingerly, since they are almost always focused on *problems*. Even though investigation reports on veterans usually originated in directives from the State Council and the Central Military Commission, it is possible that some local officials exaggerated certain circumstances in order to make a compelling case for devoting more attention to local veterans' affairs (even when the introductory paragraphs of these reports lauded these efforts). To assess just how extensive these problems are, researchers should look for corroborating evidence from other sources (interviews, the press, gazetteers, *neibu* books), regions, or other documents in the archives (work reports, policy statements). On many occasions I have "tested" my evidence and arguments with friends and colleagues in China, many of whom confirmed that the treatment of veterans was generally "not good."

WORK REPORTS

Most of us complain at one time or another about bureaucracy, but researchers should always remain thankful that bureaucrats have meetings and routinely issue reports and summaries of what they are doing (or say they are doing). PRC archives are full of this type of document; they were issued quarterly, bi-annually, and annually, often in multiple drafts for each bureaucracy involved in a particular problem. This means, for instance, that one can access materials on more sensitive organizations, such as courts or the PLA, by looking for those that were copied by these units and sent to other, less sensitive bureaucracies, such as Civil Affairs or the Women's Federation. This sort of document is generally a broad-stroked summary and critique of an agency's work, broken down by subcategories. (For instance, Civil Affairs will be broken down into sections on disaster relief, refugees, local elections, veterans, and minorities.) Compared to investigation reports, work summaries have a great deal more empty verbiage (*kong hua*) and provide a far less rich sense of context and specifics of a problem. Because of this, they can be read fairly quickly, especially compared to handwritten minutes or investigation reports. Work summaries start off by providing basic information (e.g., how many veterans were taken in by a city, where they came from, whether they were party or CYL members), continue with two or three examples of success (typically about model individuals praising the party/Mao), and then shift into critique mode. The transition between sections two and three is clearly marked by the word "however" (*danshi*). Weighing which of this information is closest to the truth of the matter can be a bit challenging: to me, at least, the "achievements" often sound too exaggerated and unrealistic, but the "problem" section can also be overly harsh. I have generally discounted examples of "models" in the achievement section and waited for further confirmation from other sources to determine whether the "problems" in these summaries were pervasive. My overall sense is that the "problems" section is generally closer to the truth, however, if only because the Chinese government has a well-known tendency to exaggerate good news and underreport negative information. If the summary report lists five problems, there were probably a lot more that were never reported.

POLICY DOCUMENTS

Since archives are repositories of official activity, policy documents unsurprisingly represent a substantial share of their content. Although not as comprehensive as central archives, researchers can still find most all important policy documents relevant to research in large provincial archives or in archives in cities that have provincial status (Shanghai or Tianjin, for example). In some respects, archives at that level are even better for looking at issues of policy *implementation*, since they receive key policies and reports from the center (these sometimes include material from other provinces), devise their own policy documents, and are given materials from districts (*qu*), suburban (*jiaoqu*) areas, and rural counties. The Shanghai Municipal Archive includes many documents from the center, as well as reports from its own agencies and committees, villages on the outskirts of the city, and counties as far as sixty miles away. If one does not have the time to work in a rural archive, or would rather avoid the hassle of securing permission and letters of introduction, it is still possible to conduct a rural–urban comparison in a large municipal archive.

In sum, archival documents, like any other source, have advantages and disadvantages. They are government sources, after all, and need to be treated with some caution and used in conjunction with other data sources. Although I was not able to take advantage of oral histories of veterans—a primary source in the study of veterans in democracies and more open societies (including Russia)—this source would be the ideal complement to archives. At the time I undertook this project, unsupervised interviews with veterans were not possible. Moreover, over time, access to some archives became more restricted as well. My hope is that in the near future scholars will be able to take advantage of dozens of provincial and country archives (to point out regional or even sub-county variations) as well as interview war veterans before they pass away. Time is running out.

NOTES

1. This is important because most indexes provide only the title of the document, so searching for keywords referring to a specific place or for minutes can save a great deal of time and hassle.

Appendix B

Selected Character List

afei	阿飞
anzhi	安置
baofu	包袱
benqian	本钱
bianxiang	变相
bijiao hunluan	比较混乱
bing pi	兵痞
bu hao xiang chu de ren	不好相处的人
bu licai	不理睬
bu yong bu cai	不用不睬
buqi zuoyong	不起作用
bu wen, bu wen	不闻, 不问
chongjin	冲进
choushi	仇视
chunchong	蠢虫
ci huo	次货
cong nali lai, hui dao nali qu	从那里来, 回到那里去
dacai xiaoyong	大材小用
daigeng	代耕
daji wuru	打击侮辱
diaocha baogao	调查报告

dian ji	惦记
dingqi dingliang	定期定量
dou hui xiang	都回乡
fabao	法宝
fanshen	翻身
fayanquan	发言权
fuyuan junren	复员军人
ge he	隔阂
gongchen ziju sixiang	功臣自居思想
gongkai	公开
gongling	工龄
gua yang tou, mai gou rou, chou lilun duo	挂羊头, 卖狗肉, 臭理论多
guangrong	光荣
guyong bing	雇佣兵
haohun	好混
heshang bing	和尚兵
huxiang qiaobuqi	互相瞧不起
jianshe junren	建设军人
jiao'ao	骄傲
jiedai anzhi fuyuan tuiwu junren bangongsh i	接待安置复员退伍军人办公室
jieji yiyi fenzi	阶级异议分子
jing er yuan	敬而远
jiuji mi	救济米
jueda duoshu	绝大多数
junling	军龄
junshu	军属
kan bu guan	看不惯
kaiyou	揩油
kumen	苦闷
laji	垃圾
lan ren	懒人
lie taitai	烈太太

lieshu	烈属
liewang	烈王
linshi gong	临时工
luan tan lian'ai	乱谈恋爱
mangmu wailiu	盲目外流
mabi	麻痹
maochong	冒充
Minzheng jianbao	民政简报
momian shalü	磨面杀驴
nan chan	难缠
nan lingdao	难领导
nan gao	难搞
nannong	难弄
naode xiong jiejue le, bu nao de bu jieju le	闹得凶解决 了,不闹得不解决了
naoshi	闹事
nimen dou shi jiefang jun shu shu	你们都是解放军叔叔
nimen shi bu shi you kanzhong le wo de xifer	你们是不是又看中了我的媳妇儿
nimen you shenme liaobuqi	你们有什么了不起
paichi	排斥
pinjunzhuyi	平均主义
pubian youdai	普遍优待
qiaobuqi	瞧不起
qisi	气死
qiyi	起义
rentong	认同
you sa jiang sa (Qingpu dialect)	有什么讲什么
shengshu	生疏
shiwu gongzuo	事务工作
suosui	琐碎
tiaoti	挑剔

ti yijian	提意见
tiaopi	调皮
tuiwu junren	退伍军人
wangben	忘本
wufa chuli	无法处理
xicheng yanxiang, *xigong, yannong*	喜城厌农， 喜工厌农
xin dou sangle	心都丧了
xuerou guanxi	血肉关系
xuetu	学徒
xuwei	虚伪
yan e	厌恶
yanfan	厌烦
yingong	因公
yongjun, youshu	拥军优属
youdai laodong ri	优待劳动日
youfu chu	优抚处
youli de difang	有利的地方
yuanji anzhi	原籍安置
zhishifenzi zuo tianxia	知识分子座天下
zhuanye junren	转业军人
zhuanye junguan	转业军官
zhuang gouxiong	装狗熊
zisi toujun	自私投军
ziyou zhe	自由者
zongjie baogao	总结报告
zui ke'ai	最可爱
zui kelian	最可怜

Appendix C

Source Material

ARCHIVES

National Archives of the United States, College Park, Maryland
Israel Defense Forces Archives, Givatai'im, Israel
Ma'ariv Archives, Tel Aviv, Israel
Israel State Archives, Jerusalem, Israel
Republic of China, Ministry of Justice–Bureau of Investigation Archives, Xindian, Taiwan
Shanghai Municipal Archives [SMA], PRC
Qingpu District Archives [QA], Shanghai, PRC
Shandong Provincial Archives [SA], Jinan, PRC
Dongcheng District Archives [DDA], Beijing, PRC
Chuxiong Prefectural Archives [CXA], Yunnan, PRC

SELECTED BIBLIOGRAPHY

Aguilar, Paloma. "Agents of Memory: Spanish Civil War Veterans and Disabled Soldiers," pp. 84–103. In Jay Winter and Emmanuel Sivan, eds., *War and Remembrance in the 20th Century*. Cambridge: Cambridge University Press, 2000.

Allsup, Carl. *The American G.I. Forum: Origins and Evolution*. Austin: Center for Mexican-American Studies, University of Texas, 1982.

Almog, Oz, and Haim Watzman, trans. *The Sabra: The Creation of the New Jew*. Berkeley: University of California Press, 2000.

Alston, Richard. *Soldier and Society in Roman Egypt: A Social History*. London: Routledge, 1998.

Aminzade, Ron, Jack Goldstone, and Elizabeth Perry. "Leadership Dynamics and Dynamics of Contention," pp. 126–54. In Ronald Aminzade et al., eds., *Silence and Voice in the Study of Contentious Politics*. Cambridge: Cambridge University Press, 2001.

Andreski, Stanislav. *Military Organization and Society*. London: Routledge and Kegan Paul, 1967.

Bao, Ninh, and Phan Thanh Hao, trans. *The Sorrow of War: A Novel of North Vietnam*. New York: Riverhead Books, 1996.

Bardach, Eugene. *The Implementation Game*. Cambridge: MIT Press, 1974.

Bartov, Omer. "The Nation in Arms: German and France, 1789–1939," *History Today* 44, no. 9 (September 1994): 27–33.

Ben-Ari, Eyal. "Tests of Soldierhood, Trials of Manhood: Military Service and Male Ideals in Israel," pp. 239–68. In Daniel Maman, Eyal Ben-Ari, and Zeev Rosenhek, eds., *Military, State and Society in Israel*. New Brunswick: Transaction, 2001.

Ben-Eliezer, Uri. *The Making of Israel Militarism*. Bloomington: University of Indiana Press, 1998.

———. "A Nation-in-Arms: State, Nation, and Militarism in Israel's First Years." *Comparative Studies in Society and History* 37, no. 2 (1995): 264–85.

Bensel, Richard Franklin. "Politics Is Thicker than Blood: Union and Confederate Veterans in the U.S. House of Representatives in the Late Nineteenth Century," pp. 253–77. In Diane E. Davis and Anthony W. Pereira, eds., *Irregular Armed Forces and Their Role in Politics and State Formation*. Cambridge: Cambridge University Press, 2003.

Berezin, Mabel. *Making the Fascist Self: The Political Culture of Interwar Italy*. Ithaca: Cornell University Press, 1997.

Berns, Walter. *Making Patriots*. Chicago: University of Chicago Press, 2001.

Bernstein, Thomas P., and Xiaobo Lü. *Taxation with Representation in Contemporary Rural China*. Cambridge: Cambridge University Press, 2003.

Biess, Frank. *Homecomings: Returning POWs and the Legacies of Defeat in Postwar Germany*. Princeton: Princeton University Press, 2006.

Bilmes, Linda. "Soldiers Returning from Iraq and Afghanistan: The Long-Term Costs of Providing Veterans Medical Care and Disability Benefits." KSG (Kennedy School of Government) Faculty Research Working Paper Series RWP07-001, January 2007.

Bilu, Yoram, and Eliezer Witztum. "War-Related Loss and Suffering in Israeli Society: An Historical Perspective." *Israel Studies* 5, no. 2 (Fall 2000): 1–31.

Black, John, and Charles Hyson. "Postwar Soldier Settlement." *Quarterly Journal of Economics* 59, no. 1 (November, 1944): 1–35.

Blight, David. *Race and Reunion: The Civil War in American Memory*. Cambridge: Belknap, 2001.

Bodnar, John, ed. *Bonds of Affection: Americans Define Their Patriotism*. Princeton: Princeton University Press, 1996.

Bodnar, John. *Remaking America: Public Memory, Commemoration, and Patriotism in the 20th Century*. Princeton: Princeton University Press, 1992.

Bradley, James, and Ron Powers. *Flags of Our Fathers*. New York: Bantam, 2000.

Bradley, Mark P. "Contests of Memory: Remembering and Forgetting War in the Contemporary Vietnamese Cinema," pp. 196–226. In Hue-Tam Ho Tai, ed., *The Country of Memory: Remaking the Past in Late Socialist Vietnam*. Berkeley: University of California Press, 2001.

Braithwaite, John, and Toni Makkai. "Testing an Expected Utility Model of Corporate Deterrence." *Law and Society Review* 25, no. 1 (1991): 7–40.

Brook, Timothy. *Collaboration: Japanese Agents and Local Elites in Wartime China*. Cambridge: Harvard University Press, 2007.

Brooks, Jennifer. *Defining the Peace: World War II, Veterans, Race and the Remaking of the Southern Political Tradition*. Chapel Hill: University of North Carolina Press, 2004.

Brown, Jeremy. "From Resisting Communists to Resisting America: Civil War and Korean War in Southwest China, 1950–1951" pp. 105–29. In Jeremy Brown and Paul Pickowicz, eds., *Dilemmas of Victory: The Early Years of the People's Republic of China*. Cambridge: Harvard University Press, 2007.

Browne, Susan. "War-Making and U.S. State Formation: Mobilization, Demobilization, and the Inherent Ambiguities of Federalism," pp. 232–52. In Diane E. Davis and Anthony W. Pereira, eds., *Irregular Armed Forces and Their Role in Politics and State Formation*. Cambridge: Cambridge University Press, 2003.

Brubaker, Rogers. *Citizenship and Nationhood in France and Germany*. Cambridge: Harvard University Press, 1998.

Bullman, Tim, and Han Kang. "The Risk of Suicide among Wounded Vietnam Veterans." *American Journal of Public Health* 86, no. 5 (May 1996): 662–67.

Burk, James. "Citizenship Status and Military Service: The Quest for Inclusion by Minorities and Conscientious Objectors." *Armed Forces and Society* 21, no. 4 (Summer 1995): 503–29.

Camacho, Paul, and Paul Atwood. "A Review of the Literature on Veterans Published in *Armed Forces and Society*, 1974–2006." *Armed Forces and Society* 33, no. 3 (April 2007): 351–81.

Carruthers, Susan. "No One's Looking: The Disappearing Audience for War," *Media, War and Conflict* 1, no. 1 (2008): 70–76.

Centeno, Miguel. *Blood and Debt: War and the Nation-State in Latin America*. University Park: Pennsylvania State University Press, 2002.

Challener, Richard. *The French Theory of the Nation in Arms, 1866–1939*. New York: Columbia University Press, 1955.

Chan, Anita, Richard Madsen, and Jonathan Unger. *Chen Village under Mao and Deng*. Berkeley: University of California Press, 1992.

Chen, Yung-fa. *Making Revolution: The Communist Movement in Eastern and Central China, 1937–1945*. Berkeley: University of California Press, 1986.

Cheng, Sijin. "The Challenge of Conscription in an Era of Social Change," pp. 235–54. In David Finkelstein and Kristen Gunness, eds., *Civil–Military Relations*. Armonk: M.E. Sharpe, 2006.

Chowers, Eyal. "Time in Zionism: The Life and Afterlife of a Temporal Revolution." *Political Theory* 26, no. 5 (October 1998): 652–85.

Coble, Parks M. "China's 'New Remembering' of the Anti-Japanese War of Resistance, 1937–1945." *The China Quarterly* 190 (June 2007): 394–410.

Cohen, Deborah. *The War Come Home: Disabled Veterans in Britain and Germany, 1914–1939.* Berkeley: University of California Press, 2001.

Colley, Linda. *Britons: Forging the Nation, 1707–1837.* New Haven: Yale University Press, 1992.

Cook, Theodore. "The Japanese Reserve Experience: From Nation-in-Arms to Baseline Defense," pp. 259–73. In Louis Zurcher and Gwyn Harries-Jenkins (eds.), *Supplemental Military Forces.* London: Sage, 1978.

Crew, David. *Germans on Welfare: From Weimar to Hitler.* New York: Oxford University Press, 1998.

Crossley, Pamela K. *Orphan Warriors: Three Manchu Generations and the End of the Qing World.* Princeton: Princeton University Press, 1990.

Culp, Robert. *Articulating Citizenship: Civic Education and Student Politics in Southeastern China, 1912–1940.* Cambridge: Harvard University Asia Center, 2007.

Dauncey, Sarah. "Screening Disability in the PRC: The Politics of Looking Good." *China Information* 21, no. 3 (2007): 481–506.

Davies, Wallace Evan. *Patriotism on Parade: The Story of Veterans' and Hereditary Organizations in America, 1793–1900.* Cambridge: Harvard University Press, 1955.

Denton, Kirk. "Museums, Memorial Sites and Exhibitionary Culture in the People's Republic of China." *The China Quarterly* 183 (2005): 565–86.

Derthick, Martha. *Agency under Stress: The Social Security Administration in American Government.* Washington, D.C.: Brookings Institution Press, 1990.

Diamant, Neil J. *Revolutionizing the Family: Politics, Love, and Divorce in Urban and Rural China, 1949–1968.* Berkeley: University of California Press, 2000.

———. "Making Love 'Legible' in China: Politics and Society during the Enforcement of Civil Marriage Registration, 1950–1966." *Politics and Society* 29, no. 3 (June 2001): 447–480.

Dickson, Paul, and Thomas Allen. *The Bonus Army: An American Epic.* New York: Walker, 2006.

———. "Marching on History." *Smithsonian.* February 1, 2003. Online Edition.www .smithson.ianmag.com/history-archeology/marching/html.

Diehl, James. *The Thanks of the Fatherland: German Veterans after the Second World War.* Chapel Hill: University of North Carolina Press, 1993.

———. "Victors or Victims? Disabled Veterans in the Third Reich." *Journal of Modern History* 59, no. 4 (December 1987): 705–36.

Diehl, James, and Stephen Ward, eds. *The War Generation: Veterans of the First World War.* Port Washington: Kennikat, 1975.

Dittmer, John. *Local People: The Struggle for Civil Rights in Mississippi.* Urbana: University of Illinois, 1994.

Dixon, John. *The Chinese Welfare System, 1949–1979.* Westport: Praeger, 1981.

Doblin, Ernest, and Claire Pohly. "The Social Composition of the Nazi Leadership." *American Journal of Sociology* 51, no. 1 (July 1945): 42–49.

Dower, John. *Embracing Defeat: Japan in the Wake of World War II.* New York: W.W. Norton, 1999.

Dreyer, June. "The Demobilization of PLA Servicemen and Their Integration into Civilian Life," pp. 297–330. In June Dreyer, ed., *Chinese Defense and Foreign Policy*. New York: Paragon House, 1989.

Druckman, Daniel. "Social–Psychological Aspects of Nationalism," pp. 47–98. In John Comeroff and Paul Stern, eds., *Perspectives on Nationalism and War*. Amsterdam: Gordon and Breach, 1995.

Dunn, Ethel. "Disabled Russian War Veterans: Surviving the Collapse of the Soviet Union," pp. 253–68. In David Gerber, ed., *Disabled Veterans in History*. Ann Arbor: University of Michigan Press, 2000.

Dutton, Michael. *Policing Chinese Politics: A History*. Durham: Duke University Press, 2005.

Edele, Mark. "A 'Generation of Victors'? Soviet Second World War Veterans from Demobilization to Organization, 1941–1956." Ph.D. dissertation, Department of History, University of Chicago, 2004.

———. "Soviet Veterans as an Entitlement Group, 1945–1955." *Slavic Review* 65, no. 1 (Spring 2006): 111–37.

Eghigian, Greg A. "The Politics of Victimization: Social Pensioners and the German Social State in the Inflation of 1914–1924." *Central European History* 26 (1993): 375–404.

———. *Making Security Social: Disability, Insurance, and the Birth of the Social Entitlement State in Germany*. Ann Arbor: University of Michigan Press, 2000.

Elliot, Mark. *The Manchu Way: The Eight Banners and Ethnic Identity in Late Imperial China*. Stanford: Stanford University Press, 2001.

Ellis, Joseph. *Founding Brothers: The Revolutionary Generation*. New York: Vintage, 2002.

England, Robert. *Discharged: A Commentary of Civil Reestablishment of Veterans in Canada*. Toronto: McMillan, 1943.

Epp, Charles. *The Rights Revolution: Lawyers, Activists, and Supreme Courts in Comparative Perspective*. Chicago: University of Chicago Press, 1998.

Esherick, Joseph."War and Revolution: Chinese Society during the 1940s." *Twentieth Century China* 27, no. 1 (November 2001): 1–37.

Esherick, Joseph, and Many Rankin, eds. *Chinese Local Elites and Patterns of Dominance*. Berkeley: University of California Press, 1993.

Fan, Yu-Wen. "Becoming a Civilian: Mainland Chinese Soldiers/Veterans and the State in Taiwan, 1949–2001," Ph.D. dissertation, Department of Sociology, New School for Social Research, 1995.

Feng, Chen. "Industrial Restructuring and Workers Resistance in China." *Modern China* 29, no. 2 (April 2003): 237–62.

Fewsmith, Joseph. "China's Defense Budget," pp. 202–13. In David Finkelstein and Kristen Gunness, eds., *Civil–Military Relations*. Armonk: M.E. Sharpe, 2006.

Fitzgerald, John. *Awakening China: Politics, Culture, and Class in the Nationalist Revolution*. Stanford: Stanford University Press, 1998.

———. "The Nationless State: The Search for a Nation in Modern Chinese Nationalism," pp. 56–85. In Jonathon Unger, ed., *Chinese Nationalism*. Armonk: M.E. Sharpe, 1996.

Fleche, Andre. "'Shoulder to Shoulder as Comrades Tried': Black and White Union Veterans and Civil War Memory." *Civil War History* 51, no. 2 (June 2005): 175–201.

Fleischer, Doris Zames, and Frieda Zames. *The Disability Rights Movement: From Charity to Confrontation.* Philadelphia: Temple University Press, 2001.

Fletcher, George. *Loyalty: An Essay on the Morality of Relationships.* New York: Oxford University Press, 1993.

Fligstein, Neil. "Who Served in the Military, 1940–73," *Armed Forces and Society* 6, no. 2 (Winter 1980): 297–312.

Forrest, Alan. "La Patrie en danger: The French Revolution and the First Levée en masse," pp. 8–32. In Daniel Moran and Arthur Waldron, eds., *The People in Arms.* Cambridge: Cambridge University Press, 2006.

Franco, Jeré. "Empowering the World War II Native American Veteran: Postwar Civil Rights." *Wicazo Sa Review* 9, no. 1 (Spring 1993): 32–37.

Frazier, Mark W. *The Making of the Chinese Industrial Workplace: State, Revolution and Labor Management.* New York: Cambridge University Press, 2002.

Friedman, Edward, Paul Pickowicz, and Mark Selden. *Revolution, Resistance and Reform in Village China.* New Haven: Yale University Press, 2005.

Gal, John, and Michael Bar. "The Needed and the Needy: The Policy Legacies of Benefits for Disabled War Veterans in Israel." *Journal of Social Policy* 29, no. 4 (2000): 577–98.

Gao, James Z. "The Call of the Oases: The 'Peaceful Liberation' of Xinjiang, 1949–1953," pp. 184–204. In Jeremy Brown and Paul Pickowicz, eds., *Dilemmas of Victory: The Early Years of the People's Republic of China.* Cambridge: Harvard University Press, 2007.

Garton, Stephen. *The Cost of War: Australians Return.* Melbourne: Oxford University Press, 1996.

———. "Longing for War: Nostalgia and Australian Returned Soldiers after the First World War," pp. 222–40. In T. G. Ashplant, Graham Dawson, and Michael Roper, eds., *The Politics of War Memory and Commemoration.* London: Routledge, 2000.

Gat, Azar. "The Democratic Peace Theory Reframed: The Impact of Modernity." *World Politics* 58 (October 2005): 73–100.

———. *War in Human Civilization.* Oxford: Oxford University Press, 2006.

Gelpi, Chistopher, and Peter Feaver. "Speak Softly and Carry a Big Stick? Veterans in the Political Elite and the American Use of Force." *American Political Science Review* 96, no. 4 (2002): 779–93.

Gerber, David. "Heroes and Misfits: The Troubled Social Reintegration of Disabled Veterans in 'The Best Years of Our Lives.'" *American Quarterly* 46, no. 4 (December 1994): 545–74.

Geyer, Michael. "War and the Context of General History in an Age of Total War." *Journal of Military History* 57, no. 5 (October 1993): 145–63.

Gill, Leslie. "Creating Citizens, Making Men: The Military and Masculinity in Bolivia." *Cultural Anthropology* 12, no. 4 (November 1997): 527–50.

Gillin, Donald, and Charles Etter. "Staying On: Japanese Soldiers and Civilians in China, 1945–1949." *Journal of Asian Studies* 42, no. 3 (May 1983): 497–518.

Gittings, John. *The Role of the Chinese Army.* London: Oxford University Press, 1967.

Glassberg, David and J. Michael Moore. "Patriotism in Orange: The Memory of World War I in a Massachusetts Town," pp. 160–90. In John Bodnar, ed., *Bonds of Affection: Americans Define their Patriotism.* Princeton University Press, 1996.

Glatthaar, Joseph. *Forged in Battle: The Civil War Alliance of Black Soldiers and White Officers.* New York: The Free Press, 1990.

Glazer, Myron, and Penina Migdal Glazer. *The Whistleblowers: Exposing Corruption in Government and Industry.* New York: Basic Books, 1989.

Goldhammer, Jesse. *The Headless Republic: Sacrificial Violence in Modern French Thought.* Ithaca: Cornell University Press, 2005.

Goldsworthy, Adrian. *Caesar: Life of a Colossus.* New Haven: Yale University Press, 2006.

Goodman, Bryna. "Networks of News: Power, Language and the Transnational Dimensions of the Chinese Press, 1850–1949." *The China Review* 4, no. 1 (Spring 2004): 1–10.

Goodman, David S. G. *Social and Political Change in Revolutionary China.* Lanham: Rowman & Littlefield, 2000.

Granjo, Paulo. "The Homecomer: Postwar Cleansing Rituals in Mozambique." *Armed Forces and Society* 33, no. 3 (April 2007): 382–95.

Greenstein, Lewis. "The Impact of Military Service in World War I on Africans: The Nandi of Kenya." *Journal of Modern African Studies* 16, no. 3 (September 1978): 495–507.

Gries, Peter. *China's New Nationalism: Pride, Politics and Diplomacy.* Berkeley: University of California Press, 2004.

Grodzins, Martin. *The Loyal and the Disloyal: Social Boundaries of Patriotism and Treason.* Chicago: University of Chicago Press, 1956.

Guowuyuan jundui ganbu anzhi gongzuo xiaozu bangongshi, ed., *Jundui ganbu zhuanye fuyuan gongzuo wenjian huibian.* Beijing: Laodong renshi chubanshe, 1983.

Ha, Jin. *War Trash.* New York: Pantheon, 2004.

Hall, Peter. "Policy Paradigms, Social Learning and the State: The Case of Economic Policymaking in Britain." *Comparative Politics* 25, no. 3 (April 1993): 275–96.

Harding, Harry. *China's Second Revolution: Reform after Mao.* Washington, D.C.: Brookings Institution Press, 1987.

Hartmann, Susan. *The Home Front and Beyond: American Women in the 1940s.* Boston: Twayne, 1982.

Heineman, Elisabeth. "The Hour of the Woman: Memories of Germany's 'Crisis Years' and West German National Identity." *American Historical Review* 101, no. 2 (April 1996): 354–95.

Hobsen, Barbara. "Women's Collective Agency, Power Resources, and the Framing of Citizenship Rights," pp. 149–78. In Michael Hanagan and Charles Tilly, eds., *Extending Citizenship, Reconfiguring States.* Lanham: Rowman & Littlefield, 1999.

Hogeland, William. *The Whiskey Rebellion: George Washington, Alexander Hamilton, and the Frontier Rebels Who Challenged America's Newfound Sovereignty.* New York: Simon and Schuster, 2006.

Homer, and Robert Fagles, trans. *The Iliad*. New York: Viking, 1990.

Honig, Emily. *Creating Chinese Ethnicity: Subei People in Shanghai, 1850–1980*. New Haven: Yale University Press, 1992.

Hood, Steven J. *Dragons Entangled: Indochina and the China–Vietnam War*. Armonk: M.E. Sharpe, 1992.

Hoogendoorn, Mandy, "Remembering and Forgetting the Finnish Civil War." *Journal of Finnish Studies* 3, no. 1 (May 1999): 28–49.

Huang, Ray. *1587: A Year of No Significance*. New Haven: Yale University Press, 1981.

Hudson, Valerie, and Andrea Den Boer. "A Surplus of Men, A Deficit of Peace: Security and Sex Ratios in Asia's Largest States." *International Security* 26, no. 4 (Spring 2002): 5–38.

Hung, Chang-tai. "Mao's Parades: State Spectacles in China in the 1950s." *The China Quarterly* 190 (June 2007): 411–31.

———. "Oil Paintings and Politics: Weaving a Heroic Tale of the Chinese Communist Revolution." *Comparative Studies in Society and History* 49, no. 4 (October 2007): 783–814.

———. "The Cult of the Red Martyr: Politics of Commemoration in China." *Journal of Contemporary History* 43, no. 2 (2008): 279–304.

Hunt, Andrew. *A History of Vietnam Veterans Against the War*. New York: New York University Press, 1999.

Israel, Adrienne. "Measuring the War Experience: Ghanaian Soldiers in World War II." *Journal of African Studies* 25, no. 1 (March 1987): 159–68.

———. "Ex-Servicemen at the Crossroads: Protest and Politics in Post-War Ghana." *Journal of Modern African Studies* 30, no. 2 (June 1992): 359–68.

Janowitz, Morris. "Military Institutions and Citizenship in Western Societies." *Armed Forces and Society* 2, no. 2 (February 1976): 185–204.

———. "Observations on the Sociology of Citizenship: Obligations and Rights." *Social Forces* 59, no. 1 (September 1980): 1–24.

Jefferson, Robert F. "Enabled Courage: Race, Disability and Black World War II Veterans in Postwar America." *The Historian* 65, no. 5 (2003): 1102–24.

Jensen, Laura. "Constructing and Entitling America's Original Veterans," pp. 35–62. In Helen Ingram and Anne Schneider, eds., *Deserving and Entitled: Social Constructions and Public Policy*. Albany: SUNY Press, 2005.

Jessup, Mary Frost. *The Public Reaction to the Returned Serviceman after World War I*. Washington, DC: U.S. Department of Labor, 1944.

Jin, Qiu. *The Culture of Power: The Lin Biao Incident in the Cultural Revolution*. Stanford: Stanford University Press, 1999.

Joffe, Ellis. "The Chinese Army after the Cultural Revolution: The Effects of Intervention." *The China Quarterly* 55 (Summer 1973): 450–77.

Johnson, Wray. "Black American Radicalism and the First World War: The Secret Files of the Military Intelligence Division." *Armed Forces and Society* 26, no. 1 (Fall 1999): 27–53.

Kaplan, Danny. *The Men We Loved: Male Friendship and Nationalism in Israeli Culture*. New York: Berghahn Books, 2006.

Karsten, Peter. *Soldiers and Society: The Effects of Military Service on American Life*. Westport: Greenwood Press, 1978.

Kasza, Gregory. *One World of Welfare: Japan in Comparative Perspective*. Ithaca: Cornell University Press, 2006.

———. "War and Comparative Politics." *Comparative Politics* 28, no. 3 (April 1996): 355–73.

Kateb, George. "Is Patriotism a Mistake?" *Social Research* 67, no. 4 (2000): 901–24.

Katriel, Tamar. *Talking Straight:* Dugri *Speech in Israeli Sabra Culture*. Cambridge: Cambridge University Press, 1986.

Kau, Michael Y. M., and John K. Leung, eds. *The Writings of Mao Zedong, 1949–1976*, Vol. 1, *September 1949–December 1955*. Armonk: M.E. Sharpe, 1986.

Kaufman, Herbert. *The Administrative Behavior of Federal Bureau Chiefs*. Washington, D.C.: Brookings Institution Press, 1981.

Keegan, John. *The Face of Battle: A Study of Agincourt, Waterloo and the Somme*. New York: Viking, 1976.

Keep, John. *Soldiers of the Czar: Army and Society in Russia, 1492–1874*. Oxford: Oxford University Press, 1985.

Kelly, John D. "Diaspora and World War, Blood and Nation in Fiji and Hawai'i." *Public Culture* 7 (1995): 475–97.

Keppie, L. *Colonisation and Veteran Settlement in Italy, 47–14 B.C.* London: British School at Rome, 1983.

Keren, Michael. "Commemoration and National Identity: A Comparison between the Making of the Anzac and Palmach Legends." *Israel Studies Forum* 19, no. 3 (Fall 2004): 9–27.

Kestnbaum, Meyer. "Citizenship and Compulsory Military Service: The Revolutionary Origins of Conscription in the United States." *Armed Forces and Society* 27, no. 1 (Fall 2000): 7–36.

Kivlehan-Wise, Maryanne. "Demobilization and Resettlement: The Challenge of Downsizing the People's Liberation Army," pp. 255–69. In David Finkelstein and Kristin Gunness, eds., *Civil–Military Relations in Today's China*. Armonk: M.E. Sharpe, 2007.

Knight, Alan. "Peasants into Patriots: Thoughts on the Making of the Mexican Nation." *Mexican Studies/Estudios Mexicanos* 10, no. 3 (Winter 1994): 135–61.

Koenker, Diane. "Urbanization and Deurbanization during the Russian Revolution and Civil War." *Journal of Modern History* 57, no. 3 (September 1985): 424–50.

Kohrman, Matthew. *Bodies of Difference: Experiences of Disability and Institutional Advocacy in the Making of Modern China*. Berkeley: University of California Press, 2005.

Koven, Seth. "Remembering and Dismemberment: Crippled Children, Wounded Soldiers and the Great War in Great Britain." *American Historical Review* 99, no. 4 (October 1994): 1167–1202.

Kravetz, Shlomo, Shlomo Katz, and David Albez. "Attitudes toward Israeli War Veterans with Disabilities: Combat versus Noncombat Military Service and Responsibility for the Disability." *Rehabilitation Counseling Bulletin* 37, no. 4 (1994): 371–79.

Krebs, Ronald. *Fighting for Rights: Military Service and the Politics of Citizenship.* Ithaca: Cornell University Press, 2006.

Kristianson, G. L. *The Politics of Patriotism: The Pressure Group Activities of the Returned Servicemen's League.* Canberra: Australia National University Press, 1966.

Land, Isaac. "Bread and Arsenic: Citizenship from the Bottom Up in Georgian London." *Journal of Social History* 39, no. 1 (Fall 2005): 89–110.

Lary, Diana. "One Province's Experience of War: Guangxi, 1937–1945," pp. 314–34. In Stephen MacKinnon, Diana Lary, and Ezra Vogel, eds., *China at War*. Stanford: Stanford University Press, 2007.

———. *Warlord Soldiers: Chinese Common Soldiers, 1911–1937*. Cambridge: Cambridge University Press, 1985.

Lary, Diana, and Stephen MacKinnon, eds. *Scars of War: The Impact of Warfare on Modern China*. Vancouver: University of British Columbia Press, 2001.

Lawson, Melinda. *Patriot Fires: Forging a New American Nationalism in the Civil War North*. Lawrence: University Press of Kansas, 2002.

Lebel, Udi. *Ha'derech el ha'pantheon: Etzel, Lehi vi'gvulot ha'zikaron ha'yisraeli.* Jerusalem: Carmel, 2007.

Lee, Hong Yung. *The Politics of the Chinese Cultural Revolution: A Case Study.* Berkeley: University of California Press, 1978.

Lee, K. A., G. E. Vaillant, W. C. Torrey, and G. H. Elder. "A 50-Year Prospective Study of the Psychological Sequelae of World War II Combat." *American Journal of Psychiatry* 152, no. 4 (1995): 516–22.

Lee, Sing, and Arthur Kleinman. "Suicide as Resistance in Chinese Society," pp. 289–311. In Elizabeth Perry and Mark Selden, eds., *Chinese Society: Change, Conflict and Resistance*. New York: RoutledgeCurzon, 2003.

Leese, Peter. "Problems Returning Home: The British Psychological Casualties of the Great War." *The Historical Journal* 40, no. 4 (1990): 1055–67.

Leff, Mark H. "The Politics of Sacrifice on the American Home Front in World War II." *The Journal of American History* 77, no. 4 (March 1991): 1296–1318.

Lei, Guang. "Realpolitik Nationalism: International Sources of Chinese Nationalism." *Modern China* 31, no. 4 (October 2005): 487–514.

Levi, Margaret. *Consent, Dissent and Patriotism*. Cambridge: Cambridge University Press, 1997.

Li, Cheng. *China's Leaders: The New Generation*. Lanham: Rowman & Littlefield, 2001.

Li, Lianjiang. "Political Trust in Rural China." *Modern China* 30, no. 2 (April 2004): 228–58.

Li, Xiaobing. *A History of the Modern Chinese Army*. Lexington: University Press of Kentucky, 2007.

Liang, Heng, and Judith Shapiro. *Son of the Revolution*. New York: Viking, 1984.

Lieberthal, Kenneth, and Michel Oksenberg. *Policy Making in China: Leaders, Structures and Processes*. Princeton: Princeton University Press, 1988.

Liebman, Charles, and Eliezer Don-Yehiya. *Civil Religion in Israel: Traditional Judaism and Political Culture in the Jewish State*. Berkeley: University of California Press, 1983.

Linderman, Gerald. *Embattled Courage: The Experience of Combat in the American Civil War*. New York: Free Press, 1987.

———. *The World within War: America's Combat Experience in World War II*. Cambridge: Harvard University Press, 1997.

Link, Perry. *Evening Chats in Beijing: Probing China's Predicament*. New York: W.W. Norton, 1992.

Lipsky, Michael. *Street-Level Bureaucracy: Dilemmas of the Individual in Public Service*. New York: Russell Sage, 1980.

Lisio, Donald. "United States: Bread and Butter Politics," pp. 38–58. In James Diehl and Stephen Ward, eds., *The War Generation: Veterans of the First World War*. Port Washington: Kennikat, 1975.

Liu, Binyan. *A Higher Kind of Loyalty*. New York: Pantheon, 1990.

Liu, F. F. *A Military History of China, 1924–1949*. Princeton: Princeton University Press, 1956.

Lockenour, Jay. *Soldiers as Citizens: Former Wehrmacht Officers in the Federal Republic of Germany, 1945–1955*. Lincoln: University of Nebraska Press, 2001.

Lockhart, Greg. "In Lieu of the Levée en masse: Mass Mobilization in Vietnam," pp. 208–33. In Daniel Moran and Arthur Waldron, eds., *The People in Arms: Military Myth and National Mobilization since the French Revolution*. Cambridge: Cambridge University Press, 2002.

Logue, Larry M. "Union Veterans and Their Government: The Effects of Public Policies on Private Lives." *Journal of Interdisciplinary History* 22, no. 3 (1992): 411–34.

Lü, Xiaobo. *Cadres and Corruption: The Organizational Involution of the Chinese Communist Party*. Stanford: Stanford University Press, 2000.

Luo, Pingfei. *Anzhi guanli*. Beijing: Zhongguo shehui chubanshe, 1996.

Lynn, John. "The Embattled Future of Academic Military History." *The Journal of Military History* 61, no. 4 (October 1997): 777–89.

MacFarquhar, Roderick. *The Origins of the Cultural Revolution, Vol. 3: The Coming of the Cataclysm, 1961–1966*. New York: Columbia University Press, 1997.

MacFarquhar, Roderick, and Michael Schoenhals. *Mao's Last Revolution*. Cambridge: Harvard University Press, 2006.

MacKinnon, Stephen. "Conclusion: Wartime China," pp. 335–51. In Stephen MacKinnon, Diana Lary, and Ezra Vogel, eds., *China at War: Regions of China, 1937–1945*. Stanford: Stanford University Press, 2007.

———. "Refugee Flight at the Outset of the Anti-Japanese War," pp. 118–35. In Diana Lary and Stephen MacKinnon, eds., *Scars of War: The Impact of Warfare on Modern China*. Vancouver: University of British Columbia Press, 2001.

MacKinnon, Stephen, Diana Lary, and Ezra Vogel, eds. *China at War: Regions of China, 1937–45*. Stanford: Stanford University Press, 2007.

Madsen, Richard. *Morality and Power in a Chinese Village*. Berkeley: University of California Press, 1984.

Malarney, Shaun K. "'The Fatherland Remembers Your Sacrifice': Commemorating War Death in North Vietnam," pp. 46–76. In Hue-Tam Ho Tai, ed., *The Country of Memory: Remaking the Past in Late Socialist Vietnam*. Berkeley: University of California Press, 2001.

Mann, John Cecil. "The Settlement of Veterans in the Roman Empire." Ph.D. dissertation, University of London, 1956.

Mann, Michael. "The Autonomous Power of the State: Its Origins, Mechanisms and Results," pp. 109–36. In John Hall, ed., *States in History*. Oxford: Basil Blackwell, 1986.

Marshall, Douglas. "Soldier Settlement in Agriculture." *The Journal of Land and Public Utility Economics* 20, no. 3 (August 1944): 270–78.

Marten, James. "Exempt from the Ordinary Rules of Life: Researching Postwar Adjustment Problems of Union Veterans." *Civil War History* 47, no. 1 (March 2001): 57–70.

Matthews, James. "Clock Towers for the Colonized: Demobilization of the Nigerian Military and the Readjustment of Its Veterans to Civilian Life, 1918–1925." *International Journal of African Historical Studies* 14, no. 2 (1981): 254–71.

Mauldin, Bill. *Back Home*. New York: William Sloane, 1947.

McCann, Michael. *Rights at Work: Pay Equity Reform and the Politics of Legal Mobilization*. Chicago: University of Chicago Press, 1994.

McClintock, Megan. "Binding Up the Nation's Wounds: Nationalism, Civil War Pensions, and American Families, 1861–1890." Ph.D. dissertation, Department of History, Rutgers University, 1994.

———. "Civil War Pensions and the Reconstruction of Union Families." *Journal of American History* 83, no. 2 (September 1996): 456–80.

McConnell, Stuart. "Who Joined the Grand Army? Three Case Studies in the Construction of Union Veteranhood, 1866–1900," pp. 139–70. In Maris Vinovskis, ed., *Toward a Social History of the American Civil War*. Cambridge: Cambridge University Press, 1990.

———. "Reading the Flag: A Reconsideration of Patriotic Cults of the 1890s," pp. 102–19. In John Bodnar, ed., *Bonds of Affection: Americans Define Their Patriotism*. Princeton: Princeton University Press, 1996.

McDonald, Forrest. "The Relation of the French Peasant Veterans of the American Revolution to the Fall of Feudalism in France, 1789–1792," pp. 337–48. In Peter Karsten, ed., *The Military–State–Society Symbiosis*. New York: Garland, 1998.

McMillen, Neil. "How Mississippi's Black Veterans Remember World War II," pp. 93–110. In Neil McMillen, ed., *Remaking Dixie: The Impact of World War II on the American South*. Jackson: University Press of Mississippi, 1997.

———. "Introduction," p. xiii. In Neil McMillen, ed., *Remaking Dixie: The Impact of World War II on the American South*. Jackson: University Press of Mississippi, 1997.

Meijer, Jan. "Town and Country in the Civil War," pp. 259–81. In Richard Pipes, ed., *Revolutionary Russia*. Cambridge: Harvard University Press, 1968.

Meisner, Maurice. *Marxism, Maoism and Utopianism: Eight Essays*. Madison: University of Wisconsin Press, 1982.

Merker, Peter, "The Guomindang Regions of Jiangxi," pp. 288–312. In Stephen MacKinnon, Diana Lary, and Ezra Vogel (eds.), *China at War: Regions of China, 1937–1945*. Stanford: Stanford University Press, 2007.

Merridale, Catherine. *Ivan's War: Life and Death in the Red Army, 1939–1945*. New York: Picador, 2006.

Mershon, Sherie, and Steven Schlossman. *Foxholes and Color Lines: Desegregating the U.S. Armed Forces*. Baltimore: Johns Hopkins University Press, 1998.

Mertha, Andrew. *The Politics of Piracy: Intellectual Property in Contemporary China*. Ithaca: Cornell University Press, 2005.

Mettler, Suzanne. *Soldiers to Citizens: The G.I. Bill and the Making of the Greatest Generation*. Oxford: Oxford University Press, 2005.

Migdal, Joel. "The State in Society: An Approach to Struggles for Domination," pp. 7–36. In Joel Migdal, Atul Kohli, and Vivienne Shue, eds., *State Power and Social Forces: Domination and Transformation in the Third World*. Cambridge: Cambridge University Press, 1994.

Mo, Yan, and Howard Goldblatt, trans. *The Garlic Ballads*. New York: Viking, 1995.

Modell, John, and Timothy Haggerty. "The Social Impact of War." *Annual Review of Sociology* 17 (1991): 205–224.

Moon, Seungsook. *Militarized Modernity and Gendered Citizenship in South Korea*. Durham: Duke University Press, 2005.

Moore, Deborah Dash. *GI Jews: How World War II Changed a Generation*. Cambridge: Belknap, 2004.

Morris, Andrew. *Marrow of the Nation: A History of Sport and Physical Culture in Republican China*. Berkeley: University of California Press, 2004.

Morton, Desmond, and Glenn Wright. *Winning the Second Battle: Canadian Veterans and the Return to Civilian Life, 1915–1930*. Toronto: University of Toronto Press, 1987.

Mosch, Theodore R. *The G.I. Bill: A Breakthrough in Educational and Social Policy in the United States*. Hicksville, NY: Exposition Press, 1975.

Mosse, George L. *The Nationalization of the Masses: Political Symbolism and Mass Movements in Germany from the Napoleonic Wars through the Third Reich*. Ithaca: Cornell University Press, 1975.

———. *The Fascist Revolution: Toward a General Theory of Fascism*. New York: Howard Fertig, 1999.

———. "Max Nordau: Liberalism and the New Jew," pp. 161–75. In George L. Mosse, ed., *Confronting the Nation: Jewish and Western Nationalism*. Hanover: Brandeis University Press, 1993.

Murphy, Rachel. *How Migrant Labor Is Changing Rural China*. Cambridge: Cambridge University Press, 2002.

Nair, Elizabeth. "Nation-Building through Conscript Service in Singapore," pp. 101–7. In Daniella Ashkenazy, ed., *The Military in the Service of Society and Democracy: The Challenge of the Dual-Role Military*. Westport: Greenwood Press, 1994.

Nakamura, Karen. *Deaf in Japan: Signing and the Politics of Identity*. Ithaca: Cornell University Press, 2006.

Nash, Gary B. *The Unknown American Revolution*. New York: Penguin, 2005.

Naughton, Barry. "Cities in the Chinese Economic System," pp. 61–89. In Deborah S. Davis, Richard Kraus, Barry Naughton, and Elizaabeth J. Perry, eds., *Urban Spaces in Contemporary China: The Potential for Autonomy and Community in Post-Mao China*. Washington, DC: Woodrow Wilson Center Press, 1995.

Nee, Victor. "Between Center and Locality: State, Militia and Village," pp. 223–43. In David Mozingo and Victor Nee, eds., *State and Society in Contemporary China*. Ithaca: Cornell University Press, 1983.

O'Brien, Kevin J. "Villagers, Elections and Citizenship," pp. 212–31. In Merle Goldman and Elizabeth Perry, eds., *The Meanings of Citizenship in Modern China*. Cambridge: Harvard University Press, 2002.

O'Brien, Kevin, and Li Lianjiang. *Rightful Resistance in Rural China*. Cambridge: Cambridge University Press, 2006.

———. "Suing the Local State," pp. 31–53. In Neil J. Diamant, Stanley B. Lubman, and Kevin J. O'Brien, eds., *Engaging the Law in China*. Stanford: Stanford University Press: 2005.

———. "The Politics of Lodging Complaints in Rural China." *The China Quarterly* 143 (1995): 756–83.

———. "Selective Policy Implementation in Rural China." *Comparative Politics* 31, no. 2 (January 1999): 167–86.

O'Connor, Pam, and Brian O'Connor. *In Two Fields: Soldier Settlement in the South East of South Australia*. Millicent: S.E. Soldiers Committee, 1991.

O'Leary, Cecilia. "Blood Brotherhood: The Racialization of Patriotism, 1865–1918," pp. 53–81. In John Bodnar, ed., *Bonds of Affection*. Princeton: Princeton University Press, 1996.

———. *To Die For: The Paradox of American Patriotism*. Princeton: Princeton University Press, 1999.

Oi, Jean. *Rural China Takes Off: The Institutional Foundations of Economic Reform*. Berkeley: University of California Press, 1999.

Onkst. David. "First a Negro . . . Incidentally a Veteran." *Journal of Social History* 31, no. 3 (Spring 1998): 517–43.

Pateman, Carole. *The Problem of Political Obligation: A Critical Analysis of Liberal Theory*. Berkeley: University of California Press, 1985.

Pennington, Lee. "Protecting the Wounded: Japanese Disabled Veterans on the Homefront, 1937–1945." Paper presented at the Annual Meeting of the Association for Asian Studies, March 31–April 3, 2005.

Perry, Elizabeth. *Rebels and Revolutionaries in North China, 1845–1945*. Stanford: Stanford University Press, 1980.

———. *Patrolling the Revolution: Worker Militias, Citizenship, and the Modern Chinese State*. Lanham: Rowman & Littlefield, 2006.

———. "The Shanghai Strike Wave of 1957." *China Quarterly* 137 (March 1994): 1–27.

———. "Chinese Conceptions of 'Rights': From Mencius to Mao and Now." *Perspectives on Politics* 6, no. 1 (March 2008): 37–50.

Perry, Elizabeth, and Li Xun. *Proletarian Power: Shanghai in the Cultural Revolution*. Boulder: Westview, 1997.

———. "Revolutionary Rudeness: The Language of Red Guards and Rebel Workers in China's Cultural Revolution." *Indiana East Asian Working Paper Series on Language and Politics in Modern China* 2 (Summer 1993).

Piehler, G. Kurt. "The War Dead and the Gold Star: American Commemoration of the

First World War," pp. 168–85. In John Gillis, ed., *Commemorations: The Politics of National Identity*. Princeton: Princeton University Press, 1994.

Pipes, Richard. "The Origins of Bolshevism: The Intellectual Evolution of Young Lenin," pp. 26–62. In Richard Pipes, ed., *Revolutionary Russia*. Cambridge: Harvard University Press, 1968.

Porter, Bruce. *War and the Rise of the State: The Military Foundations of Modern Politics*. New York: Free Press, 1994.

Posen, Barry. "Nationalism, the Mass Army, and Military Power." *International Security* 18, no. 2 (Fall 1993): 80–124.

Pressman, Jeffrey, and Aaron Wildavsky. *Implementation*. Berkeley: University of California Press, 1973.

Preston, Rosemary. "Integrating Fighters after War: Reflections on the Namibian Experience, 1989–1993." *Journal of Southern African Studies* 23, no. 3 (1997): 453–72.

Prost, Antoine, and Helen McPhail, trans. *In the Wake of War: 'Les Anciens Combattants' and French Society*. Providence: Berg, 1992.

Ramos, Henry A. J. *The American G.I. Forum: In Pursuit of the Dream, 1948–1983*. Houston: Arte Publico Press, 1998.

Rao, B. Shiva. "After the War in India." *Pacific Affairs* 18, no. 2 (June 1945): 169–79.

Reese, Peter. *Homecoming Heroes: An Account of the Reassimilation of British Military Personnel into Civilian Life*. London: L. Cooper, 1992.

Reid, Richard. "Government Policy, Prejudice, and the Experience of Black Civil War Soldiers and Their Families." *Journal of Family History* 27, no. 4 (2002): 374–98.

Reiss, Matthias. "Bronzed Bodies behind Barbed Wire: Masculinity and the Treatment of German Prisoners of War in the United States during World War II." *The Journal of Military History* 69, no. 2 (April 2005): 475–504.

Resch, John. *Suffering Soldiers: Revolutionary War Veterans, Moral Sentiment and Political Culture in the Early Republic*. Amherst: University of Massachusetts Press, 1999.

Rhoads, Edward. *Manchus and Han: Ethnic Relations and Political Power in Late Qing and Early Republican China 1861–1928*. Seattle: University of Washington Press, 2000.

Riggs, Fred W. *The Consulting Firm, the U.S. Aid Agency and the Chinese Veterans Program*. Syracuse: Inter-University Case Study Program, 1970.

Rohlf, Greg. "Dreams of Oil and Fertile Fields: The Rush to Qinghai in the 1950s." *Modern China* 29, no. 4 (October 2003): 455–89.

Roisman, Florence Wagman. "National Ingratitude: The Egregious Deficiencies of the United States' Housing Programs for Veterans and the 'Public Scandal' of Veterans' Homelessness." *Indiana Law Review*, 38, no. 1 (2005): 105–76.

Rosenberg, Gerald. *Hollow Hope: Can Courts Bring About Social Change?* Chicago: University of Chicago Press, 1991.

Rousseau, Jean-Jacques, and Willmoore Kendall, trans. *The Government of Poland*. Indianapolis: Hackett, 1985.

Sabatier, Paul. "Top-Down and Bottom-Up Approaches to Implementation Research: A Critical Analysis and Suggested Synthesis." *Journal of Public Policy* 6, no. 1 (January 1986): 21–48.

Salyer, Lucy E. "Baptism by Fire: Race, Military Service and U.S. Citizenship Policy, 1918–1935." *Journal of American History* 90, no. 3 (December 2004): 847–76.

Sanborn, Joshua. *Drafting the Russian Nation: Military Conscription, Total War and Mass Politics, 1905–1925.* Dekalb: Northern Illinois University Press, 2003.

Schneider, Anne, and Helen Ingram, eds. *Deserving and Entitled: Social Construction and Public Policy.* Albany: SUNY Press, 2005.

Schram, Stuart, ed. *Chairman Mao Talks to the People: Talks and Letters, 1956–1971.* New York: Pantheon, 1974.

———. *The Political Thought of Mao Tse-tung.* New York: Praeger, 1963.

Segal, David R. *Recruiting for Uncle Sam: Citizenship and Military Manpower Policy.* Lawrence: University of Kansas Press, 1989.

———. "Citizenship and Military Service in the United States and the Soviet Union." *Contemporary Sociology* 17, no. 2 (1988): 184–86.

Segal, Gerald. *Defending China.* Oxford: Oxford University Press, 1985.

Seraphim, Franziska. *War Memory and Social Politics in Japan, 1945–2005.* Cambridge: Harvard University Asia Center, 2006.

Shaffer, Donald R. *After the Glory: The Struggles of Black Civil War Veterans.* Lawrence: University of Kansas Press, 2004.

Shaffer, Donald. "'I Do Not Suppose That Uncle Sam Looks at the Skin': African-Americans and the Civil War Pension System." *Civil War History* 46, no. 2 (2000): 132–47.

Shamgar-Handelman, Lea. "Administering to War Widows in Israel: The Birth of a Social Category." *Social Analysis* 9 (1981): 24–47.

———. *Israeli War Widows: Beyond the Glory of Heroism.* South Hadley: Bergin & Garvey, 1986.

Shay, Jonathan. *Achilles in Vietnam: Combat Trauma and the Undoing of Character.* New York: Atheneum, 1994.

———. *Odysseus in America: Combat Trauma and the Trials of Homecoming.* New York: Scribner, 2003.

Shichor, Yitzhak. "Demobilization: The Dialectics of PLA Troop Reduction." *The China Quarterly* 146 (June 1996): 336–59.

Shih, Victor, Wei Shan, and Mingxing Lu. "The Central Committee Past and Present: A Method for Quantifying Elite Biographies." Paper presented at the Workshop on Methods and Sources in Chinese Politics, University of Michigan–Ann Arbor, November 3–5, 2006.

Shuetz, Alfred. "The Homecomer." *American Journal of Sociology* 50, no. 5 (March 1945): 369–76.

Siegel, Mona. "History Is the Opposite of Forgetting: The Limits of Memory and the Lessons of History in Interwar France." *Journal of Modern History* 74, no. 4 (2002): 770–800.

Skelly, Alan. *The Victorian Army at Home.* Montreal: McGill-Queens University Press, 1977.

Skocpol, Theda. *Protecting Soldiers and Mothers: The Political Origins of Social Policy in the United States*. Cambridge: Belknap, 1992.

———. "Will 9/11 and the War on Terror Revitalize American Civic Democracy?" *PS: Political Science and Politics* 35, no. 3 (September 2002): 537–40.

Smethurst, Richard J. *A Prewar Basis for Japanese Militarism: The Army and the Rural Community*. Berkeley: University of California Press, 1974.

Smith, Adam. *The Theory of Moral Sentiments*. New York: Cosimo, 2007.

Smith, Rogers. *Civic Ideals: Conflicting Visions of Citizenship in U.S. History*. New Haven: Yale University Press, 1997.

Snyder, R. Claire. *Citizen-Soldiers and Manly Warriors: Military Service and Gender in the Civic Republic Tradition*. Lanham: Rowman & Littlefield, 1999.

Solinger, Dorothy. *Contesting Citizenship in Urban China: Peasant Migrants, the State and the Logic of the Market*. Berkeley: University of California, 1999.

Sommer, Matthew. *Sex, Law and Society in Late Imperial China*. Stanford: Stanford University Press, 2000.

Sophocles, and Carl Phillips, trans. *Philoctetes*. New York: Oxford University Press, 2003.

Sosna, Morton. "Introduction," pp. xiii–2. In Neil McMillen, ed., *Remaking Dixie*. Jackson: University of Mississippi Press, 1997.

Spector, Ronald. *In the Ruins of Empire: The Japanese Surrender and the Battle for Postwar Asia*. New York: Random House, 2007.

Stacey, Judith. *Patriarchy and Socialist Revolution in China*. Berkeley: University of California, 1983.

Stockdale, Melissa. "United in Gratitude: Honoring Soldiers and Defining the Nation in Russia's Great War." *Kritika: Explorations in Russian and Eurasian History* 7, no. 3 (Summer 2006): 459–85.

Stouffer, Samuel et al. *The American Soldier: Combat and Its Aftermath*, vols. I & II. Princeton: Princeton University Press, 1949.

Stranahan, Patricia. *Underground: The Shanghai Communist Party and the Politics of Survival*. Lanham: Rowman & Littlefield, 1998.

Strand, David. "Protest in Beijing: Civil Society and the Public Sphere in China." *Problems of Communism* 39, no. 3 (1990): 1–19.

Strauss, Julia. "Introduction: In Search of PRC History," pp. 1–15. In Julia Strauss, ed., *The History of the PRC, 1949–1976*. Cambridge: Cambridge University Press, 2007.

———. "Paternalist Terror: The Campaign to Suppress Counterrevolutionaries and Regime Consolidation in the People's Republic of China, 1950–1953." *Comparative Studies in Society and History* 44, no. 1 (January 2002): 80–105.

Tai, Hue-Tam Ho. "Faces of Remembering and Forgetting," pp. 167–95. In Hue-Tam Ho Tai, ed., *The Country of Memory: Remaking the Past in Late Socialist Vietnam*. Berkeley: University of California Press, 2001.

Tamir, Yael. "Reflections on Patriotism," pp. 23–43. In Daniel Bar-tal and Ervin Staub, eds., *Patriotism in the Lives of Individuals and Nations*. Chicago: Nelson Hall, 1997.

Tang, Edward. "Writing the American Revolution: War Veterans in the Nineteenth-Century Cultural Memory." *Journal of American Studies* 32 (1998): 63–80.

Taylor, Carl. "The Veteran in Agriculture." *Annals of the American Academy of Political and Social Science* 238 (March 1945): 48–55.

Taylor, Charles. "Cross-Purposes: The Liberal Communitarian Debate," pp. 159–82. In Nancy L. Rosenblum, ed., *Liberalism and the Moral Life*. Cambridge: Harvard University Press, 1989.

Teiwes, Frederick, and Warren Sun. *The Tragedy of Lin Biao: Riding the Tiger during the Cultural Revolution*. Honolulu: University of Hawai'i Press, 1996.

Thaxton Jr., Ralph. *Salt of the Earth: The Political Origins of Peasant Protest and Communist Revolution in China*. Berkeley: University of California Press, 1997.

———. *Catastrophe and Contention in Rural China: Mao's Great Leap Forward Famine and the Origins of Righteous Resistance in Da Fo Village*. Cambridge: Cambridge University Press, 2008.

Thornton, Patricia M. *Disciplining the State: Virtue, Violence and State-Making in Modern China*. Cambridge: Harvard University Asia Center, 2007.

Tikhonov, Vladimir. "Masculinizing the Nation: Gender Ideologies in Traditional Korea and in the 1890s–1900s Korean Enlightenment Discourse." *Journal of Asian Studies* 66, no. 4 (November 2007): 1029–65.

Tilly, Charles. *Coercion, Capital, and European States, AD 990–1992*. Cambridge: Blackwell, 1990.

Titmuss, Richard. *Essays on 'The Welfare State.'* New Haven: Yale University Press, 1959.

Tsou, Tang. *America's Failure in China, 1941–1950*. Chicago: University of Chicago Press, 1963.

Truesdell, Barbara. "Exalting U.S. Ness: Patriotic Rituals of the Daughters of the American Revolution," pp. 273–89. In John Bodnar, ed., *Bonds of Affection: Americans Define Their Patriotism*. Princeton: Princeton University Press, 1996.

Turner, Karen Gottschang (with Phan Thanh Hao). *Even the Women Must Fight: Memories of War from North Vietnam*. New York: John Wiley and Sons, 1999.

Tyler, Tom. *Why People Obey the Law*. New Haven: Yale University Press, 1990.

U, Eddy. "The Making of *zhishifenzi*: The Critical Impact of the Registration of Unemployed Intellectuals in the Early PRC." *China Quarterly* 173 (March 2003): 100–121.

Unger, Jonathan. "Whither China? Yang Xiguang, Red Capitalists, and the Social Turmoil of the Cultural Revolution." *Modern China* 17, no. 1 (January 1991): 3–37.

Unger, Jonathan, ed. *Chinese Nationalism*. Armonk: M.E. Sharpe, 1996.

University of Chicago Committee on Human Development. *The American Veteran Back Home: A Study of Veteran Readjustment*. New York: Longmans, Green and Co., 1951.

Vagts, Alfred. *A History of Militarism*. New York: Meridian, 1959.

van de Ven, Hans. "War in the Making of Modern China." *Modern Asian Studies* 30, no. 4 (1996): 737–56.

———. *War and Nationalism in China, 1925–1945*. London: RoutledgeCurzon, 2003.

van Ells, Mark. *To Hear Only Thunder Again*. Lanham: Lexington Books, 2001.

van Meter, Donald, and Carl Von Horn. "The Policy Implementation Process: A Conceptual Framework." *Administration and Society* 6 (February 1975): 445–88.

Vigoda, Eran, and Fani Yovel, *Bitsua Hamigzar hatziburi biYisrael*. Haifa: Department of Political Science and Center for the Study of Organization and Manpower, 2001.

Vinovskis, Maris. "Have Social Historians Lost the Civil War? Some Preliminary Demographic Speculations," pp. 1–30. In Maris Vinovskis, ed., *Toward a Social History of the American Civil War: Exploratory Essays*. Cambridge: Cambridge University Press, 1990.

Viroli, Maurizio. *For Love of Country: An Essay on Patriotism and Nationalism*. Oxford: Clarendon, 1995.

Vogel, Ezra. *Canton under Communism: Programs and Politics in a Provincial Capital, 1949–1968*. New York: Harper and Row, 1971.

von Hagen, Mark. "The levee en masse from Russian Empire to Soviet Union," pp. 159–88. In Daniel Moran and Arthur Waldron, eds., *The People in Arms*. Cambridge: Cambridge University Press, 2003.

Wakeman Jr., Frederic. "'Cleanup': The New Order in Shanghai," pp. 21–58. In Jeremy Brown and Paul Pickowicz, eds., *Dilemmas of Victory: The Early Years of the People's Republic of China*. Cambridge: Harvard University Press, 2007.

Walder, Andrew. *Communist Neotraditionalism: Work and Authority in Chinese Society*. Berkeley: University of California Press, 1986.

Waldron, Arthur. "China's New Remembering of WWII: The Case of Zhang Zizhong." *Modern Asian Studies* 30, no. 4 (1996): 945–78.

———. "From Jaurès to Mao: The levée en masse in China," pp. 189–207. In Daniel Moran and Arthur Waldron, eds., *The People in Arms*. Cambridge: Cambridge University Press, 2003.

———. "Looking Backward: The People in Arms and the Transformation of War," pp. 256–62. In Daniel Moran and Arthur Waldron, eds., *The People in Arms*. Cambridge: Cambridge University Press, 2003.

Walzer, Michael. *Obligations: Essays on Disobedience, War and Citizenship*. Cambridge: Harvard University Press, 1970.

Ward, Stephen. "Introduction," pp. 3–9. In James Diehl and Stephen Ward, eds., *The War Generation: Veterans of the First World War*. Port Washington: Kennikat, 1975.

Weber, Eugen. *Peasants into Frenchmen: The Modernization of Rural France, 1870–1914*. Stanford: Stanford University Press, 1976.

Weiner, Amir. *Making Sense of War: The Second World War and the Fate of the Bolshevik Revolution*. Princeton: Princeton University Press, 2001.

Weston, Timothy. *The Power of Position: Beijing University, Intellectuals and Chinese Political Culture, 1898–1929*. Berkeley: University of California Press, 2004.

White, Gordon. "The Politics of Demobilized Soldiers from Liberation to the Cultural Revolution." *The China Quarterly* 82 (June 1980): 187–213.

———. "The Politics of Economic Reform in Chinese Industry: The Introduction of the Labour Contract System," *The China Quarterly* 111 (September 1987): 365–89.

White III, Lynn T. *Unstately Power, Vol. II*. Armonk: M.E. Sharpe, 1998.

————. *Policies of Chaos*. Princeton: Princeton University Press, 1989.

Whiting, Susan. *Power and Wealth in Rural China: The Political Economy of Institutional Change*. Cambridge: Cambridge University Press, 2001.

Wilson, James Q. *Bureaucracy: What Government Agencies Do and Why They Do It*. New York: The Free Press, 1989.

Wirtshafter, Elise. "Social Misfits: Veterans and Soldiers Families in Servile Russia." *Journal of Military History* 59, no. 2 (April 1995): 215–35.

Wong, Linda. *Marginalization and Social Welfare in China*. London: Routledge, 1998.

Wong, R. Bin. "Citizenship in Chinese History," pp. 97–122. In Michael Hanagan and Charles Tilly, eds., *Extending Citizenship, Reconfiguring States*. Lanham: Rowan & Littlefield, 1999.

Yang, Ruizong. "Taiwan diqu yu dalu diqu tuiwu junren anzhi zhidu bijiao yanjiu." Ph.D. dissertation, National Taiwan University, Department of East Asian Studies, 1998.

Yu, Jianrong. "Organized Struggles of the Peasants and Political Risks Involved: An Investigation in County H of Hunan Province." *Zhanlue yu guanli*. May 1, 2003: 1–16.

Yue, Daiyun, and Carolyn Wakeman. *To the Storm: The Odysseus of a Revolutionary Chinese Woman*. Berkeley: University of California, 1985.

Yue, Daiyun. *Intellectuals in Chinese Fiction*. Berkeley: Institute of East Asian Studies, 1988.

Zhang, Jishun. "Cultural Consumption and Popular Reception of the West in Shanghai, 1950–1966." *The Chinese Historical Review* 12, no. 2 (Spring 2005): 101–20.

Zhang, Li. *Strangers in the City: Reconfigurations of Space, Power and Social Networks within China's Floating Population*. Stanford: Stanford University Press, 2001.

Zhang, Xiaoming. "China's 1979 War with Vietnam: A Reassessment." *The China Quarterly* 184 (2005): 851–74.

Ziemann, Benjamin, and Alex Skinner, trans. *War Experiences in Rural Germany, 1914–1923*. Oxford: Berg, 2007.

Index

adultery: cadres having affairs with fiancées and wives of soldiers, 307; commission by veterans, 280

affirmative action: hiring or rehiring returning veterans, 153

Afghanistan War: failure to prepare for returning veterans, 406; inadequate care of disabled veterans, 403

Africa, post-independence conflicts, 3

African-Americans, 1, 8, 28, 84

agricultural production: agricultural competence of veterans, 57; assignment of veterans to work in agriculture, 68, 370; collectivization, 82, 369; daigeng "substitute tilling" program, 328; environmental problems, 80; Household Responsibility System, 363; junshu and lieshu, neglect of, 327; modernizing agriculture with resettled veterans, 369; percentage of veterans returning to, 67, 70, 369; poor skills of some veterans, 82; surplus of rural labor, 76; veterans ignoring importance of, 76

anti-war sentiment, families of soldiers, 343

an zhi (resettlement): implementing policy problematic, 66; resettlement of veterans, 66

apprenticeships for veterans, 171, 180

Australia: veterans organizations, 230; veterans rewarded with land, 59

begging, impoverished veterans, 78, 81

Beijing, 9, 80, 159, 206, 316, 360, 392

benefits for veterans: administering benefits, 201; conscripts, 373; depriving "counterrevolutionary" veterans of benefits, 268; difficulties in implementing programs, 202; effort to improve salaries and benefits, 179; failure to receive, 272; land confiscations to benefit veterans, 57; land grants awarded to veterans, 56; loan guarantees provided to veterans, 59; revoked pensions, 273; veterans considered entitled to benefits, 55; volunteer soldiers, 373

bonuses, World War I veterans, 2

Bonus March, 2, 5, 136

bureaucracy and veterans: administration and public policy, 201; allies of veterans, 237; civil affairs in comparative perspective, 216;

military families, 212; crimes leading to family problems, 280; junshu, 32, 312, 315, 318, 320, 323, 328; lack of respect for military families, 313; lieshu, 32, 313, 316, 318, 320, 323, 328; mistreatment of families by cadres, 311; problems leading to suicide, 261; suicides related to family problems, 287; veterans losing families, 260; veterans with family problems, 255

famine: migrations to cities in famine years, 75; "push" and "pull" factors for migration to cities, 76

Finland, 238

"Four Modernizations" campaign, 359, 374

Fujian Province, 157, 364, 390

Germany: reintegration of rural veterans after WWI, 60; veterans' welcome after WWII, 84; World War I veterans, 2

Ghana, veterans moving to urban settings, 59

GI Bill, 2, 8, 24, 58, 201, 387

grants to veterans: land grants as rewards for service, 56; Roman Senate, failure to provide, 1; Union veterans, 2; World War I veterans, 2; World War II veterans, 2

Great Britain: allies of veterans, 237; resettlement of veterans, 58; veterans organizations, 230

Great Leap Forward: criticism of failures of, 113; establishment of communes during, 262; migrations during famine years, 75; veterans returning to rural areas during, 67

Great Patriotic War, 101

Grieving Hearts Army (GHA), 364, 366, 374

Guangdong Province, 80, 187, 228, 363

Guangxi Province, 83, 228, 362, 364

Guizhou Province, 228, 361, 364, 377

Guomindang: alliance with CCP against Japan, 10; alliance with the United States, 11; attack on CCP during "Northern Expedition," 9; civil war with Communists, 62; conscription in WWII, 11; creation of agency for veterans, 235; failure to plan for demobilization of veterans, 3; power base in cities, 63; work for Nationalist soldiers, 121

Hainan Province, 391

Health Ministry, control of medicine and care for veterans, 270

Hebei Province, 67, 228, 357, 390

Henan Province, 67, 116, 259

Household Responsibility System, agricultural production, 363

housing for veterans: allocation process for housing, 180; expediting construction for retired cadres, 369; habitability of available housing, 182; lack of housing available for veterans, 82; rural areas, 182

Hubei Province, 379, 389

Hunan Province, 106, 228, 357, 389, 391

identities of veterans: belief that respect due, 104; change of identity, 102; disdain for local officials, 107; hero status, 103; individual identities, 101; view of local cadres, 107

illnesses. *See* health problems

infanticide, shortage of women due to, 260

intellectuals, veterans' view that intellectuals in control, 104

Interior Ministry: clarification of aid eligibility, 207; depriving disabled veterans of benefits, 268

Iraq War: failure to prepare for returning veterans, 406; inadequate care of disabled veterans, 403

Israel, struggle for rights among

About the Author

Neil J. Diamant is associate professor of Asian law and society at Dickinson College and chair of the department of political science. He is author of *Revolutionizing the Family: Politics, Love, and Divorce in Urban and Rural China, 1949-1968* (University of California Press, 2000) and a co-editor (with Kevin J. O'Brien and Stanley Lubman) of *Engaging the Law in China: State, Society and Possibilities for Justice* (Stanford University Press, 2005). Before joining the Dickinson faculty, he taught Chinese politics at Tel Aviv University in Israel. His articles on various aspects of Chinese law and society have appeared in *The Journal of Conflict Resolution*, *The Journal of East Asian Studies*, *Politics and Society*, *The Law and Society Review* and *The China Quarterly*, among others. He received his Ph.D. in political science from the University of California, Berkeley.